The Humanities
Volume I

The Humanities

Cultural Roots and Continuities

Fourth Edition

Volume I

Three Cultural Roots

Mary Ann Frese Witt
North Carolina State University at Raleigh

Charlotte Vestal Brown
North Carolina State University at Raleigh

Roberta Ann Dunbar
University of North Carolina at Chapel Hill

Frank Tirro
Yale University

Ronald G. Witt
Duke University

With the collaboration of
Herbert L. Bodman, Jr.
University of North Carolina at Chapel Hill

D. C. Heath and Company
Lexington, Massachusetts   Toronto

Address editorial correspondence to:

D. C. Heath and Company
125 Spring Street
Lexington, MA 02173

Acquisitions Editor: Paul Smith
Developmental Editor: Linda Bieze
Production Editor: Martha Wetherill
Designer: Henry Rachlin
Photo Researcher: Sharon Donahue
Production Coordinator: Richard Tonachel
Permissions Editor: Margaret Roll

Drawings by Eugene Wilson Brown, A.I.A.

Preface

Changes in this Edition

The fourth edition of *The Humanities: Cultural Roots and Continuities* has benefited from the suggestions of readers, professors, and teachers from a wide variety of geographical locations and teaching situations, as well as from our own rethinking of the problems involved in presenting the humanities and cultural roots. Although the format and the spirit of the book remain basically the same, we have made some important changes.

The most significant of these involves an expansion of the concept of "roots." Although the book still reflects our conviction that the Greco-Roman and Judeo-Christian traditions form the basis of the Western humanities, the addition of new Chapters 1 and 2 on Mesopotamia and Egypt highlights the fact that these Western traditions have their own roots in more ancient civilizations. In an effort to emphasize somewhat more the influence of non-Western cultures on Western cultures, we have expanded the medieval section to include a new Chapter 9 on Byzantium and Islam. These new chapters feature many works of art and reading selections, including portions of the *Epic of Gilgamesh*, the "Negative Confession" from the *Egyptian Book of the Dead*, Egyptian love poetry, selections from Justinian's *The Digest*, and portions of the Islamic *Quran*.

In part because of these additions, and because of requests from readers, the present Volume II begins with the Italian Renaissance instead of with the seventeenth century. Also because of these changes, we have consolidated some of the chapters in Volume II. In addition, readings have been added to both volumes, often at the request of readers. New selections include Book 11 of Homer's *Odyssey*, the story of Pygmalion and Galatea from Ovid's *Metamorphoses*, texts from early Church fathers St. Jerome and St. Augustine, sonnets of Petrarch, the Seneca Falls "Declaration of Rights and Sentiments," Franz Kafka's "A Country Doctor," the Prologue from Ralph Ellison's *Invisible Man*, excerpts from Roland Barthes's "The Death of the Author," and Ishmael Reed's "beware: do not read this poem."

The content of all the chapters—and particularly of Chapter 35 dealing with the contemporary world—has been thoroughly reviewed and revised when necessary. For greater accessibility, we have grouped all of the readings at the end of each chapter.

Focus of the Book

Our commitment to a truly interdisciplinary introduction to the humanities through the concept of "cultural roots" remains the same. We feel that in an introductory humanities course the student's personal growth should take place on three levels—historical, aesthetic, and philosophical. The overall purpose of the two volumes can best be described by breaking it down into these three categories.

The Historical Level

We stress the concept of "cultural roots" because one cannot understand the culture in which one lives without some notion of what went into its making. Therefore, we have made every effort here to link the "roots" discussed to aspects of the contemporary American cultural environment. This can be a knotty problem because such links can sometimes be too facile, and we also would like students to discover that cultures remote in time or space can be worth studying simply for themselves. We do not in any way claim to present, let alone discuss, all of the myriad cultural roots that compose the background of today's students. Such a claim would be far beyond the scope of a single introductory humanities course.

Volume I focuses on three traditions—Greco-Roman, Judeo-Christian, and West African—while also exploring *their* roots in the ancient civilizations of Mesopotamia and Egypt and looking briefly at some other influences, such as that of Islam. African culture, a long-neglected field, is now studied more as a significant root of African-American art and thought. The cultures of Africa and the West have intertwined and influenced each other for many centuries. In addition, the study of African culture offers the opportunity to study some fundamental aspects of the humanities in a truly interdisciplinary context, often in contrast to their counterparts in the West.

In our examination of these three cultural roots, we have attempted to focus on certain periods and monuments rather than to survey everything. For example, the focus for the Greco-Roman root is on Athens during the fifth century B.C. This means that some significant works of classical Greek drama, sculpture, and architecture can be examined rather extensively, in relation to each other, while archaic Greece and the entire civilization of Rome receive a briefer treatment. Similarly, in our treatment of West Africa, we have chosen to focus on the culture of the Yoruba people, rather than to survey all of the cultures from this part of the world. While we study the "root" of the Judeo-Christian tradition in the Bible, with selections from the Old and New Testaments, we focus on the relations of arts and thought in the Gothic cathedral, with the specific example of Chartres, during the European Middle Ages. The addition of the chapter on Byzantium and Islam helps to clarify the context of this focal culture.

If we pursue the same metaphor, Volume II might be called "stems, leaves, and flowers." Here, too, we have attempted to focus and spread out more than to survey and spread thin. In our exploration of the Renaissance and Reformation periods we emphasize the fusion of the Greco-Roman and Judeo-Christian roots and focus on the development of humanism in fifteenth-century Italy and its diffusion in the north. The court of Louis XIV in the seventeenth century, the Enlightenment in France and America, the romantic movement, the Industrial Revolution, the modernist movement, and the controversial notion of post-modernism all provide centers around which the many interrelated facets of the humanities can be discussed. As in previous editions, our choice of texts and art works reflects a commitment to recognize the contributions of women, African-Americans, and Hispanic-Americans to the Western humanities.

The Aesthetic Level

On the whole, we follow the same "focal" principle in the aesthetic domain. In presenting music, we operate on the assumption that a student will retain more from listening to and analyzing an entire work than from reading music history and theory and hearing snippets. In the presentation of major works of literature and art in the focal periods, we assume that it is more useful for a student to look at the whole of Chartres cathedral than to skim the history of medieval art, and to read all of *Oedipus Rex* rather than bits and summaries from several Greek tragedies. With lengthy works, such as epics and novels, this is, of course, not possible. We have thus chosen portions of the *Iliad,* the *Aeneid,* and *The Divine Comedy* that are significant in themselves and representative of the whole.

Dance, an often-neglected art form, is given more extensive treatment here than in other humanities texts. Entire dance compositions can, of course, be appreciated only in live performance or film, and we suggest that instructors exploit those resources as much as possible. Although some art forms may seem unfamiliar to students at the beginning, it has been our experience that a long introductory chapter on how to look, listen, and read is largely wasted; therefore, we cover such matters in the introductions to individual works. Questions on the nature of genre are considered in the cultural context in which they originated, notably in ancient Greece. We place much importance on study questions that require the student to read, look, and listen carefully.

Although we try to avoid jargon, we feel that some knowledge of the technical vocabulary of criticism in the art is essential for literate discussion. Difficult or unfamiliar terms appear in italics the first time they are used in any given chapter, indicating that they are defined in the Glossary.

The Philosophical Level

It may well be objected that we compromise the focal method in our presentation of philosophy, because no entire philosophical works appear in the book. This is largely due to considerations of space; but it is also true that, when dealing with a work in terms of certain fundamental ideas rather than in terms of aesthetic wholeness, the "snippet" method is not objectionable. Beginning humanities students are probably not ready to read Aristotle's *Ethics* in its entirety, but they should be able to see how Aristotle's ideas are essential to the cultural roots of the modern world.

The student's personal growth in the philosophical area means, however, something much broader than his or her contact with formal philosophy. The (ideal) student—whose historical awareness is increased by an understanding of cultural roots and whose aesthetic sensitivity is heightened by personal confrontation with a variety of works of art—should also be able to grow intellectually through contact with diverse ideas. A humanities course should enable students to refine their thinking on the basic questions that affect all human beings, to formulate more clearly their personal values, and to discuss these with intellectual rigor rather than in vaporous "bull" sessions. Instructors should welcome debates that might arise from comparing Genesis and African mythology, the issue of women's role in society in Aristophanes's *Lysistrata* and in John Stuart Mill's *The Subjection of Women,* or the relative merits of realistic and abstract art or tonal and atonal music. They and their students will find many more such issues for debate.

Individual instructors will decide which aspect of the humanities they wish to emphasize. We believe that this book offers enough flexibility to be useful for a variety of approaches.

Supplements to the Text

To facilitate teaching and study, we provide a package of supplements available to all who adopt this text. It includes an *Instructor's Guide* with advice for using this text and suggestions for approaching the study of various art forms, a *Study Guide* for each volume for students to reinforce their learning of the text's content, a *Test Item File* for instructors to use in building their own chapter tests and examinations, and a set of slides that includes many of the works of fine art discussed in the text to facilitate class discussion. A single-volume Brief Version of the text is also available. It contains the same instructional text, illustrations, and chapter organization of the two-volume edition, excluding only the primary-source reading selections. It is well suited for one-semester courses.

Mary Ann Frese Witt
Charlotte Vestal Brown
Roberta Ann Dunbar
Frank Tirro
Ronald G. Witt

Acknowledgments

Many people have contributed time, work, ideas, and encouragement to the creation of this book. Gratitude is due, first of all, to those who provided their own research and writing: In Volume I, Professor emeritus Herbert Bodman of the University of North Carolina at Chapel Hill wrote the material on Byzantium and Islam, and Professor Edmund Reiss wrote the sections on courtly love and on medieval English poetry. In Volume II, Professor Ernest Mason of North Carolina Central University wrote the introduction to Freud as well as the material on African-American culture, and Professor John Kelly of North Carolina State University wrote the sections on Latin American culture. Professor emeritus Alan Gonzalez of North Carolina State University wrote the material on the Spanish baroque.

The plan for the first (1980) edition of *The Humanities* grew out of the four years I spent initiating and directing an interdisciplinary humanities program at North Carolina Central University in Durham. It would not have been possible without the stimulation and aid of my students and colleagues there. The late Professor Charles Ray and Dean Cecil Patterson provided me with the time, encouragement, and wherewithal to create the program. The professors who worked closely with me—Elizabeth Lee, Phyllis Lotchin, Ernest Mason, Norman Pendergraft, Earl Sanders, Winifred Stoelting, and Randolph Umberger—have all left their mark on this book. The generous support of the Kenan Foundation, which provided the humanities program with a four-year grant, enabled me to research and compile much of the material. The Kenan Foundation also gave me the opportunity to attend numerous conferences on the humanities. The workshops given at North Carolina Central university by Clifford Johnson, of the Institute for Services to Education, also provided inspiration.

The fourth edition manuscript benefited greatly from readings and criticisms by experts and users. The authors wish to thank Dr. John Brinkman and Dr. Emily Teeter of the Oriental Institute of the University of Chicago for their careful work with the chapters on Mesopotamia and Egypt.

We are also grateful to the instructors who reviewed all of or portions of this book: Henry C. Allan, Jr., Moraine Valley Community College; Lawrence Aufderheide, Lakeland Community College; H. Guy Bensusan, Northern Arizona University; Dion K. Brown, Polk Community College; Thomas J. Cleman, Northern Arizona University; Paula A. Drewek, Macomb Community College; Gunar Freibergs, Los Angeles Valley College; Ann M. Green, Jackson Community College; Mark Hawkins, Foothill College; Mary Kay Kramp, Alverno College; Rodney Oakes, Los Angeles Harbor College; Christine E. Oliver, Savannah State College; Helen C. Othow, Saint Augustine's College; Cornelius A. Page, San Diego Mesa College; William A. Pasch, Clayton State College; Joan Sevick, Nassau Community College; Robert Williams, Bethune-Cookman College. Thanks are due also to Bruce McNair for his painstaking assistance in updating the *Instructor's Guide*.

The authors are especially grateful to Linda Bieze of D. C. Heath for her scrupulous and insightful editing as well as her patience, Martha Wetherill of D. C. Heath for her careful work with the publishing process, and Shira Eisenman for her helpful assistance. The guidance of Paul Smith of D. C. Heath has been essential to the conception and the completion of this new edition.

My collaborating authors deserve many thanks for their fine work and their support over the years.

Mary Ann Frese Witt

Contents

COLOR ILLUSTRATIONS

MAPS

Chronicle of Events

	EGYPT	MESOPOTAMIA-SYRIA-PALESTINE	GREECE
3200 B.C.			
3100	Union of North and South Egypt (3150)		
3000			
2900		Sumerian city-states	
2800		Successive waves of Semites occupy Palestine	
2700			
2600	Old Kingdom (2686–2182)		
2500	Pyramids of Cheops, Chephren, and Mycerinus	Gilgamesh of Uruk	
2400			
2300	Settlement of Kerma	Agade dynasty established by Sargon (2340)	
2200			
2100	Intermediate Period (2181–2134) Middle Kingdom (2134–1782)	*Epic of Gilgamesh* (?)	
2000			Minoan Palace construction begins on Island of Crete
1900		Phoenician (Canaanite) city culture	
1800			
1700	Second Intermediate Period (1782–1570)	Babylonian Dynasty established: Hammurabi (1792)	
1600	New Kingdom (1570–1070)		High point of Minoan civilization (1600–1400)
1500		Hittites destroy Babylon	
1400	Hatshepsut (1498–1483)		
1300	Amenophis IV (Akhenaton) (1350–1334)	Phoenicians develop alphabet Hebrews enter Palestine	Destruction of Minoan palace Mycenaean expansion
1200		Phoenicians flourish (1200–900)	
1100			Traditional date for sack of Troy (1184)
1000	Third Intermediate Revival (1070–664)	Early biblical books written Saul made King of Hebrews (1025)	Greek colonies on Aegean Coast and Greek colonies in Asia Minor established

	AFRICA	MESOPOTAMIA-SYRIA-PALESTINE	ROME	GREEK POLITICAL EVENTS	GREEK CULTURAL EVENTS	
1000 B.C.		Biblical texts written David King of Hebrews (1000–961) Assyrian empire begins Solomon (961–922)				
900		Hebrew kingdom divides into Israel and Judah (922) Assyria conquers Phoenicians and Israel (876–605)				
800	Napata rules Kush (800–270)		Traditional date for founding of Rome (753)		Homer?	
700	Kushite kings of Egypt (780–656)			Beginning of *polis*		
600		Nineveh falls (612) Neo-Babylonian Empire of Nebuchadnezzar (604–562)			Sappho (c. 600) Beginning of Drama and Panathenian Festivals	*Archaic Age (750–480)*
	Persia conquers Egypt (525)	Jews taken captive to Babylon (586) Persians take Babylon (539) Jews return home (538) Darius of Persia (521–486)	Kings expelled and Republic created (509)		Aeschylus (525–456)	
500				Persian Wars (499–479) Pericles (498–427)	Euripides (480–406) Thucydides (470–400) Socrates (470–399) Building of Parthenon (447–432)	*Classical Age (480–350)*
				Peloponnesian War (431–404)	Plato (427–347) Aristophanes's *Lysistrata* (411) Sophocles's *Oedipus* (406)	
400				Philip of Macedon (382–336) Alexander of Macedon (the Great) (356–323)	Aristotle (384–322)	
	Alexander conquers Egypt (332) Greek dynasty rules (331–304)		Vigorous program of Roman conquest of Italy begins (343)		Epicurus (342–270) Zeno (336–264) and founding of Stoic school	*Hellenistic Age (350–150)*
300	Meroe rules Kush (270 B.C.–350 A.D.)		I Punic War (264–241) Sardinia and Corsica annexed (238) II Punic War (218–201)			

	AFRICA	MESOPOTAMIA-SYRIA-PALESTINE	ROME	GREEK POLITICAL EVENTS	GREEK CULTURAL EVENTS
200	Nok civilization at its height (200 B.C.–200 A.D.)		Terence (195–159)	Rome begins conquest of Greece	
	Carthage sacked (146) Rome conquers North Africa		III Punic War (149–146)		
100			Cicero (106–43) Caesar (100–44) Lucretius (99–55)		
		Occupation of Israel by Romans (63)			
		Reign of Herod the Great in Palestine (37 B.C.–4 A.D.)	Horace's *Satires* (35–29) Virgil's *Aeneid* (29–19) Augustus begins reign (27)		

	AFRICA	ROMAN EMPIRE
A.D.		Birth of Jesus Christ
		Death of Augustus (14) Conquest of Britain (43–51)
		Death of Paul (c. 62–64) Persecution of Christians by Nero (64)
		Sack of Jerusalem (70)
100		Juvenal's *Satires* (c. 100) Roman Pantheon built (188–125)
200		Plotinus (205–270) and Neo-Platonism
		Period of disorder (235–284)
300		Reforms of Diocletian (285–305)

	AFRICA	WESTERN EUROPE	EASTERN EUROPE AND MIDDLE EAST
400		Augustine, *Confessions* Alaric sacks Rome (410) Vandals sack Rome (455) Traditional date for end of Western Empire (476) Franks invade Gaul (486)	Byzantium consolidates hold on area
500		Lombards invade Italy (568)	Justinian (483–555) extends empire in East and temporarily conquers part of Italy, Africa and Spain—codifies Roman Law
600	Moslem conquest of Africa		Muhammad begins preaching (610) Muhammad dies (632)
700	Empire of Ghana (700–1230)		Dome of the Rock (completed 692)

	AFRICA	WESTERN EUROPE	EASTERN EUROPE AND MIDDLE EAST
700		Moslem conquest of Spain (711) Defeat of Moslems at Poitiers (732)	Iconoclasts begin century-long campaign against images Abbasid Calephate established (750–1258) at Baghdad Spanish amirate establishes independence at Cordova (756)
800		Charlemagne (768–814) Second period of invasions (c. 800–950): Northmen, Hungarians, and Saracens	
900			Final restoration of images (843)
1000	Beginnings of Benin	Northmen establish Normandy (911) Otto I founds German Empire (962) First systematic teaching of Aristotle's *Logic* (975) Hugh Capet King of France (987) Great mosque of Cordoba completed	
1050		Building of St. Sernin—Romanesque (11th and 12th centuries)	Spanish amirate splinters (1031) into small kingdoms
1100		Norman invasion of England (1066) St. Bernard (1090–1153) First Crusade (1095)	East-West schism (1054)
1150		*Play of Daniel* (12th century) Rebuilding of St. Denis on new lines—early Gothic	
1200	Revolt of Mande peoples against Ghana (c. 1200) and rise of Mali Empire	Bernart de Ventadorn (late 12th century) Marie de France (late 12th century) Chartres Cathedral begun (1194)	Saladin, Kurdish ruler, captures Jerusalem from crusaders (1187)
1250		Mongol invasion of Russia European embassy sent to China St. Louis (1214–1270) Aquinas (1225–1274)	Conquest of Constantinople by Fourth Crusade (1204) Fall of Latin kingdom (1211)
1300	Mansa Musa pilgrimage to Mecca (1324) Exploration of Canaries (1330s and 1340s)	Giotto (1276–1337) Dante's *Divine Comedy* (1300–1321) Petrarch (1304–1374) Boccaccio (1310–1375) Hundred Years War begins (1337) First appearance of Black Death (1348–1350)	Expansion of Ottoman Turks in Greece and elsewhere in Balkans (1308–1337)
1350		The Alhambra (c. 1354–1391) Bruni (1370–1444) Brunelleschi (1377–1446) Chaucer's *Canterbury Tales* (1390–1400)	Unsuccessful siege of Constantinople by Turks (1397–1402)
1400		Masaccio (1401–1428) Henry the Navigator founds navigation school at Sagres (1419) Piero della Francesca (1420–1492) Jeanne d'Arc burned (1431) Medici dominate Florence (1434) Alberti's *On Painting* (1435) Leonardo da Vinci (1442–1519) Botticelli (1444–1510) Lorenzo il Magnifico (1449–1492)	
1450	John Affonso d'Aveiro visits Benin (1485–1486)	Pico della Mirandola (1463–1494) Isaac's *On the Death of Lorenzo* Erasmus (1466?–1536) Spanish Inquisition established (1478) Columbus reaches America (1492) DaGama sails for India (1497)	Fall of Constantinople (1453)

Romanesque Style (11th and 12th centuries)

Gothic Style (12th–15th centuries)

Renaissance Style (15th and 16th centuries)

	AFRICA	EUROPE	EUROPEAN CULTURE	NEW WORLD
1500	Duarte Pacheco Pereira's *Esmeraldo de situ orbis* (1507) Benin at the height of its power (16th and 17th centuries)		Michelangelo's *David* (1504) Raphael's *School of Athens* (1510–1511) Machiavelli's *Prince* (1513) First edition of Erasmus's *Colloquies* (1516) Luther publishes German *New Testament* (1521)	First black slaves in New World (1505) Magellan circumnavigates the globe (1519) Cortez in Mexico (1519–1521) Verrazano establishes French claims in North America (1524)
1525		Peasants' Revolt in Germany (1525) Henry VIII declares himself head of Church of England (1534) Jesuit Order founded (1540) Council of Trent (1545–1563)	First edition of Calvin's *Institutes* (1536) Copernicus's *Revolution of Heavenly Bodies* (1543)	
1550		Peace of Augsburg legalizes Lutheranism in Germany (1555) Reign of Queen Elizabeth I of England (1558–1603) Wars of Religion begin in France (1561) Massacre of French Protestants (1572)	Titian (1477–1576) Bruegel (1520–1569)	Building of St. Augustine in Florida (1565)
1575		Defeat of Spanish Armada (1588) Edict of Nantes (1598)	First edition of Montaigne's *Essays* (1580–1588) Shakespeare (1564–1616) Kepler (1571–1630) Caravaggio's *Calling of St. Matthew* (1599–1600)	
1600		Thirty Years War begins (1618)	Rubens's *Raising of the Cross* (1609–1610) Giambattista Marino (1569–1625) John Donne (1572–1631) Descartes (1596–1650) Corneille (1606–1684) Bacon's *Novum Organum* (1620)	Settlement at Jamestown (1607) Founding of Quebec (1608) First slaves in Virginia (1619) Plymouth colony established (1620)
1625		Civil War in England begins (1643) Peace of Westphalia in Germany (1648)	Harvey demonstrates circulation of blood (1628) French Academy founded (1635) Tirsa de Molina's *The Trickster of Seville* (1635) Galileo's *Discourse on Two New Sciences* (1638) Richard Crashaw (1612–1649)	
1650				

Renaissance Style (15th and 16th centuries)

	AFRICA	EUROPE	EUROPEAN CULTURE	NEW WORLD
1650			Hobbes' *Leviathan* (1651) Rome's Cornaro Chapel (1645–1652) Rembrandt (1606–1669) Milton (1609–1674) Lully (1632–1687) Royal Society of London created (1662) Construction of Versailles begins (1669) Molière's *Le Bourgeois Gentilhomme* (1670) Robert Boyle (1627–1691)	
		Restoration of English Monarchy (1660) Louis XIV (1638–1715) Louis revokes Edict of Nantes (1685)		New York City taken by English from Dutch (1664)
			Newton publishes *Mathematical Principles* (1687) Locke's *An Essay Concerning Human Understanding* (1690)	
1700	Foundation of Ashanti Confederacy (1701)	Union of Scotland and England (1707) War of Spanish Succession (1701–1713) Hanover (Windsor) dynasty begins in England (1714)	Darby cokes coal (1709) Johann Sebastian Bach (1685–1750)	Salem Witch Trials (1692)
1725			Building of Hôtel Soubise (1732) Kay's Flying Shuttle (1733) English repeal laws against witchcraft (1736) Great Awakening (1730s) Handel's *Messiah* (1742) Montesquieu's *Spirit of the Laws* (1748)	Georgia, last of original thirteen colonies, founded (1733)
1750		War of Austrian Succession (1740–1748)		
		Death of George II (1760)	Volume I of the *Encyclopédie* (1751) Mozart (1756–1791) Rousseau's *On the Origins of Inequality* (1755) Voltaire's *Candide* (1759) First blast furnace (1761) Rousseau's *Social Contract* (1762) Watt patents steam engine (1769)	French and Indian War (1754–1763) English take Quebec (1759) English acquire Canada by Treaty of Paris (1763) Boston Massacre (1770)
1775		Accession of Louis XVI (1774)	Schiller (1759–1805)	Revolutionary War begins (1775)
		Meeting of Estates General (May, 1789) Taking of Bastille (July, 1789) Fall of Robespierre (1794) Napoleon's coup d'état (1799)	Goethe's *Werther* (1787) Wollstonecraft's *Vindication of Rights of Women* (1792)	Treaty of Paris ends war (1783) Constitution goes into effect (1789) Washington dies (1799)
1800	Rise of Fulani Empire (19th century) Britain abolishes slave trade (1807)	Napoleon Consul for life (1802) Napoleon crowned Emperor (1804) End of Holy Roman Empire (1806)	David (1748–1825) Madame de Staël (1766–1817) Wordsworth (1770–1850) Constable (1776–1837)	Jefferson elected President (1801)
1810				

	AFRICA	EUROPE	EUROPEAN CULTURE	NEW WORLD
1810			Stephenson's locomotive (1814) Byron (1788–1824) Goya *Executions of the 3rd of May* (1814)	War of 1812 (1812–1814)
	France abolishes slave trade (1815)	Defeat of Napoleon and Congress of Vienna (1815) Industrialization of England (1815–1850)		Founding of *North American Review* (1815)
1820			Blake (1757–1827)	
	Liberia established (1832)	Greek War of Independence (1821–1829)	Beethoven's *Ninth Symphony* (1824) Heine (1797–1856)	
1830	France annexes Algeria (1830)	Revolutions in France, Germany, Italy, Belgium, and Poland (1830) Industrialization of France and Belgium (1830–1860) Industrialization of Germany (1840–1870)		
1840			Delacroix (1799–1863) Dickens's *Old Curiosity Shop* (1840) *Giselle* (1841) Chopin (1810–1849) Turner's *Rain, Steam, and Speed* (1845) Marx-Engels's *Communist Manifesto* (1848)	Emerson (1803–1882) Poe (1809–1849) Seneca Falls convention (1844)
		Revolutions in France, Italy, Germany, and Austria (1848)		Mexican War (1846–1848) Gold discovered in California (1848)
1850	Livingstone at Victoria Falls (1853–1856)	Second Empire founded in France (1852) Crimean War (1855)	Crystal Palace (1851) Millet (1814–1875) Courbet's *Manifesto* (1855) Baudelaire (1821–1867) Darwin's *Origin of Species* (1859)	Walt Whitman (1819–1892)
1860		Foundation of Kingdom of Italy (1860) Emancipation of serfs in Russia (1861) Creation of Dual Monarchy Austria-Hungary (1867)	Mill's *On Subjection of Women* (1861) Ford Maddox Brown's *Work* (1862–1863) van Gogh (1853–1890)	Civil War (1861–1865) Emily Dickinson (1830–1886) Period of Reconstruction (1867–1877)
	Opening of Suez Canal (1869)			
1870		Franco-Prussian War (1870–1871) German Empire and Third French Republic created (1871)	Nietzsche (1844–1900) Monet's *Impressions: Sunrise* (1873) Gauguin (1848–1903)	Stephen Crane (1871–1900)
	Brazza explores Lower Congo (1875)	Dual Alliance: Germany and Austria-Hungary (1879)		
1880	France occupies Tunisia (1881) Britain occupies Egypt (1882) Germans in Togo and Cameroon (1886) Gold found in South Africa (1886) Rhodes establishes Rhodesia (1889–1891)	Triple Alliance: Germany, Austria-Hungary, and Italy (1882) German-Russian Reinsurance Treaty (1887)	Dostoevsky's *Brothers Karamazov* (1880) Mallarmé (1842–1898) Verlaine (1844–1896) Rimbaud (1854–1891)	William Dean Howells (1837–1920) Henry James (1843–1916)
1890				

	AFRICA	INTERNATIONAL POLITICS	EUROPEAN CULTURE	AMERICAN CULTURE
1890	French annex Guinea and Ivory Coast (1893)	Industrialization of Russia (1890–1914)	Cézanne (1839–1906)	Reliance Building (1891)
		Franco-Russian Alliance (1894)		Spanish-American War (1898) Chesnutt's *The Conjure Woman* (1899)
1900	British conquest of N. Nigeria (1900–1903)	Entente Cordiale: France and Great Britain (1902)	Matisse (1869–1954) Apollinaire (1880–1918)	Louis H. Sullivan (1856–1924)
1910		First Russian Revolution (1905)	Picasso's *Les demoiselles d'Avignon* (1907)	
	Morocco becomes French protectorate (1912) Conquest of German colonies (1914–1915)	Balkan Wars (1912–1913) First World War (1914–1918) Russian Revolution (1917) Treaty of Versailles (1919) German Weimar Republic created (1919)	Duchamp's *Nude Descending a Staircase* (1912) Mondrian (1872–1944) Kandinsky's *On the Spiritual in Art* (1912) Stravinsky's *Rite of Spring* (1913) Kirchner's *Street* (1914) Bauhaus founded (1919)	Armory Show (1913) U.S. declares war on Germany and Austria-Hungary (1917) Harlem Renaissance (1919–1932)
1920		Irish Free State (1922) Mussolini establishes Fascism in Italy (1922) Great Depression begins (1929)	Kafka (1883–1924) Nijinsky (1890–1950) Hitler's *Mein Kampf* (1925–1926) Spengler's *Decline of the West* (1926–1928) Lipchitz' *Figure* (1926–1928) Brancusi's *Bird in Space* (1928)	W. E. B. Du Bois (1868–1963) Mariano Azuela (1873–1952) Davis's *Egg Beater No. 1* (1927) Stock Market Crash (1929)
1930	Nigerian youth movement begins (early 1930s) Italy conquers Ethiopia (1936)	Hitler rises to power (1933) Official rearmament of Germany (1935) Spanish Civil War (1936–1939) Second World War begins (1939)	Freud's *Civilization and Its Discontents* (1930) Le Corbusier's *Villa Savoye* (1929–1930) Malraux's *La Condition humaine* (1933) James Joyce (1882–1941) Virginia Woolf (1882–1941) Picasso's *Guernica* (1937)	Shahn's *Passion of Sacco and Vanzetti* (1930) New Deal begins (1933) Louis Armstrong (1900–1971) Claude McKay (1890–1948) Jean Toomer (1894–1967) Georgia O'Keeffe (1887–1986)
1940	Ethiopia liberated (1941) Léopold Sédar Senghor (b. 1903) Léon Damas (1912–1987) Aimé Césaire (b. 1913)	Formation of United Nations (1945) Fourth French Republic established (1945) Communist takeover in E. Europe (1946–1948) China becomes communist (1949)	Giacometti (1901–1966) Sartre (1905–1980) Simone de Beauvoir (1908–1986)	Welles's *Citizen Kane* (1941) Japanese attack Pearl Harbor (1941) Albert Einstein (1879–1955) T. S. Eliot (1888–1965) E. E. Cummings (1894–1962) Richard Wright (1908–1960) Jackson Pollock (1912–1956) Charley Parker (1920–1955)
1950	Algerian War begins (1954) Morocco and Tunisia freed (1955) Ghana first colony to gain independence (1957) Guinea independent (1958) Frantz Fanon (1925–1961) David Diop (1927–1960)	Korean War (1950–1953) Russian Sputnik (1957) Common Market (1957) de Gaulle's Fifth Republic (1958)	Camus (1913–1960) Charlie Chaplin (1889–1977) Arrabal's *Picnic on the Battlefield* (1952) Beckett's *Endgame* (1957) Primo Levi *If This Is a Man* (1958)	Frank Lloyd Wright (1869–1959) Ezra Pound (1885–1972) Langston Hughes (1902–1967) Duke Ellington (1899–1974) Martha Graham (1895–1991) Jorge Luis Borges (1899–1986)
1960				

	AFRICA	INTERNATIONAL POLITICS	EUROPEAN CULTURE	AMERICAN CULTURE
1960	Nigeria and most French colonies independent (1960) Algeria and Tanganyika freed (1962)	Berlin Wall (1961) Beginning of Russia-China split (1962) Great Cultural Revolution in China (1966)	Jean Genet (1910–1985) Roland Barthes (1915–1980)	Ralph Ellison (b. 1914) Katherine Dunham (b. 1919) Kurt Vonnegut, Jr. (b. 1922) James Baldwin (1924–1987) Miles Davis (1926–1991) Ornette Coleman (b. 1930)
1970	Dennis Brutus (b. 1924)			
	Amin gains power in Uganda (1971) Breakdown of Portuguese African Empire (1974) Wathiong'O Ngugi (b. 1938) Soweto Uprising (1976)	Withdrawal of U.S. from Vietnam (1972) Oil prices rise (1973) Shah leaves Iran and Khomeini takes power (1979) Russian troops sent to Afghanistan (1979)	Michel Foucault (1926–1984) Jacques Derrida (b. 1930)	Adrienne Rich (b. 1929) Andy Warhol (1931–1987) Alvin Ailey (1931–1992) LeRoi Jones (b. 1934) Nikki Giovanni (b. 1943) Judy Chicago's *The Dinner Party* (1979)
1980	Rhodesia becomes Zimbabwe (1980) Prolonged famine (1981) Liberation struggles continue in Africa (1988)	Polish solidarity movement repressed (1981) Marcos ousted in Philippines (1986) Chernobyl nuclear explosion (1986) USA-USSR agreement on medium-range strategic force (1988) Berlin Wall falls (1989)	Salman Rushdie (b. 1947)	Ernesto Cardenal (b. 1925) John Barth (b. 1930) Alice Walker (b. 1944) Leonard Bernstein (1918–1990)
1990	South Africa repeals all racial laws (1991)	Gulf War (1991) Commonwealth of independent states replaces USSR (1991)		
2000				

Rethinking the Humanities and Cultural Roots

Controversy Over the Humanities

Recent years have witnessed an outpouring of articles, books, speeches, and conferences on the teaching of the humanities in schools and universities. After a period of relative neglect, when technical and professional education seemed to attract most attention, the nature of the humanities and the way in which they are taught has become the subject of comment and attack from a variety of positions. What is all the fuss about?

Briefly and simply stated, the humanities are the object of conflict between what have been called, erroneously perhaps, the "cultural right" and the "cultural left." In the former camp, writers such as Allan Bloom (*The Closing of the American Mind*), E. D. Hirsch, Jr. (*Cultural Literacy*), Dinesh D'Souza (*Illiberal Education*) and their proponents in the popular press argue for a "return" to a curriculum based on the reading of books generally recognized as great and the formation of a common cultural heritage. In the latter group, a number of professors and critics of various persuasions (many represented in a volume entitled *The Politics of Liberal Education* edited by Darryl J. Gless and Barbara Herrnstein Smith) uphold constant challenge to and redefinition of the notion of great books or great works of art. They point out that the growing diversity of American students with regard to race, economic class, religion, language, and gender justifies the rethinking and reshaping of a curriculum designed for a privileged white male elite. Some believe that the humanities should include "low" or "pop" culture along with "high" culture. The battle came to a head in 1988 over Stanford University's decision to open its Western Civilization core course to include works from non-Western civilizations, minority cultures, and by women. The debate continues to rage. Caught in the middle, in a sense, are the teachers, students, and textbook writers who must decide on a pragmatic level what to include in and how to approach courses designated as "humanities." Whatever their persuasion, however, most would agree that the debate itself has raised some important issues and that awareness of these may enhance the critical thinking of humanities students.

Canons

"Canons in conflict" and "debate over decanonization" are phrases used to describe contention over the humanities. Since the idea of either setting up or doing away with a canon of great works is a central issue, it may be useful to understand the meaning of "canon." The word in Greek meant "rod," "ruler," or "standard" and seems to have been used first by scholars at the library of Alexandria in the third century B.C. to designate a list they made of the best examples of Greek literature. A similar canon, based like the Greek one on literary merit, was later made for Latin literature. Inclusion of books in the biblical canon, however, was based on religious doctrine rather than on aesthetics. The formation of canons, or lists of books that educated people should read, continued throughout the Middle Ages, the Renaissance, and the modern era in Europe and then in America. The books included on these lists, however, changed consistently. Various writings in Hebrew, Greek, and Latin dominated the Western canon through the nineteenth century. It is only recently that works in modern languages such as English were admitted and very recently that anything in translation could be acceptable. There has never been a stable, unchanging canon. It would seem that each generation reestablishes canons for itself, dropping works that no longer speak to its concerns, adding new ones, rereading the traditional ones with new questions. In our time, however, there is a greater plurality of voices speaking to the issue of canons.

Development of the Humanities

The establishment of the humanities as a body of knowledge occurred in Italy some five hundred years ago. The Renaissance humanists, reacting against a curriculum dominated by theology in the Middle Ages, passionately devoted themselves to reading Latin and Greek secular texts, because they believed that human-centered inquiry should be revived. The studies that they called the humanities—in Latin, *studia humanitatis*—thus centered on the literature of antiquity.

This focus on the human did not mean, however, that "man was the measure of all things." The humanists considered the human individual the finest creature in God's creation and, like God, a maker, a doer, a creative force. Nonetheless, humans remained creatures, mortal and imperfect. The humanists' criticism of much medieval education was that it had concentrated on "man" as intellect outside a time frame. The human being was a product of history and a close study of the past, especially of the ancient Greek and Roman world, in which human achievement seemed to have been maximized, could guide people in the present and toward the future. Nor did the lessons of history contradict the truths found in the humanists' ultimate source of truth, the Holy Scriptures. For the humanists, moreover, the emotional component of human nature had to be recognized as a reality, and this recognition was the foundation for ethical development through the use of eloquence. Studying the writings of the ancients, models of eloquence, not only stimulated the mind but also aroused the passions to pursue the good. Having learned the lessons of effective presentation from the ancients, the humanists themselves not only helped others to lead a higher moral life but also, by conveying the message of Scripture, made their audience better Christians.

In spite of their affirmation of the basic dignity of all human beings, the Renaissance humanists definitely believed that some were more "human" than others. People who studied the humanities, according to them, actually acquired more "humanity," not only because they were able to think for themselves more creatively and to express themselves more fully but also because they acquired a deeper understanding of people. Ideally, this kind of humanistic growth should be available to all. In practice, however, it was available only to those with enough wealth, family support, or adequate patronage to have a certain amount of leisure. Moreover, the program of humanistic studies was, with a few notable exceptions, a male monopoly.

It is only fair to point out that people who called themselves humanists, in both Europe and America, have at times associated themselves with cultural élitism, blind worship of tradition, class oppression, and racism. Yet the study of the humanities has also served to stimulate creative men and women to redefine the humanist spirit for their own time. Seventeenth-century humanists in Europe allied themselves with scientists to fight for the liberty of the questioning human mind against the dictates of established authority. Eighteenth-century humanists, speaking out for religious tolerance, for liberty, equality, and fraternity,

helped to create revolutions. Nineteenth-century humanists struggled to save the human spirit from threatening industrial growth and technical progress. They also considerably broadened the areas encompassed by humanistic study through the creation of new fields such as folklore, comparative religion, art history, and music history. Pioneers in Oriental and African studies began the process of making us aware that the study of the humanities can include artistic and philosophical creations from traditions other than the Western one. Humanists such as the many intellectuals who fled Nazi Germany in the 1930s reaffirmed the humanistic demand for freedom of intellectual inquiry and artistic expression, as well as the opposition to oppression, intolerance, and fanaticism in all its forms. Humanists today (who, in contrast to the caricatured "secular humanists" defined by certain religious groups, may be deeply religious) continue to struggle against dogmatism and narrow definitions of truth. One humanistic value seems to be a commitment to the fullest possible development of the intellectual, moral, and aesthetic faculties of individual human beings, along with a belief that the study of the humanities may at least contribute to that endeavor.

The Humanities Today

We have come a long way from a study confined to Greek and Roman literature, but these are still relevant to our present concerns. A line from the Roman poet Terence, a slave of African origins, might in fact define an ideal modern humanist.

Homo sum; humani nihil a me alienum puto.
(I am a man; I hold nothing human foreign to me.)

The interest in everything human covers a very broad range indeed. It means inquiry into the world's cultures and into the wide range of disciplines and creations focused on human beings. The National Endowment for the Humanities has formulated a partial list of areas in the humanities:

The humanities include, but are not limited to: history, philosophy, languages, linguistics, literature, archaeology, jurisprudence, history and criticism of the arts, ethics, comparative religion, and those aspects of the social sciences employing historical or philosophical approaches. This last category includes political theory, international relations, and other subjects primarily concerned with questions of quality and value rather than methodologies.

Contemporary technology continues to expand the scope of the humanities to include productions in film, television, computer, and other electronic media.

What, it may well be asked, can the study of the humanities do for a student in the final years of the twentieth century? We are no longer certain, as the Renaissance humanists were, that the study of the humanities will make one a better or "more human" person. Yet the study of the humanities should involve a process of individual growth and self-knowledge valid today as it was hundreds of years ago. Involvement with the humanities means stretching and expanding one's capacity for thought, sensitivity, and creativity. It means searching for the answers to fundamental questions, such as: What are good and evil? What is the nature of God? What constitutes the good life and the just society? What is beauty? What is love?

The study of the humanities will not provide readymade answers to these or other questions, but it will provide contact with minds and imaginations that have pondered them, and it should help students to think more sharply and more critically. Understanding developed through work in the humanities may, it is hoped, change lives as well as ideas.

The Interdisciplinary Humanities

In this introductory text we cannot pretend to deal with all of the fields mentioned above. Our focus will be on literature, art history, cultural history, and music, with some attention to philosophy, dance, theater arts, and film. The interdisciplinary method of approaching the humanities stresses their relationships but at the same time makes clear the limits and boundaries of each discipline.

What justifies studying a poem or story, a building, a statue, a dance, a musical composition, and a work of philosophy together? One reason often given is enriched understanding of a particular human culture: for example, the study of the masks, dances, poetry, music, and religion of the Yoruba people will give more insight into their culture than will the study of their poetry alone. Another reason lies in the fact that the comparative method enables one art form to shed light on another. A third, more general, reason is that all of these enable us to understand more about the human spirit and its creative capacity.

The various disciplines in the humanities are all concerned with human values, beliefs, and emotions and with the way in which these are expressed through human creations. Philosophy and religion embody more or less systematically organized values and beliefs, whereas works of art (in literature, painting, music, or other) embody the creative expression of these values and beliefs. But these distinctions are not hard and fast. A philosophical tract may also be artistic, and a play or a statue may open up new dimensions in philosophy. The study of cultural history—of values and beliefs prevalent at certain times and places—helps to bind the humanities together, even if a given artist may *oppose* prevailing values and systems.

What do the arts have in common? Let us suppose that for the creation of a work of art, basically two elements are needed: some kind of raw material and a creative mind. Some examples from the Western tradition come to mind: Michelangelo and a block of marble, Shakespeare and the English language, Beethoven and the tones of the scale and instruments of the orchestra. The artist works on the raw material, giving it shape and form. The finished product then bears the imprint of the artist's individual genius, but it also shows the influence of the cultural tradition and the era from which it comes. The combination of these will constitute its style. The work of art will also have a certain subject matter, structure, and theme that will be composed of the "fundamentals" of the art form used. All of these can be analyzed, step by step. A technical analysis of a work of art, though a necessary and useful step in the process of understanding, is still only a means to an end. The end can be called "aesthetic awareness"—the expansion of one's capacity to perceive meaning in art and react to it.

A humanistic education presupposes a willingness to open the mind and senses to the unfamiliar and to judge only after attempting to understand. And the interdisciplinary method invites speculation and comparisons that transcend traditional boundaries.

Culture and Cultural Roots

Culture, a word that has acquired many meanings in recent years, is in need of some definition. We all feel that we belong to a group culture, whose values we may either defend or reject; and in the educational process (broadly speaking, not limited to schooling) we also acquire an individual culture. We may also classify certain works as belonging to "popular" or to "high" culture.

It may be useful to look at the root meaning of the word. In Latin, the verb *colere* means "to cultivate or till," and the noun *cultura,* "soil cultivation." Our word *agriculture* comes from this root and from the Latin word for *field.* Language often grows by metaphors, and here the word culture, applied to human beings, suggests that the human mind, especially the mind of a child, is like a field that must be tilled, fertilized, planted, and *cultivated* by parents, teachers, and other influential members of the society in which the child lives. Applied to an adult, it implies the acquisition of learning and knowledge not merely for their practical value but also for the growth of the mind in its intellectual, moral, and aesthetic capacities. It is in this sense that the African American poet Dudley Randall, describing the beliefs of the humanist W. E. B. DuBois, speaks of "the right to cultivate the brain."[1] We are, of course, vitally concerned with culture in this sense of individual development in the humanities. The Renaissance humanists believed, as we have seen, that this sort of culture was best acquired through the study of Greek and Latin literature. For most humanists today, the study of any and all of the fields considered to be humanistic may further this goal.

If the humanities are concerned with culture in an individual sense, they are also concerned with it in a social or sociological sense. Let us return for a moment to the comparison between the child's mind and the farmer's field. As it is cultivated, that mind not only develops as an individual, but it also acquires certain habits, values, beliefs, ways of thinking, seeing, feeling, and expressing that attach the child to a certain culture. When we use the word in this sense, it might help to think of its meaning in the biological sciences. Certain types of bacteria growing in certain types of environments are called "cultures." When we extend this notion to human beings, we are aware of what it means to speak of a Western culture, an Oriental culture, an African culture. More specifically, we may speak of Slavic or Latin culture, of Ibo or Bantu culture, of Japanese culture. We may speak of American culture, or we may break it down into African-American culture, Italian American culture, Midwestern culture, urban culture, rural culture, and so on. We may make other categories such as youth culture, female culture, male culture, and Baptist culture. There are, in other words, a variety of ways to slice the cultural pie.

Anthropologists looking at a culture are interested in its language, religion, social customs, food, and clothing; its moral and philosophical beliefs; its political, economic, and familial systems; and its plastic arts, poetry, tales, music, and dance. Humanists are interested in all of these things too, but primarily in a given culture's intellectual and artistic achievements. Ideally, in the study of the humanities, we should combine the two meanings of the word *culture* discussed here: we should both acquire individual culture and learn about a social culture. In reading a Greek tragedy or examining a piece of African sculpture, we learn something about the values, beliefs, and sense of beauty of a culture remote from us in time or space; but we also cultivate our own minds in the present through new aesthetic experiences and contact with unfamiliar ideas. Human beings differ from bacteria in that they can flourish and develop through exposure to cultures different from their own.

The matter of tracing one's own cultural roots can be extremely complex. On the American continent, particularly, where so many of us have several different ethnic origins, we have all been influenced by a number of cultures. Although most would agree that the Greco-Roman and Judeo-Christian traditions still form the basis of American culture, particularly in the humanities, we are beginning to understand more fully the impact of other, diverse cultural traditions. These include native American, far eastern, Arabian, and Nordic, to name only a few. We cannot, of course, study all possible cultural roots in an introductory course in the humanities. We hope that students will begin to explore their own cultural roots more fully by asking questions such as "what lies at the root of the ways in which I think, perceive, and express myself?" or "what are the origins of the books, films, TV programs, buildings, music, and visual stimuli of my culture?"

Not every one of you who reads this book will agree that all of the works presented here form part of your "cultural roots." Nevertheless, if you are willing to experience them openly and creatively, they will become part of your personal culture.

---

[1]In "Booker T. and W.E.B." The relevant lines are: "Some men rejoice in skill of hand, /And some in cultivating land, /But there are others who maintain /The right to cultivate the brain."

PART ONE

Earliest Civilizations

Mesopotamia

Revolutions in the Land Between Two Rivers

ince the beginning of human existence on this planet it has been generally agreed that three enormous revolutions have transformed the nature of our lives: the shift from hunting and gathering to food production, the birth of the city, and industrialization. The last revolution occurred relatively recently in the late eighteenth and early nineteenth centuries of our era in western Europe. The other two began in the Near East on the banks of the Tigris and Euphrates rivers between 9000 and 3000 B.C.

We can think of ancient Mesopotamia (the name means "between rivers"), the area now roughly equivalent to modern Iraq, as being divided into two zones. In the north were the foothills shut in to the north and east by the Taurus and Zagros mountains; below them to the south was the low and level plain. The plain was crossed by the Tigris and the Euphrates rivers, which came out of the mountains, sloped southward for five hundred miles, and poured into the Persian Gulf. Whereas the northern third of the plain had substantial rainfall, the southern two-thirds consisted largely of barren desert except along the banks of the life-giving waters of the two rivers. Here, by contrast with the wastelands stretching beyond, the land, built up by deposits of topsoil carried along by the Tigris and Euphrates, was one of the most fertile areas in the world. (See map.)

Agriculture

The first revolution, that involving the domestication of animals such as sheep, cattle, and goats, and the cultivation of barley and wheat, began in the foothills of Mesopotamia about 9000 B.C. No longer compelled to keep contantly moving in search of food, families and groups of families could now build permanent shelters against the weather and fortifications against

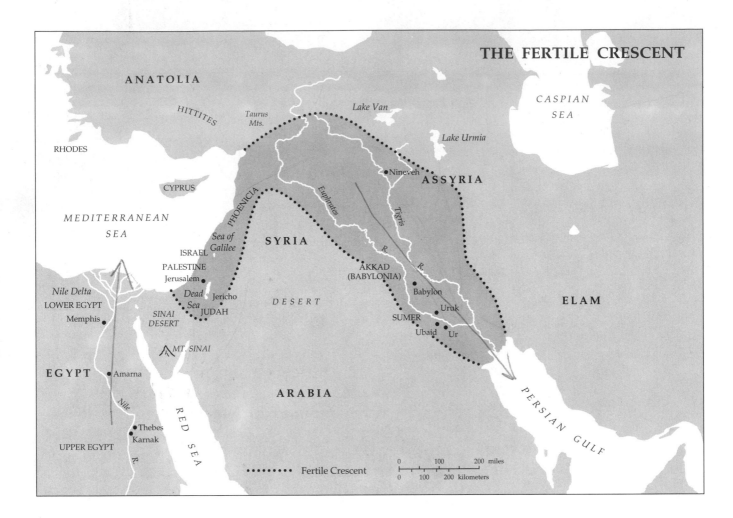

THE FERTILE CRESCENT

ANATOLIA

HITTITES   Taurus Mts.   Lake Van

RHODES

CASPIAN SEA

Lake Urmia

Nineveh   ASSYRIA

CYPRUS

MEDITERRANEAN SEA

PHOENICIA

Sea of Galilee   SYRIA

Euphrates

Tigris

ISRAEL

PALESTINE

Jerusalem   Dead Sea   Jericho   JUDAH

AKKAD (BABYLONIA)

DESERT

Babylon

R.

R.

Uruk

SUMER

Ubaid   Ur

ELAM

Nile Delta   LOWER EGYPT

Memphis

SINAI DESERT

MT. SINAI

EGYPT   Amarna

Nile

ARABIA

RED SEA

R.

Thebes   Karnak

UPPER EGYPT

PERSIAN GULF

•••••• Fertile Crescent

0   100   200 miles

0   100   200 kilometers

hostile people and animals. Because of more favorable living conditions, population increased, and by 6000 B.C., settlers were moving out of the foothills down into the two river valleys, where the rich land promised more abundant harvests.

To exploit the possibilities of the land, however, pioneers had to work and contrive. Of the two rivers, the Tigris was the more difficult to navigate. Both, however, overflowed their banks in March and April, just during harvesting season, occasionally carrying away fields and whole settlements. In the intense heat of the plain, moreover, the fields, which had been flooded in spring, were often parched for moisture by summer. Thus, settlers had to learn to harness the rivers by using canals and dikes so as to maintain a steady flow of water to the fields even when nature gave too much or too little. Archaeological evidence suggests that the beginnings of artificial irrigation came around 3400 B.C., coincident with the appearance of the first cities on the southern banks of the Euphrates. Among the first was Uruk (called Erech in the biblical Old Testament), controlled by the Sumerians, a people whose origins remain unknown.

Urbanization

With the founding of cities came an acceleration of cultural and technological developments, bringing into being the first urban and literate civilization. Urbanization, the second great revolution in human existence, with its specialization of arts and professions and its exchange with distant regions, vastly enriched life. A large grouping of people, moreover, had a greater chance of permanence than a village vulnerable to the first attackers.

The three centuries from 3400 to 3100 B.C. mark the appearance of several of the arts of civilization: a calendar based on observation of the movements of celestial bodies, the first writing, and monumental architecture. Preoccupation with laying out canals and irrigation ditches encouraged the creation of arithmetic, geometry, and the art of surveying. Increased urbanization also led to important developments in architecture. The art of building could move from the construction of simple shelters and monuments for sacred places to specific types of houses and elaborate temples.

By 2900 B.C. the banks of the Euphrates River were occupied by at least twelve fiercely independent city-states. The pattern of the river delayed the creation of central government for centuries, however. The Euphrates broke up midway in its course into six channels and then recombined lower down. As it neared the Persian Gulf, moreover, it created a great area of marshland. This kind of landscape furnished natural defenses of cities and towns against an ambitious conquerer and nourished local independence.

By the beginning of the third millennium (3000 B.C.) the area was inhabited by a variety of different ethnic groups, one of which was Semitic. However, the Sumerians, a non-Semitic people, appear to have dominated in the cities and they gave their name to the area. Their language had already taken written form at Uruk, and it became the written language of the whole area. Independent of one another, these Sumerian cities frequently warred among themselves over land and especially over water rights. The rise of Sargon, who established a Semitic dynasty at Agade about 2340 B.C., temporarily brought to an end this period of political independence by establishing a central government in Mesopotamia lasting about a century.

The Sumerian City   In Sumer the city constituted the principal unit of organization. In the first centuries of city life political control appears to have rested in the hands of an assembly as it had previously in the village communities. There also seems to have been a council of elders, which gave direction to the business of the assembly and executed its commands. In times of trouble a leader was elected for the duration of the emergency, usually caused by the outbreak of war, and at the end of the trouble he was expected to resign. But when emergencies persisted or war followed war it proved easy for the leader to retain control so that by the last centuries of the Sumerian period these cities were ruled by kings from hereditary dynasties. Since they were originally elected, Sumerian kings, unlike the Egyptian pharaohs, were not regarded as living gods. The most celebrated of these early kings, Gilgamesh, king of Uruk about 2600 B.C., was said to have had a partially divine origin, yet the texts written about him, as we will see, recount that he suffered and died.

Sumerian Architecture and Art

A Sumerian myth about the moon god Nanna begins as follows:

Behold the bond of Heaven and Earth, the city . . .
Behold the kindly wall, the city . . .

. . . its pure river . . .
its quay where the boats stand
Behold the Pulal, its well of good water
Behold the Idnunbirdu, its pure canal . . .[1]

This fragment indicates something of the pride that the Sumerians took in their cities and also the importance of boundaries in architecture for the definition of living space. The high city walls of hard clay bricks enclosed individual private houses, shops, streets, shrines, temples, and the royal palace. Houses had only doors and tiny windows on the street. The life of the family was lived around an inner courtyard during the day, and at night, during the hot months, the family slept on the flat roof of the house. Houses of the prosperous were usually two floors high with a balcony around the courtyard. Pottery pipes buried deep in the ground carried away sewage and oil lamps were used for light.

The Temple

Early temples were freestanding shrines with a table for offerings and a niche for the statue of the god or goddess to be worshiped there. As urban centers developed, however, each adopted its own particular deity. The city then belonged to the patron god or goddess whom the inhabitants served as he or she provided for the city. This idea affected the architecture of the temple, which became the heart of a socially sustaining complex of workshops and storehouses as well as a dwelling for the patron deity. Each temple was the household of a god or goddess who had a hierarchy of people and subordinate deities to serve him or her, from the high priest down through the diviners, exorcists, and musicians to the slaves who swept the courtyard. Associated with the temple building were granaries and workshops where artisans produced goods for consumption in the temple and for sale in the city and abroad. Outside the city walls lay large estates that grew crops and animals for the same purposes. Finally, the king and individuals made offerings from their private estates that supplemented the temple's own resources. Throughout the city there were also smaller temples for lesser deities.

To create a space set apart from the dense urban fabric, the temple complex within the walled city was itself walled. Eventually, this complex gave rise to a distinctive form, the *ziggurat* or temple-tower (Fig. 1-1). A ziggurat was created by stacking as many as seven layers of earth, with each succeeding layer

---

[1]The Oriental Institute, the University of Chicago.

1-1 *The White Temple on its Ziggurat, Uruk (present-day Warka, Iraq), c. 3500–3000 B.C. (Courtesy, German Archaeological Institute, Berlin)*

becoming smaller and connected to the layer beneath it by ramps and stairs. As they grew, the ziggurats incorporated previously built smaller temples. At the top of this symbolic mountain—an intermediate territory between the earth and the sky—lay the temple, the place of the god's *epiphany* or appearance. Earth gods could dwell within such a temple, sky gods could stop off for a ritual meal, and the god or goddess of the city could reside there. One ziggurat was named the House of the Mountain, Mountain of the Storm, Bond between Heaven and Earth.

The idea that the ziggurat represents a sacred mountain that raises the temple on high and makes it visible from afar can be seen in the great ziggurat of Ur-Nammu at Ur (c. 2100 B.C.), a stepped pyramid in a number of levels, three of which survive (Fig. 1-2). The core was mudbrick, with the exterior faces made of baked brick set in bitumen mortar. Three stairways formed an approach on the northeast side, one set at right angles to the building, the other two leaning against the wall. They met at the foot of a gateway to a

1-2 *Ziggurat of King Ur-Nammu, Ur, c. 2100 B.C. (Hirmer Fotoarchiv, Munich) with reconstructed view.*

0   50   100

great stairway, which ran straight up to the front of the temple door. Planted trees graced the upper terraces, colored tiles supplied further decoration, and *weep holes* cut into the fabric allowed interior moisture to seep out. At some sites exterior walls were curved slightly and battered inward; at others the walls were whitewashed. In later periods glazed bricks would create distinctive, bright-colored surfaces that sparkled in the sun.

The distinctive structure of a sacred mountain—the ziggurat—in the flat, low-lying plains of Mesopotamia necessitated a winding journey along the processional way to the altar of the god. One writer has called it "reverential climbing"; another the bent-axis approach in which the object of the pilgrimage is not only hidden from view but also demands many steps and turns before the approach to the god can be made. It will be interesting to compare this processional way with that of the Egyptians, who lined up different architectural spaces on a long axis to create a processional way with a variety of architectural experiences. "Reverential climbing" also forms an important aspect of many Greek temple complexes, discussed in Chapter 4. The winding approach has some parallels with the Minoan Labyrinth or maze of Bronze Age Crete (3000–1100 B.C.), which has been interpreted as an ascending way made flat.

Sumerian Art

The city, the temple, and the palace complexes were all means for rulers, religious or secular, to give physical, objective expression to power, just as the individual's dwelling describes something about his or her place in society. As the forms of the Sumerian city and its buildings provide us with our first encounter with a fairly complete building language, so the wonderful artifacts from Sumer introduce us to an artistic language. Objects made by Sumerian artists derive from a cluster of shared ideas or traditions about the way to depict the human figure, the landscape, and events. To be sure, the objects were never thought of as "art objects" in our sense of the term. Rather, they were highly functional, while still aesthetically pleasing, like the cave paintings or carvings of prehistoric people. The objects that have been preserved help us understand the powers that shaped life in the land between the rivers.

The art objects can be roughly divided into three major categories: ritual objects, objects of state, and personal objects. Among the earliest three-dimensional survivals are a stunning collection of marble

1-3   *Statuettes from the Abu Temple, Tell Asmar, c. 2700–2500 B.C., marble. (The Iraq Museum, Baghdad and the Oriental Institute, University of Chicago)*

statuettes from the Abu Temple at Tell Asmar, c. 2700–2500 B.C. (Fig. 1-3). The tallest figure (about 30 inches) represents Abu, god of vegetation; the next tallest, a mother goddess. The next largest figures are priests and the smallest are worshipers. The cylindrical bodies, scarcely differentiated by gender, with their uplifted heads and their hands clasped on the breast, create powerful images and feelings. The symmetry and abstraction of the human form, concealed within the long skirt, and the reduction and stylization of textures to represent cloth and hair, reinforce the riveting aspect of the faces dominated by the vast eyes, whose cavities would once have been inlaid with colored stone or enamel. These are not silent figures; they seem to speak, if in unfamiliar sounds, as they stare open-eyed, offering constant supplication to their god on behalf of their donors.

A panel from the Standard of Ur, c. 2500 B.C. shows Scenes from War (Fig. 1-4), a seemingly full-time business in this period. The people depicted here bear a strong resemblence to those from Tell Asmar, and many of the same artistic ideas are used: repetition, simplification, and abstraction. The standard depicts an image of war that is both organized and brutal.

The experience engendered by these artifacts is quite different from that created by an offering stand from Ur (Color Plate I). Here a wooden, gold-fleeced male goat made of a wood core overlaid with metal stands upright before a golden, flowering tree. The bearded face, bright eyes, curling horns, and springing

1-4 *A panel from the* Royal Standard of Ur, *sounding box of a musical instrument, decorated with mosaic in shell, lapis lazuli, and set in bitumen, showing* Scenes from War, *c. 2600* B.C., *18½" × 8". (Reproduced by Courtesy of the Trustees of the British Museum)*

flowers are filled with energy and power, perhaps the power of the god Tammuz, the male principle in nature. The maker of this stand has used artistic principles similar to those of the Tell Asmar statuettes. The figure is abstracted, the fleece reduced to repeated curling patterns. However, the more pliant materials, carved wood overlaid with thin sheets of gold, create a lively creature who glitters with life and energy.

Sumerian Mythology, Religion, and Worship

The terms *myth* and *mythology*, used in a variety of ways, need some clarification. In popular usage, a myth designates something that the person using the word believes to be untrue even though many people may accept it as true. Thus we speak of myths created by advertising or the myth of pure and honest government. Used by psychologists, anthropologists, or literary critics, however, the word has a much broader meaning, one that is nearly the opposite of its popular one. It comes from the Greek word *mythos*, which can mean "a word" or "a story." Every culture in the world has or has had a set of stories passed down orally from one generation to the next that are called its myths; the body of a culture's myths is its mythology. Myths differ from legends in that they are not usually based on historical events situated in time. Myths take place outside of historical time, in what students of mythology call "sacred time" and the Australian aborigines call "dream time." They often attempt to explain the origins of some phenomenon of nature such as the creation of humankind or why the sun rises and sets. Their characters are gods, sacred beings, or semidivine heroes and heroines. Studies in comparative mythology show that many figures such as the sky god, the earth goddess, the vegetation god, the divine child, and the virgin mother are, with different names and in various forms, found in widely divergent cultures that apparently had no influence on each other. Calling such figures *archetypes,* the psychologist Carl Gustav Jung postulated a "collective unconscious" from which human beings draw their vital myths.

Far from being a pack of lies, as popular usage would have it, the myths of a particular culture represent for that culture the deepest form of truth—a reality that is lived and practiced through ritual. For those outside of the culture they may also portray profound human truths, whether in a psychological, sociological, or spiritual sense. Thus we may distinguish between mythological truth and factual truth.

The notion of "mythological truth" also informs the way in which Western culture views its own religions. After the work of Charles Darwin and of biblical criticism in the nineteenth century, many believing Jews and Christians found that they could no longer accept the account of the origin of the world and of humanity given in Genesis to be true in a literal sense; and yet most believers today accept it as true in a symbolic, religious, or mythological sense. Religion, of course, is much more than a particular set of myths, although these are part of it. The word means a "binding together" and implies a system of beliefs, rituals, and standards of conduct. Great world religions such as Judaism, Christianity, Islam, Hinduism, and Buddhism have given human beings a core of meaning to their lives outlasting political change, scientific discoveries, and other cultural developments. The religion of ancient Mesopotamia, despite its fascinating mythology, was not one of these.

It is somewhat difficult to generalize about the religion of the Mesopotamians since they had numerous gods and goddesses whose names and attributes shifted according to city and era. However, the Sumerian concept of creation seems to be as follows. The primeval sea, which may have existed eternally, begat the cosmic mountain consisting of heaven and earth united. The Sumerian word for universe, *an-ki*, literally means "heaven-earth," and denotes the god An and the goddess Ki. From their union was born Enlil, the air god, who is usually depicted as the most powerful god of the pantheon. From An and Ki also sprang

Ninhursag, or Aruru, the Great Mother or goddess of procreation, and Enki, or Ea, the god of flowing water. Many other gods and goddesses were born from these, but the most important for our purposes are Shamash the sun god and Inanna (Sumerian) or Ishtar (Semitic), the goddess of love and war. Human beings were created so that the gods would have servants, or as the Babylonian creation epic puts it, "Man shall be charged with the service of the gods, that they might be at ease." There was no one creator god, but the Great Mother goddess, perhaps like a potter, is usually depicted as creating human beings out of clay. In addition to the patron deity of the city, each person had his or her own personal deity.

The Mesopotamians' idea of an afterlife was quite different from that of other religious traditions. Although they believed in an underworld where something of the person survived after death, this was a place neither of punishment nor of reward, but (so it seems in the *Epic of Gilgamesh*) a dark, dusty cave where the crowded shades of the dead bumped into each other like bats. Those dead remembered and cared for by loved ones still on earth fared better than those who were forgotten, but death brought with it no promise of a better life. Only one man, Utanapishtim, and one woman, his wife, were given immortality by the gods. Utanapishtim is in many ways the equivalent of the biblical Noah: as in the Bible when the great flood destroyed humanity, Utanapishtim built an ark with a pair of each species so that the world would be peopled again after its destruction. He and his wife were said to reside in the mountain of the gods. This story figures importantly in the *Epic of Gilgamesh.*

Since the Sumerians believed that the gods had created humans to serve them, one of the duties of the temple staff was to make sure that the statues of the gods were fed regularly. If properly cared for, the gods would bring wealth and power to the city that worshiped them. Writing in about 2250 B.C., a poet praising the generosity of Inanna, goddess of love and patron of his city Agade, captures the belief in these lines:

Inanna filled Agade, her home, with gold.
She filled the radiant house, her home, with silver.
She filled the storerooms with barley, bronze, and
   lumps of lapis lazuli...
She gave its elderly women the gift of good counsel.
She gave its elderly men the gift of wise counsel.
She gave its young girls the joy of dancing.
She gave its young men the strength of weapons.
She gave its little ones a joyful heart...

The ships at the wharves were an awesome sight.
All the lands around rested in security.
The people saw beautiful things.
The king, Naram-Sin, shone forth like the sun on the
   holy throne of Agade.[2]

Several times a day in an elaborate ritual the god was served an abundant meal. Course after course was set before the statue to the accompaniment of music and the sprinkling of incense. The hands of the god were washed both before and after meals. Here is the daily menu of the god Anu at Uruk:

12 vessels of wine	2 bulls	4 wild boars
2 vessels of milk	1 bullock	3 ostrich eggs
108 vessels of beer	8 lambs	3 duck eggs[3]
243 loaves of bread	60 birds	
29 bushels of dates	3 cranes	
21 rams	7 ducks	

At special festivals unusual cakes were also offered. Except for leaving offerings with the priests for the divine meal, however, private individuals had nothing to do with this cult. The only time they came into contact with the gods was when the deities' statues were brought out of the temple and were carried through the streets in procession.

Sumerian Music

Dancing, as the poem above indicates, was considered one of the joys of city life. Pictorial evidence, as well as fragments of instruments excavated from the royal cemetery at Ur, suggests that music was also an important part of religious and civic life in Sumer. We can no longer hear the sounds as they were performed thousands of years ago, but we can reconstruct the instruments, imagine the sounds and rhythms, and visualize the rituals of court and temple. From approximately 2500 B.C., harps were made in the form of a boat with a keel-shaped soundbox and eleven to fifteen strings that slanted up to the neck, which ran up like a mast from the prow (Figs. 1-5, 1-6). A decorative cap of silver or gold at the end of the neck gives some indication of the value placed on the instrument. Although we know that copper and gold pegs were used to secure and tighten the strings, we will never be able to discover the exact tunings this instrument enjoyed.

In Sumer the bull was a symbol of fertility and divine power, and another musical instrument, the

[2] The Oriental Institute, the University of Chicago.
[3] The Oriental Institute, the University of Chicago.

1-5 *Sumerian characters, representing boat-shaped harps, copied from stone tablets, c. 2800* B.C. *(From Wilhelm Stauder,* Die Harfen und Leiern der Sumerer, *Frankfurt, 1957)*

1-6 *Reconstruction of a boat-shaped harp from the Royal Cemetery at Ur, c. 2600–2350* B.C. *(Reproduced by Courtesy of the Trustees of the British Museum)*

1-7 *Reconstruction of a silver Sumerian lyre from the Royal Cemetery at Ur, c. 2600–2350* B.C. *(Reproduced by Courtesy of the Trustees of the British Museum)*

lyre, was fashioned on its figure. The bull's body could act as the resonant soundbox with two necks and a cross brace rising to stretch the strings, but instruments in the shape of a bull's head alone, with two large horns rising symmetrically on each side to stretch the strings, were also used in performance during the Sumerian period (Fig. 1-7). Dancing girls used clappers to provide rhythmic accompaniment for their dance, and eventually drums and wind instruments made their appearance as well.

It is unlikely that concerts of music, as we know them today—public concerts by professional musicians in spaces designated for music—took place in antiquity, for such events are neither described nor pictured. We also know nothing about independent instrumental music in Sumer. We believe music was inseparably linked to the recitation or intonation of poetry used for ritual occasions. Music was used in the daily celebration of temple rites, during the annual holy festivals, and on special occasions such as a birth in the royal family, a marriage of rulers or gods, the construction of a palace or temple, or the burial of a head of state. The words of hymns and laments are preserved in cuneiform texts, but no melodies were recorded in writing, for not only was there no developed system of notation (a means to indicate pitch and duration), but the melodies were considered priestly secrets to be transmitted orally from elder to neophyte.

Literacy and Literature in Mesopotamia

One of the great inventions of Mesopotamian civilization was the art of writing. The very earliest writing system (using clay tokens) dates back before 7000 B.C.; the first setting of words on tablets occurs about 3400 B.C. Their written language was at first constituted partly of pictures, but later the Sumerians developed a system of signs in which each sign seems to have represented a single word. Dominated by wedge shapes, their writing system is called cuneiform, from the Latin word *cuneus,* "wedge" (see Fig. 1-8, a tablet of *Gilgamesh*). The writing was done on soft clay tablets with a reed stylus. The earliest tablets that we possess are economic records and vocabulary lists for training scribes. Later, writing was used for legal transactions, receipts, historical records such as lists of kings, sacred texts, and works of literature. Letters were sent by wrapping a tablet in a clay envelope, sealing it with a cylinder seal, and having a messenger deliver it. The earliest writings were in Sumerian; after the conquest of Sargon about 2340 B.C. (see below), Akkadian became the dominant language. Not until the 1850s did scholars decipher the complex cuneiform script.

Mastering the art of cuneiform writing was not an easy task, and the majority of the population, including royalty, was illiterate. Reading and writing were the tasks of specialized scribes, which included both men and women. To become a scribe, one had to begin to attend school as a child. In one surviving clay tablet called "School Days," from the eighteenth or seventeenth century B.C., a pupil describes life at school. Here are two excerpts:

The days I spend in school are as follows:
My vacation days are three days a month,
Various festivals are three days a month,
That leaves twenty-four days a month in which I sit
  in school.

My mother gave me two pieces of bread and I went
  to school.
In school the supervisor asked me, why are you late?
I was afraid. My heart was pounding.

1-8 *A fragment of the eleventh tablet of the* Epic of Gilgamesh, *Nineveh, showing cuneiform writing, c. 800–600 B.C., clay, 5¼″ × 5¾″ × 1¼″. (Reproduced by Courtesy of the Trustees of the British Museum)*

I entered into the presence of the masters.
I bowed down, and I recited my tablet to the Master
  of the school.
He said, "You are going to be beaten because you
  left out some lines."[4]

In the course of their training, scribes copied texts from the traditional writings of Mesopotamia. Roughly two hundred thousand lines of these writings were preserved in the library of Ashurbanipal, an Assyrian king of the seventh century B.C. They include myths, laments, songs, and proverbs. For the modern reader, the most interesting are the tablets that form the *Epic of Gilgamesh,* discussed below. Other surviving examples include "The Instructions of Shuruppak," the earliest copies of which date from 2500 B.C., which contains about 280 proverbs consisting of the king's advice to his son. Among them: "Heaven is far away, but earth is precious." (You will notice how this might be applied to *Gilgamesh.*) "Love maintains a

---

[4]The Oriental Institute, the University of Chicago.

1-9 The Slaying of Humbaba. *An impression of a Neo-Assyrian period cylinder seal, c. 9th–8th century B.C. (Reproduced with the permission of Dr. Leonard Gorelick)*

family." "Do not speak arrogantly to your mother; you will be hated." Songs praising kings were frequent, as were praise songs or prayers to the gods.

The *Epic of Gilgamesh,* the most important literary work from Mesopotamia that has come down to us, concerns a historical and legendary figure who was probably king of the city of Uruk around 2600 B.C. Gilgamesh was revered as a great hero, and the various legends that grew up about him were written in both the Sumerian and Akkadian languages. Although the first clay tablets about Gilgamesh may have been written not long after his actual rule, we have no existing texts written before 2100 B.C. What has come to be known as the "standard version" of the Gilgamesh story consists of eleven cuneiform tablets in Akkadian, written in the first millennium B.C. (see Fig. 1-8). Some scholars believe that they were originally written by a single author, Sinlequeunninni, a priest at Uruk in the fourteenth century B.C. Unfortunately, we do not have any complete version of the story of Gilgamesh; many of the clay tablets are broken, so that several parts are missing, but it is hoped that these may eventually still be discovered. Yet the basic story line is clear. Gilgamesh, who established Uruk as the supreme city in Mesopotamia, was thought to be two-thirds divine and one-third human. Renowned for both his strength and his beauty, he nonetheless overstepped the boundaries of his duties as king by oppressing the young men and women of the city. The gods decide to create a counterpart to Gilgamesh with Enkidu, the "wild man," who lives with animals. A trapper, who finds that Enkidu is disturbing his hunting, devises a plan to strip him of his animal powers. He goes to Gilgamesh

and asks for a love-priestess or temple prostitute. The woman, who stays with Enkidu for "six days and seven nights," begins to "civilize" him. She also leads him to Gilgamesh, and after a wrestling match that Gilgamesh wins, the two become close friends, indeed brothers, since Gilgamesh's mother adopts Enkidu. They decide to go off on an expedition to kill the monster Humbaba, the guardian of the Cedar Forest. Despite Gilgamesh's terrifying dreams and Enkidu's fear, they continue their journey, urged on by the sun god Shamash, and Gilgamesh finally kills the monster (Fig. 1-9).

Once they are back in Uruk, the goddess of love and patron of the city, Ishtar, smitten with Gilgamesh's strength and beauty, asks him to become her husband. Gilgamesh, however, refuses, citing the terrible fate that has befallen all of Ishtar's many lovers. Insulted, the goddess convinces her father, Anu, to send the Bull of Heaven to punish Gilgamesh, but Enkidu and Gilgamesh succeed in slaying the bull. The gods decide to kill Enkidu in revenge. After a long illness, watched over by his devoted friend, Enkidu succumbs to death and Gilgamesh to a profound grief. Fearing his own death as well as mourning his friend, Gilgamesh decides to undertake a journey to meet Utanapishtim, the only human to have been granted immortal life, in order to learn from him his secret. He reaches the mountain of the gods but is warned of the impossibility of his quest by all the creatures he meets. He nevertheless succeeds in reaching Utanapishtim, who tells him a "secret of the gods," the story of the Flood resembling the account in Genesis. Utanapishtim's wife persuades her husband to give

Gilgamesh a plant that will make him young again, but on the way home he loses it to a snake. At the end, Gilgamesh returns to Uruk to continue his reign. Although he has learned that there is no immortality, he has also learned to value the accomplishments of earthly life such as the construction and ruling of a great city.

What kind of a poem is *Gilgamesh?* The word *epic,* although invented by the Greeks considerably later to characterize the *Iliad* and the *Odyssey* of Homer, may be used to classify this first story of a cultural hero, as well as many other such stories from around the world. The epic is centered on a human rather than a divine figure, and recounts the famous deeds of a hero important to the audience. Yet the hero may also undertake a quest and in so doing face anguish and loneliness resembling a kind of symbolic death and rebirth. Often this journey involves a visit to the underworld or to the realm of the gods. The *Epic of Gilgamesh* may be divided into two parts, the first celebrating the hero's strength and exploits and the second recounting his "dark night of the soul" and his quest. Although remote and strange to us in many ways, *Gilgamesh* nevertheless speaks vividly to the modern reader.

Semitic Kingdoms

About 2340 B.C., Sargon, cupbearer of the Sumerian governor of Kish, overthrew the Sumerian power and took control of the city. His people, the Akkadians, were Semitic and lived north of the main concentration of Sumerian cities. During his long reign (he is reported to have ruled for fifty-six years) Akkadian, also written in cuneiform, became the official language of the area, although scribes still learned Sumerian as a "classical" language. Soon after assuming power Sargon created a new capital city, Agade, which was to become the center of an enormous empire.

Indeed, before his death, Sargon conquered all of southern and northern Mesopotamia and moved with his armies into Syria and Anatolia, which is now part of modern Turkey. His grandson, Naram-Sin (praised in the poem on page 9) is reported to have pushed these conquests into the eastern Mediterranean. The victory stele of Naram-Sin (Fig. 1-10) shows the king above the ranks of his soldiers as well as the defeated, who plead for mercy. Larger than all the other figures, Naram-Sin wears the horned crown usually reserved for the gods. Only the top of the mountain and the celestial bodies, his "good stars," appear above him. The carving shows that the Akkadians absorbed the

1-10 *Stele of King Naram Sin, from Susa, Iran, c. 2300–2200 B.C., sandstone, height 78", Louvre, Paris. (Copyright PHOTO Réunion des Musées Nationaux)*

artistic language of the Sumerians just as they appropriated their writing, and they turned that language to the glorification of the king.

Both Sargon and Naram-Sin are remembered in the annals of this region for the next fifteen hundred years as the greatest conquerors in history. Domination of such an enormous territory, however, required genius, and under their less fortunate successors the kingdom of Akkad decayed. Ferocious tribes from the mountains, the Gutians, burned Agade itself about 2150 B.C. and for about fifty years central power disappeared. There was a brief revival of Sumerian power centered at Ur about 2100 B.C. but it lasted only a century. The destruction of Ur about 2000 B.C. by the Elamites marked the end of Sumerian political power in Mesopotamia. By 1800 B.C., the Amorites had captured all of old Sumer as well as some of Sargon's foreign possessions and set up the First Dynasty of Babylon.

The Babylonians

Among the greatest of these Babylonian rulers was Hammurabi, who became king in 1792 B.C. The literally thousands of written records surviving from his reign reveal the city of Babylon on the southern Euphrates as a great center for international trade. Precious stones from the Persian Gulf, cotton cloth from India, and exotic spices from Egypt competed for purchasers in the city's bazaars. Of all the written documents of the period, perhaps the most important is the Code of Hammurabi, recorded on an eight-foot-high block of basalt stone covered with writing in horizontal columns. At the top of the block Hammurabi is depicted in the act of receiving the symbols of kingship from Shamash, the sun god and lawgiver (Fig. 1-11). Stylistically, the Babylonians did little to change the artistic language of their predecessors. The figure of Hammurabi has the same intense gaze that recalls the oversized eyes of the Sumerians from Tell Asmar (Fig. 1-3). But the gift that Hammurabi receives is nothing less than a code of the 282 laws written on the block below.

The Code of Hammurabi is not, as was once believed, the oldest law code known to humanity, for earlier ones have been discovered in Mesopotamia. It is still, however, the most complete set of laws surviving from these centuries. Essentially motivated by the spirit of retaliation, "an eye for an eye," Hammurabi's laws paid no attention to intentionality. For example (218): "If a surgeon performed a major operation on a citizen with a bronze lancet and has caused the death of this citizen...his hand shall be cut off." Or again (229): "If a builder built a house for a citizen but did not make his work strong, so that the house collapsed and has caused the death of its owner, that architect shall be put to death." A few other laws from the code concerning the family and property follow:

> 117 If a citizen's debt falls due and he sells his wife, son, or daughter, or if he himself is bound over to service, the debt-slaves shall work in the house of their creditor for three years; in the fourth year they shall be given their freedom.

> 124 If a man give to another silver, gold, or anything else on deposit in the presence of witnesses,

1-11 *Stele of Law Code of Hammurabi, c. 1792–1750 B.C., 7" × 9". (Copyright PHOTO Réunion des Musées Nationaux)*

and the latter deny it, the custodian shall be proven guilty and shall double whatever he has disputed and repay it.

> 129 If the wife of a man has been caught lying with another man, they shall be bound and thrown into the water. If the husband of the woman would allow his wife to live, then the king may allow his subject [the male offender] to live.

> 130 If a man force the betrothed of another who has not known a male and is living in her father's house, ... that man shall be put to death and that woman shall go free.

> 138 If a man divorces his wife who has not borne him children, he shall give her money to the amount of her marriage settlement, and he shall make good to her the dowry which she brought from her father's house and then he may divorce her.

Compare these laws to similar ones in the Bible, such as those in the book of Deuteronomy, and to our own legal system.

Development of the Palace In Sumerian times, the royal palace with its many courtyards was a more elaborate form of the private house. Although the king had the power to tax his people, in normal times he, like the gods, maintained himself and his court from the goods produced in royal workshops around the

1. **Entrance**
2. **Courtyards**
3. **Audience Hall**
4. **Royal Chapel**
5. **Archives**
6. **Throne Room**
7. **Courtyard and Royal Apartments**

N

0   50   100   200

1-12   *Plan of the royal palace complex at Mari (present-day Tel Nariri, Syria), c. 1775 B.C.*

palace and from his estates lying outside the wall. Because the territories governed by the individual Sumerian kings were diminutive and their tax base small, they did not have the resources to build great palaces, and the temple or ziggurat was the most important architectural feature of the city. During the reign of Sargon of Akkad and his successors (2340–2180 B.C.), the kingship achieved a new importance. By the time of the Babylonians, the increased powers of kingship were expressed in a palace architecture that rivaled the temple complex in its glorification of the sovereign.

The royal palace at Mari (Tel Hariri, Syria), built during the Old Babylonian period about 1775 B.C. (Fig. 1-12), shows a vast number of rooms arranged around three courtyards: one for public gatherings with access to a large audience hall, a second that was the focus for the archives and elaborately decorated throne room, and a third that was smaller and the focus of the private royal apartments. The complex borrowed much from the city form but was more orderly and hierarchical, providing a physical setting that reinforced the power of the king through security, inaccessibility, and regimentation of his contact with the public. Although the Mesopotamians never believed, as did the Egyptians, that the king was actually divine, they did come to believe that the institution of kingship was sent from the gods to humanity.

Assyria

The kingdom of Babylon lasted until about 1600 B.C., when it fell to the Hittites, invading from Syria. Recognized by its invaders as superior, however, the Mesopotamian culture remained strong throughout the following five-hundred-year period because it was embraced by its conquerors. The rise of Assyria between 1000 and 900 B.C. brought an end to Hittite domination over the region.

By contrast with the Babylonian kingdom in southern Mesopotamia, Assyria was located in the northern third of the plain, where sufficient rainfall obviated the need for irrigation. A land naturally hospitable to human life, Assyria still suffered from its proximity to the mountains. Perpetually open to attack from mountain tribes eager to seize booty, the Assyrian peasants had become as adroit at using the sword and bow as they were at the hoe and plow.

The new Assyrian kingdom, centered on Nineveh, used these peasant warriors to build one of the greatest empires of the ancient world. Within the previous thousand years, warfare in these regions had undergone several changes. The use of iron weapons, much stronger than bronze, became common. The horse appeared in Mesopotamia sometime shortly after 2000 B.C., making possible the creation of cavalry. The Hyksos (see Chapter 2, on Egypt) had, within a few centuries, tied the horse to a light cart to create the battle chariot.

Integrating these new inventions into a military force composed of hardy peasant warriors, Assyria set out to rule the world. Absolutely ruthless against their enemies, the Assyrians became the terror of the Middle East. When King Ashurnasirpal (883–859 B.C.) overcame a conspiracy of princes in Syria, for example, he made their punishment a public spectacle and boasted of its brutality:

> I built a pillar over against his city gate and I flayed all the chiefs who had revolted, and I covered the pillar with their skin. Some I walled up within the pillar, some I impaled upon the pillar on stakes, and others I bound to stakes round about the pillar.... And I cut the limbs of the officers, of the royal officers who had rebelled....
>
> Many captives from among them I burned with fire, and many I took as living captives. From some I cut off their noses, their fingers, of many I put out the eyes. I made one pillar of the living and another of the dead, and I bound their heads to tree trunks round about the city. Their young men and maidens I burned in the fire.[5]

They also conducted a policy of massive deportations, transferring Hittite mountain people to the southern desert regions of Syria and placing Syrians in the mountains. At its height, this terrifying power controlled an empire reaching from the Arabian Peninsula across Mesopotamia and including parts of Anatolia, all of Syria and Palestine, and a great part of Egypt.

Assyrian Palace Art   The palace of Sargon II at Khorsabad, built in the eighth century B.C., reveals the extent to which the palace building has become a passion with Mesopotamian rulers. The Assyrian palace is no longer a part of the city but is set adjacent to the city walls within its own walls and the ziggurat is reduced to an ornament within the complex (Fig. 1-13). The plan of the palace is very much like the one at Mari (Fig. 1-12). The approach to the palace is through the city, up a board ramp, across an open court, through a small passage, and into a court decorated with larger-than-life-size reliefs of the king and his court facing the long, narrow throne room. Here the throne sits on a base decorated with reliefs of the bodies of the victims of Sargon II.

The Assyrians also demonstrated their awe for king and conquest in the bas-reliefs that decorated

their palace. Assyrian court artists transformed the pictorial language of the Sumerians and the Babylonians into visual records of the conquests of their kings to adorn acres of limestone or alabaster palace walls. In these the whole apparatus of the Assyrian war machine can be studied as they appear like one comic strip above the other: archers, slingers, chariots, marching warriors, the sad parade of captives, and, on the bottom strip, the dead. Many of these reliefs are of uneven quality and can be monotonous, but not those of the royal lion hunt.

Ashurnasirpal II Killing Lions, from Nimrud (Calah), about 883–859 B.C., depicts a lion as heroic as the king (Fig. 1-14). Knowing that the lions were captured and let loose for this event does not tarnish the power with which the sculptor presents the scene. The profiled figures are carved in low relief, but this only enhances the energetic pose of the king with drawn bow that contrasts with the more regular upright warriors who advance in step behind the lion. The horses pull away, each nose just beyond the other, to leap over the recumbent wounded lion while another lion rears to attack. The power and energy of the event are further enhanced by the stylized, abstracted depiction of sinew and muscle in both man and beast.

Two hundred years later another court artist would create another lion hunt, this time at Nineveh. *The Dying Lioness* (c. 668–627 B.C.; Fig. 1-15) is an incredibly powerful image that arouses strong feelings of pathos. The artist has observed and recorded the lion's dead hindquarters and the head lifted in pain, but the presentation seems to represent all such noble animals. Other reliefs, like that of a *Herd of Fleeing Gazelles* (Fig. 1-16), produce a similar feeling, as if the artist empathizes with the animals as they flee from hunters.

Decline of Assyria   The power, the terror, and the armed might of the Assyrian empire did not prevent the recurrence of rebellions, and every Assyrian king spent most of his life waging either external or civil wars. Gradually, in the seventh century B.C., the rebels, aided by outside forces, were able successfully to detach pieces of the empire. The most effective group of allies were the Babylonians, whose homeland was in the southern part of Mesopotamia, and the Medes, a nomadic horse-riding people living on the high Persian plateau. Finally, in 612 B.C., the coalition successfully conquered and leveled Nineveh itself. The biblical prophet Ezekiel celebrated the destruction of Israel's oppressors, the Assyrians, by declaring "all of them slain, fallen by the sword which caused terror in the land of the living."

---

[5]In Georges Roux, *Ancient Iraq* (New York: Allen & Unwin, 1964), p. 2.

1-13 *Reconstructed view of the palace of Sargon II at Khorsabad, and plan of the inner palace precincts, c. 742–706 B.C.*

1. **Edge of Platform**
2. **Entrance**
3. **Entrance Court**
4. **Temples**
5. **Ziggurat**
6. **Court of Honor**
7. **Throne Room**

1-14   King Ashurnasirpal II Killing Lions, *from the Palace of King Ashurnasirpal II, Nimrud, c. 883–859* B.C., *alabaster relief, 39″ × 100″. (Reproduced by Courtesy of the Trustees of the British Museum)*

1-15   Dying Lioness *(detail of* The Great Lion Hunt*), from the Palace of King Ashurbanipal, Nineveh, c. 668–627* B.C., *alabaster relief, height 13¾″. (Reproduced by Courtesy of the Trustees of the British Museum)*

1-16 Herd of Fleeing Gazelles, *(detail of a relief) from the Palace of King Ashurbanipal, Nineveh, c. 668–627* B.C., *alabaster, height 20⅞". (Reproduced by Courtesy of the Trustees of the British Museum)*

The Second Babylonia

The allies divided the lands of Assyria between them: the Medes took all the territories east and north of the Tigris, and the Babylonians took the rest. With their capital located at a restored Babylon, it appeared that the Babylonians would be able to restore the ancient cultural domination exercised by previous Mesopotamian societies over much of the world. Babylonia's greatest king, Nebuchadnezzar II (604–562 B.C.), embellished the old city with great monuments, the greatest of which was a new palace for his Median wife. Rising to a height of about 350 feet, the building consisted of a series of vaulted terraces, each one of which, watered by a system of hydraulic pumps, supported trees and gardens. The city during these years numbered about one hundred thousand people and occupied an area of twenty-five hundred acres, about five times the size of ancient Athens at the height of its development in the fifth century B.C.

This was a history-conscious society, one that endeavored to restore the culture of the Sumerian, Akkadian, and Old Babylonian periods. It was also a progressive society that made marked advances in astronomy. In fact, the Babylonians' interest in creating a more accurate calendar and improving navigation by astronomical research laid the basis for the modern science of astronomy. Their use of some of the information for prophecy, however, was to connect the Chaldean name with astrology for the next two thousand years.

Babylonian Music

Cosmology was also important in Babylonian musical theory, for the association of gods and stars, the connection between astronomy and mathematics, and the significance of number and proportion in music gave rise to a music theory relating these elements. The holy instruments of the temple, especially the long-necked lute, had strings whose lengths were proportional to pitch. The scales and intervals also demonstrated mathematical precision. In Babylonia, temple schools for music developed alongside schools for other academic disciplines, and temple musicians were admitted to the profession only after about three years of instruction and rigorous examination. The musician was required to perform on a number of instruments, memorize sacred texts and melodies, and demonstrate a proficiency in Sumerian even after this language had become obsolete for everyday use.

The End of Mesopotamian Civilization

For all its glory, the new Babylonian kingdom was conquered by Cyrus of Persia in 550 B.C. The conquest of Babylon and the subjection of Mesopotamia to a new Persian power farther to the east marked the beginning of a new era. The river valleys of the Tigris and Euphrates, with their great mixture of different peoples, had for almost three thousand years been the generator of civilization for a large part of the world. Now having lost its political integrity, Mesopotamia ceased to be a creative force. Yet its cultural heritage had become an endowment for a vastly larger territory than that enclosed within the boundaries of its successive kingdoms. Mesopotamian building traditions, artistic conventions, legal, religious, and scientific ideas, and the art of writing became part of the resources of the other peoples dwelling near the Mediterranean Sea. Along with the other great early civilization—that of Egypt, to which we will turn in Chapter 2—Mesopotamia brought nourishment to the developing cultures of Crete, Greece, and their successors in the West.

READING SELECTION

FROM THE *Epic of Gilgamesh*

Translation by Maureen Gallery Kovacs

Since we will see similar journeys in the *Odyssey*, the *Aeneid*, and the *Divine Comedy*, we have chosen to focus on Gilgamesh's visit to the dwelling of the gods in the selections below. Refer to the introduction to and summary of *Gilgamesh* on pages 12–13.

Tablet I

The Legacy

He who has seen everything, I will make known to
    the lands.
I will teach about him who experienced all things . . .
Anu granted him the totality of knowledge of all.
He saw the Secret, discovered the Hidden,
he brought information of the time before the
    Flood.   5
He went on a distant journey, pushing himself to
    exhaustion,
but then was brought to peace.
He carved on a stone stela all of his toils,
and built the wall of Uruk-Haven,
the wall of the sacred Eanna Temple, the holy
    sanctuary.   10
Look at its wall which gleams like copper,
inspect its inner wall, the likes of which no one can
    equal!
Take hold of the threshold stone—it dates from
    ancient times!
Go close to the Eanna Temple, the residence of
    Ishtar, *Godess of Love + War*
such as no later king or man ever equaled!   15
Go up on the wall of Uruk and walk around,
examine its foundation, inspect its brickwork
    thoroughly.
Is not even the core of the brick structure made of
    kiln-fired brick,

and did not the Seven Sages themselves lay out its
    plans?
One league city, one league palm gardens, one league
    lowlands, the open area of the Ishtar Temple,   20
three leagues and the open area of Uruk the wall
    encloses.
Find the copper tablet box,
open . . . its lock of bronze,
undo the fastening of its secret opening.
Take and read out from the lapis lazuli tablet   25
how Gilgamesh went through every hardship.

Gilgamesh

Supreme over other kings, lordly in appearance,
he is the hero, born of Uruk, the goring wild bull.
He walks out in front, the leader,
and walks at the rear, trusted by his companions.   30
Mighty net, protector of his people,
raging flood-wave who destroys even walls of stone!
Offspring of Lugalbanda, Gilgamesh is strong to
    perfection,
son of the august cow, Rimat-Ninsun, . . . Gilgamesh
    is awesome to perfection.
It was he who opened the mountain passes,   35
who dug wells on the flank of the mountain.
It was he who crossed the ocean, the vast seas, to the
    rising sun,
who explored the world regions, seeking life.
It was he who reached by his own sheer strength
    Utanapishtim, the Faraway,
who restored the sanctuaries (or: cities) that the
    Flood had destroyed!   40
. . . for teeming mankind.
Who can compare with him in kingliness?
Who can say like Gilgamesh: "I am King!"?
Whose name, from the day of his birth, was called
    "Gilgamesh"?
Two-thirds of him is god, one-third of him is
    human.   45
The Great Goddess [Aruru] designed the model for
    his body,

she prepared his form...
...beautiful, handsomest of men,
...perfect...

Tablet IX

[after the death of Enkidu]

The Quest

Over his friend, Enkidu, Gilgamesh cried bitterly,
   roaming the wilderness.
     "I am going to die!—am I not like Enkidu?!
     Deep sadness penetrates my core,
     I fear death, and now roam the wilderness—
     I will set out to the region of Utanapishtim, son
       of Ubartutu, and will go with utmost
       dispatch!   5
     When I arrived at mountain passes at nightfall,
     I saw lions, and I was terrified!
     I raised my head in prayer to Sin,
     to...the Great Lady of the gods my
       supplications poured forth, 'Save me...!'"

The Scorpion-Beings

The mountain is called Mashu.   10
When he reached Mount Mashu,
which daily guards the rising and setting of the Sun,
above which only the dome of the heavens reaches,
and whose flank reaches as far as the Netherworld
   below,
there were Scorpion-beings watching over its gate.
Trembling terror they inspire, the sight of them is
   death,   15
their frightening aura sweeps over the mountains.
At the rising and setting they watch over the Sun.
When Gilgamesh saw them, trembling terror
   blanketed his face,
but he pulled himself together and drew near to
   them.
The scorpion-being called out to his female: 20
     "He who comes to us, his body is the flesh of
       gods!"
The scorpion-being, his female, answered him:
     "(Only) two-thirds of him is a god, one-third is
       human."
The male scorpion-being called out,
saying to the offspring of the gods: 25
     "Why have you traveled so distant a journey?

Why have you come here to me,
   over rivers whose crossing is treacherous?
I want to learn your..."
...

[26 lines are missing here. When the text resumes
Gilgamesh is speaking.]

     "I have come on account of my ancestor
       Utanapishtim,   30
     who joined the Assembly of the Gods, and was
       given eternal life.
     About Death and Life I must ask him!"
The scorpion-being spoke to Gilgamesh..., saying:
     "Never has there been, Gilgamesh, a mortal
       man who could do that.
     No one has crossed through the mountains,   35
     for twelve leagues it is darkness throughout—
     dense is the darkness, and light there is none...."

[67 lines are missing, in which Gilgamesh convinces the scorpion-being to allow him passage.]

     "Though it be in deep sadness and pain,
     in cold or heat...
     gasping after breath...I will go on!   40
     Now! Open the Gate!"
The scorpion-being spoke to Gilgamesh, saying:
     "Go on, Gilgamesh, fear not!
     The Mashu mountains I give to you freely,
     the mountains, the ranges, you may
       traverse...   45
     In safety may your feet carry you...."

The Journey Through the Night

...As soon as Gilgamesh heard this
he heeded the utterances of the scorpion-being.
Along the Road of the Sun° he journeyed—
one league he traveled...,   50
dense was the darkness, light there was none.
Neither what lies ahead nor behind does it allow
   him to see....

[Gilgamesh travels for ten leagues in darkness.]

---

⁴⁹The Road of the Sun refers to the course of the sun through the
Netherworld at night.

Eleven leagues he traveled and came out before the
sun(rise).
Twelve leagues he traveled and it grew brilliant.

The Jeweled Garden

Before him there were trees of precious stones,   55
and he went straight to look at them.
The tree bears carnelian as its fruit,
laden with clusters (of jewels), dazzling to behold,
—it bears lapis lazuli as foliage,
bearing fruit, a delight to look upon.   60

Tablet X

The Tavern-Keeper by the Sea

The tavern-keeper Siduri who lives by the
seashore,...
She is covered with a veil...
Gilgamesh was roving about...
wearing a skin,...
having the flesh of the gods in his body,   5
but sadness deep within him,
looking like one who has been traveling a long
distance.
The tavern-keeper was gazing off into the distance,
puzzling to herself, she said,
wondering to herself: 10
    "That fellow is surely a murderer!
    Where is he heading?..."
As soon as the tavern-keeper saw him, she bolted her
door,
bolted her gate, bolted the lock.
But at her noise Gilgamesh pricked up his ears,   15
lifted his chin (to look about) and then laid his eyes
on her.
Gilgamesh spoke to the tavern-keeper, saying:
    "Tavern-keeper, what have you seen that made
    you bolt your door,
      bolt your gate, bolt the lock?
    If you do not let me in I will break your door,
    and smash the lock!..."   20
Gilgamesh said to the tavern-keeper:
    "I am Gilgamesh, I killed the Guardian!
    I destroyed Humbaba who lived in the Cedar
      Forest,
    I slew lions in the mountain passes!
    I grappled with the Bull that came down from
      heaven, and killed him."   25
The tavern-keeper spoke to Gilgamesh, saying:
    "If you are Gilgamesh, who killed the Guardian,

who destroyed Humbaba who lived in the
    Cedar Forest,
who slew lions in the mountain passes,
who grappled with the Bull that came down
    from heaven, and killed him,   30
why are your cheeks emaciated, your expression
    desolate?
Why is your heart so wretched, your features so
    haggard?
Why is there such sadness deep within you?
Why do you look like one who has been
    traveling a long distance
so that ice and heat have seared your face?   35
...you roam the wilderness?"°
Gilgamesh spoke to her, to the tavern-keeper he
said:
    "Tavern-keeper, should not my cheeks be
    emaciated?
    Should my heart not be wretched, my features
    not haggard?
    Should there not be sadness deep within me?   40

    Should I not look like one who has been
    traveling a long distance,
    and should ice and heat not have seared my
    face?
    ..., should I not roam the wilderness?
    My friend, the wild ass who chased the wild
    donkey, panther of the wilderness,
    Enkidu, the wild ass who chased the wild
    donkey, panther of the wilderness,   45
    we joined together, and went up into the
    mountain.
    We grappled with and killed the Bull of Heaven,

36In the Old Babylonian version, the tavern-keeper offers her
insights on the true goal of life, which is not to escape death, but
to enjoy the normal, if transitory, pleasures of life.
    "Gilgamesh, where are you wandering?
    The life that you are seeking all around you will not find.
    When the gods created mankind
    they fixed Death for mankind,
    and held back Life in their own hands.
    Now you, Gilgamesh, let your belly be full!
    Be happy day and night,
    of each day make a party,
    dance in circles day and night!
    Let your clothes be sparkling clean,
    let your head be clean, wash yourself with water!
    Attend to the little one who holds onto your hand,
    let a wife delight in your embrace.
    This is the (true) task of *mankind*."
(Some restore the last words differently, as "this is the task of
womankind," and take it to refer to intercourse as the natural duty
of women, as it was for the harlot in Tablet I.)

we destroyed Humbaba who lived in the Cedar
  Forest,
we slew lions in the mountain passes!
My friend, whom I love deeply, who went
  through every hardship with me,   50
Enkidu, whom I love deeply, who went through
  every hardship with me,
the fate of mankind has overtaken him.
Six days and seven nights I mourned over him
and would not allow him to be buried
until a maggot fell out of his nose.   55
I was terrified by his appearance,
I began to fear death, and so roam the
  wilderness.
The issue of my friend oppresses me,
so I have been roaming long trails through the
  wilderness.
The issue of Enkidu, my friend, oppresses me, 60
so I have been roaming long roads through the
  wilderness.
How can I stay silent, how can I be still?
My friend whom I love has turned to clay.
Am I not like him? Will I lie down, never to get
  up again?"
Gilgamesh spoke to the tavern-keeper, saying: 65
  "So now, tavern-keeper, what is the way to
    Utanapishtim?
  What are its markers? Give them to me! Give
    me the markers!
  If possible, I will cross the sea;
  if not, I will roam through the wilderness."
The tavern-keeper spoke to Gilgamesh, saying: 70
  "There has never been, Gilgamesh, any passage
    whatever,
  there has never been anyone since days of yore
    who crossed the sea.
  The (only) one who crosses the sea is valiant
    Shamash, except for him who can cross?
  The crossing is difficult, its ways are
    treacherous—
  and in between are the Waters of Death that bar
    its approaches!   75
  And even if, Gilgamesh, you should cross the
    sea,
  when you reach the Waters of Death what
    would you do?
  Gilgamesh, over there is Urshanabi, the
    ferryman of Utanapishtim.
  . . .
  Go on, let him see your face.
  If possible, cross with him;   80
  if not, you should turn back."

[Gilgamesh convinces the ferryman to take him.]

The Waters of Death

. . .
Gilgamesh and Urshanabi boarded the boat,
Gilgamesh launched the *magillu*-boat° and they
  sailed away.
By the third day they had traveled a stretch of a
  month and a half, and
Urshanabi arrived at the Waters of Death.   85
Urshanabi said to Gilgamesh:
  "Hold back, Gilgamesh, take a punting pole,
    but your hand must not pass over the Waters
    of Death . . . !
  Take a second, Gilgamesh, a third, and a fourth
    pole,
  take a fifth, Gilgamesh, a sixth, and a seventh
    pole,   90
  take an eighth, Gilgamesh, a ninth, and a tenth
    pole,
  take an eleventh, Gilgamesh, and a twelfth
    pole!"
In twice 60 rods Gilgamesh had used up the punting
  poles.
Then he loosened his waist-cloth . . .
Gilgamesh stripped off his garment   95
and held it up on the mast with his arms.

[Gilgamesh comes to Utanapishtim, who asks him
the same questions as the tavern keeper. Gilgamesh
gives the same answers. See pages 23–24.]

. . .
  "Enkidu, my friend whom I love, has turned to
    clay!
  Am I not like him? Will I lie down never to get
    up again?"
Gilgamesh spoke to Utanapishtim, saying:
  "That is why I must go on, to see Utanapishtim
    whom they call 'The Faraway.'°   100
  I went circling through all the mountains,
  I traversed treacherous mountains, and crossed
    all the seas—
  that is why sweet sleep has not mellowed my
    face,
  through sleepless striving I am strained,
  my muscles are filled with pain.   105
  I had not yet reached the tavern-keeper's area

---

83 *Magillu* is the name of a boat taken from mythology.

100 Apparently Gilgamesh has not yet realized that he is already
talking with Utanapishtim, whom he expected to look very
different from an ordinary human being. It is only after Utanapishtim's soliloquy on death that Gilgamesh realizes whom he
is speaking to.

before my clothing gave out.
　I killed bear, hyena, lion, panther, tiger, stag,
　　red-stag, and beasts of the wilderness;
　I ate their meat and wrapped their skins around
　　me...."
Utanapishtim spoke to Gilgamesh, saying:
　...
　You have toiled without cease, and what have
　　you got?...   110
　Through toil you wear yourself out,
　you fill your body with grief,
　your long lifetime you are bringing near (to a
　　premature end)
　No one can see death,
　no one can see the face of death,   115
　no one can hear the voice of death,
　yet there is savage death that snaps off
　　mankind.
　For how long do we build a household?
　For how long do we seal a document?
　For how long do brothers share the
　　inheritance?   120
　For how long is there to be jealousy in the land?
　For how long has the river risen and brought
　　the overflowing waters,
　so that dragonflies drift down the river?
　The face that could gaze upon the face of the
　　Sun
　has never existed ever.   125
　How alike are the sleeping and the dead.
　The image of Death cannot be depicted.
　Yes, you are a human being, a man!
　After Enlil had pronounced the blessing,°
　the Anunnaki, the Great Gods, assembled.   130
　Mammetum, she who fashions destiny,
　　determined destiny with them.
　They established Death and Life,
　but they did not make known 'the days of
　　death.'"°

[Utanapishtim now tells the story of the Flood,
explaining how he escaped from death.]

---

¹²⁹Finishing his soliloquy on life and death, Utanapishtim here
　reveals how death came to be the fate of mankind, and implicitly
　how Utanapishtim himself was spared. This is apparently the
　"secret of the gods" that Gilgamesh has been seeking. These last
　five lines refer to the "Myth of Atrahasis" (Atrahasis = Uta-
　napishtim), in which Enlil grudgingly allows the pious Atrahasis,
　who escaped the Flood, to live for eternity, but Enlil and the
　other gods then establish death for all other humans as a neces-
　sary means of population control. The Flood story is retold at
　length in Tablet XI.
¹³³The "days of death" probably means the day on which an
　individual's death will occur, although some interpret the line to
　mean "they did not fix a limit to death."

Tablet XI

A Second Chance at Life

The wife of Utanapishtim the Faraway said to him:
　"Gilgamesh came here exhausted and worn out.
　　What can you give him so that he can return to
　　his land (with honor)?"
Then Gilgamesh raised a punting pole
and drew the boat to shore.   5
Utanapishtim spoke to Gilgamesh, saying:
　"Gilgamesh, you came here exhausted and worn
　　out.
　What can I give you so you can return to your
　　land?
　I will disclose to you a thing that is hidden,
　　Gilgamesh,
　...
　There is a plant...like a boxthorn,   10
　whose thorns will prick your hand like a rose.
　If your hands reach that plant you will become
　　a young man again."
Hearing this, Gilgamesh opened a conduit...
and attached heavy stones to his feet.
They dragged him down, to the Apsu° they pulled
　him.   15
He took the plant, though it pricked his hand,
and cut the heavy stones from his feet,
letting the waves throw him onto its shores.
Gilgamesh spoke to Urshanabi, the ferryman,
　saying:
　"Urshanabi, this plant is a plant against
　　decay   20
　by which a man can attain his survival
　I will bring it to Uruk-Haven,
　and have an old man eat the plant to test it.
　The plant's name is 'The Old Man Becomes a
　　Young Man.'°
　Then I will eat it and return to the condition of
　　my youth."   25
At twenty leagues they broke for some food,
at thirty leagues they stopped for the night.
Seeing a spring and how cool its waters were,
Gilgamesh went down and was bathing in the
　water.
A snake smelled the fragrance of the plant,   30
silently came up and carried off the plant.
While going back it sloughed off its casing.
At that point Gilgamesh sat down, weeping,
his tears streaming over the side of his nose.

---

¹⁵Abyss(?).
²⁴The same as the apparent meaning of the name "Gilgamesh."

"Counsel me, O ferryman Urshanabi!   35
For whom have my arms labored, Urshanabi?
For whom has my heart's blood roiled?
I have not secured any good deed for myself,
but done a good deed for the 'lion of the
    ground'!°

Deeds over Death

...
At twenty leagues they broke for some food,   40
at thirty leagues they stopped for the night.
They arrived in Uruk-Haven.
Gilgamesh said to Urshanabi, the ferryman:
    "Go up, Urshanabi, onto the wall of Uruk and
        walk around.
    Examine its foundation, inspect its brickwork
        thoroughly—   45
    is not (even the core of) the brick structure of
        kiln-fired brick,
    and did not the Seven Sages themselves lay out
        its plan?
    One league city, one league palm gardens, one
        league lowlands, the open area of the Ishtar
        Temple,
    three leagues and the open area of Uruk the
        wall encloses."

COMMENTS AND QUESTIONS

1. The Western *epic* traditionally begins by describing the theme and stating the story the poet intends to tell. Does this apply to *Gilgamesh?*

2. Another characteristic of the *epic* is that it begins *in medias res,* in the "middle of things," rather than, like the folk tale or myth, at the beginning, or "once upon a time." Is this true of *Gilgamesh?*

3. What does the description of Uruk indicate about the Mesopotamian attitude toward cities?

4. We cannot know if Gilgamesh stories were told orally before they were written down, but it seems probable. We are fairly certain that this was the case with the Homeric epics. Repetitions of key words and phrases and the use of *epithets,* or adjectival phrases defining a character, may indicate orality. What effect does the repeated description of Gilgamesh's condition during his grief produce in the written text?

5. Describe the world of the gods that Gilgamesh enters. Can you attribute any symbolic value to the creatures that he encounters?

6. What is the role of women as goddesses and priestesses here? Note that, contrary to the Adam and Eve story, it is the male who makes the mistake that loses eternal life. (Gilgamesh loses the plant.) What accounts for this?

7. What is the "lesson" that Gilgamesh learns from Utanapishtim?

8. What is the effect of repeating the description of the city in the first and last tablets?

9. Some readers, comparing *Gilgamesh* to other epics, consider it pessimistic or depressing because Gilgamesh's grief is not consoled by a faith in life after death. Others consider it life-affirming, and close to modern concerns, because Gilgamesh after his painful quest learns the value of life on earth. What is your opinion?

---

³⁹This scene is an etiological story of how the snake came to shed its old skin—after eating a "plant of rejuvenation."

Egypt and the Kingdom of Kush

While Mesopotamia was the product of two rivers, the Tigris and Euphrates, Egypt, in the words of the fifth-century B.C. Greek historian Herodotus, was "the gift of the Nile." Although settlement along the Nile developed fairly early, population on its banks began to rise significantly only in the sixth millennium as the Sahara region, hitherto a land of lakes and forests, became increasingly dry. Over the next two thousand years, during which the desiccation of the Sahara steadily increased, most of its former inhabitants scattered in different directions. Some groups moved into moister areas toward the south. Others moved east as far as the Nile valley. Still others pushed north into Syria and Palestine and further east into Mesopotamia. In this last region late in the fourth millennium it was these people, identified in the previous chapter as Semites, who joined with the Sumerians coming from the east to build the first cities.

The Nile

The Nile proved even more favorable for human habitation than the Euphrates and the Tigris. Rising deep in the African highlands in Uganda and Ethiopia, the river travels 4,000 miles north to the Mediterranean Sea. In its last 675 miles it creates the land of Egypt. Beginning at the first cataract at Aswan, the river descends slowly for 500 miles to Memphis (near modern Cairo), where it divides into many shallow branches, growing ever wider and shallower through a 60-mile-wide marsh until its many mouths empty into the Mediterranean (see map). Unlike its Mesopotamian counterparts, the Nile moves calmly, making navigation easy. Boats going north toward the Mediterranean are carried along by the current, and those going south use the wind to face the water's flow. Also, whereas the Mesopotamian rivers often crest when the planting season has passed, destroying crops in the fields, the annual flooding of the Nile begins at about the same time each summer and, unlike the rise of the Tigris and Euphrates rivers, that of the Nile is generally not destructive.

The predictability of the inundation was crucial to the rise of Egyptian civilization. It made agriculture nearly effortless, for each year, as the flood receded at planting time, a fresh layer of rich silt was left on the fields. Seeds were scattered on the nutrient-rich banks, and very little effort was required to produce several crops each year. In contrast to Mesopotamia, the Nile valley did not experience problems with sanitization or nutrient depletion of the agricultural lands.

However, the annual inundation of the Nile may actually have delayed the development of agriculture there by comparison with Mesopotamia. The natural supply of fish, wild animals, and wild grains was so rich that people did not need to work hard to feed themselves. Only as population became more dense along the river, with the increasing immigration from the Sahara after 5000 B.C., were collective efforts undertaken, as in Mesopotamia a few centuries earlier, to construct dikes and canals both to direct water to the fields and to preserve it as long as possible.

The First and Second Dynasties (3150–2686 B.C.)

Protected from hostile intrusions by deserts stretching off to the east and west, by the Mediterranean to the north and the river cataracts to the south, Egypt enjoyed long periods of tranquillity denied the Sumerian states, periods that allowed it to work out its own destiny. Because easy navigation of the river gave access to the whole country bordering the Nile, central government rose there early. Several centuries before 3000 B.C. the settlements along the river became divided into two countries ruled by separate kings: Upper Egypt, which began at the first cataract and ran north as far as Memphis, and Lower Egypt, taking in the area from Memphis to the sea. By about 3150 B.C. the whole length of the river lay under the control of a certain Menes, the founder of the First Dynasty of Egyptian pharaohs, who, uniting the country, established his government at Memphis near the border between Upper and Lower Egypt. Thus, five hundred years before Sargon (2371–2316 B.C.) unified Mesopotamia, Egypt had a central government with a single capital for the whole country.

From the earliest period, the pharaoh, as ruler of Egypt, was considered to be the protector of natural forces such as the Nile inundation, rain, fertility, and other aspects of life. His personal welfare was so intimately tied to the welfare of the whole society that his will deserved unquestioned obedience. Although the identification of his divine parentage changed over time, in the early period no one disputed that he was himself a god. Early Mesopotamian rulers, whose original powers arose out of a popular assembly, could well envy the Egyptian pharaohs, and even later, when royal absolutism became accepted in Mesopotamia, a tradition of the divinity of the ruler never took deep root.

Egyptian Historical Periods

Around 300 B.C. an Egyptian priest, Manetho, divided Egyptian history into thirty dynasties, but most of the divisions are arbitrary and do not reflect any real change. For example, the kings of the Fourth and Fifth dynasties are certainly of the same family and tradition, and there is no apparent reason to make a division between the two periods. Modern historians group the dynasties into larger periods called "kingdoms." Each of the three kingdoms is separated by an "intermediate period." The following major divisions are treated in this book:

> The Archaic Period (Dynasties 1–2, 3150–2686 B.C.)
>
> The Old Kingdom (Dynasties 3–6, 2686–2181 B.C.)
>
> The First Intermediate Period (Dynasties 7–11, 2181–2134 B.C.)
>
> The Middle Kingdom (Dynasty 12, 2134–1782 B.C.)
>
> The Second Intermediate Period (Dynasties 13–17, 1782–1570 B.C.)
>
> The New Kingdom (Dynasties 18–20, 1570–1070 B.C.)
>
> The Third Intermediate Period (Dynasties 21–25, 1070–664 B.C.)
>
> The Late Period (Dynasties 26–31, 664–332 B.C.)
>
> The Ptolemaic Period (Dynasties 27–30, 332–30 B.C.)

The Old Kingdom (2686–2181 B.C.)

Few specific historical events are known about the history of Egypt before the Third Dynasty, but from this time records become numerous. Egyptian society

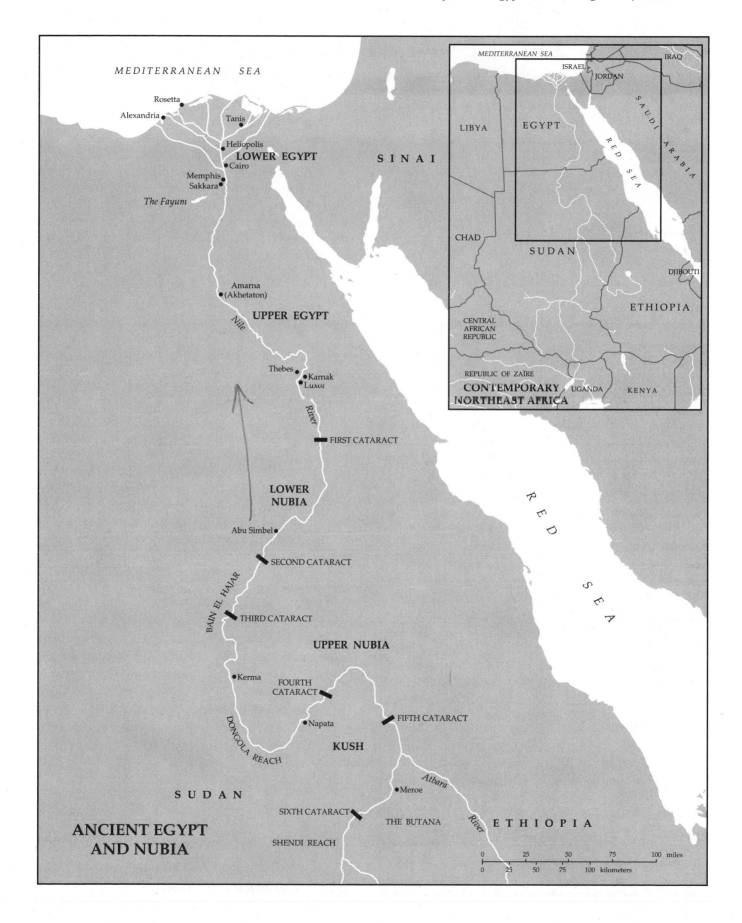

MEDITERRANEAN   SEA

Rosetta

Alexandria

Tanis

Heliopolis

LOWER EGYPT

Cairo

Memphis

Sakkara

The Fayum

Nile

Amarna
(Akhetaton)

UPPER EGYPT

Thebes

Karnak

Luxor

River

FIRST CATARACT

**LOWER
NUBIA**

Abu Simbel

SECOND CATARACT

BAIN EL HAJAR

THIRD CATARACT

UPPER NUBIA

Kerma

FOURTH
CATARACT

FIFTH CATARACT

DONGOLA REACH

Napata

KUSH

Atbara

Meroe

SUDAN

SIXTH CATARACT

THE BUTANA

River

**ANCIENT EGYPT
AND NUBIA**

SHENDI REACH

S I N A I

ETHIOPIA

R
E
D

S
E
A

MEDITERRANEAN SEA

ISRAEL

JORDAN

IRAQ

LIBYA

EGYPT

SAUDI
ARABIA

RED SEA

CHAD

SUDAN

DJIBOUTI

CENTRAL
AFRICAN
REPUBLIC

ETHIOPIA

REPUBLIC OF ZAÏRE

UGANDA

KENYA

**CONTEMPORARY
NORTHEAST AFRICA**

0   25   50   75   100 miles

0   25   50   75   100 kilometers

was closely governed by the pharaoh's officials who were charged with justice, management of water and food resources, collecting taxes, and keeping royal records. Both Upper and Lower Egypt were divided into administrative units called *nomes,* each headed by a *nomarch,* whose office was hereditary. Finally, all aspects of government activity were coordinated by a powerful official called the *vizier.* Initially a prince of the royal blood, by the Third Dynasty this official could be chosen from among the ranks of the nobility.

Egyptian Writing

An administrative organization as complex as that of ancient Egypt would have been impossible to maintain had it not been for the existence of writing and teams of scribes to staff the various departments. Like the Mesopotamians, the Egyptians seem to have first used writing as a practical means of recording historical events and government and business transactions and, later, for scientific and literary purposes. The Egyptians developed three forms of writing. These were later named by the Greeks (and the English words have retained the Greek origins) *hieroglyphic, hieratic,* and *demotic* (Fig. 2-1). Hieroglyphics began as a form of picture writing, but eventually a hieroglyphic symbol could represent a letter, a sound, a whole idea, or all three. The elaborate hieroglyphs, which were time-

consuming to write, were reserved for formal uses, such as inscriptions on temples and tombs and for some literary and religious texts. A simplified cursive form, called hieratic, was employed for everyday use because it could be written more rapidly. Hieratic was rarely used on stone surfaces, but was common on papyrus and flakes of pottery or stone called *ostraca,* which were the ancient equivalent of scratch paper.

In the three thousand years that the ancient Egyptian language was employed, the language underwent many changes. By 600 B.C. the demotic script, or the people's script (from the Greek *demos,* for "people"), was employed. It is very cursive, and although the language is essentially a close variant of that written in hieroglyphs, six new letters that expressed sounds in the Greek alphabet were added to the Egyptian signs. This was necessary, for in that time Egypt was in contact with Greece, and scribes had to write Greek personal names and titles in Egyptian records. An even later form of the Egyptian language, Coptic, is written in Greek letters. It is still employed as the liturgical language of the Egyptian Christian (Coptic) church.

It was not until 1822 that moderns were able to translate the ancient Egyptian language. In that year a young French scholar, Jean-François Champollion, published his research on the inscriptions that are engraved on the Rosetta Stone (Fig. 2-2). This slab of basalt is incised with a temple decree written in Greek and in hieroglyphic and demotic Egyptian scripts. Champollion was the first to recognize that the three scripts contained the same message. By matching up often-repeating words, he was able to determine the phonetic value of many of the demotic and then the hieroglyphic signs. From that time, the study of Egyptology flourished as the words of the ancient Egyptians came to life.

As in Mesopotamia, most Egyptian writing was done by scribes who attended special schools. Although most of the student scribes were from wealthy families and most were boys, there were exceptions, and being literate was the key to social advancement. The strictness of the schools is evident from this piece of advice given to a student: "O scribe, don't be idle, or you will be punished straightaway. Don't give your heart to pleasures, or you will fail. Write with your hand, recite with your mouth, and speak with those more knowledgeable than you. Don't be idle or you will be beaten. The youth has ears on his back and he hears when he is beaten. Pay attention!" Another papyrus advises the student on the advantages of being a scribe. "Your body will be sleek; your hand will be soft.... You call for one; a thousand answer you. You

2-1 *Three forms of Egyptian writing. (From G. Möller, in* Zeitschrift des Deutschen Vereins für Buchwesen und Schrifttum, *ii, 1919, 78)*

HIEROGLYPHIC					HIEROGLYPHIC BOOK-SCRIPT	HIERATIC			DEMOTIC
2900-2800 B.C.	2700-2800 B.C.	2000-1800 B.C.	c.1500 B.C.	500-100 B.C.	c.1500 B.C.	c.1900 B.C.	c.1300 B.C.	c.200 B.C.	400-100 B.C.

2-2 *The Rosetta Stone, Egyptian, 196 B.C., British Museum, London. (Bildarchiv Preussischer Kulturbesitz, Berlin)*

stride freely on the road. You will not be like a hired ox. You are in front of others."[1]

Scribes learned to write with reed pens dipped in colored pigment or in an ink made of soot. *Papyrus*, a paperlike substance made of overlapped fibers, was used, but since it was expensive its use was reserved for purposes such as official documents and funerary texts. More frequently, scribes wrote on flat flakes of limestone or broken bits of pottery. Scribes were a very important element in society, for literacy was highly valued in ancient Egypt. Scribes were employed by the local and central governments, and they would hire themselves out to write personal letters and to compose lengthy biographies and prayers that might be carved in stone tombs or on statues.

Egyptian Religion

Egyptian religious beliefs are very complex and difficult to understand because there were hundreds of

---

[1]Miriam Lichtheim, ed., *Ancient Egyptian Literature: A Book of Readings*, vol. 2: *The New Kingdom* (Berkeley: University of California Press, 1976), p. 171.

gods, and these gods combined temporarily to form other deities. So, too, the real "power" or association of some of the important gods is unclear. Specific gods rose in importance in certain times and then retreated into relative obscurity in other years.

Another difficulty is that the Egyptian religious beliefs grew through accretion rather than through evolution. In other words, no beliefs were discarded, but they were added to or kept alongside other seemingly contradictory beliefs. For example, there are several myths about the creation of the gods and people because the Egyptians' fluid religious beliefs admitted each equally, rather than replacing one with another.

A further feature of the Egyptian pantheon is that although gods were created by combining one god with another, such as the fusion of Amon (also spelled Amen or Amun) and Ra (Re) to become Amon-Ra, the same general cast of gods was revered for the three thousand years of Egyptian history. When the Greeks conquered Egypt, in 332 B.C. with Alexander the Great, many Egyptian gods were adopted by the Greeks. For example, the Greek god Hermes was associated with the ancient Egyptian god Thoth, a god of writing and wisdom.

A major characteristic of Egyptian gods is their generally benevolent nature. In general, the ancient Egyptians did not fear their gods, as was often the case in Mesopotamia. We have many letters and hymns that express the comfort that the gods gave to worshipers. The oldest Egyptian gods were protectors of particular cities or provinces, and these continued to be worshiped throughout Egyptian history. Among these early gods was the sun god Ra (Color Plate III), whose earliest cult center was at Heliopolis, near modern Cairo. In the Heliopolitan myth of creation it is recorded that Ra created himself out of his mother, Nun, the primordial waters. He then created the air god Shu, the moisture goddess Tefnut, the earth god Geb, and the sky goddess Nut. From Geb and Nut were born gods and goddesses in human form: Set, Nephthys, Osiris, and Isis.

Ra was among the most important gods in the Old Kingdom, and the religious beliefs surrounding the king were based on the solar theology of that god. By the middle of the Old Kingdom (Fourth Dynasty), the belief that the pharaoh was semidivine was firmly established, and a primary title of the king from that time onward was the "son of Ra."

However, this was only one aspect of the divine associations of the king. From the very earliest time, the living king was associated with the falcon god Horus. On his death he was equated with the god Osiris, the father of Horus. In this way, the royal succession was enforced by myth, for each new king, whether or not he was actually related to his predecessor by birth, succeeded his father as the new Osiris. In that fashion the ancient Egyptians created a myth that there had been a single line of kings in orderly succession for most of Egypt's history.

The myths surrounding Horus and Osiris entered into other aspects of religion and morality as well. The legend recounts that Osiris was the first king of Egypt. According to the legend, Set, the brother of Osiris, killed the king, dismembered his body, and cast the pieces into the Nile. Osiris' faithful wife, Isis, collected the pieces, wrapped them as a mummy, and later conceived their son, Horus. This story became the basis not only for the family relationship of Horus and Osiris, which was associated with the king, but also for a model for the Egyptian family and role models of the dutiful wife and son. The characteristic fertility of Osiris, who was able to engender a son even after his death, gave rise to the idea of Osiris as the god of fertility and rebirth.

The Afterlife   One of the most important religious implications of the Osirian myth was the promise of personal immortality. From the Old Kingdom onward through Egyptian history, it was thought that on death, one became equated with the god Osiris, and like that god, the individual was reborn again in the afterlife. Several requirements, however, had to be met for this rebirth. The spirit of the deceased had to pass a judgment before the tribunal of the gods to prove that the soul (envisioned as the human heart) was free from sin. He or she had to recite a long "negative confession" containing statements such as "I did not harm anyone" and "I did not defy any god." The next procedure was for the person's heart to be weighed against the feather of Maat, goddess of truth. If the scale did not balance, the person would be devoured by the monster Ammit and die a permanent death, but if it did balance, he or she would be admitted to the presence of Isis and Osiris and live forever.

Egyptian faith in the afterlife contrasts sharply with that of the Mesopotamians for whom even Gilgamesh, part divine, faced extinction with the death of his body. No other aspect of the Egyptian mentality is more important in understanding the culture of this civilization of the Nile than its confidence that the spirit survived death. The Egyptian Book of the Dead contains a wealth of rituals and secret magic formulas to help individuals pass into the afterlife.

2-3   Imhotep. *Funerary complex of King Zoser with step pyramid, Saqqara, c. 2750 B.C., limestone. (Art Resource, NY)*

Pyramids: The Zoser Pyramid Complex

When compared with the closely grouped cities of contemporary Mesopotamia, the cities of Egypt lay widely separated from one another along the Nile. Although tremendous resources were lavished on the palaces of the Old Kingdom, these structures, built of mudbrick, have not survived. On the other hand, the pyramids, built of stone, continue to testify to the appropriateness of the title given them in antiquity as "first great wonder of the world."

While the ziggurat at Ur was a temple that replicated a mountain for access to the gods (Chapter 1, Fig. 1-2), the stepped pyramid at Saqqara was a tomb for the Old Kingdom pharaoh Zoser (Fig. 2-3). It stood at the heart of a vast necropolis site surrounded by many nonroyal tombs. Like the ziggurat, the pyramid had its origins in a traditional building vocabulary of mudbrick, reeds, and timber. Zoser's complex, however, was built of limestone, and the architect's name, Imhotep, was chiseled on a statue base. Notice other comparisons and contrasts between Mesopotamian and Egyptian architecture as you study the pyramids. What do these say about the values and beliefs of the two ancient civilizations?

Prior to the building of the pyramid complex of King Zoser, the typical tomb was a simple pit in the ground, which was then covered over with a mound of earth. This mound over the burial evolved into a rectangular or squarish superstructure called a *mastaba* (Arabic for "bench"). In the early Old Kingdom, bench-shaped mastabas became more and more elaborate, and the once-simple mound over the burial mound developed into a houselike structure with rooms decorated with funerary offering scenes. The activities in these scenes were thought to be able to provide the deceased with provisions in the afterlife. Most mastabas had special chambers where a stone or wooden statue of the deceased was stored, and a funerary chapel for the spirit (*ka*) of the deceased.

A major innovation of the Zoser complex is the form of the king's tomb. Prior to this time, tombs were built in the bench-shaped mastaba. The tomb of King Zoser was originally in this form, with underground passages for the burial of the king and his family. However, his chief architect and chief administrator (vizier), Imhotep, is credited with elaborating on the mastaba, stacking mastaba on mastaba to form a stepped pyramid.

King Zoser's tomb is composed of the pyramid resting on a terrace surrounded by buildings and enclosed within a stone wall, originally thirty-three feet high and nearly a third of a mile around (Fig. 2-4). The complex is something like a huge movie set, for although there are many buildings within the walls of the complex, they are all false fronts, and although they have doors, they are only representations of doors. It is thought that all these buildings were to serve the spirit of the king in the afterlife. The complex was built to commemorate the worship and memory of the king after his death and to make it possible for the king to enact rituals of renewal in the afterlife.

The true pyramid evolved from the design of Zoser's stepped pyramid tomb. The best-known true pyramids are the tombs of Cheops, Chephren, and Mycerinus (c. 2600–2500 B.C.). These tombs, a few miles north of Saqqara, were not isolated, for they stood in the middle of a vast necropolis of mastaba tombs built for the royal family and administrators. The royal pyramid was only one part of the royal tomb complex, which was composed of a mortuary temple on the east side and a long, covered causeway leading to another valley temple. Processions of priests would have come on the river to the valley temple and, from there, up through the causeway to the pyramid itself. The elements of the royal funerary complex can still be seen in the Chephren complex, which is also marked by the famous Sphinx, a portrait of the king shown with the body of a lion. This general style of pyramid

1. **Enclosing Wall**
2. **Entrance**
3. **Entry Hall with Columns**
4. **Grand Court**
5. **Heb-Seb Court**
6. **House of the South**
7. **House of the North**
8. **Court of the Serdab**
9. **Serdab**
10. **Mortuary Temple**
11. **Step Pyramid**
12. **Sarcophagus Chamber**
13. **Original Mastaba**

2-4   *Reconstructed view and partial plan of the funerary complex of King Zoser at Saqqara.*

2-5   *Pyramids of Mycerinus, Chephren, and Cheops, Giza, Egypt, limestone, height of Cheops pyramid c. 480'. (Hirmer Fotoarchiv, Munich)*

2-6   Portrait Panel of Hesy-ra, *from Saqqara, c. 2660 B.C., wood, height 45", Egyptian Museum, Cairo. (Hirmer Fotoarchiv, Munich)*

complex was retained for the burials of the kings of the Old and Middle kingdoms (Fig. 2-5).

Sculpture

As the architecture of the Zoser complex both builds on and creates a new tradition, so the sculptural decoration at the tomb has artifacts whose forms will show artistic conventions that will endure until the end of the Old Kingdom.

The wood tomb panels of *Hesira* (c. 2750 B.C.) (Fig. 2-6), a scribe and a physician, show him with other attributes of his authority. He is rendered with head, legs, and hips in profile, whereas the eyes and shoulders are presented as if seen *frontally*. This artistic principle of frontality is expressed in the head of the relief and in the convention that shows the body's weight evenly distributed on both legs, the left leg

advanced. Presentation of the human figure in this way may have been created to ensure that all the necessary parts could be seen and would therefore be present in the afterlife. The wood would have been brightly painted, but the paint would not alter the carved surfaces, which render the figure noble and dignified.

Other examples of sculpture from the Old Kingdom, such as the bust of Prince Ankhhaf (c. 2550 B.C.) (Fig. 2-7) or the *Seated Scribe* (c. 2400 B.C.) (Fig. 2-8), illustrate the range possible within these conventions. Both figures are somewhat idealized—that is, they are presented without obvious blemishes, wrinkles, or other distracting individualized characteristics; yet both sculptures also clearly capture the personality and presence of the figure. The prince's skin, and the skin folds under his eyes and around his mouth, convey maturity and a thoughtful, almost melancholy mood. The scribe is bright, alert, and intense. Egyptian representations of human beings like this contrast sharply with the sculpture of Greece, which hardly knows individuals, and seem more like the sculptures of the Romans, whose public figures have public, familiar faces.

2-7   *Bust of Ankh-haef, Egyptian, 4th Dynasty from Giza chapel, sculpture, limestone; partially molded in plaster. H: 0.506. (Harvard University-MFA Expedition. Courtesy, Museum of Fine Arts, Boston)*

2-8   Seated Scribe, *from Saqqara, c. 2400* B.C., *painted limestone, height 21". (The Louvre, Paris)*

The Middle Kingdom (2134–1782 B.C.)

The causes behind the breakup of the Old Kingdom and the three-hundred-year period of confusion that followed are difficult to ascertain. Order was finally restored by the Eleventh Dynasty rulers Mentuhetep II (2065–2060 B.C.) and his son Mentuhetep III (2060–2010 B.C.), under whom Egypt returned to its former position as the dominant power of the region.

After a long struggle Mentuhetep III and his successors were able to make the office of nomarch a royal appointment. Enormous efforts were expended to restore the irrigation works neglected for centuries and to improve water supply. Associated closely with Thebes, both these monarchs encouraged the worship of Amon-Ra, the sun god of Thebes. These pharaohs and their successors showered Amon-Ra with treasures and properties in thanks for the prosperity and conquests abroad that marked the first centuries of the Middle Kingdom.

The pharaohs of the Middle Kingdom showed themselves much more expansionist than those of the Old. During the centuries of the Middle Kingdom, Egypt not only subjugated Nubia and the Sudan but

advanced Egypt's boundaries into Palestine. Sesotris I (1887–1850 B.C.) and his son Amenemhat III (1850–1800 B.C.) share the credit for having made the large desert area of the Fayum to the west of the Lower Nile into a valuable agricultural resource through irrigation. Amenemhat III also built the largest habitable structure ever constructed in ancient Egypt, his palace of Hawara. Already in ruins when visited by the Greek historian Herodotus in the fifth century B.C., the palace of three thousand rooms seemed to him to be a second Labyrinth, the legendary abode of the Cretan Minotaur.

The decay of the Middle Kingdom has so far eluded explanation by scholars. It is clear that the Middle Kingdom traditions were disrupted by the infiltration of the Hyksos, people from Palestine, who established their capital at Avaris in the eastern Delta. Records from this time reflect an alliance between the Hyksos in the north and the Nubians in the south. The domination of the Hyksos was not so much military as economic, as indicated by records of taxes and tribute demanded of the native Egyptian population.

The Hyksos, whose name is a corruption of the title "foreign kings," had a lasting impact on Egypt. The psychological effect of proud Egypt being dominated by foreigners was never forgotten, and this disgrace became a theme in pessimistic literature of the time. The Hyksos also forever changed Egypt by the introduction of new technology: the compound bow, the chariot, a style of bronze dagger, and new agricultural techniques. Ironically, the military innovations allowed the Egyptians of the New Kingdom to dominate the homelands of the Hyksos.

The Hyksos were expelled by a line of rulers at the end of the Seventeenth Dynasty in Thebes in Upper Egypt. Their expulsion marked the beginning of the glorious period called the New Kingdom.

The New Kingdom (1570–1070 B.C.)

In the New Kingdom, Egypt was the dominant power in the entire Near East. It was a time of cultural achievement as well. From the onset of the Eighteenth Dynasty, the pharaohs dedicated their energies to the conquest of Nubia to the south and the entire eastern Mediterranean area. By the middle of the dynasty, Egypt maintained garrisons throughout these regions, and under Thutmose III (c. 1504–1450 B.C.), called the "Napoleon of Egypt," Egyptian armies campaigned across the Euphrates River in Mesopotamia. The end of the dynasty was devoted to consolidating the political gains, and also to incredible accomplishments in architecture, sculpture, and painting.

Queen Hatshepsut (c. 1503–1482 B.C.)

Hatshepsut was the daughter, sister, and wife of pharaohs. As the widow and half sister of Thutmose II, she ruled as regent for her nephew, Thutmose III, when he was a young boy. After four years, she adopted the full title of king rather than of queen and ruled in her own right. Although many aspects of her reign suggest that her nephew was co-regent with her, her usurpation of royal rituals was unprecedented. She executed the duties of any male king, sending military campaigns to Nubia and Palestine, and acting as a patron of extravagant arts and architecture. After her death, Thutmose III, perhaps out of frustration at being denied the sole rule, attempted to destroy many of Hatshepsut's monuments.

The Temple of Hatshepsut at Deir el Bahari   In the time of Hatshepsut, the rulers of Egypt no longer were buried in pyramids. Their tombs were in chambers cut deep into the rock faces of the Valley of the Kings in Thebes. A mortuary temple that was built during their lifetime to serve as a monument to their memory and a religious center was separated from the tomb and was located on the valley floor over the hills from the Valley of the Kings (Fig. 2-9).

The mortuary temple of Hatshepsut at Deir el Bahari in Thebes is in stark contrast to the Old and Middle Kingdom pyramid complexes. The lines are linear with strong, heavy columns (round posts) and *piers* (square posts) that were used, along with walls, to define and divide spaces and to carry the great *lintels* and *slabs* that provided for the roofs. Columns might be fluted and painted or carved. Some ended in bell-shaped floral capitals; others had budlike bulbous tops. Walls were carved, painted, and decorated with elaborate reliefs. The physical energy and engineering skill required to erect these buildings is still impressive (Fig. 2-10).

It is thought that an adviser to the queen named Senmut was the architect of much of the temple at Deir el Bahari. The Hatshepsut complex rises in three successive stages and two great courtyards to end at the cliffs. The faces of the two lower terraces are carried on square pillars. The walls of the colonnade of the second terrace are painted with scenes of an expedition to obtain myrrh trees. Chapels are dedicated to the jackal-headed Anubis, lord of cemeteries, and to

2-9   *Senmut. Funerary temple of Queen Hatshepsut, Deir el Bahari, c. 1480 B.C. (Hirmer Fotoarchiv, Munich)*

2-10   *Perspective view and plan of the funerary complex of Queen Hatshepsut.*

1. **Hathor Chapel**
2. **Amon Chapel**
3. **Sun Court and Altar**
4. **Funerary Chamber**

the cow goddess Hathor, who is associated with love and death. Above this second colonnade were colossal statues of Hatshepsut as Osiris. Behind these statues is the uppermost terrace and the inner sanctuary cut deep into the rock of the mountain. The processional way—up ramps and through courts—recalls the processional way from the river to the pyramids at Giza. Here, however, space is shared among the divine ruler and the divinities themselves.

Monumental Writing   The walls of the tomb are decorated with hieroglyphic inscriptions that praise the queen and the god Amon. Partially destroyed by her nephew, the series recounts Hatshepsut's divine paternity and the legitimacy of her claim to the throne. The union of the god Amon with Queen Ahmose, Hatshepsut's mother, is described as follows: "When he came before her, she rejoiced at the sight of his beauty, his love passed into her limbs, which the fragrance of the god flooded." Amon then declares, "Khnemet-Amon-Hatshepsut shall be the name of this my daughter, whom I have placed in thy body. . . . She shall exercise the excellent kingship in this whole land. My soul is hers . . . , my crown is hers, that she may rule the Two Lands, that she may lead all the living."[2]

---

[2]Quoted in J. H. Breasted, *Ancient Records of Egypt,* vol. 2 (Chicago: University of Chicago Press, 1906), pp. 80–81.

Queen Hatshepsut also erected four obelisks in the temple of Amon at Karnak. One of these, in pink granite, still stands, and is, at 97.5 feet, the highest standing obelisk in Egypt. The queen's inscription incised on the shaft tells us that the obelisks were gilded with the finest gold. Part of the inscription is in prose, part in poetry. In the poetic portion she stresses her divine origins to legitimate her rule as well as praises her accomplishments as ruler.

The Amarna Period

This period includes the reigns of Amenophis III and IV as well as Tutankhamun (c. 1386–1325 B.C.). In the reign of Amenophis III (c. 1386–1349 B.C.), the Egyptian court came in closer and more consistent contact with Mesopotamia. This contact is best recorded by a group of documents called the "Amarna letters," correspondence written to the king of Egypt from the kings of Assyria, Babylonia, and the Hittites. The letters indicate that these lands maintained diplomatic relations with each other. This was a period of great cultural achievement and prosperity in Egypt, brought about primarily by a century of military campaigns by the pharaohs of the Eighteenth Dynasty. During the second half of the reign of Amenophis III, the kingdom was at peace and the state resources were directed toward massive temple and palace building projects.

Because of the increased contact with the southern and eastern areas, Egypt had become a multicultural and multiracial society. Inhabitants from Nubia in particular were assimilated into Egyptian culture and stood equally alongside native Egyptians in the bureaucracy and society. This period also saw the rise of the sun god Aten (also spelled Aton). Unlike other Egyptian gods, Aten was not represented as a man or an animal, but only as the round disk of the sun. Under Amenophis III, the priesthood of Aten grew in importance and strength.

Under Amenophis IV (c. 1350–1334 B.C.) the god Aten was elevated to a new prominence. In the early years of the king's reign, he built temples to the god in the precinct of the god Amon-Ra at Karnak. Although the motivation of Amenophis IV is not clear, by year five of his reign he professed his special allegiance to Aten by changing his throne name from Amenophis (the Greek form for "the one who satisfies Amon") to Akhenaton ("the one who is beneficial to Aten"). Shortly afterward, Akhenaton and his wife, Nefertiti, moved the administrative center of Egypt from Thebes to a new site, called Tell el Amarna, in the middle of Egypt. The dedication decrees of the city indicate that the king wished to establish a city that was associated with no other god. From this time through the end of his reign, there was deliberate attempt to erase the mention of other gods in the pantheon. Crews of workers were dispatched to temples to hack away the stone hieroglyphs that invoked the names of other gods. Although this appears to be an early form of *monotheism*, there are many indications that Akhenaton himself was considered to be divine and of a status nearly equal to Aten. His praise for his sole god, the Aten, is best summed up in the "Hymn to the Aten."

Akhenaton's refusal to accept the worship of other deities not only did honor to Aten but also provided the pharaoh with the wealth to continue his ambitious building projects for the new worship. With Amon-Ra suppressed, the rich revenues from the lands held by his priesthood were now diverted into the royal treasure. On the other hand, Akhenaton's policies made him hated by the religious establishment of the country, which the populace, deprived of the reassuring contact with their gods through rites and processions, probably supported wholeheartedly. The priests could accept Aten as another god but not that he alone was divine.

Akhenaton reigned for seventeen years. During the last of those years, there was political unrest in Mesopotamia and Palestine, and the Egyptian armies were less effective in maintaining Egypt's hold on its colonies. Its foreign domains were diminished and were not revived for a century.

Shortly after the death of Akhenaton, a young boy named Tutankhaton, perhaps the son of Akhenaton and a secondary queen, came to the throne. By the third year of his reign he modified his name to replace the Aten element with that of the old god Amon and adopted the name Tutankhamun. Under his rule the city of Amarna was abandoned and *polytheistic* beliefs were again adopted through the society.

Art Under Akhenaton   The radical changes in theology and society during Akhenaton's reign are paralleled by equally radical changes in art. Sculptures of the pharaoh from the Aten temple at Karnak show not the heroic, athletic, idealized figure, but a dreamy-eyed, heavy-lipped face and almost feminine body (Fig. 2-11). In an incised relief (Fig. 2-12) from Tell el Amarna, Akhenaton, Queen Nefertiti, and a daughter

2-11   *King Akhenaton, from the Temple of Aten, Karnak (fragment). c. 1360 B.C., sandstone, height 60¼". Egyptian Museum, Cairo. (Hirmer Fotoarchiv, Munich)*

2-12   King Akhenaton and His Family sacrificing to Aten, *from Tell el Amarna, Egypt, c. 1360 B.C., limestone relief. Egyptian Museum, Cairo. (Hirmer Fotoarchiv, Munich)*

sacrifice to the Aten, and we see the same kind of style applied to all three actors in this scene. The bust of Nefertiti, a model found in a sculptor's studio in Amarna, presents us with a queen beautiful, regal, and self-contained (Color Plate II).

Decay of the New Kingdom

Under Tutankhamun's successors Egypt returned to its warlike stance, aggressively defending its expanded borders, which ran from the south deep within Nubia, east across the Arabian Desert to the Euphrates, and then west again including Syria and Palestine. At the same time new threats to Egyptian stability appeared on Egypt's western and northern flanks from the rise of a strong power in Libya and the appearance of the Sea People, motley groups of pirates composed of tribes from Asia Minor, many of whom would later be called Hellenes, the name of the ancient Greeks.

The Nineteenth Dynasty saw the restoration of the great Egyptian kingdoms in Palestine with the annual military campaigns of kings Seti I and Rameses II (Rameses the Great), both of the Nineteenth Dynasty, and Rameses III of the Twentieth Dynasty. However, after the death of Rameses III (c. 1151 B.C.), renewed invasions from the west and from the Mediterranean islands placed Egypt in a defensive position, causing it to withdraw most of the troops that had formerly maintained its colonies and garrisons in Palestine and Syria.

The Third Intermediate Period and the Late Period (1070–332 B.C.)

For much of the seven hundred years between 1095 B.C. and the end of the fourth century B.C., Egypt survived as a divided country. The pharaoh in the north, at the new administrative center named Tanis, was challenged by princes and military leaders in the south and in Middle Egypt. This lack of central authority weakened Egypt's ability to protect its interests along the Mediterranean coast.

Two Libyan dynasties ruled Lower and much of Upper Egypt between 950 and 780 B.C. Unity was restored to Egypt by the kings of Kush from Nubia (see page 42), who, at the request of beleaguered rulers in Thebes, invaded Egypt. These Kushite kings of the Twenty-fifth Dynasty (c. 780–656 B.C.) dressed in imitation of the Egyptian pharaohs and worshiped Amon, to whom they built great temples in their homeland. Although many of the Nubian kings did not reside in Egypt, they ruled the land by means of their daughters, whom they installed as "God's Wives of Amon" in Thebes (Fig. 2-13). These women who ruled as virtual kings were forbidden to marry, for their children would be potential rivals to the Egyptian throne.

The Kushite dynasty was overthrown by the Assyrian army of Ashurbanipal, who entered Egypt and sacked Thebes in 667 B.C. When the Assyrians withdrew to their homeland to attend to threats from the Medes and Persians, they installed a family of administrators who later overthrew their Assyrian

2-13   *Alabaster statue of the Divine Consort Amenirdis I, sister of King Shabaka, from the Chapel of Osiris Nebankh at north Karnak, c. 710 B.C. (Egyptian Museum, Cairo)*

masters to establish the Twenty-sixth Dynasty, also called the Saite period.

The Saite period (664–525 B.C.), the last independent Egyptian dynasty, was a time of relative peace, prosperity, and considerable achievement in building. Under the Saite kings, Egypt was further drawn into the greater sphere of the New East. Foreign soldiers from Greece and Phoenicia were drafted into the Egyptian army, and trading colonies expressly for Greeks and other nationalities were established in the Delta area. However, there seems to have been some resistance among the native population to the Hellenizing tendencies of the Saite rulers.

Egypt, like most of the ancient Middle East, fell to the Persians, who annexed the country as a province or *satrapy* of its empire in 525 B.C. Although the Persians were expelled in 405 B.C., the brief and troubled reigns of a series of Egyptian rulers could not give peace to the country, and after a brief second occupation by

Persia between 341 and 332 B.C., Egyptian rebels called in Alexander the Great.

The Ptolemaic Period (332–30 B.C.)

Alexander was viewed as a savior for Egypt. He adopted Egyptian royal titles and allowed the temples and administration to function as they were before the Persian conquest. With the death of Alexander in 323 B.C., his vast empire was divided among his generals. Egypt fell to Ptolemy I, a Macedonian, for whom the Ptolemaic period is named. During the next centuries of Greek rule at least the upper classes of the Nile valley became culturally a part of the Hellenistic society, which dominated the Mediterranean from Syria to Spain. In 30 B.C. Cleopatra VII, the last of the Ptolemaic dynasty, allied herself with Antony in his struggle with Octavian for control of Julius Caesar's empire and, defeated, killed herself. With her death Egypt became incorporated into the Roman Empire.

Egyptian Music

The abundance and variety of music making in ancient Egypt is recorded in the wall paintings and artifacts of Egyptian tombs, as well as in the literature about its kings and gods. Also, the classical authors Plutarch, Strabo, and Plato inform us at a late date, during and after the decline of the Egyptian empire, about the excellence of Egyptian musical standards, the nature of some instruments, performance practices, and the richness and importance of Egyptian musical life. However, although we have the poetry of some ancient Egyptian song texts and specific references to instruments that accompanied the singing, we have not the least trace of musical notation to reveal or suggest what the music actually sounded like. We can play the reconstructions of some ancient Egyptian instruments, but we cannot know the beat, the melody, the tempo, or the tuning. At best, we can imagine elaborate temple ceremonies, ritual song and dance, and musical entertainment in the palaces.

Some instruments are described or depicted as early as the Old Kingdom (c. 2686–2181 B.C.), and these seem to have a continuous history of use: the end-blown flute (much like a recorder), a single-reed pipe (roughly similar in principle to a clarinet), the harp, and the sistrum, an Egyptian rattle of great significance in mythology, ritual, and everyday practice. (See Fig. 2-14.) Osiris, god of the lower world and judge of the dead, is known as the sistrum player, and he apparently carried this instrument with him as he

2-14 *Musician animals with double-reed pipes, lute, lyre, and harp; reconstruction of a detail from a papyrus, c. 1320–1200 B.C. (Cat. 2031, CGT 55001, Collezione Drovetti, Museo Egizio, Torino)*

2-15 *Egyptian, scene on papyrus showing sistrum. Museo Egizio, Torino. (Alinari/Art Resource, NY)*

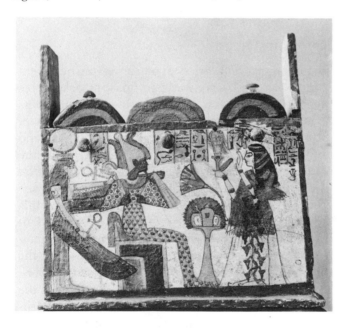

civilized the world. (See Fig. 2-15.) Plutarch, writing that the inhabitants of Busiris and Lycopolis did not use the trumpet because its performance resembled the braying of an ass, also implies that such an instrument was present and probably in use somewhere else. During the Ptolemaic period, Strabo informs us, the aulos, an oboelike instrument with a double reed, performed licentious music. We see a similarity in

practice to the music of classical Greece, for the aulos was an instrument associated with the orgies of the Dionysian festivals. Even before the Old Kingdom, we infer some musical practice suggested by the record of prehistoric dancing in rock drawings and on pottery figures. Then the record of the tomb illustrations from the Old and Middle kingdoms show us singers, dancers, and players of string, wind, and percussion instruments, principally the harp, flute, and sistrum. A variety of new instruments appear during the New Kingdom, including the lute, lyre, drums, tambourine, and trumpet. Because music was clearly so important in the religious and cultural life of Egypt, and also because the Egyptian kingdoms were so powerful and influential over a vast time period, we must assume that Egyptian music played a significant role in the development of music in the classical world of Greece and Rome, even though we do not yet know much about those specific relationships.

Nubia and the Kingdom of Kush

Ancient Egypt's continuing wealth and power depended on the relations between the state and the rest of Africa as well as on those with Asia. Fragmentary and uneven as our evidence is concerning Egypt's ties to the Saharan and Libyan peoples in the west, to the Nubians in the south, and to Punt in the east, attempting to understand them will improve our knowledge of the influence that other African cultures and Egypt had on each other. Perhaps the most important contacts were to the south, with Nubia, an area within the modern African country of Sudan. Nubia is a region whose history is distinct, but at times so intertwined with that of Egypt as to be one.

Historical Background

Nubia is a geographical term referring to that part of the Nile valley in Egypt and Sudan that extends between the first and sixth cataracts. From the time of the late Old Kingdom on through the Middle Kingdom, Egyptians referred to the area above the first cataract as Kush. Settlements in this region appeared as early as 2300 B.C. at a site called Kerma. Modern scholarship uses the name Kush to refer to the kingdom that entered history under King Kashta around 800 B.C. and that dominated the middle reaches of the Nile for over a thousand years from its two centers, Napata (800–270 B.C.) and Meroe (270 B.C.–A.D. 350).

Nubia's wealth in cattle, precious metals, copper, iron, and jewels led to lively trade with Egypt and brought about a fusion of their cultural features. We will deal briefly here with the two cultural centers at Napata and Meroe.

The Napatan Period (750–270 B.C.)   Napata owed its origin to its location at the head of a major track, the Bayuda road, which ran overland to avoid a particularly difficult stretch of the Nile between the fifth and the fourth cataracts. Under the New Kingdom, Napata became a religious and bureaucratic center about the year 1400 B.C. The location of the town is uncertain, but the complex of burial grounds, pyramids, and temples at El Kurru and Nuri near Jebal Barkal are identified with Napata.

In the eighth century B.C., a succession of kings—Kashta, Piye, and Shabaqo—spearheaded campaigns from Napata. In 750 B.C., Piye (also called Piankhi) led his armies north of the first cataract and finally captured the city of Memphis. Thirty-six years later his brother Shabaqo completed the conquest and unification of Egypt. Shabaqo was the first Nubian king to reside in the ancient capital of Memphis.

For the next fifty years, until the capture and sack of Thebes by the Assyrian king Ashurbanipal in 663 B.C., this Kushite dynasty—as Egypt's Twenty-fifth Dynasty—provided a brilliant flash of energy amid the declining years of pharaonic Egypt. Two sons of Piye, Shabataka (700–690 B.C.) and the fabled Taharqa (690–664 B.C.), succeeded Shabaqo. They restored pride in Egypt's glorious past by a refurbishing and building program in both Egypt and Nubia. After the Assyrian invasion, the Kushite kings withdrew to Napata, where the kingdom flourished until the city was destroyed in 591 B.C. by the armies of the Egyptian king Psammetik II. In the fifth and fourth centuries B.C., Kush's center shifted upstream to Meroe, which developed a culture even more distinct from Egypt's than that of Napata.

Analysis of the archaeological sites suggests that Napata remained important as a religious center associated with the deity Amon-Ra long after the rulers of Kush came to reside in Meroe during the fifth century B.C. At least kings and queens of Meroe continued to be buried near Napata until the third century B.C.

The Meroitic Period (270 B.C.–A.D. 350)   Meroe provides greater evidence of state development and urbanization. The city, at least three-quarters of a kilometer by one kilometer in size, harbored a palace precinct that contained numerous stores, baths, domestic quarters, and reception rooms. There were many temples, and major ones for Amon, Isis, and Apedemak the lion god are prominent sources of our knowledge of Kush's history during the Meroitic period. Far from Egypt, Meroe's culture moved further away from the Egyptian models so prominent in Napata. But the kings were in frequent contact with Ptolemaic and Roman Egypt: a major agricultural, manufacturing, and trade center for the Meroitic period developed far to the north of the capital city near the third cataract—in easy reach of Egyptian sites downstream. Indeed, this was the region that preserved remnants of Kush's culture after the fall of Meroe in the fourth century A.D., as seen in the Nubian features of the tombs at Ballana and Qustul. It was also the first Nubian region to convert to Christianity (in A.D. 543). As we examine other features of Kushite culture, notice that some are more characteristic of Napata, others of Meroe. Given the great extent of the kingdom in both time and space, the resilience of a conservative core of values and institutions is remarkable.

Population and Social Structure

The entire population of the Nile valley was distinct from other areas by the time of early dynastic Egypt. The skin color of people in the middle reaches of the Nile valley was dark: Nubians were often distinguished both from Egyptians and from other Africans to the south. Iconographic distinctions may account for some of these differences. But scholars agree in general that although Libyans, Southwest Asians, and Africans from other areas to the south were present, the peoples of the region were probably ancestral to those called Nubian today. The social structure of Kushite society seems to have been strictly stratified on the basis of wealth. At the top was the ruling class, composed of the king, members of the royal family, palace officials, the priests and priestesses of the temples, and perhaps the provincial bureaucrats. Elaborate residences and associated buildings dominated the urban landscape; fine pottery, tools, clothing, leather goods, shell, bone and ivory jewelry, and other grave goods were early markers of these differences in wealth.

At the bottom of the social hierarchy were slaves, captured through warfare and raids on the surrounding desert peoples. Donated in very large numbers to the temples, they were also settled as colonists to occupy newly conquered territory. Their work as gardeners, builders, and preparers of irrigation canals and beds was probably the greatest source of their value.

Inscriptions relating to slavery feature women more than men, suggesting that domestic service must have been an important activity as well. Slaves were exported from Nubia to Egypt and the Mediterranean in large numbers during Roman times. How far back in time the systematic trading of slaves goes, however, is unknown.

The majority of the population in between these two social poles probably consisted of free cultivators and herders. The visual prominence of the latter, and the symbolic importance of cattle and other animals in graves and on temple reliefs, are mute testimony to the nomadic origins of the civilization of the middle Nile. A middle class of low-ranking bureaucrats, artisans, and merchants must have existed, but the evidence for their distinctiveness as a class is scant. Artisans were imported from Egypt from time to time, and clearly left their mark on material culture—they introduced the pottery wheel, which remained a preserve of men, distinct from the indigenous pottery made by women. It is unlikely that immigrants ever formed more than a small percentage of the artisan group, for the production of the elaborate silver and gold jewelry, ivory carvings of animal motifs, weaving, leather working, basketry, decorated pottery and furniture making, all requiring the skill of specialists, reflects a visible blend of the alien and indigenous in their design and manufacture.

Politics and Religion

In Kush, as in Egypt, politics and religion inspired the artistic works that provide us with the evidence of Kush's past. During the Napatan period, the legacy of Egyptian values and religion, imported during the New Kingdom, is obvious. Moreover, when the kings from Kush ruled over Egypt during the Twenty-fifth Dynasty, their commitment to Egyptian institutions, especially their veneration of the Egyptian "state god" Amon-Ra, was an important strategy to establish their legitimacy. Despite these indications of Egyptian cultural power, the picture of the Kushite monarchy that emerges from inscriptions, reliefs, tombs, and other archaeological remains distinguishes it from Egyptian forms in a number of ways. Succession to the kingship passed through the maternal line, with the succession often going to a younger brother of the preceding monarch as opposed to his son, as was the case in Egypt. The ruler was chosen from among the appropriate candidates for his personal qualities— his wealth, power, and success in animal husbandry

being important—by designated figures of the realm. The queen mother and military officials appear to have been the most important electors. Occasional clashes between kings and temple priests recorded in inscriptions suggest that although Kushite monarchs may have had more absolute control than pharaohs, they nevertheless were held in check by the priests and the electors at the court.

One of the unique features of the monarchy that contrasts with Egypt was the singular role played by royal women. The queen mothers played important roles both in the selection of the king and in the coronation rituals, which created a bond between the king and the gods. During the Twenty-fifth Dynasty, the kings' daughters or sisters held the title of *Dewat Neter,* chief priestess to the god Amon at Thebes. This bestowed on them great economic wealth and authority: they received numerous allotments of revenues and tribute in kind, and during the ruler's absence the chief priestess acted as ruler of the country. After the loss of Egypt, inscriptions show that royal women continued to play important roles in the temples of Amon at Napata. Thus Anlamani (623–593 B.C.) dedicated each of his four sisters to be sistrum players in the temples of Amon at Napata, Sanam, Kawa, and Tebo. The sistrum, an ancient Egyptian percussion instrument, became the priestess's sign of office (see Fig. 2-15).

The importance of queen mothers seems to have increased during the Meroitic period. Known as *Candaces* (the term comes from transcriptions of Meroitic *KDKE* by classical authors), they hold a prominence in the scenes on temple walls that places them second only to the king. For a period of time beginning in the second century B.C. in Meroe, there was a series of reigning queens, the first of whom was Shanakdakhete (c. 170–160 B.C.). The Candaces were evidently well-known figures in the ancient world, as may be seen from the biblical reference to them in Acts 8:26–28. The apostle Philip encountered "an Ethiopian [Ethiopian in Greek means black], a eunuch, a minister of Candace the queen of the Ethiopians, in charge of all her treasure, [who] had come to Jerusalem to worship and was returning; seated in his chariot, he was reading the prophet Isaiah."

Although the monarchy was buttressed by an ideology that during the early period drew heavily on Egyptian principles, the flow of religious ideas between Kush and Egypt may have been in two directions: by the end of the Old Kingdom, at least one deity from Africa beyond the Nile, Dedun, provider of incense, had been added to the Egyptian pantheon. In

Napata, the numerous prayers and praises of Amon, the ram god, on stelae and temple walls testify to the importance of that Egyptian god in Kush. As we have seen earlier in this chapter, the sisters and daughters of Kush's rulers during the Twenty-fifth Dynasty often held the title of chief priestess in the Amon temple at Thebes. Amon's historic association with Kush survived the shift of the capital to Meroe, although a temple in Amon's honor was built there only during the last century before our era. Isis, Horus, Thoth, Arensnuphis, and Satis were other Egyptian deities that were worshiped there as well. But the dominant figure in the religious thought of the Meroitic period was the lion god, Apedemek. A warrior deity, Apedemek originated in the southern part of Kush and rose to prominence with Meroe. Representations of lions and lion heads are found in temples all over the region. Another Meroitic god that had no counterpart in Egypt is Sebiumeker, a creator god, whose colossal image is paired with that of Arensnuphis as protective figures on the façade of Temple 300 in the Great Enclosure at Musawwarat es-Sufra, a major temple complex of the Meroitic period. One could conclude that Kushite religion was eclectic and open; this fact enabled the religious system to absorb new peoples and local deities without calling into question the legitimacy of the entire framework.

Language and Writing in Napata and Meroe

Egyptian was the diplomatic language of Kush during the hegemony of Napata, and it is through the inscriptions on temples and stelae that some record of Kushite thought and modes of expression are preserved. Among these are the inscriptions of two rulers, Piye and Taharqa.

Piye came to the throne in Napata in 751 B.C. and ruled until 716 B.C. During his long reign, he led successful military campaigns as far north as the Delta, which enabled his successors to eventually unite Egypt and Nubia under the Kushite or Twenty-fifth Dynasty. The Victory Stela of Piye, fashioned in magnificent gray granite with a rounded top, contains a remarkable and lengthy historical account of Piye's campaign of conquest rich with details of military and diplomatic conventions. The first of the two excerpts below shows the importance of the Egyptian god Amon in the religious life of Kush. The text contains Piye's instructions to his army as to their conduct on entering Thebes en route to the campaign against Memphis and other principalities in the north. Following his charge to the army, the narrative recalls the army's response to their leader.

"When you have reached Thebes at Ipet-sut, go into the water. Cleanse yourselves in the river; wear the best linen. Rest the bow; loosen the arrow. Boast not to the lord of might, for the brave has no might without him [Amon]. He makes the weak-armed strong-armed, so that the many flee before the few, and a single one conquers a thousand men! Sprinkle yourselves with water of his altars; kiss the earth before his face. Say to him:

'Give us the way,
May we fight in the shade of your arm!
The troop you sent, when it charges,
May the many tremble before it!'

Then they placed themselves on their bellies before his majesty:

"It is your name that makes our strength,
Your counsel brings your army into port;
Your bread is in our bellies on every way,
Your beer quenches our thirst.
It is your valor that gives us strength,
There is dread when your name is recalled;
No army wins with a cowardly leader,
Who is your equal there?

You are the mighty King who acts with his arms,
The chief of the work of war!"[3]

The second excerpt comes near the end of the narrative of the campaign when the last of Piye's enemies were surrendering and he headed for home. Together with the last part of the selection above, it illustrates the manner in which Kushite kings were eulogized. The use of praise names, and the characterization of rulers in terms of both beauty and fierceness, are features typical of praise poetry throughout Africa. The frequent use of cattle metaphors reflects the importance of pastoralism in the life (or certainly in the history) of Kush. Notice also how food taboos and circumcision are used to distinguish royalty and those with access to the king.

Final Surrenders, Piye Returns to Nubia

One came to say to his majesty: "Hut-Sobk has opened its gate; Meten has thrown itself on its belly. No nome is shut against his majesty, of the nomes of the south and the north. The west, the east, and the islands in the midst are on their bellies

---

[3]Miriam Lichtheim, ed., *Ancient Egyptian Literature: A Book of Readings*, vol. 3: *The Late Period* (Berkeley: University of California Press, 1980), pp. 69–70.

in fear of him, and are sending their goods to where his majesty is, like the subjects of the palace."

At dawn of the next day there came the two rulers of Upper Egypt and the two rulers of Lower Egypt, the uraeus wearers, to kiss the ground to the might of his majesty. Now the kings and counts of Lower Egypt who came to see his majesty's beauty, their legs were the legs of women. They could not enter the palace because they were uncircumcised and were eaters of fish, which is an abomination to the palace. But the King *Namart* entered the palace because he was clean and did not eat fish. The three stood there while the one entered the palace.

Then the ships were loaded with silver, gold, copper, and clothing; everything of Lower Egypt, every product of Syria, and all plants of god's land. His majesty sailed south, his heart joyful, and all those near him shouting. West and East took up the announcement, shouting around his majesty. This was their song of jubilation:

> "O mighty ruler, O mighty ruler,
> Piye, mighty ruler!
> Your return having taken Lower Egypt,
> You made bulls into women!
> Joyful is the mother who bore you,
> The man who begot you!
> They valley dwellers worship her,
> The cow that bore the bull!
> You are eternal,
> Your might abides,
> O ruler loved of Thebes!"[4]

The Stela of Tanis

King Taharqa erected a stela in Tanis, in the northeastern Delta, to commemorate the arrival of his mother from the south at the time of Taharqa's coronation in Lower Egypt. It is interesting because it reflects both the affection of a son for his mother, from whom he had long been separated, and the honor conventionally bestowed on the queen mother.

> The queen-mother was in Napata.... Now I had been separated from her as a youth of twenty years, accompanying his majesty when he came to the Northland (Delta). Then she went north to the Northland where I was after a long period of years, and she found me crowned as king upon the throne of Horus. I had taken the diadems of Re, and I had assumed the double serpent-crest, as . . . the protection of my limbs. She rejoiced greatly when she saw the beauty of his majesty, as Isis saw her son, Horus, crowned upon the throne . . . while he was a youth

in the marsh. . . . They bowed to the ground to this King's-Mother. . . . Their old as well as their young ones gave praise to this King's-Mother, saying: Isis hath . . . [seen] her son, King of Upper and Lower Egypt, Taharka, living forever. . . .[5]

After the capital of Kush was moved south to Meroe in the sixth century B.C., Egyptian inscriptions declined and by the third century B.C. were replaced by Meroitic ones, written first in hieroglyphs, then in cursive (see Fig. 2-16). There is much debate about the origin of Meroitic: some scholars believe it is a member of the Afro-Asiatic family of languages, others that it belongs to the great family of Sudanic (or Nilo-Saharan) languages. The earliest Meroitic inscription that can be dated is on a temple at Naqa from the reign of Queen Shanakdakhete; the latest has been set at early in the second century A.D. The phonetic value of Meroitic was worked out during the first decade of the twentieth century, but to this day the meaning of Meroitic remains elusive, thereby depriving us of a major historical and literary source covering four hundred years of Meroe's past.

The barriers that remain to our understanding of the Meroitic language leave us with few indications of the nature of Meroitic literature. However, on the walls of the lion temple at Musawwarat es-Sufra there are two inscriptions that, although written in Egyptian, are about the two gods that were Meroitic in origin. The first, a prayer to Apedemek, reflects an awareness of formal features of Egyptian religious texts. But the way in which the author addresses Apedemek with a range of fearsome *epithets* parallels the praise name tradition of oral literature in other parts of the African continent (see Chapter 13).

> Thou art greeted, Apedemek, lord of Naqa; great god, lord of Musawwarat es-Sofra; splendid god, at the head of Nubia. Lion of the south, strong of arm. Great god, the one who comes to those who call him. The one who carries (?) the secret, concealed in his being, who was not seen by any eye. Who is a companion for men and women, who will not be hindered in heaven and earth. Who procures nourishment for all men, in this his name "Perfect Awakener." The one who hurls his hot breath against his enemy, in this his name "Great of Power." Who kills the enemy.... The one who punishes all who commit crimes against him. Who prepares the place for those who give themselves to

⁴Ibid., p. 80

⁵Breasted, *Ancient Records of Egypt*, vol. 4, pp. 456–57.

1. Netekamani

   Egyptian

   Meroitic

2. Amanitare

   Egyptian

   Meroitic

≈ = n	:	Egyptian ∼ = n
🐦 = m	:	Egyptian 🦅 = m
🐦 = g or k	:	acrophonic from Egyptian 🐦 = gb or kk
◡ = t	:	Egyptian ◡ = t
𓀀 = i	:	Egyptian 𓀀 = i ; HI in Old Coptic
◡ = t	:	uncertain, possibly Egyptian ◡ = ta
▭ = r or l	:	Egyptian ◡ = r
β = y	:	Egyptian 𓏭 = y

2-16a *Names of King Netekamani and Queen Amanitare in Egyptian and Meroitic. (From P. L. Shinnie,* Meroe: A Civilization of the Sudan, © *Thames and Hudson, Ltd.)*

2-16b *Meroitic and Egyptian equivalents for some consonants. (From P. L. Shinnie,* Meroe: A Civilization of the Sudan, © *Thames and Hudson, Ltd.)*

him. Who gives to those who call to him. Lord of life, great in his sight.[6]

In the second text, it is the god Sebiumeker himself who speaks; and its content suggests a religious conception original to Meroe.

> I give you everything which comes forth by night, everything which happens by day. I give to you the years of the sun, and the months of the moon in joy. So speaks Sebiumeker [spelling changed] lord of Musawwarat es-Sofra, who gives life like the sun god for ever.[7]

The Art of Napata and Meroe

The arts of the kingdom of Kush achieved distinction in many areas: human and figurative sculpture; architecture—particularly the construction of tombs, temples, and palaces; engraved friezes on the walls of tombs and temples; and a fine array of metal, glass, decorated pottery, and inlaid crafted objects used as burial goods. All of these give us telling glimpses into ritual and utilitarian features of life. By now it will not be surprising to read that Egyptian influence is more clearly seen in the art of the Napatan period, whereas Meroitic forms owe much less to the artists of Egypt. Yet clearly Kushite characteristics appear in Napatan art, and traces of Egyptian style and clear evidence of

contact with Egypt were found in Meroe. The examples selected for study here have been chosen for their fine quality, with an eye to showing differences between Napatan and Meroitic art, and to illustrate changes in style and content over Nubia's history.

Bronze of Shabaqo   The fine, solid cast bronze figure of King Shabaqo (716–701 B.C.) (Fig. 2-17) is one of the earliest sculpted images we have of Kushite kings that reflect their distinctive regalia and sculptural style. The kneeling figure poses in a balanced, *frontal* posture, the arms in a gesture of offering with palms vertical. The features typical of regal attire include the close-fitting cap with the double uraei (serpent crests symbolizing the union of Kush and Egypt); the necklace with three ram's-head pendants (symbol of the god Amon), surmounted by a serpent crest and sun disk; wide bracelets and armbands; and the short kilt. The king's name is inscribed on the buckle of the waistband. Typical of Kushite figure modeling are the muscular torso and smooth round face distinguished by the "Kushite fold" extending horizontally out from the nose and accentuating the high cheekbones.

Granite Statue of King Aspelta (600–580 B.C.)   In the early seventh century B.C. King Taharqa commissioned a massive granite statue (4.18 meters high) for the great temple of Amon at Jebel Barkal. This figure of King Aspelta, also from Jebel Barkal, is comparable (Fig. 2-18). Although reminiscent of Egyptian figures in stance, this statue is typically Kushite in the rounded face and muscular torso and the distinctive regalia. In

---

[6]P. L. Shinnie, *Meroe: A Civilization of the Sudan* (New York: Praeger, 1967), p. 143.

[7]Ibid., p. 144. Translation from German by Shinnie.

2-17 King Shabaqo Offering, *Dynasty XXV, late eighth century* B.C., *bronze, solid cast, height 15.6 cm, width 3.4 cm. (National Archaeological Museum, Athens)*

addition, the crown is surmounted by the double towering feathers characteristic of the headdress of Amon, god of Thebes, who, as we have seen, was at the center of Napatan religion.

Plan of the Temple at Kawa King Taharqa was the great builder of the Twenty-fifth Dynasty. In Egypt he constructed the colossal columns at all four of the cardinal points of the great temple of Amon at Karnak. But his main accomplishments were in Nubia, where he refurbished the great temple at Jebel Barkal, and constructed nearly identical temples for Amon at Sanam, Tebo, and Kawa. Although these temples were designed following Egyptian prototypes and constructed by builders imported from Memphis, their

2-18 *King Aspelta, Kingdom of Kush, c. 600–580* B.C., *black granite. (Courtesy, Museum of Fine Arts, Boston. Gift of Frederick Chase.)*

2-19   *Plan of the Amon Temple at Kawa, built by King Taharqa, Napatan Period, 690–664* B.C.

construction of stone faced with mud brick was original. The processional way at Kawa was bordered by stone rams representing the sacred animal of Amon, each of which protected a statuette of Taharqa. Within the temple (see Fig. 2-19), mud brick walls linking some of the columns with each other or with the inside walls were constructed as worksites for the manufacture of *ushabti* figures (votive figures used in burials) and other commercial activities. The *pronaos* contained an offering table for the god, while the *sanctuary* housed the sacred bark on its pedestal. Both the temple and the adjacent town were enclosed by a wall,

also probably constructed at Taharqa's bidding. The richness of inscriptions at Kawa suggests that it was second in importance only to Jebel Barkal as a religious center for the Napatan kings.

The Swimming Girl   The exceptional skill of artisans' work with metals and ceramics during the Napatan period is revealed in a small but stunningly beautiful object found among the tomb goods at Sanam: a swimming girl, lying prone and holding a small basin in her outstretched arms (Fig. 2-20). The figure was probably used for dispensing myrrh or wine in cult or

2-20   Swimming Girl with Basin, *faience, length 10.8 cm, height 2.8 cm, width 2.3 cm, eighth to seventh century* B.C. *(Collection Ashmolean Museum)*

2-21 *Relief from the pyramid chapel of Nahirqa. (Drawing by Lucinda Rodd. From P. L. Shinnie,* Meroe: A Civilization of the Sudan, © *Thames and Hudson, Ltd.)*

2-22 *Engraving from Richard Lepsius,* Denkmaeler aus Aegypten und Nubien, *1848, depicting Natakamani, King of Meroe, early 1st century* A.D., *from the west wall of the Lion Temple at Naqa, Sudan. (Photo courtesy of Timothy Kendall)*

burial ceremonies. The fashioning of the girl's head and face reflects the distinctive Kushite fold, full mouth, and relatively large ears typical of Napatan figures from the eighth to the seventh century B.C.

Friezes from Meroe   Although the art of the Meroitic period was as diverse in type as that of Napata, the reliefs on temples and chapels are the primary focus of study here. Ranging over a six-hundred-year period from roughly the late fourth century B.C. to the third century A.D., they provide ample evidence of changes in Meroitic styles over time. A frequent theme throughout the period was a scene like that in the pyramid chapel of Queen Nahirqa (186–177 B.C.) (Fig. 2-21). It consists of a king seated on a throne with lion-shaped armrests. Standing protectively behind the ruler is the goddess Isis and sometimes, as in this example, other members of the royal family. Nahirqa, the queen, is seated behind the unnamed king and in front of Isis, whose outstretched wings shelter them both. The king wears the distinctive banded cap highlighted by the uraeus in front and flowing streamers down the back, the transverse fringed tunic with a wide collar, and armbands. Notice the queen's beaded collar and pendant, and her finely modeled coiffure. This version is particularly interesting because of its graceful line, the detail, and the earliest use of small figures bearing palm branches, a feature that became ubiquitous thereafter. The stylistic use of contrasts in

size to denote marked differences in status is a trait that will also be seen later in the plaques of the Benin kingdom in West Africa. Another characteristic is the repetition of a symbol to underline its importance, seen here in the repetition of the uraeus in the crown of Isis and the dominant upper border as well as in the king's crown to convey an aura of great power.

A common scene in lion temples, and borne out in the two most important examples at Musawwarat es-Sufra and at Naqa, is a profile of the king standing with arms bent at the elbow, palms forward in a gesture of worship before the lion god Apedemek. In the relief at Naqa of King Natakamani (12 B.C.–A.D.

12) (Fig. 2-22), we can identify a number of features common to Meroitic iconography and style as well as contrasts with earlier forms. The king's costume bears some similarity to the one in the relief of Nahirqa, but is more elaborate and fussy: instead of one necklace, he appears to wear three, one of which has a lion-god pendant. Elaborately carved armbands cover the forearm from above the wrist to the elbow, in addition to the armbands worn just below the shoulder. Neck rings, a sometime feature of Meroitic figurative sculpture that is also seen in West Africa, are just visible. The *hemhem*-crown—consisting of various numbers of highly stylized serpents—was widely used in reliefs, sculpture, and jewelry throughout the Meroitic period. A gradual simplification of forms together with emphasis on some aspects over others developed over time in Meroitic art. Greater stress on eyes and the shift from naturalism toward abstraction are two examples seen here. Queens are portrayed with ample proportions, whereas goddesses are slender (look again at the figure of the goddess Isis in comparison to that of the queen in Fig. 2-21). Other iconographic changes included a shift from unnaturally slender human forms to short, stocky ones. Clothing, which was a cardinal indicator of social status, also changed: the royal sash, originally quite narrow, grew wider in the first century B.C. and continued to expand for another one hundred years.

The Napatan tradition persisted until the second century A.D. Nevertheless, around the beginning of the Christian era, new types of relief and other artistic changes during the reign of King Natakamani and the Candace Amanitore signaled an important new tradition of art that continued side by side with the older Napatan one. The reasons for these changes remain obscure, but their presence highlights the complex nature of cultural forms in Kush's past.

Shield Ring with Udjat Eye   The shield ring (shown in Fig. 2-23) was found with several others in the tomb of Queen Amanishakheto (41–12 B.C.) in the North Cemetery at Meroe and serves as a final point of synthesis for our study of Kushite art. It is made in two parts of gold and fused-glass inlays. The hollow upper part contains a sun disk, flanked by uraei and containing an inlaid udjat eye fashioned in gold wire (the udjat eye stands for the ultimate symbolic rendering of the fire-spitting serpent Wadjet from the Delta as the eye of Ra). The disk has atop it a crowned uraeus and a hemhem-crown. The six hollow ornaments on the bottom were surrounded by glass inlay within a rectangle bordered with three gold cords. Although reflecting the shift toward stylization typical of the subperiod, this tiny object is richly endowed with splendid media and overlapping Egyptian and indigenous symbolism, forming a fitting end to the study of the art of Kush.

Kush and the Rest of Africa

The precise ways in which Kush (and Egypt, for that matter) influenced the rest of ancient Africa may never be known. We have stressed the importance of trade to Kush's economy; it acted as one of the corridors through which goods from the heart of Africa reached the outside world. The idea once popular among historians that Kush was the filter through which the rest of Africa acquired iron-working technology and political and religious ideas has been modified somewhat. Research suggests that Kush's role may have been more important for some areas than for others, and that independent innovation as well as alternative sources for borrowing have played significant roles in the evolution of material culture elsewhere on the continent.

2-23 *Ring with Udjat-Eye, late 1st century* B.C. *Gold with fused-glass inlays, h: 5.1 cm, w: 3.0 cm. (Museum expedition. Courtesy, Museum of Fine Arts, Boston)*

Scholars like the late Cheikh Anta Diop have also pointed to important similarities between Egyptian and Kushite ideas and institutions associated with kingship, and those of certain West African peoples. Moreover, the Yoruba and Ashanti, to name only two, include in their traditions stories of eastern origins. Archaeological excavations along the east-west trade routes may one day provide tangible evidence of the nature of past contacts between Kush and West Africa. On the other hand, the long history of north-south trade is better documented, and suggests that cultural features might well have traveled to the Great Lakes region of the continent. On balance, it seems more appropriate to acknowledge the incomparable value of the Nile valley civilizations for what they were: testimony to the ingenuity of the human community in ancient times to succeed not only in surviving profound environmental change but in becoming the progenitors of culture. Egypt and Nubia benefited greatly from their differences over the centuries; the rest of the world stands in their debt for the contributions they fashioned and passed on to their neighbors along Mediterranean shores and elsewhere.

Egyptian literature includes royal monumental inscriptions, some of which are hymns of victory, hymns to the gods, and poems in praise of the pharaoh. Poetic narrations of battles may be compared to the *epic*, although there is nothing extant from Egypt of the size of the *Epic of Gilgamesh*. There is a substantial body of "wisdom literature," containing words of advice, which probably influenced the books of Proverbs and Deuteronomy in the Bible. Tales, both mythical and realistic, were well developed, as was lyric poetry, although love poetry does not appear until the period of the New Kingdom.

The Book of the Dead, with its spells of protection and transformation, shows a characteristic mixing of morality with magic. The Negative Confession reprinted here, forty-two statements to forty-two different gods on commandments *not* broken, made by souls in their passage to the afterlife, is reminiscent of the Ten Commandments in the Old Testament book of Exodus.

The Instruction of Ptah-hotep

Translation by F. L. Griffith

The author of these maxims, who lived during the Old Kingdom, around 2450 B.C., was the vizier of a pharaoh. The author is instructing his son in the rules of behavior and morality. Whereas in later Egyptian literature religion and morality are always intertwined, here the emphasis seems to be more on the social and practical aspects of morality.

Title and Aim

Beginning of the maxims of good words spoken by the...mayor and vizier, Ptah-hotep, teaching the ignorant to know according to the standard of good words, expounding the profit to him who shall listen to it, and the injury to him who shall transgress it. He said to his son:

Intellectual Snobbery

Be not arrogant because of your knowledge, and be not puffed up because you are a learned man. Take counsel with the ignorant as with the learned, for the limits of art cannot be reached, and no artist is perfect in his skills. Good speech is more hidden than the precious greenstone, and yet it is found among slave girls at the millstones....

Leadership and "Maat"

If you are a leader, commanding the conduct of many, seek out every good aim, so that your policy may be without error. A great thing is truth [*maat*], enduring and surviving; it has not been upset since the time of Osiris. He who departs from its laws is punished. It is the right path for him who knows nothing. Wrongdoing has never brought its venture safe to port. Evil may win riches, but it is the strength of truth that it endures long, and a man can say, "I learned it from my father."...

Relations with Women

If you wish to prolong friendship in a house into which you enter as master, brother or friend, or any place that you enter, beware of approaching the women. No place in which that is done prospers. There is no wisdom in it. A thousand men are turned aside from their own good because of a little moment, like a dream, by tasting which death is reached....He who fails because of lusting after women, no plan of his will succeed.

Greed

If you want your conduct to be good, free from every evil, then beware of greed. It is an evil and incurable sickness. No man can live with it; it causes divisions between fathers and mothers, and between brothers of the same mother; it parts wife and husband; it is a gathering of every evil, a bag of everything hateful. A man thrives if his conduct is right. He who follows the right course wins wealth thereby. But the greedy man has no tomb....

Marriage

If you are prosperous you should establish a household and love your wife as is fitting. Fill her belly and clothe her back. Oil is the tonic for her body. Make her heart glad as long as you live. She is a profitable field for her lord....

Conduct in Council

If you are a worthy man sitting in the council of his lord, confine your attention to excellence. Silence is more valuable than chatter. Speak only when you know you can resolve difficulties. He who gives good counsel is an artist, for speech is more difficult than any craft....

Behavior in Changed Circumstances

If you are now great after being humble and rich after being poor in the city that you know, do not boast because of what happened to you in the past. Be not miserly with your wealth, which has come to you by the god's gift. You are no different from another to whom the same has happened.

Obedience to a Superior

Bend your back to him who is over you, your superior in the administration; then your house will endure by reason of its property, and your reward will come in due season. Wretched is he who opposes his superior, for one lives only so long as he is gracious....

Conclusion

May you succeed me, may your body be sound, may the king be well pleased with all that is done, and may you spend many years of life! It is no small thing that I have done on earth; I have spent one hundred and ten years of life, which the king gave me, and with rewards greater than those of the ancestors, by doing right for the king until death.

COMMENTS AND QUESTIONS

1. The concept of "Maat" is primarily a religious one. How is it applied here in terms of morality?

2. What seems to be Ptah-hotep's view of women?

3. What aspects of this advice would you consider to be still applicable today?

FROM THE *Book of the Dead*

Translation by E. Wallis Budge

The Negative Confession

The confession takes place in the hall of double Maat, or the hall of the goddesses Isis and Nephthys, who stand for right and truth. In the hall are forty-two other gods. The soul to be judged addresses a negative statement to each one of them.

Some of the stages in the judgment of the soul can be seen in the illustration on the papyrus of the Negative Confession (Fig. 2-24). In the top band the Maat goddesses are seated on thrones, holding scepters. In the second band a deceased person stands before the god Osiris with both hands raised in adoration. The third represents a scale with a heart (the conscience of the dead person) on one end and a feather (representing Maat, right and truth) on the other. The god Anubis is testing the balance, and the monster Am-met stands close by. In the fourth band the god Thoth, with the head of an ibis, is seated on a pedestal, painting a large Maat feather.

1. "Hail, thou whose strides are long, who comest forth from Ånnu (Heliopolis), I have not done iniquity.

2. "Hail, thou who art embraced by flame, who comest forth from Kher-āḥa, I have not robbed with violence.

3. "Hail, thou divine Nose (Fenti), who comest forth from Khemennu (Hermopolis), I have not done violence [to any man].

4. "Hail, thou who eatest shades, who comest forth from the place where the Nile riseth,[1] I have not committed theft.

5. "Hail, Neḥa-ḥāu, who comest forth from Re-stau, I have not slain man or woman.

6. "Hail, thou double Lion-god, who comest forth from heaven, I have not made light the bushel.

7. "Hail, thou whose two eyes are like flint, who comest forth from Sekhem (Letopolis), I have not acted deceitfully.

---

[1] The *qerti* or caverns out of which flowed the Nile were thought to be situated between Aswân and Philae.

2-24 *Four panels from* The Negative Confession. *Papyrus of Nebseni, no. 9,900, sheet 30. (Courtesy of the Trustees of the British Museum)*

8. "Hail, thou Flame, who comest forth as [thou] goest back, I have not purloined the things which belong unto God.

9. "Hail, thou Crusher of bones, who comest forth from Suten-ḥenen (Heracleopolis), I have not uttered falsehood.

10. "Hail, thou who makest the flame to wax strong, who comest forth from Ḥet-ka-Ptaḥ (Memphis), I have not carried away food.

11. "Hail, Qerti (i.e., the two sources of the Nile), who come forth from Àmentet, I have not uttered evil words.

12. "Hail, thou whose teeth shine, who comest forth from Ta-she (i.e., the Fayyûm), I have attacked no man.

13. "Hail, thou who dost consume blood, who comest forth from the house of slaughter, I have not killed the beasts [which are the property of God].

14. "Hail, thou who dost consume the entrails, who comest forth from the *mābet* chamber, I have not acted deceitfully.

15. "Hail, thou god of Right and Truth, who comest forth from the city of double Maāti, I have not laid waste the lands which have been ploughed (?).

16. "Hail, thou who goest backwards, who comest forth from the city of Bast (Bubastis), I have never pried into matters [to make mischief].

17. "Hail, Āati, who comest forth from Ànnu (Heliopolis), I have not set my mouth in motion [against any man].

18. "Hail, thou who art doubly evil, who comest forth from the nome of Āti,[2] I have not given way to wrath concerning myself without a cause.

19. "Hail, thou serpent Uamenti, who comest forth from the house of slaughter, I have not defiled the wife of a man.

20. "Hail, thou who lookest upon what is brought to him, who comest forth from the Temple of Àmsu, I have not committed any sin against purity.

21. "Hail, Chief of the divine Princes, who comest forth from the city of Nehatu,[3] I have not struck fear [into any man].

22. "Hail, Khemi (i.e., Destroyer), who comest forth from the Lake of Ḳaui (Khas?), I have not encroached upon [sacred times and seasons].

23. "Hail, thou who orderest speech, who comest forth from Urit, I have not been a man of anger.

24. "Hail, thou Child, who comest forth from the Lake of Ḥeq-āt,[4] I have not made myself deaf to the words of right and truth.

25. "Hail, thou disposer of speech, who comest forth from the city of Unes,[5] I have not stirred up strife.

26. "Hail, Basti, who comest forth from the Secret city, I have made no [man] to weep.

27. "Hail, thou whose face is [turned] backwards, who comest forth from the Dwelling, I have not

---

[2] I.e., the ninth nome of Lower Egypt, the capital of which was Per Àusar or Busiris.

[3] The "city of the sycamore"; a name of a city of Upper Egypt.

[4] The thirteenth nome of Lower Egypt.

[5] The metropolis of the nineteenth nome of Upper Egypt.

committed acts of impurity, neither have I lain with men.

28. "Hail, Leg of fire, who comest forth from Ākhekhu, I have not eaten my heart.[6]

29. "Hail, Kenemti, who comest forth from [the city of] Kenemet, I have abused [no man].

30. "Hail, thou who bringest thine offering, who comest forth from the city of Sau (Saïs), I have not acted with violence.

31. "Hail, thou lord of faces, who comest forth from the city of Tchefet, I have not judged hastily.

32. "Hail, thou who givest knowledge, who comest forth from Unth, I have not........, and I have not taken vengeance upon the god.

33. "Hail, thou lord of two horns, who comest forth from Satiu, I have not multiplied [my] speech overmuch.

34. "Hail, Nefer-Tem, who comest forth from Ḥet-ka-Ptaḥ (Memphis), I have not acted with deceit, and I have not worked wickedness.

35. "Hail, Tem-Sep, who comest forth from Ṭaṭṭu, I have not uttered curses [on the king].

36. "Hail, thou whose heart doth labour, who comest forth from the city of Ṭebti, I have not fouled (?) water.

37. "Hail, Ahi of the water, who comest forth from Nu, I have not made haughty my voice.

38. "Hail, thou who givest commands to mankind, who comest forth from [Sau (?)], I have not cursed the god.

39. "Hail, Neḥeb-nefert, who comest forth from the Lake of Nefer (?), I have not behaved with insolence.

40. "Hail, Neḥeb-kau, who comest forth from [thy] city, I have not sought for distinctions.

41. "Hail, thou whose head is holy, who comest forth from [thy] habitation, I have not increased my wealth, except with such things as are [justly] mine own possessions.

42. "Hail, thou who bringest thine own arm, who comest forth from Āukert (underworld), I have not thought scorn of the god who is in my city."

QUESTIONS

1. Enumerate the actions that are prohibited under Egyptian religious codes. Under what general categories do they fall?

2. Compare these categories of prohibition with the "thou shalt not" prohibitions in the biblical Ten Commandments (see Chapter 8).

3. Why are forty-two gods necessary here in addition to the two goddesses of Maat?

4. Can you define more precisely the concept of "Maat" after reading this confession?

Monumental Inscription by Queen Hatshepsut

Translation by Miriam Lichtheim

Speech of the Queen

I have done this with a loving heart for my father
   Amun;
Initiated in his secret of the beginning,
Acquainted with his beneficent might,
I did not forget whatever he had ordained.
My majesty knows his divinity,
I acted under his command;
It was he who led me,
I did not plan a work without his doing.

. . .

It is the King himself who says:
I declare before the folk who shall be in the future,
Who shall observe the monument I made for my
   father,
Who shall speak in discussion,
Who shall look to posterity—
It was when I sat in the palace,
And thought of my maker,
That my heart led me to make for him
Two obelisks of electrum,[1]
Whose summits would reach the heavens,
In the august hall of columns,
Between the two great portals of the King,
The Strong Bull, King Aakheperkare, the Horus
   triumphant.
Now my heart turns to and fro,
In thinking what will the people say,
They who shall see my monument in after years,
And shall speak of what I have done.

. . .

I swear, as I am loved of Re,
As Amun, my father, favors me,
As my nostrils are refreshed with life and dominion,

---

[6]I.e., "lost my temper and become angry."

[1]A fine alloy of gold. [Ed.]

As I wear the white crown,
As I appear with the red crown,
As the Two Lords have joined their portions for me,
As I rule this land like the son of Isis,
As I am mighty like the son of Nut,
As Re rests in the evening bark,
As he prevails in the morning bark,
As he joins his two mothers in the god's ship,
As sky endures, as his creation lasts,
As I shall be eternal like an undying star,
As I shall rest in life like Atum—
So as regards these two great obelisks,
Wrought with electrum by my majesty for my father
    Amun,
In order that my name may endure in this temple,
For eternity and everlastingness,
They are each of one block of hard granite,
Without seam, without joining together!

. . .

Not shall he who hears it say,
"It is a boast," what I have said;
Rather say, "How like her it is,
She is devoted to her father!"
Lo, the god knows me well,
Amun, Lord of Thrones-of-the-Two-Lands;
He made me rule Black Land and Red Land as
    reward,
No one rebels against me in all lands.
All foreign lands are my subjects,
He placed my border at the limits of heaven,
What Aten[2] encircles labors for me.
He gave it to him who came from him,
Knowing I would rule it for him.
I am his daughter in very truth,
Who serves him, who knows what he ordains.
My reward from my father is life-stability-rule,
On the Horus throne of all the living, eternally like
    Re.

QUESTIONS

1. Describe Hatshepsut's attitude toward her "father," the god Amon. Does it seem to you religious or political?

2. What seems to be the function of the obelisk here?

3. How does the queen praise herself? What is her goal in doing this?

AMENHOTEP IV (AKHENATON)

The Great Hymn to the Aten

Translation by Miriam Lichtheim

The long text columns begin at the top of the wall.
Below the text are the kneeling relief figures of Ay
and his wife.

Splendid you rise in heaven's lightland,
O living Aten, creator of life!
When you have dawned in eastern lightland,
You fill every land with your beauty.
You are beauteous, great, radiant,
High over every land;
Your rays embrace the lands,
To the limit of all that you made.
Being Re, you reach their limits,
You bend them (for) the son whom you love;
Though you are far, your rays are on earth,
Though one sees you, your strides are unseen.

When you set in western lightland,
Earth is in darkness as if in death;
One sleeps in chambers, heads covered,
One eye does not see another.
Were they robbed of their goods,
That are under their heads,
People would not remark it.
Every lion comes from its den,
All the serpents bite;
Darkness hovers, earth is silent,
As their maker rests in lightland.

Earth brightens when you dawn in lightland,
When you shine as Aten of daytime;
As you dispel the dark,
As you cast your rays,
The Two Lands are in festivity.
Awake they stand on their feet,
You have roused them;
Bodies cleansed, clothed,
Their arms adore your appearance.
The entire land sets out to work,
All beasts browse on their herbs;
Trees, herbs are sprouting,
Birds fly from their nests,
Their wings greeting your *ka*.[1]
All flocks frisk on their feet,
All that fly up and alight,
They live when you dawn for them.

---

[2]The sun disk.

[1]Living spirit or soul. [Ed.]

Ships fare north, fare south as well,
Roads lie open when you rise;
The fish in the river dart before you,
Your rays are in the midst of the sea.

Who makes seed grow in women,
Who creates people from sperm;
Who feeds the son in his mother's womb,
Who soothes him to still his tears.
Nurse in the womb,
Giver of breath,
To nourish all that he made.
When he comes from the womb to breathe,
On the day of his birth,
You open wide his mouth,
You supply his needs.
When the chick in the egg speaks in the shell,
You give him breath within to sustain him;
When you have made him complete,
To break out from the egg,
He comes out from the egg,
To announce his completion,
Walking on his legs he comes from it.

How many are your deeds,
Though hidden from sight,
O Sole God beside whom there is none!
You made the earth as you wished, you alone,
All peoples, herds, and flocks;
All upon earth that walk on legs,
All on high that fly on wings,
The lands of Khor and Kush,
The land of Egypt.
You set every man in his place,
You supply their needs;
Everyone has his food,
His lifetime is counted.
Their tongues differ in speech,
Their characters likewise;
Their skins are distinct,
For you distinguished the peoples.

You made Hapy in *dat*,[2]
You bring him when you will,
To nourish the people,
For you made them for yourself.
Lord of all who toils for them,
Lord of all lands who shines for them,

Aten of daytime, great in glory!
All distant lands, you make them live,
You made a heavenly Hapy descend for them;
He makes waves on the mountains like the sea,
To drench their fields and their towns.
How excellent are your ways, O Lord of eternity!
A Hapy from heaven for foreign peoples,
And all lands' creatures that walk on legs,
For Egypt the Hapy who comes from *dat*.

Your rays nurse all fields,
When you shine they live, they grow for you;
You made the seasons to foster all that you made,
Winter to cool them, heat that they taste you.
You made the far sky to shine therein,
To behold all that you made;
You alone, shining in your form of living Aten,
Risen, radiant, distant, near.
You made millions of forms from yourself alone,
Towns, villages, fields, the river's course;
All eyes observe you upon them,
For you are the Aten of daytime on high.

. . .

You are in my heart,
There is no other who knows you,
Only your son, *Neferkheprure, Sole-one-of-Re,*
Whom you have taught your ways and your might.
(Those on) earth come from your hand as you made
   them,
When you have dawned they live,
When you set they die;
You yourself are lifetime, one lives by you.
All eyes are on (your) beauty until you set,
All labor ceases when you rest in the west;
When you rise you stir [everyone] for the King,
Every leg is on the move since you founded the earth.
You rouse them for your son who came from your
   body,
The King who lives by Maat,[3] the Lord of the Two
   Lands,
Neferkheprure, Sole-one-of-Re,
The Son of Re who lives by Maat, the Lord of crowns,
Akhenaten, great in his lifetime;
(And) the great Queen whom he loves, the Lady of
   the Two Lands,
Nefer-nefru-Aten Nefertiti, living forever.

---

[2]Hapy, the inundating Nile, emerges from the netherworld (*dat*) to
   nourish Egypt, while foreign peoples are sustained by a "Nile from
   heaven" that descends as rain. [Translator's note.]

---

[3]Truth and justice. [Ed.]

COMMENTS AND QUESTIONS

1. What indications are there in the poem that Akhenaton believed in one universal god?

2. What are the attributes of this god?

3. What is the *tone* of this poem?

4. What imagery does the poet use to convey his adoration of Aten?

5. This poem has been compared to the biblical Psalms (see Chapter 8). Do you see any similarities?

6. What indications do you see of the cosmopolitanism, or multicultural and multiracial society, that characterized Akhenaton's reign?

7. Look at the sculpture of the king and his family offering to the Aten (Fig. 2-13). In what sense do they illustrate or correspond to the poem?

Egyptian Love Poetry

The *lyric* as a style of writing may have been first defined in Greece (see Chapter 3), but it was practiced earlier by the Egyptians and by the Hebrews (see "The Song of Songs," Chapter 8). Poems, almost certainly words meant to be accompanied by music, emphasizing personal feeling and in particular romantic love, flourished in the New Kingdom. We do not know who the authors were, but they seem to have been both men and women and were perhaps scribes. Since we are still ignorant of Egyptian *prosody,* poetic rendering of these often fragmentary verses into a modern language—always a difficult task—is based somewhat on guesswork. As opposed to a literal translation, we prefer the work of a modern American poet, Noel Stock. In these poetic adaptations, Stock continues the work of Ezra Pound, who died before he was able to complete them. Pound, who was interested in poetic traditions from all over the world, did not read ancient Egyptian but worked closely with an Italian Egyptologist. The adaptations seem to capture the intensity and directness of these highly emotional but not sentimental poems.

I

Diving and swimming with you here
Gives me the chance I've been waiting for:
To show my looks
Before an appreciative eye.

My bathing suit of the best material,
The finest sheer,
Now that it's wet
Notice the transparency,
How it clings.

Let us admit, I find you attractive.
I swim away, but soon I'm back,
Splashing, chattering,
Any excuse at all to join your party.

Look! a redfish flashed through my fingers!
You'll see it better
If you come over here,
Near me.

II

Nothing, nothing can keep me from my love
Standing on the other shore.

Not even old crocodile
There on the sandbank between us
Can keep us apart.

I go in spite of him,
I walk upon the waves,
Her love flows back across the water,
Turning waves to solid earth
For me to walk on.

The river is our Enchanted Sea.

III

To have seen her
To have seen her approaching
Such beauty is
Joy in my heart forever.
Nor time eternal take back
What she has brought to me.

IV

When she welcomes me
Arms open wide
I feel as some traveller returning
From the far land of Punt.

All things change; the mind, the senses,
Into perfume rich and strange.

And when she parts her lips to kiss
My head is light, I am drunk without beer.[1]

V

If I were one of her females
Always in attendance
(Never a step away)
I would be able to admire
The resplendence
Of her body
Entire.

If I were her laundryman, for a month,
I would be able to wash from her veils
The perfumes that linger.

I would be willing to settle for less
And be her ring, the seal on her finger.

Pleasant Songs of the Sweetheart Who Meets You in the Fields

I

You, mine, my love,
My heart strives to reach the heights of your love.

See, sweet, the bird-trap set with my own hand.

See the birds of Punt,
Perfume a-wing
Like a shower of myrrh
Descending on Egypt.

Let us watch my handiwork,
The two of us, together in the fields.

II

The shrill of the wild goose
Unable to resist
The temptation of my bait.

While I, in a tangle of love,
Unable to break free,
Must watch the bird carry away my nets.

And when my mother returns, loaded with birds,
And finds me empty-handed,
What shall I say?

---

[1]The most common drink in ancient Egypt. [Ed.]

That I caught no birds?
That I myself was caught in your net?

III

Even when the birds rise
Wave mass on wave mass in great flight
I see nothing, I am blind
Caught up as I am and carried away
Two hearts obedient in their beating
My life caught up with yours
Your beauty the binding.

IV

Without your love, my heart would beat no more;
Without your love, sweet cake seems only salt;
Without your love, sweet "shedeh" turns to bile.
O listen, darling, my heart's life needs your love;
For when you breathe, mine is the heart that beats.

V

With candour I confess my love;
I love you, yes, and wish to love you closer;
As mistress of your house,
Your arm placed over mine.

Alas your eyes are loose.
I tell my heart: "My lord
Has moved away. During
The night moved away
And left me. I am like a tomb."

And I wonder: Is there no sensation
Left, when you come to me?
Nothing at all?

Alas those eyes which lead you astray,
Forever on the loose.
And yet I confess with candour
That no matter where else they roam
If they roam towards me
I enter into life.

VI

The swallow sings "Dawn,
        Whither fadeth the dawn?"

So fades my happy night
My love in bed beside me.

Imagine my joy at his whisper:
"I'll never leave you," he said.
"Your hand in mine we'll stroll
In every beautiful path."

Moreover he lets the world know
That I am first among his women
And my heart grieves no longer.

VII

Head out the door—
Is he coming?

Ears alert for his step,
And a heart that never stops talking about him.

A messenger:
"I'm not well..."
Why doesn't he come straight out
And tell me
He's found another girl.

One more heart to suffer.

VIII

I writhe so for lost love
Half my hair has fallen in grief.

I am having my hair recurled and set,
Ready, just in case...

COMMENTS AND QUESTIONS

1. One of these lyric cycles (groups of poems) may have been written by a man and the other by a woman (although stylistically, both are the work of the translator). What similarities and differences in the expression and the nature of love do you find between the two?

2. What images specific to Egypt and what depictions of Egyptian life do you find in these poems?

3. How does the narrator in the first cycle use the image of water? How does he portray himself?

4. How does the narrator in the second cycle use the image of birds? What is her attitude toward her rivals?

5. Do you notice a musical quality in these poems? Can you be specific? To what kind of music would you set them? Refer to the section on Egyptian music.

6. Compare these love lyrics to modern songs or poems that are especially meaningful to you.

Ancient Civilizations

The development of agriculture, one of the most important revolutions in human existence, was the foundation of the great civilizations of the Tigris-Euphrates and the Nile. Beginning about 3400 B.C., after six thousand years of agricultural development, the Mesopotamians, followed closely by the Egyptians, formed the increasing population generated by this new mode of food production into societies organized around cities. From that point on, although later peoples introduced many changes in urban and rural modes of life, their accomplishments were essentially exploitations of the original revolutionary combination of agriculture and urbanization.

The City

The creation of the city between 3200 and 3000 B.C. presupposed a degree of efficiency in food production that permitted some members of society to be exempted from cultivation of the fields to perform other tasks. Within the city wall were centered the religious and governmental agencies of the people as well as the major stores of food. Whereas commerce tended to play a minor role in Egyptian cities, Mesopotamian cities developed very early a sophisticated trade network initially between themselves and later with foreign areas. The work of many urban dwellers was devoted to commercial life.

Political Life

Initially governed by an assembly of male city-dwellers, Sumerian cities developed a monarchy about 3000 B.C. Nonetheless, until the conquests of Sargon in 2340 B.C., cities remained largely independent from one another. Although the rulers of Mesopotamia endeavored to establish their own divinity, they were largely unsuccessful. On the other hand, from the beginning of the political organization of Egypt the country was ruled by monarchs called King of Upper and Lower Egypt who later adopted the title pharaoh.

These rulers rested their authority to govern on their claimed divine origin, and throughout a three-thousand-year period this claim remained largely uncontested. Nubians from the kingdom of Kush ruled Egypt during the Twenty-fifth Dynasty, bringing with them a slightly different concept of the monarchy. Although the Egyptian queen Hatshepsut ruled as sole monarch, Kush, given the importance of the Candaces and the daughters of the king, seemed in general to accord more power to women.

Religion

In both Mesopotamia and Egypt, religious concerns were intertwined with political ones from the beginning. Both societies had a complicated variety of gods, but in Egypt the sun god, Amon-Ra, emerged as the official chief god and ancestor of the pharaohs. The first great constructions within the Sumerian cities along the Euphrates were the ziggurat temples designed as residences of the patron gods of the city. At the same time in Egypt, the main common goal of the society was to provide a proper burial monument for the pharaoh, who on his death would return to his divine family. As the belief in the immortality of the soul became diffused throughout Egyptian society with the spread of the worship of Osiris, however, the interest in a proper burial became a preoccupying personal concern for all. By contrast the Mesopotamian deemphasis on the afterlife encouraged the population to focus attention on the here-and-now. A type of *monotheism* emerged in Egypt in the reign of Akhenaton, but thereafter the Egyptians returned to the worship of many gods.

Art and Music

As in most traditional societies, art in these ancient civilizations was not an independent activity but was intimately connected to its religious or social function. The ziggurat expressed devotion to the patron god, the power of the ruler, and the pride in the city characteristic of Mesopotamia. Assyrian art tended to emphasize political and military power over religious devotion. Egyptian pyramids, with their elaborate systems of preparation for the afterlife, show striking and significant developments in architecture. In sculpture, the Mesopotamian style tended to be more fluid and lifelike than the monumental, *frontal* Egyptian one. Although Egyptian sculpture and painting underwent a significant transformation under Akhenaton, on the whole they changed very little, reflecting a conservative and stable society. The kingdom of Kush, adapting Egyptian artistic forms to its own needs and evolving others independently, also created a less rigid style in sculpture. We know much less about ancient music than about ancient art, but we do have evidence that string and wind instrumetns were developed in Mesopotamia and in Egypt. Music was probably an important part of religious ceremonies and civic festivals. It was also used to accompany poetry.

Writing and Literature

The art of writing is surely one of this period's great contributions to civilization. Although the first written tablets that have been discovered are from Sumer, writing seems to have developed independently in both Mesopotamia and Egypt. Both societies instituted schools to train scribes, but literacy was perhaps more widespread among the upper classes in Egypt. Writing was first used as a record of economic transactions, then for other documents, letters, and sacred and literary texts. Letters were exchanged between Mesopotamia and Egypt under the New Kingdom. For us, the two most important written works from Mesopotamian culture are the *Epic of Gilgamesh* and the legal code of Hammurabi. Gilgamesh may be called the first epic hero of Western civilization, and his journey to the realm of the gods in quest of immortal life is, as we shall see, a theme that will be repeated and varied in the epics of Greece, Rome, and Europe. Egyptian literature, in addition to tales, historical writings, and proverbs, has given us a variety of poetry. Hymns such as the "Hymn to the Sun" and the love lyrics anticipate some of the devotional and lyric poetry of Greece and Rome. Because Meroitic has not yet been deciphered, we know much less about literature from Kush, but those texts that we do have (written in Egyptian hieroglyphics) demonstrate features perhaps linking them to the typically African praise poem, a form that will be studied in the unit on medieval and modern western Africa. The reciprocal influences between Egypt and the rest of Africa are still a matter of scholarly discussion and debate.

For most of three thousand years, these great riverine societies acted as sources of cultural innovation for peoples in Europe, other parts of Africa, and the Middle East. However, in the last centuries of their existence the kingdoms of the Nile and the Tigris-Euphrates valleys, fixed on rehearsing their past achievements and copying earlier forms, were superseded by a series of new powers that had learned the lessons they were taught only too well.

At this point we could look in a number of directions. We could consider the evolution of the Persian and Indian civilization generated largely by the rich mix of the native culture of the Indus valley with those of Egypt and Mesopotamia. If we looked farther east, to China, which appears to have developed independently of other areas, we would in fact have to begin again. Eventually, we will explore western Africa as a cultural root. But our present goal is to examine the culture that grew up around the Mediterranean and gave rise to the two primary cultural roots of Western civilization: the Greco-Roman and the Judeo-Christian. After the societies of river valleys, then, we now turn to those of the great inland sea.

PART TWO

The Greco-Roman and Judeo-Christian Roots

Early Greece

he civilization of ancient Greece, which we can date roughly from about the eighth century to the first century B.C., and the civilization of ancient Rome, lasting from about the first century B.C. to the fifth century A.D., are often referred to collectively as *Greco-Roman* or as *classical*. This should not be interpreted to mean that their cultures were identical. There are many points of contrast, and, although the Romans assimilated a good deal of Greek culture, they added many unique features of their own. Still, they do share a common cluster of ways of thinking and creating that differ from those of other ancient cultures and that have clearly influenced the development of the Western humanistic tradition. Both Greeks and Romans gave human reason, in forms like rule by law and discussion through philosophy, more importance than mystical experience or reliance on tradition. In literature, art, and architecture, both cultures stressed balance, proportion, simplicity, and nobility as their criteria for beauty. Yet their view of human beings was not cold or merely rationalistic. The whole person was very much in view; and, if reason was to dominate the passions, the emotional, ecstatic side of human nature was also recognized as essential.

It is quite possible to argue that Western culture, particularly North American culture, has been more influenced by the Romans than by the Greeks. Yet we have chosen to focus attention here on Greek culture for three reasons: (1) the Greeks obviously came first and laid the basis for the later culture; (2) Greek culture was more concentrated and it is somewhat easier to get a coherent view of its lifestyle, art, and thought; and (3) in many instances the Greek cultural monuments, especially the tragedies, are more alive and significant for us today than are their Roman counterparts. We will devote most attention to the "classical" phase of Greek culture; but, to avoid confusion, it is necessary to remember that *all* of Greco-Roman culture is sometimes called classical, as when we speak of classical languages (Greek and Latin) or classical literature. The word was first adopted by the Renaissance humanists, who used it in the sense of "first class" or "best" because they considered the artistic and literary style of the ancient Greeks and Romans as the model for all good art. That ideal model was generally accepted until the nineteenth century in the West. Now we also use the term *classical* to refer to the particular phase of Greek art and literature that, according to most historians of Greek culture, most perfectly expresses the ideals of the Greek aesthetic and the Greek view of life— Athens in the fifth century B.C., specifically 480–404. We will define the classical *canons* more specifically when examining the creations from this phase. First, however, it will be necessary to examine briefly the rise of Greek civilization and some important prior cultural developments.

Hellenism: The Rise of Greek Culture

What was so important about a small Mediterranean civilization that flourished over two thousand years ago in a country we now call Greece?

In the context of world history, Greek civilization is a relative latecomer. Not only did the civilizations of Mesopotamia and Egypt precede it in the Mediterranean by thousands of years, but also highly developed civilizations in the Indus valley and in China flourished while the peoples of Greece still lived in primitive conditions. In their written literature, painting, sculpture, music, and science, the Greeks were often indebted to Mesopotamia and, especially, to Egypt. Yet the ways in which they developed the humanities and sciences were unique. Those developments are significant for our search for cultural roots because the Greeks were the first to express themselves in ways that can be designated as characteristically Western.

There is a more specific reason that the culture of the ancient Greeks is especially important to the study of the humanities. Theirs was the first culture that we can truly call humanistic. The Greeks were the first to be interested in, and indeed to glorify, human beings simply as human beings—for themselves and their own unique qualities rather than because of their place in a religious, familial, or social order. This stress on the value of the individual made Greek culture less conservative than its predecessors. In contrast with the stable, slowly changing, and long-lasting Egyptian

culture, Greek culture changed rapidly and was short-lived.

Unfortunately, it used to be fairly commonplace for Western historians to assume that because the Greeks were different they were better, or because their culture changed more rapidly they contributed more to the development of the human spirit. We are now perhaps better able to see that the restless, dynamic character of Western culture has created its own problems, and also that we have much to learn from the older cultures of the rest of the world. At the risk of making too great a generalization, we might say that a religious sense of life, or the sense of being in touch with a supernatural, spiritual world, and the use of signs or suggestion to convey this in art, have characterized the African and Asiatic contributions to world culture. Philosophy, or the rational analysis of problems from a human point of view, and a corresponding naturalism in art have been the legacies of the Greeks and their successors, the Romans.

Crete

How did the Hellenes (the Greeks) develop their particular form of culture? The first civilization to exist in the country now called Greece developed on the island of Crete in the Mediterranean Sea around 2000 B.C. (See map.) The island's location between Egypt and mainland Greece is symbolic of its role in helping to transmit one culture to the other. The Minoans, as they were called, after their legendary king, Minos, seem to have developed trade with Egypt and to have led peaceful and creative lives. The form of government in Crete was apparently matriarchal; that is, it was ruled by a queen whose husband, the king, was ritually sacrificed each year. A mother-earth goddess was the principal deity in Minoan religion. A modern African scholar has interpreted the importance given to the female principle in Crete as evidence that Minoan civilization is basically African in its origins. Whether or not this theory is true, the matriarchal emphasis in Minoan culture certainly contrasts with the male-dominated later Greek culture.

Minoan artists used natural forms—plants, animals, fish, and fowl—to decorate walls, pottery, and gems. Their loosely structured, vividly colorful designs suggest a deep love for, and profound observation of, nature. The unfortified, elaborate, and labyrinthine palaces at Knossos (Fig. 3-1), Phaistos, and Mallia contrast sharply with the hierarchical, ceremonial, ritualistic tomb and temple complexes of Egypt. Built of wood, mudbrick, and stone, the multileveled palaces

CLASSICAL GREECE

had light wells, folding doors, and winding stairs that connected apartments, ceremonial rooms, workshops, and storage areas. The beautiful *frescoes,* seal stones, jewelry, and other artifacts suggest a lifestyle in which satisfaction and pleasure were more important than ceremonial or military discipline.

In 1400 B.C. Crete was conquered by a more war-like people, the first we can truly call Greek. Wandering tribes from Europe, settling in mainland Greece, eventually developed a rich civilization centered in the city of Mycenae, which flourished between 1600 and 1200 B.C. This civilization is referred to either as Achaean, from the name of its principal tribe, or Mycenaean, from the name of the city. Within it a

number of kings ruled over small, independent states. The most famous of these kings were Agamemnon, who ruled in Mycenae with Queen Clytemnestra, and his brother Menelaus, who ruled in Sparta with Helen. Their names have become familiar to us because of the legend of the Trojan War. According to this legend Helen, the most beautiful woman in the world, ran away from her husband with Paris, the son of Priam, king of Troy. Troy was located in Asia Minor, and its ruins have been excavated in what is now Turkey. Determined to recapture Helen, the kings of Greece raised a huge fleet of ships commanded by Agamemnon. They sailed for Troy and remained there for nine years, fighting and plundering but unable to take the

3-1   *Knossos, Crete, Palace, East Wing. (Eugene Brown)*

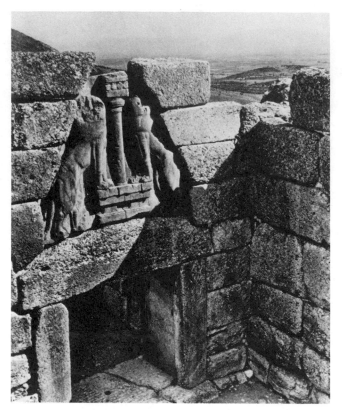

3-2   *Mycenae, Lion Gate, c. 1250 B.C. (Eugene Brown)*

city. In the tenth year Agamemnon quarreled with his most powerful fighter, Achilles. As Achilles and his followers withdrew from the fighting, the brother of Paris, Hektor, began to lead the Trojans toward victory. Achilles then returned to battle, succeeding in entering Troy; he killed Hektor but was soon killed himself. Although the Greeks were aided by powerful new allies such as Memnon, the black prince from Ethiopia, and Penthisilea, queen of the Amazons, with her female warriors, Troy still continued to hold out. It was finally overcome by a ruse devised by the "wily" Greek, Odysseus. The Greeks, pretending to acknowledge defeat, actually boarded their ships to prepare for departure, leaving behind them a huge wooden horse as an offering to the gods. The horse was, in fact, full of armed Greek soldiers. When the Trojans, overcome with curiosity, took it into their city, the Greeks came out and set fire to Troy. Thus the will of the gods was accomplished: Troy was subdued by the Achaeans, and Helen returned to Menelaus. Historians today believe that the Trojan War (c. 1200 B.C.) was actually fought, but probably for economic reasons. More important for our cultural roots is the legendary material that has spawned a wealth of Western literature, beginning with the *Iliad* and the *Odyssey*.

Mycenae

The Mycenaean age of Greek culture, about which we have little factual information, is often called the heroic age because most of the heroic deeds such as the Trojan War that were later written and sung about took place then. In contrast to matriarchal Crete, it was a masculine-oriented and male-ruled society. The painting, sculpture, and architecture of Mycenae

affirm this orientation. The citadel (Fig. 3-2) at Mycenae, overlooking the plain and visible from the sea, was heavily fortified. One entered it through the Lion Gate, so called for its monumental *relief sculpture* of two lions. The king's palace dominated the entire complex. A rectangular building with a deep porch on its narrow end, it contained a main room where the king received dignitaries, held court, and entertained. Frescoes of shields and warriors decorated the walls. The heraldic lions at the gate and the massive scale of the masonry create an image of power controlled by will, solemnity, and ritual.

Mycenae, "rich in gold," was eventually destroyed by uncivilized invaders from the north, the Dorians. The next four hundred years are often called the "dark ages" of Greece. We know little about this period except that what would later become the classical city-states—Athens, Corinth, Argos, and finally Sparta—were beginning to emerge as centers of power.

The Archaic Period

The next epoch of Greek culture is sometimes referred to as the Archaic period. *Archaic* refers to something in its initial stages. This period, which we can date from approximately 700 to 480 B.C., indeed saw the beginnings of several forms of Greek culture. In politics the unit of the city-state, or *polis,* was formed; and the type of government known as *democracy,* which means in Greek "rule by the people," evolved. In architecture the Doric temple was created, and in sculpture the first freestanding human figures appeared. Greek vase painting was also developed during this time, and the first people who can properly be called philosophers began to speculate and reason about the nature of the universe. Early forms of drama evolved throughout this period; and Thespis, the founder of Greek drama as we know it, won the first dramatic contest in Athens in the sixth century B.C. We will discuss all of these forms in connection with their classical stages in the next chapter. Here we look at two elements of Greek culture that reached a kind of culmination in the Archaic period: religion and poetry—specifically the forms of the *epic* and the *lyric.*

Greek Religion and Mythology

The Greeks, in contrast with the ancient peoples of India and the ancient Hebrews, did not have what we might call a religious genius. They seem to have been too much oriented toward this world to have devised either a great theology or a literature of mystical experience. Unlike the early Hindu scriptures or the Bible, the stories of the gods on Mount Olympus have given rise to no enduring religion. Why, then, have these stories been so appealing to people for so many generations, and why are names of gods and goddesses like Zeus, Apollo, and Aphrodite still familiar to us? Unlike the Hebrew, Muslim, and Christian God, who belongs to a realm inaccessible to humans except through faith, the Greek gods are comprehensible to human beings. They may be seen as a kind of wish fulfillment—they are like us but powerful, beautiful, and immortal; they live "at ease." Created through prescientific attempts to explain the universe, they embody deep, intuitive understandings of human psychology.

Like those of the Mesopotamians and the Egyptians, the Greek *pantheon* ("all the gods") is considerable, and it is not possible to mention the names of all the gods and goddesses here. Instead, we will look briefly at the Greek myth of the origin of the world and at some of the major deities.

The Greeks believed that the universe was created from Chaos, a great mass in which everything now existing was jumbled. The first beings to spring forth were a female divinity, earth (Gaea), and a male divinity, heaven (Uranus). It is worth noting here that nearly all myths of creation and religious systems except Judaism and Christianity have seen the need for a divine female role in creation. The children of Gaea and Uranus were the Titans, the first gods, whose leader was Cronos (Saturn, in Latin). (The Romans largely assimilated Greek religion, and all of the Greek gods and goddesses are probably more familiar under their Latin names, which appear here in parentheses.) Cronos was deposed by his son Zeus (Jupiter). Zeus became lord of the heavens, his brother Poseidon (Neptune) lord of the sea, and their brother Dis (Pluto) lord of the underworld, or the realm of the dead. Hera (Juno), the wife of Zeus, was goddess of childbirth and protector of married women. Because the family of Zeus was said to live on Mount Olympus, its members were called the Olympian gods and goddesses. Some of the others are these:

Athena (Minerva), patron of the city of Athens and goddess of wisdom. She sprang full-grown from the head of Zeus.

Phoebus Apollo, god of the sun, reason, music, and medicine. He established the oracle at Delphi where the Greeks went to receive enigmatic prophecies about their future. He is associated with two Greek sayings: "Know thyself" and "Nothing in excess."

Dionysus (Bacchus), god of wine, ecstasy, fertility, and the theater.

Aphrodite (Venus), goddess of love and beauty. She caused amorous complications among gods and mortals as well as great happiness. Her son Eros (Cupid) was well known for shooting his arrows in the wrong place at the wrong time.

There were, of course, other gods and goddesses in the Olympian pantheon as well as demigods and semidivine heroes, but none of them, not even Zeus, was all-powerful in the way of the Jewish and Christian God. Above the gods was a concept of fate, or destiny. It was believed that every individual on earth had a *moira,* or pattern of life, to fulfill. Although the gods could predict what it would be, they did not directly intervene. Just how it would be fulfilled depended on the individual's character and the choices that he or she made during life. We will see how this problem of the relations between humans, gods, and fate is examined in the tragedy *Oedipus Rex.*

Greek religion was practiced throughout the "heroic" or Mycenaean age but was not systematically written down and explained until the Archaic period. Religious practices consisted of the sacrifice of animals and the pouring of libations (usually wine or oil) to the gods. Each god or goddess had a temple where his or her sacred image was kept and the gifts of the worshipers were stored. The rites usually took place before, not within, the temple. Thus the building and the area around it became a sanctuary. Here statues and *stele* (standing slabs of stone, painted or carved) were placed as offerings and commemoratives of events such as victories. Some of the important sanctuaries, like Delphi, belonged to all Greeks and had statues, stele, and small treasuries to hold offerings from each of the great city-states. Others, like the Athenian Acropolis, were the manifestation of the power and glory of a particular city.

The gods, for the Greeks, could take part in human affairs. This divine intervention is also reflected in the close association of a particular divinity with a city. Athens and Athena are the most famous example: Athena was said to be directly involved with the evolution of Athenian law and justice. Thus religious observances became intermingled with political life in a complex way that enhanced the city's vitality and cohesiveness.

Long before Athens became the principal Greek city, the epic poems of Homer show to what extent the Greek gods were seen as involved with human activities.

Homer and the Epic

The poet Homer, who probably lived around 800 B.C., has been traditionally revered as the first writer of Western literature. Yet he was not a writer at all in the sense that we use the word today, and it is possible that he did not even know how to read and write. Homer belonged to an oral tradition, the nature of which we will study more fully in the chapter on African literature, and he was "a singer of tales." He composed, rather than wrote, his poems, probably basing them on a long tradition of singers who recited stories about the Trojan War, accompanied by the music of a stringed instrument, the lyre. The original purpose of this *epic* poetry was to "sing the famous deeds of men": to teach people in a pleasurable way about the great heroes of their culture. It should be stressed that Homer's poetry is not folk poetry—it is highly polished poetry, composed according to strict rules, but it was composed orally. It is probable that the Meso-potamian *Epic of Gilgamesh* was also originally composed orally; this is also true of other early epics. Oral epics are still being transmitted in the Balkan countries of Europe and in Africa. The *Epic of Sundiata* (Chapter 13) is an example of an epic from a living oral tradition. When we read Homer, we are reading an English text translated from an ancient Greek text that is a written version of the chanted oral epic. We do not know who decided to write down the Homeric poems or why and when this was done, but that act was in itself a momentous event for our cultural history. Homer's two great epics, the *Iliad* and the *Odyssey*, have been translated by generations of poets and scholars and are still widely read. They have also been instrumental in the creation of a long tradition of written epics.

The epic as a literary type was first defined by the first critic of Western literature, Aristotle (384–322 B.C.) in the *Poetics* (see Chapter 6). Using Aristotle's definition, Thrall, Hibbard, and Holman in their *Handbook to Literature* define the epic for the modern reader thus: "A long narrative poem in elevated style presenting characters of high position in a series of adventures which form an organic whole through their relation to a central figure of heroic proportions and through their development of episodes important to the history of a nation of race."[1] There are four important elements to retain from this definition: style, hero, action, and culture. In spite of its folk origins, the epic uses a noble rhythmic pattern or *meter* (in Greek the six-foot line, dactylic hexameter) and intricate figures of speech. The epic hero, although he may have human faults, must be almost superhuman in courage, strength, and greatness of character. Epic actions often include great wars and range over an entire country or continent. Supernatural beings, in Homer's case the gods, are usually involved in these actions. The actions must be important ones in the history of a nation or race and the hero in some sense a savior of that nation or race. Thus the hero is not only a great individual but also a culture-hero. Achilles, the hero of the *Iliad*, exemplifies what Homer perceived to be the greatness of the Greeks, and he is instrumental in an event highly significant for their culture: the downfall of Troy.

The Homeric poems were written down and read years after they were composed. The epic became a

---

[1] William Flint Thrall, Addison Hibbard, and C. Hugh Holman, *A Handbook to Literature* (New York: The Odyssey Press, 1960), pp. 174–75.

written form in Western literature with the Latin poet Virgil's *Aeneid* (Chapter 7). Important examples of the epic in English literature are *Beowulf* and Milton's *Paradise Lost*. The epic as a literary form began to die out in the nineteenth century when it was replaced by the novel. In American culture the film industry attempted to take over the form—think how many movies have been advertised as "epic." Even this form seems to be on its way out in the contemporary world. It could be argued that our culture no longer produces events and heroes of "epic" proportions.

Both of Homer's epics are concerned with the Trojan War. The *Iliad* (Greek for "Song of Troy") depicts the war itself, and the *Odyssey* depicts the long and adventurous return home of the hero of the Trojan horse episode, Odysseus. The *Iliad* has thus been called the epic of war and the *Odyssey* the epic of peace; yet both investigate the nature of these two fundamental states of human society. The *Iliad* presents war in both its terror and its glory. Through our own experience of these matters we can, as modern readers, relate to Homer's vivid portrayal of the human urge for violence and the human yearning for peace.

The *Iliad*

The opening lines of Homer's first epic tell the reader (or listener) exactly what the poet intends to do, and set the tone for the rest.

> Sing, goddess, the anger of Peleus' son Achilleus
> and its devastation, which put pains thousandfold
>   upon the Achaians,
> hurled in their multitudes to the house of Hades
>   strong souls
> of heroes, but gave their bodies to be the delicate
>   feasting
> of dogs, of all birds, and the will of Zeus was
>   accomplished
> since that time when first there stood in division of
>   conflict
> Atreus' son the lord of men and brilliant Achilleus.

The translator of this passage, Richmond Lattimore, has attempted to render in English the stately rhythm of the Greek hexameter. You should be able to count six beats in each line. Even this short passage reveals Homer's attention to realistic detail—the line about the dead bodies—and his use of *epithets* or repeated modifiers that succinctly characterize a person or thing, such as "lord of men" for Atreus' son, Agamemnon, and "brilliant" for Achilles (Achilleus). One of the most famous of these (not in this passage) is "the rosy-fingered dawn."

The goddess invoked by Homer is the muse, who was supposed to inspire the poet to sing. The poem's subject as stated is not the general one of the war but the immediate one of the anger of Achilles. Yet the poet branches out from this internal theme of the individual character of his hero to the external one of the war and its destruction. He then extends his point of view to an even more universal one—this war and its outcome were the will of the supreme god, Zeus. The introduction is rounded out by a return to the original subject. We now learn that Achilles was angry because of a conflict with Agamemnon, and the poet is ready to begin his tale.

These three levels—which we might call the internal, the external, and the universal—remain in interplay throughout the *Iliad*. The story begins with an explanation of how Achilles came to be angry with Agamemnon. Briefly, Achilles feels that he has been dishonored because Agamemnon took from him his war prize and concubine, a girl named Briseis. We are in the tenth year of the Trojan War, and Achilles withdraws himself from the fighting to prove to the Greeks how necessary he is to them. The gods become involved in this personal quarrel when Achilles prays to his mother, Thetis, a sea divinity, to let the Greeks be defeated in his absence; she carries his prayer to Zeus. This is the situation at the end of the first book of the *Iliad*. Books 2–7 describe the fighting between the Greeks and Trojans and develop individual characters, human and divine. By the end of Book 8 the Greek leaders are discouraged, and Agamemnon offers to give Briseis back to Achilles, along with many other gifts, if he will rejoin the fighting. Achilles is too angry to accept. It is only when his best friend, Patroklos, has been killed by Hektor, son of King Priam of Troy, that he is moved to return to battle. He succeeds in driving the Trojans back, slays Hektor, and drags his body behind his chariot. The Greeks hold an elaborate funeral for Patroklos. The body of Hektor remains unburied, a sign of dishonor; but, when King Priam comes to Achilles to ask for his son's body, Achilles takes pity on the old man and the *Iliad* ends with the Trojans' funeral for Hektor.

The *Odyssey*

The opening lines of the second Homeric epic also state the subject and introduce the hero. The translator here is Robert Fitzgerald.

> Sing in me, Muse, and through me tell the story
> of that man skilled in all ways of contending,
> the wanderer, harried for years on end,

after he plundered the stronghold
on the proud height of Troy.
                              He saw the townlands
and learned the minds of many distant men,
and weathered many bitter nights and days
in his deep heart at sea, while he fought only
to save his life, to bring his shipmates home.
But not by will nor valor could he save them,
for their own recklessness destroyed them all—
children and fools, they killed and feasted on
the cattle of Lord Hêlios, the Sun,
and he who moves all day through heaven
took from their eyes the dawn of their return.

Of these adventures, Muse, daughter of Zeus,
tell us in our time, lift the great song again.
Begin when all the rest who left behind them
headlong death in battle or at sea
had long ago returned, while he alone still hungered
for home and wife. Her ladyship Kalypso
clung to him in her sea-hollowed caves—
a nymph, immortal and most beautiful,
who craved him for her own.
                              And when long years and seasons
wheeling brought around that point of time
ordained for him to make his passage homeward,
trials and dangers, even so, attended him
even in Ithaka, near those he loved.
Yet all the gods had pitied Lord Odysseus,
all but Poseidon, raging cold and rough
against the brave king till he came ashore
at last on his own land.

Here we learn that the *Odyssey* takes place after the Trojan War and that it tells the story of the wanderings (by sea) and adventures of Odysseus, a man skilled in argumentation and verbal art. Because of his cleverness, Odysseus survived, whereas his shipmates, because of their foolishness, were destroyed. Although goddesses and exotic and beautiful women love Odysseus and try to retain him, his guiding passion continues to be to return home to his wife Penelope and his son Telemakos in Ithaka. The *Odyssey* tells of his adventures during his return, which takes ten years.

The poem begins with the goddess Athena's plea to her father, Zeus, to save Odysseus. It then tells of the adventures of Telemakos as he searches for his father, whom he has never known, since he was a baby when Odysseus left for the Trojan War. The bulk of the epic, however, consists of Odysseus' narration of his and his companions' many adventures, which include combat with one-eyed giants (Odysseus, characteristically, tricks them), overcoming the powers of magic charms and enchanting witches, and a visit to the realm of the dead. At the end, Odysseus returns at last to Ithaka,

slays the suitors who are attempting to usurp his kingdom and his wife, and is reunited with his household and the ever-faithful Penelope. Thus the tale ends happily.

Because of the fairy-tale, romantic quality of several of its episodes, some scholars believe that ancient Asiatic and African legends may be embedded in the *Odyssey*. It seems almost certain that there is some oriental influence and quite probable that the author of the poem was acquainted with the *Epic of Gilgamesh*. The atmosphere of the *Odyssey* is indeed quite different from that of the *Iliad*—for one thing its protagonist is a wise and seasoned middle-aged man instead of an exuberant and "wrathful" young man. Critics have called it a "romance" or "the first novel" rather than an epic; the poet Robert Graves believed that its author was a woman. There is, of course, no conclusive evidence that "Homer" wrote both poems, yet this was the tradition followed by the Greeks. In fact, reading the two Homeric epics formed the core of classical Greek education. In spite of the differences in tone and content, there is no compelling reason to conclude that the two great epics of the Trojan War, although their oral sources may have been different, were not written down by an accomplished poet named Homer.

The Lyric

With Homer, the individual poet begins to make his personal voice heard, even in the context of singing the deeds of heroes and great social events. But the trend toward individual expression of personal sentiment so characteristic of modern poetry came to perfection with the development of the *lyric* about two centuries after Homer. We use the word today for words set to music (song lyrics) or to describe a particular kind of poetry, characterized by a subjective presentation of an intense emotion, often (but not necessarily) love. Even if not set to music, lyric poetry usually has a musical effect on the listener or reader.

The love lyric, as we have seen, was already developed in Egypt. But we know much more about Greek lyric poetry. The lyric in Greece was inseparable from music; melody and rhythm were tied intimately to the words of the poem. The word meant simply "accompanied by the lyre," a stringed musical instrument (see Fig. 3-3) used in the cult of Apollo. The earliest lyric poets were primarily musicians who simultaneously composed both words and music. Their musical pieces (all of which have been lost) were probably simple tunes; at least, they lacked any har-

3-3 *Vase representing imaginary portraits of Alcaeus and Sappho holding lyres, c. 470 B.C. (Courtesy, Staatliche Antikensammlungen und Glyptothek, Munich)*

mony in the modern sense. Lyric poetry developed along two lines: choric and monodic. The choral songs, sung by groups and usually performed at religious or festive occasions, were accompanied by dancing. The combined arts of the choral spoken word, music, and dance would develop into the choruses of classical Greek drama. The monodic (one voice, solo) lyric was performed at less formal occasions, sometimes at weddings, and used more personal and colloquial language.

The lyric spirit seems to have developed almost in opposition to the heroic, warlike ethos of earlier times. A fragment from the man who is generally considered the first lyric poet, Archilochos, makes this clear. Archilochos, who probably lived during the late eighth century B.C., fought as a mercenary soldier in the colonization of the Aegean island of Thasos. The Greek warrior was typically told to come home carrying his shield or *being* carried *on* it; loss of the shield meant loss of manly honor. But Archilochos presents a different view:

> Well, what if some barbaric Thracian glories
>   in the perfect shield I left under a bush?
> I was sorry to leave it—but I saved my skin.
>   Does it matter? O hell, I'll get a better one.

The lyric was to develop primarily in the islands of the Aegean sea and on the coast of Asia Minor, where a peaceful, refined, graceful, and aristocratic life flourished. Most renowned for its lyric poetry was the island of Lesbos where the greatest poet of this period, Sappho, and her friend and fellow poet Alcaeus, flourished.

HOMER

FROM THE *Iliad*

Translation by Richmond Lattimore

Although no one selection can adequately represent the scope and power of the *Iliad*, Book 6 shows the contrast between its glorification of war and its portrayal of human tenderness and opposition to war. Although this book does not mention the principal hero, Achilles, it does develop the character of his opponent, the more mature and, to the modern reader, probably more sympathetic Hektor, the leader of the Trojans. The accounts of battle and of the various slayings of Greeks and Trojans, although an important aspect of the epic style, may not have much fascination for us. However, the drama of Hektor's encounter with Paris and Helen, the cause of the war that brought about so much suffering, and Hektor's subsequent farewell to his beloved wife Andromache and his small son have an undeniable and universal emotional impact.

Book 6

So the grim encounter of Achaians° and Trojans was left
to itself, and the battle veered greatly now one way, now in another,
over the plain as they guided their bronze spears at each other
in the space between the waters of Xanthos and Simoeis.
   First Telamonian Aias, that bastion of the Achaians,   5
broke the Trojan battalions and brought light to his own company,
striking down the man who was far the best of the Thracians,

Akamas, the huge and mighty, the son of Eussoros.
Throwing first, he struck the horn of the horse-haired helmet
and the bronze spear-point fixed in his forehead and drove inward   10
through the bone; and a mist of darkness clouded both eyes.

Diomedes° of the great war cry cut down Axylos,
Teuthras' son, who had been a dweller in strong-founded Arisbe,
a man rich in substance and a friend to all humanity
since in his house by the wayside he entertained all comers.   15
Yet there was none of these now to stand before him and keep off
the sad destruction, and Diomedes stripped life from both of them,
Axylos and his henchman Kalesios, who was the driver
guiding his horses; so down to the underworld went both men.

Now Euryalos° slaughtered Opheltios and Dresos,   20
and went in pursuit of Aisepos and Pedasos, those whom the naiad
nymph Abarbare had born to blameless Boukolion.
Boukolion himself was the son of haughty Laomedon,°
eldest born, but his mother conceived him in darkness and secrecy.

1Achaians: Greeks.

12Diomedes: Son of Tydeus, lord of Argos, one of the greatest of the Achaian fighters, prominent in battle until wounded by Paris.

20Euryalos: Leader, with Diomedes and Sthenelos, of the men of Argos.

23Laomedon: King of Troy, son of Ilos, and father of Priam.

While shepherding his flocks he lay with the nymph
   and loved her,   25
and she conceiving bore him twin boys. But now
   Mekisteos'
son° unstrung the strength of these and the limbs in
   their glory,
Euryalos, and stripped the armour away from their
   shoulders.

Polypoites the stubborn in battle cut down Astyalos,
while Odysseus° slaughtered one from Perkote,
   Pidytes,   30
with the bronze spear, and great Aretaon was killed
   by Teukros.
Nestor's° son Antilochos with the shining shaft killed
Ableros; the lord of men, Agamemnon,° brought
   death to Elatos,
whose home had been on the shores of Satnioeis'
   lovely waters,
sheer Pedasos. And Leitos the fighter caught
   Phylakos   35
as he ran away; and Eurypylos made an end of
   Melanthios.

Now Menelaos° of the great war cry captured
   Adrestos
alive; for his two horses bolting over the level land
got entangled in a tamarisk growth, and shattered
   the curving
chariot at the tip of the pole; so they broken free
   went   40
on toward the city, where many beside stampeded in
   terror.
So Adrestos was whirled beside the wheel from the
   chariot
headlong into the dust on his face; and the son of
   Atreus,
Menelaos, with the far-shadowed spear in his hand,
   stood over him.

But Adrestos, catching him by the knees, supplicated: 45
"Take me alive, son of Atreus, and take appropriate
   ransom.
In my rich father's house the treasures lie piled in
   abundance;
bronze is there, and gold, and difficultly wrought
   iron,
and my father would make you glad with abundant
   repayment
were he to hear that I am alive by the ships of the
   Achaians."   50

So he spoke, and moved the spirit inside Menelaos.
And now he was on the point of handing him to a
   henchman
to lead back to the fast Achaian ships; but
   Agamemnon
came on the run to join him and spoke his word of
   argument:
"Dear brother, o Menelaos, are you concerned so
   tenderly   55
with these people? Did you in your house get the
   best of treatment
from the Trojans? No, let not one of them go free of
   sudden
death and our hands; not the young man child that
   the mother carries
still in her body, not even he, but let all of Ilion's°
people perish, utterly blotted out and unmourned
   for."   60

The hero spoke like this, and bent the heart of his
   brother
since he urged justice. Menelaos shoved with his
   hand Adrestos
the warrior back from him, and powerful
   Agamemnon
stabbed him in the side and, as he writhed over,
   Atreides,
setting his heel upon the midriff, wrenched out the
   ash spear.   65

Nestor in a great voice cried out to the men of
   Argos:
"O beloved Danaan fighters, henchmen of Ares,
let no man any more hand back with his eye on the
   plunder

26–27 Mekisteos' son: Euryalos.

30 Odysseus: Son of Laertes, lord of Ithaka and the neighbouring islands, great fighter and counselor, close friend of Agamemnon.

32 Nestor: Leader of the Pylians, once a great warrior and still active as a commander and counselor.

33 Agamemnon: Son of Atreus (therefore sometimes called Atreides), brother of Menelaos, king of Mykenai, and chief leader of the Achaians.

37 Menelaos: Son of Atreus, brother of Agamemnon, first husband of Helen, lord of Lakedaimon.

---

59 Ilion: Troy, the city of Ilos.

designing to take all the spoil he can gather back to
   the vessels;
let us kill the men now, and afterwards at your
   leisure   70
all along the plain you can plunder the perished
   corpses."

So he spoke, and stirred the spirit and strength in
   each man.
Then once more would the Trojans have climbed
   back into Ilion's
wall, subdued by terror before the warlike Achaians,
had not Priam's° son, Helenos, best by far of the
   augurs,   75
stood beside Aineias and Hektor° and spoken a
   word to them:
"Hektor and Aineias, on you beyond others is
   leaning
the battle-work of Trojans and Lykians, since you
   are our greatest
in every course we take, whether it be in thought or
   in fighting:
stand your ground here; visit your people every-
   where; hold them   80
fast by the gates, before they tumble into their women's
   arms, and become to our enemies a thing to take
   joy in.
Afterwards, when you have set all the battalions in
   motion,
the rest of us will stand fast here and fight with the
   Danaans
though we are very hard hit indeed; necessity forces
   us;   85
but you, Hektor, go back again to the city, and there
   tell
your mother and mine to assemble all the ladies of
   honour
at the temple of gray-eyed Athene high on the
   citadel;
there opening with a key the door to the sacred
   chamber
let her take a robe, which seems to her the largest
   and loveliest   90
in the great house, and that which is far her dearest
   possession,
and lay it along the knees of Athene the lovely
   haired. Let her

promise to dedicate within the shrine twelve heifers,
yearlings, never broken, if only she will have pity
on the town of Troy, and the Trojan wives, and their
   innocent children.   95
So she might hold back from sacred Ilion the son of
   Tydeus,°
that wild spear-fighter, the strong one who drives
   men to thoughts of terror,
who I say now is become the strongest of all the
   Achaians.
For never did we so fear Achilleus even, that leader
of men, who they say was born of a goddess. This
   man has gone clean   100
berserk, so that no one can match his warcraft
   against him."

So he spoke, and Hektor did not disobey his brother,
but at once in all his armour leapt to the ground
   from his chariot
and shaking two sharp spears in his hands ranged
   over the whole host
stirring them up to fight and waking the ghastly
   warfare.   105
So they whirled about and stood their ground
   against the Achaians,
and the Argives° gave way backward and stopped
   their slaughtering,
and thought some one of the immortals must have
   descended
from the starry sky to stand by the Trojans, the way
   they rallied.
But Hektor lifted his voice and cried aloud to the
   Trojans: 110
"You high-hearted Trojans and far-renowned
   companions,
be men now, dear friends, and remember your
   furious valour
until I can go back again to Ilion, and there tell
the elder men who sit as counsellors, and our own
   wives,
to make their prayer to the immortals and promise
   them hecatombs."   115

So spoke Hektor of the shining helm, and departed;
and against his ankles as against his neck clashed the
   dark ox-hide,
the rim running round the edge of the great shield
   massive in the middle.

75Priam: Son of Laomedon, king of Troy, father of Hektor, Paris,
   and many other children.
76Hektor: Son of Priam, field commander of the Trojans and their
   greatest fighter.

96Tydeus: Father of Diomedes.
107Argives: The same as Achaians.

Now Glaukos, sprung of Hippolochos, and the son
　of Tydeus
came together in the space between the two armies,
　battle-bent.   120
Now as these advancing came to one place and
　encountered,
first to speak was Diomedes of the great war cry:
"Who among mortal men are you, good friend?
　Since never
before have I seen you in the fighting where men win
　glory,
yet now you have come striding far out in front of all
　others   125
in your great heart, who have dared stand up to my
　spear far-shadowing.
Yet unhappy are those whose sons match warcraft
　against me.
But if you are some one of the immortals come
　down from the bright sky,
know that I will not fight against any god of the
　heaven,
since even the son of Dryas, Lykourgos the powerful,
　did not   130
live long; he who tried to fight with the gods of the
　bright sky,
who once drove the fosterers of rapturous Dionysos
headlong down the sacred Nyseian hill, and all of
　them
shed and scattered their wands on the ground,
　stricken with an ox-goad
by murderous Lykourgos, while Dionysos in
　terror   135
dived into the salt surf, and Thetis took him to her
　bosom,
frightened, with the strong shivers upon him at the
　man's blustering.
But the gods who live at their ease were angered
　with Lykourgos,
and the son of Kronos° struck him to blindness, nor
　did he live long
afterwards, since he was hated by all the immortals.
Therefore neither would I be willing to fight with 141
　the blessed
gods; but if you are one of those mortals who eat
　what the soil yields,
come nearer, so that sooner you may reach your
　appointed destruction."

Then in turn the shining son of Hippolochos
　answered:

139Son of Kronos: Zeus.

"High-hearted son of Tydeus, why ask of my
　generation?   145
As is the generation of leaves, so is that of humanity.
The wind scatters the leaves on the ground, but the
　live timber
burgeons with leaves again in the season of spring
　returning.
So one generation of men will grow while another
dies. Yet if you wish to learn all this and be
　certain   150
of my genealogy: there are plenty of men who know
　it.
There is a city, Ephyre, in the corner of horse-
　pasturing
Argos; there lived Sisyphos, that sharpest of all men,
Sisyphos, Aiolos' son, and he had a son named
　Glaukos,
and Glaukos in turn sired Bellerophontes the
　blameless.   155
To Bellerophontes the gods granted beauty and
　desirable
manhood; but Proitos in anger devised evil things
　against him,
and drove him out of his own domain, since he was
　far greater,
from the Argive country Zeus had broken to the
　sway of his sceptre.
Beautiful Anteia the wife of Proitos was stricken   160
with passion to lie in love with him, and yet she
　could not
beguile valiant Bellerophontes, whose will was
　virtuous.
So she went to Proitos the king and uttered her
　falsehood:
'Would you be killed, o Proitos? Then murder
　Bellerophontes
who tried to lie with me in love, though I was
　unwilling.'   165
So she spoke, and anger took hold of the king at her
　story.
He shrank from killing him, since his heart was
　awed by such action,
but sent him away to Lykia, and handed him
　murderous symbols,
which he inscribed in a folding tablet, enough to
　destroy life,
and told him to show it to his wife's father, that he
　might perish.   170
Bellerophontes went to Lykia in the blameless
　convoy
of the gods; when he came to the running stream of
　Xanthos, and Lykia,

the lord of wide Lykia tendered him full-hearted
    honour.
Nine days he entertained him with sacrifice of nine
    oxen,
but afterwards when the rose fingers of the tenth
    dawn showed, then   175
he began to question him, and asked to be shown
    the symbols,
whatever he might be carrying from his son-in-law,
    Proitos.
Then after he had been given his son-in-law's wicked
    symbols
first he sent him away with orders to kill the
    Chimaira
none might approach; a thing of immortal make, not
    human,   180
lion-fronted and snake behind, a goat in the middle,
and snorting out the breath of the terrible flame of
    bright fire.
He killed the Chimaira, obeying the portents of the
    immortals.
Next after this he fought against the glorious
    Solymoi,°
and this he thought was the strongest battle with
    men that he entered;   185
but third he slaughtered the Amazons,° who fight
    men in battle.
Now as he came back the king spun another
    entangling
treachery; for choosing the bravest men in wide
    Lykia
he laid a trap, but these men never came home
    thereafter
since all of them were killed by blameless
    Bellerophontes.   190
Then when the king knew him for the powerful
    stock of the god,
he detained him there, and offered him the hand of
    his daughter,
and gave him half of all the kingly privilege. Thereto
the men of Lykia cut out a piece of land, surpassing
all others, fine ploughland and orchard for him to
    administer.   195
His bride bore three children to valiant Bellero-
    phontes,
Isandros and Hippolochos and Laodameia.
Laodameia lay in love beside Zeus of the counsels

and bore him godlike Sarpedon of the brazen
    helmet.
But after Bellerophontes was hated by all the
    immortals,   200
he wandered alone about the plain of Aleios, eating
his heart out, skulking aside from the trodden track
    of humanity.
As for Isandros his son, Ares the insatiate of fighting
killed him in close battle against the glorious
    Solymoi,
while Artemis° of the golden reins killed the
    daughter in anger.   205
But Hippolochos begot me, and I claim that he is my
    father;
he sent me to Troy, and urged upon me repeated
    injunctions,
to be always among the bravest, and hold my head
    above others,
not shaming the generation of my fathers, who were
the greatest men in Ephyre and again in wide
    Lykia.   210
Such is my generation and the blood I claim to be
    born from."

He spoke, and Diomedes of the great war cry was
    gladdened.
He drove his spear deep into the prospering earth,
    and in winning
words of friendliness he spoke to the shepherd of the
    people:
"See now, you are my guest friend from far in the
    time of our fathers.   215
Brilliant Oineus once was host to Bellerophontes
the blameless, in his halls, and twenty days he
    detained him,
and these two gave to each other fine gifts in token
    of friendship.
Oineus gave his guest a war belt bright with the red
    dye,
Bellerophontes a golden and double-handled
    drinking-cup,   220
a thing I left behind in my house when I came on my
    journey.
Tydeus, though, I cannot remember, since I was little
when he left me, that time the people of the
    Achaians perished
in Thebe. Therefore I am your friend and host in the
    heart of Argos;
you are mine in Lykia, when I come to your
    country.   225

184Solymoi: Tribe in Asia Minor.

186Amazons: A race of warrior women who invaded Asia Minor.

205Artemis: Sister of Apollo.

Let us avoid each other's spears, even in the close
   fighting.
There are plenty of Trojans and famed companions
   in battle for me
to kill, whom the god sends me, or those I run down
   with my swift feet,
many Achaians for you to slaughter, if you can do it.
But let us exchange our armour, so that these others
   may know   230
how we claim to be guests and friends from the days
   of our fathers."

So they spoke, and both springing down from
   behind their horses
gripped each other's hands and exchanged the
   promise of friendship;
but Zeus the son of Kronos stole away the wits of
   Glaukos
who exchanged with Diomedes the son of Tydeus
   armour   235
of gold for bronze, for nine oxens' worth the worth
   of a hundred.

Now as Hektor had come to the Skaian gates and
   the oak tree,
all the wives of the Trojans and their daughters came
   running about him
to ask after their sons, after their brothers and
   neighbours,
their husbands; and he told them to pray to the
   immortals,   240
all, in turn; but there were sorrows in store for many.

Now he entered the wonderfully built palace of
   Priam.
This was fashioned with smooth-stone cloister
   walks, and within it
were embodied fifty sleeping chambers of smoothed
   stone
built so as to connect with each other; and within
   these slept   245
each beside his own wedded wife, the sons of Priam.
In the same inner court on the opposite side, to face
   these,
lay the twelve close smooth-stone sleeping chambers
   of his daughters
built so as to connect with each other; and within
   these slept,
each beside his own wedded wife, the sons of
   Priam.   250
There there came to meet Hektor his bountiful
   mother

with Laodike, the loveliest looking of all her
   daughters.
She clung to his hand and called him by name and
   spoke to him: "Why then,
child, have you come here and left behind the bold
   battle?
Surely it is these accursed sons of the Achaians who
   wear you   255
out, as they fight close to the city, and the spirit
   stirred you
to return, and from the peak of the citadel lift your
   hands, praying
to Zeus. But stay while I bring you honey-sweet
   wine, to pour out
a libation to father Zeus and the other immortals,
first, and afterwards if you will drink yourself, be
   strengthened.   260
In a tired man, wine will bring back his strength to
   its bigness,
in a man tired as you are tired, defending your
   neighbours."

Tall Hektor of the shining helm spoke to her
   answering:
"My honoured mother, lift not to me the kindly
   sweet wine,
for fear you stagger my strength and make me forget
   my courage;   265
and with hands unwashed I would take shame to
   pour the glittering
wine to Zeus; there is no means for a man to pray to
   the dark-misted
son of Kronos, with blood and muck all spattered
   upon him.
But go yourself to the temple of the spoiler Athene,
assembling the ladies of honour, and with things to
   be sacrificed,   270
and take a robe, which seems to you the largest and
   loveliest
in the great house, and that which is far your dearest
   possession.
Lay this along the knees of Athene the lovely haired.
   Also
promise to dedicate within the shrine twelve heifers,
yearlings, never broken, if only she will have pity 275
on the town of Troy, and the Trojan wives, and their
   innocent children,
if she will hold back from sacred Ilion the son of
   Tydeus,
that wild spear-fighter, the strong one who drives
   men to thoughts of terror.
So go yourself to the temple of the spoiler Athene,

while I go in search of Paris,° to call him, if he will
    listen   280
to anything I tell him. How I wish at this moment
    the earth might
open beneath him. The Olympian let him live, a
    great sorrow
to the Trojans, and high-hearted Priam and all of his
    children.
If only I could see him gone down to the house of
    the death god,
then I could say my heart had forgotten its joyless
    affliction."   285

So he spoke, and she going into the great house
    called out
to her handmaidens, who assembled throughout the
    city the highborn
women; while she descended into the fragrant store-
    chamber.
There lay the elaborately wrought robes, the work of
    Sidonian
women, whom Alexandros° himself, the godlike, had
    brought home   290
from the land of Sidon, crossing the wide sea, on
    that journey
when he brought back also gloriously descended
    Helen.°
Hekabe° lifted out one and took it as gift to Athene,
that which was the loveliest in design and the largest,
and shone like a star. It lay beneath the others. She
    went on   295
her way, and a throng of noble women hastened
    about her.

When these had come to Athene's temple on the
    peak of the citadel,
Theano° of the fair cheeks opened the door for them,
    daughter
of Kisseus, and wife of Antenor, breaker of horses,
she whom the Trojans had established to be Athene's
    priestess.   300

With a wailing cry all lifted up their hands to
    Athene,
and Theano of the fair cheeks taking up the robe
    laid it
along the knees of Athene the lovely haired, and
    praying
she supplicated the daughter of powerful Zeus: "O
    lady,
Athene, our city's defender, shining among
    goddesses: 305
break the spear of Diomedes, and grant that the man
    be
hurled on his face in front of the Skaian gates; so
    may we
instantly dedicate within your shrine twelve heifers,
yearlings, never broken, if only you will have pity
on the town of Troy, and the Trojan wives, and their
    innocent children."   310

She spoke in prayer, but Pallas Athene turned her
    head from her.

So they made their prayer to the daughter of Zeus
    the powerful.
But Hektor went away to the house of Alexandros, [Paris]
a splendid place he had built himself, with the men
    who at that time
were the best men for craftsmanship in the generous
    Troad,   315
who had made him a sleeping room and a hall and a
    courtyard
near the houses of Hektor and Priam, on the peak of
    the citadel.
There entered Hektor beloved of Zeus, in his hand
    holding
the eleven-cubit-long spear, whose shaft was tipped
    with a shining
bronze spearhead, and a ring of gold was hooped to
    hold it.   320
He found the man in his chamber busy with his
    splendid armour,
the corselet and the shield, and turning in his hands
    the curved bow,
while Helen of Argos was sitting among her
    attendant women
directing the magnificent work done by her
    handmaidens.

But Hektor saw him, and in words of shame he
    rebuked him: 325
"Strange man! It is not fair to keep in your heart this
    coldness.

---

280 Paris: Son of Priam and Hekabe, who carried Helen from
    Lakedaimon.
290 Alexandros: Another, and in the Iliad more usual, name for
    Paris.
292 Helen: Wife of Menelaos who ran away with Paris, the cause of
    the war.
293 Hekabe: Daughter of Dymas, Priam's queen.
298 Theano: Priestess of Athene.

The people are dying around the city and around the
   steep wall
as they fight hard; and it is for you that this war
   with its clamour
has flared up about our city. You yourself would
   fight with another
whom you saw anywhere hanging back from the
   hateful encounter.   330
Up then, to keep our town from burning at once in
   the hot fire."

Then in answer the godlike Alexandros spoke to
   him:
"Hektor, seeing you have scolded me rightly, not
   beyond measure,
therefore I will tell, and you in turn understand and
   listen.
It was not so much in coldness and bitter will
   toward the Trojans   335
that I sat in my room, but I wished to give myself
   over to sorrow.
But just now with soft words my wife was winning
   me over
and urging me into the fight, and that way seems to
   me also
the better one. Victory passes back and forth
   between men.
Come then, wait for me now while I put on my
   armour of battle,   340
or go, and I will follow, and I think I can overtake
   you."

He spoke, but Hektor of the shining helm gave him
   no answer,
but Helen spoke to him in words of endearment:
   "Brother
by marriage to me, who am a nasty bitch evil-
   intriguing,
how I wish that on that day when my mother first
   bore me   345
the foul whirlwind of the storm had caught me away
   and swept me
to the mountain, or into the wash of the sea deep-
   thundering
where the waves would have swept me away before
   all these things had happened.
Yet since the gods had brought it about that these
   vile things must be,
I wish I had been the wife of a better man than this
   is,   350
one who knew modesty and all things of shame that
   men say.

But this man's heart is no steadfast thing, nor yet will
   it be so
ever hereafter; for that I think he shall take the
   consequence.
But come now, come in and rest on this chair, my
   brother,
since it is on your heart beyond all that the hard
   work has fallen   355
for the sake of dishonoured me and the blind act of
   Alexandros,
us two, on whom Zeus set a vile destiny, so that
   hereafter
we shall be made into things of song for the men of
   the future."

Then tall Hektor of the shining helm answered her:
   "Do not, Helen,
make me sit with you, though you love me. You will
   not persuade me.   360
Already my heart within is hastening me to defend
the Trojans, who when I am away long greatly to
   have me.
Rather rouse this man, and let himself also be swift
   to action
so he may overtake me while I am still in the city.
For I am going first to my own house, so I can
   visit   365
my own people, my beloved wife and my son, who is
   little,
since I do not know if ever again I shall come back
   this way,
or whether the gods will strike me down at the
   hands of the Achaians."

So speaking Hektor of the shining helm departed
and in speed made his way to his own well-
   established dwelling,   370
but failed to find in the house Andromache of the
   white arms;
for she, with the child, and followed by one fair-
   robed attendant,
had taken her place on the tower in lamentation,
   and tearful.
When he saw no sign of his perfect wife within the
   house, Hektor
stopped in his way on the threshold and spoke
   among the handmaidens: 375
"Come then, tell me truthfully as you may,
   handmaidens:
where has Andromache of the white arms gone? Is
   she
with any of the sisters of her lord or the wives of his
   brothers?

Or has she gone to the house of Athene, where all
    the other
lovely-haired women of Troy propitiate the grim
    goddess?"   380

Then in turn the hard-working housekeeper gave
    him an answer:
"Hektor, since you have urged me to tell you the
    truth, she is not
with any of the sisters of her lord or the wives of his
    brothers,
nor has she gone to the house of Athene, where all
    the other
lovely-haired women of Troy propitiate the grim
    goddess,   385
but she has gone to the great bastion of Ilion,
    because she heard that
the Trojans were losing, and great grew the strength
    of the Achaians.
Therefore she has gone in speed to the wall, like a
    woman
gone mad, and a nurse attending her carries the
    baby."

So the housekeeper spoke, and Hektor hastened
    from his home   390
backward by the way he had come through the well-
    laid streets. So
as he had come to the gates on his way through the
    great city,
the Skaian gates, whereby he would issue into the
    plain, there
at last his own generous wife came running to meet
    him,
Andromache, the daughter of high-hearted
    Eëtion;   395
Eëtion, who had dwelt underneath wooded Plakos,
in Thebe below Plakos, lord over the Kilikian
    people.
It was his daughter who was given to Hektor of the
    bronze helm.
She came to him there, and beside her went an
    attendant carrying
the boy in the fold of her bosom, a little child, only a
    baby,   400
Hektor's son, the admired, beautiful as a star
    shining,
whom Hektor called Skamandrios, but all of the
    others
Astyanax—lord of the city; since Hektor alone saved
    Ilion.
Hektor smiled in silence as he looked on his son, but
    she,

Andromache stood close beside him, letting her tears
    fall,   405
and clung to his hand and called him by name and
    spoke to him: "Dearest,
your own great strength will be your death, and you
    have no pity
on your little son, nor on me, ill-starred, who soon
    must be your widow;
for presently the Achaians, gathering together,
will set upon you and kill you; and for me it would
    be far better   410
to sink into the earth when I have lost you, for there
    is no other
consolation for me after you have gone to your
    destiny—
only grief; since I have no father, no honoured
    mother.
It was brilliant Achilleus who slew my father, Eëtion,
when he stormed the strong-founded citadel of the
    Kilikians,   415
Thebe of the towering gates. He killed Eëtion
but did not strip his armour, for his heart respected
    the dead man,
but burned the body in all its elaborate war-gear
and piled a grave mound over it, and the nymphs of
    the mountains,
daughters of Zeus of the aegis, planted elm trees
    about it.   420
And they who were my seven brothers in the great
    house all went
upon a single day down into the house of the death
    god,
for swift-footed brilliant Achilleus slaughtered all of
    them
as they were tending their white sheep and their
    lumbering oxen;
and when he had led my mother, who was queen
    under wooded Plakos,   425
here, along with all his other possessions, Achilleus
released her again, accepting ransom beyond count,
    but Artemis
of the showering arrows struck her down in the halls
    of her father.
Hektor, thus you are father to me, and my honoured
    mother,
you are my brother, and you it is who are my young
    husband.   430
Please take pity upon me then, stay here on the
    rampart,
that you may not leave your child an orphan, your
    wife a widow,
but draw your people up by the fig tree, there where
    the city

is openest to attack, and where the wall may be
mounted.
Three times their bravest came that way, and fought
there to storm it   435
about the two Aiantes and renowned Idomeneus,
about the two Atreidai and the fighting son of
Tydeus.
Either some man well skilled in prophetic arts had
spoken,
or the very spirit within themselves had stirred them
to the onslaught."

Then tall Hektor of the shining helm answered her:
"All these   440
things are in my mind also, lady; yet I would feel
deep shame
before the Trojans, and the Trojan women with
trailing garments,
if like a coward I were to shrink aside from the
fighting;
and the spirit will not let me, since I have learned to
be valiant
and to fight always among the foremost ranks of the
Trojans,   445
winning for my own self great glory, and for my
father.
For I know this thing well in my heart, and my mind
knows it:
there will come a day when sacred Ilion shall perish,
and Priam, and the people of Priam of the strong
ash spear.
But it is not so much the pain to come of the Trojans
that troubles me, not even of Priam the king nor   451
Hekabe,
not the thought of my brothers who in their
numbers and valour
shall drop in the dust under the hands of men who
hate them,
as troubles me the thought of you, when some
bronze-armoured
Achaian leads you off, taking away your day of
liberty,   455
in tears; and in Argos you must work at the loom of
another,
and carry water from the spring Messeis or
Hypereia,
all unwilling, but strong will be the necessity upon
you;
and some day seeing you shedding tears a man will
say of you:
'This is the wife of Hektor, who was ever the bravest
fighter   460
of the Trojans, breakers of horses, in the days when

they fought about Ilion.'
So will one speak of you; and for you it will be yet a
fresh grief,
to be widowed of such a man who could fight off the
day of your slavery.
But may I be dead and the piled earth hide me under
before I
hear you crying and know by this that they drag you
captive."   465

So speaking glorious Hektor held out his arms to his
baby,
who shrank back to his fair-girdled nurse's bosom
screaming, and frightened at the aspect of his own
father,
terrified as he saw the bronze and the crest with its
horse-hair,
nodding dreadfully, as he thought, from the peak of
the helmet.   470
Then his beloved father laughed out, and his
honoured mother,
and at once glorious Hektor lifted from his head the
helmet
and laid it in all its shining upon the ground. Then
taking
up his dear son he tossed him about in his arms, and
kissed him,
and lifted his voice in prayer to Zeus and the other
immortals: 475
"Zeus, and you other immortals, grant that this boy,
who is my son,
may be as I am, pre-eminent among the Trojans,
great in strength, as am I, and rule strongly over
Ilion;
and some day let them say of him: 'He is better by
far than his father,'
as he comes in from the fighting; and let him kill his
enemy   480
and bring home the blooded spoils, and delight the
heart of his mother."

So speaking he set his child again in the arms of his
beloved
wife, who took him back again to her fragrant
bosom
smiling in her tears; and her husband saw, and took
pity upon her,
and stroked her with his hand, and called her by
name and spoke to her: 485
"Poor Andromache! Why does your heart sorrow so
much for me?
No man is going to hurl me to Hades, unless it is
fated,

but as for fate, I think that no man yet has escaped it
once it has taken its first form, neither brave man
    nor coward.
Go therefore back to our house, and take up your
    own work,   490
the loom and the distaff, and see to it that your
    handmaidens
ply their work also; but the men must see to the
    fighting,
all men who are the people of Ilion, but I beyond
    others."

So glorious Hektor spoke and again took up the
    helmet
with its crest of horse-hair, while his beloved wife
    went homeward,   495
turning to look back on the way, letting the live tears
    fall.
And as she came in speed into the well-settled
    household
of Hektor the slayer of men, she found numbers of
    handmaidens
within, and her coming stirred all of them into
    lamentation.
So they mourned in his house over Hektor while he
    was living   500
still, for they thought he would never again come
    back from the fighting
alive, escaping the Achaian hands and their violence.

But Paris in turn did not linger long in his high
    house,
but when he had put on his glorious armour with
    bronze elaborate
he ran in the confidence of his quick feet through the
    city.   505
As when some stalled horse who has been corn-fed
    at the manger
breaking free of his rope gallops over the plain in
    thunder
to his accustomed bathing place in a sweet-running
    river
and in the pride of his strength holds high his head,
    and the mane floats
over his shoulders; sure of his glorious strength, the
    quick knees   510
carry him to the loved places and the pasture of
    horses;
so from uttermost Pergamos° came Paris, the son of

Priam, shining in all his armour of war as the sun
    shines,
laughing aloud, and his quick feet carried him;
    suddenly thereafter
he came on brilliant Hektor, his brother, where he
    yet lingered   515
before turning away from the place where he had
    talked with his lady.
It was Alexandros the godlike who first spoke to
    him:
"Brother, I fear that I have held back your haste, by
    being
slow on the way, not coming in time, as you
    commanded me."

Then tall Hektor of the shining helm spoke to him in
    answer: 520
"Strange man! There is no way that one, giving
    judgment in fairness,
could dishonour your work in battle, since you are a
    strong man.
But of your own accord you hang back, unwilling.
    And my heart
is grieved in its thought, when I hear shameful things
    spoken about you
by the Trojans, who undergo hard fighting for your
    sake.   525
Let us go now; some day hereafter we will make all
    right
with the immortal gods in the sky, if Zeus ever grant
    it,
setting up to them in our houses the wine-bowl of
    liberty
after we have driven out of Troy the strong-greaved
    Achaians."

COMMENTS AND QUESTIONS

1. Point out the *epithets* used in this book. What is
   their effect?

2. What stories are told within the main story? What
   purpose do they serve?

3. How does the couple Paris/Helen contrast with
   the couple Hektor/Andromache?

4. The concept of fate will be an important one in
   our study of Greek tragedy. What notion of fate is
   elaborated here?

5. What role do the gods play in this book?

512Pergamos: The citadel of Troy (also Pergamon).

FROM THE *Odyssey*

Translation by Robert Fitzgerald

Odysseus, now a guest on the island kingdom of Phaiákia, is the narrator at this point in the poem. He tells the king, Alkínoös, that he and his companions recently left the island of the enchantress Kirke, where they had spent a year. Urged by Kirke, they sailed off to find the realm of the dead, located at the limits of the ocean where the sun never shines. There Odysseus was to learn of his destiny from the prophet Tiresias. In the text that follows, Odysseus tells how he invoked the shades of the dead, met Tiresias, heard his prophecy, and spoke with other shades, including those of his mother, Agamemnon, and Achilles. He observed how the wicked are punished for their various sins on earth, then he left the realm of the dead, and sailed off again. You may wish to reread the selection from the *Epic of Gilgamesh* to compare the two versions of the epic hero's voyage to the underworld. It is possible that Homer may have directly or indirectly known of that part of *Gilgamesh*. The selections from the *Aeneid* (Chapter 7) and *The Divine Comedy* (Chapter 11) will give us two other points of comparison for this important theme.

Book 11

"We bore down on the ship at the sea's edge
and launched her on the salt immortal sea,
stepping our mast and spar in the black ship;
embarked the ram and ewe and went aboard
in tears, with bitter and sore dread upon us.   5
But now a breeze came up for us astern—
a canvas-bellying landbreeze, hale shipmate
sent by the singing nymph with sun-bright hair;
so we màde fast the braces, took our thwarts,
and let the wind and steersman work the ship   10
with full sail spread all day above our coursing,
till the sun dipped, and all the ways grew dark
upon the fathomless unresting sea.

                                    By night
our ship ran onward toward the Ocean's bourne,
the realm and region of the Men of Winter,   15
hidden in mist and cloud. Never the flaming
eye of Hêlios° lights on those men
at morning, when he climbs the sky of stars,
nor in descending earthward out of heaven;
ruinous night being rove over those wretches.   20
We made the land, put ram and ewe ashore,

—————
17 *Hêlios:* The sun god (perhaps of Egyptian origin). [Ed.]

and took our way along the Ocean stream
to find the place foretold for us by Kirkê.
There Perimêdês and Eurýlokhos
pinioned the sacred beasts. With my drawn blade   25
I spaded up the votive pit, and poured
libations round it to the unnumbered dead:
sweet milk and honey, then sweet wine, and last
clear water; and I scattered barley down.
Then I addressed the blurred and breathless dead, 30
vowing to slaughter my best heifer for them
before she calved, at home in Ithaka,
and burn the choice bits on the altar fire;
as for Teirêsias, I swore to sacrifice
a black lamb, handsomest of all our flock.   35
Thus to assuage the nations of the dead
I pledged these rites, then slashed the lamb and ewe,
letting their black blood stream into the wellpit.
Now the souls gathered, stirring out of Erebos,
brides and young men, and men grown old in
   pain,   40
and tender girls whose hearts were new to grief;
many were there, too, torn by brazen lanceheads,
battle-slain, bearing still their bloody gear.
From every side they came and sought the pit
with rustling cries; and I grew sick with fear.   45
But presently I gave command to my officers
to flay those sheep the bronze cut down, and make
burnt offerings of flesh to the gods below—
to sovereign Death, to pale Perséphonê.
Meanwhile I crouched with my drawn sword to
   keep   50
the surging phantoms from the bloody pit
till I should know the presence of Teirêsias.

One shade came first—Elpênor, of our company,
who lay unburied still on the wide earth
as we had left him—dead in Kirkê's hall,   55
untouched, unmourned, when other cares compelled us.
Now when I saw him there I wept for pity
and called out to him:

                              'How is this, Elpênor,
how could you journey to the western gloom
swifter afoot than I in the black lugger?'   60

He sighed, and answered:

                              'Son of great Laërtês,
Odysseus, master mariner and soldier,
bad luck shadowed me, and no kindly power;
ignoble death I drank with so much wine.
I slept on Kirkê's roof, then could not see   65
the long steep backward ladder, coming down,

and fell that height. My neck bone, buckled under,
snapped, and my spirit found this well of dark.
Now hear the grace I pray for, in the name
of those back in the world, not here—your wife   70
and father, he who gave you bread in childhood,
and your own child, your only son, Telémakhos,
long ago left at home.

                   When you make sail
and put these lodgings of dim Death behind,
you will moor ship, I know, upon Aiaia Island;   75
there, O my lord, remember me, I pray,
do not abandon me unwept, unburied,
to tempt the gods' wrath, while you sail for home;
but fire my corpse, and all the gear I had,
and build a cairn for me above the breakers—   80
an unknown sailor's mark for men to come.
Heap up the mound there, and implant upon it
the oar I pulled in life with my companions.'

He ceased, and I replied:

                       'Unhappy spirit,
I promise you the barrow and the burial.'   85

So we conversed, and grimly, at a distance,
with my long sword between, guarding the blood,
while the faint image of the lad spoke on.
Now came the soul of Antikleía, dead,
my mother, daughter of Autólykos,   90
dead now, though living still when I took ship
for holy Troy. Seeing this ghost I grieved,
but held her off, through pang on pang of tears,
till I should know the presence of Teirêsias.
Soon from the dark that prince of Thebes came
    forward   95
bearing a golden staff; and he addressed me:

'Son of Laërtês and the gods of old,
Odysseus, master of land ways and sea ways,
why leave the blazing sun, O man of woe,
to see the cold dead and the joyless region?   100
Stand clear, put up your sword;
let me but taste of blood, I shall speak true.'

At this I stepped aside, and in the scabbard
let my long sword ring home to the pommel silver,
as he bent down to the sombre blood. Then
    spoke   105
the prince of those with gift of speech:

                     'Great captain,
a fair wind and the honey lights of home
are all you seek. But anguish lies ahead;
the god who thunders on the land prepares it,

not to be shaken from your track, implacable,   110
in rancor for the son whose eye you blinded.
One narrow strait may take you through his blows:
denial of yourself, restraint of shipmates.
When you make landfall on Thrinakia° first
and quit the violet sea, dark on the land   115
you'll find the grazing herds of Hêlios
by whom all things are seen, all speech is known.
Avoid those kine, hold fast to your intent,
and hard seafaring brings you all to Ithaka.
But if you raid the beeves, I see destruction   120
for ship and crew. Though you survive alone,
bereft of all companions, lost for years,
under strange sail shall you come home, to find
your own house filled with trouble: insolent men
eating your livestock as they court your lady.   125
Aye, you shall make those men atone in blood!
But after you have dealt out death—in open
combat or by stealth—to all the suitors,
go overland on foot, and take an oar,
until one day you come where men have lived   130
with meat unsalted, never known the sea,
nor seen seagoing ships, with crimson bows
and oars that fledge light hulls for dipping flight.
The spot will soon be plain to you, and I
can tell you how: some passerby will say,   135
"What winnowing fan is that upon your shoulder?"
Halt, and implant your smooth oar in the turf
and make fair sacrifice to Lord Poseidon:
a ram, a bull, a great buck boar; turn back,
and carry out pure hekatombs at home   140
to all wide heaven's lords, the undying gods,
to each in order. Then a seaborne death
soft as this hand of mist will come upon you
when you are wearied out with rich old age,
your country folk in blessed peace around you.   145
And all this shall be just as I foretell.'

When he had done, I said at once,

                           'Teirêsias,
my life runs on then as the gods have spun it.
But come, now, tell me this; make this thing clear:
I see my mother's ghost among the dead   150
sitting in silence near the blood. Not once
has she glanced this way toward her son, nor
    spoken.
Tell me, my lord,
may she in some way come to know my presence?'

---

114 *Thrinakia:* Sicily (the island of three corners). [Ed.]

To this he answered:

                    'I shall make it clear
in a few words and simply. Any dead man   156
whom you allow to enter where the blood is
will speak to you, and speak the truth; but those
deprived will grow remote again and fade.'

When he had prophesied, Teirêsias' shade   160
retired lordly to the halls of Death;
but I stood fast until my mother stirred,
moving to sip the black blood; then she knew me
and called out sorrowfully to me:

                          'Child,
how could you cross alive into this gloom   165
at the world's end?—No sight for living eyes;
great currents run between, desolate waters,
the Ocean first, where no man goes a journey
without ship's timber under him.

                       Say, now,
is it from Troy, still wandering, after years,   170
that you come here with ship and company?
Have you not gone at all to Ithaka?
Have you not seen your lady in your hall?'

She put these questions, and I answered her:

'Mother, I came here, driven to the land of death   175
in want of prophecy from Teirêsias' shade;
nor have I yet coasted Akhaia's hills
nor touched my own land, but have had hard roving
since first I joined Lord Agamémnon's host
by sea for Ilion, the wild horse country,   180
to fight the men of Troy.
But come now, tell me this, and tell me clearly,
what was the bane that pinned you down in Death?
Some ravaging long illness, or mild arrows
a-flying down one day from Artemis?   185
Tell me of Father, tell me of the son
I left behind me; have they still my place,
my honors, or have other men assumed them?
Do they not say that I shall come no more?
And tell me of my wife: how runs her thought,   190
still with her child, still keeping our domains,
or bride again to the best of the Akhaians?'

To this my noble mother quickly answered:

'Still with her child indeed she is, poor heart,
still in your palace hall. Forlorn her nights   195
and days go by, her life used up in weeping.
But no man takes your honored place. Telémakhos
has care of all your garden plots and fields,

and holds the public honor of a magistrate,
feasting and being feasted. But your father   200
is country bound and comes to town no more.
He owns no bedding, rugs, or fleecy mantles,
but lies down, winter nights, among the slaves,
rolled in old cloaks for cover, near the embers.
Or when the heat comes at the end of summer,   205
the fallen leaves, all round his vineyard plot,
heaped into windows, make his lowly bed.
He lies now even so, with aching heart,
and longs for your return, while age comes on him.
So I, too, pined away, so doom befell me,   210
not that the keen-eyed huntress with her shafts
had marked me down and shot to kill me; not
that illness overtook me—no true illness
wasting the body to undo the spirit;
only my loneliness for you, Odysseus,   215
for your kind heart and counsel, gentle Odysseus,
took my own life away.'

                        I bit my lip,
rising perplexed, with longing to embrace her,
and tried three times, putting my arms around her,
but she went sifting through my hands, impalpable
as shadows are, and wavering like a dream.   221
Now this embittered all the pain I bore,
and I cried in the darkness:

                       'O my mother,
will you not stay, be still, here in my arms,
may we not, in this place of Death, as well,   225
hold one another, touch with love, and taste
salt tears' relief, the twinge of welling tears?
Or is this all hallucination, sent
against me by the iron queen, Perséphonê,   229
to make me groan again?'

                   My noble mother
answered quickly:

                      'O my child—alas,
most sorely tried of men—great Zeus's daughter,
Perséphonê, knits no illusion for you.
All mortals meet this judgment when they die.
No flesh and bone are here, none bound by
   sinew,   235
since the bright-hearted pyre consumed them
   down—
the white bones long examinate—to ash;
dreamlike the soul flies, insubstantial.

You must crave sunlight soon.
                    Note all things strange
seen here, to tell your lady in after days.'   240

So went our talk; then other shadows came,
ladies in company, sent by Perséphonê—
consorts or daughters of illustrious men—
crowding about the black blood.

                      I took thought
how best to separate and question them,   245
and saw no help for it, but drew once more
the long bright edge of broadsword from my hip,
that none should sip the blood in company
but one by one, in order; so it fell
that each declared her lineage and name.   250

Here was great loveliness of ghosts! I saw
before them all, that princess of great ladies,
Tyro, Salmoneus' daughter, as she told me,
and queen to Krêtheus, a son of Aiolos.
She had gone daft for the river Enipeus,   255
most graceful of all running streams, and ranged
all day by Enipeus' limpid side,
whose form the foaming girdler of the islands,
the god who makes earth tremble, took and so
lay down with her where he went flooding
    seaward,   260
their bower a purple billow, arching round
to hide them in a sea-vale, god and lady.

Now when his pleasure was complete, the god
spoke to her softly, holding fast her hand:

'Dear mortal, go in joy! At the turn of seasons,   265
winter to summer, you shall bear me sons;
no lovemaking of gods can be in vain.
Nurse our sweet children tenderly, and rear them.
Home with you now, and hold your tongue, and tell
no one your lover's name—though I am yours,   270
Poseidon, lord of surf that makes earth tremble.'

He plunged away into the deep sea swell,
and she grew big with Pelias and Neleus,
powerful vassals, in their time, of Zeus.
Pelias lived on broad Iolkos seaboard   275
rich in flocks, and Neleus at Pylos.
As for the sons borne by that queen of women
to Krêtheus, their names were Aison, Pherês,
and Amytháon, expert charioteer.

Next after her I saw Antiopê,   280
daughter of Ásopos. She too could boast
a god for lover, having lain with Zeus
and borne two sons to him: Amphion and
Zêthos, who founded Thebes, the upper city,
and built the ancient citadel. They sheltered   285
no life upon that plain, for all their power,
without a fortress wall.

                      And next I saw
Amphitrion's true wife, Alkmênê, mother,
as all men know, of lionish Heraklês,
conceived when she lay close in Zeus's arms;   290
and Megarê, high-hearted Kreon's daughter,
wife of Amphitrion's unwearying son.

I saw the mother of Oidipous, Epikastê,°
whose great unwitting deed it was
to marry her own son. He took that prize   295
from a slain father; presently the gods
brought all to light that made the famous story.

But by their fearsome wills he kept his throne
in dearest Thebes, all through his evil days,
while she descended to the place of Death,   300
god of the locked and iron door. Steep down
from a high rafter, throttled in her noose,
she swung, carried away by pain, and left him
endless agony from a mother's Furies....

[Odysseus tells of other noble women he saw.]

But how name all the women I beheld there,   305
daughters and wives of kings? The starry night
wanes long before I close.

                    Here, or aboard ship,
amid the crew, the hour for sleep has come.
Our sailing is the gods' affair and yours."

Then he fell silent. Down the shadowy hall   310
the enchanted banqueters were still. Only
the queen with ivory pale arms, Arêtê, spoke,
saying to all the silent men:

                        "Phaiákians,
how does he stand, now, in your eyes, this captain,
the look and bulk of him, the inward poise?   315
He is my guest, but each one shares that honor.
Be in no haste to send him on his way
or scant your bounty in his need. Remember
how rich, by heaven's will, your possessions are."

Then Ekhenêos, the old soldier, eldest   320
of all Phaiákians, added his word:

"Friends, here was nothing but our own thought
    spoken,
the mark hit square. Our duties to her majesty.

---

293 *Oidipous, Epikaste:* Greek spellings for Oedipus and Jocasta
(see Chapter 5). [Ed.]

For what is to be said and done,
we wait upon Alkínoös' command." 325

At this the king's voice rang:

"I so command,
as sure as it is I who, while I live,
rule the sea rovers of Phaiákia. Our friend
longs to put out for home, but let him be
content to rest here one more day, until 330
I see all gifts bestowed. And every man
will take thought for his launching and his voyage,
I most of all, for I am master here."

Odysseus, the great tactician, answered:

"Alkínoös, king and admiration of men, 335
even a year's delay, if you should urge it,
in loading gifts and furnishing for sea—
I too could wish it; better far that I
return with some largesse of wealth about me—
I shall be thought more worthy of love and courtesy 340
by every man who greets me home in Ithaka."

The king said:

"As to that, one word, Odysseus:
from all we see, we take you for no swindler—
though the dark earth be patient of so many,
scattered everywhere, baiting their traps with lies 345
of old times and of places no one knows.
You speak with art, but your intent is honest.
The Argive troubles, and your own troubles,
you told as a poet would, a man who knows the world.
But now come tell me this: among the dead 350
did you meet any of your peers, companions
who sailed with you and met their doom at Troy?
Here's a long night—an endless night—before us,
and no time yet for sleep, not in this hall.
Recall the past deeds and the strange adventures. 355
I could stay up until the sacred Dawn
as long as you might wish to tell your story."

Odysseus the great tactician answered:

"Alkínoös, king and admiration of men,
there is a time for story telling; there is 360
also a time for sleep. But even so,
if, indeed, listening be still your pleasure,
I must not grudge my part. Other and sadder
tales there are to tell, of my companions,
of some who came through all the Trojan spears, 365
clangor and groan of war,

only to find a brutal death at home—
and a bad wife behind it.

After Perséphonê,
icy and pale, dispersed the shades of women,
the soul of Agamémnon, son of Atreus, 370
came before me, sombre in the gloom,
and others gathered round, all who were with him
when death and doom struck in Aigísthos' hall.
Sipping the black blood, the tall shade perceived me,
and cried out sharply, breaking into tears; 375
then tried to stretch his hands toward me, but could not,
being bereft of all the reach and power
he once felt in the great torque of his arms.
Gazing at him, and stirred, I wept for pity,
and spoke across to him:

'O son of Atreus,
illustrious Lord Marshal, Agamémnon, 381
what was the doom that brought you low in death?
Were you at sea, aboard ship, and Poseidon
blew up a wicked squall to send you under,
or were you cattle-raiding on the mainland 385
or in a fight for some strongpoint, or women,
when the foe hit you to your mortal hurt?'

But he replied at once:

'Son of Laërtês,
Odysseus, master of land ways and sea ways,
neither did I go down with some good ship 390
in any gale Poseidon blew, nor die
upon the mainland, hurt by foes in battle.
It was Aigísthos who designed my death,
he and my heartless wife, and killed me, after
feeding me, like an ox felled at the trough. 395
That was my miserable end—and with me
my fellows butchered, like so many swine
killed for some troop, or feast, or wedding banquet
in a great landholder's household. In your day
you have seen men, and hundreds, die in war, 400
in the bloody press, or downed in single combat,
but these were murders you would catch your breath at:
think of us fallen, all our throats cut, winebowl
brimming, tables laden on every side,
while blood ran smoking over the whole floor. 405
In my extremity I heard Kassandra,
Priam's daughter, piteously crying
as the traitress Klytaimnéstra made to kill her
along with me. I heaved up from the ground
and got my hands around the blade, but she 410
eluded me, that whore. Nor would she close
my two eyes as my soul swam to the underworld
or shut my lips. There is no being more fell,

more bestial than a wife in such an action,
and what an action that one planned!   415
The murder of her husband and her lord.
Great god, I thought my children and my slaves
at least would give me welcome. But that woman,
plotting a thing so low, defiled herself
and all her sex, all women yet to come,   420
even those few who may be virtuous.'

He paused then, and I answered:

        'Foul and dreadful.
That was the way that Zeus who views the wide world
vented his hatred on the sons of Atreus—
intrigues of women, even from the start.
          Myriads
died by Helen's fault, and Klytaimnéstra   426
plotted against you half the world away.'

And he at once said:

        'Let it be a warning
even to you. Indulge a woman never,
and never tell her all you know. Some things   430
a man may tell, some he should cover up.
Not that I see a risk for you, Odysseus,
of death at your wife's hands. She is too wise,
too clear-eyed, sees alternatives too well,
Penélopê, Ikários' daughter—   435
that young bride whom we left behind—think of it!—
when we sailed off to war. The baby boy
still cradled at her breast—now he must be
a grown man, and a lucky one. By heaven,
you'll see him yet, and he'll embrace his father   440
with old fashioned respect, and rightly.
          My own
lady never let me glut my eyes
on my own son, but bled me to death first.
One thing I will advise, on second thought;
stow it away and ponder it.
         Land your ship
in secret on your island; give no warning.   446
The day of faithful wives is gone forever.

But tell me, have you any word at all
about my son's life? Gone to Orkhómenos
or sandy Pylos, can he be? Or waiting   450
with Meneláos in the plain of Sparta?
Death on earth has not yet taken Orestês.'

But I could only answer:

        'Son of Atreus,
why do you ask these questions of me? Neither

news of home have I, nor news of him,   455
alive or dead. And empty words are evil.'

So we exchanged our speech, in bitterness,
weighed down by grief, and tears welled in our eyes,
when there appeared the spirit of Akhilleus,
son of Peleus; then Patróklos' shade,   460
and then Antílokhos, and then Aias,
first among all the Danaans in strength
and bodily beauty, next to prince Akhilleus.
Now that great runner, grandson of Aíakhos,
recognized me and called across to me: 465

'Son of Laërtês and the gods of old,
Odysseus, master mariner and soldier,
old knife, what next? What greater feat remains
for you to put your mind on, after this?
How did you find your way down to the dark   470
where these dimwitted dead are camped forever,
the after images of used-up men?'

            I answered:

'Akhilleus, Peleus' son, strongest of all
among the Akhaians, I had need of foresight
such as Teirêsias alone could give   475
to help me, homeward bound for the crags of Ithaka.
I have not yet coasted Akhaia, not yet
touched my land; my life is all adversity.
But was there ever a man more blest by fortune
than you, Akhilleus? Can there ever be?   480
We ranked you with immortals in your lifetime,
we Argives did, and here your power is royal
among the dead men's shades. Think, then, Akhilleus:
you need not be so pained by death.'

            To this
he answered swiftly:

       'Let me hear no smooth talk
of death from you, Odysseus, light of councils.   486
Better, I say, to break sod as a farm hand
for some poor country man, on iron rations,
than lord it over all the exhausted dead.
Tell me, what news of the prince my son: did he   490
come after me to make a name in battle
or could it be he did not? Do you know
if rank and honor still belong to Peleus
in the towns of the Myrmidons? Or now, may be,
Hellas and Phthia spurn him, seeing old age   495
fetters him, hand and foot. I cannot help him
under the sun's rays, cannot be that man
I was on Troy's wide seaboard, in those days
when I made bastion for the Argives

and put an army's best men in the dust.   500
Were I but whole again, could I go now
to my father's house, one hour would do to make
my passion and my hands no man could hold
hateful to any who shoulder him aside.'

Now when he paused I answered:

                                             'Of all that—
of Peleus' life, that is—I know nothing;   506
but happily I can tell you the whole story
of Neoptólemos, as you require.
In my own ship I brought him out from Skyros
to join the Akhaians under arms.

                                           And I can tell
in every council before Troy thereafter   511
your son spoke first and always to the point;
no one but Nestor and I could out-debate him.
And when we formed against the Trojan line
he never hung back in the mass, but ranged   515
far forward of his troops—no man could touch him
for gallantry. Aye, scores went down before him
in hard fights man to man. I shall not tell
all about each, or name them all—the long
roster of enemies he put out of action,   520
taking the shock of charges on the Argives.
But what a champion his lance ran through
in Eurýpulos the son of Télephos! Keteians
in throngs around that captain also died—
all because Priam's gifts had won his mother   525
to send the lad to battle; and I thought
Memnon alone in splendor ever outshone him.

But one fact more: while our picked Argive crew
still rode that hollow horse Epeios built,
and when the whole thing lay with me, to open   530
the trapdoor of the ambuscade or not,
at that point our Danaan lords and soldiers
wiped their eyes, and their knees began to quake,
all but Neoptólemos. I never saw
his tanned cheek change color or his hand   535
brush one tear away. Rather he prayed me,
hand on hilt, to sortie, and he gripped
his tough spear, bent on havoc for the Trojans.
And when we had pierced and sacked Priam's tall city
he loaded his choice plunder and embarked   540
with no scar on him; not a spear had grazed him
nor the sword's edge in close work—common wounds
one gets in war. Arês in his mad fits
knows no favorites.'

                                      But I said no more,
for he had gone off striding the field of asphodel,   545

the ghost of our great runner, Akhilleus Aiákidês,
glorying in what I told him of his son.

Now other souls of mournful dead stood by,
each with his troubled questioning, but one
remained alone, apart: the son of Télamon,   550
Aîas, it was—the great shade burning still
because I had won favor on the beachhead
in rivalry over Akhilleus' arms.
The Lady Thetis, mother of Akhilleus,
laid out for us the dead man's battle gear,   555
and Trojan children, with Athena,
named the Danaan fittest to own them. Would
god I had not borne the palm that day!
For earth took Aîas then to hold forever,
the handsomest and, in all feats of war,   560
noblest of the Danaans after Akhilleus.
Gently therefore I called across to him:

'Aîas, dear son of royal Télamon,
you would not then forget, even in death,
your fury with me over those accurst   565
calamitous arms?—and so they were, a bane
sent by the gods upon the Argive host.
For when you died by your own hand we lost
a tower, formidable in war. All we Akhaians
mourn you forever, as we do Akhilleus;   570
and no one bears the blame but Zeus.
He fixed that doom for you because he frowned
on the whole expedition of our spearmen.
My lord, come nearer, listen to our story!
Conquer your indignation and your pride.'   575

But he gave no reply, and turned away,
following other ghosts toward Erebos.
Who knows if in that darkness he might still
have spoken, and I answered?

                                       But my heart
longed, after this, to see the dead elsewhere.   580
And now there came before my eyes Minos,°
the son of Zeus, enthroned, holding a golden staff,
dealing out justice among ghostly pleaders
arrayed about the broad doorways of Death.

And then I glimpsed Orion, the huge hunter,   585
gripping his club, studded with bronze, unbreakable,
with wild beasts he had overpowered in life
on lonely mountainsides, now brought to bay
on fields of asphodel.

---

581 *Minos:* King of Crete who after his death was made judge in the
realm of the dead. [Ed.]

And I saw Tityos,
the son of Gaia, lying   590
abandoned over nine square rods of plain.
Vultures, hunched above him, left and right,
rifling his belly, stabbed into the liver,
and he could never push them off.
                                              This hulk
had once committed rape of Zeus's mistress,   595
Lêto, in her glory, when she crossed
the open grass of Panopeus toward Pytho.

Then I saw Tántalos put to the torture:
in a cool pond he stood, lapped round by water
clear to the chin, and being athirst he burned   600
to slake his dry weasand with drink, though drink
he would not ever again. For when the old man
put his lips down to the sheet of water
it vanished round his feet, gulped underground,
and black mud baked there in a wind from hell.   605
Boughs, too, drooped low above him, big with fruit,
pear trees, pomegranates, brilliant apples,
luscious figs, and olives ripe and dark;
but if he stretched his hand for one, the wind
under the dark sky tossed the bough beyond
   him.   610

Then Sísyphos in torment I beheld
being roustabout to a tremendous boulder.
Leaning with both arms braced and legs driving,
he heaved it toward a height, and almost over,
but then a Power spun him round and sent   615
the cruel boulder bounding again to the plain.
Whereon the man bent down again to toil,
dripping sweat, and the dust rose overhead.
Next I saw manifest the power of Heraklês—
a phantom, this, for he himself has gone   620
feasting amid the gods, reclining soft
with Hêbê of the ravishing pale ankles,
daughter of Zeus and Hêra, shod in gold.
But, in my vision, all the dead around him
cried like affrighted birds; like Night itself   625
he loomed with naked bow and nocked arrow
and glances terrible as continual archery.
My hackles rose at the gold swordbelt he wore
sweeping across him: gorgeous intaglio
of savage bears, boars, lions with wildfire eyes, 630
swordfights, battle, slaughter, and sudden death—
the smith who had that belt in him, I hope
he never made, and never will make, another.
The eyes of the vast figure rested on me,
and of a sudden he said in kindly tones: 635

'Son of Laërtês and the gods of old,
Odysseus, master mariner and soldier,
under a cloud, you too? Destined to grinding
labors like my own in the sunny world?
Son of Kroníon Zeus or not, how many   640
days I sweated out, being bound in servitude
to a man far worse than I, a rough master!
He made me hunt this place one time
to get the watchdog of the dead: no more
perilous task, he thought, could be; but I   645
brought back that beast, up from the underworld;
Hermês and grey-eyed Athena showed the way.'

And Heraklês, down the vistas of the dead,
faded from sight; but I stood fast, awaiting
other great souls who perished in times past.   650
I should have met, then, god-begotten Theseus
and Peirithoös, whom both I longed to see,
but first came shades in thousands, rustling
in a pandemonium of whispers, blown together,
and the horror took me that Perséphonê   655
had brought from darker hell some saurian death's head.
I whirled then, made for the ship, shouted to crewmen
to get aboard and cast off the stern hawsers,
an order soon obeyed. They took their thwarts,
and the ship went leaping toward the stream of
   Ocean   670
first under oars, then with a following wind...."

QUESTIONS

1. What, exactly, is Tiresias' prophecy and what is Odysseus' attitude toward it?

2. How would you characterize Homer's vision of the afterlife here? Compare it with that in the *Epic of Gilgamesh* and with that in other myths and religions with which you are familiar.

3. What is Achilles' attitude toward death? How might this typify a Greek point of view?

4. How does Homer's poetry communicate the pathos in the meeting between Odysseus and the shade of his mother?

5. What different *tones* do you find in this selection? What justifies the changes in tone?

6. What kinds of punishment are recounted here and how do they fit the sins? We will return to this question when reading Virgil and Dante.

SAPPHO

Selected Lyric Poems and Fragments

Translation by Willis Barnstone

Sappho, who was born around 605 B.C., was something like the headmistress of a school of girls that was devoted to poetry and to the service of the goddess of love and beauty, Aphrodite. The term *lesbian* comes from the island Lesbos, Sappho's home, and its customs, and it is true that Sappho formed passionate attachments to her pupils. A wife and mother, Sappho also wrote poems about love between men and women. Unfortunately, most of Sappho's poetry has come down to us only in fragments; in fact, only two poems, "Seizure" and "A Prayer to Aphrodite," both printed below, have remained intact. Sappho developed a metric stanza that became known as the "Sapphic" and was adopted by later lyric poets. Here is a rendering of a Sapphic stanza in English. The symbol (‾) stands for a long beat and (˘) for a short one.

The musical equivalent would be

♩♪|♩♩|♩♫|♩♪|♩♩   for the first three lines
♫♫|♩♩   for the last line

Faded every violet, all the roses
Gone the promise glorious, and the victim,
Broken in this anger of Aphrodite,
Yields to the victor.

Even with this fixed meter, the poetry of Sappho seems straightforward, spontaneous, almost simple. She wrote without reservation about her personal world of emotions, and her apparently plain images have great evocative power. Perhaps most important for us is that in a world dominated by men she was an independent woman and sang proudly about the woman's sphere in which she lived. In keeping with the new lyric spirit, she glorified her world of intimate emotions and friendships and her cult of Aphrodite as superior to politics or warfare.

A Prayer to Aphrodite

On your dappled throne, Aphrodite,
sly eternal daughter of Zeus,
I beg you: do not crush me with grief,

but come to me now—as once
you heard my far cry, and yielded,
slipping from your father's house

to yoke the birds to your gold
chariot, and came. Handsome swallows
brought you swiftly to the dark earth,

their wings whipping the middle sky.
Happy, with deathless lips, you smiled:
"What is wrong, why have you called me?

What does your mad heart desire?
Whom shall I make love you, Sappho,
who is turning her back on you?

Let her run away, soon she'll chase you;
refuse your gifts, soon she'll give them.
She will love you, though unwillingly."

Then come to me now and free me
from fearful agony. Labor
for my mad heart, and be my ally.

Seizure

To me that man equals a god
as he sits before you and listens
closely to your sweet voice

and lovely laughter—which troubles
the heart in my ribs. For Brocheo,
when I look at you my voice fails,

my tongue is broken and thin fire
runs like a thief through my body.
My eyes are dead to light, my ears

pound, and sweat pours down over me.
I shudder, I am paler than grass,
and am intimate with dying—but

I must suffer everything, being poor.

To Aphrodite of the Flowers, at Knossos

Come to the holy temple of the virgins
where the pleasant grove of apple trees
circles an altar smoking with frankincense.

The roses leave shadows on the ground
and cool springs murmur through apple branches
where shuddering leaves pour down profound sleep.

In that meadow where horses have grown
glossy, and all spring flowers grow wild,
the anise shoots fill the air with aroma.

And there our queen Aphrodite pours
celestial nectar in the gold cups,
which she fills gracefully with sudden joy.

A Letter to Atthis (I)

My Atthis, although our dear Anaktoria
lives in distant Sardis,
she thinks of us constantly, and

of the life we shared in days when for her
you were a splendid goddess,
and your singing gave her deep joy.

Now she shines among Lydian women as
when the red-fingered moon
rises after sunset, erasing

stars around her, and pouring light equally
across the salt sea
and over densely flowered fields;

and lucent dew spreads on the earth to quicken
roses and fragile thyme
and the sweet-blooming honey-lotus.

Now while our darling wanders she remembers
lovely Atthis' love,
and longing sinks deep in her breast.

She cries loudly for us to come! We hear,
for the night's many tongues
carry her cry across the sea.

To Anaktoria, Now a Soldier's Wife in Lydia

Some say cavalry and some would claim
infantry or a fleet of long oars
is the supreme sight on the black earth.
    I say it is

the girl you love. And easily proved.
Did not Helen, who was queen of mortal

beauty, choose as first among mankind the very
    scourge

of Trojan honor? Haunted by Love
she forgot kinsmen, her own dear child,
and wandered off to a remote country.
    O weak and fitful

Woman bending before any man:
So Anaktoria, although you are
Far, do not forget your loving friends.
    And I for one

Would rather listen to your soft step
and see your radiant face—than watch
all the dazzling horsemen and armored
    Hoplites of Lydia.

Full Moon

The glow and beauty of the stars
are nothing near the splendid moon
when in her roundness she burns silver
about the world.

Then

In gold sandals
dawn like a thief
fell upon me.

Shrill Song

When sun sprays the earth
with straight-falling flames,
a cricket rubs his wings,
scraping up thin sweet song.

QUESTIONS

1. Contrast Sappho's view of the story of the origins of the Trojan War in "To Anaktoria" with Homer's.

2. What is the nature of love expressed in "Seizure" and "A Prayer to Aphrodite"?

3. What other emotions associated with love can you find in these poems?

4. What *images* does Sappho use? What effects do they have?

5. What themes besides love do you find in these poems?

Classical Greece: Life and Art

The time between the world of Homer and Sappho and the world of "classical" Athens saw a growth in the population of Greece, greater material prosperity, and shifts in political power. The city-states in Mycenaean times had been governed by kings, but control had then passed to the nobles; now, in the seventh century B.C., a rising merchant class began to make its power felt. Through revolutions against the nobles, this class assumed control in several of the city-states through a strong man or *tyrant*. This word originally had no bad connotations; but, as these men began to depend more and more on force to impose their wills, the word took on its modern significance. Other governments soon replaced the tyrannies. The form of government that arose in the city-state of Athens was called *democracy*, which means in Greek "rule by the people." Athens' rival city-state, Sparta, did not go through the tyrant stage but retained an aristocratic government or *oligarchy*, which means in Greek "rule by the few." The relative advantages and disadvantages of these two opposing forms of government became an important theme in Greek thought during the period with which we are concerned here.

Athens and Sparta began as allies in a series of wars that were decisive for the political, economic, and cultural importance that Greece was to assume. Persia, the last great power of the Middle East (see Chapter 1), controlled an empire stretching from India and the Asiatic steppes to the Aegean and the Nile. Naturally, the Persians attempted to annex the tiny land of Greece to their empire. The surprise on all sides was great when the Greek allies, led by the Athenians, defeated the mighty Persian army, led by King Xerxes, at the naval battle of Salamis in 480 B.C. Prior to the battle, however, the Athenians themselves had had to evacuate their city before the advancing Persians. Xerxes took the city and burned the Acropolis but, defeated at Salamis, was forced to abandon Athens and return to Persia.

The Greeks saw this battle not only as a great military victory but, perhaps more important, as a cultural one. Persia represented to the Athenians in particular all the values that were anti-Greek. The Persian empire, with its political hierarchy and remote, powerful king at the top, was a far cry from the small state with its "rule by the people." Another negative value that the Persians represented is summed up by the Greek word *hubris*. This is best translated as arrogance, unbridled ambition, or stepping out of the boundaries that the gods have set for people. Xerxes' ambition to conquer the world and his manner of acting and treating himself more like a god than a man were seen to be examples of hubris. In the example of Xerxes' defeat, the Greeks could see a rhythm of tragedy: hubris leads people into folly, or actions that are contrary to reason; such acts bring on *nemesis*. Nemesis was the name of a Greek goddess, but the word is translated as retribution, punishment, or disaster. A tragedy written by Aeschylus in 472 B.C. entitled *The Persians* showed just this cycle. In opposition, the Greeks upheld an ideal they called *sophrosyne*, which means wisdom and moderation. It is perhaps best expressed by the famous motto of the oracle at Delphi: "Nothing in excess." We will see the importance of this concept to the art and thought that we call classical.

Politics and Life in Ancient Athens

Greek culture was concentrated in the *polis* (from which comes the word *politics*), a city-state. Territorially, the polis included the city and the surrounding countryside; but, as it was customarily observed, no citizen should live more than a day's walk from the center. The contrast between the care lavished on public buildings and the humble construction of private houses demonstrates the important role of the polis in the lives of its citizens. The market, the courts, the temples were the focuses of activity, not private gardens and domiciles. It was generally believed that people could realize their humanity only through participation in political processes. The polis provided the religious forms and the moral and cultural values that gave meaning and fullness to a citizen's existence. Citizenship was a privilege acquired by males through birth; normally both one's father and mother had to be natives of the state. Citizenship guaranteed membership in a political community and at least some share in the government of the polis. Whereas in more aristocratic city-states participation was often limited to membership in an assembly with minimal powers, in fifth-century Athens every citizen over twenty-five was eligible for the whole range of state offices, which were filled for short terms either by election or by drawing lots.

All policy decisions and laws were made by the Assembly of the People, composed of the whole body of male citizens. Day-to-day matters and the responsibility of preparing an agenda for the frequent meetings of the Assembly were in the hands of a Council of Five Hundred. Chosen annually by lot, this council functioned by means of a rotating committee meeting daily. A variety of magistrates performed specialized tasks relating to finance and military matters, but the closely defined powers delegated them allowed almost no room for personal initiative. Ultimately, all public officials were responsible to the Assembly, and anyone wishing to exert political authority in the state had to do so through leadership within that body.

Despite its democratic constitution, Athens, like all Greek city-states (and all ancient societies), endorsed slaveholding. Slaves numbered about 90,000, while citizens and their families made up about 150,000 and foreigners about 35,000. A majority of the slaves were employed in domestic service, but about 50,000 worked in industry and another 10,000 (surely the most unfortunate) toiled in the silver mines of Laurion. Apart from the mines, Athenian slavery was not oppressive. Citizens worked alongside slaves in industrial production, and it was usually difficult to distinguish slaves from free people by their dress. In a society where the productive capacity was low and consumption needs relatively simple, the use of slaves was motivated by a desire not for the luxurious life but rather for the creation of an amount of leisure so that citizens could carry out their duties as members of the polis.

The status of women in this society is a matter of debate. They were not citizens, nor did they have rights in law. Marriage seems to have meant the passing from the protection of the father to that of the husband. Wives were expected to remain at home to supervise their households and children. The women free to attend gatherings of men outside the home were either prostitutes or high-class courtesans—foreign women called *hetaerae*. On the other hand, tender scenes between husband and wife depicted on funeral vases suggest the existence of deep ties of affection between some married couples. Representations of strong, intelligent women in Greek tragedy and comedy indicate that such women, at least in the upper class, did exist; but, on the whole, we must think of Greek women as excluded from active roles in the community. A female political leader such as Queen Hatshepsut or, even more, the Candaces of Kush would have been unthinkable in fifth-century Greek society.

The great age of Athens fell between the end of the Persian War in 480 B.C. and the end of the Peloponnesian War in 404 B.C., when Athens was defeated by Sparta. The Peloponnesian War is so called because Sparta is located in that section of Greece called the Peloponnesus (see map, Chapter 3). As rivals for commercial power and representatives of conflicting political ideologies, the two cities of Athens and Sparta came to an inevitable clash. The Athenian Thucydides, one of the first historians of Western culture, has given us both a chronicle of the war between the two city-states and a vision of the workings of history in his *History of the Peloponnesian War,* probably completed about 400 B.C. His history is conceived in terms related to classical tragedy. In particular, he sees the reckless Athenian attack on the city of Syracuse in Sicily as a manifestation of hubris, which led to the downfall of the Athenians.

Thucydides' view of human history, like that of other Greek historians of his generation, was modeled on nature, which for them was a spectacle of incessant change. Indeed, human history changed more violently than anything else in their experience. Although not deriving an historical law, they believed that in the general scheme of change certain causes normally produced specific effects. Particularly, excessive action in one direction produced a violent reaction in the other. Thus examples of history could be used to teach individuals to control their emotional life so that they would resist excess and avoid disaster. In the case of political leaders, the consequences of lack of self-control could ruin not only themselves but their people. While stressing the use of reason to control human destiny, the Hellenic historians, however, saw in human history no general pattern, no direction, only ceaseless change.

Classical Greek Architecture

When the Athenians returned to Athens after their triumph over Xerxes at Salamis, they found a ravaged city. On the Acropolis, temples had been burned, statues toppled, and inscriptions destroyed or defaced. After the city rebuilt its fortifications, its leaders began

the great rebuilding project on the Acropolis. This activity not only built morale, as Pericles said, but also provided jobs. The majestic buildings on the Acropolis, now ruined by time and subsequent wars, are the results of Pericles' building program. They and the sculpture adorning them constitute the best models for the ideals of the classical style (Fig. 4-1)

Like all cultural monuments, the buildings on the Acropolis have a history. To understand the accomplishments of the expert builders and artisans who created the buildings, it is necessary to know something of the origins of Greek architecture.

Origins of Greek Architecture

Beginnings in Greece were humble, as they had been in Mesopotamia and Egypt. The first temples built by the Greeks were simple rectangular boxes, sometimes curved at one end. The ground plan would show a room whose walls extend to flank the doorway. This room, called a *naos,* was for the cult statue, and the extended walls made an entrance porch, the *pronaos;* together they formed the *cella.* Beams for the roof rested on the top edge of the cella walls and, when crossed to form a triangular shape, could carry a wooden gable or ridge pole that followed the long axis of the cella, leaving an open triangular space at each end, the *pediment.* The roof would slope down from the center to the sides, creating a deep overhang. Any openings, such as doors or windows, would be made by using posts and lintels. The combinations of posts and lintels would also carry the weight of the roof (Fig. 4-2).

A comparison of this form with Mesopotamian or Egyptian temples shows a basic similarity—a room for the statue separated from the public. The Greeks enclosed the cult statue in the cella and soon surrounded it with rows of columns or posts on all four sides to create a *colonnade.* Ceremonies took place outside at an altar placed on the long axis of the building that faced east.

The experience of this form diverges radically from that of the sacred mountain, the ziggurat, which rises as a great mass, and is also unlike the long processions from dark to light to dark of the Egyptian temple complex, which may have influenced the Greek columnar orders. Our bodies respond differently to the columns and roof of the Greek form from how they do to the heavy monoliths of Egypt. The Greeks used the smooth mass of the exterior wall and the great downward pressing weight of the roof with its overhang to contrast with the dynamic power of the upward-thrusting posts or columns. Similarly, the

4-1   *Athens, Acropolis, general view. (Courtesy, TWA)*

rhythm of light and dark created by the columns against the smooth cella walls also plays a part in our perception of the temple.

The Greek Temple

The architectural factor that became the most significant formal element of the Greek temple was the shape and scale of the column and its combination with other specific features—its *capital* (the cushion and flat block under the lintel) and the lintel, or *entablature*, above. The two most important combinations or *orders* are the *Doric* and the *Ionic*. Documents

4-2   *Basic post-and-lintel construction.*

RIDGE BEAM

PRINCIPAL RAFTER

TIE BEAM

KINGPOST

WALLPLATE

LINTEL

POST

tell us that the Doric order evolved in the Dorian Peloponnesus. The Ionic order was first found in Asia Minor. Both were used by the Greeks of the fifth century (Fig. 4-3).

Observing the orders side by side, you can see that there is a difference in the height and thickness of the column, the presence or absence of a base for the column, the forms of the capital, and the lintel and *frieze* above the column. Vitruvius, a first-century B.C. Roman who wrote a treatise on architecture, tells us that the Doric was the most ancient order and was serious, grave, dignified, and masculine. The slender, lighter, more elegant Ionic was considered feminine. Femininity, in this case, was not associated with the gender of the gods but with the universal aspects of the female principle.

The Parthenon   The temple form, a cella with a colonnade on all four sides, became the rule for major temples; but its builders enriched and elaborated it, as we will see in the Parthenon. The Parthenon, built between 477 and 438 B.C., was designed and executed under the direction of Ictinus and Kallicrates, expert builders (Figs. 4-4, 4-5). The sculptural program was directed by the sculptor Phideas, who did some images himself and was solely responsible for the cult statue of Athena, placed in the cella. Tradition dictated that the temple be Doric; this one has six columns on its ends and seventeen down each flank. Located on the highest point of the Acropolis, the third temple to Athena Parthenos on that site, it was the crown of the com-

4-3   *Classical Greek orders.*

plex. Forms originally built in mudbrick and wood, then in local stone, were now interpreted in gleaming white marble. The *pediment* on the west end, facing the sea, had its triangular space filled with sculptures depicting the story of Athena's rivalry with Poseidon for the homage of the city. The sculpture of the east pediment showed Athena's birth. The *metopes,* the spaces between the ends of the lateral beams of the roof, above the lintel, were sculpted in *low relief* with scenes from the Trojan War, the Battle of Gods and Giants, Lapiths and Centaurs, Greeks and Amazons, all historical allusions to the Greeks' struggle with the Persians—allegories for the struggle between light and darkness, civilization and barbarism. At the top of the cella walls was a sculpted frieze, showing the procession of the Panathenaea, the festival held every four years to honor Athena. Finally, the whole building was painted and polished. Capitals and moldings received color: blue, red, and gilding. Sculpture was given natural coloring; weapons, horse tack, shields, and other objects were bronze, brass, or gold. Within the cella,

the gold and ivory cult statue was placed at the far end from the door.

Surrounded by terraces, trees, statues, and stelae, as well as the other buildings that soon rose around it, the Parthenon dominated the Acropolis. The entire complex was so moving that even the embittered Spartans did not destroy it when they finally defeated the Athenians in 404 B.C. Time and wars following the fall of the Roman Empire ravaged the site, the worst destruction being the Venetian bombardment of 1678.

Even in the ruined state in which the Parthenon stands today, one senses an order of intractable stone formed into an ideal relationship between weight and support, repose and response, symmetry and rhythm. These characteristics recall the system of balances in Pericles' *Funeral Oration* or the search for a mean between passion and will, intuition and reason, that we will observe in Greek philosophy. Perhaps we can better understand the Parthenon by looking now at Greek sculpture, whose origins lie in the same past and

4-4   *Athens, Acropolis, the Parthenon. (Greek National Tourist Organization)*

Greek Sculpture

whose possibilities, like the temple form, seem completely realized by the late fifth century.

Just as the architecture of Mesopotamia with its processional ways suggests comparisons with the ascension up the Acropolis, so the sculpture of Egypt provides comparisons with that of Greece. The Egyptians produced three-dimensional sculpture carved from solid blocks of stone. The Greeks learned from those techniques just as they learned from the formal, frontal, and almost ideal nature of Egyptian sculpture. In the developing culture of Greece its sculpture seems born of two almost contradictory desires: the desire to attain complete naturalism and the desire to make the figures ideal types. The gods and goddesses, votive figures, and even the more personalized portraits seem both human and divine.

4-5   *Athens, Acropolis, Groundplan.*

A **Propylaea**
B **Statue of Athena**
C **Parthenon**
D **Erectheum**
E **Site of Older Parthenon**
F **Temple of Athena Nike**

4-6   Kouros of Sounion, *c. 600* B.C. *(National Archae-ological Museum, Athens)*

Archaic Sculpture

The *Kouros* of Sounion (*kouros* is Greek for "youth," a standing male nude) was made in the *Archaic* period about 600 B.C. (Fig. 4-6). Over life size (ten feet), this freestanding male nude is characteristic of many such figures that exhibit some attempt to appear natural but are still confined to the stone block from which they were carved. One foot steps forward, but the body weight does not shift. The body itself is really perceived as a columnar shape in which anatomical details are arranged in a symmetrical, stylized way.

Beginning with the head, the face, jawline, ears, and back of the head are seen as almost separate flat sections. The forehead, eyebrow ridge, and nose form one smooth plane, and the eyes are simplified into a wide open stare, the eyelids marked only by a groove. Similarly, the shoulders and chest flow into another smooth plane, where slight ridges, grooves, and swellings incorrectly delineate the body but are formally pleasing and symmetrical. The hip joint and the hips are reduced to one generalized swell into the thighs.

Kneecaps are rigid designs, and the calves have some incised ridges for musculature. The spinal column is almost perfectly straight, and shoulder blades are incised grooves. The arms mask the sides of the body, and the clenched fists make the arms seem to press in toward the body.

The total impression is one of a compact, sculptural solid. It is a memorable and commanding form that deserves our attention because it is a familiar form—a human body—transformed into something timeless. The *Kouros* can be walked around and studied, touched and compared mentally with the surface, texture, articulation, and movement of our own bodies. When we compare the flexible elbow, the soft flesh behind the knee, the loose, floating oval kneecap, and the soft ridges behind the neck and ears with those of this figure, we begin to realize that although the statue is *not* lifelike, its own symmetry, the incised ridges, and the contrast between the way it is and what it seems to be—a human body—create a pleasing and enlightening experience. The *Kouros*, made to commemorate an event, inhabits a space different from our own, and we, like it, are confined to a different place and space. The columnar *Kore*, a female, is equally rigid and posed, yet the symmetry, balance, and harmony of the drapery of the figure, the hair, and the very stylized face are pleasing (Fig. 4-7).

Early Classical Sculpture

The *Kritios Boy* found on the Acropolis was made about 480 B.C. (Fig. 4-8). How different he seems from the previous figures! The body now moves and turns—weight flows into one leg as the figure poses and balances. The body has become a flexible, smooth-muscled, and tactile form. One feels that a touch would reveal a yielding surface of skin and flesh. The body is perceived in the round; it reaches outside the imaginary lines of the block from which it was carved. Yet, because of its perfection, the sculpture remains separate from us. Not a blemish or scar, an undeveloped muscle or unhappy emotion breaks the graceful forms of the body and face. Our own form would rarely compare favorably with this athletic perfection that seems to speak of self-restraint and control; perpetual youth and self-awareness. This is humanity idealized into what one *might* become.

These figures should be compared to the Mesopotamian burial figures and to those of Egypt (see Chapters 1 and 2). What difference does the presence of the nude body make? Do you see similarities in the way faces and expressions are treated?

4-7   Kore *from Auxerre, Louvre, Paris, (Copyright PHOTO Réunion des Musées Nationaux)*

4-8   Kritios Boy, *c. 480* B.C. *(Acropolis Museum, Athens)*

4-9   Mounted Horses, *followed by* Men on Foot, *detail of Panathenaic procession from Parthenon frieze, 432* B.C. *(Reproduced by Courtesy of the Trustees of the British Museum)*

4-10 Dionysus *from the east pediment of the Parthenon, c. 438–432 B.C. (Reproduced by Courtesy of the Trustees of the British Museum)*

Classical Sculpture

The development of freestanding figures toward this expressive perfection is paralleled in other kinds of sculpture. The frieze of the Panathenaic procession gives us more insight into the qualities of the ideal and the real that combine to make the expressive and dramatic scenes of classical art. The frieze has a rhythm that grows like that of an anthem.

On the southeast side, where the procession begins, figures stand or begin to walk slowly. Riders hold their horses, and the sacrificial beasts are readied. As the procession moves along the south flank and turns the western corner, the participants move more rapidly, clustering together. In the section illustrated here (Fig. 4-9), horses and riders, bodies mingling in the low sculpted relief, seem to push eagerly forward. Cloaks blow in the wind; manes and hair are breeze-tossed. As the procession reaches the east end, movement becomes quiet and figures halt in the presence of the gods and goddesses on Mount Olympus. The participants are almost anonymous, the ideally beautiful youths and maids of a procession still going on. The older priest-celebrants will always remain so, as will for all time the gods watching the ceremony.

In the blasted, broken fragments that remain from the Parthenon's pedimental sculptures, scholars and students of Greek sculpture see some of the most beautiful forms of the fifth century. Yet it is difficult for us, as novices, to penetrate the veil of destruction and time that lies over these forms. Only in the *Dionysus* (Fig. 4-10) or the now headless figures of the goddesses from the pediment can we begin to perceive the magnificent beauty of the body, perfectly harmonized with an expressive ideal (Fig. 4-11). The three women sit, lean, and recline to fit the space of the triangular pediment. Their bodies are substantial, weighty volumes. Their clothes do not conceal, but cling, turn, reveal, and emphasize the physical presence of these figures.

4-11 Three Goddesses *from the east pediment of the Parthenon, c. 438–432 B.C. (Reproduced by Courtesy of the Trustees of the British Museum)*

4-12 Polykleitos, *Spearbearer, bronze, (Ludwig-Maximilians-Universitat, Munich)*

Let us now concentrate on a single classical sculpture, *The Spearbearer* by Polykleitos (Fig. 4-12). This figure is a bronze sculpture (the Greeks worked in bronze as much as stone), but the medium does not deny a comparison with the *Kritios Boy.* Of the two figures, which seems more confined in an imaginary blocklike space? How is movement suggested? Of the two bodies, which is more convincingly lifelike, which is more nearly perfect? Compare both works with a present-day athlete of the same general build. What does this tell you about the classical ideal? What is the mental or emotional state of each figure? Is it appealing? Does it enhance or contrast with the forms of the figures? What devices, like the material itself, help maintain the figures' physical and psychological distance?

Classical Architecture and Sculpture Compared

Just as *The Spearbearer* harmonizes nature—the real with the ideal, of what one might be—the Parthenon harmonizes the forces of gravity and weight and the characteristics of the building system itself into a perfect balance of vertical and horizontal, compression and support (Fig. 4-4). The Parthenon's colonnade is not too tall or it would seem spindly; the columns are not too thick or they would be stumpy; the spaces between the columns are not too great or the rhythm they create would be broken; the lintels are not too long; neither are the capitals too large or small. The floor rises slightly to the center on both the long and short axis; the columns lean inward ever so slightly to counter visually the outward, downward pressure of the roof. The columns at the corner are slightly larger since they, as Vitruvius says, would seem too slender because they must be seen against light from both sides. The columns themselves swell slightly as though in vigorous, elastic response to the downward pressure of the roof. Greek architects grasped these fine points in the way that sculptors came to know the body. As head, neck, and chest become understood, as surface dissolves so that muscles swell and move rather than appear as ridges and grooves, as the body turns in space and becomes free of the solid compact mass of stone, so the Parthenon is lifted from the intractable marble to sit lightly in its landscape, its mass balanced between the reality of gravity and a thrust into bright light. To be seen from all sides, experienced during ceremonies, the building is like an ideal body, completely harmonious, self-aware and whole, mysterious and moving.

Other Classical Greek Buildings

The temple form is a complete entity with its traditional, ritual, and formal demands; nevertheless, we should remember that it was not the only type of Greek building. There were theaters, meeting houses, and the colonnaded porticoes of the marketplace. Moreover, the basic temple form itself was capable of elaborate variation, and it is in this context that we should see the Parthenon. Two buildings on the Acropolis help us to do so.

Built after the Parthenon, the Propylaea is a monumental gateway providing a secondary focus for processions, bridging the physical changes in the levels of entry and creating a place of passage from which one can focus on the sanctuary (Fig. 4-13). The expert

4-13 *Acropolis, Propylaea from the west. (Alinari/Art Resource, NY)*

4-14 *Athens, Acropolis, Erechtheion, the porch of the Maidens, Caryatides, from the west side. (Greek National Tourist Organization)*

builders employed the Doric and Ionic orders; on the porticoes and exterior passages the Doric order gives substance to the idea of gateway and entrance. As the levels change, the interior Ionic columns stretch upward easily to carry the roof and visually lighten its weight. The complete gateway once acted also as entrance to the two wings, which were picture galleries containing scenes of Athenian victories.

The Erechtheum, on the north side of the Parthenon, is a very irregular but equally harmonious adjustment of building to its site and to the variety of functions it had to serve (Fig. 4-14). A number of shrines and ancient artifacts of the city had to be accommodated. To the east was a shallow Ionic portico; on the north side was a deeper, richer Ionic porch for entry to the rooms that contained ancient relics; on the south side was the Porch of the Maidens, its flat roof supported by columns transformed into maidens, the *caryatid* order. Instead of a uniform building with a single *gable,* there are intersecting gables and two stories united with one. The Ionic order not only stretches but, along the west side, is also flattened into half-columns that unite the north and south porches, minimizing the change in location and in scale. Each porch has its own symmetry; but, in the balance of each against each, harmony is attained by the contrast of height and weight, openness and enclosure, shallowness and depth.

Greek architecture and sculpture were accompanied and enhanced by all the other arts: painting, music, dance, and drama. We know about painting only through written accounts, surviving vase painting, and later Roman copies of Greek work. But we do know that other arts shared in the conquest of space and movement and that, after the Parthenon, the builder's art continued to grow, flourish, and change. New needs inspired new ideas that provided a growing and changing art. After the Peloponnesian War new states acquired power and wealth; their ideals and beliefs were manifested in sculpture, painting, and building.

From Classical to Hellenistic Sculpture

The Cnidian *Aphrodite,* made in the fourth century B.C., was among the first nude female sculptures. The original statue was carved by the Greek Praxiteles for Aphrodite's important shrine on the island of Cnidos. The ideal female form had evolved at the same time as the ideal male form, and portraying the goddess nude had become widely accepted. The *Aphrodite* illustrated here (Fig. 4-15) is a Roman copy of the Greek original and lacks the sensual liveliness that writers ascribed to the original. But the artist's realization of the ideal female as a relaxed, elegant figure, unabashed by her nudity, which is so wonderfully revealed as she steps from the bath, fueled the imagination of artists for many centuries. This ideal was revived again by the Italian artists of the fifteenth century in their search for the classical female prototype. The later Roman

4-15   Praxiteles, Aphrodite of Cnidos, *c. 350 B.C., Vatican Museums, Rome. (Alinari/Art Resource, NY)*

4-16   Aphrodite of Cyrene, *from North Africa, early first century B.C., marble. (Hirmer Fotoarchiv, Munich)*

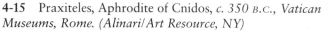

Aphrodite from Cyrene, in North Africa (Fig. 4-16), relies on the same hipshot pose, general proportions, and support of the water jar and drapery as does the *Aphrodite* from Cnidos. Compare these figures with each other and with *The Spearbearer* (Fig. 4-12). How has the Greek ideal been extended to women? Is there any change from the previous centuries?

Another example of later Greek art is the great Altar of Zeus at Pergamon (Fig. 4-17). It was part of an architectural complex radically different from that of the Athenian Acropolis, and the form of the altar itself gives an idea of the many ways in which the Greek columnar orders and architectural details could be used to create new buildings and public spaces. The actual space of the altar is raised above the frieze, which has come down off the walls of the temple and out to the steps where the figures could be more easily seen and understood. The figures themselves are much more dramatic and graphically expressive than those of the *Panathenae.* Consider the striking differences of

scale, depth of relief, and movement of figures (Fig. 4-18). In this detail of Zeus fighting three giants, the forms themselves seem almost trapped by the architectural framework, and as they struggle with each other they also seem to struggle to be free of the stones from which they are carved. The swirling drapery and heavy muscular bodies of these figures have an emotional power quite different from the calm mien imparted by sculptors of earlier generations.

For centuries, authorities in the field held that the diffusion of artists and builders, along with the evolution of new and more complex forms, represented a decline in the power and quality of Greek art and architecture, which reached its highest state in the classical period. Although modern scholarship questions this judgment against Hellenistic art (the term used to refer to the art of the third and second centuries B.C.), it is a tribute to the classical period that its goals and forms could provide sources and ideas for two millennia.

4-17 *Altar of Zeus, Pergamon, c. 181–159* B.C., *Staatliche Museen zu Berlin. (Bildarchiv Preussischer Kulturbesitz, Berlin)*

4-18 *Detail from Altar of Zeus,* Zeus Fighting Three Giants, *Staatliche Museen zu Berlin. (Bildarchiv Preussischer Kulturbesitz, Berlin)*

READING SELECTION

THUCYDIDES

Pericles' Funeral Oration

Translation by Benjamin Jowett

The most famous passage of Thucydides' *History of the Peloponnesian War* is a funeral oration for some young Athenian soldiers by the Athenian statesman Pericles. Pericles, who headed the Athenian democracy during its greatest (classical) period, speaks for the young men who died. He does so by praising the way of life for which they gave their own lives.

I will speak first of our ancestors, for it is right and becoming that now, when we are lamenting the dead, a tribute should be paid to their memory. There has never been a time when they did not inhabit this land, which by their valor they have handed down from generation to generation, and we have received from them a free state. But if they were worthy of praise, still more were our fathers, who added to their inheritance, and after many a struggle transmitted to us their sons this great empire. And we ourselves assembled here today, who are still most of us in the vigor of life, have chiefly done the work of improvement, and have richly endowed our city with all things, so that she is sufficient for herself both in peace and war. Of the military exploits by which our various possessions were acquired, or of the energy with which we or our fathers drove back the tide of war, Hellenic or Barbarian, I will not speak; for the tale would be long and is familiar to you. But before I praise the dead, I should like to point out by what principles of action we rose to power, and under what institutions and through what manner of life our empire became great. For I conceive that such thoughts are not unsuited to the occasion, and that this numerous assembly of citizens and strangers may profitably listen to them.

Our form of government does not enter into rivalry with the institutions of others. We do not copy our neighbors, but are an example to them. It is true that we are called a democracy, for the administration is in the hands of the many and not of the few. But while the law secures equal justice to all alike in their private disputes, the claim of excellence is also recognized; and when a citizen is in any way distinguished, he is preferred to the public service, not as a matter of privilege, but as the reward of merit. Neither is poverty a bar, but a man may benefit his country whatever be the obscurity of his condition. There is no exclusiveness in our public life, and in our private intercourse we are not suspicious of one another, nor angry with our neighbor if he does what he likes; we do not put on sour looks at him which, though harmless, are not pleasant. While we are thus unconstrained in our private intercourse, a spirit of reverence pervades our public acts; we are prevented from doing wrong by respect for authority and for the laws, having an especial regard to those which are ordained for the protection of the injured as well as to those unwritten laws which bring upon the transgressor of them the reprobation of the general sentiment.

And we have not forgotten to provide for our weary spirits many relaxations from toil; we have regular games and sacrifices throughout the year; at home the style of our life is refined; and the delight which we daily feel in all these things helps to banish melancholy. Because of the greatness of our city the fruits of the whole earth flow in upon us; so that we enjoy the goods of other countries as fseely as of our own.

Then, again, our military training is in many respects superior to that of our adversaries. Our city is thrown open to the world, and we never expel a foreigner or prevent him from seeing or learning anything of which the secret if revealed to an enemy might profit him. We rely not upon management or trickery, but upon our own hearts and hands. And in the matter of education, whereas they from early youth are always undergoing laborious exercises which are to make them brave, we live at ease, and yet are equally ready to face the perils which they face. And here is the proof. The Lacedaemonians come into Attica not by themselves, but with their whole confederacy following; we go alone into a neighbor's country; and although our opponents are fighting for their homes and we on a foreign soil, we have seldom any difficulty in overcoming them. Our enemies have never yet felt our united strength; the care of a navy divides our attention, and on land we are obliged to send our own citizens everywhere. But they, if they meet and defeat a part of our army, are as proud as if they had routed us all, and when defeated they pretend to have been vanquished by us all.

If then we prefer to meet danger with a light heart but without laborious training, and with a courage which is gained by habit and not enforced by law, are we not greatly the gainers? Since we do not anticipate the pain, although, when the hour comes, we can be as brave as those who never allow themselves to rest; and thus too our city is equally admirable in peace and in war. For we are lovers of the beautiful, yet simple in our tastes, and we cultivate the mind without loss of manliness. Wealth we employ, not for talk and ostentation, but when there is a real use for it. To avow poverty with us is no disgrace: the true disgrace is in doing nothing to avoid it. An Athenian citizen does not neglect the state because he takes care of his own household; and even those of us who are engaged in business have a very fair idea of politics. We alone regard a man who takes no interest in public affairs, not as a harmless, but as a useless character; and if few of us are originators, we are all sound judges of a policy. The great impediment to action is, in our opinion, not discussion, but the want of that knowledge which is gained by discussion preparatory to action. For we have a peculiar power of thinking before we act and of acting too, whereas other men are courageous from ignorance but hesitate upon reflection. And they are surely to be esteemed the bravest spirits who, having the clearest sense both of the pains and pleasures of life, do not on that account shrink from danger. In doing good, again, we are unlike others; we make our friends by conferring, not by receiving favors. Now he who confers a favor is the firmer friend, because he would fain by kindness keep alive the memory of an

obligation; but the recipient is colder in his feelings, because he knows that in requiting another's generosity he will not be winning gratitude, but only paying a debt. We alone do good to our neighbors not upon a calculation of interest, but in the confidence of freedom and in a frank and fearless spirit. To sum up: I say that Athens is the school of Hellas, and that the individual Athenian in his own person seems to have the power of adapting himself to the most varied forms of action with the utmost versatility and grace. This is no passing and idle word, but truth and fact; and the assertion is verified by the position to which these qualities have raised the state. For in the hour of trial Athens alone among her contemporaries is superior to the report of her. No enemy who comes against her is indignant at the reverses which he sustains at the hands of such a city; no subject complains that his masters are unworthy of him. And we shall assuredly not be without witnesses; there are mighty monuments of our power which will make us the wonder of this and of succeeding ages; we shall not need the praises of Homer or of any other panegyrist whose poetry may please for the moment, although his representation of the facts will not bear the light of day. For we have compelled every land and every sea to open a path for our valor, and have everywhere planted eternal memorials of our friendship and of our enmity. Such is the city for whose sake these men nobly fought and died; they could not bear the thought that she might be taken from them; and every one of us who survive should gladly toil on her behalf.

COMMENTS AND QUESTIONS

1. Thucydides, through his spokesman Pericles, is defining a balanced system of government in a style that is also balanced. Define and point out the balances in style and content.

2. Where does Pericles describe the Athenian taste in art, and what is it?

3. What are the potential disadvantages of a democracy, and how does Athenian democracy avoid these disadvantages, according to Pericles?

4. How does Athenian democracy compare with modern democracies?

Classical Greece: Drama

Along with its creativity in the visual arts, the age of Pericles saw a flourishing of drama. Drama, as we know it in the West, is in fact a creation of the Greeks. Theatergoing was more than a festive activity for Athenians; it was regarded as an important part of a citizen's education and was supported by the state. *Tragedies and comedies,* as well as other theatrical events, were performed annually at the festival of Dionysus, the god of wine, fertility, and ecstasy. The Athenian theatergoer, rather than going out for an evening's entertainment as we do, would devote a whole day to this activity. During the festival of Dionysus, which lasted for several days, business activities would cease, prisoners would be released from jail, and everyone—young, old, rich, poor, male, female, free, slave—would congregate at daybreak in a type of outdoor auditorium from which our football stadiums have been developed. There they would sit on stone benches, often to watch three tragedies, a *satyr play* (a grotesque skit in which the actors wore horses' tails and ears), and a comedy. The ruins of the theater of Dionysus on the Acropolis and the better-preserved theater at Epidaurus (Fig. 5-1) give us a clear idea of the circular orchestra, where the chorus sang and danced, and the *theatron,* the horseshoe-shaped area for the audience. A *skene,* or backdrop against which the actors performed, would have been set up in the back of the orchestra, facing the audience. Acoustics in this theater are still remarkable. A clear voice from the orchestra is deflected by the stone sides and can be heard without any form of artificial amplification.

Even though the Athenian theatergoer's experience was different from ours, it is recognizable to us because it is at the base of our own experience with the theater. We are all familiar with actors who act out a story and come into conflict with each other, but fifth-century B.C. Athens was, as far as we

5-1   *Epidaurus, theater from above. Polykleitos the Younger, c. 350 B.C. (Eugene Brown)*

know, the first place in the world where this type of performance had been or was being staged. How did it come to be? Was the drama someone's invention or a longstanding development? It should be stated immediately that no one knows the definitive answer to this question. We can best examine it in relation to the two principal forms themselves, tragedy and comedy.

The Development of Tragedy

Tragedy developed into a full-fledged dramatic form sometime before the classical age and earlier than comedy. Τραγωιδια (*tragoidia*) in Greek comes from words meaning "goat" and "song." For this reason it has been assumed that tragedy developed from "goat songs" or choric performances similar to, or identical with, the grotesque satyr plays mentioned earlier. According to this theory, the serious play that we now know as tragedy would have begun as a kind of ecstatic comedy, perhaps far from Athens, in the Peloponnesus. Since tragedy was performed at the festival of Dionysus, many have also assumed that it grew out of some sort of religious ritual. According to one of these theories, the chants of the priest and the response of the worshipers gave rise to the actors and chorus

respectively. Another theory holds that Greek tragedy had nothing to do with religious rituals but was essentially the creation of the first man of the theater, Thespis, who created drama out of poetic recitations of stories from Homer.

The tragedies written by Thespis probably featured only one actor, along with a chorus. The actor, who probably represented an epic hero from Homer, would have to present his own story, which would be concentrated on his *pathos*, or suffering. The chorus would begin the play with a hymn to the gods and end with a lamentation over the hero. The *aulos*, a type of oboe and the characteristic instrument of the Dionysian cult, was employed in the performance of elegies, or songs of mourning; and it is likely that it was also used for instrumental preludes and interludes in the drama. In between the short scenes or *episodes* during which the hero spoke, the chorus would sing lyrics as a comment on his sufferings.

The Role of Music and Dance in Tragedy

From the beginning, tragedy was intimately associated with the arts of music and dance. The Greek word for *chorus*, which comes from the verb "to dance," indicates that the choruses were originally groups of dancers as well as singers (all men, as were the actors). It is probable that individual actors danced, too. Although there is little evidence on what the dances were like, we do know that they were mimetic; that is, they mimed or imitated the action of the play. The use of the hands was very important in expressing emotion, just as it is in oriental dancing today.

Music, instrumental as well as choral, also played an important role in creating emotional effects in tragedy. Just as the lyre was the instrument of lyric poetry, the aulos, a double-reeded wind instrument, was seen as most appropriate for tragedy. It had a shrill, piercing tone, perhaps associated with the ecstatic worship of Dionysus. The Greeks composed music in several *modes,* scales whose organization of notes differs from our modern major and minor system. Each mode was said to produce a special kind of feeling. In modern music, we distinguish between the forceful major mode and the wistful or melancholy minor mode. The Greek theory of modes was more complicated. The Dorian mode was considered manly and strong, appropriate for the training of young men, whereas the emotional Mixolydian mode was considered piercing and suitable for lamentations. Both, however, were appropriate for tragedy. The Greeks, as we will see in the section on philosophy, had great faith in the ability of music to influence and mold the characters of human beings. Unfortunately, very little Greek music remains—none from the classical period—so we can only conjecture what the total spectacle of an Athenian drama would have been like.

The Principal Greek Tragedians

Aeschylus The first tragedian whose plays are known to us is Aeschylus, who lived from 525 to 456 B.C. and thus participated in the growth and the glory of Athens. He was proud of having fought at the battle of Marathon. Aeschylus had the genius to add a second actor to the tragic form; thus, in his plays two actors appear at once on the stage. There is still a principal hero, whose sufferings are the main subject of the tragedy, but now he can be seen interacting with other human beings. The chorus, though, is still of major importance in the dramas of Aeschylus, who was himself a musician and was said to have been most attentive in fitting his choral songs to music. Aeschylus' most famous work is the trilogy, or series of three plays, entitled the *Oresteia* (Orestes plays). The first play in the trilogy is *Agamemnon*, the name of the king of Mycenae and leader of the Greeks in the Trojan War.

In the play Agamemnon returns from the war, a glorious hero, only to be murdered by his wife, Clytemnestra. In the second play, *The Libation Bearers*, Agamemnon's son, Orestes, avenges his father's death by killing his mother and her lover. In the final part of the trilogy Orestes is pursued by the Eumenides, horrible furies who torment him because of the slaying of his mother; but he is finally put on trial, judged, and acquitted by Athena, the patron goddess of Athens. The outcome of the trilogy shows the belief in law and the new system of justice developing in Athens.

Aeschylus wrote about ninety tragedies altogether. Besides the *Oresteia* those that survive are *The Persians, Seven Against Thebes, Prometheus Bound,* and *The Suppliants.* The plots of all of Aeschylus' tragedies are extremely simple, and the characters are not what we would call "well rounded," but rather embodiments of a single passion. Everything is concentrated on the tragic event and the emotional and spiritual meaning of that event. This simplicity and concentration is, as we have seen in other art forms, part of what we mean by classical. Aeschylus' plays, in their spareness and grandeur, have been compared to early classical sculpture such as the *Kritios Boy* (Fig. 4-8).

Sophocles (496–406 B.C.) Sophocles, a younger contemporary of Aeschylus, further developed the tragic form by adding a third actor. During his long life he wrote about 125 plays, of which only eight have come down to us. Of these, the best known are the plays of the Oedipus cycle: *Antigone, Oedipus Rex,* and *Oedipus at Colonus.* Unlike the *Oresteia,* these plays were not written as a trilogy but at different points of Sophocles' career. They are thus meant to be performed as individual plays. It is *Oedipus Rex,* the most renowned of all Greek tragedies, that we will study in detail here. Sophocles' characters, while maintaining a sense of classical balance and restraint, seem more human and alive than those of Aeschylus. They may be compared to "high" classical sculpture. The chorus has less importance relative to the actors than in Aeschylus' drama, but we should bear in mind that music and dance still played a vital role. Sophocles was himself a dancer.

Euripides (480–406 B.C.) The next great tragedian, Euripides, began to break out of the limits of classicism by creating more realistic characters and more complex plots. The traditional critical judgment on Euripides and his older contemporary holds that "Sophocles shows man as he ought to be and Euripides shows man as he is." Euripides' interest in individual psychology and in extreme real-life situations makes him in many ways closer to modern sensibilities. Although, like all ancient Greek playwrights, he uses old myths as the basis for his plots, Euripides appears to many readers as a religious skeptic or even an atheist. Euripides also wrote an *Orestes,* which differs considerably from the trilogy by Aeschylus. Like all great psychological writers, he had a considerable interest in women, as shown in plays such as *Hippolytus,* which treats the myth of Phaedra driven mad by love, *The Trojan Women,* and *Medea.* The realism, emotionalism, and individuality of Euripides' characters make them comparable to postclassical or Hellenistic sculptures.

Oedipus: Legend and Tragedy

It is Sophocles, among these three tragedians, who now seems most representative of the cultural spirit of Athens in its classical, Periclean age. His *Oedipus Tyrannus,* or, using the Latin word for king, *Oedipus Rex,* was probably first performed soon after a plague that swept over Athens in 429 B.C. Although the action is set in Greece's remote, legendary past in the city of Thebes, the Athenian audience would have identified immediately with the plague that has fallen like a curse on that city as the play opens. Through the writings of Aristotle, *Oedipus Rex* has come to stand for the most nearly perfect example of classical tragedy in the Western humanistic tradition.

One important notion to bear in mind while reading a Greek tragedy is that, unlike modern audiences, the Greeks who attended the festival of Dionysus did not attend a play for its plot suspense or to find out "what happens next." Today, when recommending a movie to friends, we do not tell the plot for fear of spoiling it for them. Greek tragedies were all based on myths or legends that the theatergoers already knew. Thus, when they went to see *Oedipus,* they did not wonder what the play would be about but rather what Sophocles had done with an old, familiar story. Since the tragedies at the festival of Dionysus were presented as a contest, the judges would also choose the best three tragedies on the basis of how well the already given material had been worked into dramatic form. It will therefore be useful to know something about the myth of Oedipus before approaching the tragedy.

The story takes place in a much earlier period of Greek history, when the city-states had been ruled by kings. The city of Thebes, it was told, was ruled by King Laius (Laïos) and his queen, Jocasta (Iokastê). Thebes was founded by Laius' ancestor Cadmus, who was cursed by the gods and told that all of his descendants would receive some form of this curse. Thus Laius was told by a prophet of the god Apollo that he and Jocasta would bear a son who would kill his father and marry his mother. Hoping to avert this fate, the king and queen asked one of their shepherds to take their firstborn son to Mount Cithaeron (Kithairon) near Thebes, to leave the baby to be exposed to die. The shepherd, out of pity for the child, gave him to a slave from the Greek city of Corinth, on the other side of the mountain, hoping that he would remain in that city and thus have no chance to fulfill the dreadful prophecy. The child is, of course, Oedipus, whose name means "swollen foot," a deformity he acquired from the pins put in his feet when he was left to die. He grows up believing that he is the natural son of King Polybus (Polybos) and Queen Meropê of Corinth, but one day he, too, receives a prophecy declaring that he will kill his father and marry his mother. He then flees Corinth and vows never to see his parents again.

During his travels Oedipus arrives at the outskirts of Thebes. There he gets into a quarrel with an old man whom he kills in a fit of anger—the man is Laius. He then finds that Thebes is under the control of a monster called the Sphinx, who has stationed herself outside the city and demands a yearly tribute from its citizens. Her power over Thebes can be overcome only if someone answers her riddle: "What walks on four legs in the morning, on two in the afternoon, and on three in the evening and is strongest when it uses the fewest number of legs?" Oedipus solves the riddle: the answer is *man,* who crawls on all fours as a baby, walks on two legs as an adult, and with a stick as an old man. Oedipus is hailed in Thebes as the savior of the city and given the hand of Laius' widow, Queen Jocasta, in marriage. Sophocles' play opens several years after this event, at a time when the city is again in peril and the people again look to Oedipus to help them. This time the trouble is a plague, a disease that is spreading among the people of Thebes, killing many of them.

The legend of Oedipus, no doubt originally an oral tale, contains many of the elements found in familiar folk or fairy tales—the curse, the prophecies, the riddle, and the hero-savior. There are numerous imaginable ways of treating this material. Sophocles' task was to mold it into the form of tragedy.

Unlike the oral folk tale that opens with "once upon a time," Sophocles does not begin the story at the beginning. Since Homer, it has been the rule in Western drama and fiction to begin "in the middle of things." *Oedipus* begins in the midst of a tense situation that demands a solution: a plague is raging; what will the king do? In fact, Sophocles begins his story after the important events have already occurred. The action of the play takes place in less than a day; yet the entire life of Oedipus, from his birth to his preparation for death, is brought into the development. Also, although we hear about Corinth and other parts of Thebes, the stage setting is in only one place—just outside the palace of the king and queen. There is only one plot or action in the play—no subplots or other distractions. There is certainly no comic relief, as found in Shakespeare. This simplicity of structure and unity of tone contribute to the play's classical quality. Just as in the Parthenon or the statue of *The Spearbearer,* everything nonessential is stripped away. What is left is a clear and balanced presentation of the essence of an aspect of life, rather than a realistic "slice of life." Part of the force and the impact of Greek tragedy lies in this classical simplicity.

Humanism and Tragedy

During the great classical age of Athens, intellectuals, intrigued with new developments in science and philosophy, began to challenge the old, accepted religious beliefs. In art, in politics, as in thought, human beings were upstaging the gods. The philosopher Protagoras summed up the new attitude with the phrase "man is the measure of all things." Confidence in human abilities and powers has perhaps never been greater than at this time. We see this in *Oedipus* in the hero's self-confidence at the beginning of the play. The people of Thebes who look to him as their savior treat him almost like a god. We see an extreme confidence in human reason and a denial of the power of the gods over people in Iokastê's scoffing at prophecies. But here, as in other aspects, Sophocles portrays a balance between extremes. The outcome of the tragedy shows that the gods, or fate, have the last word, but it certainly does not show people to be little puppets whose destiny is simply to obey the divine will. Oedipus is "blind" in that he does not recognize the limits set by divine power, but great in that he struggles to find the truth through his own individual human reason. Sophocles wanted to warn his fellow Athenians not to neglect religion, but he also wanted to demonstrate to them the greatness of human character and intelligence. Sophocles' faith in humanity, or his "humanism," is perhaps best exemplified in the famous choral ode in another of his tragedies, *Antigone* (translated by Elizabeth Wyckoff):

> Many the wonders but nothing walks stranger than
>   man.
> This thing crosses the sea in the winter's storm,

> making his path through the roaring waves.
> And she, the greatest of gods, the earth—
> ageless she is, and unwearied—he wears her away
> as the ploughs go up and down from year to year
> and his mules turn up the soil.

> Gay nations of birds he snares and leads,
> wild beast tribes and the salty brood of the sea,
> with the twisted mesh of his nets, this clever man.
> He controls with craft the beasts of the open air,
> walkers on hills. The horse with his shaggy mane
> he holds and harnesses, yoked about the neck,
> and the strong bull of the mountain.

> Language, and thought like the wind
> and the feelings that make the town;
> he has taught himself, and shelter against the cold,
> refuge from rain. He can always help himself.
> He faces no future helpless. There's only death
> that he cannot find an escape from. He has con-
>   trived
> refuge from illnesses once beyond all cure.

> Clever beyond all dreams
> the inventive craft that he has
> which may drive him one time or another to well or
>   ill.

Classical tragedy shows that a belief in the dignity and greatness of human beings is not incompatible with a full awareness of their limitations.

Greek Comedy

Tragedy, according to the philosopher Aristotle, provides a release for the emotions of pity and terror. Spectators pity the unfortunate protagonist and fear that they themselves might undergo a disaster, thus purging themselves of those emotions. Whatever else went on at the festival of Dionysus, it must have offered an opportunity for the release of pent-up feelings. The people who attended it "let off steam" in all sorts of ways—first of all by feeling liberated from the everyday world of work and duty. There was drinking, feasting, carousing. At the plays themselves the idea was to participate emotionally as a spectator rather than merely to view passively. The Greeks, like most peoples of the world, recognized society's need for a true holiday, or festival—a time of collective celebration and liberation. The way that a culture celebrates, or organizes its festivals, says a great deal about its values. (Bear this in mind as we study festivals in medieval and Renaissance Europe and in Africa.) One might well ask if our contemporary society recognizes this need adequately. Do people who spend their days off at home watching television experience a release and liberation from the everyday world? Is there a basic difference between the theatrical and the media experience? Or do we provide other, communal ceremonies of celebration?

Comedy is one response to the human need to "let go" or to transcend the everyday world. Human beings, if they remain truly human, never lose the childlike need to play, and they certainly need to be able to laugh at their own and at others' shortcomings and to remember that life is not all earnestness and work. If we transcend the everyday world with tragedy through an almost religious sense of awe, we transcend it with comedy through our laughter. We laugh at comic characters either because they are quick, witty, and always able to outsmart the "bad guys" or, on the contrary, because they are always getting into trouble. Comedy is often worked out on the level of *action,* whereas tragedy is often worked out on the level of *thought.* Whereas tragic writers tend to view people in the context of a universal human condition, comic writers often take a hard look at their immediate society, satirizing its customs and institutions. For this reason, it will be useful to look at the development of comedy in Greece and at the society in which the comic playwright Aristophanes lived.

The word *comedy* comes from *komos,* which means "revel." It seems probable that fertility rituals and celebrations are at the origins of comedy. From the earliest days of Greece, groups of men, revelers, would go around from village to village, wearing huge artificial phalluses, telling jokes (often obscene ones), singing, and dancing. The community would participate in the revels. These were not only for fun but also intended to increase fertility—in the land, in people, in animals. Worship of the phallus as a symbol of fertility is common among all "primitive" peoples, and Freud and Jung have shown that phallic symbols appear in the dreams of "civilized" people as well. Often the

komos would end with some sort of sexual union—a ritual orgy, a pairing off with mates, or a marriage. This was not meant to encourage free sex on all occasions but to ensure fertility.

We do not know exactly how comedy as an art form grew from these revels, but it was recognized as such at the festival of Dionysus in Athens around 486 B.C., thus later than tragedy. Aristophanes, the only Greek classical comic author whose works survive, composed "old comedies." In his comedies, many of the old ritual features of the *komos*—the big phalluses, padding, animal costumes, grotesque masks, colloquial speech, and obscene jokes—are retained. There are often two choruses in opposition to each other (in *Lysistrata,* the choruses of old men and old women). Certainly, music and dance were of great importance. Of course, the purpose was no longer to promote fertility but to entertain people.

The situations in old comedy are often fantastic ones (in some, such as *The Birds* and *The Frogs,* the characters are dressed like animals), but the people or the institutions made fun of were real enough. About a hundred years after Aristophanes we find "new comedy," in the hands of its most famous practitioner, Menander, without phalluses, grotesque costumes, or indecent jokes. The new comedy was realistic rather than fantastic—it reflected everyday life and created stock, yet individualized characters. New comedy, such as that practiced by the Romans Plautus and Terence, is more similar to the comedies of manners with which we are familiar in modern theater, films, and television. The situations in new comedy often arise from misunderstandings, there is often a great deal of verbal play and wit, and the endings are happy. New comedy has lost touch with its origins in ritual fertility except that—even today—it often ends with a marriage or a happy love.

READING SELECTIONS

SOPHOCLES

Oedipus Rex

Translation by Dudley Fitts and Robert Fitzgerald

As we saw on page 116, most of the story of Oedipus has taken place before the play begins. What, then, *is* the plot or action of this tragedy? Most of it lies in the discovery of previous events. In this sense it resembles a detective story that opens after the crime has been committed. Oedipus begins by trying to find the answer to the question, "Who killed King Laius?" He ends by asking, and then answering, a much more profound question, "Who am I?" His tragedy, or his downfall, occurs when he finds the answer to his questions. As you read the play, notice how Sophocles builds up to the climactic point step by step. Try to determine, too, what emotional effect the tragic discovery of Oedipus has on you, the reader or spectator, and whether or not this changes by the end of the play. Notice how Sophocles has interpreted and portrayed the character of Oedipus. Finally, try to define for yourself what constitutes the personal tragedy of Oedipus and what makes the play a tragedy.

CHARACTERS

OEDIPUS, *King of Thebes, supposed son of Polybos and Meropê, King and Queen of Corinth*
IOKASTÊ, *wife of Oedipus and widow of the late King Laïos*
KREON, *brother of Iokastê, a prince of Thebes*
TEIRESIAS, *a blind seer who serves Apollo*
PRIEST
MESSENGER, *from Corinth*
SHEPHERD, *former servant of Laïos*
SECOND MESSENGER, *from the palace*
CHORUS OF THEBAN ELDERS
CHORAGOS, *leader of the Chorus*
ANTIGONE *and* ISMENE, *young daughters of Oedipus and Iokastê. They appear in the Éxodos but do not speak.*
SUPPLIANTS, GUARDS, SERVANTS

THE SCENE. *Before the palace of* OEDIPUS, *King of Thebes. A central door and two lateral doors open onto a platform which runs the length of the façade. On the platform, right and left, are altars; and three steps lead down into the orchêstra or chorus-ground. At the beginning of the action these steps are crowded by suppliants who have brought branches and chaplets of olive leaves and who sit in various attitudes of despair.* OEDIPUS *enters.*

PROLOGUE

OEDIPUS My children, generations of the living
In the line of Kadmos,[1] nursed at his ancient hearth:
Why have you strewn yourselves before these altars
In supplication, with your boughs and garlands?
The breath of incense rises from the city
With a sound of prayer and lamentation.
                                        Children,
I would not have you speak through messengers,
And therefore I have come myself to hear you—
I, Oedipus, who bear the famous name.
(*To a* PRIEST) You, there, since you are eldest in the
    company,
Speak for them all, tell me what preys upon you,
Whether you come in dread, or crave some blessing:
Tell me, and never doubt that I will help you
In every way I can; I should be heartless
Were I not moved to find you suppliant here.
PRIEST Great Oedipus, O powerful king of Thebes!
You see how all the ages of our people
Cling to your altar steps: here are boys
Who can barely stand alone, and here are priests
By weight of age, as I am a priest of God,
And young men chosen from those yet unmarried;
As for the others, all that multitude,
They wait with olive chaplets in the squares,

---

[1]Founder of Thebes.

At the two shrines of Pallas, and where Apollo
Speaks in the glowing embers.
                                    Your own eyes
Must tell you: Thebes is tossed on a murdering sea
And can not lift her head from the death surge.
A rust consumes the buds and fruits of the earth;
The herds are sick; children die unborn,
And labor is vain. The god of plague and pyre
Raids like detestable lightning through the city,
And all the house of Kadmos is laid waste,
All emptied, and all darkened: Death alone
Battens upon the misery of Thebes.

You are not one of the immortal gods, we know;
Yet we have come to you to make our prayer
As to the man surest in mortal ways
And wisest in the ways of God. You saved us
From the Sphinx, that flinty singer, and the tribute
We paid to her so long; yet you were never
Better informed than we, nor could we teach you:
A god's touch, it seems, enabled you to help us.

Therefore, O mighty power, we turn to you:
Find us our safety, find us a remedy,
Whether by counsel of the gods or of men.
A king of wisdom tested in the past
Can act in a time of troubles, and act well.
Noblest of men, restore
Life to your city! Think how all men call you
Liberator for your boldness long ago;
Ah, when your years of kingship are remembered,
Let them not say *We rose, but later fell—*
Keep the State from going down in the storm!
Once, years ago, with happy augury,
You brought us fortune; be the same again!
No man questions your power to rule the land:
But rule over men, not over a dead city!
Ships are only hulls, high walls are nothing,
When no life moves in the empty passageways.

OEDIPUS   Poor children! You may be sure I know
All that you longed for in your coming here.
I know that you are deathly sick; and yet,
Sick as you are, not one is as sick as I.
Each of you suffers in himself alone
His anguish, not another's; but my spirit
Groans for the city, for myself, for you.

I was not sleeping, you are not waking me.
No, I have been in tears for a long while
And in my restless thought walked many ways.
In all my search I found one remedy,
And I have adopted it: I have sent Kreon,
Son of Menoikeus, brother of the queen,

To Delphi, Apollo's place of revelation,
To learn there, if he can,
What act or pledge of mine may save the city.
I have counted the days, and now, this very day,
I am troubled, for he has overstayed his time.
What is he doing? He has been gone too long.
Yet whenever he comes back, I should do ill
Not to take any action the god orders.

PRIEST   It is a timely promise. At this instant
They tell me Kreon is here.

OEDIPUS   O Lord Apollo!
May his news be fair as his face is radiant!

PRIEST   Good news, I gather! he is crowned with bay,
The chaplet is thick with berries.

OEDIPUS   We shall soon know;
He is near enough to hear us now.

(*Enter* KREON)

                                        O prince:
Brother: son of Menoikeus:
What answer do you bring us from the god?

KREON   A strong one. I can tell you, great afflictions
Will turn out well, if they are taken well.

OEDIPUS   What was the oracle? These vague words
Leave me still hanging between hope and fear.

KREON   Is it your pleasure to hear me with all these
Gathered around us? I am prepared to speak,
But should we not go in?

OEDIPUS   Speak to them all,
It is for them I suffer, more than for myself.

KREON   Then I will tell you what I heard at Delphi.
In plain words
The god commands us to expel from the land of
    Thebes
An old defilement we are sheltering:
It is a deathly thing, beyond cure;
We must not let it feed upon us longer.

OEDIPUS   What defilement? How shall we rid
ourselves of it?

KREON   By exile or death, blood for blood. It was
Murder that brought the plague-wind on the city.

OEDIPUS   Murder of whom? Surely the god has
named him?

KREON   My lord: Laïos once ruled this land,
Before you came to govern us.

OEDIPUS   I know;
I learned of him from others; I never saw him.

KREON   He was murdered; and Apollo commands us
now
To take revenge upon whoever killed him.

OEDIPUS   Upon whom? Where are they? Where shall
we find a clue
To solve that crime, after so many years?

KREON   Here in this land, he said. Search reveals
   Things that escape an inattentive man.
OEDIPUS   Tell me: Was Laïos murdered in his house,
   Or in the fields, or in some foreign country?
KREON   He said he planned to make a pilgrimage.
   He did not come home again.
OEDIPUS   And was there no one,
   No witness, no companion, to tell what happened?
KREON   They were all killed but one, and he got away
   So frightened that he could remember one thing
     only.
OEDIPUS   What was the one thing? One may be the
     key
   To everything, if we resolve to use it.
KREON   He said that a band of highwaymen attacked
   them,
   Outnumbered them, and overwhelmed the king.
OEDIPUS   Strange, that a highwayman should be so
   daring—
   Unless some faction here bribed him to do it.
KREON   We thought of that. But after Laïos' death
   New troubles arose and we had no avenger.
OEDIPUS   What troubles could prevent your hunting
   down the killers?
KREON   The riddling Sphinx's song
   Made us deaf to all mysteries but her own.
OEDIPUS   Then once more I must bring what is dark
   to light.
   It is most fitting that Apollo shows,
   As you do, this compunction for the dead.
   You shall see how I stand by you, as I should,
   Avenging this country and the god as well,
   And not as though it were for some distant friend,
   But for my own sake, to be rid of evil.
   Whoever killed King Laïos might—who knows?—
   Lay violent hands even on me—and soon.
   I act for the murdered king in my own interest.

   Come, then, my children: leave the altar steps,
   Lift up your olive boughs!
               One of you go
   And summon the people of Kadmos to gather here.
   I will do all that I can; you may tell them that.

(*Exit a* PAGE)

   So, with the help of God,
   We shall be saved—or else indeed we are lost.
PRIEST   Let us rise, children. It was for this we came,
   And now the king has promised it.
   Phoibos[2] has sent us an oracle; may he descend
   Himself to save us and drive out the plague.

---

[2]Apollo.

(*Exeunt* OEDIPUS *and* KREON *into the palace by the central door. The* PRIEST *and the* SUPPLIANTS *disperse R and L. After a short pause the* CHORUS *enters the orchestra*)

PARODOS[3]

Strophe 1

CHORUS   What is God singing in his profound
   Delphi of gold and shadow?
   What oracle for Thebes, the sunwhipped city?
   Fear unjoints me, the roots of my heart tremble.
   Now I remember, O Healer, your power, and
     wonder:
   Will you send doom like a sudden cloud, or weave it
   Like nightfall of the past?
   Speak to me, tell me, O
   Child of golden Hope, immortal Voice.

Antistrophe 1

Let me pray to Athenê, the immortal daughter of
   Zeus,
And to Artemis her sister
Who keeps her famous throne in the market ring,
And to Apollo, archer from distant heaven—
O gods, descend! Like three streams leap against
The fires of our grief, the fires of darkness;
Be swift to bring us rest!
As in the old time from the brilliant house
Of air you stepped to save us, come again!

Strophe 2

Now our afflictions have no end,
Now all our stricken host lies down
And no man fights off death with his mind;
The noble plowland bears no grain,
And groaning mothers can not bear—
See, how our lives like birds take wing,

---

[3]The *parados* is the song or ode chanted by the chorus on its entry. It is accompanied by dancing and music played on an oboe. The chorus, in this play, represents elders of the city of Thebes. They remain on stage (on a level lower than the principal actors) for the remainder of the play. The choral odes and dances serve to separate one scene from another (there was no curtain in Greek theater) as well as to comment on the action, reinforce the emotion, and interpret the situation. The chorus also performs dance movements during certain portions of the scenes themselves. *Strophe* and *antistrophe* are terms denoting the movement and countermovement of the chorus from one side of its playing area to the other. When the chorus participates in dialogue with the other characters, the lines are spoken by the Choragos, its leader.

Like sparks that fly when a fire soars,
To the shore of the god of evening.

Antistrophe 2

The plague burns on, it is pitiless,
Though pallid children laden with death
Lie unwept in the stony ways,
And old gray women by every path
Flock to the strand about the altars
There to strike their breasts and cry
Worship of Phoibos in wailing prayers:
Be kind, God's golden child!

Strophe 3

There are no swords in this attack by fire,
No shields, but we are ringed with cries.
Send the besieger plunging from our homes
Into the vast sea-room of the Atlantic
Or into the waves that foam eastward of Thrace—
For the day ravages what the night spares—
Destroy our enemy, lord of the thunder!
Let him be riven by lightning from heaven!

Antistrophe 3

Phoibos Apollo, stretch the sun's bowstring,
That golden cord, until it sing for us,
Flashing arrows in heaven!
                              Artemis, Huntress,
Race with flaring lights upon our mountains!
O scarlet god, O golden-banded brow,
O Theban Bacchos in a storm of Maenads,

(*Enter* OEDIPUS, C)

Whirl upon Death, that all the Undying hate!
Come with blinding torches, come in joy!

SCENE 1

OEDIPUS   Is this your prayer? It may be answered. Come,
Listen to me, act as the crisis demands,
And you shall have relief from all these evils.

Until now I was a stranger to this tale,
As I had been a stranger to the crime.
Could I track down the murderer without a clue?
But now, friends,
As one who became a citizen after the murder,
I make this proclamation to all Thebans:
If any man knows by whose hand Laïos, son of
    Labdakos,

Met his death, I direct that man to tell me
    everything,
No matter what he fears for having so long
    withheld it.
Let it stand as promised that no further trouble
Will come to him, but he may leave the land in
    safety.

Moreover: If anyone knows the murderer to be
    foreign,
Let him not keep silent: he shall have his reward
    from me.
However, if he does conceal it; if any man
Fearing for his friend or for himself disobeys this
    edict,
Hear what I propose to do:

I solemnly forbid the people of this country,
Where power and throne are mine, ever to receive
    that man
Or speak to him, no matter who he is, or let him
Join in sacrifice, lustration, or in prayer.
I decree that he be driven from every house,
Being, as he is, corruption itself to us: the Delphic
Voice of Apollo has pronounced this revelation.
Thus I associate myself with the oracle
And take the side of the murdered king.

As for the criminal, I pray to God—
Whether it be a lurking thief, or one of a number—
I pray that that man's life be consumed in evil and
    wretchedness.
And as for me, this curse applies no less
If it should turn out that the culprit is my guest here,
Sharing my hearth.
                        You have heard the penalty.
I lay it on you now to attend to this
For my sake, for Apollo's, for the sick
Sterile city that heaven has abandoned.
Suppose the oracle had given you no command:
Should this defilement go uncleansed for ever?
You should have found the murderer: your king,
A noble king, had been destroyed!
                                        Now I,
Having the power that he held before me,
Having his bed, begetting children there
Upon his wife, as he would have, had he lived—
Their son would have been my children's brother,
If Laïos had had luck in fatherhood!
(And now his bad fortune has struck him down)—
I say I take the son's part, just as though
I were his son, to press the fight for him
And see it won! I'll find the hand that brought

Death to Labdakos' and Polydoros' child,
Heir of Kadmos' and Agenor's line.[4]
And as for those who fail me,
May the gods deny them the fruit of the earth,
Fruit of the womb, and may they rot utterly!
Let them be wretched as we are wretched, and worse!

For you, for loyal Thebans, and for all
Who find my actions right, I pray the favor
Of justice, and of all the immortal gods.

CHORAGOS   Since I am under oath, my lord, I swear
I did not do the murder, I can not name
The murderer. Phoibos ordained the search;
Why did he not say who the culprit was?

OEDIPUS   An honest question. But no man in the
world
Can make the gods do more than the gods will.

CHORAGOS   There is an alternative, I think—

OEDIPUS   Tell me.
Any or all, you must not fail to tell me.

CHORAGOS   A lord clairvoyant to the lord Apollo,
As we all know, is the skilled Teiresias.
One might learn much about this from him,
Oedipus.

OEDIPUS   I am not wasting time:
Kreon spoke of this, and I have sent for him—
Twice, in fact; it is strange that he is not here.

CHORAGOS   The other matter—that old report—
seems useless.

OEDIPUS   What was that? I am interested in all reports.

CHORAGOS   The king was said to have been killed
by highwaymen.

OEDIPUS   I know. But we have no witnesses to that.

CHORAGOS   If the killer can feel a particle of dread,
Your curse will bring him out of hiding!

OEDIPUS   No.
The man who dared that act will fear no curse.

(*Enter the blind seer* TEIRESIAS, *led by a* PAGE)

CHORAGOS   But there is one man who may detect
the criminal.
This is Teiresias, this is the holy prophet
In whom, alone of all men, truth was born.

OEDIPUS   Teiresias: seer: student of mysteries,
Of all that's taught and all that no man tells,
Secrets of Heaven and secrets of the earth:
Blind though you are, you know the city lies
Sick with plague; and from this plague, my lord,
We find that you alone can guard or save us.

Possibly you did not hear the messengers?
Apollo, when we sent to him,
Sent us back word that this great pestilence
Would lift, but only if we established clearly
The identity of those who murdered Laïos.
They must be killed or exiled.
Can you use
Birdflight[5] or any art of divination
To purify yourself, and Thebes, and me
From this contagion? We are in your hands.
There is no fairer duty
Than that of helping others in distress.

TEIRESIAS   How dreadful knowledge of the truth
can be
When there's no help in truth! I knew this well,
But did not act on it: else I should not have come.

OEDIPUS   What is troubling you? Why are your eyes
so cold?

TEIRESIAS   Let me go home. Bear your own fate,
and I'll
Bear mine. It is better so: trust what I say.

OEDIPUS   What you say is ungracious and unhelpful
To your native country. Do not refuse to speak.

TEIRESIAS   When it comes to speech, your own is
neither temperate
Nor opportune. I wish to be more prudent.

OEDIPUS   In God's name, we all beg you—

TEIRESIAS   You are all ignorant.
No; I will never tell you what I know.
Now it is my misery; then, it would be yours.

OEDIPUS   What! You do know something, and will
not tell us?
You would betray us all and wreck the State?

TEIRESIAS   I do not intend to torture myself, or you.
Why persist in asking? You will not persuade me.

OEDIPUS   What a wicked old man you are! You'd
try a stone's
Patience! Out with it! Have you no feeling at all?

TEIRESIAS   You call me unfeeling. If you could only
see
The nature of your own feelings . . .

OEDIPUS   Why,
Who would not feel as I do? Who could endure
Your arrogance toward the city?

TEIRESIAS   What does it matter?
Whether I speak or not, it is bound to come.

OEDIPUS   Then, if "it" is bound to come, you are
bound to tell me.

TEIRESIAS   No, I will not go on. Rage as you please.

---

[4]Father, grandfather, great-grandfather, and great-great-grand-father of Laïos.

[5]Prophets predicted the future or divined the unknown by observing the flight of birds.

OEDIPUS   Rage? Why not!
                    And I'll tell you what I think:
You planned it, you had it done, you all but
Killed him with your own hands: if you had eyes,
I'd say the crime was yours, and yours alone.

TEIRESIAS   So? I charge you, then,
Abide by the proclamation you have made:
From this day forth
Never speak again to these men or to me;
You yourself are the pollution of this country.

OEDIPUS   You dare say that! Can you possibly think
   you have
Some way of going free, after such insolence?

TEIRESIAS   I have gone free. It is the truth sustains me.

OEDIPUS   Who taught you shamelessness? It was
   not your craft.

TEIRESIAS   You did. You made me speak. I did not
   want to.

OEDIPUS   Speak what? Let me hear it again more
   clearly.

TEIRESIAS   Was it not clear before? Are you
   tempting me?

OEDIPUS   I did not understand it. Say it again.

TEIRESIAS   I say that you are the murderer whom
   you seek.

OEDIPUS   Now twice you have spat out infamy.
   You'll pay for it!

TEIRESIAS   Would you care for more? Do you wish
   to be really angry?

OEDIPUS   Say what you will. Whatever you say is
   worthless.

TEIRESIAS   I say you live in hideous shame with those
Most dear to you. You can not see the evil.

OEDIPUS   Can you go on babbling like this for ever?

TEIRESIAS   I can, if there is power in truth.

OEDIPUS   There is:
But not for you, not for you,
You sightless, witless, senseless, mad old man!

TEIRESIAS   You are the madman. There is no one here
Who will not curse you soon, as you curse me.

OEDIPUS   You child of total night! I would not
   touch you;
Neither would any man who sees the sun.

TEIRESIAS   True: it is not from you my fate will come.
That lies within Apollo's competence,
As it is his concern.

OEDIPUS   Tell me, who made
These fine discoveries? Kreon? or someone else?

TEIRESIAS   Kreon is no threat. You weave your own
   doom.

OEDIPUS   Wealth, power, craft of statesmanship!
Kingly position, everywhere admired!
What savage envy is stored up against these,
If Kreon, whom I trusted, Kreon my friend,

For this great office which the city once
Put in my hands unsought—if for this power
Kreon desires in secret to destroy me!

He has bought this decrepit fortune-teller, this
Collector of dirty pennies, this prophet fraud—
Why, he is no more clairvoyant than I am!
                             Tell us:
Has your mystic mummery ever approached the
   truth?
When that hellcat the Sphinx was performing here,
What help were you to these people?
Her magic was not for the first man who came
   along:
It demanded a real exorcist. Your birds—
What good were they? or the gods, for the matter
   of that?
But I came by,
Oedipus, the simple man, who knows nothing—
I thought it out for myself, no birds helped me!
And this is the man you think you can destroy,
That you may be close to Kreon when he's king!
Well, you and your friend Kreon, it seems to me,
Will suffer most. If you were not an old man,
You would have paid already for your plot.

CHORAGOS   We can not see that his words or yours
Have been spoken except in anger, Oedipus,
And of anger we have no need. How to accomplish
The god's will best: that is what most concerns us.

TEIRESIAS   You are a king. But where argument's
   concerned
I am your man, as much a king as you.
I am not your servant, but Apollo's.
I have no need of Kreon or Kreon's name.

Listen to me. You mock my blindness, do you?
But I say that you, with both your eyes, are blind:
You can not see the wretchedness of your life,
Nor in whose house you live, no, nor with whom.
Who are your father and mother? Can you tell me?
You do not even know the blind wrongs
That you have done them, on earth and in the
   world below.
But the double lash of your parents' curse will
   whip you
Out of this land some day, with only night
Upon your precious eyes.
Your cries then—where will they not be heard?
What fastness of Kithairon[6] will not echo them?
And that bridal-descant of yours—you'll know it
   then,

---

[6]The mountain where Oedipus was taken to be exposed as an infant.

The song they sang when you came here to Thebes
And found your misguided berthing.
All this, and more, that you can not guess at now,
Will bring you to yourself among your children.

Be angry, then. Curse Kreon. Curse my words.
I tell you, no man that walks upon the earth
Shall be rooted out more horribly than you.

OEDIPUS   Am I to bear this from him?—Damnation
Take you! Out of this place! Out of my sight!

TEIRESIAS   I would not have come at all if you had
    not asked me.

OEDIPUS   Could I have told that you'd talk
    nonsense, that
You'd come here to make a fool of yourself, and of
    me?

TEIRESIAS   A fool? Your parents thought me
    sane enough.

OEDIPUS   My parents again!—Wait: who were
    my parents?

TEIRESIAS   This day will give you a father, and
    break your heart.

OEDIPUS   Your infantile riddles! Your damned
    abracadabra!

TEIRESIAS   You were a great man once at solving
    riddles.

OEDIPUS   Mock me with that if you like; you will
    find it true.

TEIRESIAS   It was true enough. It brought about
    your ruin.

OEDIPUS   But if it saved this town?

TEIRESIAS (*to the* PAGE)   Boy, give me your hand.

OEDIPUS   Yes, boy; lead him away.
                    —While you are here
We can do nothing. Go; leave us in peace.

TEIRESIAS   I will go when I have said what I have to
    say.
How can you hurt me? And I tell you again:
The man you have been looking for all this time,
The damned man, the murderer of Laïos,
That man is in Thebes. To your mind he is foreign-
    born,
But it will soon be shown that he is a Theban,
A revelation that will fail to please.
                    A blind man,
Who has his eyes now; a penniless man, who is
    rich now;
And he will go tapping the strange earth with his
    staff.
To the children with whom he lives now he will be
Brother and father—the very same; to her
Who bore him, son and husband—the very same
Who came to his father's bed, wet with his father's
    blood.

Enough. Go think that over.
If later you find error in what I have said,
You may say that I have no skill in prophecy.

(*Exit* TEIRESIAS, *led by his* PAGE. OEDIPUS *goes into
the palace*)

ODE 1

Strophe 1

CHORUS   The Delphic stone of prophecies
Remembers ancient regicide
And a still bloody hand.
That killer's hour of flight has come.
He must be stronger than riderless
Coursers of untiring wind,
For the son[7] of Zeus armed with his father's thunder
Leaps in lightning after him;
And the Furies hold his track, the sad Furies.

Antistrophe 1

Holy Parnassos'[8] peak of snow
Flashes and blinds that secret man,
That all shall hunt him down:
Though he may roam the forest shade
Like a bull gone wild from pasture
To rage through glooms of stone.
Doom comes down on him; flight will not avail him;
For the world's heart calls him desolate,
And the immortal voices follow, for ever follow.

Strophe 2

But now a wilder thing is heard
From the old man skilled at hearing Fate in the
    wing-beat of a bird.
Bewildered as a blown bird, my soul hovers and
    can not find
Foothold in this debate, or any reason or rest of
    mind.
But no man ever brought—none can bring
Proof of strife between Thebes' royal house,
Labdakos' line, and the son of Polybos;
And never until now has any man brought word
Of Laïos' dark death staining Oedipus the King.

Antistrophe 2

Divine Zeus and Apollo hold
Perfect intelligence alone of all tales ever told;

---

[7]Apollo.
[8]Mountain sacred to Apollo.

And well though this diviner works, he works in
  his own night;
No man can judge that rough unknown or trust in
  second sight,
For wisdom changes hands among the wise.
Shall I believe my great lord criminal
At a raging word that a blind old man let fall?
I saw him, when the carrion woman[9] faced him of
  old,
Prove his heroic mind. These evil words are lies.

SCENE II

KREON   Men of Thebes:
  I am told that heavy accusations
  Have been brought against me by King Oedipus.

  I am not the kind of man to bear this tamely.

  If in these present difficulties
  He holds me accountable for any harm to him
  Through anything I have said or done—why, then,
  I do not value life in this dishonor.
  It is not as though this rumor touched upon
  Some private indiscretion. The matter is grave.
  The fact is that I am being called disloyal
  To the State, to my fellow citizens, to my friends.
CHORAGOS   He may have spoken in anger, not from
  his mind.
KREON   But did you not hear him say I was the one
  Who seduced the old prophet into lying?
CHORAGOS   The thing was said: I do not know how
  seriously.
KREON   But you were watching him! Were his eyes
  steady?
Did he look like a man in his right mind?
CHORAGOS   I do not know.
  I can not judge the behavior of great men.
  But here is the king himself.

(*Enter* OEDIPUS)

OEDIPUS   So you dared come back.
  Why? How brazen of you to come to my house,
  You murderer!
                  Do you think I do not know
  That you plotted to kill me, plotted to steal my
  throne?
  Tell me, in God's name: am I coward, a fool,
  That you should dream you could accomplish this?

_____
[9]The Sphinx.

A fool who could not see your slippery game?
A coward, not to fight back when I saw it?
You are the fool, Kreon, are you not? hoping
Without support or friends to get a throne?
Thrones may be won or bought: you could do
  neither.
KREON   Now listen to me. You have talked; let me
  talk, too.
You can not judge unless you know the facts.
OEDIPUS   You speak well: there is one fact; but I find
  it hard
To learn from the deadliest enemy I have.
KREON   That above all I must dispute with you.
OEDIPUS   That above all I will not hear you deny.
KREON   If you think there is anything good in being
  stubborn
Against all reason, then I say you are wrong.
OEDIPUS   If you think a man can sin against his own
  kind
And not be punished for it, I say you are mad.
KREON   I agree. But tell me: What have I done to you?
OEDIPUS   You advised me to send for that wizard, did
  you not?
KREON   I did. I should do it again.
OEDIPUS   Very well. Now tell me:
  How long has it been since Laïos—
KREON   What of Laïos?
OEDIPUS   Since he vanished in that onset by the road?
KREON   It was long ago, a long time.
OEDIPUS   And this prophet,
  Was he practicing here then?
KREON   He was; and with honor, as now.
OEDIPUS   Did he speak of me at that time?
KREON   He never did,
  At least, not when I was present.
OEDIPUS   But . . . the enquiry?
  I suppose you held one?
KREON   We did, but we learned nothing.
OEDIPUS   Why did the prophet not speak against me
  then?
KREON   I do not know; and I am the kind of man
  Who holds his tongue when he has no facts to go on.
OEDIPUS   There's one fact that you know, and you
  could tell it.
KREON   What fact is that? If I know it, you shall have
  it.
OEDIPUS   If he were not involved with you, he could
  not say
  That it was I who murdered Laïos.
KREON   If he says that, you are the one that knows
  it!—
But now it is my turn to question you.

OEDIPUS   Put your questions. I am no murderer.
KREON   First, then: You married my sister?
OEDIPUS   I married your sister.
KREON   And you rule the kingdom equally with her?
OEDIPUS   Everything that she wants she has from me.
KREON   And I am the third, equal to both of you?
OEDIPUS   That is why I call you a bad friend.
KREON   No. Reason it out, as I have done.
   Think of this first: Would any sane man prefer
   Power, with all a king's anxieties,
   To that same power and the grace of sleep?
   Certainly not I.
   I have never longed for the king's power—only his
     rights.
   Would any wise man differ from me in this?
   As matters stand, I have my way in everything
   With your consent, and no responsibilities.
   If I were king, I should be a slave to policy.

   How could I desire a scepter more
   Than what is now mine—untroubled influence?
   No, I have not gone mad; I need no honors,
   Except those with the perquisites I have now.
   I am welcome everywhere; every man salutes me,
   And those who want your favor seek my ear,
   Since I know how to manage what they ask.
   Should I exchange this ease for that anxiety?
   Besides, no sober mind is treasonable.
   I hate anarchy
   And never would deal with any man who likes it.
   Test what I have said. Go to the priestess
   At Delphi, ask if I quoted her correctly.
   And as for this other thing: if I am found
   Guilty of treason with Teiresias,
   Then sentence me to death. You have my word
   It is a sentence I should cast my vote for—
   But not without evidence!
               You do wrong
   When you take good men for bad, bad men for good.
   A true friend thrown aside—why, life itself
   Is not more precious!
            In time you will know this well:
   For time, and time alone, will show the just man,
   Though scoundrels are discovered in a day.
CHORAGOS   This is well said, and a prudent man
     would ponder it.
   Judgments too quickly formed are dangerous.
OEDIPUS   But is he not quick in his duplicity?
   And shall I not be quick to parry him?
   Would you have me stand still, hold my peace, and
     let
   This man win everything, through my inaction?

KREON   And you want—what is it, then? To banish
   me?
OEDIPUS   No, not exile. It is your death I want,
   So that all the world may see what treason means.
KREON   You will persist, then? You will not believe
   me?
OEDIPUS   How can I believe you?
KREON   Then you are a fool.
OEDIPUS   To save myself?
KREON   In justice, think of me.
OEDIPUS   You are evil incarnate.
KREON   But suppose that you are wrong?
OEDIPUS   Still I must rule.
KREON   But not if you rule badly.
OEDIPUS   O city, city!
KREON   It is my city, too!
CHORAGOS   Now, my lords, be still. I see the queen,
   Iokastê, coming from her palace chambers;
   And it is time she came, for the sake of you both.
   This dreadful quarrel can be resolved through her.

(*Enter* IOKASTÊ)

IOKASTÊ   Poor foolish men, what wicked din is this?
   With Thebes sick to death, is it not shameful
   That you should rake some private quarrel up?
   (*To* OEDIPUS) Come into the house.
              —And you, Kreon, go now:
   Let us have no more of this tumult over nothing.
KREON   Nothing? No, sister: what your husband
   plans for me
   Is one of two great evils: exile or death.
OEDIPUS   He is right.
        Why, woman I have caught him squarely
   Plotting against my life.
KREON   No! Let me die
   Accurst if ever I have wished you harm!
IOKASTÊ   Ah, believe it, Oedipus!
   In the name of the gods, respect this oath of his
   For my sake, for the sake of these people here!

Strophe 1

CHORAGOS   Open your mind to her, my lord. Be
   ruled by her, I beg you!
OEDIPUS   What would you have me do?
CHORAGOS   Respect Kreon's word. He has never
   spoken like a fool,
   And now he has sworn an oath.
OEDIPUS   You know what you ask?
CHORAGOS   I do.
OEDIPUS   Speak on, then.

CHORAGOS   A friend so sworn should not be baited so,
In blind malice, and without final proof.
OEDIPUS   You are aware, I hope, that what you say
Means death for me, or exile at the least.

Strophe 2

CHORAGOS   No, I swear by Helios, first in Heaven!
May I die friendless and accurst,
The worst of deaths, if ever I meant that!
It is the withering fields
That hurt my sick heart:
Must we bear all these ills,
And now your bad blood as well?
OEDIPUS   Then let him go. And let me die, if I must,
Or be driven by him in shame from the land of
Thebes.
It is your unhappiness, and not his talk,
That touches me.
As for him—
Wherever he goes, hatred will follow him.
KREON   Ugly in yielding, as you were ugly in rage!
Natures like yours chiefly torment themselves.
OEDIPUS   Can you not go? Can you not leave me?
KREON   I can.
You do not know me; but the city knows me,
And in its eyes I am just, if not in yours.

(*Exit* KREON)

Antistrophe 1

CHORAGOS   Lady Iokastê, did you not ask the King
to go to his chambers?
IOKASTÊ   First tell me what has happened.
CHORAGOS   There was suspicion without evidence;
yet it rankled
As even false charges will.
IOKASTÊ   On both sides?
CHORAGOS   On both.
IOKASTÊ   But what was said?
CHORAGOS   Oh let it rest, let it be done with!
Have we not suffered enough?
OEDIPUS   You see to what your decency has brought
you:
You have made difficulties where my heart saw
none.

Antistrophe 2

CHORAGOS   Oedipus, it is not once only I have told
you—
You must know I should count myself unwise

To the point of madness, should I now forsake you—
You, under whose hand,
In the storm of another time,
Our dear land sailed out free.
But now stand fast at the helm!
IOKASTÊ   In God's name, Oedipus, inform your wife
as well:
Why are you so set in this hard anger?
OEDIPUS   I will tell you, for none of these men
deserves
My confidence as you do. It is Kreon's work,
His treachery, his plotting against me.
IOKASTÊ   Go on, if you can make this clear to me.
OEDIPUS   He charges me with the murder of Laïos.
IOKASTÊ   Has he some knowledge? Or does he speak
from hearsay?
OEDIPUS   He would not commit himself to such a
charge,
But he has brought in that damnable soothsayer
To tell his story.
IOKASTÊ   Set your mind at rest.
If it is a question of soothsayers, I tell you
That you will find no man whose craft gives
knowledge
Of the unknowable.
Here is my proof:
An oracle was reported to Laïos once
(I will not say from Phoibos himself, but from
His appointed ministers, at any rate)
That his doom would be death at the hands of his
own son—
His son, born of his flesh and of mine!

Now, you remember the story: Laïos was killed
By marauding strangers where three highways meet;
But his child had not been three days in this world
Before the king had pierced the baby's ankles
And left him to die on a lonely mountainside.

Thus, Apollo never caused that child
To kill his father, and it was not Laïos' fate
To die at the hands of his son, as he had feared.
This is what prophets and prophecies are worth!
Have no dread of them.
It is God himself
Who can show us what he wills, in his own way.
OEDIPUS   How strange a shadowy memory crossed
my mind,
Just now while you were speaking; it chilled my
heart.
IOKASTÊ   What do you mean? What memory do you
speak of?

OEDIPUS   If I understand you, Laïos was killed
  At a place where three roads meet.
IOKASTÊ   So it was said;
  We have no later story.
OEDIPUS   Where did it happen?
IOKASTÊ   Phokis, it is called: at a place where the
    Theban Way
  Divides into the roads toward Delphi and Daulia.
OEDIPUS   When?
IOKASTÊ   We had the news not long before you came
  And proved the right to your succession here.
OEDIPUS   Ah, what net has God been weaving for me?
IOKASTÊ   Oedipus! Why does this trouble you?
OEDIPUS   Do not ask me yet.
  First, tell me how Laïos looked, and tell me
  How old he was.
IOKASTÊ   He was tall, his hair just touched
  With white; his form was not unlike your own.
OEDIPUS   I think that I myself may be accurst
  By my own ignorant edict.
IOKASTÊ   You speak strangely.
  It makes me tremble to look at you, my king.
OEDIPUS   I am not sure that the blind man can not see.
  But I should know better if you were to tell me—
IOKASTÊ   Anything—though I dread to hear you ask
    it.
OEDIPUS   Was the king lightly escorted, or did he ride
  With a large company, as a ruler should?
IOKASTÊ   There were five men with him in all: one
    was a herald.
  And a single chariot, which he was driving.
OEDIPUS   Alas, that makes it plain enough!
                                    But who—
  Who told you how it happened?
IOKASTÊ   A household servant,
  The only one to escape.
OEDIPUS   And is he still
  A servant of ours?
IOKASTÊ   No; for when he came back at last
  And found you enthroned in the place of the dead
    king,
  He came to me, touched my hand with his, and
    begged
  That I would send him away to the frontier district
  Where only the shepherds go—
  As far away from the city as I could send him.
  I granted his prayer; for although the man was a
    slave,
  He had earned more than this favor at my hands.
OEDIPUS   Can he be called back quickly?
IOKASTÊ   Easily.
  But why?

OEDIPUS   I have taken too much upon myself
  Without enquiry; therefore I wish to consult him.
IOKASTÊ   Then he shall come.
                                But am I not one also
  To whom you might confide these fears of yours?
OEDIPUS   That is your right; it will not be denied you,
  Now least of all; for I have reached a pitch
  Of wild foreboding. Is there anyone
  To whom I should sooner speak?

  Polybos of Corinth is my father.
  My mother is a Dorian: Meropê.
  I grew up chief among the men of Corinth
  Until a strange thing happened—
  Not worth my passion, it may be, but strange.
  At a feast, a drunken man maundering in his cups
  Cried out that I am not my father's son![10]

  I contained myself that night, though I felt anger
  And a sinking heart. The next day I visited
  My father and mother, and questioned them. They
    stormed,
  Calling it all the slanderous rant of a fool;
  And this relieved me. Yet the suspicion
  Remained always aching in my mind;
  I knew there was talk; I could not rest;
  And finally, saying nothing to my parents,
  I went to the shrine at Delphi.
  The god dismissed my question without reply;
  He spoke of other things.
                                Some were clear,
  Full of wretchedness, dreadful, unbearable:
  As, that I should lie with my own mother, breed
  Children from whom all men would turn their eyes;
  And that I should be my father's murderer.

  I heard all this, and fled. And from that day
  Corinth to me was only in the stars
  Descending in that quarter of the sky,
  As I wandered farther and farther on my way
  To a land where I should never see the evil
  Sung by the oracle. And I came to this country
  Where, so you say, King Laïos was killed.

  I will tell you all that happened there, my lady.

---

[10]Oedipus perhaps interprets this as an allegation that he is a
bastard, the son of Meropê but not of Polybos. The implication,
at any rate, is that he is not of royal birth, not the legitimate heir to
the throne of Corinth.

There were three highways
Coming together at a place I passed;
And there a herald came towards me, and a chariot
Drawn by horses, with a man such as you describe
Seated in it. The groom leading the horses
Forced me off the road at his lord's command;
But as this charioteer lurched over towards me
I struck him in my rage. The old man saw me
And brought his double goad down upon my head
As I came abreast.

           He was paid back, and more!
Swinging my club in this right hand I knocked him
Out of his car, and he rolled on the ground.

                     I killed him.
I killed them all.
Now if that stranger and Laïos were—kin,
Where is a man more miserable than I?
More hated by the gods? Citizen and alien alike
Must never shelter me or speak to me—
I must be shunned by all.

               And I myself
Pronounced this malediction upon myself!

Think of it: I have touched you with these hands,
These hands that killed your husband. What
    defilement!

Am I all evil, then? It must be so,
Since I must flee from Thebes, yet never again
See my own countrymen, my own country,
For fear of joining my mother in marriage
And killing Polybos, my father.

                   Ah,
If I was created so, born to this fate,
Who could deny the savagery of God?

O holy majesty of heavenly powers!
May I never see that day! Never!
Rather let me vanish from the race of men
Than know the abomination destined me!
CHORAGOS   We too, my lord, have felt dismay at this.
  But there is hope: you have yet to hear the shepherd.
OEDIPUS   Indeed, I fear no other hope is left me.
IOKASTÊ   What do you hope from him when he
  comes?
OEDIPUS   This much:
  If his account of the murder tallies with yours,
  Then I am cleared.
IOKASTÊ   What was it that I said
  Of such importance?
OEDIPUS   Why, "marauders," you said,
  Killed the king, according to this man's story.

If he maintains that still, if there were several,
Clearly the guilt is not mine: I was alone.
But if he says one man, singlehanded, did it,
Then the evidence all points to me.
IOKASTÊ   You may be sure that he said there were
  several;
  And can he call back that story now? He can not.
  The whole city heard it as plainly as I.
  But suppose he alters some detail of it:
  He can not ever show that Laïos' death
  Fulfilled the oracle: for Apollo said
  My child was doomed to kill him; and my child—
  Poor baby!—it was my child that died first.
  No. From now on, where oracles are concerned,
  I would not waste a second thought on any.
OEDIPUS   You may be right.
                But come: let someone go
  For the shepherd at once. This matter must be
  settled.
IOKASTÊ   I will send for him.
  I would not wish to cross you in anything,
  And surely not in this.—Let us go in.

(*Exeunt into the palace*)

ODE II

Strophe 1

CHORUS   Let me be reverent in the ways of right,
  Lowly the paths I journey on;
  Let all my words and actions keep
  The laws of the pure universe
  From highest Heaven handed down.
  For Heaven is their bright nurse,
  Those generations of the realms of light;
  Ah, never of mortal kind were they begot,
  Nor are they slaves of memory, lost in sleep:
  Their Father is greater than Time, and ages not.

Antistrophe 1

The tyrant is a child of Pride
Who drinks from his great sickening cup
Recklessness and vanity,
Until from his high crest headlong
He plummets to the dust of hope.
That strong man is not strong.
But let no fair ambition be denied;
May God protect the wrestler for the State
In government, in comely policy,
Who will fear God, and on His ordinance wait.

Strophe 2

Haughtiness and the high hand of disdain
Tempt and outrage God's holy law;
And any mortal who dares hold
No immortal Power in awe
Will be caught up in a net of pain:
The price for which his levity is sold.
Let each man take due earnings, then,
And keep his hands from holy things,
And from blasphemy stand apart—
Else the crackling blast of heaven
Blows on his head, and on his desperate heart.
Though fools will honor impious men,
In their cities no tragic poet sings.

Antistrophe 2

Shall we lose faith in Delphi's obscurities,
We who have heard the world's core
Discredited, and the sacred wood
Of Zeus at Elis praised no more?
The deeds and the strange prophecies
Must make a pattern yet to be understood.
Zeus, if indeed you are lord of all,
Throned in light over night and day,
Mirror this in your endless mind:
Our masters call the oracle
Words on the wind, and the Delphic vision blind!
Their hearts no longer know Apollo,
And reverence for the gods has died away.

SCENE III

(*Enter* IOKASTÊ)

IOKASTÊ   Princes of Thebes, it has occurred to me
To visit the altars of the gods, bearing
These branches as a suppliant, and this incense.
Our king is not himself: his noble soul
Is overwrought with fantasies of dread,
Else he would consider
The new prophecies in the light of the old.
He will listen to any voice that speaks disaster,
And my advice goes for nothing.

(*She approaches the altar, R*)

To you, then, Apollo,
Lycéan lord, since you are nearest, I turn in prayer.
Receive these offerings, and grant us deliverance
From defilement. Our hearts are heavy with fear
When we see our leader distracted, as helpless sailors
Are terrified by the confusion of their helmsman.

(*Enter* MESSENGER)

MESSENGER   Friends, no doubt you can direct me:
Where shall I find the house of Oedipus,
Or, better still, where is the king himself?
CHORAGOS   It is this very place, stranger; he is inside.
This is his wife and mother of his children.
MESSENGER   I wish her happiness in a happy house,
Blest in all the fulfillment of her marriage.
IOKASTÊ   I wish as much for you: your courtesy
Deserves a like good fortune. But now, tell me:
Why have you come? What have you to say to us?
MESSENGER   Good news, my lady, for your house
and your husband.
IOKASTÊ   What news? Who sent you here?
MESSENGER   I am from Corinth.
The news I bring ought to mean joy for you,
Though it may be you will find some grief in it.
IOKASTÊ   What is it? How can it touch us in both
ways?
MESSENGER   The word is that the people of the
Isthmus
Intend to call Oedipus to be their king.
IOKASTÊ   But old King Polybos—is he not reigning
still?
MESSENGER   No. Death holds him in his sepulchre.
IOKASTÊ   What are you saying? Polybos is dead?
MESSENGER   If I am not telling the truth, may I die
myself.
IOKASTÊ (*to a* MAIDSERVANT)   Go in, go quickly;
tell this to your master.

O riddlers of God's will, where are you now!
This was the man whom Oedipus, long ago,
Feared so, fled so, in dread of destroying him—
But it was another fate by which he died.

(*Enter* OEDIPUS, C)

OEDIPUS   Dearest Iokastê, why have you sent for me?
IOKASTÊ   Listen to what this man says, and then tell
me
What has become of the solemn prophecies.
OEDIPUS   Who is this man? What is his news for me?
IOKASTÊ   He has come from Corinth to announce
your father's death!
OEDIPUS   Is it true, stranger? Tell me in your own
words.
MESSENGER   I can not say it more clearly: the king
is dead.
OEDIPUS   Was it by treason? Or by an attack of illness?
MESSENGER   A little thing brings old men to their rest.
OEDIPUS   It was sickness, then?

MESSENGER   Yes, and his many years.

OEDIPUS   Ah!
Why should a man respect the Pythian hearth,[11] or
Give heed to the birds that jangle above his head?
They prophesied that I should kill Polybos,
Kill my own father; but he is dead and buried,
And I am here—I never touched him, never,
Unless he died of grief for my departure,
And thus, in a sense, through me. No. Polybos
Has packed the oracles off with him underground.
They are empty words.

IOKASTÊ   Had I not told you so?

OEDIPUS   You had; it was my faint heart that
betrayed me.

IOKASTÊ   From now on never think of those things
again.

OEDIPUS   And yet—must I not fear my mother's
bed?

IOKASTÊ   Why should anyone in this world be afraid,
Since Fate rules us and nothing can be foreseen?
A man should live only for the present day.

Have no more fear of sleeping with your mother:
How many men, in dreams, have lain with their
mothers!
No reasonable man is troubled by such things.

OEDIPUS   That is true; only—
If only my mother were not still alive!
But she is alive. I can not help my dread.

IOKASTÊ   Yet this news of your father's death is
wonderful.

OEDIPUS   Wonderful. But I fear the living woman.

MESSENGER   Tell me, who is this woman that you fear?

OEDIPUS   It is Meropê, man; the wife of King Polybos.

MESSENGER   Meropê? Why should you be afraid of her?

OEDIPUS   An oracle of the gods, a dreadful saying.

MESSENGER   Can you tell me about it or are you
sworn to silence?

OEDIPUS   I can tell you, and I will.
Apollo said through his prophet that I was the man
Who should marry his own mother, shed his
father's blood
With his own hands. And so, for all these years
I have kept clear of Corinth, and no harm has
come—
Though it would have been sweet to see my
parents again.

MESSENGER   And is this the fear that drove you out
of Corinth?

OEDIPUS   Would you have me kill my father?

MESSENGER   As for that
You must be reassured by the news I gave you.

OEDIPUS   If you could reassure me, I would reward
you.

MESSENGER   I had that in mind, I will confess: I
thought
I could count on you when you returned to Corinth.

OEDIPUS   No: I will never go near my parents again.

MESSENGER   Ah, son, you still do not know what
you are doing—

OEDIPUS   What do you mean? In the name of God
tell me!

MESSENGER   —if these are your reasons for not
going home.

OEDIPUS   I tell you, I fear the oracle may come true.

MESSENGER   And guilt may come upon you
through your parents?

OEDIPUS   That is the dread that is always in my heart.

MESSENGER   Can you not see that all your fears are
groundless?

OEDIPUS   Groundless? Am I not my parents' son?

MESSENGER   Polybos was not your father.

OEDIPUS   Not my father?

MESSENGER   No more your father than the man
speaking to you.

OEDIPUS   But you are nothing to me!

MESSENGER   Neither was he.

OEDIPUS   Then why did he call me son?

MESSENGER   I will tell you:
Long ago he had you from my hands, as a gift.

OEDIPUS   Then how could he love me so, if I was
not his?

MESSENGER   He had no children, and his heart
turned to you.

OEDIPUS   What of you? Did you buy me? Did you
find me by chance?

MESSENGER   I came upon you in the woody vales of
Kithairon.

OEDIPUS   And what were you doing there?

MESSENGER   Tending my flocks.

OEDIPUS   A wandering shepherd?

MESSENGER   But your savior, son, that day.

OEDIPUS   From what did you save me?

MESSENGER   Your ankles should tell you that.

OEDIPUS   Ah, stranger, why do you speak of that
childhood pain?

MESSENGER   I pulled the skewer that pinned your
feet together.

OEDIPUS   I have had the mark as long as I can
remember.

MESSENGER   That was why you were given the
name you bear.

---

[11]Delphi.

OEDIPUS   God! Was it my father or my mother who
did it?
Tell me!
MESSENGER   I do not know. The man who gave you
to me
Can tell you better than I.
OEDIPUS   It was not you that found me, but another?
MESSENGER   It was another shepherd gave you to me.
OEDIPUS   Who was he? Can you tell me who he was?
MESSENGER   I think he was said to be one of Laïos'
people.
OEDIPUS   You mean the Laïos who was king here
years ago?
MESSENGER   Yes; King Laïos; and the man was one
of his herdsmen.
OEDIPUS   Is he still alive? Can I see him?
MESSENGER   These men here
Know best about such things.
OEDIPUS   Does anyone here
Know this shepherd that he is talking about?
Have you seen him in the fields, or in the town?
If you have, tell me. It is time things were made
plain.
CHORAGOS   I think the man he means is that same
shepherd
You have already asked to see. Iokastê perhaps
Could tell you something.
OEDIPUS   Do you know anything
About him, Lady? Is he the man we have summoned?
Is that the man this shepherd means?
IOKASTÊ   Why think of him?
Forget this herdsman. Forget it all.
This talk is a waste of time.
OEDIPUS   How can you say that,
When the clues to my true birth are in my hands?
IOKASTÊ   For God's love, let us have no more
questioning!
Is your life nothing to you?
My own is pain enough for me to bear.
OEDIPUS   You need not worry. Suppose my mother
a slave,
And born of slaves: no baseness can touch you.
IOKASTÊ   Listen to me, I beg you: do not do this thing!
OEDIPUS   I will not listen; the truth must be made
known.
IOKASTÊ   Everything that I say is for your own good!
OEDIPUS   My own good
Snaps my patience, then! I want none of it.
IOKASTÊ   You are fatally wrong! May you never
learn who you are!
OEDIPUS   Go, one of you, and bring the shepherd here.
Let us leave this woman to brag of her royal name.
IOKASTÊ   Ah, miserable!

That is the only word I have for you now.
That is the only word I can ever have.

(*Exit into the palace*)

CHORAGOS   Why has she left us, Oedipus? Why has
she gone
In such a passion of sorrow? I fear this silence:
Something dreadful may come of it.
OEDIPUS   Let it come!
However base my birth, I must know about it.
The Queen, like a woman, is perhaps ashamed
To think of my low origin. But I
Am a child of Luck; I can not be dishonored.
Luck is my mother; the passing months, my
brothers,
Have seen me rich and poor.
                            If this is so,
How could I wish that I were someone else?
How could I not be glad to know my birth?

ODE III

Strophe

CHORUS   If ever the coming time were known
To my heart's pondering,
Kithairon, now by Heaven I see the torches
At the festival of the next full moon,
And see the dance, and hear the choir sing
A grace to your gentle shade:
Mountain where Oedipus was found,
O mountain guard of a noble race!
May the god[12] who heals us lend his aid,
And let that glory come to pass
For our king's cradling-ground.

Antistrophe

Of the nymphs that flower beyond the years,
Who bore you,[13] royal child,
To Pan of the hills or the timberline Apollo,
Cold in delight where the upland clears,
Or Hermês for whom Kyllenê's heights are piled?
Or flushed as evening cloud,
Great Dionysos, roamer of mountains,
He—was it he who found you there,
And caught you up in his own proud

---

[12]Apollo.

[13]The chorus is suggesting that perhaps Oedipus is the son of one of
the immortal nymphs and of a god—Pan, Apollo, Hermes, or
Dionysus. The "sweet god-ravisher" (below) is the presumed
mother.

Arms from the sweet god-ravisher
Who laughed by the Muses' fountains?

SCENE IV

OEDIPUS   Sirs: though I do not know the man,
I think I see him coming, this shepherd we want:
He is old, like our friend here, and the men
Bringing him seem to be servants of my house.
But you can tell, if you have ever seen him.

(*Enter* SHEPHERD *escorted by* SERVANTS)

CHORAGOS   I know him, he was Laïos' man. You
can trust him.
OEDIPUS   Tell me first, you from Corinth: is this the
shepherd
We were discussing?
MESSENGER   This is the very man.
OEDIPUS (*to* SHEPHERD)   Come here. No, look at me.
You must answer
Everything I ask.—You belonged to Laïos?
SHEPHERD   Yes: born his slave, brought up in his
house.
OEDIPUS   Tell me: what kind of work did you do for
him?
SHEPHERD   I was a shepherd of his, most of my life.
OEDIPUS   Where mainly did you go for pasturage?
SHEPHERD   Sometimes Kithairon, sometimes the
hills near-by.
OEDIPUS   Do you remember ever seeing this man
out there?
SHEPHERD   What would he be doing there? This man?
OEDIPUS   This man standing here. Have you ever
seen him before?
SHEPHERD   No. At least, not to my recollection.
MESSENGER   And that is not strange, my lord. But
I'll refresh
His memory: he must remember when we two
Spent three whole seasons together, March to
September,
On Kithairon or thereabouts. He had two flocks;
I had one. Each autumn I'd drive mine home
And he would go back with his to Laïos' sheepfold.—
Is this not true, just as I have described it?
SHEPHERD   True, yes; but it was all so long ago.
MESSENGER   Well, then: do you remember, back in
those days,
That you gave me a baby boy to bring up as my own?
SHEPHERD   What if I did? What are you trying to say?
MESSENGER   King Oedipus was once that little child.
SHEPHERD   Damn you, hold your tongue!
OEDIPUS   No more of that!
It is your tongue needs watching, not this man's.

SHEPHERD   My king, my master, what is it I have
done wrong?
OEDIPUS   You have not answered his question about
the boy.
SHEPHERD   He does not know...He is only making
trouble...
OEDIPUS   Come, speak plainly, or it will go hard
with you.
SHEPHERD   In God's name, do not torture an old man!
OEDIPUS   Come here, one of you; bind his arms
behind him.
SHEPHERD   Unhappy king! What more do you wish
to learn?
OEDIPUS   Did you give this man the child he speaks
of?
SHEPHERD   I did.
And I would to God I had died that very day.
OEDIPUS   You will die now unless you speak the truth.
SHEPHERD   Yet if I speak the truth, I am worse than
dead.
OEDIPUS (*to* ATTENDANT)   He intends to draw it
out, apparently—
SHEPHERD   No! I have told you already that I gave
him the boy.
OEDIPUS   Where did you get him? From your house?
From somewhere else?
SHEPHERD   Not from mine, no. A man gave him to
me.
OEDIPUS   Is that man here? Whose house did he
belong to?
SHEPHERD   For God's love, my king, do not ask me
any more!
OEDIPUS   You are a dead man if I have to ask you
again.
SHEPHERD   Then...Then the child was from the
palace of Laïos.
OEDIPUS   A slave child? or a child of his own line?
SHEPHERD   Ah, I am on the brink of dreadful speech!
OEDIPUS   And I of dreadful hearing. Yet I must hear.
SHEPHERD   If you must be told, then...
                                    They said it was Laïos' child;
But it is your wife who can tell you about that.
OEDIPUS   My wife!—Did she give it to you?
SHEPHERD   My lord, she did.
OEDIPUS   Do you know why?
SHEPHERD   I was told to get rid of it.
OEDIPUS   Oh heartless mother!
SHEPHERD   But in dread of prophecies...
OEDIPUS   Tell me.
SHEPHERD   It was said that the boy would kill
his own father.
OEDIPUS   Then why did you give him over to this
old man?

SHEPHERD   I pitied the baby, my king,
And I thought that this man would take him far
　　away
To his own country.
　　　　　　　　He saved him—but for what a fate!
For if you are what this man says you are,
No man living is more wretched than Oedipus.
OEDIPUS   Ah God!
It was true!
　　　　　All the prophecies!
　　　　　　　　　　—Now,
O Light, may I look on you for the last time!
I, Oedipus,
Oedipus, damned in his birth, in his marriage
　　damned,
Damned in the blood he shed with his own hand!

(*He rushes into the palace*)

ODE IV

Strophe 1

CHORUS   Alas for the seed of men.
What measure shall I give these generations
That breathe on the void and are void
And exist and do not exist?
Who bears more weight of joy
Than mass of sunlight shifting in images,
Or who shall make his thought stay on
That down time drifts away?
Your splendor is all fallen.
O naked brow of wrath and tears,
O change of Oedipus!
I who saw your days call no man blest—
Your great days like ghosts gone.

Antistrophe 1

That mind was a strong bow.
Deep, how deep you drew it then, hard archer,
At a dim fearful range,
And brought dear glory down!
You overcame the stranger[14]—
The virgin with her hooking lion claws—
And though death sang, stood like a tower
To make pale Thebes take heart.
Fortress against our sorrow!
True king, giver of laws,

Majestic Oedipus!
No prince in Thebes had ever such renown,
No prince won such grace of power.

Strophe 2

And now of all men ever known
Most pitiful is this man's story:
His fortunes are most changed, his state
Fallen to a low slave's
Ground under bitter fate.
O Oedipus, most royal one!
The great door[15] that expelled you to the light
Gave at night—ah, gave night to your glory:
As to the father, to the fathering son.
All understood too late.
How could that queen whom Laïos won,
The garden that he harrowed at his height,
Be silent when that act was done?

Antistrophe 2

But all eyes fail before time's eye,
All actions come to justice there.
Though never willed, though far down the deep past,
Your bed, your dread sirings,
Are brought to book at last.
Child by Laïos doomed to die,
Then doomed to lose that fortunate little death,
Would God you never took breath in this air
That with my wailing lips I take to cry:
For I weep the world's outcast.
I was blind, and now I can tell why:
Asleep, for you had given ease of breath
To Thebes, while the false years went by.

EXODOS[16]

(*Enter, from the palace,* SECOND MESSENGER)

SECOND MESSENGER   Elders of Thebes, most
　　honored in this land,
What horrors are yours to see and hear, what weight
Of sorrow to be endured, if, true to your birth,
You venerate the line of Labdakos!
I think neither Istros nor Phasis, those great rivers,
Could purify this place of all the evil
It shelters now, or soon must bring to light—
Evil not done unconsciously, but willed.

The greatest griefs are those we cause ourselves.

---

[14] The Sphinx.

[15] Iokastê's womb.
[16] Final scene.

CHORAGOS   Surely, friend, we have grief enough already;
  What new sorrow do you mean?
SECOND MESSENGER   The queen is dead.
CHORAGOS   O miserable queen! But at whose hand?
SECOND MESSENGER   Her own.
  The full horror of what happened you can not know,
  For you did not see it; but I, who did, will tell you
  As clearly as I can how she met her death.

  When she had left us,
  In passionate silence, passing through the court,
  She ran to her apartment in the house,
  Her hair clutched by the fingers of both hands.
  She closed the doors behind her; then, by that bed
  Where long ago the fatal son was conceived—
  That son who should bring about his father's death—
  We heard her call upon Laïos, dead so many years,
  And heard her wail for the double fruit of her marriage,
  A husband by her husband, children by her child.

  Exactly how she died I do not know:
  For Oedipus burst in moaning and would not let us
  Keep vigil to the end: it was by him
  As he stormed about the room that our eyes were caught.
  From one to another of us he went, begging a sword,
  Hunting the wife who was not his wife, the mother
  Whose womb had carried his own children and himself.
  I do not know: it was none of us aided him,
  But surely one of the gods was in control!
  For with a dreadful cry
  He hurled his weight, as though wrenched out of himself,
  At the twin doors: the bolts gave, and he rushed in.
  And there we saw her hanging, her body swaying
  From the cruel cord she had noosed about her neck.
  A great sob broke from him, heartbreaking to hear,
  As he loosed the rope and lowered her to the ground.

  I would blot out from my mind what happened next!
  For the king ripped from her gown the golden brooches
  That were her ornament, and raised them, and plunged them down
  Straight into his own eyeballs, crying, "No more,
  No more shall you look on the misery about me,

The horrors of my own doing! Too long you have known
  The faces of those whom I should never have seen,
  Too long been blind to those for whom I was searching!
  From this hour, go in darkness!" And as he spoke,
  He struck at his eyes—not once, but many times;
  And the blood spattered his beard,
  Bursting from his ruined sockets like red hail.

  So from the unhappiness of two this evil has sprung,
  A curse on the man and woman alike. The old
  Happiness of the house of Labdakos
  Was happiness enough: where is it today?
  It is all wailing and ruin, disgrace, death—all
  The misery of mankind that has a name—
  And it is wholly and for ever theirs.
CHORAGOS   Is he in agony still? Is there no rest for him?
SECOND MESSENGER   He is calling for someone to open the doors wide
  So that all the children of Kadmos may look upon
  His father's murderer, his mother's—no,
  I can not say it!
                    And then he will leave Thebes,
  Self-exiled, in order that the curse
  Which he himself pronounced may depart from the house.
  He is weak, and there is none to lead him,
  So terrible is his suffering.
                    But you will see:
  Look, the doors are opening; in a moment
  You will see a thing that would crush a heart of stone.

(*The central door is opened;* OEDIPUS, *blinded, is led in*)

CHORAGOS   Dreadful indeed for men to see.
  Never have my own eyes
  Looked on a sight so full of fear.

  Oedipus!
  What madness came upon you, what daemon
  Leaped on your life with heavier
  Punishment than a mortal man can bear?
  No: I can not even
  Look at you, poor ruined one.
  And I would speak, question, ponder,
  If I were able. No.
  You make me shudder.
OEDIPUS   God. God.
  Is there a sorrow greater?
  Where shall I find harbor in this world?

My voice is hurled far on a dark wind.
What has God done to me?
CHORAGOS   Too terrible to think of, or to see.

Strophe 1

OEDIPUS   O cloud of night,
    Never to be turned away: night coming on,
    I can not tell how: night like a shroud!
    My fair winds brought me here.
                                         O God. Again
    The pain of the spikes where I had sight,
    The flooding pain
    Of memory, never to be gouged out.
CHORAGOS   This is not strange.
    You suffer it all twice over, remorse in pain,
    Pain in remorse.

Antistrophe 1

OEDIPUS   Ah dear friend
    Are you faithful even yet, you alone?
    Are you still standing near me, will you stay here,
    Patient, to care for the blind?
                                         The blind man!
    Yet even blind I know who it is attends me,
    By the voice's tone—
    Though my new darkness hide the comforter.
CHORAGOS   Oh fearful act!
    What god was it drove you to rake black
    Night across your eyes?

Strophe 2

OEDIPUS   Apollo. Apollo. Dear
    Children, the god was Apollo.
    He brought my sick, sick fate upon me.
    But the blinding hand was my own!
    How could I bear to see
    When all my sight was horror everywhere?
CHORAGOS   Everywhere; that is true.
OEDIPUS   And now what is left?
    Images? Love? A greeting even,
    Sweet to the senses? Is there anything?
    Ah, no, friends: lead me away.
    Lead me away from Thebes.
                                    Lead the great wreck
    And hell of Oedipus, whom the gods hate.
CHORAGOS   Your misery, you are not blind to that.
    Would God you had never found it out!

Antistrophe 2

OEDIPUS   Death take the man who unbound
    My feet on that hillside
    And delivered me from death to life! What life?
    If only I had died,
    This weight of monstrous doom
    Could not have dragged me and my darlings down.
CHORAGOS   I would have wished the same.
OEDIPUS   Oh never to have come here
    With my father's blood upon me! Never
    To have been the man they call his mother's
        husband!
    Oh accurst! Oh child of evil,
    To have entered that wretched bed—
                                    the selfsame one!
    More primal than sin itself, this fell to me.
CHORAGOS   I do not know what words to offer you.
    You were better dead than alive and blind.
OEDIPUS   Do not counsel me any more. This
        punishment
    That I have laid upon myself is just.
    If I had eyes,
    I do not know how I could bear the sight
    Of my father, when I came to the house of Death,
    Or my mother: for I have sinned against them both
    So vilely that I could not make my peace
    By strangling my own life.
                            Or do you think my children,
    Born as they were born, would be sweet to my eyes?
    Ah never, never! Nor this town with its high walls,
    Nor the holy images of the gods.
                                    For I,
    Thrice miserable!—Oedipus, noblest of all the line
    Of Kadmos, have condemned myself to enjoy
    These things no more, by my own malediction
    Expelling that man whom the gods declared
    To be a defilement in the house of Laïos.
    After exposing the rankness of my own guilt,
    How could I look men frankly in the eyes?
    No, I swear it,
    If I could have stifled my hearing at its source,
    I would have done it and made all this body
    A tight cell of misery, blank to light and sound:
    So I should have been safe in my dark mind
    Beyond external evil.
                            Ah Kithairon!
    Why did you shelter me? When I was cast upon you,
    Why did I not die? Then I should never
    Have shown the world my execrable birth.

Ah Polybos! Corinth, city that I believed

The ancient seat of my ancestors: how fair
I seemed, your child! And all the while this evil
Was cancerous within me!
      For I am sick
In my own being, sick in my origin.

O three roads, dark ravine, woodland and way
Where three roads met: you, drinking my father's
  blood,
My own blood, spilled by my own hand: can you
  remember
The unspeakable things I did there, and the things
I went on from there to do?
      O marriage, marriage!
That act that engendered me, and again the act
Performed by the son in the same bed—
        Ah, the net
Of incest, mingling fathers, brothers, sons,
With brides, wives, mothers: the last evil
That can be known by men: no tongue can say
How evil!
    No. For the love of God, conceal me
Somewhere far from Thebes; or kill me; or hurl me
Into the sea, away from men's eyes for ever.

Come, lead me. You need not fear to touch me.
Of all men, I alone can bear this guilt.

(*Enter* KREON)

CHORAGOS Kreon is here now. As to what you ask,
 He may decide the course to take. He only
 Is left to protect the city in your place.
OEDIPUS Alas, how can I speak to him? What right
 have I
 To beg his courtesy whom I have deeply wronged?
KREON I have not come to mock you, Oedipus,
 Or to reproach you, either. (*To* ATTENDANTS)
      —You, standing there:
 If you have lost all respect for man's dignity,
 At least respect the flame of Lord Helios:
 Do not allow this pollution to show itself
 Openly here, an affront to the earth
 And Heaven's rain and the light of day. No, take him
 Into the house as quickly as you can.
 For it is proper
 That only the close kindred see his grief.
OEDIPUS I pray you in God's name, since your
 courtesy
 Ignores my dark expectation, visiting
 With mercy this man of all men most execrable:
 Give me what I ask—for your good, not for mine.
KREON And what is it that you turn to me begging
 for?

OEDIPUS Drive me out of this country as quickly as
 may be
 To a place where no human voice can ever greet me.
KREON I should have done that before now—only,
 God's will had not been wholly revealed to me.
OEDIPUS But his command is plain: the parricide
 Must be destroyed. I am that evil man.
KREON That is the sense of it, yes; but as things are,
 We had best discover clearly what is to be done.
OEDIPUS You would learn more about a man like me?
KREON You are ready now to listen to the god.
OEDIPUS I will listen. But it is to you
 That I must turn for help. I beg you, hear me.

The woman in there—
Give her whatever funeral you think proper:
She is your sister.
    —But let me go, Kreon!
Let me purge my father's Thebes of the pollution
Of my living here, and go out to the wild hills,
To Kithairon, that has won such fame with me,
The tomb my mother and father appointed for me,
And let me die there, as they willed I should.

And yet I know
Death will not ever come to me through sickness
Or in any natural way: I have been preserved
For some unthinkable fate. But let that be.

As for my sons, you need not care for them.
They are men, they will find some way to live.
But my poor daughters, who have shared my table,
Who never before have been parted from their
 father—
Take care of them, Kreon; do this for me.

And will you let me touch them with my hands
A last time, and let us weep together?
Be kind, my lord,
Great prince, be kind!
      Could I but touch them,
They would be mine again, as when I had my eyes.

(*Enter* ANTIGONE *and* ISMENE, *attended*)

Ah, God!
Is it my dearest children I hear weeping?
Has Kreon pitied me and sent my daughters?
KREON Yes, Oedipus: I knew that they were dear to
 you
 In the old days, and know you must love them still.
OEDIPUS May God bless you for this—and be a
 friendlier
 Guardian to you than he has been to me!

Children, where are you?
Come quickly to my hands: they are your
  brother's—
Hands that have brought your father's once clear
  eyes
To this way of seeing—
                          Ah dearest ones,
I had neither sight nor knowledge then, your father
By the woman who was the source of his own life!
And I weep for you—having no strength to see you—,
I weep for you when I think of the bitterness
That men will visit upon you all your lives.
What homes, what festivals can you attend
Without being forced to depart again in tears?
And when you come to marriageable age,
Where is the man, my daughters, who would dare
Risk the bane that lies on all my children?
Is there any evil wanting? Your father killed
His father; sowed the womb of her who bore him;
Engendered you at the fount of his own existence!
That is what they will say of you.
                                    Then, whom
Can you ever marry? There are no bridegrooms for
  you,
And your lives must wither away in sterile
  dreaming.

O Kreon, son of Menoikeus!
You are the only father my daughters have,
Since we, their parents, are both of us gone for ever.
They are your own blood: you will not let them
Fall into beggary and loneliness;
You will keep them from the miseries that are mine!
Take pity on them; see, they are only children,
Friendless except for you. Promise me this,
Great prince, and give me your hand in token of it.

(KREON *clasps his right hand*)

Children:
I could say much, if you could understand me,
But as it is, I have only this prayer for you:
Live where you can, be as happy as you can—
Happier, please God, than God has made your
  father.
KREON   Enough. You have wept enough. Now go
  within.
OEDIPUS   I must; but it is hard.
KREON   Time eases all things.
OEDIPUS   You know my mind, then?
KREON   Say what you desire.
OEDIPUS   Send me from Thebes!
KREON   God grant that I may!
OEDIPUS   But since God hates me . . .

KREON   No, he will grant your wish.
OEDIPUS   You promise?
KREON   I can not speak beyond my knowledge.
OEDIPUS   Then lead me in.
KREON   Come now, and leave your children.
OEDIPUS   No! Do not take them from me!
KREON   Think no longer
That you are in command here, but rather think
How, when you were, you served your own
  destruction.

(*Exeunt into the house all but the* CHORUS; *the* CHO-
RAGOS *chants directly to the audience*)

CHORAGOS   Men of Thebes: look upon Oedipus.

This is the king who solved the famous riddle
And towered up, most powerful of men.
No mortal eyes but looked on him with envy,
Yet in the end ruin swept over him.

Let every man in mankind's frailty
Consider his last day; and let none
Presume on his good fortune until he find
Life, at his death, a memory without pain.

COMMENTS AND QUESTIONS

1. Describe Oedipus' character as fully as you can.
   To what extent is he a realistic human being and
   to what extent an ideal type?

2. What are Iokastê's religious beliefs? How does she
   serve as a foil to Oedipus?

3. What kinds of "blindness" are there in this play?
   Explain their significance.

4. Sophocles uses much tragic *irony* in this tragedy
   and in others. Irony, in this sense, means that the
   tragic figure says something "all too true," related
   to his fate, that the audience understands but that
   he does not. Find examples of tragic irony. What is
   their effect?

5. To what extent is Oedipus a puppet of the gods
   and to what extent is he a free man?

6. *Oedipus Rex* has been interpreted both as a
   glorification of humanity and as a defense of religion that points out human limitations. Which
   view seems truer in your opinion?

7. What is Oedipus' attitude at the end of the play?
   What has he learned about himself and life? What
   is the difference between a tragic view of life and a
   merely pessimistic one?

8. Look up Freud's notion of the "Oedipus complex" if you are not familiar with it. To what extent is this useful for a modern interpretation of the tragedy?

9. If you were to take the legend of Oedipus and rewrite it for the modern stage, film, or television, what would you do with it? Is a modern tragedy possible?

ARISTOPHANES

Lysistrata

Translation by Dudley Fitts

Lysistrata, first performed in 411 B.C., is essentially a comic fantasy about a real contemporary event. Athens and Sparta, as we saw in Chapter 4, were the rival leaders in a series of battles, lasting from 431 to 404 B.C., called the Peloponnesian War. Aristophanes had long been a spokesman for peace—in one of his plays he even went so far as to suggest that in some instances the Athenians had treated the Spartans unfairly. Like many other Athenians, he deplored the evolution of Athens from a democracy to a dictatorship, a seeming necessity in wartime. He was particularly opposed to the foolhardy naval expedition that the Athenians sent to Sicily in 415 B.C. This attack, which ended in defeat and brought the Athenians vast losses in ships and men, was really the turning point of the war. By the time of the writing of *Lysistrata*, it must have been apparent that the Spartans were winning the war and that a genuine negotiated peace treaty, which might have been possible earlier, was no longer possible. There are some sad underpinnings to this comedy: an idyllic dream of peace; a memory of the time when Athens and Sparta were allies and fought bravely together during the Persian War. Yet these serious concerns do not prevent *Lysistrata* from being a total comedy. Perhaps the human need to laugh at the world is even greater at times of disaster than in normal times. And perhaps Aristophanes is suggesting something that is of concern to us today: if men have been such failures at keeping peace in the world, might not women do better?

The play's title character (her name means "she who dissolves the armies") shows herself superior to the men in every way. She is the only one who keeps a cool head; she plans an effective strategy and negotiates the peace. Her plan for forcing peace negotiations—organizing the women of Athens and Sparta in a sex strike against their husbands—is highly comic but also effective. Because of its explicitness about sex, *Lysistrata* was forbidden reading in schools for a long time. Most modern readers, however, find it extremely funny. Aristophanes' comedies, because of their use of Greek dialects and plays on words, are particularly difficult to translate. In this English version, the woman from Sparta, Lampito, is given a southern accent as the American equivalent of her Spartan dialect.

CHARACTERS

LYSISTRATA
KALONIKE } *Athenian women*
MYRRHINE
LAMPITO, *a Spartan woman*
CHORUS
MAGISTRATE
KINESIAS, *husband of Myrrhine*
SPARTAN HERALD
SPARTAN AMBASSADOR
A SENTRY
ATHENIAN DRUNKARD

The supernumeraries include the BABY SON *of Kinesias;* STRATYLLIS, *a member of the hemichorus of Old Women; various individual speakers, both Spartan and Athenian.*

Until the exodos, the CHORUS *is divided into two hemichori: the first, of Old Men; the second, of Old Women. Each of these has its* CHORAGOS. *In the exodos, the hemichori return as Athenians and Spartans.*

THE SCENE.   *Athens. First, a public square; later, beneath the walls of the Acropolis; later, a courtyard within the Acropolis. Time: early in 411* B.C.

Athens; a public square; early morning; LYSISTRATA *sola.*

LYSISTRATA   If someone had invited them to a festival—
Bacchus's, say, or Pan's, or Aphrodite's, or
that Genetyllis business[1]—, you couldn't get through the streets,
what with the drums and the dancing. But now, not a woman in sight!
          Except—oh, yes!

(*Enter* KALONIKE)

Here's one, at last. Good morning, Kalonike.
KALONIKE   Good morning, Lysistrata.
                    Darling,
don't frown so! You'll ruin your face!

[1]References to cults of love and wine.

LYSISTRATA   Never mind my face.
Kalonike,
the way we women behave! Really, I don't blame the
men
for what they say about us.
KALONIKE   No; I imagine they're right.
LYSISTRATA   For example: I call a meeting
to think out a most important matter—and what
happens?
The women all stay in bed!
KALONIKE   Oh, they'll be along.
It's hard to get away, you know: a husband, a cook,
a child...Home life can be *so* demanding!
LYSISTRATA   What I have in mind is even more
demanding.
KALONIKE   Tell me: what is it?
LYSISTRATA   Something big.
KALONIKE   Goodness! *How* big?
LYSISTRATA   Big enough for all of us.
KALONIKE   But we're not all here!
LYSISTRATA   We would be, if *that's* what was up!
                              No, Kalonike,
this is something I've been turning over for nights;
and, I may say, sleepless nights.
KALONIKE   Can't be so hard, then,
if you've spent so much time on it.
LYSISTRATA   Hard or not,
it comes to this: Only we women can save Greece!
KALONIKE   Only we women? Poor Greece!
LYSISTRATA   Just the same,
it's up to us. First, we must liquidate
the Peloponnesians—
KALONIKE   Fun, fun!
LYSISTRATA   —and then the Boeotians.
KALONIKE   Oh! But not those heavenly eels![2]
LYSISTRATA   You needn't worry.
Athens shall have her sea food.—But here's the
point:
If we can get the women from those places
to join us women here, why, we can save
all Greece!
KALONIKE   But dearest Lysistrata!
How can women do a thing so austere, so
political? We belong at home. Our only armor's
our transparent saffron dresses and
our pretty little shoes!
LYSISTRATA   That's it exactly.

Those transparent saffron dresses, those little
shoes—
well, there we are!
KALONIKE   Oh?
LYSISTRATA   Not a single man would lift
his spear—
KALONIKE   I'll get my dress from the dyer's tomorrow!
LYSISTRATA   —or need a shield—
KALONIKE   The sweetest little negligée—
LYSISTRATA   —or bring out his sword.
KALONIKE   I know where I can buy
the dreamiest sandals!
LYSISTRATA   Well, so you see. Now, shouldn't
the women have come?
KALONIKE   Come? they should have *flown*!
LYSISTRATA   Athenians are always late.
                              But imagine!
There's no one here from the South Shore.
KALONIKE   They go to work early,
I can swear to that.
LYSISTRATA   And nobody from Acharnai.
They should have been here hours ago!
KALONIKE   Well, you'll get
that awful Theagenes woman: she's been having
her fortune told at Hecate's shrine.[3]
                              But look!
Someone at last! Can you see who they are?

(*Enter* MYRRHINE *and other women*)

LYSISTRATA   People from the suburbs.
KALONIKE   Yes! The entire
membership of the Suburban League!
MYRRHINE   Sorry to be late, Lysistrata.
                              Oh, come,
don't scowl so! Say something!
LYSISTRATA   My dear Myrrhine,
what is there to say? After all,
you've been pretty casual about the whole thing.
MYRRHINE   Couldn't find
my girdle in the dark, that's all.
                              But what *is*
"the whole thing"?
LYSISTRATA   Wait for the rest of them.
KALONIKE   I suppose so. But, look!
Here's Lampito!

(*Enter* LAMPITO *with women from Sparta*)

LYSISTRATA   Darling Lampito,

---

[2]Boeotia was famous for its seafood, especially its eels.

[3]Theagenes was notoriously superstitious; his practice of never leaving home without consulting Hecate is here transferred to his wife.

how pretty you are today! What a nice color!
Goodness, you look as though you could strangle a
   bull!
LAMPITO   Ah think Ah could! It's the work-out
   in the gym every day; and, of co'se that dance of ahs
   where y' kick yo' own tail.[4]
LYSISTRATA   What lovely breasts!
LAMPITO   Lawdy, when y' touch me lahk that,
   Ah feel lahk a heifer at the altar!
LYSISTRATA   And this young lady?
   Where is she from?
LAMPITO   Boeotia. Social-Register type.
LYSISTRATA   Good morning, Boeotian. You're as
      pretty as green grass.
KALONIKE   And if you look,
   you'll find that the lawn has just been cut.
LYSISTRATA   And this lady?
LAMPITO   From Corinth. But a good woman.
LYSISTRATA   Well, in Corinth
   anything's possible.
LAMPITO   But let's get to work. Which one of you
   called this meeting, and why?
LYSISTRATA   *I* did.
LAMPITO   Well then:
   what's up?
MYRRHINE   Yes, what *is* "the whole thing," after all?
LYSISTRATA   I'll tell you.—But first, one question.
MYRRHINE   Ask away!
LYSISTRATA   It's your husbands. Fathers of your
      children. Doesn't it bother you
   that they're always off with the Army? I'll stake my
      life,
   not one of you has a man in the house this minute!
KALONIKE   Mine's been in Thrace the last five
      months, keeping an eye
   on that General.[5]
MYRRHINE   Mine's been in Pylos for seven.
LAMPITO   And mahn,
   whenever he gets a *dis*charge, he goes raht back
   with that li'l ole speah of his, and enlists again!
LYSISTRATA   And not the ghost of a lover to be found!
   From the very day the war began—
                        those Milesians!
   I could skin them alive!
                  —I've not seen so much, even,
   as one of those devices they call Widow's Delight.

But there! What's important is: I've found a way
   to end the war, are you with me?
MYRRHINE   I should *say* so!
   Even if I have to pawn my best dress and
   drink up the proceeds.[6]
KALONIKE   Me, too! Even if they split me
   right up the middle, like a flounder.
LAMPITO   Ah'm shorely with you.
   Ah'd crawl up Taygetos[7] on mah knees
   if that'd bring peace.
LYSISTRATA   Then here it is.
   Women! Sisters!
   If we really want our men to make an armistice,
   we must be ready to give up—
MYRRHINE   Give up what?
   Quick, tell us!
LYSISTRATA   But *will* you?
MYRRHINE   We will, even if it kills us.
LYSISTRATA   Then we must give up sleeping with our
      men. (*Long silence*)
   Oh? So now you're sorry? Won't look at me?
   Doubtful? Pale? All teary-eyed?
                        But come: be frank with me,
   as I've certainly been with you. Will you do it?
MYRRHINE   I couldn't. No.
   Let the war go on.
KALONIKE   Nor I. Let the war go on.
LYSISTRATA   You, you little flounder,
   ready to be split up the middle?
KALONIKE   Lysistrata, no!
   I'd walk through fire for you—you *know* I
      would!—, but don't
   ask us to give up *that!* Why, there's nothing like it!
LYSISTRATA   And you?
BOEOTIAN   No. I must say *I'd* rather walk through
   fire.
LYSISTRATA   You little salamanders!
   No wonder poets write tragedies about women.
   All we want's a quick tumble!
                        But you from Sparta:
   if you stand by me, we may win yet! Will you?
   It means so much!
LAMPITO   Ah sweah, it means *too* much!
   By the Two Goddesses,[8] it does! Asking a girl
   to sleep—Heaven knows how long!—in a great big
   bed

---

[4]Among the physical exercises practiced by Greek girls was the
strenuous *bibasis,* a dance in which the dancer kicked her buttocks
with her heels.
[5]A certain Eukrates about whom nothing is known.

---

[6]Athenian women were frequently satirized for heavy drinking.
[7]A rugged mountain range in the Peloponnesus.
[8]Demeter, goddess of the harvest, and her daughter, Persephone,
queen of the Underworld; a woman's oath.

with nobody there but herself! But Ah'll stay with
you!
Peace comes first!

LYSISTRATA   Spoken like a true Spartan!

KALONIKE   But, if—
oh dear!
—if we give up what you tell us to,
will there *be* any peace?

LYSISTRATA   Why, mercy, of course there will!
We'll just sit snug in our very thinnest gowns,
perfumed and powdered from top to bottom, and
those men
simply won't stand still! And when we say No,
they'll go out of their minds! And there's your peace.
You can take my word for it.

LAMPITO   Ah seem to remember
that Colonel Menelaus threw his sword away
when he saw Helen's breast all bare.

KALONIKE   But, goodness me!
What if they just get up and leave us?

LYSISTRATA   Well,
we'd have to fall back on ourselves, of course.
But they won't.

KALONIKE   What if they drag us into the bedroom?

LYSISTRATA   Hang on to the door.

KALONIKE   What if they slap us?

LYSISTRATA   If they do, you'd better give in.
But be sulky about it. Do I have to teach you how?
You know there's no fun for men when they have to
force you.
There are millions of ways of getting them to see
reason.
Don't you worry: a man
doesn't like it unless the girl co-operates.

KALONIKE   I suppose so. Oh, all right! We'll go along!

LAMPITO   Ah imagine us Spahtans can arrange a
peace. But you
Athenians! Why, you're just war-mongerers!

LYSISTRATA   Leave that to me.
I know how to make them listen.

LAMPITO   Ah don't see how.
After all, they've got their boats; and there's lots of
money
piled up in the Acropolis.

LYSISTRATA   The Acropolis? Darling,
we're taking over the Acropolis today!
That's the older women's job. All the rest of us
are going to the Citadel to sacrifice—you
understand me?
And once there, we're in for good!

LAMPITO   Whee! Up the rebels!
Ah can see you're a good strat*ee*gist.

LYSISTRATA   Well, then, Lampito,
let's take the oath.

LAMPITO   Say it. We'll sweah.

LYSISTRATA   This is it.
—But Lord! Where's our Inner Guard? Never mind.
               —You see this
shield? Put it down there. Now bring me the victim's
entrails.

KALONIKE   But the oath?

LYSISTRATA   You remember how in Aeschylus' *Seven*[9]
they killed a sheep and swore on a shield? Well, then?

KALONIKE   But I don't see how you can swear for
peace on a shield.

LYSISTRATA   What else do you suggest?

KALONIKE   Why not a white horse?
We could swear by that.

LYSISTRATA   And where will you get a white horse?

KALONIKE   I never thought of that. *What* can we do?

MYRRHINE   I have it!
Let's set this big black wine-bowl on the ground
and pour in a gallon or so of Thasian,[10] and swear
not to add one drop of water.

LAMPITO   Ah lahk *that* oath!

LYSISTRATA   Bring the bowl and the wine-jug.

KALONIKE   Oh, what a simply *huge* one!

LYSISTRATA   Set it down; and, women, place your
hands on the gift offering.

O Goddess of Persuasion! And thou, O Loving-cup!
Look upon this our sacrifice, and
be gracious!

KALONIKE   It spills out like blood. How red and
pretty it is!

LAMPITO   And Ah must say it smells good.

MYRRHINE   Let me swear first!

KALONIKE   No, by Aphrodite, let's toss for it!

LYSISTRATA   Lampito: all of you women: come, touch
the bowl, and repeat after me:
I WILL HAVE NOTHING TO DO WITH MY
HUSBAND OR MY LOVER

KALONIKE   *I will have nothing to do with my
husband or my lover*

LYSISTRATA   THOUGH HE COME TO ME IN
PITIABLE CONDITION

KALONIKE   *Though he come to me in pitiable
condition*
(Oh, Lysistrata! This is killing me!)

---

[9]*Seven Against Thebes.*
[10]A popular wine from Thasos.

LYSISTRATA   I WILL STAY IN MY HOUSE
UNTOUCHABLE
KALONIKE   *I will stay in my house untouchable*
LYSISTRATA   IN MY THINNEST SAFFRON SILK
KALONIKE   *In my thinnest saffron silk*
LYSISTRATA   AND MAKE HIM LONG FOR ME.
KALONIKE   *And make him long for me.*
LYSISTRATA   I WILL NOT GIVE MYSELF
KALONIKE   *I will not give myself*
LYSISTRATA   AND IF HE CONSTRAINS ME
KALONIKE   *And if he constrains me*
LYSISTRATA   I WILL BE AS COLD AS ICE AND
NEVER MOVE
KALONIKE   *I will be as cold as ice and never move*
LYSISTRATA   I WILL NOT LIFT MY SLIPPERS
TOWARD THE CEILING
KALONIKE   *I will not lift my slippers toward the
ceiling*
LYSISTRATA   OR CROUCH ON ALL FOURS LIKE
THE LIONESS IN THE CARVING
KALONIKE   *Or crouch on all fours like the lioness in
the carving*
LYSISTRATA   AND IF I KEEP THIS OATH LET ME
DRINK FROM THIS BOWL
KALONIKE   *And if I keep this oath let me drink from
this bowl*
LYSISTRATA   IF NOT, LET MY OWN BOWL BE
FILLED WITH WATER.
KALONIKE   *If nop, let my own bowl be filled with
water.*
LYSISTRATA   You have all sworn?
MYRRHINE   We have.
LYSISTRATA   Then thus
I sacrifice the victim. (*Drinks largely*)
KALONIKE   Save some for us!
Here's to you, darling, and to you, and to you! It's all
for us women. (*Loud cries off-stage*)
LAMPITO   What's all *that* whoozy-goozy?
LYSISTRATA   Just what I told you.
The older women have taken the Acropolis. Now
you, Lampito,
rush back to Sparta. We'll take care of things here.
And
be sure you get organized!
                              The rest of you girls,
up to the Citadel: and mind you push in the bolts.
KALONIKE   But the men? Won't they be after us?
LYSISTRATA   Just you leave
the men to me. There's not fire enough in the world
to make me open *my* door.
KALONIKE   I hope so, by Aphrodite!
At any rate,
let's remember the League's reputation for hanging
on!

(*Exeunt*)

The hillside just under the Acropolis.

(*Enter* CHORUS OF OLD MEN *with burning torches
and braziers; much puffing and coughing*)

MALE CHORAGOS   Easy, Drakes, old friend! Don't
skin your shoulders
with those damnable big olive-branches. What a job!

Strophe 1

OLD MEN   Forward, forward, comrades! Whew!
The things that old age does to you!
Neighbor Strymodoros, would you have thought it?
We've caught it—
                              And from women, too!
Women that used to board with us, bed with us—
Now, by the gods, they've got ahead of us,
Taken the Acropolis (Heaven knows why!),
Profaned the sacred statuar-y,
                              And barred the doors,
                              The aggravating whores!
MALE CHORAGOS   Come, Philourgos, quick, pile
your brushwood
next to the wall there.
                    These traitors to Athens and to us,
we'll fry each last one of them! And the very first
will be old Lykon's wife.[11]

Antistrophe 1

OLD MEN   By Demeter I swear it—(ouch!),
I'll not perform the Kleomenes-crouch!
How he looked—and a good soldier, too—
When out he flew,
                    That filthy pouch
Of a body of his all stinking and shaggy,
Bare as an eel, except for the bag he
Covered his rear with. Lord, what a mess!
Never a bath in six years, I'd guess!
                    Unhappy Sparta,
                    With such a martyr![12]
MALE CHORAGOS   What a siege, friends! Seventeen
ranks strong
we stood at the Gate, and never a chance for a nap.
And all because of women, whom the gods hate
(and so does Euripides).
                    It's enough to make a veteran
turn in his medals from Marathon!

---

[11]Rhodia, a famous belle of the day.

[12]Kleomenes, a king of Sparta, had captured the Acropolis but had
been forced to give it up.

Strophe 2

OLD MEN   Forward, men! Just up the hillside,
      And we're there!
   Keep to the path! A yoke of oxen
      Wouldn't care
         To haul this lumber. Mind the fire,
         Or it'll die before we're higher!
            Puff! Puff!
            This smoke will strangle me, sure enough!

Antistrophe 2

   Holy Heracles, I'm blinded,
      Sure as fate!
   It's Lemnos-fire[13] we've been toting;
      And isn't it great
         To be singed by this infernal flame?
         (Laches, remember the Goddess: for shame!)
            Woof! Woof!
   A few steps more, and we're under the roof!
MALE CHORAGOS   It catches! It's blazing!
   Down with your loads!
   We'll sizzle 'em now,
   By all the gods!
   Vine-branches here, quick!
   Light 'em up,
   And in through the gate with 'em!
   If that doesn't stop
   Their nonsense—well,
   We'll smoke 'em to Hell.
   Ker*shoo!*
   (What we really need
   Is a grad-u-ate,
   Top of his class,
   From Samos Military State.[14]
   Achoo!)
   Come, do
   Your duty, you!
   Pour out your braziers,
   Embers ablaze!
   But first, Gentlemen, allow me to raise
   The paean:
            Lady
   Victory, now
   Assist thine adherents
   Here below!

   Down with women!
   Up with men!
   lo triumphe![15]
OLD MEN   Amen!

(*Enter* CHORUS OF OLD WOMEN *on the walls of the Acropolis, carrying jars of water to extinguish the fire set by the* CHORUS OF OLD MEN)

FEMALE CHORAGOS   Fire, fire!
   Quickly, quickly, women, if we're to save ourselves!

Strophe

OLD WOMEN   Nikodike, run!
   Or Kalyke's done
   To a turn, and poor Kratylla's
   Smoked like a ham.
            Damn
   These men and their wars,
   Their hateful ways!
   I nearly died before I got to the place
   Where we fill our jars:
      Slaves pushing and jostling
      Such a hustling
   I never say in all my days!

Antistrophe

   But here's water at last.
   Sisters, make haste
   And slosh it down on them,
   The silly old wrecks!
            Sex
   Almighty! What they want's
   A hot bath? Send it down!
   And thou, Athena of Athens town,
   Assist us in drowning their wheezy taunts!
      O Trito-born![16] Helmet of Gold!
      Help us to cripple their backs, the old
   Fools with their semi-incendiary brawn!

(*The* OLD MEN *capture a woman,* STRATYLLIS)

STRATYLLIS   Let me go! Let me go!
FEMALE CHORAGOS   You walking corpses,
   have you no shame?
MALE CHORAGOS   I wouldn't have believed it!
   An army of women in the Acropolis!
FEMALE CHORAGOS   So we scare you, do we?
   Grandpa, you've seen
   only our pickets yet!

---

[13] Volcanic; Mount Moschylus on the island of Lemnos was the site of Hephaestus' (Vulcan's) forge.

[14] At this time Samos was the headquarters of Athenian military activities.

---

[15] A ritual cry of triumph.

[16] Athena; according to some versions of her story, she was born at Lake Tritonis in Libya.

MALE CHORAGOS   Hey, Phaidrias!
   Help me with the necks of these jabbering hens!
FEMALE CHORAGOS   Down with your pots, girls!
      We'll need both hands
   if these antiques attack us.
MALE CHORAGOS   Want your face kicked in?
FEMALE CHORAGOS   Want to try my teeth?
MALE CHORAGOS   Look out! I've got a stick!
FEMALE CHORAGOS   You lay a half-inch of your stick
      on Stratyllis,
   And you'll never stick again!
MALE CHORAGOS   Fall apart!
FEMALE CHORAGOS   I'll chew your guts!
MALE CHORAGOS   Euripides! Master!
   How well you knew women!
FEMALE CHORAGOS   Listen to him! Rhodippe,
   up with the pots!
MALE CHORAGOS   Demolition of God,
   what good are your pots?
FEMALE CHORAGOS   You refugee from the tomb,
   What good is your fire?
MALE CHORAGOS   Good enough to make a pyre
   to barbecue you!
FEMALE CHORAGOS   We'll squizzle your kindling!
MALE CHORAGOS   You think so?
FEMALE CHORAGOS Yah! Just hang around a while!
MALE CHORAGOS   Want a touch of my torch?
FEMALE CHORAGOS   Your torch needs a bath.
MALE CHORAGOS   How about you?
FEMALE CHORAGOS   Soap for a senile bridegroom!
MALE CHORAGOS   Senile? Hold your trap!
FEMALE CHORAGOS   Just *you* try to hold it!
MALE CHORAGOS   The yammer of women!
FEMALE CHORAGOS   The yatter of men!
   But you'll never sit in the jury-box again.
MALE CHORAGOS   Gentlemen, I beg you, burn off
   that woman's hair!
FEMALE CHORAGOS   Let it come down! (*They empty
   their pots on the men*)
MALE CHORAGOS   What a way to drown!
FEMALE CHORAGOS   Hot, hey?
MALE CHORAGOS   Say,
      enough!
FEMALE CHORAGOS   Dandruff
         needs watering. I'll make you
         nice and fresh.
MALE CHORAGOS   For God's sake, you
      sluts, hold off!

(*Enter a* MAGISTRATE *accompanied by four constables*)

MAGISTRATE   These degenerate women! What a
   racket of little drums,

what a yapping for Adonis on every house-top!
It's like the time in the Assembly when I was
   listening
to a speech—out of order, as usual—by that fool
Demostratos,[17] all about troops for Sicily,
that kind of nonsense—
                  and there was his wife
trotting around in circles howling
Alas for Adonis!—
              and Demostratos insisting
we must draft every last Zakynthian that can walk—
and his wife up there on the roof,
drunk as an owl, yowling
Oh weep for Adonis!—
              and that damned ox Demostratos
mooing away through the rumpus. That's what we
   get
for putting up with this wretched woman-business!
MALE CHORAGOS   Sir, you haven't heard the half of
   it. They laughed at us!
Insulted us! They took pitchers of water
and nearly drowned us! We're still wringing out our
   clothes,
for all the world like unhousebroken brats.
MAGISTRATE   And a good thing, by Poseidon!
   Whose fault is it if these women-folk of ours
   get out of hand? We coddle them,
   we teach them to be wasteful and loose. You'll see a
      husband
   go into a jeweler's. "Look," he'll say,
   "jeweler," he'll say, "you remember that gold choker
   you made for my wife? Well, she went to a dance
      last night
   and broke the clasp. Now, I've got to go to Salamis,
   and can't be bothered. Run over to my house
      tonight,
   will you, and see if you can put it together for her."
   Or another one
   goes to a cobbler—a good strong workman, too,
   with an awl that was never meant for child's play.
      "Here,"
   he'll tell him, "one of my wife's shoes is pinching
   her little toe. Could you come up about noon
   and stretch it out for her?"
                  Well, what do you expect?
   Look at me, for example. I'm a Public Officer,

---

[17]A well-known demagogue; the speech alludes to the festival in
honor of Adonis that four years earlier had coincided with the
decision to undertake the disastrous Sicilian expedition. It was
believed that the women's madness in lamenting Adonis had
influenced the decision.

and it's one of my duties to pay off the sailors.
And where's the money? Up there in the Acropolis!
And those blasted women slam the door in my face!
But what are we waiting for?
                              —Look here, constable,
stop sniffing around for a tavern, and get us
some crowbars. We'll force their gates! As a matter
    of fact,
I'll do a little forcing myself.

(*Enter* LYSISTRATA, *above, with* MYRRHINE, KALO-
NIKE, *and the* BOEOTIAN)

LYSISTRATA   No need of forcing.
    Here I am, of my own accord. And all this talk
    about locked doors—! We don't need locked doors,
    but just the least bit of common sense.
MAGISTRATE   Is that so, ma'am!
                              —Where's my constable?
                              —Constable,
    arrest that woman, and tie her hands behind her.
LYSISTRATA   If he touches me, I swear by Artemis
    there'll be one scamp dropped from the public
    payroll tomorrow!
MAGISTRATE   Well, constable? You're not afraid, I
    suppose? Grab her,
    two of you, around the middle!
KALONIKE   No, by Pandrosos![18]
    Lay a hand on her, and I'll jump on you so hard
    your guts will come out the back door!
MAGISTRATE   That's what *you* think!
    Where's the sergeant?—Here, you: tie up that
    trollop first,
    the one with the pretty talk!
MYRRHINE   By the Moon-Goddess![19]
    Just you try it, and you'd better call a surgeon!
MAGISTRATE   Another one!
                          Officer, seize that woman!
                                      I swear
    I'll put an end to this riot!
BOEOTIAN   By the Taurian,[20]
    one inch closer and you won't have a hair on your
    head!
MAGISTRATE   Lord, what a mess! And my constables
    seem to have left me.

---

[18] One of the daughters of the founder of Athens; a woman's oath.
[19] Artemis.
[20] Again Artemis, who was worshiped at Taurica Chersonesos.

But—women get the best of us? By God, no!
                              —Scythians![21]
    Close ranks and forward march!
LYSISTRATA   "Forward," indeed!
    By the Two Goddesses, what's the sense in *that*?
    They're up against four companies of women
    armed from top to bottom.
MAGISTRATE   Forward, my Scythians!
LYSISTRATA   Forward, yourselves, dear comrades!
    You grainlettucebeanseedmarket girls!
    You garlicandonionbreadbakery girls!
    Give it to 'em! Knock 'em down! Scratch 'em!
    Tell 'em what you think of 'em! (*General mêlée; the
    Scythians yield*)
                              —Ah, that's enough!
    Sound a retreat; good soldiers don't rob the dead!
MAGISTRATE   A nice day *this* has been for the police!
LYSISTRATA   Well, there you are.—Did you really
    think we women
    would be driven like slaves? Maybe now you'll admit
    that a woman knows something about glory.
MAGISTRATE   Glory enough,
    especially glory in bottles! Dear Lord Apollo!
MALE CHORAGOS   Your Honor, there's no use
    talking to them. Words
    mean nothing whatever to wild animals like these.
    Think of the sousing they gave us! and the water
    was not, I believe, of the purest.
FEMALE CHORAGOS   You shouldn't have come after
    us. And if you try it again,
    you'll be one eye short!—Although, as a matter of
    fact,
    what I like best is just to stay at home and read,
    like a sweet little bride: never hurting a soul, no,
    never going out. But if you *must* shake hornets'
    nests,
    look out for the hornets!

Strophe

OLD MEN   Good God, what can we do?
        What are we coming to?
    These women! Who could bear it? But, for that
    matter, who
            Will find
            What they had in mind
            When they seized Cranaos' city
            And held it (more's the pity!)
    Against us men of Athens, and our police force, too?

---

[21] Athens' finest archers.

MALE CHORAGOS   We might question them, I
    suppose. But I warn you, sir,
don't believe anything you hear! It would be un-
    Athenian
not to get to the bottom of this plot.
MAGISTRATE   Very well.
My first question is this: Why, so help you God,
did you bar the gates of the Acropolis?
LYSISTRATA   Why?
To keep the money, of course. No money, no war.
MAGISTRATE   You think that money's the cause of
    war?
LYSISTRATA   I do.
Money brought about the Peisandros business[22]
and all the other attacks on the State. Well and good!
They'll not get another cent here!
MAGISTRATE   And what will you do?
LYSISTRATA   What a question! From now on, we
    intend
to control the Treasury.
MAGISTRATE   Control the Treasury!
LYSISTRATA   Why not? Does that seem strange? After
    all,
we control our household budgets.
MAGISTRATE   But that's different!
LYSISTRATA   "Different"? What do you mean?
MAGISTRATE   I mean simply this:
it's the Treasury that pays for National Defense.
LYSISTRATA   Unnecessary. We propose to abolish war!
MAGISTRATE   Good God.—And National Security?
LYSISTRATA   Leave that to us.
MAGISTRATE   You?
LYSISTRATA   Us.
MAGISTRATE   We're done for, then!
LYSISTRATA   Never mind.
We women will save you in spite of yourselves.
MAGISTRATE   What nonsense!
LYSISTRATA   If you like. But you must accept it, like it
    or not.
MAGISTRATE   Why, this is downright subversion!
LYSISTRATA   Maybe it is.
But we're going to save you, Judge.
MAGISTRATE   I don't *want* to be saved!
LYSISTRATA   Tut. The death-wish. All the more
    reason.
MAGISTRATE   But the idea of women bothering
    themselves about peace and war!
LYSISTRATA   Will you listen to me?

MAGISTRATE   Yes. But be brief, or I'll—
LYSISTRATA   This is no time for stupid threats.
MAGISTRATE   By the gods,
I'm losing my mind!
AN OLD WOMAN   That's nice. If you do, remember
you've less to lose than *we* have.
MAGISTRATE   Quiet, you old buzzard!
Now, Lysistrata: tell me what you're thinking.
LYSISTRATA   Glad to.
                        Ever since this war began
we women have been watching you men, agreeing
    with you,
keeping our thoughts to ourselves. That doesn't
    mean
we were happy: we weren't, for we saw how things
    were going;
but we'd listen to you at dinner
arguing this way and that.
                        —Oh you, and your big
Top Secrets!—
                        And then we'd grin like little patriots
(though goodness knows we didn't feel like
    grinning) and ask you:
"Dear, did the Armistice come up in Assembly
    today?"
And you'd say, "None of your business! Pipe
    down!," you'd say.
And so we would.
AN OLD WOMAN   *I* wouldn't have, by God!
MAGISTRATE   You'd have taken a beating, then!
                        —Please go on.
LYSISTRATA   Well, we'd be quiet. But then, you know,
    all at once
you men would think up something worse than ever.
Even *I* could see it was fatal. And, "Darling," I'd say,
"have you gone completely mad?" And my husband
    would look at me
and say, "Wife, you've got your weaving to attend to.
Mind your tongue, if you don't want a slap. 'War's
a man's affair!' "[23]
MAGISTRATE   Good words, and well pronounced!
LYSISTRATA   You're a fool if you think so.
                        It was hard enough
to put up with all this banquet-hall strategy.
But then we'd hear you out in the public square:
"Nobody left for the draft-quota here in Athens?"
you'd say; and, "No," someone else would say, "not
    a man!"
And so we women decided to rescue Greece.

---

[22] A politician who, even as Aristophanes was completing this play,
was bringing about the revolution of the Four Hundred, which
overthrew Athenian democracy.

---

[23] Quoted from Hektor's farewell to Andromache, *Iliad*, VI, 492.

Plate I
Ram in the Thicket,
offering stand from Ur,
about 2600 B.C. Wood,
gold, and lapis lazuli.
Height 20″.
(The University Museum,
University of Pennsylvania,
neg. #T4-33)

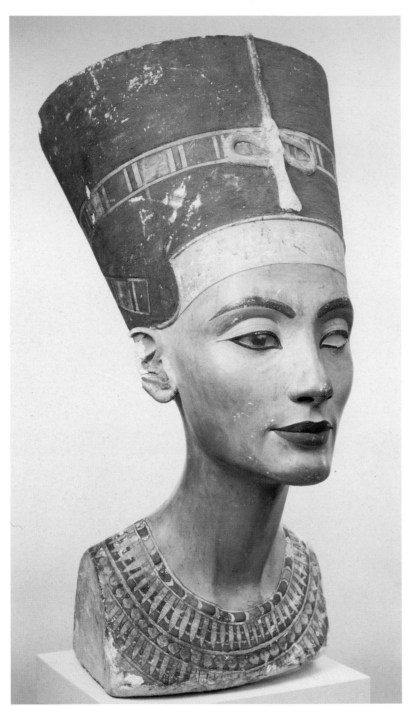

Plate II
Queen Nefertiti,
c. 1365 B.C. Painted
limestone. Height 19⅝″.
(Agyptisches Museum SMPK,
Berlin. Photograph: Bildarchiv
Preussischer Kulturbesitz,
Berlin)

Plate III
Sun God on a Lotus,
Tutankhamen, c. 1342
B.C. 18th Dynasty.
(Cairo Museum/Superstock)

Plate IV
Emperor Justinian and Attendants, mosaic, from apse of San Vitale, Ravenna, c. A.D. 547.
(Scala/Art Resource, NY)

Plate V
Apse Mosaic, Saint
Appollinaire in Classe,
Ravenna, c. A.D. 533–549.
(Scala/Art Resource, NY)

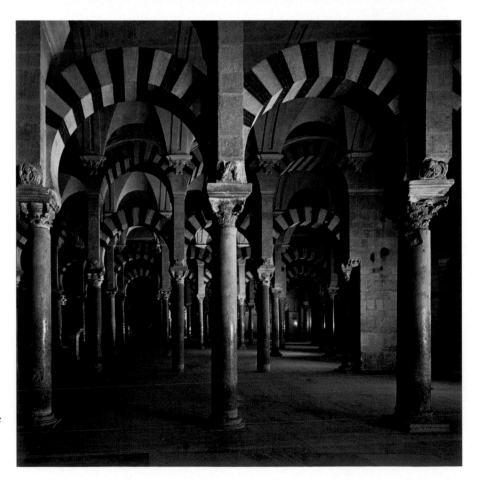

Plate VI
Interior, Great Mosque
of Cordoba, Spain,
A.D. 786.
(Scala/Art Resource, NY)

You might as well listen to us now: you'll have to, later.

MAGISTRATE *You* rescue Greece? Absurd!

LYSISTRATA You're the absurd one!

MAGISTRATE You expect me to take orders from a woman?

LYSISTRATA Heavens, if that's what's bothering you, take my veil,

here, and my girdle, and my market-basket. Go home

to your weaving and your cooking! I tell you, "War's a woman's affair!"

FEMALE CHORAGOS Down with your pitchers, comrades,

but keep them close at hand. It's time for a rally!

Antistrophe

OLD WOMEN Dance, girls, dance for peace!

Who cares if our knees

Wobble and creak? Shall we not dance for such allies as these?

Their wit! their grace! their beauty!

It's a municipal duty

To dance them luck and happiness who risk their all for Greece!

FEMALE CHORAGOS Women, remember your grandmothers! Remember, you were born

among brambles and nettles! Dance for victory!

LYSISTRATA O Eros, god of delight! O Aphrodite! Cyprian!

Drench us now with the savor of love!

Let these men, getting wind of us, dream such joy

that they'll tail us through all the provinces of Hellas!

MAGISTRATE And if we do?

LYSISTRATA Well, for one thing, we shan't have to watch you

going to market, a spear in one hand, and heaven knows

what in the other.

FEMALE CHORAGOS Nicely said, by Aphrodite!

LYSISTRATA As things stand now, you're neither men nor women.

Armor clanking with kitchen pans and pots—

you sound like a pack of Corybantes![24]

MAGISTRATE A man must do what a man must do.

LYSISTRATA So I'm told.

But to see a General, complete with Gorgon-shield,

jingling along the dock to buy a couple of herrings!

---

[24]Wild and frenzied dancers; attendants of the goddess Cybele.

FEMALE CHORAGOS *I* saw a Captain the other day—lovely fellow he was,

nice curly hair—sitting on his horse; and—can you believe it?—

he'd just bought some soup, and was pouring it into his helmet!

And there was a soldier from Thrace

swishing his lance like something out of Euripides,

and the poor fruit-store woman got so scared

that she ran away and let him have his figs free!

MAGISTRATE All this is beside the point.

Will you be so kind

as to tell me how you mean to save Greece?

LYSISTRATA Of course!

Nothing could be simpler.

MAGISTRATE I assure you, I'm all ears.

LYSISTRATA Do you know anything about weaving?

Say the yarn gets tangled: we thread it

this way and that through the skein, up and down,

until it's free. And it's like that with war.

We'll send our envoys

up and down, this way and that, all over Greece,

until it's finished.

MAGISTRATE Yarn? Thread? Skein?

Are you out of your mind? I tell you,

war is a serious business.

LYSISTRATA So serious

that I'd like to go on talking about weaving.

MAGISTRATE All right. Go ahead.

LYSISTRATA The first thing we have to do

is to wash our yarn, get the dirt out of it.

You see? Isn't there too much dirt here in Athens?

You must wash those men away.

Then our spoiled wool—

that's like your job-hunters, out for a life

of no work and big pay. Back to the basket,

citizens or not, allies or not,

or friendly immigrants!

And your colonies?

Hanks of wool lost in various places. Pull them

together, weave them into one great whole,

and our voters are clothed for ever.

MAGISTRATE It would take a woman

to reduce state questions to a matter of carding and weaving!

LYSISTRATA You fool! Who were the mothers whose sons sailed off

to fight for Athens in Sicily?

MAGISTRATE Enough!

I beg you, do not call back those memories.

LYSISTRATA And then,

instead of the love that every woman needs,

we have only our single beds, where we can dream
of our husbands off with the Army.
                              Bad enough for wives!
But what about our girls, getting older every day,
and older, and no kisses?
MAGISTRATE   Men get older, too.
LYSISTRATA   Not in the same sense.
                              A soldier's discharged,
and he may be bald and toothless, yet he'll find
a pretty young thing to go to bed with.
                              But a woman!
Her beauty is gone with the first grey hair.
She can spend her time
consulting the oracles and the fortune-tellers,
but they'll never send her a husband.
MAGISTRATE   Still, if a man can rise to the occasion—
LYSISTRATA (*Furiously*)   Rise? Rise, yourself!
Go invest in a coffin!
                              You've money enough.
                              I'll bake you
a cake for the Underworld.[25]
                              And here's your funeral
wreath! (*She pours water upon him*)
MYRRHINE   And here's another! (*More water*)
KALONIKE   And here's
my contribution! (*More water*)
LYSISTRATA   What are you waiting for?
All aboard Styx Ferry![26]
                              Charon's calling for you!
It's sailing-time: don't disrupt the schedule!
MAGISTRATE   The insolence of women! And to me!
No, by God, I'll go back to court and show
the rest of the Bench the things that might happen to
them!

(*Exit* MAGISTRATE)

LYSISTRATA   Really, I suppose we should have laid out
his corpse
on the doorstep, in the usual way.
                              But never mind!
We'll give him the rites of the dead tomorrow
morning!

(*Exit* LYSISTRATA *with* MYRRHINE *and* KALONIKE)

Strophe 1

OLD MEN   Sons of Liberty, strip off your clothes for
action! Men arise!

Shall we stand here limp and useless while old
Cleisthenes'[27] allies
Prod a herd of furious grandmas to attempt to bring
to pass
A female restoration of the Reign of Hippias?[28]
                              Forbid it, gods misogynist!
                              Return our Treasury, at least!
We must clothe ourselves and feed ourselves to face
these civic rages,
And who can do a single thing if they cut off our
wages?
MALE CHORAGOS   Gentlemen, we are disgraced
forever if we allow
these madwomen to jabber about spears and shields
and make friends with the Spartans. What's a
Spartan? a wild
wolf's a safer companion any day! No; their plan's
to bring back Dictatorship; and we won't stand for
that!
From now on, let's go armed, each one of us
a new Aristogeiton!
                              And to begin with,
I propose to poke a number of teeth
down the gullet of that harridan over there.

Antistrophe 1

OLD WOMEN   Hold your tongues, you senile bravoes,
or I swear, when you get home
Your own mothers wouldn't know you! Strip for
action, ladies, come!
I bore the holy vessels in my eighth year,[29] and at ten
I was pounding out the barley for Athena
Goddess,[30] then
                              They elected me Little Bear
                              For Artemis at Brauron Fair,[31]
I'd been made a Basket-Carrier[32] by the time I came
of age:
So trust me to advise you in this feminist rampage!
FEMALE CHORAGOS   As a woman, I pay my taxes to
the State,

---

[25] A honey cake was usually placed in the hand of the dead to be given to Cerberus, the three-headed dog guarding the gates of Hades.

[26] The Styx was the river over which Charon ferried the souls of the dead.

[27] An Athenian of notorious bisexual tendencies.

[28] Last of the Athenian tyrants. He had ruled with his brother Hipparchos until the latter's death at the hands of the patriots Aristogeiton and Harmonius; Hippias was killed later at Marathon.

[29] Four girls of high birth between the ages of seven and eleven were appointed to service in the Temple of Athena in the Acropolis.

[30] At ten a girl of aristocratic family was eligible to be Millmaid and to grind the sacred grain of Athena.

[31] Brauron was a town on the coast of Attica where a ceremony to Artemis was celebrated in which a little girl impersonated a bear.

[32] Girls carried baskets containing precious objects sacred to Athena.

though I pay them in baby boys. What do you
  contribute,
you impotent horrors? Nothing but waste:
our treasury, the so-called Glory of the Persian
  Wars,
gone! rifled! parceled out for privilege! And you
have the insolence to control public policy,
leading us all to disaster!

                  No, don't answer back
unless you want the heel of my slipper
slapped against that ugly jaw of yours!

Strophe 2

OLD MEN   What impudence!
        What malevolence!
        Comrades, make haste,
All those of you who still are sensitive below the
    waist!
          Off with your clothes, men!
          Nobody knows when
            We'll put them back on.
            Remember Leipsydrion![33]
          We may be old,
          But let's be bold!
MALE CHORAGOS   Give them an inch, and we're done
    for! We'll have them
launching boats next and planning naval strategy.
Or perhaps they fancy themselves as cavalry!
That's fair enough: women know how to ride,
they're good in the saddle. Just think of Mikon's
    paintings,[34]
all those Amazons wrestling with men! No, it's time
to bridle these wild mares!

Antistrophe 2

OLD WOMEN   Hold on, or
        You *are* done for,
        By the Two Goddesses above!
Strip, strip, my women: we've got the veterans on
    the move!
          Tangle with me, Gramps,
          And you'll have cramps
            For the rest of your days!
            No more beans! No more cheese!
          My two legs
          Will scramble your eggs!

FEMALE CHORAGOS   If Lampito stands by me, and
    that elegant
Theban girl, Ismenia—what good are *you*?
                    Pass your laws!
Laws upon laws, you decrepit legislators!
At the worst you're just a nuisance, rationing
    Boeotian eels
on the Feast of Hecate, making our girls go without!
That was statesmanship! And we'll have to put up
    with it
until some patriot slits your silly old gizzards!

(*Exeunt omnes*)

The scene shifts to a court within the Acropolis.

(*Re-enter* LYSISTRATA)

FEMALE CHORAGOS   But Lysistrata! Leader! Why
    such a grim face?
LYSISTRATA   Oh the behavior of these idiotic women!
    There's something about the female temperament
    that I can't bear!
FEMALE CHORAGOS   What in the world do you mean?
LYSISTRATA   Exactly what I say.
FEMALE CHORAGOS   What dreadful thing has
    happened?
    Come, tell us: we're all your friends.
LYSISTRATA   It isn't easy
    to say it; yet, God knows, we can't hush it up.
FEMALE CHORAGOS   Well, then? Out with it!
LYSISTRATA   To put it bluntly,
    we're desperate for men.
FEMALE CHORAGOS   Almighty God!
LYSISTRATA   Why bring God into it?—No, it's just as I
    say.
    I can't manage them any longer: they've gone man-
    crazy,
    they're all trying to get out.
                Why, look:
one of them was sneaking out the back door
over there by Pan's cave,[35] another
was sliding down the walls with rope and tackle;
another was climbing aboard a sparrow,[36] ready to
    take off
for the nearest brothel—I dragged *her* back by the
    hair!
They're all finding some reason to leave.
                Look there!
There goes another one.
              —Just a minute, you!
Where are you off to so fast?

---

[33] After the patriots had killed Hipparchos, they fled and fortified
    themselves in Leipsydrion; after a heroic defense they were forced
    to surrender.

[34] Mikon was one of the many painters who dealt with the invasion
    of Attica by the Amazons, a fabulous race of warrior-women.

[35] A grotto on the north side of the Acropolis.

[36] A bird sacred to Aphrodite; it had been harnessed to the chariot
    of the goddess.

FIRST WOMAN   I've got to get home!
I've a lot of Milesian wool, and the worms are
  spoiling it.
LYSISTRATA   Oh bother you and your worms! Get
  back inside!
FIRST WOMAN   I'll be back right away, I swear I will!
I just want to get it stretched out on my bed.
LYSISTRATA   You'll do no such thing. You'll stay right
  here.
FIRST WOMAN   And my wool?
  You want it ruined?
LYSISTRATA   Yes, for all I care.
SECOND WOMAN   Oh dear! My lovely new flax from
    Amorgos³⁷—
I left it at home, all uncarded!
LYSISTRATA   Another one!
And all she wants is someone to card her flax.
Get back in there!
SECOND WOMAN   But I swear by the Moon-Goddess,
  the minute I get it done, I'll be back!
LYSISTRATA   I say No!
If you, why not all the other women as well?
THIRD WOMAN   O Lady Eileithyia!³⁸ Radiant
    goddess! Thou
intercessor for women in childbirth! Stay, I pray
    thee,
oh stay this parturition! Shall I pollute
a sacred spot?
LYSISTRATA   And what's the matter with *you*?
THIRD WOMAN   I'm having a baby—any minute now!
LYSISTRATA   But you weren't pregnant yesterday.
THIRD WOMAN   Well, I am today!
Let me go home for a midwife, Lysistrata:
there's not much time.
LYSISTRATA   I never heard such nonsense.
What's that bulging under your cloak?
THIRD WOMAN   A little baby boy.
LYSISTRATA   It certainly isn't. But it's something
    hollow,
like a basin or—Why, it's the helmet of Athena!
And you said you were having a baby!
THIRD WOMAN   Well, I am! So there!
LYSISTRATA   Then why the helmet?
THIRD WOMAN   I was afraid that my pains
might begin here in the Acropolis; and I wanted
to drop my chick into it, just as the dear doves do.

LYSISTRATA   Lies! Evasions!—But at least one thing's
    clear:
you can't leave the place before your purification.
THIRD WOMAN   But I can't stay here in the Acropolis!
    Last night I dreamed
of a snake.³⁹
FIRST WOMAN   And those horrible owls,⁴⁰ the noise
    they make!
I can't get a bit of sleep; I'm just about dead.
LYSISTRATA   You useless girls, that's enough: Let's
    have no more lying.
Of course you want your men. But don't you
    imagine
that they want you just as much? I'll give you my
    word,
their nights must be pretty hard.
                    Just stick it out!
A little patience, that's all, and our battle's won.
I have heard an Oracle. Should you like to hear it?
FIRST WOMAN   An Oracle? Yes, tell us!
LYSISTRATA   Quiet, then.—Here
  is what it said:
IF EVER THE SWALLOWS, ESCHEWING HOOPOE-
    BIRDS,
SHALL CONSPIRE TOGETHER TO DENY
    THEM ALL ACCESS,
THEIR GRIEF IS FOREVER OVER.
                    These are the words
  from the Shrine itself.
                    AYE, AND ZEUS WILL REDRESS
THEIR WRONGS, AND SET THE LOWER ABOVE
THE HIGHER.
FIRST WOMAN   Does that mean we'll be on top?
LYSISTRATA   BUT IF THEY RETIRE,
EACH SWALLOW HER OWN WAY, FROM THIS
    HOLY PLACE,
LET THE WORLD PROCLAIM NO BIRD OF
    SORRIER GRACE
THAN THE SWALLOW.
FIRST WOMAN   I swear, *that* Oracle makes sense!
LYSISTRATA   Now, then, by all the gods,
let's show that we're bigger than these annoyances.
Back to your places! Let's not disgrace the Oracle.

(*Exeunt* LYSISTRATA *and the dissident women; the*
CHORUSES *renew their conflict*)

---

³⁷An island in the Aegean famed for its flax.
³⁸The goddess invoked by women at childbirth; it was unlawful to
  bear children on the Acropolis because it was holy ground.

³⁹The sacred snake of the Acropolis; it was never seen but was
  believed to guard the holy ground.
⁴⁰Birds sacred to Athena.

Strophe

OLD MEN   I know a little story that I learned way
   back in school
Goes like this:
Once upon a time there was a young man—and no
   fool—
Named Melanion,[41] and his
   One aversion was marriage. He loathed the very
      thought!
So he ran off to the hills, and in a special grot
Raised a dog, and spent his days
Hunting rabbits. And it says
That he never never never did come home.
It might be called a refuge *from* the womb.
All right,
      all right,
            all right!
We're as pure as young Melanion, and we hate the
   very sight
Of you sluts!
A MAN   How about a kiss, old woman?
A WOMAN   Here's an onion in your eye!
A MAN   A kick in the guts, then?
A WOMAN   Try, old bristle-tail, just try!
A MAN   Yet they say Myronides[42]
   On hands and knees
Looked just as shaggy fore and aft as I!

Antistrophe

OLD WOMEN   Well, *I* know a little story, and it's just
   as good as yours.
Goes like this:
Once there was a man named Timon[43]—a rough
   diamond, of course,
And that whiskery face of his
Looked like murder in the shrubbery. By God, he
   was a son
Of the Furies, let me tell you! And what did he do
   but run
From the world and all its ways,
Cursing mankind! And it says
That his choicest execrations as of then
Were leveled almost wholly at *old* men.

---

[41]The suitor of Atalanta, who hated men. The Chorus of Old Men
   have made him a hater of women.
[42]A famous Athenian general.
[43]A famous Athenian misanthrope.

All right,
      all right,
            all right!
But there's one thing about Timon: he could always
   stand the sight
Of us "sluts"!
A WOMAN   How about a crack in the jaw, Pop?
A MAN   I can take it, Ma—no fear!
A WOMAN   How about a kick in the face?
A MAN   You'd show your venerable rear.
A WOMAN   I may be old;
   But I've been told
That I've nothing to worry about down there!

(*Re-enter* LYSISTRATA)

LYSISTRATA   Oh, quick, girls, quick! Come here!
FEMALE CHORAGOS   What is it?
LYSISTRATA   A man!
   A man simply bulging with love!
                O Cyprian Queen,
   O Paphian, O Cythereian! Hear us and aid us!
FEMALE CHORAGOS   Where is this enemy?
LYSISTRATA   Over there, by Demeter's shrine.
FEMALE CHORAGOS   Damned if he isn't. But who *is* he?
MYRRHINE   My husband.
   Kinesias.
LYSISTRATA   Oh then, get busy! Tease him!
   Undermine him!
   Wreck him! Give him everything—kissing, tickling,
      nudging,
   whatever you generally torture him with—: give
      him everything
   except what we swore on the wine we would not
      give.
MYRRHINE   Trust me!
LYSISTRATA   I do. But I'll help you get him started.
   The rest of you women, stay back.

(*Enter* KINESIAS)

KINESIAS   Oh God! Oh my God!
   I'm stiff for lack of exercise. All I can do to stand up!
LYSISTRATA   Halt! Who are you, approaching our
   lines?
KINESIAS   Me? I.
LYSISTRATA   A man?
KINESIAS   You have eyes, haven't you?
LYSISTRATA   Go away.
KINESIAS   Who says so?
LYSISTRATA   Officer of the Day.
KINESIAS   Officer, I beg you,
   by all the gods at once, bring Myrrhine out!
LYSISTRATA   Myrrhine? And who, my good sir, are
   you?

KINESIAS   Kinesias. Last name's Pennison. Her
husband.

LYSISTRATA   Oh, of course. I beg your pardon. We're
glad to see you.
We've heard so much about you. Dearest Myrrhine
is always talking about "Kinesias"—never nibbles
an egg
or an apple without saying
"Here's to Kinesias!"

KINESIAS   Do you really mean it?

LYSISTRATA   I do.
When we're discussing men, she always says,
"Well, after all, there's nobody like Kinesias!"

KINESIAS   Good God.—Well, then, please send her
down here.

LYSISTRATA   And what do *I* get out of it?

KINESIAS   A standing promise.

LYSISTRATA   I'll take it up with her.

(*Exit* LYSISTRATA)

KINESIAS   But be quick about it!
Lord, what's life without a wife? Can't eat. Can't
sleep.
Every time I go home, the place is so empty, so
insufferably sad! Love's killing me! Oh,
hurry!

(*Enter* MANES, *a slave, with Kinesias' baby; the voice
of* MYRRHINE *is heard off-stage*)

MYRRHINE   But of course I love him! Adore him!—
but no,
he hates love. No. I won't go down.

(*Enter* MYRRHINE, *above*)

KINESIAS   Myrrhine!
Darlingest little Myrrhine! Come down quick!

MYRRHINE   Certainly not.

KINESIAS   Not? But why, Myrrhine?

MYRRHINE   Why? You don't need me.

KINESIAS   Need you? My God, *look* at me!

MYRRHINE   So long! (*Turns to go*)

KINESIAS   Myrrhine, Myrrhine, Myrrhine!
If not for my sake, for our child! (*Pinches* BABY)
                          —All right, you: pipe up!

BABY   Mummie! Mummie! Mummie!

KINESIAS   You hear that?
Pitiful, I call it. Six days now
with never a bath; no food; enough to break your
heart!

MYRRHINE   My darlingest child! What a father *you*
acquired!

KINESIAS   At least come down for his sake!

MYRRHINE   I suppose I must.
Oh, this mother business![44]

(*Exit*)

KINESIAS   How pretty she is! And younger!
She's so much nicer when she's bothered!

(MYRRHINE *enters below*)

MYRRHINE   Dearest child,
you're as sweet as your father's horrid. Give me a
kiss.

KINESIAS   Now you see how wrong it was to get
involved
in this scheming League of women. All this agony
for nothing!

MYRRHINE   Keep your hands to yourself!

KINESIAS   But our house
going to rack and ruin?

MYRRHINE   I don't care.

KINESIAS   And your knitting
all torn to pieces by the chickens? Don't you care?

MYRRHINE   Not at all.

KINESIAS   And our vows to Aphrodite?
Oh, *won't* you come back?

MYRRHINE   No.—At least, not until you men
make a treaty to end the war.

KINESIAS   Why, if that's all you want,
by God, we'll make your treaty!

MYRRHINE   Oh? Very well.
When you've done that, I'll come home. But
meanwhile,
I've sworn an oath.

KINESIAS   Don't worry.—Now, let's have fun.

MYRRHINE   No! Stop it! I said no!
                          —Although, of course,
I *do* love you.

KINESIAS   I know you do. Darling Myrrhine:
come, shall we?

MYRRHINE   Are you out of your mind? In front of the
child?

KINESIAS   Take him home, Manes.

(*Exit* MANES *with* BABY)

                          There. He's gone.
                          Come on!
There's nothing to stop us now.

MYRRHINE   You devil! But where?

KINESIAS   In Pan's cave. What could be snugger than
that?

---

[44]A line that parodies Euripides' *Iphigenia at Aulis*, 917.

MYRRHINE   But my purification before I go back to
the Citadel?

KINESIAS   There's always the Klepsydra.[45]

MYRRHINE   And my oath?

KINESIAS   Leave the oath to me.
After all, I'm the man.

MYRRHINE   Well...if you say so!
                                        I'll go find a bed.

KINESIAS   Oh, bother a bed! The ground's good
enough for me!

MYRRHINE   No. You're a bad man, but you deserve
something better than dirt.

(*Exit* MYRRHINE)

KINESIAS   What a love she is! And how thoughtful!

(*Re-enter* MYRRHINE)

MYRRHINE   Here's your bed.
Now let me get my clothes off.
                              But, good horrors!
We haven't a mattress!

KINESIAS   Oh, forget the mattress!

MYRRHINE   No.
Just lying on blankets? Too sordid!

KINESIAS   Give me a kiss.

MYRRHINE   Just a second.

(*Exit* MYRRHINE)

KINESIAS   I swear, I'll explode!

(*Re-enter* MYRRHINE)

MYRRHINE   Here's your mattress.
Go to bed now. I'll just take my dress off.
                                   But look—
where's our pillow?

KINESIAS   I don't need a pillow!

MYRRHINE   Well, *I* do.

(*Exit* MYRRHINE)

KINESIAS   I don't suppose even Heracles
would stand for this!

(*Re-enter* MYRRHINE)

MYRRHINE   There we are. Ups-a-daisy!

KINESIAS   So we are. Well, come to bed.

MYRRHINE   But I wonder:
is everything ready now?

KINESIAS   I can swear to that. Come, darling!

MYRRHINE   Just getting out of my girdle.
                           But remember, now,
what you promised about the treaty!

KINESIAS   I'll remember.

MYRRHINE   But no coverlet!

KINESIAS   Damn it, I'll be
your coverlet!

MYRRHINE   Be right back.

(*Exit* MYRRHINE)

KINESIAS   This girl and her coverlets
will be the death of me.

(*Re-enter* MYRRHINE)

MYRRHINE   Here we are. Up you go!

KINESIAS   Up? I've been up for ages!

MYRRHINE   Some perfume?

KINESIAS   No, by Apollo!

MYRRHINE   Yes, by Aphrodite!
I don't care whether you want it or not.

(*Exit* MYRRHINE)

KINESIAS   For love's sake, hurry!

(*Re-enter* MYRRHINE)

MYRRHINE   Here, in your hand. Rub it right in.

KINESIAS   Never cared for perfume.
And this is particularly strong. Still, here goes!

MYRRHINE   What a nitwit I am! I brought you the
Rhodian bottle![46]

KINESIAS   Forget it.

MYRRHINE   No trouble at all. You just wait here.

(*Exit* MYRRHINE)

KINESIAS   God damn the man who invented perfume!

(*Re-enter* MYRRHINE)

MYRRHINE   At last! The right bottle!

KINESIAS   I've got the rightest
bottle of all, and it's right here waiting for you.
Darling, forget everything else. Do come to bed!

MYRRHINE   Just let me get my shoes off.
                        —And, by the way,
you'll vote for the treaty?

KINESIAS   I'll think about it.

(MYRRHINE *runs away*)

There! That's done it! Off she runs,
with never a thought for the way I'm feeling. I must

---

[45]A sacred spring near Pan's cave.

[46]From Rhodes.

have *some*one, or I'll go mad! Myrrhine
has just about ruined me.
                    And you, strutting little soldier:
what about you? There's nothing for it, I guess,
But an expedition to old Dog-fox's[47] bordello.
OLD MEN   She's left you in a sorry state:
                    You have my sympathy.
                    What upright citizen could bear
                    Your pain? I swear, not I!
Just the look of you, with never a woman
    To come to your aid! It isn't human!
KINESIAS   The agony!
MALE CHORAGOS   Well, why not?
    She has you on the spot!
FEMALE CHORAGOS   A lovelier girl never breathed,
    you old sot!
KINESIAS   A lovelier girl? Zeus! Zeus!
                    Produce a hurricane
                    To hoist these lovely girls aloft
                    And drop them down again
    Bump on our lances! Then they'd know
        What they do that makes men suffer so.

(*Exit* KINESIAS)

(*Enter a* SPARTAN HERALD)

HERALD   Gentlemen, Ah beg you will be so kind
    as to direct me to the Central Committee.
    Ah have a communication.

(*Re-enter* MAGISTRATE)

MAGISTRATE   Are you a man,
    or a fertility symbol?
HERALD   Ah refuse to answer that question!
    Ah'm a certified herald from Sparta, and Ah've
        come
    to talk about an ahmistice.
MAGISTRATE   Then why
    that spear under your cloak?
HERALD   Ah have no speah!
MAGISTRATE   You don't walk naturally, with your
        tunic
    poked out so. You have a tumor, maybe,
    or a hernia?
HERALD   No, by Castor![48]
MAGISTRATE   Well,
    something's wrong, I can see that. And I don't like it.
HERALD   Colonel, Ah resent this.
MAGISTRATE   So I see. But what *is* it?

---

[47]Nickname for a famous procurer.
[48]One of Sparta's protective spirits.

HERALD   A scroll
    with a message from Spahta.
MAGISTRATE   Oh. I've heard about these scrolls.
    Well, then, man, speak out: How are things in
        Sparta?
HERALD   Hard, Colonel, hard! We're at a standstill.
    Can't seem to think of anything but women.
MAGISTRATE   How curious! Tell me, do you Spartans
        think
    that maybe Pan's to blame?
HERALD·   Pan? No. Lampito and her little naked
        friends.
    They won't let a man come near them.
MAGISTRATE   How are you handling it?
HERALD   Losing our minds,
    if you want to know, and walking around hunched
        over
    like men carrying candles in a gale.
    The women have sworn they'll have nothing to do
        with us
    until we get a treaty.
MAGISTRATE   Yes, I know.
    It's a general uprising, sir, in all parts of Greece.
    But as for the answer—
                    Sir: go back to Sparta
    and have them send us your Armistice Commission.
    I'll arrange things in Athens.
                    And I may say
    that my standing is good enough to make them
        listen.
HERALD   A man after mah own heart! Sir, Ah thank
    you!

(*Exit* HERALD)

Strophe

OLD MEN   Oh these women! Where will you find
                    A slavering beast that's more unkind?
                    Where a hotter fire?
            Give me a panther, any day!
            He's not so merciless as they,
                    And panthers don't conspire!

Antistrophe

OLD WOMEN   We may be hard, you silly old ass,
                    But who brought you to this stupid pass?
                    You're the ones to blame.
            Fighting with us, your oldest friends,
            Simply to serve your selfish ends—
                    Really, you have no shame!

MALE CHORAGOS   No, I'm through with women for
   ever![49]
FEMALE CHORAGOS   If you say so.
  Still, you might put some clothes on. You look too
   absurd
standing around naked. Come, get into this cloak.
MALE CHORAGOS   Thank you; you're right. I merely
  took it off
because I was in such a temper.
FEMALE CHORAGOS   That's much better
  Now you resemble a man again.
                 Why have you been so horrid?
  And look: there's some sort of insect in your eye!
Shall I take it out?
MALE CHORAGOS   An insect, is it? So that's
  what's been bothering me! Lord, yes: take it out!
FEMALE CHORAGOS   You might be more polite.
                    —But, heavens!
  What an enormous gnat!
MALE CHORAGOS   You've saved my life.
  That gnat was drilling an artesian well
in my left eye.
FEMALE CHORAGOS   Let me wipe
  those tears away!—And now: one little kiss?
MALE CHORAGOS   Over my dead body!
FEMALE CHORAGOS   You're so difficult!
MALE CHORAGOS   These impossible women! How
  they do get around us!
  The poet was right: Can't live with them, or without
   them!
  But let's be friends.
  And to celebrate, you might lead off with an Ode.

Strophe

OLD WOMEN   Let it never be said
      That my tongue is malicious:
      Both by word and by deed
  I would set an example that's noble and gracious.
    We've had sorrow and care
    Till we're sick of the tune.
    Is there anyone here
    Who would like a small loan?
      My purse is crammed,
      As you'll soon find;
  And you needn't pay me back if the Peace gets
   signed!

  I've invited to lunch
  Some Karystian rips—[50]
    An esurient bunch,
But I've ordered a menu to water their lips!
    I can still make soup
    And slaughter a pig.
  You're all coming, I hope?
  But a bath first, I beg!
    Walk right up
    As though you owned the place,
And you'll get the front door slammed to in your
  face!

(*Enter* SPARTAN AMBASSADOR, *with entourage*)

MALE CHORAGOS   The Commission has arrived
  from Sparta
            How oddly
  they're walking!
           Gentlemen, welcome to Athens!
  How is life in Laconia?
AMBASSADOR   Need we discuss that?
  Simply use your eyes.
OLD MEN   The poor man's right:
        What a sight!
AMBASSADOR   Words fail me.
  But come, gentlemen, call in your Commissioners,
  and let's get down to a peace.
MALE CHORAGOS   The state we're in! Can't bear
  a stitch below the waist. It's a kind of pelvic
  paralysis.
AN ATHENIAN   Won't somebody call Lysistrata?
  She has the answer.
A SPARTAN   Yes, there, look at him.
  Same thing.
         Seh, do y'all feel a certain strain
  early in the morning?
ATHENIAN   I do, sir. It's worse than a strain.
  A few more days, and there's nothing for us but
   Cleisthenes,
  that broken blossom!
MALE CHORAGOS   But you'd better get dressed
  Again. You know these prudes who go around
  Athens
  with chisels,
  looking for prominent statues.[51]
ATHENIAN   Sir, you are right.
SPARTAN   He certainly is! Ah'll put mah own clothes
  back on.

---

[49]Parodies lines in Euripides' *Hippolytus.*

[50]The Karystians were allies of Athens at this time, but were dis-
  dained for their primitive manners and loose morals.

[51]Statues with prominent male sexual organs, or *phalloi.*

(*Enter* ATHENIAN COMMISSIONERS)

AN ATHENIAN   They're no better off than we are!
                              —Greetings, Laconians!
SPARTAN (*To one of his own group*)   Colonel, we got
    dressed just in time.
                    Ah sweah,
    if they'd seen us the way we were, there'd have been a
        new war
    between the states.
ATHENIAN   Call the meeting to order.
                              Now, Laconians,
    what's your proposal?
AMBASSADOR   We'd lahk to consider peace.
ATHENIAN   Good. That's on our minds, too.
                        —Summon Lysistrata.
    We'll never get anywhere without her.
AMBASSADOR   Lysistrata?
    Summon Lysis-*any*body![52] Only, summon!
MALE CHORAGOS   No need to summon:
    here she is, herself.

(*Enter* LYSISTRATA)

                    Lysistrata! Lion of women!
    This is your hour to be
    hard and yielding, outspoken and sly, austere and
    gentle. You see here
    the best brains of Hellas (confused, I admit,
    by your devious charming) met as one man
    to turn the future over to you.
LYSISTRATA   That's fair enough,
    unless you men take it into your heads
    to turn to each other instead of to me. But I'd know
    soon enough if you did!
                    —Where is that goddess of Peace?
    Go, some of you: bring her here.

(*Exeunt two* SERVANTS)

                        And now,
    summon the Spartan Commission. Treat them
        courteously:
    our husbands have been lax in that respect.
    Take them by the hand, women,
    or by anything else, if they seem unwilling.
                            —Spartans:
    you stand here. Athenians: on this side. Now listen
        to me.

(*Re-enter* SERVANTS, *staggering under the weight of a
more than life-size statue of a naked woman: this is*
PEACE)

_____

[52]Lysistrata's name means "dissolver of armies."

I'm only a woman, I know; but I've a mind,
and I can distinguish between sense and foolishness.
I owe the first to my father; the rest
to the local politicians.[53] So much for that.
Now, then.
What I have to say concerns both sides in this war.
We are all Greeks.
Must I remind you of Thermopylae? of Olympia?
of Delphi? names deep in all our hearts?
And yet you men go raiding through the country,
Greek killing Greek, storming down Greek cities—
and all the time the Barbarian across the sea
is waiting for his chance.—That's my first point.
AN ATHENIAN   Lord! I can hardly contain myself!
LYSISTRATA   And you Spartans:
    Was it so long ago that Pericleides
    came here to beg our help?[54] I can see him still,
    his white face, his sombre gown. And what did he
        want?
    An army from Athens! Messenia
    was at your heels, and the sea-god splitting your
        shores.
    Well, Kimon and his men,
    four thousand infantry, marched out of here to save
        you.
    What thanks do we get? You come back to murder
        us.
ATHENIAN   Can't trust a Spartan, Lysistrata!
A SPARTAN   Ah admit it.
    When Ah look at those legs, Ah sweah Ah can't trust
        mahself!
LYSISTRATA   And you, men of Athens:
    you might remember that bad time when we were
        down,
    and an army came from Sparta
    and sent Hippias and the Thessalians
    whimpering back to the hills. That was Sparta,
    and only Sparta; without Sparta, we'd now be
    cringing helots, not walking about like free men!

(*From this point, the male responses are less to*
LYSISTRATA *than to the statue of* PEACE)

A SPARTAN   An eloquent speech!
AN ATHENIAN   An elegant construction!
LYSISTRATA   Why are we fighting each other? Why
    not make peace?
AMBASSADOR   Spahta is ready, ma'am,
    so long as we get that place back.

_____

[53]The preceding four lines are probably quoted from Euripides'
    Melanippe the Wise.
[54]In 464 B.C. during a revolt in Sparta, when an earthquake had
    just severely damaged the city.

LYSISTRATA   Place? What place?
AMBASSADOR   Ah refer to Pylos.[55]
MAGISTRATE   Not while I'm alive, by God!
LYSISTRATA   You'd better give in.
MAGISTRATE   But—what were we fighting about?
LYSISTRATA   Lots of places left.
MAGISTRATE   All right. Well, then:
  Hog Island first, and that gulf behind there, and the
    land between
  the Legs of Megara.
AMBASSADOR   Mah government objects.
LYSISTRATA   Over-ruled. Why fuss about a pair of
  legs?

(*General assent; the statue of* PEACE *is removed*)

AN ATHENIAN   Let's take off our clothes and plow
    our fields.
A SPARTAN   Ah'll fertilize mahn first, by the Heavenly
    Twins!
LYSISTRATA   And so you shall,
  once we have peace. If you are serious,
  go, both of you, and talk with your allies.
ATHENIAN   Too much talk already. We'll stand
    together!
  We've only one end in view. All that we want
  is our women: and I speak for our allies.
AMBASSADOR   Mah government concurs.
AN ATHENIAN   So does Karystos.
LYSISTRATA   Good.—But before you come inside
  to join your wives at supper, you must perform
  the usual lustration. Then we'll open
  our baskets for you, and all that we have is yours.
  But you must promise upright good behavior
  from this day on. Then each man home with his
    woman!
ATHENIAN   Let's get it over with!
SPARTAN   Lead on: Ah follow!
ATHENIAN   Quick as a cat can wink!

(*Exeunt all but the* CHORUSES)

Antistrophe

OLD WOMEN   Embroideries and
                    Twinkling ornaments and
                    Pretty dresses—I hand
  Them all over to you, and with never a qualm.
                    They'll be nice for your daughters
                    On festival days
                    When the girls bring the Goddess
                    The ritual prize.

_____
[55]A lost Spartan possession; for the moment political and sexual
  desires become confused.

Come in, one and all:
  Take what you will.
I've nothing here so tightly corked that you can't
  make it spill!
            You may search my house,
            But you'll not find
            The least thing of use,
  Unless your two eyes are keener than mine.
            Your numberless brats
            Are half starved? and your slaves?
            Courage, grandpa! I've lots
            Of grain left, and big loaves.
            I'll fill your guts,
            I'll go the whole hog;
  But if you come too close to me, remember:
  'ware the dog!

(*Exeunt* CHORUSES)

(*An* ATHENIAN DRUNKARD *approaches the gate and is
halted by a* SENTRY)

DRUNKARD   Open. The. Door.
SENTRY   Now, friend, just shove along!
  So you want to sit down! If it weren't such an old
    joke,
  I'd tickle your tail with this torch. Just the sort of
    thing
  that this kind of audience appreciates.
DRUNKARD   I. Stay. Right. Here.
SENTRY   Oh, all right. But you'll see some funny
    sights!
DRUNKARD   Bring. Them. On.
SENTRY   No, what am I thinking of?
  The gentlemen from Sparta are just coming back
    from supper.
  Get out of here, or I'll scalp you!

(*Exit* DRUNKARD)

(*The general company re-enters; the two* CHORUSES
now represent SPARTANS *and* ATHENIANS)

MAGISTRATE   I must say,
  I've never tasted a better meal. And those
    Laconians!
  They're gentlemen, by the Lord! Just goes to show:
  a drink to the wise is sufficient. And why not?
  A sober man's an ass.
  Men of Athens, mark my words: the only efficient
  Ambassador's a drunk Ambassador. Is that clear?
  Look: we go to Sparta,
  and when we get there we're dead sober. The result?
  Everyone cackling at everyone else. They make
    speeches;
  and even if we understand, we get it all wrong

when we file our reports in Athens. But today—!
Everybody's happy. Couldn't tell the difference
between *Drink to Me Only* and
the *Star Spangled Athens.*

What's a few lies,
washed down in good strong drink?

(*Re-enter* DRUNKARD)

SENTRY   God almighty,
he's back again!
DRUNKARD   I. Resume. My. Place.
A SPARTAN (*To an* ATHENIAN)   I beg you, seh,
take your instrument in your hand and play for us.
Ah'm told
you understand the in*tri*cacies of the floot?
Ah'd lahk to execute a song and dance
in honor of Athens,
                    and, of course, of Spahta.

(*The following song is a solo—an aria—accompanied
by the flute. The* CHORUS OF SPARTANS *begins a slow
dance*)

DRUNKARD   Toot. On. Your. Flute.
SPARTAN CHORAGOS   Mnemosyne,[56]
        Inspire once more the Grecian Muse
        To sing of glory glory glory without end.
        Sing Artemesion's shore,[57]
        Where Athens fluttered the Persian fleet—
        Alalai,[58] that great
        Victory! Sing Leonidis and his men,
        Those wild boars, sweat and blood
        Down in a red drench. Then, then
        The barbarians broke, though they had stood
        A myriad strong before!
                        O Artemis,
        Virgin Goddess, whose darts
        Flash in our forests: approve
        This pact of peace, and join our hearts,
        From this day on, in love.
        Huntress, descend!
LYSISTRATA   All that will come in time.
                        But now, Laconians,
take home your wives. Athenians, take yours.
Each man be kind to his woman; and you, women,
be equally kind. Never again, pray God,
shall we lose our way in such madness.

                                        —And now
let's dance our joy! (*From this point the dance
becomes general*)
CHORUS OF ATHENIANS   Dance!
                        Dance!
                            Dance, you Graces!
        Artemis, Dance!
                    Dance, Phoebus, Lord of dancing!
        Dance, Dionysus, in a scurry of Maenads!
                Dance, Zeus Thunderer!
            Dance, Lady Hera,
        Queen of the sky!
                        Dance, dance, all you gods!
        Dance for the dearest, the bringer of peace,
        Deathless Aphrodite!
LYSISTRATA   Now let us have another song from
    Sparta.
CHORUS OF SPARTANS   From Taygetos' skyey summit,
                Laconian Muse, come down!
        Sing the glories of Apollo,
                Regent of Amyclae Town.
                Sing of Leda's Twins,
                Those gallant sons,
                On the banks of Eurotas—
                    Alalai Evohe![59]
        Here's to our girls
                With their tangling curls,
                Legs a-wriggle,
                Bellies a-jiggle,
                    A riot of hair,
                A fury of feet,
        Evohe! Evohai! Evohe!
                                as they pass
            Dancing,
                    dancing,
                        dancing,
                            to greet
        Athena of the House of Brass![60]

COMMENTS AND QUESTIONS

1. Like the tragedy *Oedipus Rex,* the comedy *Lysistrata* treats a selection of events taking place in
   a relatively short time. What, exactly, happens in
   Lysistrata? How has Aristophanes arranged the
   events? Where does the climax of the play fall, and
   how is it revealed?

---

[56]Goddess of memory and mother of the Muses.

[57]Where in 480 B.C. the Athenian fleet successfully engaged the
Persians, while Leonidas and his Spartans were making their
famous stand at Thermopylae.

[58]A war cry.

[59]Now an orgiastic war cry.

[60]A famous temple on the acropolis of Sparta.

2. Is the *tone* of *Lysistrata* entirely comic, or are there tragic or serious moments?

3. Do the characters in the play seem realistic to you? What makes them comic characters?

4. Which lines in the comedy seem especially funny to you? Why? Is the sexual explicitness in *Lysistrata* comic? Compare the treatment of sex here with the deadly seriousness of pornography. What is the difference?

5. *Lysistrata* is read more and more today as a play about women's liberation. Look for arguments both for and against this view in the play. What can you surmise about the actual social conditions of Greek women from this text? If the idea of the sex strike is not very realistic, the idea of women organizing themselves to achieve common goals is. What difficulties does Lysistrata encounter in the characters of the women themselves when she attempts to organize them? Can these be compared with the differences between "liberated" women and other women today? How are men viewed in this comedy?

Classical Greece: Philosophy and Ethical Thought

Although thinkers and artists in the ancient civilizations of Africa and the Middle East had asked questions about human destiny and the universe that may be called "philosophical," the ancient Greeks were, as far as we know, the first to attempt to understand their universe as an order governed by a rational principle. The word *philosophy*, from the words *philo* and *sophia*, is in fact a Greek term that literally means "love of wisdom." From the late sixth century B.C., a group of philosophers, usually called the Pre-Socratics because they flourished before Socrates, looked beyond the arbitrary, willful gods worshiped by the masses to define a universal principle of rationality. Whereas the popular gods were like human beings, only more powerful, the philosophers were in search of a unitary principle giving order and intelligibility to the world. The most ancient of these Pre-Socratic thinkers can be considered physicists, in that they tried to locate the unitary principle in a material element. Thales (640–546? B.C.), the earliest of the group, believed the underlying element in all nature was water, whereas air and fire became the preferred choices of philosophers in later generations.

The first half of the fifth century B.C. in Greece saw the rapid breakdown of social order and government, which raised pressing questions about the individual's place in society. By mid-century, *ethical* questions became uppermost and Greek philosophy moved to focus on humanity rather than nature. The major intellectuals dominating Greece by this time were the Sophists. The Sophists promised to teach wisdom for a price. In actual fact, their lessons were aimed at teaching students the art of eloquence to enable them to win influence in the new popular governments emerging all over the peninsula. They attacked the ideal of absolute right and wrong and taught that all things were relative.

Socrates (470?–399 B.C.)

Socrates set himself to oppose the skepticism and self-interested orientation of the Sophists. He was convinced that there was an absolute set of moral laws and that most people in a confused way assumed this to be true. His general goal was to make people aware of their assumptions about what they thought they knew, not to make them skeptics but so that they might begin the pursuit of knowledge in the proper way. He believed that knowledge begins with knowing what we do *not* know. So it was that the short, powerfully built, snub-nosed man, looking very much like a wrestler, spent most of his days in the streets of Athens, his native city, asking questions of his fellow citizens. Seemingly never satisfied with the first answer, he pushed his questions to the point where his companions in the dialogues had finally to admit that they did not know what they believed they knew at the outset. He became known as the gadfly of Athens—after the little gnat that pesters its object to desperation. Finally, he appeared so threatening to the traditions of his city that he was arrested and condemned to death for his detrimental influence on the youth of Athens.

Plato (427?–347 B.C.)

Socrates never wrote a word, but his greatest disciple, Plato, wrote volumes; in many of his writings, called *Dialogues,* he immortalized Socrates by making him the voice of the philosopher in the discussion. It is impossible to be certain how much of Plato's thought was borrowed from his master. At least the technique of seeking an immutable, eternal basis for our knowledge by interrogation certainly derived from Socrates, but it was probably Plato who formulated the technique into a method. The typical dialogue begins with Socrates asking for the definition of justice, or of courage, or of virtue itself. The person questioned responds usually with confidence, giving a traditional commonsense definition. Further questioning shows the answer to be inadequate, and a second definition is proposed—only to be rejected in turn—then a third and even a fourth without any results. At length the discussant admits reluctantly to being ignorant of what he believed himself to know. Perhaps the dialogue ends there, but frequently the interrogation continues until some positive conclusions are achieved.

It would appear that Socrates' main concern was ethical, but Plato extended Socrates' method to embrace a much wider variety of philosophical problems. Through the method of interrogation, or *dialectic,* Plato eventually established the existence of two levels of reality. From eternity there were three elements in the universe: a Demiurge or creator God; a world of eternal unchanging Ideas or patterns, perfect exemplars of truth, beauty, and justice, and of all numbers, geometrical shapes, and natural things; and the receptacle, equivalent to pure space or matter. The work of the Demiurge was to model the receptacle into shapes resembling the eternal patterns of the Ideas or forms. Because the matter he worked with was mobile, his creations could never remain fixed for long; but at least the world he fashioned represented or imitated imperfectly the immutable exemplars of the transcendent world. Before this life people had lived as souls in the world of the Ideas and had beheld them in their splendor. Only like can know like: human beings could know the Ideas in this other world because they, like the Ideas, were divine.

Imprisoned at birth in a body, subject to the sensations of matter, the individual has forgotten that earlier life; nevertheless, enough remains to serve as the basis for judging experience. When we say that that thing is more beautiful than this thing, we are comparing both objects with a standard of beauty not found in our earthly experience but rather brought with us into this life from our contact in the upper world with the idea of pure beauty. The same is true with our judgment about other objects in our experience.

For Plato the soul is a divine entity, buried in a body from which at death it will escape. Because of our contact with the absolute beauty and good in a preexistence, we continue in this life to seek the experience we once had. Motivated by love of beauty and good, we strive to satisfy our needs through possession of material objects and other human beings. Only education can teach us the true end of our longing, directing our gaze away from the imperfect, transitory objects of this world to contemplation of the Ideas themselves of which these objects are but a dim reflection. Once in possession of the knowledge of mathematics, geometry, and other truths, we will come to look on our bodies and this world as a prison from which death will free us.

The psychology of the philosopher constituted the first attempt to define various aspects of the human personality. Plato believed that the human soul consists of three fundamental parts: the reason that governs, moral courage that pursues the honorable even against great obstacles, and the appetite. The third part of the soul must be kept in close confinement; otherwise it would topple reason from its seat and create chaos in the life of the soul. Moral courage, on the other hand, is the ally of reason. A loyal member of a Greek city-state, Plato was convinced that the individual could not attain moral perfection or reach the stage where reason contemplated the eternal realities while living in a corrupt community. Plato's ideal state reflects in its organization the three divisions of the soul. Like the soul it has its rational principle in the Guardians, those who govern the whole. The auxiliaries, the soldiers, correspond to moral courage; and the artisans, who do most of the hard work in the society, reflect the appetitive principle. Just as in the individual soul, the whole is in harmony when reason rules, so in the state ruled by philosophers everyone keeps his or her place, performs his or her function, and is content. In striking contrast to Athenian society's tendency to absolute male dominance, Plato specifies that males and females receive the same education from childhood and, depending on their individual abilities to learn, are ultimately assigned to one of the three classes in the state.

Aristotle (384–322 B.C.)

For Plato knowledge was essentially *deductive*, that is, it came from within the human mind and was applicable to the world. Humans brought categories of organization to experience. In his later years Plato came increasingly to conceive of the world of the Ideas in terms of mathematical relationships. From Plato derives, therefore, the conception that mathematics is the key to understanding nature. By contrast, his student Aristotle approached the universe not as a mathematician but as a biologist. Knowledge of humanity and nature in Aristotle's judgment was *inductive*. It was derived by the human intellect from nature itself.

Like Plato, Aristotle requires that knowledge, to be knowledge, must be eternally and immutably true. Accordingly, there can be knowledge only of that which is eternal and unchanging. At the same time, however, Aristotle in his mature work considered Plato's belief in a world of the Ideas to be nonsense. There are not two levels of reality—the world we know and a world of perfect Forms or Ideas; there is only one reality. But how is knowledge possible in such a world where all seems in a state of constant change? What in our experience is immutable and eternal when all about us is moving from place to place, being born, dying, becoming bigger or less, changing colors and the like? Aristotle's reply is that there is no need to postulate a world of ideal forms because this needlessly duplicates the forms already in nature. There are in the universe of Aristotle a finite if immense number of different kinds of things, which he calls forms or species. The species are eternal and never change, but they never exist apart from individual members of that species. Each individual member of the species, say of human beings, carries within him- or herself the form of humanness that makes the individual "be" what he or she is. Individuals of a species differ one from the other (that is, they are individuals) because they differ in their matter. Each is composed of a different mass of bone and flesh. Individuals are born, grow old, and die, but the form or species lives on, passing from generation to generation to all eternity. Thus Aristotle has found the eternal forms *in* the things of this world themselves. We experience them in our encounter with each of the individual representatives of the species. In sense experience my intellect has the power to grasp the eternal form in the individual. When, for example, I see a tree, I know it is a tree because my mind perceives the form of "treeness" in it. Gradually, through experience with different trees, I can develop a knowledge of the various operations of the species; this knowledge will be immutable and eternal because the species in itself never changes. What I learn generally about these trees will be true for all trees.

How does Aristotle explain the cause of change in the universe? Why do streams flow, flowers grow, and the heavenly spheres circle? Each individual thing in the universe for Aristotle moves and changes because it is attempting in this way to realize perfection in its form. Indirectly, however, God is the ultimate cause of all movement. Aristotle sets the earth at the center of the universe, ringing it round with ten revolving spheres. The innermost sphere takes the moon around the earth, the next the sun, and so on, moving outward for each of the planets until we reach the tenth sphere, which holds the fixed stars. Beyond that sphere lies God. Aristotle's God is perfect mind who exists eternally thinking only of himself and absolutely motionless. He knows nothing of the universe below him. Like him, the universe with its species is eternal. He did not create them. His only relationship to the universe is that all objects on earth and in heaven are attracted to him and attempt to imitate his perfection by being themselves perfect. To do so, they must undergo change. He is perfect and therefore unmoving. The individual members of the countless species of things must constantly strive to perfect their particular species in themselves; thus they move. Aristotle's God, consequently, is not a creator God but the underlying cause of all universal motion through the force of attraction he exerts on them.

What is the nature of humanity and human destiny in such a universe? Whereas everything in the universe consists of matter and form, in living things the form is called a soul. Plants and animals have souls, but not as complex as those of human beings. People, as opposed to all other living things, have the power to know truth. They are endowed with minds that can grasp the forms of things and can develop a body of knowledge about nature through reasoning and observation. On the basis of the axiom "like alone can know like," does the fact that the human mind can know the eternal form found in individual members of a species mean that a person's soul as opposed to other living souls is immortal? Although we cannot be certain, Aristotle seems to reject personal immortality. The part of the human mind that grasps the forms of things is specifically designated as immortal, but Aristotle describes it in such a way that it does not really belong to us individually and that, while the personal elements of our souls perish at death, it departs from us. Thus humans—like every other thing on earth—bear the species for their time; and, as this generation passes away, another rises to replace it.

If there is no afterlife for the human being, what is the nature of happiness? Aristotle replies: humanity's happiness lies in the perfection of its form as humanity. A human being is distinctive in being a rational animal; therefore, an individual's highest good lies in perfecting reason. Such perfection occurs in two areas. First of all, individuals must control their lives through reason. Such a life is a virtuous life. Honesty, courage, temperance, and the like are virtues; they are different aspects of the behavior of a rational person. The second area in which reason must be perfected to obtain happiness is in the intellectual sphere. Since human reason has the capacity to learn the truth, the rational person must study the sciences, mathematics, and divine things to fulfill human nature. Aristotle himself, following his inductive method of investigation, produced an immense number of works devoted to the widest range of subjects, including botany, zoology, astronomy, physics, rhetoric, psychology, physiology, and political science.

But the attainment of moral and intellectual virtue is not sufficient to create happiness. Aristotle willingly acknowledged that even the virtuous person could not be happy if poor or sick. Accordingly, Aristotle maintained that although virtue was the highest good for happiness, people needed both health and a degree of wealth to reach their end. The demands placed on the individual by this kind of ethic were obviously not excessively rigorous and could easily be met by the upper class of the Greek polis.

Although differing from Plato on the place of the forms and on the immortality of the human soul among other things, Aristotle was in complete agreement with the older man who had once been his teacher on the close relationship between ethics and politics. For Aristotle, as for Plato, the state was humankind written large. People were only animals outside the state; only through the state could they obtain moral and intellectual perfection. But whereas for Plato the best form of government was a monarchy ruled by a philosopher king, Aristotle, rejecting what he considered Plato's purely theoretical approach, opted for republican government as the best form of government in the world as it was. Through participation in the political life of his state, the citizen could maximize his power and talents, thereby finding happiness.

While Aristotle wrote extensively concerning the ideal man, he ignored the matter of the ideal woman. The selection from the *Politics* indicates that Aristotle shared the common prejudice of his society that woman was naturally inferior to man and not worthy of special analysis. In a treatise entitled "on the Generation of Animals," Aristotle writes that a female was simply a failed male. Nature in producing human beings aims at making a male offspring, but when the process is defective, a female is the result. Because the woman by nature is colder than the man, girls are usually born when the father is either young or old, that is, when he has not yet reached the heat of maturity or when he is past that point. This view of man as the most perfect creature in nature and of woman as a defective or second-rate man was to have long-range repercussions in Western culture. Yet one should not conclude that the ancient Greeks consistently viewed the female as inferior. The goddesses in Greek mythology, the ideal female form in sculpture, the admiration shown for Sappho, and characters such as Lysistrata in comedy and Antigone in tragedy attest to the contrary. Plato, as mentioned earlier, envisaged equality between superior men and women in *The Republic*.

The Poetics

In addition to having made enormous contributions to the fields of metaphysics, politics, and ethics, Aristotle was also the Western world's first literary critic, and his views on poetic and dramatic form continue to be influential to this day. Having before him the major works of classical Greek literature, Aristotle in the *Poetics* sought not only to define the nature of the forms of the epic, tragedy, comedy, and the dithyramb, but also to produce a kind of manual for writers who wished to write in these forms. He was also, in a sense, answering his former master Plato, who thought that poetry, with its dangerous effects on emotions, ought to be banished from the ideal republic. For Aristotle, poetry was actually superior to history, because poetry deals with the general and the philosophical, whereas history treats the particular. All poetry, for Aristotle, is an imitation (*mimesis*) of life, but this imitation involves not merely the realistic copying of a "slice of life" but the condensation of life into a form, with a beginning, a middle, and an end, resulting in both pleasure and self-knowledge for the audience. For Aristotle, tragedy, because it portrays people as better than they actually are, and because its form is the most cohesive, is superior to both comedy and epic. Indeed, most of the *Poetics* concerns tragedy, and because Aristotle apparently never finished the section on comedy, we can only speculate as to what his views on that form might have been.

READING SELECTIONS

The Allegory of the Cave

Translation by Benjamin Jowett

An important characteristic of Plato's method was to illustrate profound philosophical ideas through use of stories, in the manner of myths. The selection below is taken from *The Republic,* Plato's great dialogue on justice, illustrated by the perfect state. Commonly known as "The *Allegory* of the Cave," this passage endeavors to dramatize the predicament of humankind, which takes the shifting, temporary things of this world for ultimate reality. It also describes the problem of the philosopher, who has looked on the realm of the Ideas through contemplation and who yet has to return to live in this world among the shadows with which other people are content. The dialogue is between Socrates and Glaucon. Socrates speaks first.

"And now," I said, "let me show in a figure how far our nature is enlightened or unenlightened. Behold! Human beings living in an underground den, which has a mouth open towards the light and reaching all along the den; here they have been from their childhood, and have their legs and necks chained so that they cannot move, and can only see before them, being prevented by the chains from turning round their heads. Above and behind them a fire is blazing at a distance, and between the fire and the prisoners there is a raised way; and you will see, if you look, a low wall built along the way, like the screen which marionette players have in front of them, over which they show the puppets."

"I see."

"And do you see," I said, "men passing along the wall carrying all sorts of vessels, and statues and figures of animals made of wood and stone and various materials, which appear over the wall? Some of them are talking, others silent."

"You have shown me a strange image, and they are strange prisoners."

"Like ourselves," I replied; "and they see only their own shadows, or the shadows of one another, which the fire throws on the opposite wall of the cave?"

"True," he said; "how could they see anything but the shadows if they were never allowed to move their heads?"

"And of the objects which are being carried in like manner they would only see the shadows?"

"Yes," he said.

"And if they were able to converse with one another, would they not suppose that they were naming what was actually before them?"

"Very true."

"And suppose further that the prison had an echo which came from the other side, would they not be sure to fancy when one of the passers-by spoke that the voice which they heard came from the passing shadow?"

"No question," he replied.

"To them," I said, "the truth would be literally nothing but the shadows of the images."

"That is certain."

"And now look again, and see what will naturally follow if the prisoners are released and disabused of their error. At first, when any of them is liberated and compelled suddenly to stand up and turn his neck round and walk and look towards the light, he will suffer sharp pains; the glare will distress him, and he will be unable to see the realities of which in his former state he had seen the shadows; and then conceive someone saying to him that what he saw before was an illusion, but that now, when he is approaching nearer to being and his eye is turned towards more real existence, he has a clearer vision—what will be his reply? And you may further imagine that his instructor is pointing to the objects as they pass and requiring him to name them—will he not be perplexed? Will he not fancy that the shadows which he formerly saw are truer than the objects which are now shown to him?"

"Far truer."

"And if he is compelled to look straight at the light, will he not have a pain in his eyes which will make him turn away to take refuge in the objects of vision which he can see, and which he will conceive to be in reality clearer than the things which are now being shown to him?"[1]

"True," he said.

"And suppose once more, that he is reluctantly dragged up a steep and rugged ascent, and held fast until he is forced into the presence of the sun himself, is he not likely to be pained and irritated? When he approaches the light his eyes will be dazzled, and he will not be able to see anything at all of what are now called realities."

"Not all in a moment," he said.

"He will require to grow accustomed to the sight of the upper world. And first he will see the shadows best, next the reflections of men and other objects in the water, and then the objects themselves; then he will gaze upon the light of the moon and the stars and the spangled heaven; and he will see the sky and the stars by night better than the sun or the light of the sun by day?"

"Certainly."

"Last of all he will be able to see the sun, and not mere reflections of him in the water, but he will see him in his own proper place, and not in another; and he will contemplate him as he is."

"Certainly."

"He will then proceed to argue that this is he who gives the season and the years, and is the guardian of all that is in the visible world, and in a certain way the cause of all things which he and his fellows have been accustomed to behold?"

"Clearly," he said, "he would first see the sun and then reason about him."

"And when he remembered his old habitation, and the wisdom of the den and his fellow prisoners, do you not suppose that he would felicitate himself on the change, and pity them?"

"Certainly, he would."

"And if they were in the habit of conferring honors among themselves on those who were quickest to observe the passing shadows and to remark which of them went before, and which followed after, and which were together; and who were therefore best able to draw conclusions as to the future, do you think that he would care for such honors and glories, or envy the possessors of them? Would he not say with Homer, 'Better to be the poor servant of a poor master,' and to endure anything, rather than think as they do and live after their manner?"

"Yes," he said, "I think that he would rather suffer anything than entertain these false notions and live in this miserable manner."

"Imagine once more," I said, "such a one coming suddenly out of the sun to be replaced in his old situation;[2] would he not be certain to have his eyes full of darkness?"

"To be sure," he said.

"And if there were a contest, and he had to compete in measuring the shadows with the prisoners who had never moved out of the den, while his sight was still weak, and before his eyes had become steady (and the time which would be needed to acquire this new habit of sight might be very considerable), would he not be ridiculous? Men would say of him that up he went and down he came without his eyes; and that it was better not even to think of ascending; and if any one tried to loose another and lead him up to the light, let them only catch the offender, and they would put him to death."

"No question," he said.

"This entire allegory," I said, "you may now append, dear Glaucon, to the previous argument; the prison house is the world of sight, the light of the fire is the sun, and you will not misapprehend me if you interpret the journey upwards to be the ascent of the soul into the intellectual world according to my poor belief, which, at your desire, I have expressed—whether rightly or wrongly, God knows. But, whether true or false, my opinion is that in the world of knowledge the idea of good appears last of all, and is seen only with an effort; and, when seen, is also inferred to be the universal author of all things beautiful and right, parent of light and of the lord of light in this visible world, and the immediate source of reason and truth in the intellectual; and that this is the power upon which he who would act rationally either in public or private life must have his eye fixed."

"I agree," he said, "as far as I am able to understand you."

"Moreover," I said, "you must not wonder that those who attain to this beatific vision are unwilling

---

[1]He will think the shadows to which he is accustomed more real than the puppets behind him that caused them. The puppets in turn he will find easier to look at than the living creatures in the world of sunlight outside, of which the puppets were but copies.

[2]Or "such a one going down again and taking his old position."

to descend to human affairs; for their souls are ever hastening into the upper world where they desire to dwell; which desire of theirs is very natural, if our allegory may be trusted."

"Yes, very natural."

"And is there anything surprising in one who passes from divine contemplations to the evil state of man, misbehaving himself in a ridiculous manner; if, while his eyes are blinking and before he has become accustomed to the surrounding darkness, he is compelled to fight in courts of law, or in other places, about the images or the shadows of images of justice, and is endeavoring to meet the conceptions of those who have never yet seen absolute justice?"

"Anything but surprising," he replied.

"Anyone who has common sense will remember that the bewilderments of the eyes are of two kinds, and arise from two causes, either from coming out of the light or from going into the light, which is true of the mind's eye, quite as much as of the bodily eye; and he who remembers this when he sees anyone whose vision is perplexed and weak, will not be too ready to laugh; he will first ask whether that soul of man has come out of the brighter life, and is unable to see because unaccustomed to the dark, or having turned from darkness to the day is dazzled by excess of light. And he will count the one happy in his condition and state of being, and he will pity the other; or, if he have a mind to laugh at the soul which comes from below into the light, there will be more reason in this than in the laugh which greets him who returns from above out of the light into the den."

"That," he said, "is a very just distinction."

"But then, if I am right, certain professors of education must be wrong when they say that they can put a knowledge into the soul which was not there before, like sight into blind eyes."

"They undoubtedly say this," he replied.

"Whereas our argument shows that the power and capacity of learning exists in the soul already; and that just as the eye was unable to turn from darkness to light without the whole body, so too the instrument of knowledge can only by the movement of the whole soul be turned from the world of becoming into that of being, and learn by degrees to endure the sight of being, and of the brightest and best of being, or in other words, of the good."

QUESTIONS

1. If the artificial objects carried along the wall designate objects that we perceive in our experience with the world, what, then, do the shadows signify?

2. Why does Plato stress the difficulty that the prisoners have in looking at the light of the sun?

3. Why do prisoners receive their returning colleague as they do? What does this tell us of the position of the philosopher in society?

4. In what ways does this allegory attack contemporary Greek education?

The Death of Socrates

Translation by Benjamin Jowett

The *Phaedo* depicts Socrates' last hours. Having been tried and found guilty for corrupting the youth of Athens, he has been sentenced to die by drinking a cup of poison. As the appointed time for the execution approaches, he spends his last hours in prison philosophizing with his friends Cebes, Simmias, and Crito, proving to the satisfaction of all that the soul is immortal.

"Tell me, then, what is that of which the inherence will render the body alive?"[1]

"The soul," he replied.

"And is this always the case?"

"Yes," he said, "of course."

"Then whatever the soul possesses, to that she comes bearing life?"

"Yes, certainly."

"And is there any opposite to life?"

"There is," he said.

"And what is that?"

"Death."

"Then the soul, as has been acknowledged, will never receive the opposite of what she brings."

"Impossible," replied Cebes.

"And now," he said, "what did we just now call that principle which repels the even?"

"The odd."

"And that principle which repels the musical or the just?"

"The unmusical," he said, "and the unjust."

"And what do we call that principle which does not admit of death?"

---

[1] Or, "what is that which by its presence in the body makes it alive?"

"The immortal," he said.

"And does the soul admit of death?"

"No."

"Then the soul is immortal?"

"Yes," he said.

"And may we say that this has been proven?"

"Yes, abundantly proven, Socrates," he replied.

"Supposing that the odd were imperishable, must not three be imperishable?"

"Of course."

"And if that which is cold were imperishable, when the warm principle came attacking the snow, must not the snow have retired whole and unmelted—for it could never have perished, nor could it have remained and admitted the heat?"

"True," he said.

"Again, if the uncooling or warm principle were imperishable, the fire when assailed by cold would not have perished or have been extinguished, but would have gone away unaffected?"

"Certainly," he said.

"And the same may be said of the immortal: if the immortal is also imperishable, then the soul will be imperishable as well as immortal; but if not, some other proof of her imperishableness will have to be given."

"No other proof is needed," he said; "for if the immortal, being eternal, is liable to perish, then nothing is imperishable."

"Yes," replied Socrates, "and yet all men will agree that God, and the essential form of life, and the immortal in general, will never perish."

"Yes, all men," he said; "that is true; and what is more, gods, if I am not mistaken, as well as men."

"Seeing then that the immortal is indestructible, must not the soul, if she is immortal, be also imperishable?"

"Most certainly."

"Then when death attacks a man, the mortal portion of him may be supposed to die, but the immortal retires at the approach of death and is preserved safe and sound?"

"True."

"Then, Cebes, beyond question, the soul is immortal and imperishable, and our souls will truly exist in another world!"

"I am convinced, Socrates," said Cebes, "and have nothing more to object; but if my friend Simmias, or anyone else, has any further objection to make, he had better speak out, and not keep silence, since I do not know to what other season he can defer the discussion, if there is anything which he wants to say or to have said."

"But I have nothing more to say," replied Simmias; "nor can I see any reason for doubt after what has been said. But I still feel and cannot help feeling uncertain in my own mind, when I think of the greatness of the subject and the feebleness of man."

"Yes, Simmias," replied Socrates, "that is well said: and I may add that first principles, even if they appear certain, should be carefully considered; and when they are satisfactorily ascertained, then, with a sort of hesitating confidence in human reason, you may, I think, follow the course of the argument; and if that be plain and clear, there will be no need for any further inquiry."

"Very true."

"But then, O my friends," he said, "if the soul is really immortal, what care should be taken of her, not only in respect of the portion of time which is called life, but of eternity! And the danger of neglecting her from this point of view does indeed appear to be awful. If death had only been the end of all, the wicked would have had a good bargain in dying, for they would have been happily quit not only of their body, but of their own evil together with their souls. But now, inasmuch as the soul is manifestly immortal, there is no release or salvation from evil except the attainment of the highest virtue and wisdom. For the soul, when on her progress to the world below, takes nothing with her but nurture and education; and these are said greatly to benefit or greatly to injure the departed, at the very beginning of his journey thither....

"Wherefore, Simmias, seeing all these things, what ought not we to do that we may obtain virtue and wisdom in this life? Fair is the prize, and the hope great!

"A man of sense ought not to say, nor will I be very confident, that the description which I have given of the soul and her mansions is exactly true. But I do say that, inasmuch as the soul is shown to be immortal, he may venture to think, not improperly or unworthily, that something of the kind is true. The venture is a glorious one, and he ought to comfort himself with words like these, which is the reason why I lengthen out the tale. Wherefore, I say, let a man be of good cheer about his soul, who having cast away the pleasures and ornaments of the body as alien to him and working harm rather than good, has sought after the pleasures of knowledge; and has arrayed the soul, not in some foreign attire, but in her own proper jewels, temperance, and justice, and courage, and nobility, and truth—in these adorned she is ready to go on her journey to the world below, when her hour comes. You, Simmias and Cebes, and all other men will depart at some time or other. Me already, as a tragic poet would say, the voice of fate calls. Soon I must drink the poison; and I think that I had better repair to the bath first, in order that the women may not have the trouble of washing my body after I am dead."

When he had done speaking, Crito said: "And have you any commands for us, Socrates—anything to say about your children, or any other matter in which we can serve you?"

"Nothing particular, Crito," he replied; "only, as I have always told you, take care of yourselves; that is a service which you may be ever rendering to me and mine and to all of us, whether you promise to do so or not. But if you have no thought for yourselves, and care not to walk according to the rule which I have pre-scribed for you, not now for the first time, however much you may profess or promise at the moment, it will be of no avail."

"We will do our best," said Crito: "And in what way shall we bury you?"

"In any way that you like; but you must get hold of me, and take care that I do not run away from you."

Then he turned to us, and added with a smile: "I cannot make Crito believe that I am the same Socrates who has been talking and conducting the argument; he fancies that I am the other Socrates whom he will soon see, a dead body—and he asks, How shall he bury me? And though I have spoken many words in the endeavor to show that when I have drunk the poison I shall leave you and go to the joys of the blessed—these words of mine, with which I was comforting you and myself, have had, as I perceive, no effect upon Crito. And therefore I want you to be surety for me to him now, as at the trial he was surety to the judges for me: but let the promise be of another sort; for he was surety for me to the judges that I would remain, and you must be my surety to him that I shall not remain, but go away and depart; and then he will suffer less at my death, and not be grieved when he sees my body being burned or buried. I would not have him sorrow at my hard lot, or say at the burial, Thus we lay out Socrates, or, Thus we follow him to the grave or bury him; for false words are not only evil in themselves, but they infect the soul with evil. Be of good cheer then, my dear Crito, and say that you are burying my body only, and do with that whatever is usual, and what you think best."

When he had spoken these words, he arose and went into a chamber to bathe; Crito followed him and told us to wait. So we remained behind, talking and thinking of the subject of discourse, and also of the greatness of our sorrow; he was like a father of whom we were being bereaved, and we were about to pass the rest of our lives as orphans. When he had taken the bath his children were brought to him (he had two young sons and an elder one); and the women of his family also came, and he talked to them and gave them a few directions in the presence of Crito; then he dismissed them and returned to us.

Now the hour of sunset was near, for a good deal of time had passed while he was within. When he came out, he sat down with us again after his bath, but not much was said. Soon the jailer, who was the servant of the Eleven, entered and stood by him, saying: "To you, Socrates, whom I know to be the noblest and gentlest and best of all who ever came to this place, I will not impute the angry feelings of other men, who rage and swear at me, when, in obedience to the authorities, I bid them drink the poison—indeed, I am sure that you will not be angry with me; for others, as you are aware, and not I, are to blame. And so fare you well, and try to bear lightly what must needs be—you know my errand." Then bursting into tears he turned away and went out.

Socrates looked at him and said: "I return your good wishes, and will do as you bid." Then turning to us, he said, "How charming the man is: since I have been in prison he has always been coming to see me, and at times he would talk to me, and was as good to me as could be, and now see how generously he sor-rows on my account. We must do as he says, Crito; and therefore let the cup be brought, if the poison is pre-pared: if not, let the attendant prepare some."

"Yet," said Crito, "the sun is still upon the hill-tops, and I know that many a one has taken the draught late, and after the announcement has been made to him, he has eaten and drunk, and enjoyed the society of his beloved; do not hurry—there is time enough."

Socrates said: "Yes, Crito, and they of whom you speak are right in so acting, for they think that they will be gainers by the delay; but I am right in not following their example, for I do not think that I should gain anything by drinking the poison a little later; I should only be ridiculous in my own eyes for sparing and saving a life which is already forfeit. Please then to do as I say, and not to refuse me."

Crito made a sign to the servant, who was stand-ing by; and he went out, and having been absent for some time, returned with the jailer carrying the cup of poison. Socrates said: "You, my good friend, who are experienced in these matters, shall give me directions how I am to proceed."

The man answered: "You have only to walk about until your legs are heavy, and then to lie down, and the poison will act."

At the same time he handed the cup to Socrates, who in the easiest and gentlest manner, without the least fear or change of colour or feature, looking at the man with all his eyes, Echecrates, as his manner was, took the cup and said: "What do you say about making a libation out of this cup to any god? May I, or not?"

The man answered: "We only prepare, Socrates, just so much as we deem enough."

"I understand," he said, "but I may and must ask the gods to prosper my journey from this to the other world—even so—and so be it according to my prayer." Then raising the cup to his lips, quite readily and cheerfully he drank off the poison. And hitherto most of us had been able to control our sorrow; but now when we saw him drinking, and saw too that he had finished the draught, we could no longer forbear, and in spite of myself my own tears were flowing fast; so that I covered my face and wept, not for him, but at the thought of my own calamity in having to part from such a friend. Nor was I the first; for Crito, when he found himself unable to restrain his tears, had got up, and I followed; and at that moment, Apollodorus, who had been weeping all the time, broke out in a loud and passionate cry which made cowards of us all.

Socrates alone retained his calmness: "What is this strange outcry?" he said. "I sent away the women mainly in order that they might not misbehave in this way, for I have been told that a man should die in peace. Be quiet then, and have patience." When we heard his words we were ashamed, and refrained our tears; and he walked about until, as he said, his legs began to fail, and then he lay on his back, according to the directions, and the man who gave him the poison now and then looked at his feet and legs; and after a while he pressed his foot hard, and asked him if he could feel; and he said, "No"; and then his leg, and so upwards and upwards, and showed us that he was cold and stiff. And he felt them himself, and said: "When the poison reaches the heart, that will be the end." He was beginning to grow cold about the groin, when he uncovered his face, for he had covered himself up, and said—they were his last words—he said: "Crito, I owe a cock to Asclepius;[2] will you remember to pay the debt?"

"The debt shall be paid," said Crito; "is there anything else?" There was no answer to this question; but in a minute or two a movement was heard, and the attendants uncovered him; his eyes were set, and Crito closed his eyes and mouth.

Such was the end, Echecrates, of our friend; concerning whom I may truly say, that of all the men of his time whom I have known, he was the wisest and justest and best.

COMMENTS AND QUESTIONS

1. What is Socrates' proof for the immortality of the soul? On what premises is it based?
2. The death of Socrates has served for twenty-five hundred years as the humanistic example of how a person should die. Is it a relevant example for our age?
3. What moral values does Socrates uphold?

ARISTOTLE

FROM THE *Politics*

Translation by Benjamin Jowett

In the *Politics,* Aristotle describes the state as a self-sufficient community based on a union of villages, each one more or less composed of a large family. If the family is a natural institution, so, for Aristotle, is the state, because it is the culminating organization toward which political life tends. Only at the state level can the human community be self-sufficient and individuals live a truly virtuous life. Put another way, the state is prior to the family, not because it actually existed before the family, but because the desire to form a state is innate in humans and constitutes the driving force in political organization. Fathers rule over their families as kings rule over their subjects. Women and slaves are subordinate. Moreover, the passage reflects the low opinion the Hellenic Greeks had of the "barbarians"—that is, male and female non-Greeks—whom they considered to be slaves by nature and unworthy of freedom. Although the passage does not say so explicitly, it prepares the way for Aristotle's assertion that, while the government of the family or village is royal, that of the state ought to be republican. Ideally, male family heads participate in a constitutional government and alternate between ruling and obeying.

He who thus considers things in their first growth and origin, whether a state or anything else, will obtain the clearest view of them. In the first place there must be a union of those who cannot exist without each other; namely, of male and female, that the race may continue (and this is a union which is formed, not of deliberate purpose, but because, in common with other animals and with plants, mankind have a natural

---

[2]The god of medicine and healing. Sick people sacrificed roosters to him to be cured. Socrates apparently means that death cures the sickness of life.

desire to leave behind them an image of themselves), and of natural ruler and subject, that both may be preserved. For that which can foresee by the exercise of mind is by nature intended to be lord and master, and that which can with its body give effect to such foresight is a subject, and by nature a slave; hence master and slave have the same interest. Now nature has distinguished between the female and the slave. For she is not niggardly, like the smith who fashions the Delphian knife for many uses; she makes each thing for a single use, and every instrument is best made when intended for one and not for many uses. But among barbarians no distinction is made between women and slaves, because there is no natural ruler among them: they are a community of slaves, male and female. Wherefore the poets say—

> It is meet that Hellenes should rule over barbarians;

as if they thought that the barbarian and the slave were by nature one.

Out of these two relationships between man and woman, master and slave, the first thing to arise is the family, and Hesiod is right when he says—

> First house and wife and an ox for the plough,

for the ox is the poor man's slave. The family is the association established by nature for the supply of men's everyday wants, and the members of it are called by Charondas "companions of the cupboard," and by Epimenides the Cretan, "companions of the manger." But when several families are united, and the association aims at something more than the supply of daily needs, the first society to be formed is the village. And the most natural form of the village appears to be that of a colony from the family, composed of the children and grandchildren, who are said to be "suckled with the same milk." And this is the reason why Hellenic states were originally governed by kings; because the Hellenes were under royal rule before they came together, as the barbarians still are. Every family is ruled by the eldest, and therefore in the colonies of the family the kingly form of government prevailed because they were of the same blood. As Homer says:

> Each one gives law to his children and to his wives.

For they lived dispersedly, as was the manner in ancient times. Wherefore men say that the Gods have a king, because they themselves either are or were in ancient times under the rule of a king. For they imagine, not only the forms of the Gods, but their ways of life to be like their own....

Now, that man is more of a political animal than bees or any other gregarious animals is evident.

Nature, as we often say, makes nothing in vain, and man is the only animal whom she has endowed with the gift of speech. And whereas mere voice is but an indication of pleasure or pain, and is therefore found in other animals (for their nature attains to the perception of pleasure and pain and the intimation of them to one another, and no further), the power of speech is intended to set forth the expedient and inexpedient, and therefore likewise the just and the unjust. And it is a characteristic of man that he alone has any sense of good and evil, of just and unjust, and the like, and the association of living beings who have this sense makes a family and a state.

Further, the state is by nature clearly prior to the family and to the individual, since the whole is of necessity prior to the part; for example, if the whole body be destroyed, there will be no foot or hand, except in an equivocal sense, as we might speak of a stone hand; for when destroyed the hand will be no better than that. But things are defined by their working and power; and we ought not to say that they are the same when they no longer have their proper quality, but only that they have the same name. The proof that the state is a creation of nature and prior to the individual is that the individual, when isolated, is not self-sufficing; and therefore he is like a part in relation to the whole. But he who is unable to live in society, or who has no need because he is sufficient for himself, must be either a beast or a god: he is no part of a state. A social instinct is implanted in all men by nature, and yet he who first founded the state was the greatest of benefactors. For man, when perfected, is the best of animals, but, when separated from law and justice, he is the worst of all; since armed injustice is the more dangerous, and he is equipped at birth with arms, meant to be used by intelligence and virtue, which he may use for the worst ends. Wherefore, if he have not virtue, he is the most unholy and the most savage of animals, and the most full of lust and gluttony. But justice is the bond of men in states for the administration of justice, which is the determination of what is just, is the principle of order in political society.

QUESTIONS

1. What, for Aristotle, makes certain men the masters of women and other men?

2. According to Aristotle, for what purpose did nature create woman?

3. What does Aristotle mean when he speaks of the state as the "final cause" of political life?

4. Why does Aristotle think that man within the state is the best of all animals and outside the state the worst?

The High-Minded Man

Translation by F. H. Peters

Aristotle's discussion of high-mindedness presents the philosopher's ideal of the happy man in some detail. Virtue for Aristotle was fundamentally a mean between two extremes. Self-esteem was a mean between arrogance and humility. Generosity held the middle place between spendthriftiness and stinginess. The other virtues are similarly defined. Obviously again the classical ideal of balance, "nothing too much," is at work in Aristotle's ethics. The high-minded person must most of all cultivate the virtue of prudence: the ability to measure each situation and to determine the correct course of action. He must be able to establish the correct middle course for appropriate action. The resultant picture of the gentleman is very different from that of the later Christian ideal. We are clearly dealing with a male member of the upper classes, affluent, confident, calculating, and disdainful of members of the lower classes, who have no hope of matching his standards of conduct. This selection is from the *Nicomachean Ethics.*

High-mindedness would seem from its very name to have to do with great things; let us first ascertain what these are.

It will make no difference whether we consider the quality itself, or the man who exhibits the quality.

By a high-minded man we seem to mean one who claims much and deserves much: for he who claims much without deserving it is a fool; but the possessor of a virtue is never foolish or silly. The man we have described, then, is high-minded.

He who deserves little and claims little is temperate [or modest], but not high-minded: for high-mindedness [or greatness of soul] implies greatness, just as beauty implies stature; small men may be neat and well proportioned, but cannot be called beautiful.

He who claims much without deserving it is vain (though not every one who claims more than he deserves is vain).

He who claims less than he deserves is little-minded, whether his deserts be great or moderate, or

whether they be small and he claims still less: but this little-mindedness is most conspicuous in him whose deserts are great; for what would he do if his deserts were less than they are?

The high-minded man, then, in respect of the greatness of his deserts occupies an extreme position, but in that he behaves as he ought, observes the mean; for he claims that which he deserves, while all the others claim too much or too little.

But now if he deserves much and claims much, and most of all deserves and claims the greatest things, there will be one thing with which he will be especially concerned. For desert has reference to external good things. Now, the greatest of external good things we may assume to be that which we render to the Gods as their due, and that which people in high stations most desire, and which is the prize appointed for the noblest deeds. But the thing that answers to this description is honour, which, we may safely say, is the greatest of all external goods. Honours and dishonours, therefore, are the field in which the high-minded man behaves as he ought.

And indeed we may see, without going about to prove it, that honour is what high-minded men are concerned with; for it is honour that great men claim and deserve.

The little-minded man falls short, whether we compare his claims with his own deserts or with what the high-minded man claims for himself.

The vain or conceited man exceeds what is due to himself, though he does not exceed the high-minded man in his claims.

But the high-minded man, as he deserves the greatest things, must be a perfectly good or excellent man; for the better man always deserves the greater things, and the best possible man the greatest possible things. The really high-minded man, therefore, must be a good or excellent man. And indeed greatness in every virtue or excellence would seem to be necessarily implied in being a high-minded or great-souled man.

It would be equally inconsistent with the high-minded man's character to run along swinging his arms, and to commit an act of injustice; for what thing is there for love of which he would do anything unseemly, seeing that all things are of little account to him? . . .

. . . The gifts of fortune also are commonly thought to contribute to high-mindedness. For those who are well born are thought worthy of honour, and those who are powerful or wealthy; for they are in a position of superiority, and that which is superior in any good thing is always held in greater honour. And so these things do make people more high-minded in a sense; for such people find honour from some. But in strictness it is only the good man that is worthy of honour, though he that has both goodness and good fortune is commonly thought to be more worthy of honour. Those, however, who have these good things without virtue, neither have any just claim to great things, nor are properly to be called high-minded, for neither is possible without complete virtue....

The high-minded man is not quick to run into petty dangers, and indeed does not love danger, since there are few things that he much values; but he is ready to incur a great danger, and whenever he does so is unsparing of his life, as a thing that is not worth keeping at all costs.

It is his nature to confer benefits, but he is ashamed to receive them; for the former is the part of a superior, the latter of an inferior. And when he has received a benefit, he is apt to confer a greater in return; for thus his creditor will become his debtor and be in the position of a recipient of his favour.

It is thought, moreover, that such men remember those on whom they have conferred favours better than those from whom they have received them; for the recipient of a benefit is inferior to the benefactor, but such a man wishes to be in the position of a superior. So he likes to be reminded of the one, but dislikes to be reminded of the other....

It is characteristic of the high-minded man, again, never or reluctantly to ask favours, but to be ready to confer them, and to be lofty in his behaviour to those who are high in station and favoured by fortune, but affable to those of the middle ranks; for it is a difficult thing and a dignified thing to assert superiority over the former, but easy to assert it over the latter. A haughty demeanour in dealing with the great is quite consistent with good breeding, but in dealing with those of low estate is brutal, like showing off one's strength upon a cripple.

Another of his characteristics is not to rush in wherever honour is to be won, nor to go where others take the lead, but to hold aloof and to shun an enterprise, except when great honour is to be gained, or a great work to be done—not to do many things, but great things and notable.

Again, he must be open in his hate and in his love; for concealment shows fear.

He must care for truth more than for what men will think of him, and speak and act openly; he will not hesitate to say all that he thinks, as he looks down upon mankind. So he will speak the truth, except when he speaks ironically; and irony he will employ in speaking to the generality of men.

Another of his characteristics is that he cannot fashion his life to suit another, except he be a friend, for that is servile: and so all flatterers or hangers on of great men are of a slavish nature, and men of low natures become flatterers.

Nor is he easily moved to admiration; for nothing is great to him.

He readily forgets injuries; for it is not consistent with his character to brood on the past, especially on past injuries, but rather to overlook them.

He is no gossip; he will neither talk about himself nor about others; for he cares not that men should praise him, nor that others should be blamed (though, on the other hand, he is not very ready to bestow praise); and so he is not apt to speak evil of others, not even of his enemies, except with the express purpose of giving offence.

When an event happens that cannot be helped or is of slight importance, he is the last man in the world to cry out or to beg for help; for that is the conduct of a man who thinks these events very important.

He loves to possess beautiful things that bring no profit, rather than useful things that pay; for this is characteristic of the man whose resources are in himself.

Further, the character of the high-minded man seems to require that his gait should be slow, his voice deep, his speech measured; for a man is not likely to be in a hurry when there are few things in which he is deeply interested, nor excited when he holds nothing to be of very great importance: and these are the causes of a high voice and rapid movements.

This, then, is the character of the high-minded man.

But he that is deficient in this quality is called little-minded; he that exceeds, vain or conceited.

QUESTIONS

1. Would you like to have this man for a friend?
2. How would a Christian criticize this ideal?
3. What information about Greek social structure does this passage give us?

FROM THE *Poetics*

Translation by Benjamin Jowett and Thomas Twining

The selections reprinted here deal primarily with tragedy but also with the comparison of tragic to epic poetry.

From Book Second: Of Tragedy

I. Of the species of poetry which imitates in hexameters, and of comedy, we shall speak hereafter. Let us now consider Tragedy; collecting first, from what has been already said, its true and essential definition.

Tragedy, then, is an imitation of some action that is important, entire, and of a proper magnitude—by language, embellished and rendered pleasurable, but by different means in different parts—in the way, not of narration, but of action—effecting through pity and terror the correction and refinement of such passions.

By pleasurable language I mean a language that has the embellishments of rhythm, melody, and metre. And I add, by different means in different parts, because in some parts metre alone is employed, in others, melody. . . .

Again, tragedy being an imitation of an action, and the persons employed in that action being necessarily characterized by their manners and their sentiments, since it is from these that actions themselves derive their character, it follows that there must also be manners and sentiments as the two causes of actions, and, consequently, of the happiness or unhappiness of all men. The imitation of the action is the fable: for by fable I now mean the contexture of incidents, or the plot. By manners, I mean whatever marks the characters of the persons; by sentiments, whatever they say, whether proving anything, or delivering a general sentiment, etc.

Hence all tragedy must necessarily contain six parts, which together constitute its peculiar character or quality: fable, manners, diction, sentiments, decoration, and music. Of these parts, two relate to the means, one to the manner, and three to the object of imitation. And these are all. These specific parts, if we may so call them, have been employed by most poets, and are all to be found in almost every tragedy. . . .

III. But of all these parts the most important is the combination of incidents or the fable. Because tragedy is an imitation, not of men, but of actions—of life, of happiness and unhappiness; for happiness consists in action, and the supreme good itself, the very end of life, is action of a certain kind—not quality. Now the manners of men constitute only their quality or characters; but it is by their actions that they are happy, or the contrary. Tragedy, therefore, does not imitate action for the sake of imitating manners, but in the imitation of action that of manners is of course involved. So that the action and the fable are the end of tragedy; and in everything the end is of principal importance. . . .

Add to this, that those parts of tragedy by means of which it becomes most interesting and affecting are parts of the fable; I mean revolutions and discoveries. . . .

IV. These things being thus adjusted, let us go on to examine in what manner the fable should be constructed; since this is the first and most important part of tragedy.

Now we have defined tragedy to be an imitation of an action that is complete and entire; and that has also a certain magnitude; for a thing may be entire and a whole, and yet not be of any magnitude.

(1) By entire I mean that which has a beginning, a middle, and an end. A beginning is that which does not necessarily suppose anything before it, but which requires something to follow it. An end, on the contrary, is that which supposes something to precede it, either necessarily or probably, but which nothing is required to follow. A middle is that which both supposes something to precede and requires something to follow. The poet, therefore, who would construct his fable properly is not at liberty to begin or end where he pleases, but must conform to these definitions. . . .

In general, we may say that an action is sufficiently extended when it is long enough to admit of a change of fortune, from happy to unhappy, or the reverse, brought about by a succession, necessary or probable, of well-connected incidents. . . .

VII. Of simple fables or actions, the episodic are the worst. I call that an episodic fable, the episodes of which follow each other without any probable or necessary connection; a fault into which bad poets are betrayed by their want of skill, and good poets by the players: for in order to accommodate their pieces to the purposes of rival performers in the dramatic contests, they spin out the action beyond their powers, and are thus frequently forced to break the connection and continuity of its parts.

But tragedy is an imitation, not only of a complete action, but also of an action exciting terror and pity. Now that purpose is best answered by such events as are not only unexpected, but unexpected consequences of each other: for, by this means, they will have more of the wonderful than if they appeared to be the effects of chance; since we find that, among events merely casual, those are the most wonderful and striking which seem to imply design: as when, for instance, the statue of Mitys at Argos killed the very man who had murdered Mitys, by falling down upon him as he was surveying it; events of this kind not having the appearance of accident. It follows, then, that such fables as are formed on these principles must be the best. . . .

IX. A revolution is a change (such as has already been mentioned) into the reverse of what is expected from the circumstances of the action; and that produced, as we have said, by probable or necessary consequence.

Thus, in the *Oedipus,* the messenger, meaning to make Oedipus happy, and to relieve him from the dread he was under with respect to his mother, by making known to him his real birth, produces an effect directly contrary to his intention. . . .

A discovery—as, indeed, the word implies—is a change from unknown to known, happening between those characters whose happiness or unhappiness forms the catastrophe of the drama, and terminating in friendship or enmity.

The best sort of discovery is that which is accompanied by a revolution as in the *Oedipus.* . . .

XI. The order of the subject leads us to consider, in the next place, what the poet should aim at and what avoid in the construction of his fable; and by what means the purpose of tragedy may be best effected.

Now since it is requisite to the perfection of a tragedy that its plot should be of the complicated, not of the simple kind, and that it should imitate such actions as excite terror and pity (this being the peculiar property of the tragic imitation), it follows evidently, in the first place, that the change from prosperity to adversity should not be represented as happening to a virtuous character; for this raises disgust rather than terror or compassion. Neither should the contrary change, from adversity to prosperity, be exhibited in a vicious character: this, of all plans, is the most opposite to the genius of tragedy, having no one property that it ought to have; for it is neither gratifying in a

moral view, nor affecting, nor terrible. Nor, again, should the fall of a very bad man from prosperous to adverse fortune by represented: because, though such a subject may be pleasing from its moral tendency, it will produce neither pity nor terror. For our pity is excited by misfortunes undeservedly suffered, and our terror by some resemblance between the suffered, and our terror by some resemblance between the sufferer and ourselves. Neither of these effects will, therefore, be produced by such an event.

There remains, then, for our choice, the character between these extremes: that of a person neither eminently virtuous or just, nor yet involved in misfortune by deliberate vice or villainy, but by some error of human frailty; and this person should also be someone of high fame and flourishing prosperity. For example, Oedipus, Thyestes, or other illustrious men of such families.

XII. Hence it appears that, to be well constructed, a fable, contrary to the opinion of some, should be single rather than double; that the change of fortune should not be from adverse to prosperous, but the reverse; and that it should be the consequence, not of vice, but of some great frailty, in a character such as has been described, or better rather than worse. . . .

XVIII. Every tragedy consists of two parts—the complication and the development. The complication is often formed by incidents supposed prior to the action, and by a part, also, of those that are within the action; the rest form the development. I call complication all that is between the beginning of the piece and the last part, where the change of fortune commences; development all between the beginning of that change and the conclusion. Thus, in the *Lynceus* of Theodectes, the events antecedent to the action and the seizure of the child constitute the complication; the development is from the accusation of murder to the end.

From Book Third: Of the Epic Poem

II. The epic poem differs from tragedy in the length of its plan and in its metre.

With respect to length a sufficient measure has already been assigned. It should be such as to admit of our comprehending at one view the beginning and the end, and this would be the case if the epic poem were reduced from its ancient length, so as not to exceed that of such a number of tragedies as are performed successively at one hearing. But there is a circumstance in the nature of epic poetry which affords it peculiar latitude in the extension of its plan. It is not in the power of tragedy to imitate several different actions performed at the same time; it can imitate only that one which occupies the stage, and in which the actors are employed. But the epic imitation, being narrative, admits of many such simultaneous incidents, properly related to the subject, which swell the poem to a considerable size.

From Book Fifth: Of the Superiority of Tragic to Epic Poetry

III. Tragedy has the advantage in the following respects: It possesses all that is possessed by the epic; it might even adopt its metre: and to this it makes no inconsiderable addition, in the music and the decoration; by the latter of which the illusion is heightened, and the pleasure arising from the action is rendered more sensible and striking.

It has the advantage of greater clearness and distinctness of impression, as well in reading as in representation.

It has also that of attaining the end of its imitation in a shorter compass: for the effect is more pleasurable when produced by a short and close series of impressions, than when weakened by diffusion through a long extent of time; as the *Oedipus* of Sophocles, for example, would be if it were drawn out to the length of the Iliad.

Further: there is less unity in all epic imitation, as appears from this—that any epic poem will furnish matter for several tragedies. For, supposing the poet to choose a fable strictly one, the consequence must be

either that his poem, if proportionably contracted, will appear curtailed and defective, or, if extended to the usual length, will become weak and, as it were, diluted. If, on the other hand, we suppose him to employ several fables—that is, a fable composed of several actions—his imitation is no longer strictly one. The Iliad, for example, and the Odyssey contain many such subordinate parts, each of which has a certain magnitude and unity of its own; yet is the construction of those poems as perfect, and as nearly approaching to the imitation of a single action, as possible.

COMMENTS AND QUESTIONS

1. What does Aristotle consider to be the most important part of tragedy and why?

2. Note that Aristotle often uses Sophocles' *Oedipus* as his example of the ideal tragedy. Show how the concept "discovery" applies to the tragedy of Oedipus.

3. Aristotle contends that the ideal tragic figure becomes involved in misfortune not by deliberate villainy but "by some error of human frailty." Does this apply to Oedipus in your opinion? Why or why not? What other views of the tragic hero, besides those of Aristotle, are possible?

4. In Aristotle's view, what differentiates the epic from tragedy and why is tragedy superior?

5. How would you apply Aristotle's categories to modern forms (film, novel, television drama, and so on)?

The Culture of Rome

Hellenistic and Roman History and Thought

Hellenistic Empires

Already before the deaths of Plato and Aristotle, their political philosophies, assuming as they did the existence of the independent city-state, were becoming out of date. Athens was conquered by Sparta in 404 B.C., and for about thirty years Sparta controlled the leadership of the Greek city-state system. Sparta, however, was neither intellectually suited nor powerful enough to carry such a burden, and in 371 B.C. the Spartans were defeated by the Thebans, who in turn became the leading military force in Greece. But the Greek city-states were so isolated and divided by rivalries that they fell easy prey to the armies of Philip II of Macedon, a kingdom in the northern part of the Aegean peninsula. By 338 B.C. almost all Greece was under Philip's control, and, when he died in 336 B.C., his place was taken by his son Alexander (356–323 B.C.). With Alexander, the West took the offensive against the East. The armies of Macedon and Greece invaded and conquered the Persian empire, and Greek rule was established in the Near East, including all of Mesopotamia, and in Egypt. Educated in the ideas of Greek culture partially instilled in him by Aristotle, who acted as his tutor for a time, Alexander diffused the civilization and language of Greece wherever his armies went (see map).

In the process, Greek culture became more cosmopolitan and sophisticated while remaining essentially Greek. Because of this modification in the character of Greek life, the age beginning with Alexander is referred to as Greeklike, or Hellenistic. The graceful nudity of the *Cnidian Aphrodite* and the dramatic power of the frieze for the Pergamon altar (Figs. 4-15 and 4-18) are examples of the expansion and transformation of Greek art. In philosophy, in contrast to the wide-ranging interest of earlier thinkers, there was a

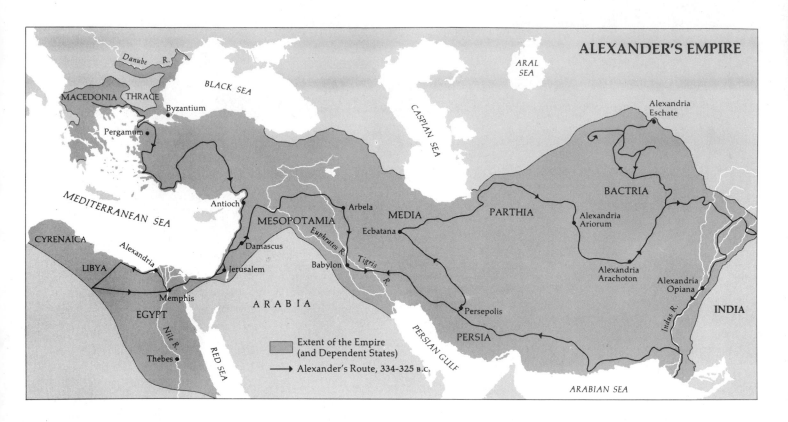

tendency toward specialization. Euclid produced his masterful geometrical treatise, *The Elements;* Archimedes did basic work in statistics and hydrostatics; great advances were also made in biology, astronomy, geography, and city planning.

The expansion of the frontiers of Greek culture, moreover, had a dissolving effect on the political and cultural shell around the individual created by the polis. Individuals came increasingly to live on their own. They found themselves in a larger, more international community than the one they had known. The sharp distinction drawn by Hellenic culture between the Greek, free by nature, and the barbarian, by nature a slave, broke down. However, freedom from the encompassing pressures of the integrated life of the polis made people uneasy. Eastern religions extending hope of personal immortality became popular. These beliefs often centered on a suffering god, who through his earthly death extended to his worshipers the hope of everlasting life. People in the Hellenistic empire also turned to philosophies focusing on the ethical conduct of the individual and providing a vision of political association more adapted to a period of world empire. These philosophies themselves gradually became more religious in nature.

Stoicism

Among the variety of new philosophical movements rising at the end of the fourth century, the one with the greatest future was Stoicism. First taught by Zeno (322–264 B.C.) at Athens, the Stoic doctrine maintained that the principle of the world was reason. Reason was a divine essence that lay behind everything occurring in the universe and was the ultimate cause of all that happened. This rational principle was the Stoic God. The human being was a rational creature whose soul, moreover, was a particle of that divine reason. Thus all people were equal, one to the other, because each, whether slave or free, man or woman, was a particle of the same divine substance. Divine reason operated according to certain laws. If individuals carefully examined their consciences, they would see in themselves, as particles of divine reason, the same laws. Every individual, moreover, if he or she submitted himself or herself to an honest examination, would produce the same conclusions: that it was wrong to kill, to steal, to hurt another human being. Thus for the Stoic, at the basis of every human mind lay the same principle of ethical action, a natural law, which was common to world reason and the individual reason of humans. What better kind of philosophy was there for a world state?

What of human happiness? Since the cause of the world was pure reason, everything had to happen for the best. Divine reason was not a cold indifferent force but rather a providential goodness that aimed for the good of the whole. Human beings must learn to accept this external world as it is. The individual should not regret failures and lose control in times of success. Rather, the individual must welcome everything calmly. To do so was to put oneself in accord with world reason and to follow one's own nature, which was essentially reason. Furthermore, because the principle of divine reason was beneficent, so the individual, truly following his or her own nature, would also be a force for good in the world and especially for other human beings. This doctrine gave a strong social direction to followers of the school.

The early doctrine of the Stoics pictured the ethical ideal as apathy, indifference to all that was not concerned with virtue. The wise person was to do his or her duty regardless of the personal costs. Other "goods" of the soul, health and wealth (which for Aristotle were necessary for happiness), were irrelevant for the Stoic. Nor did the Stoic expect eternal reward. At death the individual human soul of good and evil people alike would fall back into the reservoir of divine reason whence it came. With the centuries, however, Stoicism became less harsh, more reconciled to human weaknesses. By the first century B.C., adherents of the school rejected the ideal of apathy as inhuman and admitted that, if not "goods," health and wealth were nonetheless useful for happiness. Increasingly, Stoics also came to believe in some kind of personal immortality of the human soul even though it was difficult to reconcile that belief with the general structure of their thought.

The Rise of Rome

The great Macedonian empire of Alexander was unstable. When, after his death in 323, it was divided among his generals, disintegration set in. Throughout most of the third century B.C. a power vacuum existed in the Mediterranean area. By the beginning of the second century B.C., Rome gradually came to fill it. Founded sometime in the eighth century B.C. (the mythical date is 753 B.C.), Rome developed slowly. Only after five hundred years—after numerous wars and a series of annexation and treaty agreements—did Rome finally become mistress of Italy, around 260 B.C.

But from there Roman frontiers expanded quickly. The Romans first expanded toward the south and west to Sicily and Spain, bringing themselves into conflict with Carthage, the great maritime power on the northern coast of Africa. They then moved toward the east, where by the mid-second century they had destroyed the kingdom of Macedon and annexed Greece as the province of Achaia. By 100 B.C., Rome was for all practical purposes mistress of the Mediterranean.

In the following century and a half the major interest of the state was to push back the frontiers from the coasts of the inland sea. On the east Rome expanded into Arabia, the Levant, and Persian territory; on the south into the deserts of North Africa and Egypt; on the north into southern Germany and southern Russia; while Roman legions from Gaul invaded and conquered England. At the height of its empire in the century after Christ, Rome controlled most of western Europe, the Middle East, and North Africa. To the north stretched the German forests, to the east the decaying Persian empire, to the south the deserts of Africa, and to the west Ireland and the ocean (see map).

Italy, like Greece, had an area where political power was divided among numerous little city-states. Rome had been only one of a number in central Italy; and, as the city expanded its authority, Rome merely absorbed one city-state after another. In its subsequent expansion outside of Italy, Rome followed very much the same policy of preserving the city-states as the local center of government; where no such organization existed, Rome created the city-state afresh. By the first century B.C. the Roman Empire consisted of a grouping of dependent city-states into provinces, the governors of which were officials sent out from the city council (called the Senate) of the supreme city-state, Rome.

The ancient Romans, unlike the Greeks, were not given to speculation and abstract thinking. They were a practical people, religiously tolerant, ferocious fighters, and devoutly patriotic. But they proved themselves very adaptable. If initially the Romans conquered Greece, they in their turn were conquered by Greek culture. Especially attractive to the Romans, now moving to a position of ruling a good portion of the world, was the philosophy of Stoicism, with its stern insistence on duty. The Stoic conception of humanity as a particle of divine reason, moreover, provided the Romans with just the sort of theoretical background for a legal system designed to integrate the disparate territories of the world state.

Roman Law

The Roman world, consisting of myriads of city-states, big and little kingdoms, was a legal nightmare. Each of these areas had its own law code, and the task of the conqueror was to develop some kind of legal system that would provide justice for the whole. From at least the first century B.C. on, Roman jurists began transforming the Stoic conception of a natural law present in the consciousness of all into practical forms. This task took centuries, and the final codification of Roman law was not finished until centuries after the Roman Empire in the West had fallen to the barbarians. While allowing each of the city-states to keep its own peculiar set of laws, the Roman state in matters of basic law and procedure forced all parts of its territory from England to Asia to follow the principles of the law of nations, the *jus gentium*, those principles of justice derived by Roman jurists and statesmen from the abstract natural law found in human consciousness. With time, following Rome's example, the individual city-states in other than basic principles of law tended as well to follow the law of Rome.

Cicero (106–43 B.C.)

Perhaps the most eloquent testimony to the faith in the essential equality of all human beings is found in the writings of the great Roman statesman Marcus Tullius Cicero. By Cicero's time, the old Roman Republic, centered on the Roman Senate, was creaking at the joints with aristocratic factions struggling for domination of the world state. The most gifted orator of his day, Cicero used his eloquence to defend the republican institutions from the twin threats of dictatorship and anarchy. He lived to realize that his political work was a failure and, dying, could only hope that the coming monarchy would be benevolent. Despite a busy political career, Cicero found time to translate the terminology and ideas of Greek philosophers into Latin and composed numerous philosophical works of his own. Although skeptical of the validity of vast systems of thought found in many philosophers such as Plato and Aristotle, Cicero was vitally concerned with moral or ethical philosophy. He fervently believed that the eloquence of the orator, joined with moral philosophy, could have a tremendously positive effect on the hearts and minds of human beings. In a series of books primarily devoted to ethics and politics, *On Duties, On the Republic,* and *On the Laws,* he captured the Stoics' cosmopolitan vision of humanity, using their conception of natural law as the background against which to judge the legal institutions and customs of his world. His God was the Stoic divine reason, and humanity, being essentially rational, was a particle of God. God's reason is right reason and right reason applied to the world is God's law. Sharing reason with God, all human beings can know this law and thus distinguish the just from the unjust.

Intimately connected with the theme of justice in this passage is that of the dignity of humanity, who, in possession of consciousness of the law, is akin to the gods. Cicero, like the ancient philosophers before him, looked on the human predicament as essentially one of ignorance. In Cicero's case, humanity was divine but had lowered itself by commitment to the passions. The salvation of the individual lay in becoming aware of one's true nature and of training oneself to conform with the commandments of reason. Thus, as for Plato, Aristotle, and the Stoics, human happiness was within a person's grasp. The task of the philosopher was to educate individuals in the truth; the rest was up to them.

The Questions of Slavery and Women

Despite what might appear as the revolutionary tendencies of these doctrines of the basic equality of people and their common human dignity, neither Cicero nor his Stoic predecessors intended them to be attacks on the institution of slavery in their society. As opposed to Plato and Aristotle—who generally considered the state to be natural to human beings and political life to be the means by which the individual realizes humanity—these later thinkers maintained that the state was a creation brought into being to meet the needs of individuals who were already human beings. By the time of Cicero it was widely believed that humanity had originally existed in a state of nature without formal government. Without property and forced subjection, people had led lives of peace and harmony. At some point when this tranquillity was disrupted by passion, the state was instituted as a means for restoring peace. Both slavery and property were essential ingredients of the new order. Thus, although slavery was not natural, it was a necessary institution designed to fit a corrupted human nature and was consequently legitimate. The only practical corollary of the doctrines of equality and human dignity in regard to the

institution of slavery itself was the admonition to slaveholders to be humane with their chattels and to treat them more as hired workers than as possessions.

Until the late republican period the condition of women in Rome differed very little from that of their Greek counterparts. Under the control of her father or a male relative until marriage, the woman was subject to her husband thereafter. Were her husband to die or divorce her, she passed back under the authority of her own family. Not only did her family choose her husband but, although he had the right to divorce her, she had no such possibility.

By the time of Cicero the status of women had improved considerably. It then became common for women to choose their own husbands, and women as well as men could obtain divorces. In the first century of the Empire women were also granted extensive control over the management of their own property. Although the freedom of women often became the subject of criticism by conservatives loyal to the "old republican values" who blamed it for the high divorce rate—at least among members of the upper classes—the imperial society of the first and second centuries A.D. furnishes many historical examples of deep attachment between husband and wife unmatched by anything comparable in ancient Greece.

From Republic to Empire

Although Stoic beliefs continued to dominate the mentality of the Roman upper class in the centuries immediately after Cicero, the nature of Roman government was significantly altered at the center. The Roman Republic had been founded in 509 B.C. with the expulsion of the kings who had ruled the city-state since its founding in the eighth century B.C. Despite the expansion of Rome from a tiny power to the capital of a world government, the republican government had proved very durable. In the process, the original constitution, which had centered on a Senate composed of members of the upper or patrician class, had been modified to appease the demands of the lower classes, or plebeians, to have a share in political power. By the first century B.C., however, the republican institutions were breaking down under the pressure of groups of men competing for power in the state. Cicero struggled valiantly to preserve the old republican traditions, but in his lifetime he saw a number of individuals emerge briefly as de facto rulers of Rome. Had Julius Caesar (100–44 B.C.) not been assassinated, it seems likely that he eventually would have imposed himself on the state as its official master. As it was, after Caesar was murdered in 44 B.C., Rome had to suffer almost two decades of civil war before his nephew Octavius (whose title was Augustus Caesar) succeeded in establishing his authority.

Augustus Caesar (63 B.C.–A.D. 14)

Although Augustus was designated as *imperator* among other titles, *imperator* merely meant that he was leader of the army. The title *princeps* ("foremost") best describes his place in the state. He was the first citizen of Rome. He had no wish to become a despot and honestly endeavored to restore the old republican institutions, especially the Senate, to a position of power and honor. In his own hands were concentrated the direction of the army and control over most state finance. He also directly appointed governors to a number of provinces. On the other hand, all public business was debated by the Senate, the *princeps* frequently consulted the Senate on policy, and the senators ruled over a number of provinces and held high positions in both the army and imperial civil service. Although gradually over the next two hundred years the *princeps* assumed more power at the expense of the Senate, he usually tried to maintain at least the trappings of the republican institutions.

With the establishment of the Principate, the empire remained, as before, organized around hundreds of cities with the territory attached to them; it stayed so to the end of the imperial period, but now for the first time there was a truly unified authority at the center. In the last century of the Republic the Roman senators sent out as governors of the provinces had often treated their charges as a means for self-enrichment. With Augustus and his successors the provincials felt that there was an overseer in the capital to whom they could appeal for justice. Although a number of the emperors, such as Caligula and Nero, were probably madmen, on the whole the provinces saw their general condition improve with the Principate. The Roman world, moreover, was tired of years of civil war and longed for peace. With Augustus' assumption of power as *princeps* began a two-hundred-year period of peace, the *Pax Romana,* which Gibbon, the eighteenth-century author of *The Decline and Fall of the Roman Empire,* characterized as "perhaps the happiest period in the history of the human race."

Roman Art and Architecture

The practical, orderly aspects of Roman life are reflected in Roman art and architecture. Although they adopted Greek forms and techniques, the Romans used their statues and buildings not primarily in pursuit of ideal beauty but to proclaim the Roman system to the world.

Roman Sculpture

A bronze from the first century B.C., called the *Arringatore* (*The Orator*) presents a man who may have been a Roman official (Fig. 7-1). He stands before us as he might have stood in the forum any day of the week. His stance is simple and straightforward, as is the rendering of his features; here is a particular person, a physiognomy that could belong to no one but himself. He is not an ideal politician of any sort.

The realism that we see in *The Orator* is also evident in the many surviving portrait busts and heads. The Egyptians created many wonderful portraits as a means to portray the person for his or her afterlife. The Greeks did not accept the idea of portrait busts or heads, feeling that these detached objects were too reminiscent of a decapitated body. The Romans, like the Egyptians, took portrait masks of the deceased; but unlike the Egyptians, who made these visages part of the ritual of the tomb, the Romans preserved the masks at home and brought them out for ceremonies. The patrician families sought to preserve their identity from generation to generation in this way.

By the time of Augustus the Romans had absorbed much from the Greek artists. Nevertheless, it is the combination of realism and the imperial ideal that makes distinctive portraits.

We know Augustus Caesar from statues, coins, and gems. As emperor he was priest-king, military leader, and ruler. It was important that he be represented in all the facets of his power not only to secure it for himself but also to make it legitimate. The statue of Augustus found at the imperial villa of Prima Porta is an excellent example of the military type of portrait (Fig. 7-2). Dressed in very decorative armor but without boots (therefore probably made after his death when he had been made a god and did not need boots), he stands alert but at ease, addressing his troops. The features are distinctively those of the emperor, virile and youthful. He has been ennobled and idealized by the absence of age, flaws, or any of the other makings of a fallible human. Compare the statue with *The Spearbearer* and *The Orator.* What has been taken from each, and what has been left behind in this effort to present Augustus, Imperator?

The *Ara Pacis Augustae* (the Altar of the Peace of Augustus), probably begun in 13 B.C., was made to

7-1 Arringatore, *The Orator from Sanguineto, 1st century. Archaeological Museum, Florence. (Alinari/Art Resource, NY)*

7-2 Augustus of Prima Porta, *c. 20 B.C. Vatican Museum, Rome. (Alinari/Art Resource, NY)*

commemorate the peace brought about by the imperial might of Rome (Fig. 7-3). It is useful to compare it with the frieze of the Panathenaic festival (Fig. 4-9). At first sight it recalls the frieze, but there are subtle differences. First, the Greek procession is presented as an institutionalized event without regard to the particular individuals who participate. The *Ara Pacis* commemorates one specific historical moment—the moment when the altar was begun. Second, the figures of the *Ara Pacis* are more closely crowded together, as if they had indeed just gathered, giving them an air of immediacy and realism absent in the formal rhythms of the Parthenon frieze. Concentration is not directed toward the focal event but on the interaction between those who make up the event. This frieze has a false calm that seems comparable to the nobility and wisdom that overlay the ruthless Augustus. It was power and decisiveness that made the Empire.

In the reliefs of *The Spoils from the Temple at Jerusalem* (Fig. 7-4) on the Arch of Titus, we confront an almost reportorial scene of victory. The conquering Romans return to the city with captives and treasure, including the great sacred menorah (seven-branched candelabra) from the temple. The sculpture is carved in low relief, and the space is filled with people and objects. This somewhat crowded quality gives the relief an air of urgency and energy that seems to symbolize the power of Rome. This is not myth or allegory but the direct reality of success. To the Roman mind this record of victory will ensure an immortality of which no divinity is capable. No Athenian of the fifth century would have dared to so memorialize himself.

Roman Architecture

As the Romans learned from the Greeks, so they also learned from other tribes and nations. The Roman system of building probably came from the Etruscans, a powerful tribe that lived in the peninsula until they were conquered by the Romans. It is not clear whether the Etruscans learned arcuated construction from the Mesopotamians or whether they discovered the advantages of building with arches for themselves. Employed by the Romans, the wall, post, lintel, and arch produced a major building system that would be carried across Europe.

As a building system the true arch is a combination of *pier* (post) and a semicircle of material that replaces the *lintel* (Fig. 7-5). The arch itself is made of stones or bricks cut to fit so that they help hold each other in place. Erecting an arch requires a wooden scaffold with an arch-shaped top called a *centering*. This will

7-3 *Imperial Procession from the* Ara Pacis *frieze, Rome. (Alinari/Art Resource, NY)*

support the arch while all the sections are being put into place. When the last top, center stone, the *keystone,* is inserted, the centering can be moved to the next arch. The diagram shows how an arch exerts pressure outward and downward, necessitating pressure at those points to keep it from falling apart.

A series of arches produces a *barrel vault.* The weight of the vault rests equally along the wall. When two barrel vaults intersect at right angles, a *groin vault* results (Fig. 7-5); the weight of the vault then rests on the corner piers instead of along the wall, which can then be opened up for doors and windows. An arch rotated in space 360 degrees produces a *dome.* Like a barrel vault, a dome's weight rests equally on the wall, which is its circumference.

To this potentially very rich collection of forms the Romans added a much cheaper, faster means of building—brick and rubble masonry fill. To make this, a sticky liquid mass is poured into a form in which small rocks, gravel, and stones are introduced to give greater density and strength. When dried, the surface is covered with plaster or a thin layer of marble or granite called a *veneer.*

The types of building that assumed great importance in Rome are not the same as those that were important for fifth-century Athens. When we think of Athens, we see the great Acropolian complex of sacred buildings towering over the city. The Roman city seems more of a piece, less divided between sacred and secular. The Romans were among the first to develop city planning on an extensive basis, and their methods of planning are in themselves a significant guide to their values.

If we had a Roman town or city perfectly planned and preserved, we would see first that the city itself was a rectangle, bounded by walls and traversed by major streets at right angles to each other (Fig. 7-6). These major streets were oriented to the cardinal points of the compass and traversed by other streets, also at exact right angles: this formed a grid pattern of city blocks, which were assigned different functions for living, markets, and areas of entertainment. The town would be reached by well-laid Roman roads and, if need be, fed water by aqueducts, like the Pont du Gard, still standing outside Nîmes in southern France (Fig. 7-7). At the center would be a *forum.*

7-4 The Spoils from the Temple at Jerusalem, *Arch of Titus, Rome. (Alinari/Art Resource, NY)*

7-5a   *Roman Arch*

7-5b   *Action of Forces in Arch*

7-5c   *Barrel Vault*

7-5d   *Groin Vault*

7-6   *Ideal Roman City, Groundplan*

1 **Forum**
2 **Theater**
3 **Public Baths**
4 **Market**
5 **Temple**
6 **Typical Residential Block**

7-7   *Roman Aqueduct, Pont du Gard at Nîmes, France, 1st century. (T. Lipscomb—Scala/Art Resource, NY)*

7-8   *Maison Carrée, Nîmes, France c. 19 B.C. (Giraudon/Art Resource, NY)*

The forum began as an open space with a rostrum for public speeches; but under Julius, then Augustus Caesar, it became a place for a temple with surrounding walkways. In time it included a law court (*basilica*). The forum was for the reading of proclamations, the promulgation of laws, and the celebration of triumphs and religious rites. It was a visible sign of Roman conquest, law, and administration.

The temple in the forum might have been dedicated to Jupiter or to the emperor. One of the best preserved Roman temples is the late republican Maison Carrée in southern France (Fig. 7-8). It is interesting to compare it with the Parthenon. The Roman temple has columns, a portico, and a gable roof; but what are the major visible differences? The raised basement or podium with its long flight of steps, the absence of a colonnade, the much deeper portico, and the attached half-round columns on its sides and back all contrast with the Parthenon. What does this suggest to you? Look at the plan of the forum illus-

trated above (Fig. 7-6). Where is the temple in the complex? What role does it play in the space? The temple was not the focus of the complex, but a part, among several important buildings, in a system.

In a different section of the perfectly planned imaginary Roman city, we would find the buildings for entertainment—baths, theaters, and an arena. Although not the most perfect surviving example, the Colosseum in Rome is certainly the most famous of the great amphitheaters (Fig. 7-9). Here spectacles and gladiatorial combat took place. A view of the interior of the building shows that the Colosseum is essentially made up of a series of groin vaults and barrel vaults on massive walls that support tiers of seats and provide passageways (Fig. 7-10). But the arches that open to the outside are framed with half-round columns of Greek orders—the Doric, the Ionic, and another, the Corinthian (Fig. 7-11). These have been applied to the piers between the arches for articulation and decoration. No longer supporting a lintel, the columns are used to emphasize the scale and height of the exterior. It is appropriate that the most massive, the Doric, is on the bottom, while at the topmost tier we find a thin, flattened column, a *pilaster*, with a rich flat capital. This use of the column is radically different from that employed by the Greeks. The Colosseum is not sacred at all, but a setting for human sports.

7-9   Colosseum, Rome. (Alinari/Art Resource, NY)

7-11   Exterior Arches, Colosseum, Rome. (Alinari/Art Resource, NY)

7-10   Colosseum Interior. (Alinari/Art Resource, NY)

7-12   *Front view of Pantheon, Rome.*

The Romans, in short, transformed whatever seemed adequate to fulfill their needs. Another example is the Pantheon, a temple to all the planetary deities, dedicated in Rome about A.D. 118–125 (Fig. 7-12). The plan (Fig. 7-13) shows us a great round, domed space contained within massive walls. Attached to the front is a deep portico that looks like one end of a Greek temple. The combination of circular and rectangular forms is among the first such combinations—a solution to give a sense of direction and ennobled entry to a round and therefore nondirectional space.

The Pantheon also presents us with the first important interior architectural space (Fig. 7-14). The dome rises above the floor, and the only light spills in through the oculus, a round eye in the ceiling. This great hollow space creates a very different experience from the outdoor sanctuary of the Greeks or the Roman forum. It recalls the dome of heaven, the overarching sky; it seems to float or be suspended rather than to depend on the usual weight and support of the post and lintel system of building. The vital soaring quality of this majestic space and its accompanying technology will be influential for many centuries.

The creation of great interiors joins with the Greek forms to make a rich supply of ideas. The basilica, another element of the forum, was also a majestic interior space, with long interior colonnades. Half-domes rose above the curved ends where judges sat to dispense the law (Fig. 7-15). This vision of earthly power and administration of justice could be allied with the sacred architecture of Greece to form a complex series of symbols and ideas.

7-13   *Pantheon, Rome. Groundplan and Section.*

7-14   *Giovanni Paolo Panini,* The Interior of the Pantheon, *c. 1740, oil on canvas, 50½″ × 39″. (Samuel H. Kress Collection, Copyright 1992. National Gallery of Art, Washington, D.C.)*

7-15   Basilica of Maxentius, Rome, with Groundplan. (Photo: Alinari/Art Resource, NY)

Roman Literature

As in other aspects of their culture, the Romans looked to Greek models for their literature. Greek literature began before the Greeks as a people had any political importance; with Rome it was the opposite. The Romans had been too busy organizing, building, and conquering to write; they began to do so only when, in the third century B.C., they dominated Greece and discovered Greek literature. The first real example of a literary work in Latin is a translation of Homer's *Odyssey*. Toward the end of the third century Plautus put some Greek "new comedies" into Latin, but his bawdy plays, such as *The Braggart Soldier*, have something distinctively Roman about them. The plays of Terence (195–159 B.C.), who was a slave of African origins, are more subdued and more subtle in their humor, closer to the Greek ideal of new comedy. At the time of Terence, more and more Roman men of letters were seriously studying Greek literature.

Roman oratory and rhetoric, of which Cicero's work is an example, arose during the first century B.C. This was also the time of the great philosophical poet Lucretius, who explained the philosophy of Epicureanism (a philosophy opposed to Stoicism) in a long poem entitled *De rerum natura* (*On the Nature of Things*). Catullus, a poet who admired and imitated Sappho, gave the Latin language a new lyric power.

Virgil (70–19 B.C.) and the Aeneid

Rome's greatest poet was undoubtedly Virgil, whose Latin name is Publius Vergilius Maro. During Virgil's lifetime Julius Caesar was murdered and Augustus Caesar became the first of Rome's emperors. The years of Augustus' reign (27 B.C.–A.D. 14), known as the Augustan Age, were viewed both by contemporaries and by later generations as Rome's golden years, comparable to Periclean Athens. These years indeed saw not only tremendous political and administrative achievements but also the finest Roman accomplishments in literature, as in other aspects of art and life. In the early years of this new era, Virgil wrote the great epic of Rome, the *Aeneid*, named for its hero, Aeneas.

Highly conscious of living at a period of time when his native city was mistress of most of the known world and her glory was at its height, Virgil set out to write an epic poem in praise of Rome. Some even believe that Augustus might have commissioned him to write it. For an epic, there was only one model to which he could turn—Homer. Although Virgil's poem resembles both the *Iliad* and the *Odyssey* in that it is about a hero in battle and the wanderings of a hero

and uses many similar literary devices, it differs in two basic ways. First, it is a literary, *written* work instead of an oral, *composed* one. Meant to be read instead of heard, it inaugurates the tradition of the written epic in Western literature. Second, Virgil's hero, Aeneas, is much less of an individual than is either Achilles or Odysseus. Homer's heroes represented the values of their culture in their own particular manner, but Virgil's hero seems to embody the values of his culture. Unlike Achilles or Odysseus, Aeneas is always sacrificing personal honor, glory, and happiness to something greater—and the "something greater" that seems to rule over the entire epic is the destiny of Rome.

As in the case of the *Iliad*, the first lines of the *Aeneid* tell us a great deal about the poem as a whole. Here is the opening sentence in the original Latin:

> Arma, virumque cano, Troiae qui primus ab oris
> Italiam, fato profugus, Lavinaque venit
> litora—

Here are the first seven lines put into twelve lines of English (Latin is a more concise language) by a modern translator, Allen Mandelbaum:

> I sing of arms and of a man: his fate
> had made him fugitive; he was the first
> to journey from the coasts of Troy as far
> as Italy and the Lavinian shores.
> Across the lands and waters he was battered
> beneath the violence of High Ones, for
> the savage Juno's unforgetting anger;
> and many sufferings were his in war—
> until he brought a city into being
> and carried in his gods to Latium;
> from this have come the Latin race, the lords
> of Alba, and the ramparts of high Rome.

The outline of the story of Aeneas and Aeneas' place as an instrument of Roman destiny is presented in these opening lines. First Virgil gives his subject, "*arms*" and "*a man*," as Homer's subject was "the anger of Achilles." The *Aeneid* is about both war and the struggles of Aeneas. Aeneas was predestined by Fate, a concept that looms larger than the gods, to come from Troy to Italy. According to legend he was a Trojan who, after the Trojan War, escaped from his defeated city, piously carrying his old father on his shoulders. After long years of various hardships and delays, he at last arrived in Italy. There he married Lavinia, the daughter of King Latinus, thus uniting the Trojan people with the native Latin people to found the Roman race. Aeneas' enemy in his wanderings and struggles is Juno, queen of the gods and rival of Aeneas' mother, Venus. His protector is the king of the gods, Jupiter, who, allied with Fate, is assured victory in the end. Every act of Aeneas will be determined by the destiny marked out for him. He is not a mere puppet of Jupiter; but, since he is conscious that he has a greater will to accomplish, he struggles against the traps laid for him by Juno and sacrifices personal happiness and comfort to the greater good. Virgil's prologue goes beyond the scope of the *Aeneid* itself, which ends with a duel between Aeneas and one of his Italian opponents. Aeneas founds the city of Lavinium with his bride *after* the close of the epic. Thirty years later his son establishes a new city, Alba Longa. Some three hundred years after that, Romulus and Remus, princes of Alba, found Rome, which will ultimately rule over not only all of Italy but most of the known world. This perspective puts Aeneas in his proper place. He is not a mere individual; he is an instrument of the great destiny of Rome.

Like Odysseus, Aeneas travels to the underworld to learn of his destiny. He returns from there inspired with love for the future greatness of his people. He is now more Roman than Trojan, and the rest of the epic is devoted to his feats in arms necessary to the founding of Rome.

The cultural values asserted in this epic are clearly Roman. The Romans were on the whole a practical people, conscious that their real genius was not in the cult of individualism or in art for its own sake, but in the art of administrating and ruling. They did not see their imperialism in moralistic terms, as did European imperialists in Africa and Asia in the nineteenth century, who believed that destiny had sent them to "civilize" heathens. The Romans knew that the cultures they ruled in Greece, the Near East, and North Africa were in most cases more highly developed than their own. But they knew, too, that they gave the world an unparalleled peace and a system of law that could not have been obtained without their particular kind of imperialism. Europeans often compare Americans to ancient Romans because of the practical, administrative genius of both. The United States has even been accused of trying to establish a *pax americana*.

Ovid (43 B.C.–A.D. 17/18)

Although he highly esteemed Virgil, Virgil's younger contemporary Ovid (Publius Ovidius Naso) realized that his own poetic talents were not fitted for the stately epic but rather for the celebration of amorous fantasy and sensual pleasure. His youthful *Art of Love*, a cynical poetic treatise on seduction, immediately established him as one of the leading poets of Augustan Rome. His association with this immoral poem together with a rumor of his involvement in the lascivious behavior of Augustus' granddaughter, Julia,

helps to explain his banishment from Rome in A.D. 8. Ovid's exile by the emperor to the distant shores of the Black Sea was a living death for the pleasure-loving poet of the capital. Despite his dispatch home of an unending flood of poetry lamenting his wretchedness, he remained under banishment until his death.

Finished in rough draft before his departure from Rome, Ovid's great poem the *Metamorphoses* was completed in the first years of his exile. Essentially a narrative of twelve thousand lines in Latin hexameter divided into fifteen books, the poem recounts two hundred legends and myths arranged chronologically. Although some of these stories were well known at the time, Ovid saved for future generations dozens of others almost forgotten in his own generation. Indeed, the *Metamorphoses* constitutes our major single source for such material.

As the title suggests, Ovid chose for his organizational theme the changes of state commonly experienced by divine and human actors in these ancient stories. Two examples are the transformation of Zeus into the bull that carried off the maiden Europa and of Daphne, who became a tree to ward off the lusty embrace of Apollo. Ovid's keen eye for natural beauty and his power to bring to life the fantastic world of gods, demigods, and heroes has made the *Metamorphoses* one of the most delightful writings produced by the ancient world.

Horace (65–8 B.C.)

Another great poet of the Augustan Age was Horace (Quintus Horatius Flaccus). Horace was the son of an uneducated freedman (a former slave) who saw to it that his son received the best schooling that Rome could provide. Horace was in his early years an ardent republican but became just as ardent a supporter of the emperor. He is, in fact, often called Augustus' "poet laureate" because his later poems celebrate the emperor's policies and ideals. Interested in literary criticism and theory, among other things, Horace formulated the basic tenet for Roman poets: poetry must be both *dulce* (pleasing) and *utile* (useful). The poem should combine patriotic, moral, or philosophical messages with sensuous beauty of rhythm and language. This idea that poetry should be useful is certainly more Roman than Greek.

Satire

Horace wrote lyrics (the *Epodes* and *Odes*) as well as the *Epistles*, including *The Art of Poetry*. He also excelled in the uniquely Roman genre of *satire*. Although satire as a mode of human expression had been in existence long before the Romans, the Romans developed it into a literary form, just as the Greeks did for comedy. The nonliterary origins of the mode are related to those of the *komos*. The desire to ridicule, or to expose human vices and follies, seems universal. In certain cultures, the process of ridiculing one's enemy with particularly vicious words was believed to have magical effects. It could actually injure enemies or even cause them to kill themselves and thus be used as a weapon of war. Pre-Islamic Arabs, especially women, used invectives hurled against their enemies as magical, deadly curses. We still use words like *caustic, biting,* and *venomous* to describe words used in satire and ridicule. The magical and ritual origins of satire are evident here if we bear in mind that such descriptions were for many peoples not merely *metaphorical.*

The ancient Greeks also seem to have used satire for magical purposes. At the phallic ceremonies, which we mentioned in connection with old comedy, two ritual purposes were involved. One ceremony was intended to ensure fertility of land and people through the power of the phallus; the other was to expel evil spirits and influence through abuse. Out of the latter practice grew a tradition of composing *iambs,* short invective verses directed against a particular person. The practice of this kind of satire certainly influenced old comedy. Aristophanes held many important public figures, including Socrates and Euripides, up to devastating ridicule. In *Lysistrata* the invectives that the choruses of old men and old women hurl against each other are in the same satirical tradition.

No word for satire as such existed until the Romans gave it one: *satura,* which means both "full" and "a mixture of different things." In comparison to more refined and subtle forms of literature, satire is down-to-earth, hearty, and full of all kinds of things, like a good stew. For example, the satires of Horace contain lyrical poetry, philosophical arguments, folk tales, descriptions of everyday life, slapstick comedy, and obscene jokes. It is not surprising that this literary type should have developed among a people whose tastes were more practical and realistic than contemplative and abstract. Although the Roman writers of satire no longer believed in its magical effects, they believed that the function of satire to expose the vices and follies of individuals and society could be greatly therapeutic.

Roman verse satire is, then, a particular literary form. Satires were written in hexameters, the six-foot Latin line, and are of two types. One, represented by Horace, is mild, humorous, and fundamentally optimistic. Horace claimed that the actions of some of his contemporaries impelled him to satirize—"fools rush into my head, and so I write"—but that his purpose was to enable the "fools" to reform by exposing their foolishness rather than to punish them. The second type is best represented by the later Roman writer Juvenal (died c. A.D. 130), who lived in a period when Roman society was more corrupt. Juvenal's satire is truly biting: it exposes and castigates. Satirists like Juvenal seem to believe that evil is inherent in human nature and in the structure of society. It can be identified but not easily cured. These two types of satire—we might call them simply optimistic and pessimistic—can be found throughout the history of literature, in stage and media entertainment, and in ordinary conversation.

READING SELECTIONS

CICERO

FROM *On the Laws*

Translation by Clinton Walker Keyes

The selection from *On the Laws* concerns the nature of justice. Cicero (M, for Marcus) is the major speaker of the dialogue. His friend Atticus (A) is the other. Against the argument that the law is a matter of convenience and custom, Cicero maintains that it is rooted in the consciences of all peoples.

M.... That animal which we call man, endowed with foresight and quick intelligence, complex, keen, possessing memory, full of reason and prudence, has been given a certain distinguished status by the supreme God who created him; for he is the only one among so many different kinds and varieties of living beings who has a share in reason and thought, while all the rest are deprived of it. But what is more divine, I will not say in man only, but in all heaven and earth, than reason? And reason, when it is full grown and perfected, is rightly called wisdom. Therefore, since there is nothing better than reason, and since it exists both in man and God, the first common possession of man and God is reason. But those who have reason in common must also have right reason in common. And since right reason is Law, we must believe that men have Law also in common with the gods. Further, those who share Law must also share Justice; and those who share these are to be regarded as members of the same commonwealth. If indeed they obey the same authorities and powers, this is true in a far greater degree; but as a matter of fact they do obey this celestial system, the divine mind, and the God of transcendent power. Hence we must now conceive of this whole universe as one commonwealth of which both gods and men are members.

And just as in States distinctions in legal status are made on account of the blood relationships of families, according to a system which I shall take up in its proper place, so in the universe the same thing holds true, but on a scale much vaster and more splendid, so that men are grouped with Gods on the basis of blood relationship and descent. For when the nature of man is examined, the theory is usually advanced (and in all probability it is correct) that through constant changes and revolutions in the heavens, a time came which was suitable for sowing the seed of the human race. And when this seed was scattered and sown over the earth, it was granted the divine gift of the soul. For while the other elements of which man consists were derived from what is mortal, and are therefore fragile and perishable, the soul was generated in us by God. Hence we are justified in saying that there is a blood relationship between ourselves and the celestial beings; or we may call it a common ancestry or origin. Therefore among all the varieties of living beings, there is no creature except man which has any knowledge of God, and among men themselves there is no race either so highly civilized or so savage as not to know that it must believe in a god, even if it does not know in what sort of god it ought to believe. Thus it is clear that man recognizes God because, in a way, he remembers and recognizes the source from which he sprang.

Moreover, virtue exists in man and God alike, but in no other creature besides; virtue, however, is nothing else than Nature perfected and developed to its highest point; therefore there is a likeness between man and God. As this is true, what relationship could be closer or clearer than this one? For this reason, Nature has lavishly yielded such a wealth of things adapted to man's convenience and use that what she produces seems intended as a gift to us, and not brought forth by chance; and this is true, not only of what the fertile earth bountifully bestows in the form of grain and fruit, but also of the animals; for it is clear that some of them have been created to be man's slaves, some to supply him with their products, and others to serve as his food. Moreover innumerable arts have been discovered through the teachings of Nature; for it is by a skilful imitation of her that reason has acquired the necessities of life. Nature has likewise not only equipped man himself with nimbleness of thought, but has also given him the senses, to be, as it were, his attendants and messengers; she has laid bare the obscure and none too [obvious] meanings of a great many things, to serve as the foundations of knowledge, as we may call them; and she has granted us a bodily form which is convenient and well suited to the human mind. For while she has bent the other creatures down toward their food, she has made man alone erect, and has challenged him to look up toward heaven, as being, so to speak, akin to him, and his first home. In addition, she has so formed his features as to portray therein the character that lies hidden deep within him; for not only do the eyes declare with exceeding clearness the innermost feelings of our hearts, but also the countenance, as we Romans call it, which can be found in no living thing save man, reveals the character. (The Greeks are familiar with the meaning which this word "countenance" conveys, though they have no name for it.) I will pass over the special faculties and aptitudes of the other parts of the body, such as the varying tones of the voice and the power of speech, which is the most effective promoter of human intercourse; for all these things are not in keeping with our present discussion or the time at our disposal; and besides, this topic has been adequately treated, as it seems to me, by Scipio in the books which you have read. But, whereas God has begotten and equipped man, desiring him to be the chief of all created things, it should now be evident, without going into all the details, that Nature, alone and unaided, goes a step farther; for, with no guide to point the way, she starts with those things whose character she has learned through the rudimentary beginnings of intelligence, and, alone and unaided, strengthens and perfects the faculty of reason.

A. Ye immortal gods, how far back you go to find the origins of Justice! And you discourse so eloquently that I not only have no desire to hasten on to the consideration of the civil law, concerning which I was expecting you to speak, but I should have no objection to your spending even the entire day on your present topic; for the matters which you have taken up, no doubt, merely as preparatory to another subject, are of greater import than the subject itself to which they form an introduction.

M. The points which are now being briefly touched upon are certainly important; but out of all the material of the philosophers' discussions, surely there comes nothing more valuable than the full realization that we are born for Justice, and that right is based, not upon men's opinions, but upon Nature. This fact will immediately be plain if you once get a clear conception of man's fellowship and union with his fellow-men. For no single thing is so like another, so exactly its counterpart, as all of us are to one another. Nay, if bad habits and false beliefs did not twist the weaker minds and turn them in whatever direction they are inclined, no one would be so like his own self as all men would be like all others. And so, however we may define man, a single definition will apply to all. This is a sufficient proof that there is no difference in kind between man and man; for if there were, one definition could not be applicable to all men; and indeed reason, which alone raises us above the level of the beasts and enables us to draw inferences, to prove and disprove, to discuss and solve problems, and to come to conclusions, is certainly common to us all, and, though varying in what it learns, at least in the capacity to learn it is invariable. For the same things are invariably perceived by the senses, and those things which stimulate the senses, stimulate them in the same way in all men; and those rudimentary beginnings of intelligence to which I have referred, which are imprinted on our minds, are imprinted on all minds alike; and speech, the mind's interpreter, though differing in the choice of words, agrees in the sentiments expressed. In fact, there is no human being of any race who, if he finds a guide, cannot attain to virtue.

The similarity of the human race is clearly marked in its evil tendencies as well as in its goodness. For pleasure also attracts all men; and even though it is an enticement to vice, yet it has some likeness to what is naturally good. For it delights us by its lightness and agreeableness; and for this reason, by an error of thought, it is embraced as something wholesome. It is through a similar misconception that we shun death as though it were a dissolution of nature, and cling to life because it keeps us in the sphere in which we were born; and that we look upon pain as one of the greatest of evils, not only because of its cruelty, but also because it seems to lead to the destruction of nature. In the same way, on account of the similarity between moral worth and renown, those who are publicly honoured are considered happy, while those who do not attain fame are thought miserable. Troubles, joys, desires, and fears haunt the minds of all men without distinction, and even if different men have different beliefs, that does not prove, for example, that it is not the same quality of superstition that besets those races which worship dogs and cats as gods, as that which torments other races. But what nation does not love courtesy, kindliness, gratitude, and remembrance of favours bestowed? What people does not hate and despise the haughty, the wicked, the cruel, and the ungrateful? Inasmuch as these considerations prove to us that the whole human race is bound together in unity, it follows, finally, that knowledge of the principles of right living is what makes men better.

QUESTIONS

1. What does Cicero mean by Law?
2. What effect would this belief have on one's approach to law and custom?
3. What is the basis of the natural equality of man?

OVID

FROM THE *Metamorphoses*

Translated by Gilbert Highet

The following story of Pygmalion from Book 10 of the *Metamorphoses* served as the plot of Bernard Shaw's play *Pygmalion*, written early in this century. The play in turn served as the plot for *My Fair Lady*, a famous musical comedy of the 1950s.

Pygmalion and Galatea

Pygmalion loathed the vices given by nature
To women's hearts: he lived a lonely life,
Shunning the thought of marriage and a wife.
Meanwhile he carved the snow-white ivory
With happy skill: he gave it beauty greater
Than any woman's: then grew amorous of it.
It was a maiden's figure—and it lived
(You thought) but dared not move for modesty.
So much did art conceal itself. The sculptor
Marvelled, and loved his beautiful pretence.
Often he touched the body, wondering
If it were ivory or flesh—he would not
Affirm it ivory. He gave it kisses,
Thinking they were returned; and he embraced it,
Feeling its body yield beneath his fingers,
Fearing the limbs he pressed would show a bruise.
Sometimes he courted it with flatteries
And charming gifts: shells and rounded stones,
And little birds, and many-colored flowers,
Lilies, and painted balls, and amber tears
Dropped from the trees: he dressed it with fine clothes,
Rings on its fingers, chains about its neck,
Light pearls for earrings, pendants on its bosom.
All made it lovely: it was lovely naked.
He laid the statue on a purple couch,
Calling it partner of his bed, laying its neck
On feather pillows, just as though it felt.

The festival of Venus crowded Cyprus;
And with broad horns gilded to do her honor,
The snowy heifers fell for sacrifice,
And incense fumed her altars. Then Pygmalion
Made sacrifice and prayed, "If the gods can give
Whatever they may wish, grant me a wife"
(not venturing "my ivory girl") "like her."
The golden goddess in her seat of power
Knew what the prayer meant and showed her favor:
Her altar blazed three times, shooting aloft.

When he returned, he went to his ivory image,
Lay on its couch and kissed it. It grew warm.
He kissed again and touched the ivory breast.
The ivory softened, and its carven firmness
Sank where he pressed it, yielded like the wax
Which in the sunlight takes a thousand shapes
From moulding fingers, while use makes it useful.
Pygmalion was aghast and feared his joy,
But like a lover touched his love again.
It was a body, beating pulse and heart.
Now he believed and in an ardent prayer
Gave thanks to Venus: pressed his mouth at last
To a living mouth. The maiden felt his kiss—
She blushed and trembled: when she raised her eyes
She saw her lover and heaven's light together.

COMMENTS AND QUESTIONS

1. Ovid stops his poem at the point where the statue of the maiden becomes alive. What do you imagine the relationship of the sculptor and his model would have been like thereafter?
2. Why is the story set in Cyprus?

Virgil

From the *Aeneid*

Translation by Allen Mandelbaum

For many readers the most interesting part of the
Aeneid is Book 4, in which Aeneas falls in love with
Dido, the queen of Carthage (Rome's great rival
city in North Africa). Aeneas' decision to leave
Dido after he has been with her for some time, and
her consequent suicide, make him a heartless
character for some readers; but Virgil intended to
show in this episode the great personal tragedies
that a public destiny like Aeneas' entails.

Book 4

Too late. The queen is caught between love's pain
and press. She feeds the wound within her veins;
she is eaten by a secret flame. Aeneas'
high name, all he has done, again, again
come like a flood. His face, his words hold fast   5
her breast. Care strips her limbs of calm and rest.

A new dawn lights the earth with Phoebus'° lamp
and banishes damp shadows from the sky
when restless Dido turns to her heart's sharer:
"Anna, my sister, what dreams make me
    shudder?   10
Who is this stranger guest come to our house?
How confident he looks, how strong his chest
and arms! I think—and I have cause—that he
is born of gods. For in the face of fear
the mean must fall. What fates have driven him!   15
What trying wars he lived to tell! Were it not
my sure, immovable decision not
to marry anyone since my first love
turned traitor, when he cheated me by death,
were I not weary of the couch and torch,   20
I might perhaps give way to this one fault.
For I must tell you, Anna, since the time
Sychaeus, my poor husband, died and my
own brother° splashed our household gods with
    blood,
Aeneas is the only man to move   25
my feelings, to overturn my shifting heart.
I know too well the signs of the old flame.
But I should call upon the earth to gape
and close above me, or on the almighty

Father to take his thunderbolt, to hurl   30
me down into the shades, the pallid shadows
and deepest night of Erebus,° before
I'd violate you, Shame, or break your laws!
For he who first had joined me to himself
has carried off my love, and may he keep it   35
and be its guardian within the grave."
She spoke. Her breast became a well of tears.

And Anna answers: "Sister, you more dear
to me than light itself, are you to lose
all of your youth in dreary loneliness,   40
and never know sweet children or the soft
rewards of Venus? Do you think that ashes
or buried Shades will care about such matters?
Until Aeneas came, there was no suitor
who moved your sad heart—not in Libya nor,   45
before, in Tyre: you always scorned Iarbas
and all the other chiefs that Africa,
a region rich in triumphs, had to offer.
How can you struggle now against a love
that is so acceptable? Have you forgotten   50
the land you settled, those who hem you in?
On one side lie the towns of the Gaetulians,
a race invincible, and the unbridled
Numidians and then the barbarous Syrtis.°
And on the other lies a barren country,   55
stripped by the drought and by Barcaean raiders,
raging both far and near. And I need not
remind you of the wars that boil in Tyre°
and of your brother's menaces and plots.
For I am sure it was the work of gods   60
and Juno that has held the Trojan galleys
fast to their course and brought them here to
    Carthage.
If you marry Aeneas, what a city
and what a kingdom, sister, you will see!   65
With Trojan arms beside us, so much greatness
must lie in wait for Punic° glory! Only
pray to the gods for their good will, and having
presented them with proper sacrifices,
be lavish with your Trojan guests and weave
excuses for delay while frenzied winter   70
storms out across the sea and shatters ships,

---

⁷Phoebus: Apollo, god of the sun.
²⁴Pygmalion.

---

³²Erebus: The god of darkness and the realm of the underworld.
⁵⁴The Gaetulians, Numidians, and Syrtians were neighboring
    African people. Iarbas was king of the Gaetylians.
⁵⁸ Tyre: A famous seaport of the Phoenicians, from which Dido fled
    with her supporters to found Carthage, a new city in Africa.
⁶⁷Punic: An equivalent of Phoenician.

while wet Orion° blows his tempest squalls
beneath a sky that is intractable."

These words of Anna fed the fire in Dido.
Hope burned away her doubt, destroyed her
    shame.   75
First they move on from shrine to shrine,
    imploring
the favor of the gods at every altar.
They slaughter chosen sheep, as is the custom,
and offer them to Ceres° the lawgiver,
to Phoebus, Father Bacchus,° and—above all—   80
to Juno,° guardian of marriage. Lovely
Dido holds the cup in her right hand;
she pours the offering herself, midway
between a milk-white heifer's horns. She studies
slit breasts of beasts and reads their throbbing
    guts.   85
But oh the ignorance of augurs! How
can vows and altars help one wild with love?

Meanwhile the supple flame devours her marrow;
within her breast the silent wound lives on.
Unhappy Dido burns. Across the city   90
she wanders in her frenzy—even as
a heedless hind hit by an arrow when
a shepherd drives for game with darts among
the Cretan woods and, unawares, from far
leaves winging steel inside her flesh; she roams   95
the forests and the wooded slopes of Dicte,°
the shaft of death still clinging to her side.
So Dido leads Aeneas around the ramparts,
displays the wealth of Sidon° and the city
ready to hand; she starts to speak, then falters   100
and stops in midspeech. Now day glides away.
Again, insane, she seeks out that same banquet,
again she prays to hear the trials of Troy,
again she hangs upon the teller's lips....

But now the guests are gone. The darkened
    moon,   105
in turn, conceals its light, the setting stars
invite to sleep; inside the vacant hall
she grieves alone and falls upon the couch

that he has left. Absent, she see, she hears
the absent one or draws Ascanius,°   110
his son and counterfeit, into her arms,
as if his shape might cheat her untellable love.

Her towers rise no more; the young of Carthage
no longer exercise at arms or build
their harbors or sure battlements for war;   115
the works are idle, broken off; the massive,
menacing rampart walls, even the crane,
defier of the sky, now lie neglected.

As soon as Jove's° dear wife sees that her Dido
is in the grip of such a scourge and that   120
no honor can withstand this madness, then
the daughter of Saturn° faces Venus:° "How
remarkable indeed: what splendid spoils
you carry off, you and your boy; how grand
and memorable is the glory if   125
one woman is beaten by the guile of two
gods. I have not been blind. I know you fear
our fortresses, you have been suspicious of
the houses of high Carthage. But what end
will come of all this hate? Let us be done   130
with wrangling. Let us make, instead of war,
an everlasting peace and plighted wedding.
You have what you were bent upon: she burns
with love; the frenzy now is in her bones.
Then let us rule this people—you and I—   135
with equal auspices; let Dido serve
a Phrygian° husband, let her give her Tyrians
and her pledged dowry into your right hand."

But Venus read behind the words of Juno
the motive she had hid: to shunt the kingdom   140
of Italy to Libyan° shores. And so
she answered Juno: "Who is mad enough
to shun the terms you offer? Who would prefer
to strive with you in war? If only fortune
favor the course you urge. For I am ruled   145
by fates and am unsure if Jupiter
would have the Trojans and the men of Tyre
become one city, if he like the mingling

72Orion: A constellation of stars related to storms.
79Ceres: Goddess of agriculture.
80Bacchus: God of wine.
81Juno: Queen of the gods and wife of Jupiter.
96Dicte: A mountain in the eastern part of Crete.
99Sidon: Ancient city of Phoenicians and mother-city of Tyre.

110Ascanius: Young son of Aeneas and his dead Trojan wife Creusa.
119Jove: Jupiter.
122Daughter of Saturn: Juno, an enemy of the Trojans.
122Venus: Goddess of love, true mother of Aeneas, and protector of
  the Trojans.
137Troy had been located on the coast of Phrygia.
141Libyan: North African.

of peoples and the writing of such treaties.
But you are his wife and it is right for you   150
to try his mind, to entreat him. Go. I'll follow."

Queen Juno answered her: "That task is mine.
But listen now while in few words I try
to tell you how I mean to bring about
this urgent matter. When tomorrow's Titan°   155
first shows his rays of light, reveals the world,
Aeneas and unhappy Dido plan
to hunt together in the forest. Then
while horsemen hurry to surround the glades
with nets, I shall pour down a black raincloud,   160
in which I have mixed hail, to awaken all
the heavens with my thundering. Their comrades
will scatter under cover of thick night.
Both Dido and the Trojan chief will reach
their shelter in the same cave. I shall be there.   165
And if I can rely on your goodwill,
I shall unite the two in certain marriage
and seal her as Aeneas' very own;
and this shall be their wedding." Cytherea°
said nothing to oppose the plan; she granted   170
what Juno wanted, smiling at its cunning.

Meanwhile Aurora rose; she left the Ocean.
And when her brightness fills the air, select
young men move from the gates with wide-
    meshed nets
and narrow snares and broad-blade hunting
    spears,   175
and then Massylian° horsemen hurry out
with strong, keen-scented hounds. But while the
    chieftains
of Carthage wait at Dido's threshold, she
still lingers in her room. Her splendid stallion,
in gold and purple, prances, proudly champing   180
his foaming bit. At last the queen appears
among the mighty crowd; upon her shoulders
she wears a robe of Sidon with embroidered
borders. Her quiver is of gold, her hair
has knots and ties of gold, a golden clasp   185
holds fast her purple cloak. Her Trojan comrades
and glad Ascanius advance behind her.
Aeneas, who is handsome past all others,
himself approaches now to join her, linking
his hunting band to hers. Just as Apollo,   190

when in the winter he abandons Lycia°
and Xanthus° streams to visit his maternal
Delos,° where he renews the dances—Cretans,
Dryopians, and painted Agathyrsi,°
mingling around the altars, shout—advances   195
upon the mountain ridges of high Cynthus°
and binds his flowing hair with gentle leaves
and braids its strands with intertwining gold;
his arrows clatter on his shoulder: no
less graceful is Aeneas as he goes;   200
an equal beauty fills his splendid face.
And when they reach the hills and pathless thickets,
the wild she-goats, dislodged from stony summits,
run down the ridges; from another slope
stags fling themselves across the open fields;   205
they mass their dusty bands in flight, forsaking
the hillsides. But the boy Ascanius
rides happy in the valleys on his fiery
stallion as he passes on his course
now stags, now goats; among the lazy herds   210
his prayer is for a foaming boar or that
a golden lion come down from the mountain.

Meanwhile confusion takes the sky, tremendous
turmoil, and on its heels, rain mixed with hail.
The scattered train of Tyre, the youth of Troy,   215
and Venus' Dardan° grandson in alarm
seek different shelters through the fields; the
    torrents
roar down the mountains. Dido and the Trojan
chieftain have reached the same cave. Primal
    Earth
and Juno, queen of marriages, together   220
now give the signal: lightning fires flash,
the upper air is witness to their mating,
and from the highest hilltops shout the nymphs.
That day was her first day of death and ruin.
For neither how things seem nor how they are
    deemed   225
moves Dido now, and she no longer thinks
of furtive love. For Dido calls it marriage,
and with this name she covers up her fault.

155Tomorrow's Titan: The sun.
169Cytherea: Another name for Venus.
176Massylian: Refers to a people of Africa.

191Lycia: An area of Asia Minor where Apollo had an oracle.
192Xanthus: A river of Lycia.
193Delos: The island where Apollo was born.
194Cretans, Dryopians, and Agathyrsi are peoples of the Mediterranean basin.
196Cynthus: A mountain on Delos.
216Dardan: Dardanus was founder of the Trojan race.

Then, swiftest of all evils, Rumor runs
straightway through Libya's mighty cities—
  Rumor,   230
whose life is speed, whose going gives her force.
Timid and small at first, she soon lifts up
her body in the air. She stalks the ground;
her head is hidden in the clouds. Provoked
to anger at the gods, her mother Earth   235
gave birth to her, last come—they say—as sister
to Coeus and Enceladus;° fast-footed
and lithe of wing, she is a terrifying
enormous monster with as many feathers
as she has sleepless eyes beneath each feather 240
(amazingly), as many sounding tongues
and mouths, and raises up as many ears.
Between the earth and skies she flies by night,
screeching across the darkness, and she never
closes her eyes in gentle sleep. By day 245
she sits as sentinel on some steep roof
or on high towers, frightening vast cities;
for she holds fast to falsehood and distortion
as often as to messages of truth.
Now she was glad. She filled the ears of all 250
with many tales. She sang of what was done
and what was fiction, chanting that Aeneas
one born of Trojan blood, had come, that lovely
Dido has deigned to join herself to him,
that now, in lust, forgetful of their kingdom, 255
they take long pleasure, fondling through the
  winter,
the slaves of squalid craving. Such reports
the filthy goddess scatters everywhere
upon the lips of men. At once she turns
her course to King Iarbas; and his spirit 260
is hot, his anger rages at her words.

Iarbas was the son of Hammon by
a ravished nymph of Garamantia.°
In his broad realm he had built a hundred
  temples,
a hundred handsome shrines for Jupiter. 265
There he had consecrated sleepless fire,
the everlasting watchman of the gods;
the soil was rich with blood of slaughtered herds,
and varied garlands flowered on the thresholds.
Insane, incited by that bitter rumor, 270
he prayed long—so they say—to Jupiter;

he stood before the altars in the presence
of gods, a suppliant with upraised hands:
"All-able Jove, to whom the Moorish nation,
feasting upon their figured couches, pour 275
Lenaean° sacrifices, do you see
these things? Or, Father, are we only trembling
for nothing when you cast your twisting thunder?
Those fires in the clouds that terrify
our souls—are they but blind and aimless
  lightning   280
that only stirs our empty mutterings?
A woman, wandering within our borders,
paid for the right to build a tiny city.
We gave her shore to till and terms of tenure.
She has refused to marry me, she has taken 285
Aeneas as a lord into her lands.
And now this second Paris, with his crew
of half-men, with his chin and greasy hair
bound up beneath a bonnet of Maeonia,°
enjoys his prey; while we bring offerings 290
to what we have believed to be your temples,
still cherishing your empty reputation."

And as he prayed and clutched the altar stone,
all-able Jupiter heard him and turned
his eyes upon the royal walls, upon 295
the lovers who had forgotten their good name.
He speaks to Mercury, commanding him:
"Be on your way, my son, call up the Zephyrs,
glide on your wings, speak to the Dardan
  chieftain
who lingers now at Tyrian Carthage, paying 300
not one jot of attention to the cities
the Fates have given him. Mercury, carry
across the speeding winds the words I urge:
his lovely mother did not promise such
a son to us; she did not save him twice 305
from Grecian arms for this—but to be master
of Italy, a land that teems with empire
and seethes with war; to father a race from
  Teucer's°
high blood, to place all earth beneath his laws.
But if the brightness of such deeds is not 310
enough to kindle him, if he cannot
attempt the task for his own fame, does he—
a father—grudge Ascanius the walls
of Rome? What is he pondering, what hope

---

²³⁷Angered at the gods for killing her children, the Titans, Earth
 bore the Giants, one of whom was Rumor.

²⁶³King Iarbas had the Egyptian god Hammon for a father and a
 nymph from the interior of Africa for a mother.

²⁷⁶Lenaean: Pertaining to Bacchus, god of wine.

²⁸⁹Maeonia: An area of Asia Minor.

³⁰⁸Teucer: An early king of Troy.

can hold him here among his enemies,   315
not caring for his own Ausonian° sons
or for Lavinian° fields. He must set sail.
And this is all; my message lies in this."

His words were ended. Mercury made ready
to follow his great father's orders. First   320
he laces on his golden sandals: winged
to bear him, swift as whirlwinds, high across
the land and water. Then he takes his wand;
with this he calls pale spirits up from Orcus°
and down to dreary Tartarus° sends others;   325
he uses this to give sleep and recall it,
and to unseal the eyes of those who have died.
His trust in this, he spurs the winds and skims
the troubled clouds. And now in flight, he sights
the summit and high sides of hardy Atlas°   330
who props up heaven with his crest—Atlas,
whose head is crowned with pines and battered by
the wind and rain and always girdled by
black clouds; his shoulders' cloak is falling snow;
above the old man's chin the rivers rush;   335
his bristling beard is stiff with ice. Here first
Cyllene's° god poised on his even wings
and halted; then he hurled himself headlong
and seaward with his body, like a bird
that, over shores and reefs where fishes throng,   340
swoops low along the surface of the waters.
Not unlike this, Cyllene's god between
the earth and heaven as he flies, cleaving
the sandy shore of Libya from the winds
that sweep from Atlas, father of his mother.   345

As soon as his winged feet have touched the
    outskirts,
he sees Aeneas founding fortresses
and fashioning new houses. And his sword
was starred with tawny jasper, and the cloak
that draped his shoulders blazed with Tyrian
    purple—   350
a gift that wealthy Dido wove for him;
she had run golden thread along the web.
And Mercury attacks at once. "Are you

now laying the foundation of high Carthage,
as servant to a woman, building her   355
a splendid city here? Are you forgetful
of what is your own kingdom, your own fate?
The very god of gods, whose power sways
both earth and heaven, sends me down to you
from bright Olympus. He himself has asked me   360
to carry these commands through the swift air:
what are you pondering or hoping for
while squandering your ease in Libyan lands?
For if the brightness of such deeds is not
enough to kindle you—if you cannot   365
attempt the task for your own fame—remember
Ascanius growing up, the hopes you hold
for Iülus,° your own heir, to whom are owed
the realm of Italy and land of Rome."
So did Cyllene's god speak out. He left   370
the sight of mortals even as he spoke
and vanished into the transparent air.

This vision stunned Aeneas, struck him dumb;
his terror held his hair erect; his voice
held fast within his jaws. He burns to flee   375
from Carthage; he would quit these pleasant
    lands,
astonished by such warnings, the command
of gods. What can he do? With what words dare
he face the frenzied queen? What openings
can he employ? His wits are split, they shift   380
here, there; they race to different places, turning
to everything. But as he hesitated,
this seemed the better plan: he calls Sergestus
and Mnestheus and the strong Serestus,° and
he asks them to equip the fleet in silence,   385
to muster their companions on the shore,
to ready all their arms, but to conceal
the reasons for this change; while he himself—
with gracious Dido still aware of nothing
and never dreaming such a love could ever   390
be broken—would try out approaches, seek
the tenderest, most tactful time for speech,
whatever dexterous way might suit his case.
And all are glad. They race to carry out
the orders of Aeneas, his commands.   395

But Dido—for who can deceive a lover?—
had caught his craftiness; she quickly sensed
what was to come; however safe they seemed,

316Ausonian: Pertaining to middle or lower Italy.

317Lavinia: A city in Latium in Middle Italy near the seacoast.

324Orcus: God of the underworld and brother of Jupiter. The
    underworld itself is sometimes called Orcus.

325Tartarus: The infernal regions.

330Atlas: A god who supports heaven on his shoulders.

337Cyllene: A mountain in Greece, birthplace of the winged god
    Mercury.

368Iülus: Another name for Ascanius.

384Sergestus, Mnestheus, and Serestus are Trojans.

she feared all things. That same unholy Rumor
brought her these hectic tidings: that the boats   400
were being armed, made fit for voyaging.
Her mind is helpless; raging frantically,
inflamed, she raves throughout the city—just
as a Bacchante when, each second year,
she is startled by the shaking of the sacred   405
emblems, the orgies urge her on, the cry
"o Bacchus" calls to her by night; Cithaeron°
incites her with its clamor. And at last
Dido attacks Aeneas with these words:

"Deceiver, did you even hope to hide   410
so harsh a crime, to leave this land of mine
without a word? Can nothing hold you back—
neither your love, the hand you pledged, nor even
the cruel death that lies in wait for Dido?
Beneath the winter sky are you preparing   415
a fleet to rush away across the deep
among the north winds, you who have no feeling?
What! Even if you were not seeking out
strange fields and unknown dwellings, even if
your ancient Troy were still erect, would you   420
return to Troy across such stormy seas?
Do you flee me? By tears, by your right hand—
this sorry self is left with nothing else—
by wedding, by the marriage we began,
if I did anything deserving of you   425
or anything of mine was sweet to you,
take pity on a fallen house, put off
your plan, I pray—if there is still place for
    prayers.
Because of you the tribes of Libya, all
the Nomad princes hate me, even my   430
own Tyrians are hostile; and for you
my honor is gone and that good name that once
was mine, my only claim to reach the stars.
My guest, to whom do you consign this dying
woman? I must say 'guest': this name is all   435
I have of one whom once I called my husband.
Then why do I live on? Until Pygmalion,
my brother, batters down my walls, until
Iarbas the Gaetulian takes me prisoner?
Had I at least before you left conceived   440
a son in me; if there were but a tiny
Aeneas playing by me in the hall,
whose face, in spite of everything, might yet

remind me of you, then indeed I should
not seem so totally abandoned, beaten."   445

Her words were ended. But Aeneas, warned
by Jove, held still his eyes; he struggled, pressed
care back within his breast. With halting words
he answers her at last: "I never shall
deny what you deserve, the kindnesses   450
that you could tell; I never shall regret
remembering Elissa° for as long
as I remember my own self, as long
as breath is king over these limbs. I'll speak
brief words that fit the case. I never hoped   455
to hide—do not imagine that—my flight;
I am not furtive. I have never held
the wedding torches as a husband; I
have never entered into such agreements.
If fate had granted me to guide my life   460
by my own auspices and to unravel
my troubles with unhampered will, then I
should cherish first the town of Troy, the sweet
remains of my own people and the tall
rooftops of Priam° would remain, my hand   465
would plant again a second Pergamus°
for my defeated men. But now Grynean°
Apollo's oracles would have me seize
great Italy, the Lycian prophecies
tell me of Italy: there is my love,   470
there is my homeland. If the fortresses
of Carthage and the vision of a city
in Libya can hold you, who are Phoenician,
why, then, begrudge the Trojans' settling on
Ausonian soil? There is no harm: it is   475
right that we, too, seek out a foreign kingdom.
For often as the night conceals the earth
with dew and shadows, often as the stars
ascend, afire, my father's anxious image
approaches me in dreams. Anchises° warns   480
and terrifies; I see the wrong I have done
to one so dear, my boy Ascanius,
whom I am cheating of Hesperia,°
the fields assigned by fate. And now the gods'
own messenger, sent down by Jove himself—   485
I call as witness both our lives—has brought

°407Cithaeron: A mountain in Greece where the rites of Bacchus are
    celebrated.

°452Elissa: Another name for Dido.

°465Priam: Late king of Troy.

°466Pergamus: Troy.

°467Grynean: Pertaining to an oracle of Apollo in Asia Minor.

°480Anchises: Aeneas' dead father.

°483Hesperia: A place of fabled orchards in the west; here it means
    Italy.

his orders through the swift air. My own eyes
have seen the god as he was entering
our walls—in broad daylight. My ears have drunk
his words. No longer set yourself and me   490
afire. Stop your quarrel. It is not
my own free will that leads to Italy."

But all the while Aeneas spoke, she stared
askance at him, her glance ran this way, that.
She scans his body with her silent eyes.   495
Then Dido thus, inflamed, denounces him:

"No goddess was your mother, false Aeneas,
And Dardanus no author of your race;
the bristling Caucasus was father to you
on his harsh crags; Hyrcanian tigresses   500
gave you their teats. And why must I dissemble?
Why hold myself in check? For greater wrongs?
For did Aeneas groan when I was weeping?
Did he once turn his eyes or, overcome,
shed tears or pity me, who was his loved one?   505
What shall I cry out first? And what shall follow?
No longer now does mighty Juno or
our Father, son of Saturn,° watch this earth
with righteous eyes. Nowhere is certain trust.
He was an outcast on the shore, in want.   510
I took him in and madly let him share
my kingdom; his lost fleet and his companions
I saved from death. Oh I am whirled along
in fire by the Furies! First the augur
Apollo, then the Lycian oracles,   515
and now, sent down by Jove himself, the gods'
own herald, carrying his horrid orders.
This seems indeed to be a work for High Ones,
a care that can disturb their calm. I do not
refute your words. I do not keep you back.   520
Go then, before the winds, to Italy.
Seek out your kingdom overseas; indeed,
if there be pious powers still, I hope
that you will drink your torments to the lees
among sea rocks and, drowning, often cry   525
the name of Dido. Then, though absent, I
shall hunt you down with blackened firebrands;
and when chill death divides my soul and body,
a Shade, I shall be present everywhere.
Depraved, you then will pay your penalties.   530
And I shall hear of it, and that report
will come to me below, among the Shadows."

508Saturn was father of both Jupiter and his wife Juno.

Her speech is broken off; heartsick, she shuns
the light of day, deserts his eyes; she turns
away, leaves him in fear and hesitation,   535
Aeneas longing still to say so much.
As Dido faints, her servants lift her up;
they carry her into her marble chamber;
they lay her body down upon the couch.

But though he longs to soften, soothe her
    sorrow   540
and turn aside her troubles with sweet words,
though groaning long and shaken in his mind
because of his great love, nevertheless
pious Aeneas carries out the gods'
instructions. Now he turns back to his fleet.   545

At this the Teucrians indeed fall to.
They launch their tall ships all along the beach;
they set their keels, well-smeared with pitch,
    afloat.
The crewmen, keen for flight, haul from the
    forest
boughs not yet stripped of leaves to serve as
    oars   550
and timbers still untrimmed. And one could see
    them
as, streaming, they rushed down from all the city:
even as ants, remembering the winter,
when they attack a giant stack of spelt
to store it in their homes; the black file swarms 555
across the fields; they haul their plunder through
the grass on narrow tracks; some strain against
the great grains with their shoulders, heaving
    hard;
some keep the columns orderly and chide
the loiterers; the whole trail boils with work.   560

What were your feelings, Dido, then? What were
the sighs you uttered at that sight, when far
and wide, from your high citadel, you saw
the beaches boil and turmoil take the waters,
with such a vast uproar before your eyes?   565
Voracious Love, to what do you not drive
the hearts of men? Again, she must outcry,
again, a suppliant, must plead with him,
must bend her pride to love—and so not die
in vain, and with some way still left untried.   570

"Anna, you see them swarm across the beaches;
from every reach around they rush to sea:
the canvas calls the breezes, and already
the boisterous crewmen crown the sterns with
    garlands.

But I was able to foresee this sorrow;   575
therefore I can endure it, sister; yet
in wretchedness I must ask you for this
one service, Anna. Treacherous Aeneas
has honored you alone, confiding even
his secret feelings unto you; and you   580
alone know all his soft approaches, moods.
My sister, go—to plead with him, to carry
this message to my arrogant enemy.
I never trafficked with the Greeks at Aulis°
to root the Trojans out, I never sent   585
a fleet to Pergamus, never disturbed
his father's ashes or Anchises' Shade,
that now Aeneas should ward off my words
from his hard ears. Where is he hurrying?
If he would only grant his wretched lover   590
this final gift: to wait for easy sailing
and favoring winds. I now no longer ask
for those old ties of marriage he betrayed,
nor that he lose his kingdom, be deprived
of lovely Latium;° I only ask   595
for empty time, a rest and truce for all
this frenzy, until fortune teaches me,
defeated, how to sorrow. I ask this—
pity your sister—as a final kindness.
When he has granted it, I shall repay   600
my debt, and with full interest, by my death."

So Dido pleads, and her poor sister carries
these lamentations, and she brings them back.
For lamentation cannot move Aeneas;
his graciousness toward any plea is gone.   605
Fate is opposed, the god makes deaf the hero's
kind ears. As when, among the Alps, north winds
will strain against each other to root out
with blasts—now on this side, now that—a stout
oak tree whose wood is full of years; the roar   610
is shattering, the trunk is shaken, and
high branches scatter on the ground; but it
still grips the rocks; as steeply as it thrusts
its crown into the upper air, so deep
the roots it reaches down to Tartarus: 615
no less than this, the hero; he is battered
on this side and on that by assiduous words;
he feels care in his mighty chest, and yet
his mind cannot be moved; the tears fall, useless.

Then maddened by the fates, unhappy Dido   620
calls out at last for death; it tires her
to see the curve of heaven. That she may
not weaken in her plan to leave the light,
she sees, while placing offerings on the altars
with burning incense—terrible to tell—   625
the consecrated liquid turning black,
the outpoured wine becoming obscene blood.
But no one learns of this, not even Anna.
And more: inside her palace she had built
a marble temple to her former husband   630
that she held dear and honored wonderfully.
She wreathed that shrine with snow-white fleeces
    and
holy-day leaves. And when the world was seized
by night, she seemed to hear the voice and words
of her dead husband, calling out to Dido.   635
Alone above the housetops, death its song,
an owl often complains and draws its long
slow call into a wailing lamentation.
More, many prophecies of ancient seers
now terrify her with their awful warnings.   640
And in her dreams it is the fierce Aeneas
himself who drives her to insanity;
she always finds herself alone, abandoned,
and wandering without companions on
an endless journey, seeking out her people,   645
her Tyrians in a deserted land:
even as Pentheus,° when he is seized by frenzy,
sees files of Furies, and a double sun
and double Thebes appear to him; or when
Orestes, son of Agamemnon, driven   650
across the stage, flees from his mother armed
with torches and black serpents; on the threshold
the awful goddesses of vengeance squat.

When she had gripped this madness in her mind
and, beaten by her grief, resolved to die,   655
she plotted with herself the means, the moment.
Her face conceals her meaning; on her brow
she sets serenity, then speaks to Anna:
"My sister, wish me well, for I have found
a way that will restore Aeneas to me   660
or free me of my love for him. Near by
the bounds of Ocean and the setting sun
lies Ethiopia, the farthest land;
there Atlas, the incomparable, turns
the heavens, studded with their glowing stars,   665

---

584 Aulis: The town in Greece where the Greek fleet set sail to attack
    Troy.
595 Latium: A town of central Italy noted above.

---

647 Pentheus: A king of the Greek city of Thebes who was driven
    mad, seeing all things double.

upon his shoulders. And I have been shown
a priestess from that land—one of the tribe
of the Massylians°—who guards the shrine
of the Hesperides; for it was she
who fed the dragon and preserved the holy   670
branches upon the tree, sprinkling moist honey
and poppy, bringing sleep. She promises
to free, with chant and spell, the minds of those
she favors but sends anguish into others.
And she can stay the waters in the rivers   675
and turn the stars upon their ways; she moves
the nightly Shades; makes earth quake underfoot
and—you will see—sends ash trees down the
     mountains.
Dear sister, I can call the gods to witness,
and you and your dear life, that I resort   680
to magic arts against my will. In secret
build up a pyre within the inner courtyard
beneath the open air, and lay upon it
the weapons of the hero. He, the traitor,
has left them hanging in my wedding
     chamber.   685
Take all of his apparel and the bridal
bed where I was undone. You must destroy
all relics of the cursed man, for so
would I, and so the priestess has commanded."
This said, she is silent and her face is pale.   690
But Anna cannot dream her sister hides
a funeral behind these novel rites;
her mind is far from thinking of such frenzy;
and she fears nothing worse than happened when
Sychaeus died. And so, she does as told.   695

But when beneath the open sky, inside
the central court, the pyre rises high
and huge, with logs of pine and planks of ilex,
the queen, not ignorant of what is coming,
then wreathes the place with garlands, crowning
     it   700
with greenery of death; and on the couch
above she sets the clothes Aeneas wore,
the sword he left, and then his effigy.
Before the circling altars the enchantress,
her hair disheveled, stands as she invokes   705
aloud three hundred gods, especially
Chaos and Erebus and Hecate,°

the triple-shaped Diana,° three-faced virgin.
And she had also sprinkled waters that
would counterfeit the fountain of Avernus;°   710
she gathered herbs cut down by brazen sickles
beneath the moonlight, juicy with the venom
of black milk; she had also found a love charm
torn from the forehead of a newborn foal
before his mother snatched it. Dido herself—   715
with salt cake in her holy hands, her girdle
unfastened, and one foot free of its sandal,
close by the altars and about to die—
now calls upon the gods and stars, who know
the fates, as witness; then she prays to any   720
power there may be, who is both just and
     watchful,
who cares for those who love without requital.

Night. And across the earth the tired bodies
were tasting tranquil sleep; the woods and savage
waters were resting and the stars had reached   725
the midpoint of their gliding fall—when all
the fields are still, and animals and colored
birds, near and far, that find their home beside
the limpid lakes or haunt the countryside
in bristling thickets, sleep in silent night.   730
But not the sorrowing Phoenician; she
can not submit to sleep, can not admit
dark night into her eyes or breast; her cares
increase; again love rises, surges in her;
she wavers on the giant tide of anger.   735
She will not let things rest but carries on;
she still revolves these thoughts within her heart:
"What can I do? Shall I, whom he has mocked,
go back again to my old suitors, begging,
seeking a wedding with Numidians whom   740
I have already often scorned as bridegrooms?
Or should I sail away on Trojan ships,
to suffer there even their harshest orders?
Shall I do so because the Trojans once
received my help, and gratefulness for such   745
old service is remembered by the mindful?
But even if I wish it, would they welcome
someone so hated to their haughty ships?
For, lost one, do you not yet know, not feel
the treason of the breed of Laomedon?°   750

---

668 Massylians: African people who guard the sacred western
     orchards, here placed in North Africa.
707 Hecate: A goddess of witchcraft and the underworld.

---

708 Diana: Goddess of the chase and the moon, identified with
     Hecate.
710 Avernus: A lake and woods near Cumae, close to which there
     allegedly was an entrance to the underworld.
750 Laomedon: Legendary ancestor of the Trojans and a notorious
     perjurer.

What then? Shall I accompany, alone,
the exultant sailors in their flight? Or call
on all my Tyrians, on all my troops
to rush upon them? How can I urge on
those I once dragged from Sidon, how can I   755
now force them back again upon the sea
and have them spread their canvas to the winds?
No; die as you deserve, and set aside
your sorrow by the sword. My sister, you,
won over by my tears—you were the first   760
to weigh me down with evils in my frenzy,
to drive me toward my enemy. And why
was it not given me to lead a guiltless
life, never knowing marriage, like a wild
beast, never to have touched such toils? I have
    not   765
held fast the faith I swore before the ashes
of my Sychaeus." This was her lament.

Aeneas on the high stern now was set
to leave; he tasted sleep; all things were ready.
And in his sleep a vision of the god   770
returned to him with that same countenance—
resembling Mercury in everything:
his voice and coloring and yellow hair
and all his handsome body, a young man's—
and seemed to bring a warning once again: 775
"You, goddess-born, how can you lie asleep
at such a crisis? Madman, can't you see
the threats around you, can't you hear the breath
of kind west winds? She conjures injuries
and awful crimes, she means to die, she stirs   780
the shifting surge of restless anger. Why
not flee this land headlong, while there is time?
You soon will see the waters churned by
    wreckage,
ferocious torches blaze, and beaches flame,
if morning finds you lingering on this coast.   785
Be on your way. Enough delays. An ever
uncertain and inconstant thing is woman."
This said, he was at one with the black night.

The sudden apparition terrifies
Aeneas. And he tears his body free   790
from sleep. He stirs his crewmen: "Quick!
    Awake!
Now man the benches, comrades, now unfurl
our sails with speed! Down from the upper air
a god was sent to urge us on again,
to rush our flight, to slice our twisted cables.   795
O holy one among the gods, we follow
your way, whoever you may be; again

rejoicing, we shall do as you command.
Be present, help us with your kindness, bring
your gracious constellations to the heavens."   800
He spoke; and from his scabbard snatches up
his glowing sword; with drawn blade, strikes the
    hawsers.
And all are just as eager, hurrying
to leave the shore; the ships conceal the sea.
They strain to churn the foam and sweep blue   805
    waters.
Now early Dawn had left Tithonus'° saffron
bed, scattering new light upon the earth.
As soon as from her lookout on the tower
the queen could see the morning whitening,
the fleet move on with level sails, the shores   810
and harbors now abandoned, without oarsmen,
she beat against her lovely breast three times,
then four, and tore her golden hair, and cried:
"O Jupiter, you let him go, a stranger
who mocked our kingdom! Will my men not
    ready   815
their weapons, hunt him down, pour from my city
and rip the galleys from their moorings? Quick!
Bring torches, spread your sails, and ply your oars!
What am I saying? Where am I? What madness
has turned awry what I had meant to do?   820
Poor Dido, does his foulness touch you now?
It should have then, when you gave him your
    scepter.
This is the right hand, this the pledge of one
who carries with him, so they say, the household
gods of his land, who bore upon his shoulders   825
his father weak with years. And could I not
have dragged his body off, and scattered him
piecemeal upon the waters, limb by limb?
Or butchered all his comrades, even served
Ascanius himself as banquet dish   830
upon his father's table? True enough—
the battle might have ended differently.
That does not matter. For, about to die,
need I fear anyone? I should have carried
my torches to his camp and filled his decks   835
with fire, destroyed the son, the father, that
whole race, and then have thrown myself upon
    them.
You, Sun, who with your flames see all that is
    done
on earth; and Juno, you, interpreter

———
806Tithonus: Husband of Aurora, the dawn.

and witness of my sorrows; Hecate,   840
invoked with shrieks, by night, at every city's
crossways; and you, the Furies; and the gods
that guard dying Elissa—hear these words
and turn your power toward my pain; as I
deserve, take up my prayers. If it must be   845
that he, a traitor, is to touch his harbor,
float to his coasts, and so the fates of Jove
demand and if this end is fixed; yet let
him suffer war and struggles with audacious
nations, and then—when banished from his
    borders   850
and torn from the embrace of Iülus—let him
beg aid and watch his people's shameful
    slaughter.
Not even when he has bent low before
an unjust peace may he enjoy his kingdom,
the light that he has wished for. Let him fall   855
before his time, unburied in the sand.
These things I plead; these final words I pour
out of my blood. Then, Tyrians, hunt down
with hatred all his sons and race to come;
send this as offering unto my ashes.   860
Do not let love or treaty tie our peoples.
May an avenger rise up from my bones,
one who will track with firebrand and sword
the Dardan settlers, now and in the future,
at any time that ways present themselves.   865
I call your shores to war against their shores,
your waves against their waves, arms with their
    arms.
Let them and their sons' sons learn what is war."

This said, she ran her mind to every side,
for she was seeking ways with which to
    slice—   870
as quickly as she can—the hated light;
and then, with these brief words, she turned to
    Barce,
Sychaeus' nurse—for Dido's own was now
black ashes in Phoenicia, her old homeland:
"Dear nurse, call here to me my sister Anna;   875
and tell her to be quick to bathe her body
with river water; see that she brings cattle
and all that is appointed for atonement.
So must my sister come; while you yourself
bind up your temples with a pious fillet.   880
I mean to offer unto Stygian Jove
the sacrifices that, as is ordained,
I have made ready and begun, to put
an end to my disquiet and commit
to flames the pyre of the Trojan chieftain."   885

So Dido spoke. And Barce hurried off;
she moved with an old woman's eagerness.

But Dido, desperate, beside herself
with awful undertakings, eyes bloodshot
and rolling, and her quivering cheeks flecked   890
with stains and pale with coming death, now
    bursts
across the inner courtyards of her palace.
She mounts in madness that high pyre, unsheathes
the Dardan sword, a gift not sought for such
an end. And when she saw the Trojan's clothes   895
and her familiar bed, she checked her thought
and tears a little, lay upon the couch
and spoke her final words: "O relics, dear
while fate and god allowed, receive my spirit
and free me from these cares; for I have lived   900
and journeyed through the course assigned by
    fortune.
And now my Shade will pass, illustrious,
beneath the earth; I have built a handsome city,
have seen my walls rise up, avenged a husband,
won satisfaction from a hostile brother: 905
o fortunate, too fortunate—if only
the ships of Troy had never touched our coasts."
She spoke and pressed her face into the couch.
"I shall die unavenged, but I shall die,"
she says. "Thus, thus, I gladly go below   910
to shadows. May the savage Dardan drink
with his own eyes this fire from the deep
and take with him the omen of my death."

Then Dido's words were done, and her
    companions
can see her fallen on the sword; the blade   915
is foaming with her blood, her hands are
    bloodstained.
Now clamor rises to the high rooftop.
Now rumor riots through the startled city.
The lamentations, keening, shrieks of women
sound through the houses; heavens echo
    mighty   920
wailings, even as if an enemy
were entering the gates, with all of Carthage
or ancient Tyre in ruins, and angry fires
rolling across the homes of men and gods.

And Anna heard. Appalled and breathless, she   925
runs, anxious, through the crowd, her nails
    wounding
her face; her fists, her breasts; she calls the dying
Dido by name: "And was it, then, for this,

my sister? Did you plan this fraud for me?
Was this the meaning waiting for me when   930
the pyre, the flames, the altar were prepared?
What shall I now, deserted, first lament?
You scorned your sister's company in death;
you should have called me to the fate you met;
the same sword pain, the same hour should have
    taken   935
the two of us away. Did my own hands
help build the pyre, and did my own voice call
upon our fathers' gods, only to find
me, heartless, far away when you lay dying?
You have destroyed yourself and me, my
    sister,   940
the people and the elders of your Sidon,
and all your city. Let me bathe your wounds
in water, and if any final breath
still lingers here, may my lips catch it up."
This said, she climbed the high steps, then she
    clasped   945
her half-dead sister to her breast, and moaning,
embraced her, dried the black blood with her
    dress.
Trying to lift her heavy eyes, the queen
falls back again. She breathes; the deep wound in
her chest is loud and hoarse. Three times she
    tried   950
to raise herself and strained, propped on her elbow;
and three times she fell back upon the couch.
Three times with wandering eyes she tried to find
high heaven's light and, when she found it,
    sighed.

But then all-able Juno pitied her   955
long sorrow and hard death and from Olympus°
sent Iris° down to free the struggling spirit
from her entwining limbs. For as she died
a death that was not merited or fated,
but miserable and before her time   960
and spurred by sudden frenzy, Proserpina°
had not yet cut a gold lock from her crown,
not yet assigned her life to Stygian° Orcus.
On saffron wings dew-glittering Iris glides
along the sky, drawing a thousand shifting   965

colors across the facing sun. She halted
above the head of Dido: "So commanded,
I take this lock as offering to Dis;°
I free you from your body." So she speaks
and cuts the lock with her right hand; at
    once   970
the warmth was gone, the life passed to the
    winds.

COMMENTS AND QUESTIONS

1. How does Juno, an enemy of the Trojans, attempt to frustrate their mission to settle in Italy? Why does Venus, protectress of the Trojans, concede so easily to Juno? How are her plans foiled?
2. Is Dido's anger against Aeneas justified?
3. What tricks does Dido use in order to have her funeral pyre prepared?
4. Throughout the Middle Ages, Dido was used as a cautionary example for Christians. Why?
5. What purposes does Virgil's extensive use of *similes* throughout the work serve?

Book 5 of the *Aeneid* recounts the journey of Aeneas from Carthage to Italy and contains an elaborate description of the funeral games for his father, Anchises. At the beginning of Book 6, Aeneas lands at Cumae and visits the Grotto of the Sibyl near the temple of Apollo. He asks the Sibyl to prophesy to him, not scattering her prophecies on leaves, as is her custom, but speaking to him directly. After her prophecy, she commands Aeneas to sacrifice and pray to the gods. She then accompanies him on a trip to the underworld where he sees many shades (including that of Dido) and witnesses both the punishments and the rewards of the afterlife. At last he reaches his father, Anchises, who reveals to him the future glory of Rome, stressing the continuity between past and future of which Aeneas is a pivotal part.

Book 6

...But she has not yet given way to Phoebus:
she rages, savage, in her cavern, tries   110
to drive the great god from her breast. So much
the more, he tires out her raving mouth;

---

956 Olympus: Mountain home of the gods.
957 Iris: Goddess of the rainbow and Juno's messenger.
961 Proserpina: Goddess of the underworld and wife of Pluto. She was supposed to cut a lock of hair from the head of the dying as an offering to the gods of the underworld.
963 Stygian: Pertaining to one of the rivers of Orcus, the underworld.

968 Dis: Pluto, god of the underworld.

he tames her wild heart, shapes by crushing force.
And now the hundred great gates of the house
swing open of their own accord. They bear   115
the answers of the priestess through the air:
"O you who are done, at last, with those great
    dangers
that lie upon the sea—worse wait on land—
the sons of Dardanus° will reach Lavinium's
kingdom (for you can now be sure of this)   120
and yet shall wish that they had never come.
I see wars, horrid wars, the Tiber° foaming
with much blood. You shall have your Simois,
your Xanthus,° and your Doric camp; already
there is in Latium° a new Achilles—   125
he, too, son of a goddess. Nor will Juno
fail anywhere to hound the Teucrians,°
while you, a beggar in your need, implore
the towns, the tribes through all of Italy!
The cause of so much Trojan misery: 130
again, a foreign bride, a foreign wedding.
Do not relent before distress, but be
far bolder than your fortune would permit.
The first path to your safety, though it seem
unlikely, shall yet be a Grecian city."   135

These are the words that from her shrine the Sibyl
of Cumae chants; and these hard oracles
come roaring from her cavern, mingling true
sayings with darkness. So Apollo urges
the reins as she raves on; he plies the spurs   140
beneath her breast. But when her frenzy is done,
her raging lips are hushed, hero Aeneas
begins: "None of the trials you tell of, virgin,
is strange or unexpected: all of these
I have foreseen and journeyed in my thought.   145
One thing I ask: since here is said to be
the gateway of the lower king and here
the marsh of overflowing Acheron,°
may it be granted me to go before
the face and presence of my dearest father?   150
Teach me the way, open the holy doors.
For through the fire, a thousand spears behind us,

I carried him upon these shoulders; from
the press of enemies I drew him on;
he was the comrade of my journeying;   155
with me he suffered all the seas and all
the threats of sky and wave—and these beyond
the power or the portion of old age—
however weak he was. Indeed, he prayed
and charged me to seek out and find your
    threshold.   160
Kind prophetess, I plead, take pity on
one who is both a father and a son;
your power touches all, and not for nothing
has Hecate assigned Avernus'° woods
to your safekeeping. For if Orpheus° could   165
recall the spirit of his wife, relying
upon his Thracian lyre's enchanting strings,
if Pollux° could redeem his brother by
the death he alternates with him, and goes
and comes time after time on this same road...   170
I need not speak of mighty Theseus° or
of Hercules. I, too, stem from high Jove."

And so Aeneas prayed, clasping the altar;
the prophetess began: "Born of the blood
of gods and son of Troy's Anchises, easy—   175
the way that leads into Avernus: day
and night the door of darkest Dis is open.
But to recall your steps, to rise again
into the upper air: that is the labor;
that is the task. A few, whom Jupiter   180
has loved in kindness or whom blazing worth
has raised to heaven as gods' sons, returned.
Through all the central region runs a forest
encircled by the black curves of Cocytus.°
But if your mind is moved by such a love,   185
so great a longing, twice to swim the lake
of Styx and twice to see black Tartarus,
and you are pleased to try this mad attempt,
then, Trojan, hear what you must first accomplish.
A bough is hidden in a shady tree;   190
its leaves and pliant stem are golden, set
aside as sacred to Proserpina.
The grove serves as its screen, and shades enclose
the bough in darkened valleys. Only he

---

[119]Sons of Dardanus: Trojans; Dardanus was the legendary
    founder of Troy.

[122]Tiber: The river in Rome.

[124]Simois and Xanthus are two Trojan rivers.

[125]Latium: The geographical region that includes Rome.

[127]Teucrians: The people who lived under the reign of Teucer, an
    ancient king of Troy.

[148]Acheron: The river in the underworld known as the "River of
    Grief."

---

[165]Orpheus: A mythical poet of Thrace who charmed his way into
    entering the underworld by playing his lyre.

[168]Pollux: Son of Jupiter. He and his twin brother, Castor, alter-
    nately spent their days in the under- and upperworlds so that
    Castor would not have to live permanently among the shades.

[171]Theseus: Son of the Athenian king Aegeus.

[184]Cocytus: River in the underworld.

may pass beneath earth's secret spaces who   195
first plucks the golden-leaved fruit of that tree.
Lovely Proserpina ordained that this
be offered her as gift. And when the first
bough is torn off, a second grows again—
with leaves of gold, again of that same metal.   200
So let your eyes search overhead; and when
the bough is found, then pluck it down by hand
as due: for if the Fates have summoned you,
the bough will break off freely, easily;
but otherwise, no power can overcome it,   205
hard iron cannot help to tear it off.
And more, the lifeless body of your friend
now lies—but you have still to learn of this—
defiling all your fleet with death, while you
still ask your destiny and linger at   210
our threshold. First, you are to carry him
to his own place of rest and burial
and bring black cattle as peace offering.
And so, at last, your eyes shall see the groves
of Styx, the lands the living never pass."   215
She spoke and then was silent. Her lips closed.

Aeneas, sad and staring, takes his way.
He leaves the cavern, thinking on the strange
events, and at his side the same concerns
disturb the true Achates° as he goes.   220
Their talk is long and varied as they walk.
Of what dead comrade did the priestess speak?
What body did she mean for them to bury?
But when they reach the shore again, they see
Misenus° on the dry beach, beaten by   225
a death he did not merit: Misenus, son
of Aeolus, a man no one surpassed
in waking warriors with his trumpet blast,
in kindling with his clang the god of war.   230
For he had been a comrade of great Hector
and famous for his clarion and spear;
with Hector he had hurried into battle.
But when Achilles, victor, stripped his leader
of life, Misenus joined himself to Dardan
Aeneas, following no lesser banner.   235
And then he fell to madness: happening
to make the waves ring with his hollow shell,
blaring, he challenges the gods to contest;
and jealous Triton—if the tale can be
believed—snatched up Misenus, dashing him   240
in foaming shoals and breakers. Now, around him,

all mourned aloud, especially the pious
Aeneas. Then they rush to carry out,
in tears, the Sibyl's orders, strive to heap
an altar for his tomb, to build it high   245
to heaven, searching through the ancient forest,
deep dens of animals. The pitch pines fall;
the ilex rings beneath ax strokes; their wedges
now cleave the trunks of ash and splintering oaks.
They roll the giant rowans down the mountain.   250

Aeneas, first in that work, also girds
himself with tools like theirs; he cheers his
    comrades.
But gazing on the giant forest, he
is sad within his heart and prays: "If only
that golden bough might show itself to us   255
upon some tree in this great wood; for in
all things that had to do with you, Misenus,
the priestess has foreseen only too truly."
No sooner was this said than from the sky
twin doves descended, there, before his eyes,   260
settling along the green grass. And the chief
of heroes recognized his mother's birds
and prayed with gladness: "Be my guides if there
is any passage, strike across the air
to that grove where the rich bough overshadows   265
the fertile ground. And you, my goddess mother,
be true to me in my uncertainty."
As he said this, he stayed his steps. He watched
for omens, for the way the birds would turn.
Then, as they fed, they flew along as far   270
as sight could follow. But when they have reached
the jaws of foul Avernus, there they rise
and swiftly glide along the liquid air;
they settle, twins, on their desired treetop.
The gleam of gold was different, flickering   275
across the boughs. As in the winter's cold,
among the woods the mistletoe—no seed
of where it grows—is green with new leaves,
    girding
the tapering stems with yellow fruit: just so
the gold leaves seemed against the dark-green
    ilex;   280
so, in the gentle wind, the thin gold leaf
was crackling. And at once Aeneas plucks it
and, eager, breaks the hesitating bough
and carries it into the Sibyl's house.

Meanwhile along the shore the Teucrians   285
were weeping for Misenus, offering
their final tributes to his thankless ashes.

220Achates: Friend and loyal companion of Aeneas.
225Misenus: Trumpeter of the Trojans.

First they build high a giant pyre, rich
with pine and planks of oak. They interweave
the sides with somber leaves, in front they set   290
funeral cypresses, with gleaming weapons
as ornament above. And some make ready
hot water, caldrons bubbling on the flames;
they bathe and then anoint their friend's cold
   body.
Their lamentation is done, they place his limbs,   295
wept on, across the bier; and over them,
they throw his purple robes, familiar clothes.
Then some, as their sad office, raised the massive
barrow and, in their fathers' manner, faces
averted, set the firebrand below.   300
The offerings of frankincense and meats
and bowls of flowing oil are heaped together
and burned. The ashes sank, the flame was still;
they washed the remnants and the thirsty embers
with wine; and Corynaeus hid the gathered   305
bones in an urn of bronze. Three times he circled
around his comrades with clear water, and
with light spray from a fruitful olive bough,
he sprinkled them and purified the Trojans
and spoke the final words. Pious Aeneas   310
sets up a mighty tomb above Misenus
bearing his arms, a trumpet and an oar;
it stands beneath a lofty promontory,
now known as Cape Misenus after him:
it keeps a name that lasts through all the ages.   315

This done, he now moves swiftly to fulfill
all the commands and warnings of the Sibyl.
There was a wide-mouthed cavern, deep and vast
and rugged, sheltered by a shadowed lake
and darkened groves; such vapor poured from
   those   320
black jaws to heaven's vault, no bird could fly
above unharmed (for which the Greeks have called
the place "Aornos," or "The Birdless"). Here
the priestess places, first, four black-backed steers;
and she pours wine upon their brows and plucks 325
the topmost hairs between their horns and these
casts on the sacred fires as offering,
calling aloud on Hecate, the queen
of heaven and of hell. Then others slit
the victims' throats and catch warm blood in
   bowls.   330
Aeneas sacrifices with his sword
a black-fleeced lamb for Night, the Furies' mother,
and Terra, her great sister; and for you,
Proserpina, he kills a barren heifer.

And then for Pluto, king of Styx, he raises   335
nocturnal altars, laying on their fires
whole carcasses of bulls; he pours fat oil
across the burning entrails. But no sooner
are dawn and brightness of the early sun
upon them than the ground roars underfoot,   340
the wooded ridges shudder, through the shadows
dogs seem to howl as Hecate draws near.
"Away, away, you uninitiated,"
the priestess shrieks, "now leave the grove: only
Aeneas move ahead, unsheathe your sword;   345
you need your courage now; you need your
   heart."
This said, she plunges, wild, into the open
cavern; but with unfaltering steps Aeneas
keeps pace beside his guide as she advances.

You gods who hold dominion over spirits;   350
you voiceless Shades; you, Phlegethon and Chaos,
immense and soundless regions of the night:
allow me to retell what I was told;
allow me by your power to disclose
things buried in the dark and deep of earth!   355

They moved along in darkness, through the
   shadows,
beneath the lonely night, and through the hollow
dwelling place of Dis, his phantom kingdom:
even as those who journey in a forest
beneath the scanty light of a changing moon,   360
when Jupiter has wrapped the sky in shadows
and black night steals the color from all things.
Before the entrance, at the jaws of Orcus,
both Grief and goading Cares have set their
   couches;
there pale Diseases dwell, and sad Old Age,   365
and Fear and Hunger, that worst counsellor,
and ugly Poverty—shapes terrible
to see—and Death and Trials; Death's brother,
   Sleep,
and all the evil Pleasures of the mind;
and War, whose fruits are death; and facing
   these,   370
the Furies' iron chambers; and mad Strife,
her serpent hair bound up with bloody garlands.

Among them stands a giant shaded elm,
a tree with spreading boughs and aged arms;
they say that is the home of empty Dreams   375
that cling, below, to every leaf. And more,
so many monstrous shapes of savage beasts
are stabled there: Centaurs and double-bodied

Scyllas;° the hundred-handed Briareus;°
the brute of Lerna, hissing horribly;   380
Chimaera armed with flames; Gorgons and
   Harpies;
and Geryon, the shade that wears three bodies.
And here Aeneas, shaken suddenly
by terror, grips his sword; he offers naked
steel and opposes those who come. Had not   385
his wise companion warned him they were only
thin lives that glide without a body in
the hollow semblance of a form, he would
in vain have torn the shadows with his blade.

Here starts the pathway to the waters of   390
Tartarean° Acheron. A whirlpool thick
with sludge, its giant eddy seething, vomits
all of its swirling sand into Cocytus.
Grim Charon is the squalid ferryman,
is guardian of these streams, these rivers; his   395
white hairs lie thick, disheveled on his chin;
his eyes are fires that stare, a filthy mantle
hangs down his shoulder by a knot. Alone,
he poles the boat and tends the sails and carries
the dead in his dark ship, old as he is;   400
but old age in a god is tough and green.

And here a multitude was rushing, swarming
shoreward, with men and mothers, bodies of
high-hearted heroes stripped of life, and boys
and unwed girls, and young men set upon   405
the pyre of death before their fathers' eyes:
thick as the leaves that with the early frost
of autumn drop and fall within the forest,
or as the birds that flock along the beaches,
in flight from frenzied seas when the chill season   410
drives them across the waves to lands of sun.
They stand; each pleads to be the first to cross
the stream; their hands reach out in longing for
the farther shore. But Charon, sullen boatman,
now takes these souls, now those; the rest he
   leaves;   415
thrusting them back, he keeps them from the
   beach.

That disarray dismays and moves Aeneas:
"O virgin, what does all this swarming mean?

---

³⁷⁹Scylla: A sea monster.
³⁷⁹Briareus: A giant with a hundred hands who engaged in battle
   against the gods.
³⁹¹Tartarean: Of the region of the underworld in which the shades
   of the evil are punished.

What do these spirits plead? And by what rule
must some keep off the bank while others sweep   420
the blue-black waters with their oars?" The words
the aged priestess speaks are brief: "Anchises'
son, certain offspring of the gods, you see
the deep pools of Cocytus and the marsh
of Styx, by whose divinity even   425
the High Ones are afraid to swear falsely.
All these you see are helpless and unburied.
That ferryman is Charon. And the waves
will only carry souls that have a tomb.
Before his bones have found their rest, no one   430
may cross the horrid shores and the hoarse waters.
They wander for a hundred years and hover
about these banks until they gain their entry,
to visit once again the pools they long for."

Anchises' son has stopped; he stays his steps   435
and ponders, pitying these unkind fates.
There he can see the sorrowing Leucaspis,
Orontes, captain of the Lycian fleet:
both dead without death's honors, for the south
   wind
had overwhelmed them, sinking ships and sailors, 440
when they were crossing stormy seas from Troy.

And there the pilot, Palinurus, passed:
lately, upon the Libyan voyage, as
he scanned the stars, he had fallen from the stern,
cast down into the center of the sea.   445
And when at last in that deep shade Aeneas
had recognized his grieving form, he was
the first to speak: "O Palinurus, what
god tore you from us, plunged you in midsea?
O tell me. For Apollo, who had never   450
been false before, in this one oracle
deceived me; he had surely prophesied
that you would be unharmed upon the waters
and reach the coastline of Ausonia.
Is this the way he keeps his word?" He answered: 455
"Anchises' son, my captain, you must know:
Apollo's tripod did not cheat, no god
hurled me into the waves. For as it happened,
the rudder that, as my appointed charge,
I clutched, to steer our course, was twisted off   460
by force; I dragged it down headlong with me.
I swear by those harsh seas that I was taken
by no fear for myself; I was afraid
your ship, without its gear, without a helmsman,
might swamp in such a surge. Three nights of
   winter,   465

along vast fields of sea, across the waters,
the south wind lashed me violently; only
on my fourth dawn, high on a wave crest, I
saw Italy, dimly. I swam toward land
slowly and was just at the point of safety—   470
my sea-drenched clothing heavy, my hooked hands
were clinging to a jagged cliffside—when
barbarians attacked me with the sword,
ignorantly thinking me a prize.
And now I am the breakers', beach winds toss
    me. . . .   475
I beg you, therefore, by the gentle light
and winds of heaven, undefeated one,
and by your father, by your growing son,
Iülus, save me from these evils: either
cast earth upon my body—for you can—   480
and seek again the port of Velia; or
if there be any way, if you are given
such power by your goddess mother (for
I cannot think that you are now prepared
to cross such mighty rivers and the marsh   485
of Styx without the gods' protection), give
your own right hand to wretched Palinurus
and take me with you past the waters, that
at least in death I find a place of rest."

But then the priestess turned on the dead pilot.   490
"Where was it, Palinurus, that you learned
such dread desire? For how can you, unburied,
look at the waves of Styx, upon the Furies'
stern river, and approach its shore, unasked?
Leave any hope that prayer can turn aside   495
the gods' decrees. But keep in memory
these words as comfort in your cruel trial:
for all around, the neighboring cities will
be goaded by the plague, a sign from heaven
to make peace with your bones; and they will
    build   500
a tomb and send their solemn sacrifices;
the place will always be named Palinurus."
These words have set his cares to rest, his sorrow
is exiled for a while from his sad heart.
The land that bears his name has made him glad.   505

The journey they began can now continue.
They near the riverbank. Even the boatman,
while floating on the Styx, had seen them coming
across the silent grove and toward the shore.
He does not wait for greeting but attacks,   510
insulting with these words: "Enough! Stop there!
Whoever you may be who make your way,
so armed, down to our waters, tell me now

why you have come. This is the land of shadows,
of Sleep and drowsy Night; no living bodies   515
can take their passage in the ship of Styx.
Indeed, I was not glad to have Alcides°
or Theseus or Pirithoüs° cross the lake,
although the three of them were sons of gods
and undefeated in their wars. Alcides   520
tried to drag off in chains the guardian
of Tartarus; he tore him, trembling, from
the king's own throne. The others tried to carry
the queen away from Pluto's wedding chamber."
Apollo's priestess answered briefly: "We   525
bring no such trickery; no need to be
disturbed; our weapons bear no violence;
for us, the mighty watchman can bark on
forever in his cavern, frightening
the bloodless shades; Proserpina can keep   530
the threshold of her uncle faithfully.
Trojan Aeneas, famed for piety
and arms, descends to meet his father, down
into the deepest shades of Erebus.
And if the image of such piety   535
is not enough to move you, then"—and here
she shows the branch concealed beneath her
    robe—
"you may yet recognize this bough." At this
the swollen heart of Charon stills its anger.
He says no more. He wonders at the sacred   540
gift of the destined wand, so long unseen,
and turns his blue-black keel toward shore. He
    clears
the other spirits from the gangways and
long benches and, meanwhile, admits the massive
Aeneas to the boat, the vessel's seams   545
groaning beneath the weight as they let in
marsh water through the chinks. At last he sets
the priestess and the soldier safe across
the stream in ugly slime and blue-gray sedge.

These regions echo with the triple-throated   550
bark of the giant Cerberus,° who crouches,
enormous, in a cavern facing them.
The Sibyl, seeing that his neck is bristling
with snakes, throws him a honeyed cake of wheat
with drugs that bring on sleep. His triple mouths 555
yawn wide with rapid hunger as he clutches
the cake she cast. His giant back falls slack

---

517 Alcides: Hercules.
518 Theseus and his friend Pirithoüs attempted to steal Proserpina
    from the underworld.
551 Cerberus: Three-headed guard dog of the gates of Hades.

along the ground; his bulk takes all the cave.
And when the beast is buried under sleep,
Aeneas gains the entrance swiftly, leaves 560
the riverbank from which no one returns.

Here voices and loud lamentations echo:
the souls of infants weeping at the very
first threshold—torn away by the black day,
deprived of their sweet life, ripped from the
   breast, 565
plunged into bitter death. And next to them
are those condemned to die upon false charges.
These places have not been assigned, indeed,
without a lot, without a judge; for here
Minos is magistrate. He shakes the urn 570
and calls on the assembly of the silent,
to learn the lives of men and their misdeeds.
The land that lies beyond belongs to those
who, although innocent, took death by their
own hands; hating the light, they threw away 575
their lives. But now they long for the upper air,
and even to bear want and trials there.
But fate refuses them: the melancholy
marshland, its ugly waters, hem them in,
the prisoners of Styx and its nine circles. 580

Nearby, spread out on every side, there lie
the Fields of Mourning: this, their given name.
And here, concealed by secret paths, are those
whom bitter love consumed with brutal waste;
a myrtle grove encloses them; their pains 585
remain with them in death. Aeneas sees
Phaedra and Procris and sad Eriphyle,
who pointed to the wounds inflicted by
her savage son; he sees Pasiphaë
and then Evadne; and Laodamia 590
and Caeneus, once a youth and now a woman,
changed back again by fate to her first shape.

Among them, wandering in that great forest,
and with her wound still fresh: Phoenician Dido.
And when the Trojan hero recognized her 595
dim shape among the shadows (just as one
who either sees or thinks he sees among
the cloud banks, when the month is young, the
   moon
rising), he wept and said with tender love:
"Unhappy Dido, then the word I had 600
was true? That you were dead? That you pursued
your final moment with the sword? Did I
bring only death to you? Queen, I swear by
the stars, the gods above, and any trust

that may be in this underearth, I was 605
unwilling when I had to leave your shores.
But those same orders of the gods that now
urge on my journey through the shadows, through
abandoned, thorny lands and deepest night,
drove me by their decrees. And I could not 610
believe that with my going I should bring
so great a grief as this. But stay your steps.
Do not retreat from me. Whom do you flee?
This is the last time fate will let us speak."

These were the words Aeneas, weeping, used, 615
trying to soothe the burning, fierce-eyed Shade.
She turned away, eyes to the ground, her face
no more moved by his speech than if she stood
as stubborn flint or some Marpessan crag.
At last she tore herself away; she fled— 620
and still his enemy—into the forest
of shadows, where Sychaeus, once her husband,
answers her sorrows, gives her love for love.
Nevertheless, Aeneas, stunned by her
unkindly fate, still follows at a distance 625
with tears and pity for her as she goes.

He struggles on his given way again.
Now they have reached the borderlands of this
first region, the secluded home of those
renowned in war. Here he encounters Tydeus, 630
Parthenopaeus, famous soldier, and
the pale shade of Adrastus; here are men
mourned in the upper world, the Dardan captains
fallen in battle. And for all of these,
on seeing them in long array, he grieves: 635
for Glaucus, Medon, and Thersilochus,
the three sons of Antenor; Polyboetes,
who was a priest of Ceres; and Idaeus,
still clinging to his chariot, his weapons.
The spirits crowd Aeneas right and left, 640
and it is not enough to see him once;
they want to linger, to keep step with him,
to learn the reasons for his visit there.
But when the Grecian chieftains and the hosts
of Agamemnon see the hero and 645
his weapons glittering across the shadows,
they tremble with an overwhelming terror;
some turn their backs in flight, as when they once
sought out their ships; some raise a thin war cry;
the voice they now have mocks their straining
   throats. 650

And here Aeneas saw the son of Priam,
Deiphobus, all of his body mangled,

his face torn savagely, his face and both
his hands, his ears lopped off his ravaged temples,
his nostrils slashed by a disgraceful wound.   655
How hard it was to recognize the trembling
Shade as he tried to hide his horrid torments.
Aeneas does not wait to hear his greeting
but with familiar accents speaks to him:
"Deiphobus, great warrior, and born   660
of Teucer's brilliant blood, who made you pay
such brutal penalties? Who was allowed
to do such violence to you? For Rumor
had told me that on that last night, worn out
by your vast slaughter of the Greeks, you sank   665
upon a heap of tangled butchery.
Then I myself raised up an empty tomb
along Rhoeteum's° shore; three times I called
loudly upon your Shade. Your name and weapons
now mark the place. I could not find you, friend,   670
or bury you, before I left, within
your native land." The son of Priam answered:

"My friend, you left no thing undone; you paid
Deiphobus and his dead Shade their due.
But I was cast into these evils by   675
my own fate and the deadly treachery
of the Laconian woman; it was she
who left me these memorials. You know
and must remember all too well how we
spent that last night among deceiving pleasures.   680
For when across high Pergamus the fatal
horse leaped and, in its pregnant belly, carried
armed infantry, she mimed a choral dance
and, shrieking in a Bacchic orgy, paced
the Phrygian women; it was she herself   685
who held a giant firebrand and, from
the citadel, called in the Danaans.
I lay, sleep-heavy, worn with cares, within
our luckless bridal chamber, taken by
a sweet, deep rest much like the peace of death.   690
And meanwhile my incomparable wife
has stripped the house of every weapon, even
removing from beneath my head my trusted
sword; and she throws the doorway open, calls
her Menelaus to my palace, hoping   695
her lover surely will be grateful for
this mighty favor, and her infamy
for old misdeeds will be forgotten. Why
delay? They burst into my room. The son
of Aeolus joins them as a companion,   700

encourager of outrage. Gods, requite
the Greeks for this if with my pious lips
I ask for satisfaction. But, in turn,
come tell me what misfortunes bring you here
alive? Have you been driven here by sea   705
wanderings or by warnings of the gods?
What fate so wearies you that you would visit
these sad and sunless dwellings, restless lands?"

But as they talked together, through the sky
Aurora with her chariot of rose   710
had passed her midpoint; and they might have
    spent
all this allotted time with words had not
the Sibyl, his companion, warned him thus:
"The night is near, Aeneas, and we waste
our time with tears. For here the road divides   715
in two directions: on the right it runs
beneath the ramparts of great Dis, this is
our highway to Elysium;° the wicked
are punished on the left—that path leads down
to godless Tartarus." Deiphobus: 720
"Do not be angry, mighty priestess, I
now leave to fill the count, return to darkness.
Go on, our glory, go; know better fates."
He said no more; his steps turned at these words.

Aeneas suddenly looks back; beneath   725
a rock upon his left he sees a broad
fortress encircled by a triple wall
and girdled by a rapid flood of flames
that rage: Tartarean Phlegethon whirling
resounding rocks. A giant gateway stands   730
in front, with solid adamantine pillars—
no force of man, not even heaven's sons,
enough to level these in war; a tower
of iron rises in the air; there sits
Tisiphone, who wears a bloody mantle.   735
She guards the entrance, sleepless night and day.
Both groans and savage scourgings echo there,
and then the clang of iron and dragging chains.

Aeneas stopped in terror, and the din
held him. "What kind of crimes are these? Virgin,   740
o speak! What penalties are paid here? What
loud lamentations fill the air?" The priestess
began: "Great captain of the Teucrians,
no innocent can cross these cursed thresholds;
but when the goddess Hecate made me   745

668Rhoeteum: Another name for Troy.

718Elysium: The region of the underworld in which those who led
    righteous lives reside.

the guardian of Avernus' groves, then she
revealed the penalties the gods decreed
and guided me through all the halls of hell.
The king of these harsh realms is Rhadamanthus
the Gnosian: he hears men's crimes and then 750
chastises and compels confession for
those guilts that anyone, rejoicing, hid—
but uselessly—within the world above,
delaying his atonement till too late,
beyond the time of death. Tisiphone 755
at once is the avenger, armed with whips;
she leaps upon the guilty, lashing them;
in her left hand she grips her gruesome vipers
and calls her savage company of sisters.
And now at last the sacred doors are opened, 760
their hinges grating horribly. You see
what kind of sentry stands before the entrance,
what shape is at the threshold? Fiercer still,
the monstrous Hydra° lives inside; her fifty
black mouths are gaping. Tartarus itself 765
then plunges downward, stretching twice as far
as is the view to heaven, high Olympus.
And here the ancient family of Earth,
the sons of Titan who had been cast down
by thunderbolts, writhe in the deepest gulf. 770
Here, too, I saw the giant bodies of
the twin sons of Aloeus, those who tried
to rip high heaven with their hands, to harry
Jove from his realms above. I saw Salmoneus:
how brutal were the penalties he paid 775
for counterfeiting Jove's own fires and
the thunders of Olympus. For he drove
four horses, brandishing a torch; he rode
triumphant through the tribes of Greece and
    through
the city in the heart of Elis, asking 780
for his own self the honor due to gods:
a madman who would mime the tempests and
inimitable thunder with the clang
of bronze and with the tramp of horn-foot horses.
But through the thick cloud banks all-able Jove 785
let fly his shaft—it was no firebrand
or smoky glare of torches: an enormous
blast of the whirlwind drove Salmoneus headlong.
And I saw Tityos, the foster child
of Earth, mother of all, his body stretched 790
on nine whole acres; and a crooked-beaked
huge vulture feeds upon his deathless liver
and guts that only grow the fruits of grief.

The vulture has his home deep in the breast
of Tityos, and there he tears his banquets 795
and gives no rest even to new-grown flesh.
And must I tell you of Ixion and
Pirithoüs, the Lapithae? Of those
who always stand beneath a hanging black
flint rock that is about to slip, to fall, 800
forever threatening? And there are those
who sit before high banquet couches, gleaming
upon supports of gold; before their eyes
a feast is spread in royal luxury,
but near at hand reclines the fiercest Fury: 805
they cannot touch the tables lest she leap
with lifted torch and thundering outcries.
And here are those who in their lives had hated
their brothers or had struck their father or
deceived a client or (the thickest swarm) 810
had brooded all alone on new-won treasure
and set no share apart for kin and friends;
those slain for their adultery; those who followed
rebellious arms or broke their pledge to masters—
imprisoned, all await their punishment. 815
And do not ask of me what penalty,
what shape or fate has overwhelmed their souls.
For some are made to roll a giant boulder,
and some are stretched along the spokes of wheels.
Sad Theseus has to sit and sit forever; 820
and miserable Phlegyas° warns them all—
his roaring voice bears witness through the
    darkness:
'Be warned, learn justice, do not scorn the gods!'
Here is one who sold his fatherland for gold
and set a tyrant over it; he made 825
and unmade laws for gain. This one assailed
the chamber of his daughter and compelled
forbidden mating. All dared horrid evil
and reached what they had dared. A hundred
    tongues,
a hundred mouths, an iron voice were not 830
enough for me to gather all the forms
of crime or tell the names of all the torments."

So did the aged priestess of Apollo
speak, and she adds, "But come now, on your way,
complete the task you chose. Let us be quick. 835
I see the walls the Cyclops° forged, the gates
with arching fronts, where we were told to place

---

764 Hydra: Fifty-headed water monster of Tartarus.

821 Phlegyas: Ruler of the Lapithae who was punished in Tartarus
for having set fire to Apollo's temple at Delphi.
836 Cyclops: The one-eyed giants in the *Odyssey*.

our gifts." She has spoken. Side by side they move
along the shaded path; and hurrying
across the space between, they near the doors.   840
Aeneas gains the entrance, and he sprinkles
his body with fresh water, then he sets
the bough across the threshold facing them.

Their tasks were now completed; they had done
all that the goddess had required of them.   845
They came upon the lands of gladness, glades
of gentleness, the Groves of Blessedness—
a gracious place. The air is generous;
the plains wear dazzling light; they have their very
own sun and their own stars. Some exercise   850
their limbs along the green gymnasiums
or grapple on the golden sand, compete
in sport, and some keep time with moving feet
to dance and chant. There, too, the Thracian
    priest,
the long-robed Orpheus, plays, accompanying   855
with seven tones; and now his fingers strike
the strings, and now his quill of ivory.

The ancient race of Teucer, too, is here,
most handsome sons, great-hearted heroes born
in better years: Assaracus and Ilus   860
and Dardanus, who founded Pergamus.
From far Aeneas wonders at their phantom
armor and chariots; their spears are planted,
fixed in the ground; their horses graze and range
freely across the plain. The very same   865
delight that once was theirs in life—in arms
and chariots and care to pasture their
sleek steeds—has followed to this underearth.

And here to right and left he can see others:
some feasting on the lawns; and some chanting   870
glad choral paeans in a fragrant laurel
grove. Starting here, Eridanus in flood
flows through a forest to the world above.
Here was the company of those who suffered
wounds, fighting for their homeland; and of
    those   875
who, while they lived their lives, served as pure
    priests:
and then the pious poets, those whose songs
were worthy of Apollo; those who had
made life more civilized with newfound arts;
and those whose merits won the memory   880
of men: all these were crowned with snow-white
    garlands.
And as they streamed around her there, the Sibyl

addressed them, and Musaeus before all—
he stood, his shoulders towering above
a thronging crowd whose eyes looked up to him: 885
"O happy souls and you the best of poets,
tell us what land, what place it is that holds
Anchises. It is for his sake we have come
across the mighty streams of Erebus."
The hero answered briefly: "None of us   890
has one fixed home: we live in shady groves
and settle on soft riverbanks and meadows
where fresh streams flow. But if the will within
your heart is bent on this, then climb the hill
and I shall show to you an easy path."   895
He spoke, and led the way, and from the ridge
he pointed out bright fields. Then they descend.

But in the deep of a green valley, father
Anchises, lost in thought, was studying
the souls of all his sons to come—though now   900
imprisoned, destined for the upper light.
And as it happened, he was telling over
the multitude of all his dear descendants,
his heroes' fates and fortunes, works and ways.
And when he saw Aeneas cross the meadow,   905
he stretched out both hands eagerly, the tears
ran down his cheeks, these words fell from his lips:

"And have you come at last, and has the pious
love that your father waited for defeated
the difficulty of the journey? Son,   910
can I look at your face, hear and return
familiar accents? So indeed I thought,
imagining this time to come, counting
the moments, and my longing did not cheat me.
What lands and what wide waters have you
    journeyed   915
to make this meeting possible? My son,
what dangers battered you? I feared the kingdom
of Libya might do so much harm to you."

Then he: "My father, it was your sad image,
so often come, that urged me to these thresholds.   920
My ships are moored on the Tyrrhenian.
O father, let me hold your right hand fast,
do not withdraw from my embrace." His face
was wet with weeping as he spoke. Three times
he tried to throw his arms around Anchises'   925
neck; and three times the Shade escaped from that
vain clasp—like light winds, or most like swift
    dreams.

Meanwhile, Aeneas in a secret valley
can see a sheltered grove and sounding forests

and thickets and the stream of Lethe° flowing   930
past tranquil dwellings. Countless tribes and
    peoples
were hovering there: as in the meadows, when
the summer is serene, the bees will settle
upon the many-colored flowers and crowd
the dazzling lilies—all the plain is murmuring.   935
The sudden sight has startled him. Aeneas,
not knowing, asks for reasons, wondering
about the rivers flowing in the distance,
the heroes swarming toward the riverbanks.
Anchises answers him: "These are the spirits   940
to whom fate owes a second body, and
they drink the waters of the river Lethe,
the care-less drafts of long forgetfulness.
How much, indeed, I longed to tell you of them,
to show them to you face to face, to number   945
all of my seed and race, that you rejoice
the more with me at finding Italy."

"But, Father, can it be that any souls
would ever leave their dwelling here to go
beneath the sky of earth, and once again   950
take on their sluggish bodies? Are they madmen?
Why this wild longing for the light of earth?"
"Son, you will have the answer; I shall not
keep you in doubt," Anchises starts and then
reveals to him each single thing in order.   955

"First, know, a soul within sustains the heaven
and earth, the plains of water, and the gleaming
globe of the moon, the Titan sun, the stars;
and mind, that pours through every member,
    mingles
with that great body. Born of these: the race   960
of men and cattle, flying things, and all
the monsters that the sea has bred beneath
its glassy surface. Fiery energy
is in these seeds, their source is heavenly;
but they are dulled by harmful bodies, blunted   965
by their own earthly limbs, their mortal members.
Because of these, they fear and long, and sorrow
and joy, they do not see the light of heaven;
they are dungeoned in their darkness and blind
    prison.
And when the final day of life deserts them,   970
then, even then, not every ill, not all
the plagues of body quit them utterly;
and this must be, for taints so long congealed
cling fast and deep in extraordinary

ways. Therefore they are schooled by punishment   975
and pay with torments for their old misdeeds:
some there are purified by air, suspended
and stretched before the empty winds; for some
the stain of guilt is washed away beneath
a mighty whirlpool or consumed by fire.   980
First each of us must suffer his own Shade;
then we are sent through wide Elysium—
a few of us will gain the Fields of Gladness—
until the finished cycle of the ages,
with lapse of days, annuls the ancient stain   985
and leaves the power of ether pure in us,
the fire of spirit simple and unsoiled.
But all the rest, when they have passed time's circle
for a millennium, are summoned by
the god to Lethe in a great assembly   990
that, free of memory, they may return
beneath the curve of the upper world, that they
may once again begin to wish for bodies."

Anchises ended, drew the Sibyl and
his son into the crowd, the murmuring throng,   995
then gained a vantage from which he could scan
all of the long array that moved toward them,
to learn their faces as they came along:

"Listen to me: my tongue will now reveal
the fame that is to come from Dardan sons   1000
and what Italian children wait for you—
bright souls that are about to take your name;
in them I shall unfold your fates. The youth
you see there, leaning on his headless spear,
by lot is nearest to the light; and he   1005
will be the first to reach the upper air
and mingle with Italian blood; an Alban,
his name is Silvius, your last-born son.
For late in your old age Lavinia,
your wife, will bear him for you in the forest;   1010
and he will be a king and father kings;
through him our race will rule in Alba Longa.°
Next Procas stands, pride of the Trojan race;
then Capys, Numitor,° and he who will
restore your name as Silvius Aeneas,   1015
remarkable for piety and arms
if he can ever gain his Alban kingdom.
What young men you see here, what powers they
display, and how they bear the civic oak
that shades their brows! For you they will
    construct   1020

930Lethe: The river of forgetfulness in the underworld.

1012Alba Longa: Mother city of Rome.
1014Procas, Capys, and Numitor are kings of Alba Longa.

Nomentum, Gabii, Fidena's city,
and with the ramparts of Collatia,
Pometia and Castrum Inui,
and Bola, Cora, they will crown the hills.
These will be names that now are nameless
    lands.°   1025

"More: Romulus,° a son of Mars. He will
join Numitor, his grandfather, on earth
when Ilia, his mother, gives him birth
out of the bloodline of Assaracus.°
You see the double plumes upon his crest: 1030
his parent Mars already marks him out
with his own emblem for the upper world.
My son, it is beneath his auspices
that famous Rome will make her boundaries
as broad as earth itself, will make her spirit   1035
the equal of Olympus, and enclose
her seven hills within a single wall,
rejoicing in her race of men: just as
the Berecynthian mother,° tower-crowned,
when, through the Phrygian cities, she rides on   1040
her chariot, glad her sons are gods, embraces
a hundred sons of sons, and every one
a heaven-dweller with his home on high.

"Now turn your two eyes here, to look upon
your Romans, your own people. Here is Caesar   1045
and all the line of Iülus that will come
beneath the mighty curve of heaven. This,
this is the man you heard so often promised—
Augustus Caesar, son of a god, who will
renew a golden age in Latium,   1050
in fields where Saturn once was king, and stretch
his rule beyond the Garamantes° and
the Indians—a land beyond the paths
of year and sun, beyond the constellations,
where on his shoulders heaven-holding Atlas   1055
revolves the axis set with blazing stars.
And even now, at his approach, the kingdom
of Caspia and land of Lake Maeotis
shudder before the oracles of gods;
the seven mouths of Nile, in terror, tremble.   1060
For even Hercules himself had never

crossed so much of the earth, not even when
he shot the brazen-footed stag and brought
peace to the groves of Erymanthus° and
made Lerna's monster quake before his arrows;   1065
nor he who guides his chariot with reins
of vine leaves, victor Bacchus, as he drives
his tigers down from Nysa's° steepest summits.
And do we, then, still hesitate to extend
our force in acts of courage? Can it be   1070
that fear forbids our settling in Ausonia?

"But who is he who stands apart, one crowned
with olive boughs and bearing offerings?
I recognize his hair and his white beard:
when called from humble Cures, a poor land,   1075
to mighty rulership, he will become
first king of Rome to found the city's laws.
And after Numa: Tullus, who will shatter
his country's idleness and wake to arms
the indolent and ranks unused to triumph.   1080
Beside him is the ever-boastful Ancus,
one even now too glad when people hail him.
And would you see the Tarquin kings?° And, too,
the haughty spirit of avenging Brutus,
the fasces° he regained? He will be first   1085
to win the power of a consul, to use
the cruel axes; though a father, for
the sake of splendid freedom he will yet
condemn his very sons who stirred new wars.
Unhappy man! However later ages   1090
may tell his acts, his love of country will
prevail, as will his passion for renown.

"Then see, far off, the Decii and Drusi;
Torquatus° of the ruthless ax; Camillus°
as he brings back the standards. But those spirits 1095
you see there—gleaming in their equal armor
and now, while night restrains them, still at
    peace—
if they but reach the light of life, how great
a war they will incite against each other,
what armies and what slaughter! There is
    Caesar,   1100

1064 Erymanthus: Mountain range in Arcadia where Hercules killed
       a legendary wild boar.
1068 Nysa: Mountain in India said to be the birthplace of Bacchus.
1083 Anchises lists the earliest kings of Rome.
1085 Fasces: Bundle of rods with ax used as Roman symbol of
       authority (root of the word *fascism*).
1094 Decii, Drusi, and Torquatus are heroic consuls.
1094 Camillus: Conqueror of the Gauls.

1024 The aforementioned are names of Italian cities.
1026 Romulus: Legendary founder of Rome.
1029 Assaracus: Anchises' grandfather.
1039 The Berecynthian mother: Cybele, the mother-goddess.
1052 Garamantes: A people in Africa.

descending from the summits of the Alps,
the fortress of Monoecus, and Pompey,
his son-in-law, arrayed against him with
the legions of the East. My sons, do not   1105
let such great wars be native to your minds,
or turn your force against your homeland's vitals:
and Caesar, be the first to show forbearance;
may you, who come from heaven's seed, born of
my blood, cast down the weapon from your hand!

"And there is Mummius, who—famous for   1110
his slaying of Achaeans, conqueror
of Corinth—will yet drive his chariot
triumphantly to the high Capitol.
There stands Aemilius Paulus, the destroyer
of Agamemnon's own Mycenae and   1115
of Argos and the sons of Aeacus,
the seed of powerful-in-arms Achilles:
he will yet avenge the Trojan elders and
Minerva's outraged altars. Who could leave
to silence you, great Cato,° or you, Cossus?°   1120
Who can ignore the Gracchi or the Scipios,°
twin thunderbolts of war, the lash of Libya;
Fabricius, so strong and with so little;
or you, Serranus, as you sow your furrow?
And Fabii, where does your prodding lead me—   1125
now weary—with your many deeds and numbers!
You are that Maximus, the only man
who, by delaying, gave us back our fortunes.
For other peoples will, I do not doubt,
still cast their bronze to breathe with softer
      features,   1130
or draw out of the marble living lines,
plead causes better, trace the ways of heaven
with wands and tell the rising constellations;
but yours will be the rulership of nations,
remember, Roman, these will be your arts: 1135
to teach the ways of peace to those you conquer,
to spare defeated peoples, tame the proud."

So, while Aeneas and the Sibyl marveled,
father Anchises spoke to them, then added:
"And see Marcellus° there, as he advances   1140
in glory, with his splendid spoils, a victor

who towers over all! A horseman, he
will set the house of Rome in order when
it is confounded by great mutiny;
he will lay low the Carthaginians   1145
and rebel Gaul; then for a third time father
Quirinus° will receive his captured arms."

At this, Aeneas had to speak; he saw
beside that Shade another—one still young,
of handsome form and gleaming arms, and yet   1150
his face had no gladness, his eyes looked down:
"Who, Father, moves beside this man? A son
or one of the great race of his sons' sons?
For how his comrades clamor as they crowd!
What presence—his! And yet, around his head   1155
black night is hovering with its sad shade!"

With rising tears Anchises answered him:
"My son, do not search out the giant sorrow
your people are to know. The Fates will only
show him to earth; but they will not allow   1160
a longer stay for him. The line of Rome,
o High Ones, would have seemed too powerful
for you, if his gifts, too, had been its own.
What cries of mourning will the Field of Mars
send out across that overwhelming city,   1165
what funerals, o Tiber, will you see
when you glide past the new-made tomb! No
      youth
born of the seed of Ilium will so
excite his Latin ancestors to hope;
the land of Romulus will never boast   1170
with so much pride of any of its sons.
I weep for righteousness, for ancient trust,
for his unconquerable hand: no one
could hope to war with him and go untouched,
whether he faced the enemy on foot   1175
or dug his foaming horse's flank with spurs.
O boy whom we lament, if only you
could break the bonds of fate and be Marcellus.
With full hands, give me lilies; let me scatter
these purple flowers, with these gifts, at least,   1180
be generous to my descendant's spirit,
complete this service, although it be useless."

And so they wander over all that region,
across the wide and misted plains, surveying
everything. And when father Anchises   1185
has shown his son each scene and fired his soul

1120Cato: Famous Roman statesman.

1120Cossus: Roman general.

1121Gracchi and Scipios are families of Roman statesmen and generals.

1140Marcellus: Roman consul who killed the king of the Gauls in battle.

1147Quirinus: The deified Romulus as god of war.

with love of coming glory, then he tells
Aeneas of the wars he must still wage,
of the Laurentians,° of Latinus'° city,
and how he is to flee or face each trial.   1190

There are two gates of Sleep: the one is said
to be of horn, through it an easy exit
is given to true Shades; the other is made
of polished ivory, perfect, glittering,
but through that way the Spirits send false
     dreams   1195
into the world above. And here Anchises,
when he is done with words, accompanies
the Sibyl and his son together; and
he sends them through the gate of ivory.
Aeneas hurries to his ships, rejoins   1200
his comrades, then he coasts along the shore
straight to Caieta's° harbor. From the prow
the anchor is cast. The sterns stand on the beach.

COMMENTS AND QUESTIONS

1. For what reason does Aeneas want to visit the underworld? Compare his quest to those of Gilgamesh and Odysseus.

2. What is the significance of the golden bough?

3. Note that the categories of shades are much more developed here than they are in either the *Epic of Gilgamesh* or the *Odyssey*. Does there seem to be a system or a plan at work here? Can you describe it?

4. What seems to be the relationship between crime and punishment here? (We will return to this question, with far more complexity, in our study of Dante.)

5. What vision of Rome does Anchises wish to impress on Aeneas? What is, according to him, the particular genius of the Roman people?

1189Laurentians: From Laurentum, a city near Rome.
1189Latinus: King of Latium and father of Aeneas' wife-to-be, Lavinia.
1202Caieta: Italian coastal city near Rome.

8

Judaism and Early Christianity

*I*n moving to another root culture of the Western world, we shift from a culture primarily centered on humanity to one primarily centered on an all-powerful, unique God. The creators of this worldview and its system of values were the ancient Hebrews, who have left their legacy in the Bible as well as in the other cultural manifestations of Judaism. Two other major religions adopted the God of the Hebrews as their own: Christianity and Islam. As Christianity developed from Judaism, it brought elements of Greco-Roman culture to bear on the Hebraic core. We will examine a few important monuments of the culture of Christianity in our focal point for Part Three, the European High Middle Ages. Before that, however, we will look briefly at the seminal Hebraic culture and at early Christianity, then at two influential cultures in the East: the empires of Christian Byzantium and of Islam.

The Ancient Hebrews and the Bible

Modern Christian versions of the Bible include the scriptures of Judaism, called the Old Testament, and the scriptures of Christianity, called the New Testament. Originally, however, the Bible referred only to the Old Testament. It can be defined as a collection of religious literature written in Hebrew (with some parts in other Middle Eastern languages) from about 1000 to 165 B.C. Like the Homeric epics, biblical literature first existed as *oral* narratives and poetry. The written Bible contains a wealth of different kinds of literature: history, short stories, drama, lyric poetry, and philosophical meditation.

What of the people who composed these greatly influential works? The Hebrews were originally a Middle Eastern tribe belonging to the racial group known as Semites, a group that includes the Arabs. Their early history can be divided into three parts: (1) the period of the patriarchs or founding fathers: Abraham, his son Isaac, and his son Jacob; (2) the captivity of the Hebrews (now called Israelites) in Egypt; and (3) the Exodus or deliverance from Egypt to the promised land of Canaan.

Abraham

Abraham, who probably lived about four thousand years ago, is traditionally looked on as the original founder of the Jewish people. His most important contribution was to establish the worship of one God—not a god of an aspect of nature or a sun god as in Mesopotamia, Egypt, and other Middle Eastern religions, but a truly personal God who took a direct interest in his chosen people, the Israelites. God himself initiates a contractual relationship with Abraham. The relationship between Abraham and his God came to be known as the covenant.

According to this agreement, God promised that Abraham's clan would be led to a new land and would become a great nation. In return, the Israelites were to place their trust and faith in God. Abraham's grandson Jacob, driven by famine out of the Israelites' land of Canaan, settled with his clan in Egypt. Although the Egyptians were originally tolerant of them, the Israelites eventually became slaves until they were delivered by Moses, around 1200 B.C.

Moses

Moses led the Israelites to Mount Sinai, where a new covenant between the God of Israel and his people was made. God revealed himself to Moses under the name of "Jahweh," which means in Hebrew "he brings into existence." Jahweh was not only the creator of everything but could also enter into history to influence the course of human events. Israel itself was a creation of divine action in time. It was felt that God not only cared for his people but ordered events for the good. History was not, as the pagans conceived of it, meaningless change or a series of endlessly repeating cycles of events. Rather, it was the means through which God revealed his will. This conception of God gave the Israelites their strong sense of destiny. They were the chosen people—God would take care of them. In the covenant at Mount Sinai, Jahweh promised his protection and gave the Israelites the Ten Commandments to follow. The first of these is, of course, "Thou shalt have no other gods before me." The principle of one supreme personal God was firmly established, as it has been in Judaism ever since.

The Kings

Moses' successor, Joshua, brought his people to the promised land of Canaan, and at that point the Israelites became a settled, rather than a nomadic, people. The next phase of their history is called the period of kings, for they had not had one king over them earlier. The first king was Saul; the second and most famous, David. David founded the capital at Jerusalem, establishing a splendid court there with a luxury never known to the Israelites previously. It is during the reign of David that the Hebrew literature we know as the Bible was first written down. Up until that time, the legends of the patriarchs, the account of the creation, and so on had been passed along orally.

Solomon

Writing of biblical literature continued under the reign of the next king, Solomon. Solomon's court and kingdom were the most lavish and splendid that Israel ever knew. He taxed the people heavily for his extravagant building and also maintained a harem—although the hundred wives attributed to him is probably an exaggeration. He was reputed to be the wisest man in the world and a poet as well. Most scholars now think that this is probably a legend and especially that the Song of Songs, the great Hebrew poem also called the Song of Solomon, was not written by Solomon but by a later author; still, it seems to fit the splendor of Solomon's court. Solomon's power and splendor did not continue after him. When he died in 922 B.C., Israel was split into two kingdoms and foreign conquests of the Israelites began again. The Jews were exiled in Babylonia, then conquered by the Egyptians, by the Syrians, and finally, shortly before the birth of Jesus, by the Romans.

Biblical Literature

Literary genres in the Old Testament include narratives of sacred history as in Genesis, laws and rules for ethical conduct as in Exodus and Leviticus, and apparently secular love poetry such as the Song of Songs. The book of Job, which deals with human suffering in a way similar to Greek tragedy but in a Hebraic context, makes an interesting comparison with *Oedipus*. The "wisdom" literature, such as the books of Proverbs and Ecclesiastes, has been influential throughout the Western tradition. For Christianity the most important books of the Old Testament were those of the prophets (see, for example, Isaiah 11), who predicted that from the house of David would come the Messiah, or Savior, who would redeem Israel and bring about an era of peace and justice on earth. It is this promise that the followers of Jesus of Nazareth found that their leader fulfilled. The hope of a Messiah yet to come, however, still remains at the core of Judaism.

Early Christianity

Jesus of Nazareth was born during the age of the emperor Augustus. Nazareth was a part of Judea, a Roman province ruled over by a Roman governor; but Judea was also the kingdom of the Jews and had a Jewish king, Herod. The followers of Jesus were all Jews and originally did not intend to establish a separate religion but to carry out a radical reform of Judaism. A powerful group centered at Jerusalem fervently believed that proselytizing should be limited only to Jews or to those who were willing to convert to Judaism, accepting circumcision along with the other rules of the faith. Opposed to this position was Saul of Tarsus, whose Roman name was Paul.

Raised in a strict orthodox Jewish family in apparently comfortable circumstances—his father was a Roman citizen—Paul initially viewed the Christians as dangerous fanatics bent on destroying Judaism, and he joined in their persecution. Then, about A.D. 35, during a journey to Jerusalem on an errand of persecution, he had a vision in which Jesus called him to his service. Transformed by the experience, Paul became an ardent Christian and for the rest of his life devoted himself to missionary work, founding churches all over the eastern half of the Roman Empire.

To the converted Paul, Jesus had died for everyone and Christians enjoyed a freedom from all laws, including those of Judaism. "All things," he wrote to the church at Corinth (1 Cor. 6:12), "are lawful for me," and, in 1 Cor. 2:15, "But he that is spiritual judgeth all things, and he himself is judged of no man." Paul was in no way proclaiming absolute license. Rather, he believed that one who had accepted the Christ (a Greek word meaning "anointed") would of his or her own accord do what was right, and that adherence to elaborate dietary practices and other rituals had no spiritual value for the believer.

Despite a number of efforts on both sides to reach a reconciliation that would allow Paul to continue his missionary work among the Gentiles and also allow the Jerusalem congregation to proselytize Jews exclusively, the issue was not settled in Paul's lifetime. Nevertheless, Paul's universalistic interpretation quickly triumphed throughout the empire, and Christianity emerged as a religion in its own right rather than as a sect of Judaism.

However, because of its broad appeal, Christianity appeared to pose a menace to Roman authority. Rome was a society founded on the institution of slavery; its upper classes could never forget the horrors of the great slave revolt of Spartacus, in the last century of the Republic, that had threatened to incite slaves throughout Italy to murder their masters. If mere yokels—workers and slaves—became preoccupied with the personal salvation of their souls and believed that they possessed truth through their religion, would this not endanger their obedience to their masters and thus the whole structure of Roman society? The new religion must be destroyed. But the more the state persecuted, the more the faith grew.

In A.D. 64 much of Rome was destroyed by fire. The emperor, Nero, may have set it himself (to clear large areas in the center city where he intended to build a new palace complex); but he blamed the destruction on the Christians, whom he accused of "hatred of the human race." Christianity then became illegal and went underground. The Christians were accused of disloyalty to the emperor; of refusing to worship the state gods; of practicing incest, black magic, and cannibalism ("eating" their god in the communion rite); and of generally causing all sorts of misfortunes. The Roman persecution of Christian martyrs is well known, especially in its popular film versions. To be Christian in Rome was to risk imprisonment or death. If this was so, why did Christianity appeal to so many people and spread so rapidly? To answer this question is also to determine why the Christians were so easily marked out for harassment by the Roman authorities, who were usually tolerant of religious differences.

Official Roman religion at the time that the Christian message was being spread was fairly similar to the Greek religion. Generally, while adding a few state gods of their own, the Romans simply took over most of the Greek gods, giving them Latin names. Like the Greek gods and goddesses, the Roman ones were blown-up people who had their favorites among mortals and their sexual adventures. To have a happy love affair, an easy childbirth, a safe trip, or a good business deal, one might pray for help to one god or another but would not expect much more of them. The average lower-class person, for example, would not get any help from the gods at the hour of death. The slave or former slave (freedman) could only hope to cross a dark river and then, as a shade, to wander eternally in the kingdom of the dead. The Elysian Fields, the realm of happiness after death, was reserved for the upper classes. This kind of religion had obviously satisfied the Romans for hundreds of years, but already in the last century of the Roman Republic before the advent of Caesar Augustus a change in religious interests was beginning to take place.

The change occurring in Greek religious and philosophical thought from the third century B.C. on has already been noted. The spread of Greek culture to the East was balanced by a gradual penetration of eastern mystery religions such as the Egyptian cult of Isis and Osiris or the Persian worship of Mithra, both of which emphasized resurrection, into Europe. These religions extended to their adherents hope for a personal immortality beyond the grave and tended to deemphasize the importance of success in this earthly life. Philosophies too, like Stoicism, increasingly came to look on God not merely as some kind of principle of rationality needed to explain the nature of the world as it was but also as a personality who exercised a providential power over human destiny.

By the reign of Augustus, while the official religion remained centered on the pagan gods, this same movement was well under way in the western half of the Roman Empire as well. It affected men and women at all levels of society. Large numbers of Romans were rejecting the classical ethos that death in the service of the motherland was the highest moral end of the citizen. Even members of the upper class began to regard the state as a primarily negative force designed to keep order so that people could go about their central task of finding spiritual fulfillment in religious worship or philosophical contemplation of a divine being who promised individual salvation.

With so many mystery religions to choose from, why did Christianity prove so attractive to so many and ultimately triumph over its competitors? The Christians saw in their victory the vindication of their claims that the Christian faith was the true religion, but there are obvious historical explanations for the rapid growth of the sect and the intensive persecution of its members.

Of the Eastern mystery religions only Christianity was exclusive. Worshipers of Isis, Mithras, or the Asiatic "Great Mother" Cybele could belong to cults worshiping these deities and at the same time sacrifice to the gods of Rome. Christians forbade any worship of other gods. More than this, they condemned all other religions as sinful and inferior. Thus, while they offered their membership eternal life, Christians also claimed that theirs was the only way to heaven. This exclusiveness must have attracted many, but it made enemies of others who could not understand Christian intolerance.

In a sense the Christians were like the Jews in their unwillingness to participate in public religious ceremonies and to take an oath of loyalty to the emperor. But Judaism was an established religion with a limited potential for membership. Christians by contrast were bursting with missionary zeal. They claimed that the souls of all, whether slave or free, Jew or Gentile, man or woman, were equal in God's sight. This message of equality, love, and charity had a tremendous attraction, especially among the poor and enslaved.

With the growth of the Christian faith, we find the first stirrings of an art that gives expression to the central ideas of the movement. Unlike the Greeks and Romans, or the Jews with their synagogues, the early Christians had no specific building or architectural setting for their celebrations. Without money or power, all they had was their sense of separateness and community within the great world. They met then in homes or rented rooms; but, as persecution grew, it became necessary to seek a safer place for the celebration of the Eucharist (Holy Communion)—the central rite that affirmed fellowship and God's presence among people.

Outside Rome were underground chambers for burial; in these catacombs the Christians met in secret. The walls were decorated with paintings that tell stories from the Old and New Testaments, especially about miracles, persecutions, and Christ's saving grace. The painting reproduced here (Fig. 8-1) shows Christ as the Good Shepherd. What is the motive behind this representation? Compare the figure with other male figures that we have seen. Is he like an emperor or more like a young athlete? This person, the Good Shepherd who "lays down" his life for his sheep, is the same Christ who speaks in the Sermon on the Mount, the New Testament text that best introduces the Christian message.

The End of Antiquity

While Christianity grew ever stronger in the first three centuries after the death of its founder, the Roman Empire itself in the third century began a rapid decline. The middle half of the century saw almost continuous civil war among at least fifty claimants to the imperial throne.

8-1   The Good Shepherd, *Catacomb of St. Callixtus, Rome.* *(Hirmer Fotoarchiv Munich)*

The decline of Rome was temporarily halted in the last quarter of the century by Diocletian (A.D. 280–305), who, through a series of reforms and careful management of resources, laid the groundwork of an imperial organization that kept the empire together for more than another hundred years. On his death the arrangement for succession broke down and rivals for the throne began a civil war. One of these was Constantine, who, in a battle in A.D. 312 with his opponent, claimed to have had a vision that converted him to Christianity.

A New Era of Christianity

With the conversion of Constantine, who won the battle and became emperor, a new era in the history of Christianity opened. Given the divisive tendencies at work in the Empire in the third century, the conversion of Constantine strikes the observer as politically opportune. In the three hundred years of its growth the Church under the pressure of persecution had created a kind of state within a state. Christians settled disputes among themselves within the Christian community; treasuries were created for the purposes of providing for the poor, orphans, and widows. By A.D. 200 almost every major city in the Empire had its bishop and its body of priests, chosen by the community. From this time as well, the bishop of Rome, the Roman pope, asserted his claim to be the spiritual leader of the whole Church. His claim rested on the scriptural passage in which Christ tells Peter, his disciple:

> Thou art Peter, and upon this rock I will build my church; and the gates of hell shall not prevail against it. And I will give unto thee the keys of the kingdom of heaven; and whatsoever thou shalt bind on earth shall be bound in heaven; and whatsoever thou shalt loose on earth shall be loosed in heaven. (Matthew 16:18–19)

Saint Peter was believed to have been the first bishop of Rome; as a result, his successors in that office were thought to have inherited this power of binding and loosing human souls on earth and in heaven. Although these claims were hotly disputed, especially by bishops in the eastern half of the Empire, by the fourth century the leadership of Rome was generally recognized in the western portion.

At the time of Constantine's conversion, only about 10 percent of the population in the Roman Empire, most of them city dwellers, were Christian. Constantine and his successors were able to support the failing imperial machine with the vital, dynamic organization of the Christian Church. From the beginning the emperors looked on the Church as another branch of the imperial government. They influenced the election of bishops and even that of the pope himself. Clerics were treated as public officials, and the emperors drew on the various Church treasures when the need arose. Thus Christianity developed into something totally different from its beginnings: from an underground sect, it became a state religion.

Christianity in its initial stages had a marked appeal for the poor and the downtrodden, but by the second century it began to exercise a strong appeal to the learned as well. The gods of Greek and Roman antiquity, as we have seen in the *Iliad* and the *Aeneid,* were often characterized by an arbitrary conduct. They were essentially willful, superior beings who protected those who worshiped them but who changed their minds so often that it was difficult to know what was expected of the believer. On the other hand, the works of ancient philosophers such as Plato, Aristotle, and Cicero show that they believed in a God of reason, a first principle of the universe who gave order in one way or another to all things. Believers, however, could not have a personal relationship with such a God as they could with the popular pagan gods. One could not pray to Plato's Idea of the Good or Aristotle's First Mover. By the second century, with large borrowings from Jewish theologians, who had done much the same thing for Jahweh, thinkers began to develop the concept of the Christian God not only as having a will, which allowed him to love and hate, but also as the ultimate principle of reason. Thus Christians could love and fear this God as the ancient pagans did their gods while at the same time knowing that belief in this God made sense of the world. Philosophers would not have to forget all they had learned about the workings of reason when they entered a church.

8-2   *Reconstruction of Old St. Peter's, Rome*

Saint Augustine (A.D. 354–430)

Perhaps the greatest theologian of the Christian Church, Aurelius Augustinus came from a family living in modest circumstances in a small town on the North African coast near Carthage. His mother, Monica, was a devout Christian, but his father converted only late in life. A brilliant speaker and writer, Augustine himself found it difficult to accept a faith whose basic text, the Bible, was so simply written and dealt with such humble people. His *Confessions,* written about A.D. 397, recounts how after a youth given to pleasure and to acquiring fame as a teacher of eloquence, he began to question his life after reading a now-lost work of Cicero. From this point on, moving from one philosophy to another, he eagerly sought the true nature of God and the soul. In none did he find the answer he sought except that Platonism introduced him to the existence of a spiritual realm of which he had been unaware. At the same time this pursuit of knowledge had had little effect on the quality of his moral life. Finally, in Milan, he tells us, he could no longer resist the call to turn to Christ, a call that he had heard since his childhood but to which, proud of his intellect and talents, he would not surrender. He then decided to abandon his profession of teaching rhetoric and devote his life to God. He recounts his conversation with his mother on his faith as they embark to return to Africa together and the death of his mother during the voyage. The rest of the book is composed primarily of meditations on scripture and on the doctrines of Christianity.

The *Confessions* is a highly significant book in the Western tradition in that it is, as far as we know, the first autobiography. The project of writing about the self, the soul and its relation to God, and the cen-

trality of conversion in life experience is itself indicative of a change in outlook brought about by Christianity. It did not seem to have occurred to the ancients that an intimate account of individual experience could be a worthy subject for literature. The autobiographical genre will be taken up by Petrarch in his *Secret,* Montaigne in his *Essays,* Rousseau in his *Confessions,* and in countless modern narratives. A work by a man steeped in the ancient humanities but convinced of the superior truth of the Christian faith, the *Confessions* marks the transition between the end of antiquity and the era intellectually dominated by Christianity.

The First Church Buildings

The alliance of Christianity with the state is immediately evident in the appearance of churches—specific complexes for the preaching, teaching, and propagation of the faith. Old Saint Peter's in Rome (Fig. 8-2) was built in the early fourth century (333). Archaeological reconstructions show us a complex of buildings—a great gate, an open courtyard, a roofed porch (*narthex*), and then the church itself—a large simple building with a central space, the *nave,* for the congregation. Parallel to the nave on each side are two passageways, *aisles.* These reinforce the directional quality of the nave that focuses on the altar at the east end, supposedly placed above the bones of Saint Peter. Columns separating the nave and aisles support the roof and walls rising above. The roofs of the aisles do not rise the full height of the nave so that there is a story left free for windows before we reach the combinations of beams called *trusses* of the roof. These windows in the *clerestory* provided light. Candles and lamps were used for night services.

A   Nave
B   Transept
C   Apse
D   Aisle
E   Atrium

8-3   *Old St. Peter's, Rome, Groundplan.*

Before the east end is reached, another space crosses the nave at right angles. The *transept* was for the pulpit and separated the nave from the altar. The semicircular east end, called the *apse,* had a half-dome above it. The clerics and the bishop would sit here during services.

In addition to the church and courtyard there was a round building called a *baptistery.* Walls were probably painted with stories like those of the catacombs. The exterior would have been fairly plain since the significant events took place in the interior space.

Compare this building plan (Fig. 8-3) with that of a Roman basilica (Fig. 7-15). How are they different? Why do you think the law court plan might have been a source for this kind of building? What is particularly Greek? Roman?

Early Christian Sculpture

Other important monuments that document the spread and power of Christianity are the numerous *sarcophagi* (caskets) that were found in Rome and in other Christian sites. Decorated with scenes from the Christian story, they emphasize the importance of its association with life, death, and afterlife. An excellent example is the sarcophagus of Junius Bassus, a Roman noble (Fig. 8-4). Along the side represented here we see scenes that will appear again and again in Christian art.

8-4   *Sarcophagus of Junius Bassus, c.* A.D. *359 Vatican Museum, Rome. (Alinari/Art Resource, NY)*

The sarcophagus is divided into two registers or rows with five scenes each; each scene is separated by a column giving each a strong architectural framework. In the top register from left to right are the sacrifice of Isaac; Saint Peter taken prisoner; Christ enthroned between Saint Peter and Saint Paul; and Christ before Pontius Pilate (the last two scenes). In the bottom register we see Job and his comforters; Adam, Eve, and the serpent (the Fall of Man); Christ's entry into Jerusalem; Daniel in the lions' den; and Saint Paul led to his martyrdom. The artist has combined Old and New Testament scenes emphasizing sin, martyrdom, and death. These are mitigated by the two central scenes—Christ the heavenly king (he sits on a personification of the firmament) and Christ the earthly king, cheered as he enters Jerusalem. How does this sculpture differ from that we have considered? Is it classical? Do you feel the presence of other needs and aims in the presentation of these scenes? How is Christ presented—youthful or dignified, imperial or divine? How do the nude bodies of Adam and Eve compare with the Greek *Spearbearer* or the Cnidian *Aphrodite?* What accounts for the differences?

If these questions are difficult to answer, it is because art and architecture were at this point in a state of transition. Artists and thinkers were searching for the best means to convey new and important ideas at a time when there were no clear patterns for the presentation of these ideas. Greek and Roman art were sources that acted as strong influences but were not the perfect match for making images of Christianity's beliefs. Moreover, what does faith, Christianity's basic tenet, look like? Visual art could only provide examples of the acts of people who had taken the path of faith.

The Founding of Constantinople

Constantine's conversion was not the only break to be made with the Roman past. He also definitively moved the capital of the Empire to the east, selecting the town of Byzantium on the Bosphorus as the site. Rome had in fact already been abandoned (for Milan) as capital. His choice reflects his awareness of the displacement of political and economic power from the western to the eastern half of the Empire by the fourth century.

The eastern provinces of Asia Minor, Egypt, and Syria were the wealthy regions of the Empire, those with prosperous cities, a dynamic cultural elite, productive agriculture, and critical pools of workers. The western provinces stood in sharp contrast. Only the North African regions were vital, and their importance was essentially as a grain supply for Rome. At the same time the nostalgia of Rome's elite for ancient republican ideas, totally impractical in these centuries, had already caused the emperors whose power had become absolute to feel more comfortable living outside the city.

Byzantium, Constantine's choice for the new capital, was an ancient but unremarkable town situated on a promontory overlooking both the Sea of Marmara and the Bosporus. On its third side was the Golden Horn, an estuary forming a magnificent harbor. Strategically, the location, almost equidistant between the Danubian and Persian frontiers, was unsurpassed. Constantine consciously created a permanent capital city, designated "New Rome," although "Constantinople" became its popular name. Although the popular language of the city was from the outset Greek, Latin remained the official language of the imperial bureaucracy until after the reign of Justinian (A.D. 527–565). Whether Greek or Latin speakers, the emperor's eastern subjects continued to regard themselves as "Romans," their empire as "Roman," and the languages they spoke as "Romanic." Only centuries later, as we shall see in the next chapter, after a major shift toward Greek culture, did the old adjective "Byzantine" reemerge to designate both the empire and its people.

The Barbarian Influence in the Western Roman Empire

On the death of Emperor Theodosius (A.D. 378–395) the Empire was divided between the late emperor's two sons. Honorius was given the western half and Arcadius the eastern. Because Germanic tribes were threatening to invade Italy, Honorius moved the capital of his half of the Empire into the marshes on the eastern coast of Italy at Ravenna, where he would be insulated from attack. But during the fifth century, as wave upon wave of German tribes passed across the northern and northeastern frontiers of the Western Empire, resistance gave way and Romans at the local level tried to make an accommodation with their German occupiers (see map).

These Germanic tribes, despite the name "barbarians" given them by the Romans, left many of the art objects and buildings they found intact. They had in fact been in contact with Roman civilization for centuries. Their intention was not to destroy a civilization but to garner its fruits for themselves.

Most of the barbarians were already Christian or were converted to Christianity soon after settling on Roman soil. Those converting in the homeland, however, had done so largely under the influence of

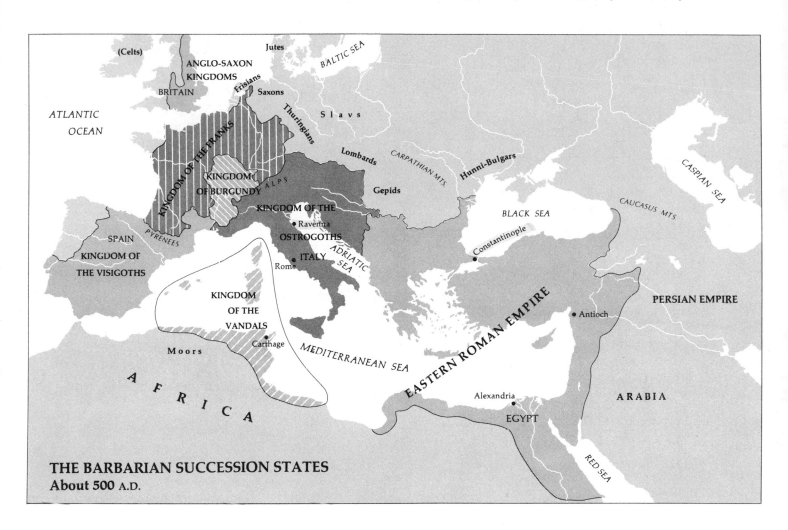

THE BARBARIAN SUCCESSION STATES
About 500 A.D.

heretical preachers and, once in the Empire, had to be converted to the Catholic faith. Although the central role of the tribal king was a religious one and war chiefs supervised military expeditions, the pressures of invading the Empire created a need for more central direction and led to a significant increase in the king's military powers. To an extent, the conversion of the various tribes to Christianity reduced the significance of the religious character of the king, but throughout most of the Middle Ages the office retained something of its sacred, priestly qualities. German kings in these newly conquered lands fully expected to control not only the churches but also another important religious institution, the monastery.

Western Monasticism

From the first century of Christianity men and women who rejected life in the world had moved out into the wilderness individually to worship God in isolation. They called themselves hermits. Others who would

have liked to withdraw from the world, however, felt unable to endure the loneliness of such a retreat or believed that isolation contradicted the Christian's duty to love one's neighbor. A communal retreat seemed to such Christians preferable to a solitary one. Thus, by the second century, communities of like-minded men and women came into existence, normally founded in remote places, and emphasizing common worship and mutual service. Often these *monasteries,* as they were eventually called, became the object of rich donations in land and money and grew to be powerful economic and political forces in the society.

Saint Jerome (A.D. 340–420), also known by his Greek name, Eusebius Hieronymus, was one of the greatest proponents of monasticism in the West. Born into a moderately wealthy Christian family in Dalmatia and educated in Rome, he was attracted to the ascetic life, but soon found the company of others a hindrance to his devotions. He retired to the Syrian desert to live as a hermit for five years. He returned to

A	Church Nave	E	Public Entrance	J	Refectory
B	Choirs	F	Guest House	K	Cloister
C	Main Altar	G	School	L	Cemetery
D	Towers	H	Abbot's House	M	Gardens, Barns

8-5   *Schematic plan for an ideal monastery at St. Gall, Switzerland, c. A.D. 819 (Drawing after a 9th century manuscript, Chapter Library, St. Gall, Switzerland)*

Rome, however, and had a major role in establishing the connection between the ascetic Christian life of withdrawal and Christian scholarship, a link that was to characterize Western monasticism. Among his many works, surely the most important was his retranslation of older Latin versions of the New Testament, completed about A.D. 388. With the help of Jewish scholars he then translated the Old Testament from Hebrew into Latin. The result of Jerome's labor was the *Vulgate*, used in the Roman Church down to the sixteenth century, when humanists undertook revisions. Yet the death of his papal patron unleashed opponents who resented his ascetic influence. Threatened with death, he left Rome for Palestine, where he built a monastery and a hospice to minister to the pilgrims of the Holy Land.

In the confusion following the disintegration of the Western Roman Empire, monasticism flourished as never before. Centers of learning sometimes as well as of piety, offering physical as well as spiritual safety, monasteries were places of refuge in a dangerous world. An ideal plan for a monastery, drawn up about A.D. 800, the Saint Gaul plan (Fig. 8-5) shows a basilica, dormitories, dining room, library, hospital, hostel, cemetery, and gardens. It resembles a small, self-contained city. Given the wealth and importance of the great monasteries, it is easy to understand why the kings in the centuries after the invasions were concerned to assert some control over the resources of these foundations and to regulate the election of abbots.

Decline of Roman Centralization

Yet, even with the support of the local churches and monasteries, the barbarian rulers after A.D. 500

proved unable to keep the old Roman institutions running. The Roman conception of political power enshrined in the imperial institutions of government was a public one; that is, the Romans considered political authority to be a series of magistracies. Obedience was owed to a magistrate not as a person but as an official representing the majesty of the Roman people. The most effective political bonds in Germanic society were, on the other hand, the personal ones between a war chief and his followers, established by an oath. The warrior obeyed the chief not because the latter represented the tribe but because the warrior had sworn to follow this particular man. As has been seen, the tendency to local autonomy had already set in under the late emperors; the coming of the barbarians only accentuated the development. In a period of insecurity, when people must seek protection wherever they can, the private conception of political power almost inevitably comes to dominate governmental relationships. By the seventh and eighth centuries a large portion of Europe's population found itself involved in a welter of political and economic relationships founded on oaths involving promises to obey or to protect.

The Germanic and surviving Roman aristocracies were the chief beneficiaries of this proliferation of power because they alone had the military might to maintain order at the local level. This group also seized control of churches and monasteries in their various regions, using them to advance their families. Whereas under the late empire and the early barbarian kings, the Church had been a tool in the hands of the central governments, now it had ten thousand masters. The papacy at Rome as well fell under the control of the Roman nobility. The effort of the Carolingian rulers of France in the eighth and early ninth centuries to reunite authority over a large expanse of territory had only a temporary effect on the process of political disintegration in most areas. Central government required a vigorous economic basis, but until the eleventh century western Europe had, generally speaking, a localized subsistence economy.

Texts from the Old Testament

King James Translation

GENESIS

The Creation

The first biblical text included here is one that may appear all too familiar, but a student of the humanities should approach it with new questions. All cultures of the world have myths of creation. Compare this Hebrew account of the beginnings of things (the meaning of the Latin word *genesis*) with the Mesopotamian, Egyptian, and Greek ones summarized in those chapters and with the West African accounts in Chapter 13. All of the biblical passages are from the King James translation of 1611, itself a cultural monument of great importance to the formation of the English language.

Chapter 1

1 In the beginning God created the heaven and the earth.

2 And the earth was without form, and void; and darkness was upon the face of the deep. And the Spirit of God moved upon the face of the waters.

3 And God said, Let there be light: and there was light.

4 And God saw the light, that it was good: and God divided the light from the darkness.

5 And God called the light Day, and the darkness he called Night. And the evening and the morning were the first day.

6 And God said, Let there be a firmament in the midst of the waters, and let it divide the waters from the waters.

7 And God made the firmament, and divided the waters which were under the firmament from the waters which were above the firmament: and it was so.

8 And God called the firmament Heaven. And the evening and the morning were the second day.

9 And God said, Let the waters under the heaven be gathered together unto one place, and let the dry land appear: and it was so.

10 And God called the dry land Earth; and the gathering together of the waters called he Seas: and God saw that it was good.

11 And God said, Let the earth bring forth grass, the herb yielding seed, and the fruit tree yielding fruit after his kind, whose seed is in itself, upon the earth: and it was so.

12 And the earth brought forth grass, and herb yielding seed after his kind, and the tree yielding fruit, whose seed was in itself, after his kind: and God saw that it was good.

13 And the evening and the morning were the third day.

14 And God said, Let there be lights in the firmament of the heaven to divide the day from the night; and let them be for signs, and for seasons, and for days, and years:

15 And let them be for lights in the firmament of the heaven to give light upon the earth: and it was so.

16 And God made two great lights; the greater light to rule the day, and the lesser light to rule the night: he made the stars also.

17 And God set them in the firmament of the heaven to give light upon the earth,

18 And to rule over the day and over the night, and to divide the light from the darkness: and God saw that it was good.

19 And the evening and the morning were the fourth day.

20 And God said, Let the waters bring forth abundantly the moving creature that hath life, and fowl that may fly above the earth in the open firmament of heaven.

21 And God created great whales, and every living creature that moveth, which the waters brought

forth abundantly, after their kind, and every winged fowl after his kind: and God saw that it was good.

22 And God blessed them, saying, Be fruitful, and multiply, and fill the waters in the seas, and let fowl multiply in the earth.

23 And the evening and the morning were the fifth day.

24 And God said, Let the earth bring forth the living creature after his kind, cattle, and creeping thing, and beast of the earth after his kind: and it was so.

25 And God made the beast of the earth after his kind, and cattle after their kind, and every thing that creepeth upon the earth after his kind: and God saw that it was good.

26 And God said, Let us make man in our image, after our likeness: and let them have dominion over the fish of the sea, and over the fowl of the air, and over the cattle, and over all the earth, and over every creeping thing that creepeth upon the earth.

27 So God created man in his own image, in the image of God created he him; male and female created he them.

28 And God blessed them, and God said unto them, Be fruitful, and multiply, and replenish the earth, and subdue it: and have dominion over the fish of the sea, and over the fowl of the air, and over every living thing that moveth upon the earth.

29 And God said, Behold, I have given you every herb bearing seed, which is upon the face of all the earth, and every tree, in the which is the fruit of a tree yielding seed; to you it shall be for meat.

30 And to every beast of the earth, and to every fowl of the air, and to every thing that creepeth upon the earth, wherein there is life, I have given every green herb for meat: and it was so.

31 And God saw every thing that he had made, and, behold, it was very good. And the evening and the morning were the sixth day.

Chapter 2

1 Thus the heavens and the earth were finished, and all the host of them.

2 And on the seventh day God ended his work which he had made; and he rested on the seventh day from all his work which he had made.

3 And God blessed the seventh day, and sanctified it: because that in it he had rested from all his work which God created and made.

4 These are the generations of the heavens and of the earth when they were created, in the day that the Lord God made the earth and the heavens,

5 And every plant of the field before it was in the earth, and every herb of the field before it grew: for the Lord God had not caused it to rain upon the earth, and there was not a man to till the ground.

6 But there went up a mist from the earth, and watered the whole face of the ground.

7 And the Lord God formed man of the dust of the ground, and breathed into his nostrils the breath of life; and man became a living soul.

8 And the Lord God planted a garden eastward in Eden; and there he put the man whom he had formed.

9 And out of the ground made the Lord God to grow every tree that is pleasant to the sight, and good for food; the tree of life also in the midst of the garden, and the tree of knowledge of good and evil.

10 And a river went out of Eden to water the garden; and from thence it was parted, and became into four heads.

11 The name of the first is Pison: that is it which compasseth the whole land of Havilah, where there is gold;

12 And the gold of that land is good: there is bdellium and the onyx stone.

13 And the name of the second river is Gihon: the same is it that compasseth the whole land of Ethiopia.

14 And the name of the third river is Hiddekel: that is it which goeth toward the east of Assyria. And the fourth river is Euphrates.

15 And the Lord God took the man, and put him into the garden of Eden to dress it and to keep it.

16 And the Lord God commanded the man, saying, Of every tree of the garden thou mayest freely eat:

17 But of the tree of the knowledge of good and evil, thou shalt not eat of it: for in the day that thou eatest thereof thou shalt surely die.

18 And the Lord God said, It is not good that the man should be alone; I will make him an help meet for him.

19 And out of the ground the Lord God formed every beast of the field, and every fowl of the air; and brought them unto Adam to see what he would call them: and whatsoever Adam called every living creature, that was the name thereof.

20 And Adam gave names to all cattle, and to the fowl of the air, and to every beast of the field; but for Adam there was not found an help meet for him.

21 And the Lord God caused a deep sleep to fall upon Adam, and he slept; and he took one of his ribs, and closed up the flesh instead thereof;

22 And the rib, which the Lord God had taken from man, made he a woman, and brought her unto the man.

23 And Adam said, This is now bone of my bones, and flesh of my flesh: she shall be called Woman, because she was taken out of man.

24 Therefore shall a man leave his father and his mother, and shall cleave unto his wife: and they shall be one flesh.

25 And they were both naked, the man and his wife, and were not ashamed.

COMMENTS AND QUESTIONS

1. The two different accounts of creation in Genesis have caused biblical scholars to believe that each was written at a different time and by a different author. What are the two accounts? Where does one end and the other begin?

2. Does God create from nothing? Does it seem that anything was there before God?

3. How does the role of the Hebrew God of creation differ from that of divinities in Mesopotamian, Egyptian, Greek, and (see Part 4) West African myths?

4. How do the two accounts of the creation of woman differ? How might these accounts have influenced ways in which we think about the nature of woman?

The Fall

The following text is central to the Judaic and Christian concepts of humanity's relationship to God and to the problem of evil. Whereas the first two chapters of Genesis show humans as a part of the totality of creation and in harmony with it, in this chapter humans, quite unlike the other living things in the created world, begin to act on their own: to make their own decisions apart from God. They have *free will:* they are given an orderly and harmonious world but are capable of creating disorder in it.

Chapter 3

1 Now the serpent was more subtil than any beast of the field which the Lord God had made. And he said unto the woman, Yea, hath God said, Ye shall not eat of every tree of the garden?

2 And the woman said unto the serpent, We may eat of the fruit of the trees of the garden:

3 But of the fruit of the tree which is in the midst of the garden, God hath said, Ye shall not eat of it, neither shall ye touch it, lest ye die.

4 And the serpent said unto the woman, Ye shall not surely die:

5 For God doth know that in the day ye eat thereof, then your eyes shall be opened, and ye shall be as gods, knowing good and evil.

6 And when the woman saw that the tree was good for food, and that it was pleasant to the eyes, and a tree to be desired to make one wise, she took of the fruit thereof, and did eat, and gave also unto her husband with her; and he did eat.

7 And the eyes of them both were opened, and they knew that they were naked; and they sewed fig leaves together, and made themselves aprons.

8 And they heard the voice of the Lord God walking in the garden in the cool of the day: and Adam and his wife hid themselves from the presence of the Lord God amongst the trees of the garden.

9 And the Lord God called unto Adam, and said unto him, Where art thou?

10 And he said, I heard thy voice in the garden, and I was afraid, because I was naked; and I hid myself.

11 And he said, Who told thee that thou wast naked? Hast thou eaten of the tree, whereof I commanded thee that thou shouldest not eat?

12 And the man said, The woman whom thou gavest to be with me, she gave me of the tree, and I did eat.

13 And the Lord God said unto the woman, What is this that thou hast done? And the woman said, The serpent beguiled me, and I did eat.

14 And the Lord God said unto the serpent, Because thou hast done this, thou art cursed above all cattle, and above every beast of the field; upon thy belly shalt thou go, and dust shalt thou eat all the days of thy life:

15 And I will put enmity between thee and the woman, and between thy seed and her seed; it shall bruise thy head, and thou shalt bruise his heel.

16 Unto the woman he said, I will greatly multiply thy sorrow and thy conception; in sorrow thou shalt bring forth children; and thy desire shall be to thy husband, and he shall rule over thee.

17 And unto Adam he said, Because thou hast hearkened unto the voice of thy wife, and hast eaten of the tree, of which I commanded thee, saying, Thou

shalt not eat of it: cursed is the ground for thy sake; in sorrow shalt thou eat of it all the days of thy life;

18 Thorns also and thistles shall it bring forth to thee; and thou shalt eat the herb of the field;

19 In the sweat of thy face shalt thou eat bread, till thou return unto the ground; for out of it wast thou taken: for dust thou art, and unto dust shalt thou return.

20 And Adam called his wife's name Eve; because she was the mother of all living.

21 Unto Adam also and to his wife did the Lord God make coats of skins, and clothed them.

22 And the Lord God said, Behold, the man is become as one of us, to know good and evil: and now, lest he put forth his hand, and take also of the tree of life, and eat, and live for ever:

23 Therefore the Lord God sent him forth from the garden of Eden, to till the ground from whence he was taken.

24 So he drove out the man; and he placed at the east of the garden of Eden Cherubims, and a flaming sword which turned every way, to keep the way of the tree of life.

QUESTIONS

1. How does this story reconcile the idea of God's infinite justice with the presence of evil in the world?

2. How does God appear in this story in relation to human beings?

3. What, specifically, tempts Eve and then Adam to eat the forbidden fruit? What does this tell you about the Hebrews' concept of the nature of human beings?

4. Compare the relationship between human curiosity and divine power here with the treatment of the same theme in *Oedipus Rex*.

5. Do you as a reader feel admiration or scorn for the human desire to eat the fruit?

The Sacrifice of Isaac

Genesis goes on to recount the rise of the tribe of Israel. The following passage is illustrative of God's relationship with his "chosen people," here in the person of their founding father, Abraham.

Chapter 22

1 And it came to pass after these things, that God did tempt Abraham, and said unto him, Abraham: and he said, Behold, here I am.

2 And he said, Take now thy son, thine only son Isaac, whom thou lovest, and get thee into the land of Moriah; and offer him there for a burnt offering upon one of the mountains which I will tell thee of.

3 And Abraham rose up early in the morning, and saddled his ass, and took two of his young men with him, and Isaac his son, and clave the wood for the burnt offering, and rose up, and went unto the place of which God had told him.

4 Then on the third day Abraham lifted up his eyes, and saw the place afar off.

5 And Abraham said unto his young men, Abide ye here with the ass; and I and the lad will go yonder and worship, and come again to you.

6 And Abraham took the wood of the burnt offering, and laid it upon Isaac his son; and he took the fire in his hand, and a knife; and they went both of them together.

7 And Isaac spake unto Abraham his father, and said, My father: and he said, Here am I, my son. And he said, Behold the fire and the wood: but where is the lamb for a burnt offering?

8 And Abraham said, My son, God will provide himself a lamb for a burnt offering: so they went both of them together.

9 And they came to the place which God had told him of; and Abraham built an altar there, and laid the wood in order, and bound Isaac his son, and laid him on the altar upon the wood.

10 And Abraham stretched forth his hand, and took the knife to slay his son.

11 And the angel of the Lord called unto him out of heaven, and said, Abraham, Abraham: and he said, Here am I.

12 And he said, Lay not thine hand upon the lad, neither do thou any thing unto him: for now I know that thou fearest God, seeing thou hast not withheld thy son, thine only son, from me.

13 And Abraham lifted up his eyes, and looked, and behold behind him a ram caught in a thicket by his horns: and Abraham went and took the ram, and offered him up for a burnt offering in the stead of his son.

14 And Abraham called the name of that place Jehovah-jireh: as it is said to this day, In the mount of the Lord it shall be seen.

15 And the angel of the Lord called unto Abraham out of heaven the second time,

16 And said, By myself have I sworn, saith the Lord, for because thou hast done this thing, and hast not withheld thy son, thine only son:

17 That in blessing I will bless thee, and in multiplying I will multiply thy seed as the stars of the heaven, and as the sand which is upon the sea shore; and thy seed shall possess the gate of his enemies;

18 And in thy seed shall all the nations of the earth be blessed; because thou hast obeyed my voice.

. . .

COMMENTS AND QUESTIONS

1. This is a *narrative*: a tight, brief and simple one based on the old principle of suspense. To understand simply how it functions as a narrative, it may be useful to break it down into parts as follows:
   a. (verses 1–6) A straightforward account of events.
   b. (verses 7–8) *Almost* a breakdown. Suspense introduced.
   c. (verses 9–12) The climax.
   d. (verses 13–18) The resolution, a happy ending.

2. Analyze the contrast between the simple way in which the events are narrated and the underlying emotions. What are these emotions, and how does the writer convey them?

3. Why is God testing Abraham? What is Abraham's reaction?

4. Would the story be more or less effective if the writer described Abraham's inner feelings in more detail?

5. What attitude on the part of humanity in relation to God is advocated here? Compare this attitude with the Greek one.

EXODUS

The Ten Commandments

As liberator and savior of Israel, God brought his people out of bondage in Egypt and into the wilderness, where he forged them into a community under the leadership of Moses. In the very first days of their desert sojourn he led them to Mount Sinai where, through Moses, he declared his offer of a covenant with them and sealed the agreement with the revelation of his laws.

Chapter 19

1 In the third month, when the children of Israel were gone forth out of the land of Egypt, the same day came they into the wilderness of Sinai.

2 For they were departed from Rephidim, and were come to the desert of Sinai, and had pitched in the wilderness; and there Israel camped before the mount.

3 And Moses went up unto God, and the Lord called unto him out of the mountain, saying, Thus shalt thou say to the house of Jacob, and tell the children of Israel;

4 Ye have seen what I did unto the Egyptians, and how I bare you on eagles' wings, and brought you unto myself.

5 Now therefore, if ye will obey my voice indeed, and keep my covenant, then ye shall be a peculiar treasure unto me above all people: for all the earth is mine:

6 And ye shall be unto me a kingdom of priests, and an holy nation. These are the words which thou shalt speak unto the children of Israel.

7 And Moses came and called for the elders of the people, and laid before their faces all these words which the Lord commanded him.

8 And all the people answered together, and said, All that the Lord hath spoken we will do. And Moses returned the words of the people unto the Lord.

9 And the Lord said unto Moses, Lo, I come unto thee in a thick cloud, that the people may hear when I speak with thee, and believe thee for ever. And Moses told the words of the people unto the Lord.

10 And the Lord said unto Moses, Go unto the people, and sanctify them to day and to morrow, and let them wash their clothes. . . .

14 And Moses went down from the mount unto the people, and sanctified the people; and they washed their clothes.

15 And he said unto the people, Be ready against the third day: come not at your wives.

16 And it came to pass on the third day in the morning, that there were thunders and lightnings, and a thick cloud upon the mount, and the voice of the trumpet exceeding loud; so that all the people that was in the camp trembled.

17 And Moses brought forth the people out of the camp to meet with God; and they stood at the nether part of the mount.

18 And mount Sinai was altogether on a smoke, because the Lord descended upon it in fire: and the smoke thereof ascended as the smoke of a furnace, and the whole mount quaked greatly.

19 And when the voice of the trumpet sounded long, and waxed louder and louder, Moses spake, and God answered him by a voice.

20 And the Lord came down upon mount Sinai, on the top of the mount; and the Lord called Moses up to the top of the mount; and Moses went up.

21 And the Lord said unto Moses, Go down, charge the people, lest they break through unto the Lord to gaze, and many of them perish.

22 And let the priests also, which come near to the Lord, sanctify themselves, lest the Lord break forth upon them.

23 And Moses said unto the Lord, The people cannot come up to mount Sinai: for thou chargedst us, saying, Set bounds about the mount, and sanctify it.

24 And the Lord said unto him, Away, get thee down, and thou shalt come up, thou, and Aaron with thee: but let not the priests and the people break through to come up unto the Lord, lest he break forth upon them.

25 So Moses went down unto the people, and spake unto them.

Chapter 20

1 And God spake all these words, saying,

2 I am the Lord thy God, which have brought thee out of the land of Egypt, out of the house of bondage.

3 Thou shalt have no other gods before me.

4 Thou shalt not make unto thee any graven image, or any likeness of any thing that is in heaven above, or that is in the earth beneath, or that is in the water under the earth:

5 Thou shalt not bow down thyself to them, nor serve them: for I the Lord thy God am a jealous God, visiting the iniquity of the fathers upon the children unto the third and fourth generation of them that hate me;

6 And shewing mercy unto thousands of them that love me, and keep my commandments.

7 Thou shalt not take the name of the Lord thy God in vain; for the Lord will not hold him guiltless that taketh his name in vain.

8 Remember the sabbath day, to keep it holy.

9 Six days shalt thou labour, and do all thy work:

10 But the seventh day is the sabbath of the Lord thy God: in it thou shalt not do any work, thou, nor thy son, nor thy daughter, thy manservant, nor thy maidservant, nor thy cattle, nor thy stranger that is within thy gates:

11 For in six days the Lord made heaven and earth, the sea, and all that in them is, and rested the seventh day: wherefore the Lord blessed the sabbath day, and hallowed it.

12 Honour thy father and thy mother: that thy days may be long upon the land which the Lord thy God giveth thee.

13 Thou shalt not kill.

14 Thou shalt not commit adultery.

15 Thou shalt not steal.

16 Thou shalt not bear false witness against thy neighbour.

17 Thou shalt not covet thy neighbour's house, thou shalt not covet thy neighbour's wife, nor his manservant, nor his maidservant, nor his ox, nor his ass, nor any thing that is thy neighbour's.

18 And all the people saw the thunderings, and the lightnings, and the noise of the trumpet, and the mountain smoking: and when the people saw it, they removed, and stood afar off.

19 And they said unto Moses, Speak thou with us, and we will hear: but let not God speak with us, lest we die.

20 And Moses said unto the people, Fear not: for God is come to prove you, and that his fear may be before your faces, that ye sin not.

21 And the people stood afar off, and Moses drew near unto the thick darkness where God was.

22 And the Lord said unto Moses, Thus thou shalt say unto the children of Israel, Ye have seen that I have talked with you from heaven. . . .

COMMENTS AND QUESTIONS

1. What previous event does God use to gain credibility for his promise?

2. What is God's promise to the Israelites?

3. In what sense is a covenant established between them and God?

4. The Ten Commandments, or Decalogue, is divided into two parts. The first four relate to the individual's relationship with God, while the last six deal with the sphere of human relationships. Why is the command to honor parents often described as the "bridge" commandment between the two parts?

5. Why, according to Moses, did God reveal himself in a cloud?

LEVITICUS

The Holiness Code

The Decalogue formed the core of Israel's law, but over the centuries an elaborate code of legislation developed around it, dealing with all aspects of ritual, moral, and civil life. The so-called Holiness Code, Leviticus 17–26, received this title because the laws it embodied were designed to preserve a level of conduct worthy of the people whom God had elected over all others. Although written down in this form in the sixth century B.C., it is presented in the Bible as part of the legislation made during the period of desert wanderings six hundred years earlier. Nonetheless, like the previous legislation of the Israelites, these laws contrast with those of other contemporary Near Eastern peoples in placing greater emphasis on people than on property. They also tend to ignore the distinctions between classes so prominent in the codes of other traditions. In its concern for the downtrodden, the Holiness Code reflects the continuing folk memory of the liberation of the Israelites themselves from bondage in Egypt. Leviticus 19 may be considered perhaps the ultimate development in ethics in the Old Testament.

Chapter 19

1 And the Lord spake unto Moses, saying,

2 Speak unto all the congregation of the children of Israel, and say unto them, Ye shall be holy: for I the Lord your God am holy.

3 Ye shall fear every man his mother, and his father, and keep my sabbaths: I am the Lord your God. . . .

9 And when ye reap the harvest of your land, thou shalt not wholly reap the corners of thy field, neither shalt thou gather the gleanings of thy harvest.

10 And thou shalt not glean thy vineyard, neither shalt thou gather every grape of thy vineyard; thou shalt leave them for the poor and stranger: I am the Lord your God.

11 Ye shall not steal, neither deal falsely, neither lie one to another.

12 And ye shall not swear by my name falsely, neither shalt thou profane the name of thy God: I am the Lord.

13 Thou shalt not defraud thy neighbour, neither rob him: the wages of him that is hired shall not abide with thee all night until the morning.

14 Thou shalt not curse the deaf, nor put a stumblingblock before the blind, but shalt fear thy God: I am the Lord.

15 Ye shall do no unrighteousness in judgment: thou shalt not respect the person of the poor, nor honour the person of the mighty: but in righteousness shalt thou judge thy neighbour.

16 Thou shalt not go up and down as a talebearer among thy people: neither shalt thou stand against the blood of thy neighbour: I am the Lord.

17 Thou shalt not hate thy brother in thine heart: thou shalt in any wise rebuke thy neighbour, and not suffer sin upon him.

18 Thou shalt not avenge, nor bear any grudge against the children of thy people, but thou shalt love thy neighbor as thyself: I am the Lord. . . .

33 And if a stranger sojourn with thee in your land, ye shall not vex him.

34 But the stranger that dwelleth with you shall be unto you as one born among you, and thou shalt love him as thyself; for ye were strangers in the land of Egypt: I am the Lord your God. . . .

QUESTIONS

1. On what grounds does God base his demand that the Israelites be holy?

2. What provisions should be made for the poor?

3. By implication, according to verse 14, how were the handicapped sometimes treated in ancient society?

4. Why should the Israelites especially be kind to strangers?

5. What comparisons can be made between these laws and those in the code of Hammurabi?

PSALMS

Psalm 8

No other Old Testament book has enjoyed the perennial success of the Psalms in appealing to readers. A few of the one hundred fifty poems composing the book may go back in some form to the period of King David in the tenth century B.C., but others were doubtless composed centuries later. These poetic works were designed to fulfill specific purposes in temple ritual. More than fifty years ago the German biblical scholar Hermann Gunkel[1] distinguished five major categories of psalms according to function: (1) hymns of praise, (2) communal laments, (3) royal psalms, (4) individual laments, and (5) individual thanksgiving psalms.

[1]Hermann Gunkel, *The Psalms,* trans. Thomas M. Horner (Philadelphia: Fortress Press, 1967.)

The following hymn of praise has as its object the praise of God, but closely associated with the idea of divine greatness here is that of the dignity of the human being. People have a unique relationship with the Creator, and to them he has committed the government of the earth. Consequently, in the biblical tradition, the worth of the individual is grounded directly in God's personal love and in the responsibilities created by that love.

1 O Jehovah, our Lord,
 How excellent is thy name in all the earth,
 Who hast set thy glory upon the heavens!
2 Out of the mouth of babes and sucklings hast thou
    established strength,
 Because of thine adversaries,
 That thou mightest still the enemy and the avenger.
3 When I consider thy heavens, the work of thy
    fingers,
 The moon and the stars, which thou hast ordained;
4 What is man, that thou art mindful of him?
 And the son of man, that thou visitest him?
5 For thou hast made him but little lower than God,
 And crownest him with glory and honor.
6 Thou makest him to have dominion over the works
    of thy hands;
 Thou hast put all things under his feet:
7 All sheep and oxen,
 Yea, and the beasts of the field,
8 The birds of the heavens, and the fish of the sea,
 Whatsoever passeth through the paths of the seas.
9 O Jehovah, our Lord,
 How excellent is thy name in all the earth!

COMMENTS AND QUESTIONS

1. What is meant by the mouths of babes and infants chanting God's glory?

2. A famous saying praising human dignity is attributed to the fifth-century B.C. Greek philosopher Protagoras: "Man is the measure of all things." Compare the basis for human dignity suggested by this statement with that in verse 4 of this psalm.

AMOS

From the mid-eighth to the sixth centuries B.C., the spiritual life of Jews was dominated by a succession of prophets. Men who considered themselves inspired by God, the prophets took it as their mission to warn kings and their people of the divine punishment to be inflicted on those who failed to fulfill the duties and moral standards imposed on the chosen people of God. Generally speaking, these were centuries of great difficulty for the Jews. They saw their kingdom—divided in two since the death of Solomon in 922 B.C.—pressured first by the Assyrians and then by the Babylonians. The northern kingdom, Israel, with its capital at Samaria, finally fell to the Assyrians in 722, while the southern kingdom, Judah, centered at Jerusalem, held out until conquered by the Babylonians in 587.

The first in this line of prophets, Amos, lived in the mid-eighth century. During his lifetime, the northern kingdom, to which he primarily directed his words, still enjoyed peace and prosperity. Landed estates expanded; costly homes were built; religious shrines were richly endowed; and the arts flourished. To Amos, however, the scrupulous insistence on religious rites, which was characteristic of the period, masked wholesale immorality: sexual liberty, oppression of the poor, bribery of judges, and corruption in government and business. Amos' emphasis on the spirit rather than the letter of religion and his burning sense of social justice also characterized the prophets who followed him.

Chapter 5

. . .

10 They hate him that reproveth in the gate, and they abhor him that speaketh uprightly.

11 Forasmuch therefore as ye trample upon the poor, and take exactions from him of wheat: ye have built houses of hewn stone, but ye shall not dwell in them: ye have planted pleasant vineyards, but ye shall not drink the wine thereof.

12 For I know how manifold are your transgressions, and how mighty are your sins—ye that afflict the just, that take a bribe, and that turn aside the needy in the gate from their right.

13 Therefore he that is prudent shall keep silence in such a time; for it is an evil time.

14 Seek good, and not evil, that ye may live; and so Jehovah, the God of hosts, will be with you, as ye say.

15 Hate the evil, and love the good, and establish justice in the gate: it may be that Jehovah, the God of hosts, will be gracious unto the remnant of Joseph.

16 Therefore thus saith Jehovah, the God of hosts, the Lord: Wailing shall be in all the broad ways; and they shall say in all the streets, Alas! alas! and they shall call the husbandman to mourning, and such as are skilful in lamentation to wailing.

17 And in all vineyards shall be wailing; for I will pass through the midst of thee, saith Jehovah.

18 Woe unto you that desire the day of Jehovah!

Wherefore would ye have the day of Jehovah? It is darkness, and not light.

19 As if a man did flee from a lion, and a bear met him; or went into the house and leaned his hand on the wall, and a serpent bit him.

20 Shall not the day of Jehovah be darkness, and not light? even very dark, and no brightness in it?

21 I hate, I despise your feasts, and I will take no delight in your solemn assemblies.

22 Yea, though ye offer me your burnt-offerings and meal-offerings, I will not accept them; neither will I regard the peace-offerings of your fat beasts.

23 Take thou away from me the noise of thy songs; for I will not hear the melody of thy viols.

24 But let justice roll down as waters, and righteousness as a mighty stream....

QUESTIONS

1. How does Amos expect his prophesy to be received? What does the prudent man say in such dangerous times?

2. What is meant in verse 12 when the poor in the gate are said to be turned aside "from their right"? What does "the gate" refer to here and elsewhere in this selection?

3. Why will the Lord not accept the sacrifices and prayers of his people?

4. What threats does Amos make?

THE SONG OF SONGS

Hebraic literature has greatly influenced our culture, primarily through the religious views that are developed in it and, along with them, a concept of morality. One book of the Bible, however, has been influential in quite different ways and represents a unique form of biblical literature. This is the Song of Songs, called in the King James Bible the Song of Solomon. Its authorship is unknown, but because of King Solomon's reputation for wisdom and poetic gifts, it was attributed to him. It is unique in the Bible in that God is never mentioned in it. What it appears to be is a passionate love poem, or more likely several love lyrics that were at some point (scholars speculate by the fifth century B.C.) collected together. Sometimes the speaker is the lover, or bridegroom, sometimes the beloved, or bride. In the course of the poems they are united, separated, sought by each other, found. The awakening of love is closely allied with the awakening of nature in springtime. The lovers celebrate each other's physical beauty and the marvel of being in love, all with a direct and sensuous imagery.

One may well ask how such a poem found its way into a collection of sacred scripture. No one has the definitive answer to this question, but it has puzzled scholars for centuries. Both Jewish and Christian commentators have attempted to explain away its sensuous, physical aspects by *allegorical* interpretations. In the Jewish tradition, the lover was said to represent Jahweh and the beloved his people, Israel. In the Christian version of the *allegory*, the lover becomes Christ; the beloved, his Church. This allegorical way of thinking came to be of great importance to the medieval Christian mentality, as we shall discover in later chapters.

More recent scholars believe that the poems in the Song of Songs are what they appear to be—celebrations of human love. They were probably originally folk poems, and they may have been sung at weddings. In any case, they have become a part of our lyric tradition and have influenced the ways in which we express love between man and woman.

Chapter 1

1 The song of songs, which is Solomon's.

2 Let him kiss me with the kisses of his mouth: for thy love is better than wine.

3 Because of the savour of thy good ointments thy name is as ointment poured forth, therefore do the virgins love thee.

4 Draw me, we will run after thee: the king hath brought me into his chambers: we will be glad and rejoice in thee, we will remember thy love more than wine: the upright love thee.

5 I am black, but comely, O ye daughters of Jerusalem, as the tents of Kedar, as the curtains of Solomon.

6 Look not upon me, because I am black, because the sun hath looked upon me: my mother's children were angry with me; they made me the keeper of the vineyards; but mine own vineyard have I not kept.

7 Tell me, O thou whom my soul loveth, where thou feedest, where thou makest thy flock to rest at noon: for why should I be as one that turneth aside by the flocks of thy companions?

8 If thou know not, O thou fairest among women, go thy way forth by the footsteps of the flock, and feed thy kids beside the shepherds' tents.

9 I have compared thee, O my love, to a company of horses in Pharaoh's chariots.

10 Thy cheeks are comely with rows of jewels, thy neck with chains of gold.

11 We will make thee borders of gold with studs of silver.

12 While the king sitteth at his table, my spikenard sendeth forth the smell thereof.

13 A bundle of myrrh is my wellbeloved unto me; he shall lie all night betwixt my breasts.

14 My beloved is unto me as a cluster of camphire in the vineyards of Engedi.

15 Behold, thou art fair, my love; behold, thou art fair; thou hast doves' eyes.

16 Behold, thou art fair, my beloved, yea, pleasant: also our bed is green.

17 The beams of our house are cedar, and our rafters of fir.

Chapter 2

1 I am the rose of Sharon, and the lily of the valleys.

2 As the lily among thorns, so is my love among the daughters.

3 As the apple tree among the trees of the wood, so is my beloved among the sons. I sat down under his shadow with great delight, and his fruit was sweet to my taste.

4 He brought me to the banqueting house, and his banner over me was love.

5 Stay me with flagons, comfort me with apples: for I am sick of love.

6 His left hand is under my head, and his right hand doth embrace me.

7 I charge you, O ye daughters of Jerusalem, by the roes, and by the hinds of the field, that ye stir not up, nor awake my love, till he please.

8 The voice of my beloved! behold, he cometh leaping upon the mountains, skipping upon the hills.

9 My beloved is like a roe or a young hart: behold, he standeth behind our wall, he looketh forth at the windows, shewing himself through the lattice.

10 My beloved spake, and said unto me, Rise up, my love, my fair one, and come away.

11 For, lo, the winter is past, the rain is over and gone;

12 The flowers appear on the earth; the time of the singing of birds is come, and the voice of the turtle is heard in our land;

13 The fig tree putteth forth her green figs, and the vines with the tender grape give a good smell. Arise, my love, my fair one, and come away.

14 O my dove, that art in the clefts of the rock, in the secret places of the stairs, let me see thy countenance, let me hear thy voice; for sweet is thy voice, and thy countenance is comely.

15 Take us the foxes, the little foxes, that spoil the vines: for our vines have tender grapes.

16 My beloved is mine, and I am his: he feedeth among the lilies.

17 Until the day break, and the shadows flee away, turn, my beloved, and be thou like a roe or a young hart upon the mountains of Bether.

COMMENTS AND QUESTIONS

1. The best-known, most often quoted part of this poem is in Chapter 2, verses 10–17. How would you explain its appeal?

2. The association between love and spring is, of course, by now an overworked cliché. Is the statement made here nevertheless still fresh and powerful?

3. Compare these love lyrics with those of the Egyptian ones in Chapter 2 and those of Sappho in Chapter 3. Which is the richest in imagery? If you were to paint your impressions of them, which would have more color and more varied *textures*?

4. How would you describe the relationship between man and woman as it appears in these two chapters of the Song of Songs?

5. Do you see any justification for the Jewish or the Christian allegorical interpretations?

Texts from the New Testament

THE GOSPEL ACCORDING TO SAINT MATTHEW

The Sermon on the Mount

In the following text, Jesus tells his followers the essentials of Christian doctrine.

Chapter 5

1 And seeing the multitudes, he went up into a mountain: and when he was set, his disciples came unto him:

2 And he opened his mouth, and taught them, saying,

3 Blessed are the poor in spirit: for theirs is the kingdom of heaven.

4 Blessed are they that mourn: for they shall be comforted.

5 Blessed are the meek: for they shall inherit the earth.

6 Blessed are they which do hunger and thirst after righteousness: for they shall be filled.

7 Blessed are the merciful: for they shall obtain mercy.

8 Blessed are the pure in heart: for they shall see God.

9 Blessed are the peacemakers: for they shall be called the children of God.

10 Blessed are they which are persecuted for righteousness' sake: for theirs is the kingdom of heaven.

11 Blessed are ye, when men shall revile you, and persecute you, and shall say all manner of evil against you falsely, for my sake.

12 Rejoice, and be exceeding glad: for great is your reward in heaven: for so persecuted they the prophets which were before you.

13 Ye are the salt of the earth: but if the salt have lost his savour, wherewith shall it be salted? it is thenceforth good for nothing, but to be cast out, and to be trodden under foot of men.

15 Ye are the light of the world. A city that is set on an hill cannot be hid.

15 Neither do men light a candle, and put it under a bushel, but on a candlestick; and it giveth light unto all that are in the house.

16 Let your light so shine before men, that they may see your good works, and glorify your Father which is in heaven.

17 Think not that I am come to destroy the law, or the prophets: I am not come to destroy, but to fulfill.

18 For verily I say unto you, Till heaven and earth pass, one jot or one tittle shall in no wise pass from the law, till all be fulfilled.

19 Whosoever therefore shall break one of these least commandments, and shall teach men so, he shall be called the least in the kingdom of heaven: but whosoever shall do and teach them, the same shall be called great in the kingdom of heaven.

20 For I say unto you, That except your righteousness shall exceed the righteousness of the scribes and Pharisees, ye shall in no case enter into the kingdom of heaven.

21 Ye have heard that it was said by them of old time, Thou shalt not kill; and whosoever shall kill shall be in danger of the judgment:

22 But I say unto you, That whosoever is angry with his brother without a cause shall be in danger of the judgment: and whosoever shall say to his brother, Raca, shall be in danger of the council: but whosoever shall say, Thou fool, shall be in danger of hell fire.

23 Therefore if thou bring thy gift to the altar, and there rememberest that thy brother hath ought against thee;

24 Leave there thy gift before the altar, and go thy way; first be reconciled to thy brother, and then come and offer thy gift.

25 Agree with thine adversary quickly, whiles thou art in the way with him; lest at any time the adversary deliver thee to the judge, and the judge deliver thee to the officer, and thou be cast into prison.

26 Verily I say unto thee, Thou shalt by no means come out thence, till thou hast paid the uttermost farthing.

27 Ye have heard that it was said by them of old time, Thou shalt not commit adultery:

28 But I say unto you, That whosoever looketh on a woman to lust after her hath committed adultery with her already in his heart.

29 And if thy right eye offend thee, pluck it out, and cast it from thee: for it is profitable for thee that one of thy members should perish, and not that thy whole body should be cast into hell.

30 And if thy right hand offend thee, cut it off, and cast it from thee: for it is profitable for thee that one of thy members should perish, and not that thy whole body should be cast into hell.

31 It hath been said, Whosoever shall put away his wife, let him give her a writing of divorcement:

32 But I say unto you, That whosoever shall put away his wife, saving for the cause of fornication, causeth her to commit adultery: and whosoever shall marry her that is divorced committeth adultery.

33 Again, ye have heard that it hath been said by them of old time, Thou shalt not forswear thyself, but shalt perform unto the Lord thine oaths:

34 But I say unto you, Swear not at all; neither by heaven; for it is God's throne:

35 Nor by the earth; for it is his footstool: neither by Jerusalem; for it is the city of the great King.

36 Neither shalt thou swear by thy head, because thou canst not make one hair white or black.

37 But let your communication be, Yea, yea; Nay, nay: for whatsoever is more than these cometh of evil.

38 Ye have heard that it hath been said, An eye for an eye, and a tooth for a tooth:

39 But I say unto you, That ye resist not evil: but whosoever shall smite thee on thy right cheek, turn to him the other also.

40 And if any man will sue thee at the law, and take away thy coat, let him have thy cloke also.

41 And whosoever shall compel thee to go a mile, go with him twain.

42 Give to him that asketh thee, and from him

that would borrow of thee turn not thou away.

43 Ye have heard that it hath been said, Thou shalt love thy neighbour, and hate thine enemy.

44 But I say unto you, Love your enemies, bless them that curse you, do good to them that hate you, and pray for them which despitefully use you, and persecute you;

45 That ye may be the children of your Father which is in heaven: for he maketh his sun to rise on the evil and on the good, and sendeth rain on the just and on the unjust.

46 For if ye love them which love you, what reward have ye? do not even the publicans the same?

47 And if ye salute your brethren only, what do ye more than others? do not even the publicans so?

48 Be ye therefore perfect, even as your Father which is in heaven is perfect.

Chapter 6

1 Take heed that ye do not your alms before men, to be seen of them: otherwise ye have no reward of your Father which is in heaven.

2 Therefore when thou doest thine alms, do not sound a trumpet before thee, as the hypocrites do in the synagogues and in the streets, that they may have glory of men. Verily I say unto you, They have their reward.

3 But when thou doest alms, let not thy left hand know what thy right hand doeth:

4 That thine alms may be in secret: and thy Father which seeth in secret himself shall reward thee openly.

5 And when thou prayest, thou shalt not be as the hypocrites are: for they love to pray standing in the synagogues and in the corners of the streets, that they may be seen of men. Verily I say unto you, They have their reward.

6 But thou, when thou prayest, enter into thy closet, and when thou hast shut thy door, pray to thy Father which is in secret; and thy Father which seeth in secret shall reward thee openly.

7 But when ye pray, use not vain repetitions, as the heathen do: for they think that they shall be heard for their much speaking.

8 Be not ye therefore like unto them: for your Father knoweth what things ye have need of, before ye ask him.

9 After this manner therefore pray ye: Our Father which art in heaven, Hallowed be thy name.

10 Thy kingdom come. Thy will be done in earth, as it is in heaven.

11 Give us this day our daily bread.

12 And forgive us our debts, as we forgive our debtors.

13 And lead us not into temptation, but deliver us from evil: For thine is the kingdom, and the power, and the glory, for ever. Amen.

14 For if ye forgive men their trespasses, your heavenly Father will also forgive you:

15 But if ye forgive not men their trespasses, neither will your Father forgive your trespasses.

16 Moreover when ye fast, be not, as the hypocrites, of a sad countenance: for they disfigure their faces, that they may appear unto men to fast. Verily I say unto you, They have their reward.

17 But thou, when thou fastest, anoint thine head, and wash thy face;

18 That thou appear not unto men to fast, but unto thy Father which is in secret: and thy Father, which seeth in secret, shall reward thee openly.

19 Lay not up for yourselves treasures upon earth, where moth and rust doth corrupt, and where thieves break through and steal:

20 But lay up for yourselves treasures in heaven, where neither moth nor rust doth corrupt, and where thieves do not break through nor steal:

21 For where your treasure is, there will your heart be also.

22 The light of the body is the eye: if therefore thine eye be single, thy whole body shall be full of light.

23 But if thine eye be evil, thy whole body shall be full of darkness. If therefore the light that is in thee be darkness, how great is that darkness!

24 No man can serve two masters: for either he will hate the one, and love the other; or else he will hold to the one, and despise the other. Ye cannot serve God and mammon.

25 Therefore I say unto you, Take no thought for your life, what ye shall eat, or what ye shall drink; nor yet for your body, what ye shall put on. Is not the life more than meat, and the body than raiment?

26 Behold the fowls of the air: for they sow not, neither do they reap, nor gather into barns; yet your heavenly Father feedeth them. Are ye not much better than they?

27 Which of you by taking thought can add one cubit unto his stature?

28 And why take ye thought for raiment? Consider the lilies of the field, how they grow; they toil not, neither do they spin:

29 And yet I say unto you, That even Solomon in all his glory was not arrayed like one of these.

30 Wherefore, if God so clothe the grass of the field, which to day is, and to morrow is cast into the

oven, shall he not much more clothe you, O ye of little faith?

31 Therefore take no thought, saying, What shall we eat? or, What shall we drink? or, Wherewithal shall we be clothed?

32 For after all these things do the Gentiles seek: for your heavenly Father knoweth that ye have need of all these things.

33 But seek ye first the kingdom of God, and his righteousness; and all these things shall be added unto you.

34 Take therefore no thought for the morrow: for the morrow shall take thought for the things of itself. Sufficient unto the day is the evil thereof.

Chapter 7

1 Judge not, that ye be not judged.

2 For with what judgment ye judge, ye shall be judged: and with what measure ye mete, it shall be measured to you again.

3 And why beholdest thou the mote that is in thy brother's eye, but considerest not the beam that is in thine own eye?

4 Or how wilt thou say to thy brother, Let me pull out the mote out of thine eye; and, behold, a beam is in thine own eye?

5 Thou hypocrite, first cast out the beam out of thine own eye; and then shalt thou see clearly to cast out the mote out of thy brother's eye.

6 Give not that which is holy unto the dogs, neither cast ye your pearls before swine, lest they trample them under their feet, and turn again and rend you.

7 Ask, and it shall be given you; seek, and ye shall find; knock, and it shall be opened unto you:

8 For every one that asketh receiveth; and he that seeketh findeth; and to him that knocketh it shall be opened.

9 Or what man is there of you, whom if his son ask bread, will he give him a stone?

10 Or if he ask a fish, will he give him a serpent?

11 If ye then, being evil, know how to give good gifts unto your children, how much more shall your Father which is in heaven give good things to them that ask him?

12 Therefore all things whatsoever ye would that men should do to you, do ye even so to them: for this is the law and the prophets.

13 Enter ye in at the strait gate: for wide is the gate, and broad is the way, that leadeth to destruction, and many there be which go in thereat:

14 Because strait is the gate, and narrow is the way, which leadeth unto life, and few there be that find it.

15 Beware of false prophets, which come to you in sheep's clothing, but inwardly they are ravening wolves.

16 Ye shall know them by their fruits. Do men gather grapes of thorns, or figs of thistles?

17 Even so every good tree bringeth forth good fruit; but a corrupt tree bringeth forth evil fruit.

18 A good tree cannot bring forth evil fruit, neither can a corrupt tree bring forth good fruit.

19 Every tree that bringeth not forth good fruit is hewn down, and cast into the fire.

20 Wherefore by their fruits ye shall know them.

21 Not every one that saith unto me, Lord, Lord, shall enter into the kingdom of heaven; but he that doeth the will of my Father which is in heaven.

22 Many will say to me in that day, Lord, Lord, have we not prophesied in thy name? and in thy name have cast out devils? and in thy name done many wonderful works?

23 And then will I profess unto them, I never knew you: depart from me, ye that work iniquity.

24 Therefore whosoever heareth these sayings of mine, and doeth them, I will liken him unto a wise man, which built his house upon a rock:

25 And the rain descended, and the floods came, and the winds blew, and beat upon that house; and it fell not: for it was founded upon a rock.

26 And every one that heareth these sayings of mine, and doeth them not, shall be likened unto a foolish man, which built his house upon the sand:

27 And the rain descended, and the floods came, and the winds blew, and beat upon that house; and it fell: and great was the fall of it.

28 And it came to pass, when Jesus had ended these sayings, the people were astonished at his doctrine:

29 For he taught them as one having authority, and not as the scribes.

QUESTIONS

1. What does Jesus demand of his followers, and what does he promise?

2. What kind of a leader, what kind of personality, is Jesus?

3. Why do you think he speaks in parables and "similitudes"? What is the effect of the comparisons made?

4. To what extent does Jesus, in his views, reject the Jewish heritage?

Saint Paul
Letter to the Ephesians

Paul has frequently been referred to as the founder of Christian theology. His mind well trained in Jewish law and clearly influenced by late Hellenistic culture, Paul was sure to offer a highly developed interpretation of what came to him as the simple faith of primitive Christianity. His emphasis on the central significance of Christ's death and resurrection for human salvation was doubtless original. By nature children of Adam, we share in the heritage of sin. We are Christ's, on the other hand, by adoption—a concept of Roman law—and thereby share in God's kingdom. Through the suffering and death of Christ, human sins are forgiven, and the belief in that redemptive act becomes the source for a new life of love: "Far be it from me to glory save in the cross of our Lord Jesus Christ" (Gal. 6:14). Christ's resurrection, moreover, is proof that Jesus was God's own son and that we, as believers, after leading a rich spiritual life, will also live eternally in paradise. Thus Paul proclaims (1 Cor. 2:2): "For I decided to know nothing... except Jesus Christ and him crucified."

Paul declares emphatically that no one has a *right* to become a child of Christ. Adoption is a gift of God, that is, an act of divine grace. God decides on whom he will bestow the privilege. The condition for the reception of grace is faith. As Paul writes (Rom. 10:9): "If thou shalt confess with thy mouth Jesus as Lord, and shalt believe in thy heart that God raised Him from the dead, thou shalt be saved." The essence of Christian life, therefore, lies in a vital, personal relationship between the individual and Christ. For Paul, Christ, the Son of God, is his Lord and Redeemer.

Chapter 2

1 And you did he make live when ye were dead through your trespasses and sins,

2 wherein ye once walked according to the course of this world, according to the prince of the power of the air, of the spirit that now worketh in the sons of disobedience;

3 among whom we also all once lived in the lusts of our flesh, doing the desires of the flesh and of the mind, and were by nature children of wrath, even as the rest:

4 but God, being rich in mercy, for his great love wherewith he loved us,

5 even when we were dead through our trespasses, made us alive together with Christ (by grace have ye been saved),

6 and raised us up with him, and made us to sit with him in the heavenly places, in Christ Jesus:

7 that in the ages to come he might show the exceeding riches of this grace in kindness toward us in Christ Jesus:

8 for by grace have ye been saved through faith; and that not of yourselves, it is the gift of God;

9 not of works, that no man should glory.

10 For we are his workmanship, created in Christ Jesus for good works, which God afore prepared that we should walk in them.

11 Wherefore remember, that once ye, the Gentiles in the flesh, who are called Uncircumcision by that which is called Circumcision, in the flesh, made by hands;

12 that ye were at that time separate from Christ, alienated from the commonwealth of Israel, and strangers from the covenants of the promise, having no hope and without God in the world.

13 But now in Christ Jesus ye that once were far off are made nigh in the blood of Christ.

14 For his is our peace, who made both one, and brake down the middle wall of partition,

15 having abolished in his flesh the enmity, even the law of commandments contained in ordinances; that he might create in himself of the two one new man, so making peace;

16 and might reconcile them both in one body unto God through the cross, having slain the enmity thereby:

17 and he came and preached peace to you that were far off, and peace to them that were nigh:

18 for through him we both have our access in one Spirit unto the Father.

19 So then ye are no more strangers and sojourners, but ye are fellow-citizens with the saints, and of the household of God,

20 being built upon the foundation of the apostles and prophets, Christ Jesus himself being the chief corner stone;

21 in whom each several building, fitly framed together, groweth into a holy temple in the Lord;

22 in whom ye also are builded together for a habitation of God in the Spirit.

Chapter 3

1 For this cause I, Paul, the prisoner of Christ Jesus in behalf of you Gentiles,

2 if so be that ye have heard of the dispensation of that grace of God which was given me to you-ward;

3 how that by revelation was made known unto me the mystery, as I wrote before in few words,

4 whereby, when ye read, ye can perceive my understanding in the mystery of Christ;

5 which in other generations was not made known unto the sons of men, as it hath now been revealed unto his holy apostles and prophets in the Spirit;

6 to wit, that the Gentiles are fellow-heirs, and fellow-members of the body, and fellow-partakers of the promise in Christ Jesus through the gospel,

7 whereof I was made a minister, according to the gift of that grace of God which was given me according to the working of his power.

8 Unto me, who am less than the least of all saints, was this grace given, to preach unto the Gentiles the unsearchable riches of Christ;

9 and to make all men see what is the dispensation of the mystery which for ages hath been hid in God who created all things;

10 to the intent that now unto the principalities and the powers in the heavenly places might be made known through the church the manifold wisdom of God,

11 according to the eternal purpose which he purposed in Christ Jesus our Lord:

12 in whom we have boldness and access in confidence through our faith in him....

COMMENTS AND QUESTIONS

1. How does Paul characterize the life of the individual before coming to Christ?

2. For what motive did God give us eternal life?

3. The Church of Ephesus in Asia Minor was composed primarily of Gentiles. How did they become, according to Paul, one with the commonwealth of Israel? That is, how was peace established between Jew and Gentile?

4. How did Christ abolish the "law of commandments and ordinances"?

First Letter to the Corinthians

At the center of the new spiritual life of the Christian is love. In the following passage from 1 Cor. 12–13, Paul strikingly dramatizes the emphasis Christ placed on the love toward God and one's neighbor that he expected from his followers.

Chapter 13

1 If I speak with the tongues of men and of angels, but have not love, I am become sounding brass, or a clanging cymbal.

2 And if I have the gift of prophecy, and know all mysteries and all knowledge; and if I have all faith, so as to remove mountains, but have not love, I am nothing.

3 And if I bestow all my goods to feed the poor, and if I give my body to be burned, but have not love, it profiteth me nothing.

4 Love suffereth long, and is kind; love envieth not; love vaunteth not itself, is not puffed up,

5 doth not behave itself unseemly; seeketh not its own, is not provoked, taketh not account of evil;

6 rejoiceth not in unrighteousness, but rejoiceth with the truth;

7 beareth all things, believeth all things, hopeth all things, endureth all things.

8 Love never faileth: but whether there be prophecies, they shall be done away; whether there be tongues, they shall cease; whether there be knowledge, it shall be done away.

9 For we know in part, and we prophesy in part;

10 but when that which is perfect is come, that which is in part shall be done away.

11 When I was a child, I spake as a child, I felt as a child, I thought as a child: now that I am become a man, I have put away childish things.

12 For now we see in a mirror, darkly; but then face to face: now I know in part; but then shall I know fully even as also I was fully known.

13 But now abideth faith, hope, love, these three; and the greatest of these is love.

QUESTIONS

1. Why are the power of tongues, prophetic powers, faith, and self-denial nothing without love?

2. What does Paul mean when he writes: "When I was a child, I spake as a child?"

Texts from the Early Church Fathers

SAINT JEROME

The Christian and the Classics

Translation by F. A. Wright

The following passage, from one of Jerome's Latin letters, describes in vivid words his struggle to forsake the pagan classics, which had clearly been an intellectual inspiration to him for many years.

Many years ago for the sake of the kingdom of heaven I cut myself off from home, parents, sister, relations, and, what was harder, from the dainty food to which I had been used. But even when I was on my way to Jerusalem to fight the good fight there, I could not bring myself to forgo the library which with great care and labour I had got together at Rome. And so, miserable man that I was, I would fast, only to read Cicero afterwards. I would spend long nights in vigil, I would shed bitter tears called from my inmost heart by the remembrance of my past sins; and then I would take up Plautus again. Whenever I returned to my right senses and began to read the prophets, their language seemed harsh and barbarous. With my blind eyes I could not see the light: but I attributed the fault not to my eyes but to the sun. While the old serpent was thus mocking me, about the middle of Lent a fever attacked my weakened body and spread through my inmost veins. It may sound incredible, but the ravages it wrought on my unhappy frame were so persistent that at last my bones scarcely held together.

Meantime preparations were made for my funeral: my whole body grew gradually cold, and life's vital warmth only lingered faintly in my poor throbbing breast. Suddenly I was caught up in the spirit and dragged before the Judge's judgment seat: and here the light was so dazzling, and the brightness shining from those who stood around so radiant, that I flung myself upon the ground and did not dare to look up. I was asked to state my condition and replied that I was a Christian. But He who presided said: "Thou liest; thou art a Ciceronian, not a Christian. 'For where thy treasure is there will thy heart be also.' "[1] Straightway I became dumb, and amid the strokes of the whip—for He had ordered me to be scourged—I was even more bitterly tortured by the fire of conscience, considering with myself the verse: "In the grave who shall give thee thanks?"[2] Yet for all that I began to cry out and to bewail myself, saying: "Have mercy upon me, O Lord, have mercy upon me": and even amid the noise of the lash my voice made itself heard. At last the bystanders fell at the knees of Him who presided, and prayed Him to pardon my youth and give me opportunity to repent of my error, on the understanding that the extreme of torture should be inflicted on me if ever I read again the works of Gentile authors. In the stress of that dread hour I should have been willing to make even larger promises, and taking oath I called upon His name: "O Lord, if ever again I possess worldly books or read them, I have denied thee."

After swearing this oath I was dismissed, and returned to the upper world. There to the surprise of all I opened my eyes again, and they were so drenched with tears, that my distress convinced even the incredulous. That this experience was no sleep nor idle dream, such as often mocks us, I call to witness the judgment seat before which I fell and the terrible verdict which I feared. May it never be my lot again to come before such a court as that! I profess that my shoulders were black and blue, and that I felt the bruises long after I awoke from my sleep. And I acknowledge that henceforth I read the books of God with a greater zeal than I had ever given before to the books of men.

QUESTIONS

1. What is so appealing to Jerome about the pagan classical authors?
2. Why and how does he struggle to liberate himself from their influence?
3. What differences between Christianity and the classical tradition emerge here?

SAINT AUGUSTINE

FROM THE *Confessions*

Translation by E. M. Blaiklock

In the first passage of the *Confessions*, Augustine looks back on his sensuous youth when he came to Carthage to study rhetoric; in the second he chastises himself for his former love of theater. The next passage recounts the experience of conversion in the garden of his house in Milan; and the final one, his last conversation with his mother, Monica.

I
Way of Restlessness

I came to Carthage where a whole frying-pan of wicked loves sputtered all around me. I was not yet in love, but I was in love with love, and with a deep-seated want I hated myself for wanting too little. I was looking for something to love, still in love with love. I hated safety and a path without snares, because I had a hunger within—for that food of the inner man, yourself, my God. Yet that hunger did not make me feel hungry. I was without appetite for incorruptible food, not because I was sated with it, but with less hunger in proportion to my emptiness. And so my soul was sick.

[1]Matthew 6:21
[2]Psalm 6:5.

Its ulcers showed, wretchedly eager to be scratched by the touch of material things which yet, if they had no life, would not be loved at all. To love and to be loved was sweet to me, the more so if I could enjoy the person of the one I loved.

I polluted, therefore, the stream of friendship with the foulness of lust, and clouded its purity with the dark hell of illicit desire. Though sordid and without honour, in my overweening pride, I longed to be a polished man about town. I plunged, too, into the love with which I sought ensnarement, my merciful God. With what gall did you in your goodness sprinkle that sweetness! I was loved. I went as far as the bondage of enjoyment. Because I so desired I was being tied in the entanglements of sorrow, just to be scourged with redhot iron rods of jealousy, suspicions, fears, bouts of rage and quarrelling.

II
The Lure of Drama

The drama enthralled me, full of representations of my own miseries and fuel for my own fire. Why does a man make himself deliberately sad over grievous and tragic events which he would not wish to suffer himself? Yet he is willing as an onlooker to suffer grief from them, and the grief itself is what he enjoys. What is that but wretched lunacy? He is the more stirred by them in proportion to his sanity. When he suffers personally it is commonly called misery. When he feels for others it is called mercy. But what source of mercy is it in imaginary situations on the stage? The hearer is not stirred to help but invited only to grieve, and he compliments the author of such fictions in proportion to his grief. And if those human catastrophes, out of ancient history or simply made up, are so presented that the spectator does not grieve, he goes off disgusted or critical. If he is moved to grief, he stays on, attentive and enjoying it. Tears and sorrows are therefore loved. To be sure we all like joyfulness. No one wants to be miserable though he likes to be sympathetic, and it is only in such case that grief is loved, because it is really without grief. This is a rill from that stream of friendship.

What is its course and flow? Why does it flow down into that torrent of boiling pitch, with its vast tides of foul lusts, into which of its own nature it is transmuted, of its own will twisted and precipitated from its heavenly clearness? Is compassion therefore to be cast aside? By no means. Let there be times when sorrows are welcomed. Beware of uncleanness, my soul, under my protecting God, the God of our fathers, to be praised and exalted for ever, beware of uncleanness. I am not now past compassion, but in those days, in the theatre, I rejoiced with lovers wickedly enjoying one another, imaginary though the situation was upon the stage. And when they lost one another, I shared their sadness with pity—in both ways enjoying it all.

VIII
Strife in the Garden

Then in that mighty conflict of my inner dwelling place, which I had strongly stirred up in the chamber of my heart, troubled in both face and mind, I assailed Alypius. I cried: "What is wrong with us? What is this you have heard? The unlearned rise and take heaven by storm, and we, with our learning, see where we wallow in flesh and blood. Are we ashamed to follow because others have gone ahead, and not ashamed not to follow at all?" Some such words I said, and my fever tore me away from him while he, looking at me with astonishment, said nothing. I did not sound like myself. Forehead, cheeks, eyes, colour, the level of my voice gave expression to my mind more than the words I uttered. A small garden was attached to our dwelling, and we had freedom to use it, as indeed, the whole house, for the master of the house, our host, did not live on the premises. To the garden, the tempest in my breast snatched me. There no one would hinder the fiery disputation I had begun against myself until its consummation, known already to you, but not to me. I was only healthily mad, dying in order to live, knowing what an evil thing I was, but not knowing what good thing I was about to be. So I went off into the garden with Alypius following close behind. His presence did not make my privacy the less, and how could he desert me in so disturbed a state? We sat as far away from the house as we could. I groaned in spirit, tempestuously indignant that I was not surrendering to your will and covenant, my God, and which all my bones, praising it to high heaven, called out to me to do. Not only to go there, but also to arrive, asked for no more than the will to go. The way was not by ships, carriages or feet. It was not so far from the house as the place to which we had gone where we were sitting. It required no more than the will to go there, a resolute and thorough act of will, not to toss and turn this way and that, a half-maimed will, struggling, one half rising, one half sinking.

In the wild passions of my irresolution, I did with my body what people sometimes want to do but cannot, either lacking the limbs, their limbs in chains, weakened by weariness, or otherwise impeded. If I tore my hair, beat my brow, clasped my knee with knitted fingers, it was because I wanted to do so. Yet I could have wanted to, and not done so, if my limbs had not been pliable enough to do my will. So much then I did when to will was not in itself to be able. And I did not what I both longed immeasurably more to do, and which soon, when I should will, I should be able to do, because soon, when I should will, I should will thoroughly. In such case power and will coincide, and willing is forthwith doing. And yet it was not done, and my body obeyed more easily the weakest willing of my mind, moving limbs as it directed, than my soul obeyed itself to carry out in the will alone, this great will which should be done.

X
Conversation with Monica

When the day was near for her departure from this life (you knew it though we did not) it happened, I think by your secret guidance, that we two should be standing alone leaning on a window. It was at Ostia-on-Tiber, and the window looked on to a courtyard garden in the house we had. Removed from the bustling crowds after the fatigue of a long journey, we were building up strength for the sea voyage. So we were conversing most pleasantly, "forgetting the things behind and reaching for those before," and speculating together in the light of present truth (which you are) about what the eternal life of the saints will be, which "eye has not seen, ear heard, nor has it come into the heart of anyone." Yet we panted, as though our hearts had lips, for those upper streams of your fountain, the fountain of life which is in your presence, so that sprinkled from it, as we are able to receive, we might set our thoughts on so vast a theme.

We agreed that the greatest imaginable delight of the senses, in the brightest conceivable bodily context, set beside the sweetness of that life, seemed not only unworthy of comparison, but not even of mention. With deeper emotion we tried to lift our thoughts to that Reality itself, covering step by step all things bodily, and heaven itself whence sun, moon and stars shine above the earth. We soared higher, and by the heart's meditation, by speech, by wonder at your work, penetrated to our naked minds and past them to reach the place where plenty never fails, from which store you feed Israel for ever with truth for food, where life is the wisdom with which all this universe is made in the past and in time yet to be. This wisdom is not created but is as it was and forever will be. Indeed, to have been and to be about to be are irrelevant terms in this

wisdom, only eternal being. While we talked and panted after it, with all our heart's outreaching we seemed just to touch it. We sighed and left captured there the firstfruits of our spirits and made our way back to the sound of our voices, where a word has both beginning and end—unlike your Word, our Lord, which endures in itself without ageing yet renewing all.

So we were saying: If for anyone the tempest of the flesh should grow still, the phantasies of the earth, the waters and the air be quietened, along with the axis of the skies, if the very soul should fall silent and transcend itself by forgetting itself with its dreams, imaginary insights, and speech, and all else taking form from the transient (for they all say to him who has ears: We made not ourselves but he who abides eternally made us), if all these, at such words, could fall silent, because they are straining their ear to their creator, and if he should speak alone, not through them, but by himself and audibly, not by human speech nor voice of angels, the sound of thunder nor obscure similitude, so that we should hear only him whom in such matters we love (in such fashion as we were straining and in swift thought touching the eternal wisdom in all things immanent) if this state could go on, leached utterly of all alien conceptions, and if this one rapture could seize, absorb, and so envelop its beholder in more inward joys, so that eternal life should be quite like that moment of understanding to which we aspired, would not this be: "Enter into the joy of your Lord"? When? When we shall rise again, though "we shall not all be changed"?

Such was our conversation though not precisely in this sequence and these words. Yet you know, Lord, that on that day, when we were speaking thus and the world grew base to us amid such conversation with its delights, she said: "Son, as for me, I find nothing in this life which delights me. I do not know what I have left to do here or why I am here, now that my hopes in this world are gone. There was one thing for which I used to desire to stay on a little in this life, to see you a Catholic Christian before I died. God has granted me this more abundantly, in that I see you his servant, all earthly happiness cast aside. What am I doing here?"

QUESTIONS

1. What are the various meanings of "love" and "friendship" in these texts?

2. What paradox does Augustine find inherent in our enjoyment of tragedy? Why does drama seem to him opposed to Christian faith?

3. What relations between mind and body appear in Augustine's account of his conversion?

4. What influences of Platonism can you find in these passages?

5. What use of rhythm and images does Augustine make and what is their effect on the reader?

The Greco-Roman and Judeo-Christian Roots

The Classical Ideal

The classical cultures, Greece and Rome, in spite of many differences, form together a unified system of cultural values and creations that has profoundly influenced the course of Western culture and is still with us today. In our focus on the "classical" phase of "classical" culture—Athens in the fifth century B.C.—we witnessed the aesthetic and moral values associated with the term. The Greek mentality of that century looks to human reason as the force giving order to the world. It is humanistic in that it stresses the dignity and worth of human individuals as such more than as part of a social or divine order. Yet it cautions against the dangers of human pride, *hubris*. "Nothing in excess" were the words of the oracle at Delphi, and we see this applied to Oedipus when he tries to outwit fate; in Pericles' description of the equilibrium between private and public good in Athens; in the historians' demonstrations of the evils entailed by extreme action; in the sculptural and architectural monuments that strive to balance or harmonize the real and the ideal; in Aristotle's golden mean. Classical art is dynamic and pleasing because its proportions and symmetry represent an attempt to harmonize forces like body and soul, humanity and the gods, reason and emotion. When a classical work is copied and calculated from reason alone, it becomes lifeless. The Greeks very much admired the power of reason, but they were deeply interested in the *whole* human being.

Greek Philosophy and Mathematics

The debt of the Greeks to Mesopotamian and Egyptian culture is a question for scholars. Stories that Plato visited Egypt as a young man and brought back with him much of its learning commonly circulated in the ancient world. Some of the Babylonian achievements in mathematics and astronomy were probably transmitted to the West through the Greeks of Asia Minor. That the earliest of the Pre-Socratic philosophers were all from this area lends strong support for such transmission.

Nonetheless, the Greeks seem to have been the first to elaborate the logical structures of our thought, structures that have become so natural to the modern mind that we take them for granted. Greek logicians laid down the basic rules for determining when arguments are valid or invalid; that is, when conclusions follow from a given set of premises and when they do not. Greek terminology still predominates in textbooks of logic. Perhaps more significantly, the Greeks were almost certainly the first to use logic and its companion mathematics for the systematic understanding of nature. These instruments of human reason were believed to work because the world was viewed as by nature intelligible and its functioning capable of being reduced to laws. Something of this same trust in the capability of human intellect to solve the mysteries of nature motivates numbers of scientists and their supporters today.

Finally, Greek philosophers endeavored to see human life within the context of a world system integrating all the elements of the universe into a consistent whole. Plato, Aristotle, Zeno, and others, confident in the powers of human reason, constructed vast synthetic structures of thought that promised to answer the basic questions surrounding human existence. Even though today we recognize the ability of the intellect to organize large segments of human experience through the use of rational powers, few would grant it such scope.

Greek Science and Politics

Modern culture owes to the ancient Greeks most of the basic categories for ordering knowledge into disciplines, such as physics, ethics, politics, and poetics (all Greek words). The Greeks also defined and distinguished the methodologies or ways of investigating truth appropriate to various disciplines. Using these methodologies, the Greeks made such advances that, in the sciences at least, western Europe was not to surpass them until after 1600. The myriad ancient Greek city-states experimented with every conceivable form of government over the centuries. Aristotle in fact wrote a now lost work on 126 different Greek constitutions. He along with other Greek political theorists provided an analysis of the basic constitutional forms of monarchy, tyranny, aristocracy, oligarchy, republican government, and democracy that still informs modern political science.

Greek and Roman Literature, Architecture, and Sculpture

Greek writers, building on previous achievements in Mesopotamia and Egypt, codified basic literary forms that influenced not only the course of Western literature but also the ways in which we think about life. The English language acknowledges its debt to Greek concepts with terms such as *epic, lyric, tragedy,* and *comedy.* The Romans adapted and modified these forms, adding an influential one of their own, *satire.*

In much the same way, Greek architectural orders and the temple form and Roman arch and dome construction are the basic elements of a major architectural language that has persisted to the present. The Romans adapted Greek sculptural and artistic forms to more practical uses: the portrait, the forum, the triumphal arch, the coliseum. Our engineering and city planning derive from Roman innovation.

Similarly, the accomplishments of the Greeks and Romans in sculpture and painting provided the archetypes for early Christian art. Later the remembered greatness of Rome was a major impetus for the artists of Renaissance Italy who sought to equal the ancients. Through the Renaissance, ideas on Greek and Roman art and architecture were to be a goad and support for artistic development in the West.

Roman Expansion of Greek Culture

Although the Greeks were undoubtedly the originators of most of the cultural forms we have been studying here, the term *Greco-Roman* makes sense because of what the Romans did with Greek culture. The parochialism of Hellenic Greece had already been broken down by the empire of Alexander in the late fourth century B.C., but the long-enduring conquests of the Romans institutionalized Greek culture among the ruling classes of a vast area from Persia to England and from the Sahara to northern Germany and the steppes of Russia.

Furthermore, the Romans added their own cultural forms to the Greek ones. The Greeks philosophized about the laws of nature, but the Romans realized them in the form of actual codes of law. Although Aristotle first defined the characteristics of republican government, the founders of the United States looked back more to Rome than to Greece for a model, because in the Roman Republic they saw a practical embodiment of the government for which the Greeks could offer only theories. Committed as they were to limited male suffrage based on property qualifications, the makers of the U.S. Constitution considered the kind of democracy found in fourth-century B.C. Athens as little short of anarchy.

Hellenic and Hebraic Ways of Thinking

Over the course of Western civilization, thinkers have attempted to compare and contrast the mentalities of the two cultures considered as "roots," the Greek and Jewish, or Hellenic and Hebraic. In an essay entitled "Culture and Anarchy," the English poet and critic Matthew Arnold defined the differences by stating that Hellenism, or the Greek mentality, aims to "see things as they really are," whereas the aim of Hebraism is "conduct and obedience." The former stresses "right thinking," individual reasoning, and logic; the latter stresses "right acting," ethical understanding, and obeying God's commandments. "Man is the measure of all things," the dictum of the Greek philosopher Protagoras, would have been inconceivable in African, Asiatic, and Near Eastern cultures such as Egypt and Mesopotamia, as well as in Israel. Although the Greeks were also aware of human frailty, the question of the Psalmist, "What is man, that thou art mindful of him?" would not have occurred to them. The Greeks assumed that human beings were the primary interest of the gods, just as the gods themselves were glorified human beings.

A more recent writer, the Scandinavian theologian Thorleif Boman, has developed further the comparisons and contrasts between Hebrew and Greek thought.[1] His major thesis is that whereas the Greek is a culture of space, the Hebrew is a culture of time. For the Hebrews, all sources of being are in God, who alone is, and who manifests his being by his words and guidance of his people in history. For the Greeks, on the other hand, truth is to be discovered by the tools of logic and geometry. Whereas the Greeks were a pri-

---

[1]Thorleif Boman, *Hebrew Thought Compared with Greek,* trans. Jules Moreau (New York: Norton Library, 1960).

marily visual people and used their art to make representations of their gods as well as of themselves, the ancient Hebrews forbade visual representation of God and human beings. Boman notes the rhythmic and dynamic properties of biblical poetry as opposed to the more visual images of Greek poetry. A literary critic, Erich Auerbach, has called biblical literature "fraught with background," or with the sense of God's presence, as opposed to the clarity and the present quality of Greek literature. All such vast syntheses, although useful, are of course open to exceptions.

Greco-Roman and Judeo-Christian Parallels

If it is possible to make a distinction between the Hellenic and Hebraic mentalities, one must remember that Christianity (and, for that matter, Judaism from the second century B.C.) was strongly influenced by Greek ways of thinking. The New Testament is itself a document of Greek literature, containing Greek philosophical terms; and the influence of Plato and Aristotle on the development of Catholic theology was enormous. Nor can one neglect the Roman contribution to Christian culture. The economic, political, and legal structures provided by the Roman Empire facilitated communication and helped make Christianity the dominant cultural influence in Europe. We have seen how the Christian church, God's house on earth, grew out of the Roman basilica.

Once this is said, however, it is nonetheless evident that certain aspects of Christianity deriving from Judaism differentiate it profoundly from the classical values of Greece and Rome. Foremost of these is the Hebraic concept of one supreme God. The God of both Jews and Christians is a creator who made the world as we know it from nothing and a law-giver who dictates to human beings, his creatures, fundamental principles of morality. Socrates determined what was right and good according to the dictates of reason; the Jew or Christian accepts the Ten Commandments or the Sermon on the Mount as moral law because it is the word of God.

Opposing itself to the values of the Greco-Roman world as a small, radical group, Christianity demanded allegiance to Christ before allegiance to the Roman emperor and the gods of the state. Yet Paul molded it into a potentially universalist faith. Once Emperor Constantine converted, Christianity was able to use the Empire to its advantage, not, of course, without making bargains with the secular world in the process.

Just as Rome had diffused the Greco-Roman culture as a part of its imperial mission in previous centuries, so in the fourth and fifth centuries the Christian Roman emperors endeavored to impose on their subjects a uniform belief in the Christian message. Although the Empire collapsed in the West by the end of this period, within the barbarian kingdoms Christianity survived its demise. In the East, where the Empire continued, the emperors fought a losing battle to keep the faithful uncontaminated by a rash of heresies that threatened both religious and civil unity. They rightly perceived these heresies as a menace to the Empire, but they were defeated in their efforts to contain them. By the seventh century a new Semitic religion, Islam, profited from this very religious discontent by carrying away a significant portion of what remained of the Roman Empire.

PART THREE

Medieval Cultures

9

The Byzantine and the Islamic Empires

*O*ut of the breakup of the Roman Empire in the fifth century rose three new political formations: the Eastern Roman Empire, which over time became known as the Byzantine Empire; the empire created by Islam; and the various states constituting western Europe. None of the three political and cultural areas developed in isolation or in a vacuum. In many ways less sophisticated than their neighbors, the Byzantines and Muslims, Europeans for centuries remained on the defensive, especially against Islam. At the same time they had frequent intellectual and economic contact with both empires. Although the Crusades beginning in 1095 marked the initial stages of a vigorous European assault on the East, into the thirteenth century the West remained largely a borrower of ideas and technology from these areas. Before tracing the rise of western European culture we will present a brief characterization of the cultures of Byzantium and Islam. This will provide a better context in which to trace the development of our European cultural root, acknowledging its debt to these two contemporary cultures as well as to ancient Greece, Rome, and the Christian and Renaissance past.

The Eastern Roman Empire or Byzantium

The Byzantine or Eastern Empire was the surviving half of the ancient Roman Empire, now centered not on Rome but on the "New Rome," the official name for Constantinople throughout the Middle Ages. Its civilization constituted a synthesis of all the intellectual, political, and religious aspects of the ancient world in its declining centuries, that is, the Latin, Hellenistic, and Christian traditions, together with the oriental culture of the revitalized Persian empire. The greatness of Byzantium lay in its preservation of the sources of ancient civilization in the period when the West

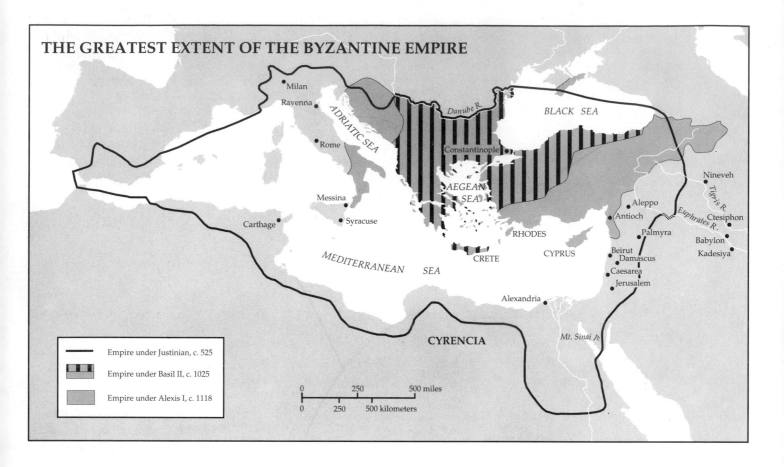

THE GREATEST EXTENT OF THE BYZANTINE EMPIRE

Empire under Justinian, c. 525

Empire under Basil II, c. 1025

Empire under Alexis I, c. 1118

experienced political, social, artistic, and intellectual decline. Of particular importance was its role as the guardian of Greek literature and Roman law for the use of distant posterity. At the same time it acted as a barricade for the West in holding off new invasions from the East and as the vital force in Christianizing the Slavic peoples on the great northern plains of eastern Europe and western Asia.

Justinian (527–565)

Byzantine history began with the reign of Justinian. The greatest of the Byzantine emperors, he was born a humble, Latin-speaking peasant in what is now a part of modern Turkey. He became emperor after the death of an uncle, an illiterate but gifted soldier, who seized the throne in Constantinople in 518. Justinian's wife, Theodora, a former prostitute of remarkable intelligence and courage, played an active role in government.

The major goals of Justinian's reign were to reassert Roman power in the West against the barbarian invaders and at the same time to expand universal Christianity into pagan lands and defend the faith against those he considered heretics. Beginning in 533, Justinian, served by two brilliant generals, undertook a military campaign that ultimately seized control from the barbarian invaders of the North African coastline, eastern Spain, and most of Italy from the barbarian occupiers. The recapture of these territories by fire and sword probably inflicted more destruction on the land than had more than a century of barbarian invasions (see map).

The expansion of Rome's new religion and its protection from heresy constituted Justinian's second goal. He supported missionary efforts to Christianize barbarians to the north in Russia and peoples as far away as China to the east. Within his kingdom religious deviation was ruthlessly suppressed. Partly a product of his strong religious beliefs, Justinian's strict religious policy toward his subjects had political overtones as well. He believed that religious conformity would augment his central control. For this reason he subordinated the patriarch of Constantinople, in theory the second most powerful cleric after the pope in Rome, to his control, while his governor at Ravenna, the Byzantine capital of Italy, closely monitored the actions of the pope himself.

This was to be the last serious effort to hold the two parts of the Roman Empire together, and it did not endure long. Within a few years of Justinian's death in 565, western European kingdoms began to develop without fear of interference from the Empire. Spain and northern and central Italy fell back into barbarian hands and the North African coast was lost to the Muslims in the seventh century. However, in one area, southern Italy, Byzantine power lasted into the eleventh century and left an indelible mark on the culture and arts of the area. The failure of the reconquest had immense significance for the papacy. Had it succeeded, the Roman pope and the Church he led would have remained captive to imperial policy, as did the patriarch in Constantinople. As it was, the pope remained relatively free without a powerful monarch in the vicinity, and from that position he ultimately was able to uphold the independence of the spiritual power, a distinctive characteristic of Christianity in western Europe.

Roman Law Codes   A more positive contribution of Justinian to western European culture related to his belief that a united Empire and Church should be accompanied by a common law. Particularly disturbing to him was the confusion in the legal system created by the lack of an integrated code of Roman law. Ancient Roman law consisted of (1) the statutes and edicts made by Roman legal agencies, including the emperor, and (2) the decisions handed down in cases by Roman judges. Over the centuries this material had come to fill many volumes, and the mass was filled with many contradictions. At the beginning of his reign Justinian resolved to integrate into one book, called the *Code,* all the Roman laws having validity in his kingdom. To this would be added two other books: the *Digest* or *Pandects,* a collection of the legal opinions of ancient legal scholars regarding the laws, and the *Institutes,* a textbook to train lawyers. Given the enormity of the enterprise, Justinian's commission of legal scholars worked with surprising rapidity and between 528 and 535 accomplished their task. The three books together with a fourth—called the *New Constitutions,* containing laws enacted after the completion of the other three—became known as the *Corpus of Civil Law.* Justinian's preface to the *Digest* explains in detail his motivation for ordering a revision of the legal books.

Subsequently, this law code circulated in western Europe as a regional code for centuries until the eleventh century, when Western scholars revived the conception of Roman law as the basic law of all peoples.

Within a few centuries it came to be accepted throughout continental Europe as the law against which all local law must be tested for validity. It still underlies the legal system of most countries in modern Western Europe.

Hagia Sophia   A great builder, Justinian endowed the cities of the Empire with new monuments, the most splendid of which, the church of Hagia Sophia (Holy Wisdom), was located in Constantinople. Its architects, Anthemius of Tralles and Isidorus of Miletus, combined the languages and skills of their artistic resources to create a fresh, new form (Fig. 9-1).

The rectangular basilican churches of Rome focused attention on the *apse* end where the altar stood. Hagia Sophia has the form of a square, topped with a great central dome, supported by two half-domes (Fig. 9-2). Four great *piers,* seventy feet high, rise from the square corners. These piers carry four great semicircular arches connected by curved, triangular-shaped membranes called *pendentives.* The pendentives join their upper edges to form the base of the central dome. The weight of the arches and dome is supported by four great *buttresses,* and the two half-domes, like the central dome, are made using traditional Roman techniques of bricks and masonry (see Chapter 7 and Fig. 9-3). The entire structure beneath the dome is enclosed in massive walls pierced with many windows. Procopius, Justinian's court historian, wrote that the church seemed to soar to heaven and rise above the city "like a huge ship anchored among them."

Procopius also tells us that artisans and precious materials came from all over the Empire. Eight porphyry columns came from Rome and eight green marble ones from Ephesus. Marble in varied colors, alabaster, and onyx were cut, fitted, carved, pierced, and veneered to cover walls and pavements in geometric patterns. No contemporary tells us whether there was any figurative, narrative mosaic decoration, but one writes: "The vaulting is formed of countless little squares of gold cemented together. And the golden stream of glittering rays pours down and strikes the eyes of men so that they can scarcely bear to look. It is as if one were to gaze upon the mid-day sun in spring, when it gilds every mountain height." The effect of light—whether from the sun or from hundreds of lamps suspended in the building—must have been otherworldly. There was a huge silver iconostasis—a screen with doors to which were attached many icons and images—that separated the sanctuary/altar from the congregation; an immense circular *ambo* (plat-

9-1 *Anthemius of Tralles and Isidorus of Miletus. Hagia Sophia, Istanbul.* A.D. *532–537. (Bildarchiv Foto Marburg, Marburg/Lahn Germany)*

9-2 *Anthemius of Tralles and Isidorus of Miletus. Interior of Hagia Sophia, Istanbul,* A.D. *532–537. (Hirmer Fotoarchiv, Munich)*

form raised on columns) that stood near the center, for preaching; and a silver *ciborium* (canopy) that stood over the altar. With all its gold and silver and its many holy relics, the church contained an immense treasure of worldly and spiritual riches. When it was completed in 537, Justinian was heard to say: "Solomon, I have surpassed thee."

Ravenna Ravenna, once the capital of Honorius, the Western Roman emperor, and now the capital of newly conquered Italy, provided Justinian's architects and artists with models for imitation for his building in Constantinople at the same time that it became the

9-3   *Plan and section of the Hagia Sophia, Istanbul.*

9-4 *Sant' Apollinare in Classe, Ravenna. Interior, nave looking toward apse,* A.D. *533–549. (Hirmer Fotoarchiv, Munich)*

9-5 *Bapistery of the Orthodox, Ravenna. (Alinari/Art Resource, NY)*

object of the emperor's passion for monumental architecture.

In Ravenna, Christians had adopted the basilican plan for many of their churches. A church like Sant' Apollinare in Classe, founded in c. 504 (Fig. 9-4), could easily be compared with Old Saint Peter's. They also erected domed buildings for baptismal rites like the Baptistery of the Orthodox (Fig. 9-5). These domed structures focused attention on the single act that occurred there and seemed ill suited to the congregations of Christians who gathered for preaching. The church of San Vitale, however, built under the patronage of Justinian and Theodora, shows how a centrally planned church like Hagia Sophia could be adapted.

The Church of San Vitale   San Vitale is an octagonal domed church (see plan and section, Fig. 9-6). The very plain redbrick exterior with deeply shaded windows and tile roofs hardly prepares one to experience the inside (Fig. 9-7). Entry is through a hall-like *narthex* placed on one side of the octagon through which one enters the church. One moves from the narthex into a two-story, vaulted *ambulatory* that is separated from the central space by seven niches formed from piers

and columns. The eighth niche ends in a half-dome that contains the apse, separated from the ambulatory by screens of columns. A third story rises above the central space, topped by a dome set on the *clerestory* beneath (Fig. 9-8).

The space is flooded with light, but light transformed by the intersecting spaces formed by columns and niches, gallery and dome, which are covered entirely in gold and vividly colored mosaics. Stories from the Old Testament that prefigure Christ fill the walls, and a youthful, idealized, imperial Christ seated on the orb of heaven appears in the half-dome above the apse. To the left and right of the chancel are Justinian and Theodora, who also stand in this immaterial space—the gold ground of the mosaic (Color Plate IV). Each faces frontally, centered among prelates and attendants. Justinian holds the bread, the body of Christ, and Theodora, in a gold cup encrusted with emeralds, the wine, his blood—the elements of the Eucharist that will be celebrated in this place. Both wear their imperial crowns, each head haloed, like the saints. The frontal poses, the glorious robes, and the

9-8 *San Vitale, Ravenna. Interior view. (Alinari/Art Resource, NY)*

9-6 *Plan and section of San Vitale, Ravenna.*

9-7 *San Vitale, Ravenna.* A.D. *c. 525–547. (Alinari/Art Resource, NY)*

trappings of state do not diminish the individuality of the faces of Justinian, Theodora, and their attendants. Although the faces and forms are rendered abstractly, the artist shows each person clearly as they both watch and participate in this ritual.

This art form—the mosaic—involves a new visual dimension and thus new conventions that allow the artist to move from depicting a naturalistic world, as in Roman painting, to a symbolic world in which saints and emperors, dead and living, share a holy space. Perhaps more than any other art that we have seen these mosaics are filled with that quiet splendor and timelessness that recall Egyptian sculpture.

Sant' Apollinare Another splendid example to be found near Ravenna is the apse decoration of the church of Sant' Apollinare in Classe, the old Roman seaport nearby. The church itself is a typical basilica with an apse. The mosaic decorations were executed between 533 and 549 (Color Plate V). The apse is divided by windows, and between the windows mosaics of deceased bishops with raised hands—a praying position—stand in niches framed by curtains. Rising from the base of the half-dome and filling nearly two-thirds of its height is a wonderful green pasture filled with stylized trees, plants, flowers, and animals. In the center stands Saint Appollinaire, and to his left and right six white sheep separated by flowering white lilies. These sheep represent the twelve disciples. Above his head, on a gold ground, floats a jeweled cross in a blue, star-studded circle. Half-length figures of Elijah and Moses are depicted on either side of the circle. This, we are to understand, symbolizes the vision of Saint Appollinaire in which he saw and understood the meaning of the Transfiguration of Christ.

Like the artists at San Vitale, the makers of this mosaic have told a story, decorated and enhanced the church's feeling, and created images that the Christian can take with him or her. Saint Appollinaire, like Justinian, is presented frontally, the sheep in profile and the figures of Elijah and Moses in an arbitrary

half-length design to indicate that they are in another place, both literally and figuratively. This represents the elaborate, wonderful, and complex symbolic language that will be used to teach, comfort, and cajole Christians for centuries to come.

Justinian's buildings at Ravenna, however, had little immediate effect on western European architecture largely because the poor economy permitted few large churches and Western artists lacked the talent for imitating such elaborate constructions. Nevertheless, when Charlemagne built himself a new capital city at Aachen, around 800, he looked to San Vitale in Ravenna as a model for his own chapel.

Venice The influence of Byzantine art on Venice came not from Ravenna but directly from Constantinople, to which Venice was closely linked by trade. Saint Mark's Cathedral in Venice, begun in 1063, is Byzantine in plan and decoration (see Fig. 9-9). The church is designed as a Greek cross—a cross with equal arms. A great dome rises above the crossing, and slightly lower domes, sheathed in wooden

9-9   St. Mark's, Venice. Begun A.D. *1063. (Alinari/Art Resource, NY)*

helmets covered by gilt copper sheeting, cap the four arms. The interior is covered with mosaics, figures on a gold ground that float above the viewer and suggest another world.

The Threat of Islam and Separation from the West

Within a hundred years of Justinian's death the forces of Islam, inflamed by a new form of monotheism, began advancing beyond their native Arabian Peninsula both toward the kingdom of Persia on the east and Byzantium on the west. By the late seventh century, the forces of Islam had occupied much of the Persian empire; had seized Syria, Palestine, and Egypt; and were working their way along the shore of North Africa toward Spain. Faced at the same time with new barbarian tribes invading the Balkans, Byzantium simply had to recognize the Muslim conquests.

Although the Empire's historians tenaciously held to the fiction of eternal Rome, all that remained by 750 were the Greek-speaking provinces of Asia Minor, the Balkans, and parts of the Italian south. In such circumstances the Greek heritage of the Byzantine Empire came to the fore. By this time the emperor himself was officially designated as *basileus,* the Greek word for "king," and the official language of the state had become Greek. By the ninth century this reorientation of culture resulted in a renaissance of art and letters inspired by ancient Greek classical influences.

Eastern Monasticism

Not only did Byzantium increasingly distinguish itself from the West by its use of Greek, but its dominant religious tendencies also encouraged a separation from Western Catholicism. Monasticism in the Eastern Roman Empire had a different flavor from that in the West. The roots of the movement in both East and West emerged from Egypt and Syria in the third century among those who desired a completely spiritual life. In those arid provinces withdrawal into the desert, first in solitude and later in communities, satisfied this need. Transplanted to the West, monasticism assumed regularized forms, devoted to worship, public service, and religious scholarship. Indeed, monasteries were in large part responsible from the fifth to the ninth centuries for the preservation of much of the Greco-Roman tradition. On the other hand, in Byzantium monks tended to be more rigorously ascetic and given to mysticism than their Western counterparts.

Although they copied manuscripts and provided some education, they tended to be highly pietistic and uninterested in scholarly and intellectual concerns.

Iconoclasm

The issue of iconoclasm in the early eighth century marked a major crisis in East-West relations. The use of images of Christ and the saints had been a common feature of religious worship throughout Christendom from the early centuries. A peculiar feature of Byzantine worship was the reverence shown to icons, or images of Christ and the saints. In a Byzantine church the icons, frescoes, and lustrous mosaics were ranged in a saintly hierarchy on the walls, culminating at the highest vault in the image of Christ Pantocrator, the All-Ruling Christ, often in the pose of judge over all humankind (Fig. 9-10). The church altar was screened from the congregation by a row of icons, each holy figure in frontal pose, luminous eyes focused on the believers. So placed, these icons were considered by the common people to be inherently rather than just symbolically holy. The twelfth-century icon of the Madonna and Child in Fig. 9-11, with its stylized, linear figure of Mary and its Christ child resembling a little man, is a good example of the Byzantine style in paint-

9-10 *Christ Pantokrater, Hosios Lonkos, Phocis, Greece, 9th century. (Michos Tzovaras/Art Resource, NY)*

9-11 Madonna and Child, *12th century Russian icon.* (Superstock)

ing. As we shall see in Chapter 16, resurgence of European interest in Byzantine painting in the late thirteenth century forms a prelude to the Renaissance.

Beginning in 717 the emperor Leo III led an attack on the veneration of icons, arguing that they were associated with paganism and also contravened the prohibition against the graven image found in Old Testament law. His command to strip the icons from the churches led to open warfare between, on one side, the emperor, most of the clergy, and the army, and on the other the monasteries and the common people, backed by the pope and the whole Western Church. Iconoclastic puritanism rocked the Empire for more than a century and almost led to a division of Christianity before dying out in futility in the late ninth century.

The defeat of the iconoclasts late in the tenth century ensured the continuity of Byzantine art with the Greco-Roman artistic tradition, which had encouraged depiction of human beings and natural objects. Had the iconoclasts won, all forms of representation in religious art in the Eastern Empire would have been forbidden and Eastern Christian art would have moved away from its Western counterpart in a direction similar to that taken by Islam (see page 274).

The Schism of 1054

The century-long struggle over iconoclasm, even if resisted by many in Byzantium itself, had almost produced a rupture in the Christian Church. This did not happen, but other sources of conflict were pushing the two areas apart. West and East had traditionally been disposed to approach the Christian faith from different viewpoints. Westerners were more legalistic, whereas Easterners were more philosophical and mystical. Westerners believed in an inherited deformity in human nature that encourages sin. On the other hand, while believing that human beings committed sin, Christians in the East did not hold to a notion of an original sin inherited from Adam and Eve. This meant that the sense of sin was deeper and the need for divine grace correspondingly greater in the West. Whereas Easterners believed religion's goal was to transform human nature and rescue it from earthliness and death, Westerners were less abstract. For them the Gospel was primarily a new law against which the believer could reckon his or her sins. Religion's aim was to help the believer establish the right relationship with God by the performance of specific acts of good.

Eastern and Western Christianity also differed in some of their rites, tradition, and theology—for example, clerics in the Eastern Church could marry—but the primary conflicts arose over differing claims for jurisdiction. For centuries the patriarch of Constantinople had been quarreling off and on with the Roman pope over the papal claim to supremacy in the Church. Constantinople, since at least the ninth century, demanded to be regarded as equal in stature to Rome. The conversion of the prince of Kiev in Russia by Byzantine missionaries during the reign of Basil II (976–1025) had substantially reinforced this claim. The eventual Christianization of all of Russia constituted the greatest religious conquest of Constantinople. Thus the patriarch of Constantinople now laid claim to the spiritual leadership of Christians in all the lands from southern Italy and the southern Balkans to the eastern borders of Asia Minor, and from the steppes of Russia south to the Christian communities living in Muslim lands in Syria, Egypt, and North Africa.

Matters came to a head in 1054, largely because of the expanding influence of the Roman papacy over the Christian churches in southern Italy. Attempts to establish peace ended in failure and Christianity divided into two churches, the Eastern or Greek Orthodox Church and Western or Roman Catholic

Church. Through later centuries the Greek Orthodox Church retained the loyalties of the vast majority of Christians in eastern Europe and it followed the expansion of Russia to the Pacific in the seventeenth and eighteenth centuries. Late-eighteenth-century Russian colonists would carry their faith to Alaska and California.

The Crusades

This split made alliance between the two halves of Christianity against the new common enemy, the Turks, almost impossible. Converting to Islam in the tenth century, the Turks, a people of central Asia, conquered Persia early in the eleventh century and by the end of that century held Palestine, Syria, and much of Asia Minor almost up to Constantinople itself. In 1095 the Byzantine emperor called on the West for aid. He had no idea that the West would respond with such enthusiasm. The First Crusade (1096–1097) marked only the beginning of a wave of military expeditions from Western countries to Palestine and Syria over the next two hundred years designed to free the Holy Places from Muslim rule. The First Crusade was largely an idealistic enterprise, but very quickly crusaders became aware of the rich opportunities for political and economic gains in these eastern lands.

After the initial expedition, in which Westerners established a kingdom in Syria and Palestine, lands claimed by the Byzantine Empire, relations between Constantinople and the Western intruders deteriorated. Finally in 1204, the Venetians, expecting great economic advantages for themselves, were able to convince the leadership of the Fourth Crusade that the only way to stabilize Western control of Palestine was to capture Constantinople. The city fell after a short seige and the Crusaders thereupon created a Latin kingdom, with Constantinople as capital, and composed of western Anatolia and parts of the Balkans. A Roman Catholic patriarch replaced the Orthodox one, who had taken flight.

The prolonged occupation of Constantinople by the Roman Catholics and their conduct in the city did little to enhance mutual understanding between the two peoples. Much of the city's gold and silver and many of its art treasures were simply seized and transported to western Europe. The four great bronze horses astride Saint Mark's Cathedral in Venice are conspicuous items of this stolen treasure. Occupying Western nobles came to appreciate the high degree of comfort enjoyed by the Byzantine upper class and to imitate them in wearing silks instead of wool and covering their stone floors with rugs, but intellectually and religiously there was almost no interchange.

Collapse of the Empire (1261–1453)

The attack on Constantinople caused a dispersion of bureaucrats, intellectuals, and artists to outlying parts of the kingdom left untouched by the Crusaders. Small independent Byzantine states formed in parts of Greece and along the Black Sea coast out of the remnants. By 1261 Michael Palaeologus, ruler of one of these little dominions, succeeded in conquering Constantinople and expelling the Westerners.

The newly established dynasty held the throne for the next 192 years but remained on the defensive throughout the whole period, its territory often extending only a few miles beyond the city walls. The most fierce among the enemies who threatened the city were the Janissaries. Originally Christian male children born in Turkish-occupied lands, they were taken from their parents at an early age, converted to Islam, and then trained to be soldiers

Byzantium as a Transmitter of Ancient Greek Culture to the West

Despite the Empire's gradual strangulation at the hands of the Turks, literature and art in the tiny Byzantine kingdom flourished. The University of Constantinople continued to function almost down to 1453, remodeled, however, by the emperor on lines resembling those of the University of Paris. The commitment of scholars to ancient Greek literature and Greek culture in general intensified in this time of trouble. The high quality of art in these centuries is brilliantly manifested by the early-fourteenth-century Church of the Chora, with its rich mosaics and frescoes.

Within the last century of Byzantium, moreover, western European scholars, primarily the Italians, awoke to the importance of ancient Greek literature and of Plato's philosophy, only fragments of which existed in Latin. From the late fourteenth century a number of young men went to Constantinople to study the language and to bring back manuscripts of Greek classics. Consequently, in the very last decades of the life of Byzantium, Italy welcomed Byzantine scholars and the books they brought with them. By 1500 the study of Greek, almost extinct in the West for a thousand years, became a part of the regular school curriculum.

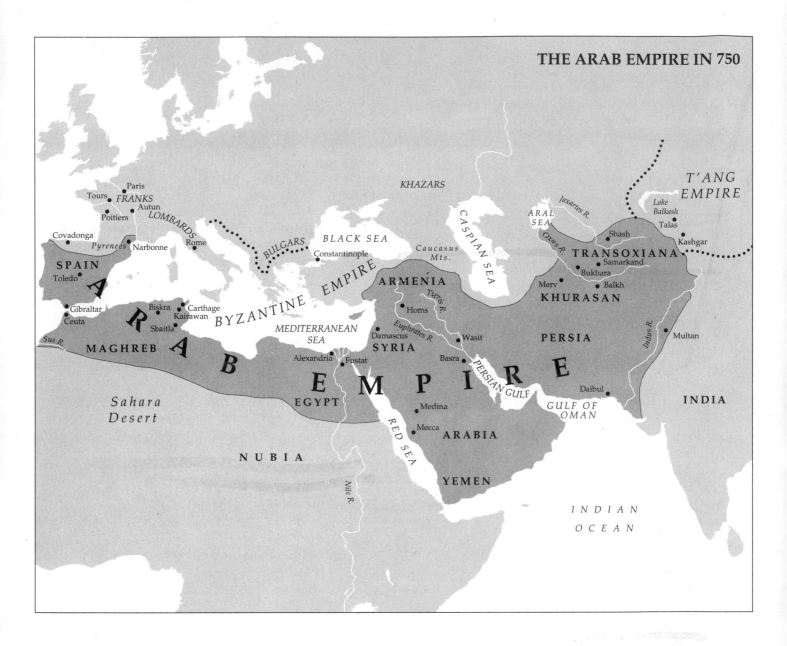

The Islamic Empire

The Early History of the Arabs

No one, least of all the Byzantine and Persian governments, anticipated the extraordinary expansion of the Arabs, an ancient Semitic people, under the banner of Islam in the seventh century of our era. The Arabian

With the entry of the Turks into Constantinople on May 29, 1453, the last citadel of what had been a major civilization became Muslim. We shall now turn to follow the development of the Muslim faith from its birth in the Arabian desert in the seventh century to its impact on the West.

peninsula was a backwater of the ancient world. Periodically, large caravans of heavily laden camels would appear in Damascus or other cities fronting on the desert to discharge exotic goods desired by the civilized world, such as spices, gums, perfumes, and aromatic woods. Occasionally, the desert frontiers of both the Byzantine and Persian empires were threatened by raids from the bedouin, Arab nomadic pastoralists. Both governments therefore made a practice of hiring friendly Arabs to keep the bedouin, to whom raiding was often a matter of existence, from plundering agricultural lands and villages on the desert fringes.

In the sixth and early seventh centuries, it is true, the cataclysmic wars between the Byzantines and Persians had led to both empires' weakening their desert frontiers. Still, who would have expected that by 732, Arab tribes would be ruling from southern France to central Asia, having eradicated the Persian empire and thrust the Byzantines back to a new frontier in Asia Minor? The course and pace of Arab expansion was nothing short of phenomenal (see map).

Islam, a New Monotheism

About the year 610, a middle-aged Arab, Muhammad, began to preach in the commercial and religious center of Mecca. When he delivered his revelations, he spoke in an Arabic different from his ordinary speech, a rhythmic prose. It was the God of the Jews and Christians speaking to him, he said. They, however, had distorted the message, so here it was again, for the last time, in its original, clear Arabic.

The message was straightforward: Be grateful to the sole God, Allah, who created you. God is all-powerful but merciful, compassionate toward weak and forgetful human beings. Worship and obey him, not those idols in the Meccan temple, the Ka'ba, which will be cleansed of paganism. There is only one God and I, Muhammad, am his Messenger. The greedy and the disobedient who fail to observe this warning will feel the wrath of God at the approaching Day of Judgment. Heed the prophets who came before me, he said, heed Abraham, Moses, Jesus, and all the others. My message only confirms what God was saying to them before their followers strayed from the truth.

Most Meccans, however, disbelieved Muhammad. He was forced eventually to leave the city in 622 and take his message to Medina, some 250 miles to the north. There an oasis wracked with civil strife welcomed him and formed a new community of Muslims, those who lived according to God's commandments, as progressively revealed to the Messenger in periodic revelations. The name of the Muslims' religion, Islam, means submission to the will of God. Years after Muhammad's death these messages from God to his Prophet were assembled in the Islamic holy book, the Quran we have today.

Apparently, the more sophisticated Arabs of the peninsula were ready for a religion more encompassing than the worship of tribal spirits residing in idols or nature. There already were Jewish and Christian Arabs. The Quran is familiar with both predecessor religions. In the eyes of Muslims, Islam is a reform of Christianity, just as the latter is a reform of Judaism in the opinion of the Christian faithful. Much of the Quran's content resembles that of the Bible. Although the Quran is addressed specifically to Arabs in their tongue, its message is cast in a universal context. The Arabs formed the core of the Muslim community.

Expansion of Islam and Conversion to the Faith

Muhammad brought Mecca into the Muslim community through an astute combination of warfare and diplomacy. In doing so, he acquired not only the religious center of western Arabia but the important talents of its merchant community as well. The Meccans provided the early leadership of Islam. The Muslims of Medina, on the other hand, found their role more in the meticulous preservation of the holy revelations.

Muhammad died in 632, throwing the Muslims into a crisis. There would be no more revelations, but new leadership in the form of a caliph, or deputy of the Messenger, continued his temporal mission. Knowing that the feuding Arab tribes would tear themselves apart, the caliph directed them outward from Arabia with results startling to the seventh-century world.

Within a century Arab tribes under the leadership of the Meccan aristocracy had penetrated deep into central Asia, even, in 751, defeating a Chinese army to halt for good the westward expansion of the Chinese empire. In 713 an Arab force had landed in the delta of the Indus River in what is now Pakistan and gradually established a Muslim colony there.

In the north a frontier zone with Byzantium came into being along the Taurus mountain range. Summer raids into Asia Minor became customary, while Constantinople came under siege from Muslim seaborne expeditionary forces several times in the seventh and eighth centuries. Failing to take the Byzantine capital, Muslim rulers lost interest in the endeavor until the Turks successfully revived the challenge in the fifteenth century. Thus Byzantium served as a shield for Europe against Muslim expansion until the Fourth Crusade shortsightedly destroyed that shield.

To the west small Arab contingents took Egypt in 639 after having defeated Byzantine soldiers in Syria. They then dashed across North Africa, accepted Berber tribes as enthusiastic converts to Islam, and with them invaded the Iberian peninsula in 711. The weak barbarian kingdom of Spain fell quickly, and Muslim armies soon found themselves in southern France, raiding out from their base at Narbonne, just across the Pyrenees.

Although France's national epic, *The Song of Roland,* celebrates the battle of Tours/Poitiers in 732 as the decisive victory of Christians over the Muslim "infidels," according to the Muslims, the Merovingian king Charles Martel defeated no more than a Muslim raiding party. In the Arabic texts the defeat is noted only as the "martyrdom" of those killed. In fact, France was beyond the limit of the Muslims' concern. Their overriding interest lay in the fertile valleys of the Iberian Peninsula, so much so that they never tried to conquer the northern mountainous parts.

From bases in North Africa the Muslims slowly crossed the Sahara desert to establish footholds in the western Sudan. They accomplished this primarily by trade, not by force of arms. The east coast of Africa, moreover, had long been a commercial partner of south Arabia. The conversion of the Arabian Peninsula to Islam merely added a new cultural dimension to an already ongoing relationship with East Africa.

By the same means, peaceful trade over centuries, the Muslim world expanded to include much of the Southeast Asian archipelago and colonies on the south China coast. There was, for example, a vigorous Muslim trading community in Canton, China, as early as the latter half of the seventh century.

Conversions among Arabs quite understandably came rapidly, among other peoples more slowly since they were not encouraged to convert. In the early years of Islam non-Arabs had to be adopted into Arab tribes, the only social structure the Arabs knew. Didn't the spectacular conquests confirm that this was an Arab religion? Non-Arab Muslims were long considered outsiders. Christians, Jews, and other monotheists were granted religious toleration and considerable autonomy provided they submitted to rule by Muslims and paid a discriminatory tax.

Cultural and Economic Assimilation

The conquerors from Arabia had much to learn from the conquered and did so eagerly. Leaving Mecca and Medina as the two holy cities of Islam, they moved the center of their empire first to the Syrian region that they knew through trade and then in the eighth century to Baghdad on the Tigris River. The agriculturally rich Mesopotamian basin and the trade routes linking the Indian Ocean and the Mediterranean Sea that converged on Baghdad produced three centuries of unparalleled prosperity. The Muslim world became a vast common market extending from sub-Saharan Africa to central Asia. The elements of a common culture imbued with Islamic values spread throughout that region and constituted "Islamic civilization."

Islamic Civilization

Above all, the core of this civilization is religious. The Word of God is everywhere, prefacing every writing, embellishing speech, adorning textiles and the walls of mosques, the places of congregational prayer. At birth the first words heard by a Muslim infant testify to the faith: "There is no god but God, Muhammad is his Messenger." They are the last words at death. Ritual prayer five times a day brings the remembrance of God persistently to the forgetful. The annual pilgrimage to Mecca, to be accomplished at least once in a lifetime, if possible, spiritually and corporally unites the Muslim world; a month of fasting from dawn to sunset disciplines the heart and mind. The giving of alms for the benefit of the community's less fortunate purifies the earnings of the donor. The affirmation of faith, the frequent prayers, the pilgrimage to Mecca, the month of fasting, and the giving of alms constitute the Five Pillars of Islam.

The entire scale of ethical values developed from the teachings of the Prophet. For example, male support of the family, including aged parents, is required as is participation in warfare in defense of Islam. Setting slaves free, providing a dower to a bride, and marriage itself are recommended for all Muslims, whereas acts such as gambling and usury are frowned on. Totally forbidden are any sort of idolatry and eating certain foods, such as pork. These ethics extend throughout the Muslim world and mold a distinct way of life, to which local custom often adapts.

Art and Architecture The art and architecture of Islam demonstrates the power with which religion can invest all things. Under the Muslim rulers, whether in Persia, North Africa, Spain, or Turkey, the prohibition against images in a religious context rendered sculpture of little importance and reduced painting to exquisite manuscript illustration and decoration for the private enjoyment of the elite. The written word—calligraphy—also achieved new heights of importance as an expressive art form found not only in manuscripts of the Quran but also in the words of the Prophet, which were inscribed on walls and carved in stone. A page from a ninth-century Quran written either in Syria or Iraq demonstrates the potent energy of a beautiful hand. The letters in Kufic script achieve a life of their own, becoming very like human forms, at prayer, with arms upraised or bodies prostrate (Fig. 9-12).

A medical textbook (1224) shows script combined with the illustration of a physician and his attendant

9-12   *Page written in Kufic script from a Quran. Syria or Iraq, c. 9th century. Illumination. (The Metropolitan Museum of Art, New York. Rogers Fund, 1937)*

9-14   Temptation of Adam and Eve, *from the* Chronology of Ancient Peoples *manuscript of al-Biruni, painted in Tabriz, Iran, 1307. Illumination, 7½" × 12½". (Edinburgh University Library)*

9-13   *Two Physicians Preparing Medicine, Iraqi painting from an Arabic translation of the* Materia Medica *of Dioscorides. Baghdad school, 1224. Opaque color and gold: paper—33.1 × 24.6 cm; painting—8.8 × 17.5 cm.*

preparing a poultice to draw out snake venom (Fig. 9-13). The figures are flattened and their forms enriched and enlivened with patterns. Nudes appear rarely and then only in a context of primeval innocence or error. For example, a fourteenth-century *Chronology of Ancient Peoples,* painted at Tabriz in Iran, and depicting the Temptation of Adam and Evil, is filled with lively decoration as well as presenting, in a very powerful but chaste way, the dilemma of these forebears (Fig. 9-14).

Manuscript illustrations were usually a secular private art form with circulation limited to the court and wealthy merchants. The Muslims created other art forms—such as ceramics, textiles, and metal work—that had wide circulation and influence.

The Mosque   As it developed, Islamic civilization found special expression in architecture. At first Muslims converted churches into their own places of prayer but soon developed their own mosque designs. They abandoned the axial orientation of the church, which focused attention on the altar, for an architectural style that encouraged equality in the presence of God.

The Prophet commanded that the faithful pray five times daily, at first facing toward Jerusalem, later toward Mecca. This admonition, combined with the principle of equality in the presence of God, produced the need for a large, undifferentiated enclosure in which the praying faithful could prostate themselves

9-15   *Dome of the Rock, Jerusalem. Late 7th century. (Art Resource, NY)*

in rows. The mosque was oriented toward Mecca, the "navel of the earth." That direction, the *qibla,* came to have a niche, the *mihrab,* to identify it for the worshipers. To the right of that niche was the *minbar,* a pulpit for the Friday sermon. Two other major architectural features are the *sahn,* a courtyard to accommodate an overflow of worshipers, and a fountain for the required ritual ablutions before prayer. Minarets, used for the muezzin's call to prayer, came into use in the eighth century but are not as essential as the other features.

Muslims also rejected any representation of animate forms in a religious setting, so the interiors of their mosques contrasted sharply with those of Byzantine churches. Instead of saintly images, any Muslim religious context was rigorously aniconic, that is, devoid of animate images. Mosques were adorned instead with intricate calligraphic bands of verses from the Quran. To write the word of God in a beautiful hand according to a variety of styles became one of the highest art forms of Islamic civilization.

None of the first mosques have survived, although Muslims realized very early that their buildings might compete with those of Christians. For example, it is said that the seventh-century Dome of the Rock (Fig. 9-15) was built in Jerusalem by the caliph 'Abd al-Malik, who, "noting the greatness of the Church of the Holy Sepulcher and its magnificence, was moved lest it should dazzle the minds of the Muslims, and hence erected above the Rock the dome which is now to be seen there," according to one scholar.

The Dome of the Rock is unique symbolically and architecturally. Completed in 692 at a time when the city's Christians still doubted the permanence of Islam, the octagonal structure is in essence a victory monument, located on a site hallowed by three faiths. Its quranic inscriptions emphasize the superiority of Islam and its interpretation of Jesus as a prophet and the son of Mary. With the passage of time, however, the original significance of the Dome of the Rock has been replaced by an association with the Prophet's alleged ascent to heaven from the rock that the sanctuary encloses.

Although it is unique, some of the forms in the Dome of the Rock can be seen in subsequent mosque architecture. Above all is the emphasis on surface decoration. The graceful, slightly pointed dome, which may have been inspired by other pointed arches found throughout the building, may be derived from Byzantine forms. The exterior, clad in veined marble set in simple patterns, recurs in many mosques; the vivid white, blue, yellow, and green tiles above the marble are sixteenth-century replacements for the original mosaics executed by the Byzantine artisans hired to build the monument.

The pointed dome and the pointed arches of the interior arcades are two features readily associated with the architecture of Islam. The pointed arch was not an unknown structural form, but the Muslims used it in ways that gave rise to new kinds of architectural articulation. The Roman semicircular or round arch required substantial support at its springing (see Fig. 7-5) because the thrust of both sides of the arch was outward and down. The two sides of the pointed arch, in contrast, lean against each other and require less pressure at the springing, which means that it does not have to be embedded in a heavy wall or roof (Fig. 9-16). The arch, in this form, began to appear where the Muslims built.

In the eighth century, gigantic mosques were erected in Cairo, Damascus, Baghdad, and Samarra. The exterior walls of the Great Mosque of al-Mutawakkil, c. 848–852, in Samarra still stand. The enclosure provided for prayer was 784 × 512 feet, a size considerably greater than that of any Christian church. The mosque's 176-foot minaret, built as a spiral of fired brick, looks very like a Mesopotamian ziggurat and may well have been inspired by one (Fig. 9-17).

The Great Mosque of Cordoba, Spain (now the cathedral), gives us some idea of the experience of the interior of these structures. Begun in the eighth century by 'Abd ar-Rahman I, it was enlarged repeatedly until the tenth century. In plan it is a huge rectangle filled with aisles, all of which are located on the qibla side of the sahn (Color Plate VI). The interior with its

9-16 *Comparison drawing: The Muslim system of building, using pointed arches (right) was highly flexible and capable of expression quite different from that of the Roman system (left).*

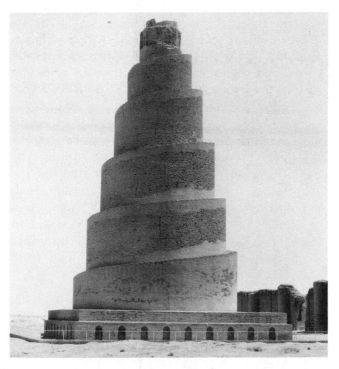

9-17 *Spiral minaret, Great Mosque of al-Mutawakkil, Samarra, Iraq. Fired brick, height 176'. (Bildarchiv Preussischer Kulturbesitz, Berlin)*

striped arches within arches seems an infinite range of spaces of equal value with a ceiling of continuous expanse. The vaults of the vestibule of the mihrab introduce another level of complexity, where the arches are interlaced and scalloped and their interior faces carved with intricate patterns (Figs. 9-18 and 9-19).

The Great Mosque of Cordoba with its rows of columns and arcades also illustrates the decoration not only found in mosques but also characteristic of palaces, one of the other major building types of Islamic civilization. The façade of the palace at Mshatta, Jordan, c. 743, is an early surviving example of the rich patterns derived by combining floral, animal, and geometric forms in fantastic repeating and symmetrical patterns that came to be known as *arabesque*. These complex patterns, with forms abstracted from nature, look like the fabulous woven textiles still produced by Muslim artists today (Fig. 9-20).

The Alhambra Palace The palaces of the Muslim rulers are epitomized and unsurpassed in the Alhambra built in Granada in the fourteenth century by the Nasrids of southern Spain who were defeated by

9-18   *Plan of the Great Mosque of Cordoba, c. A.D. 786–987, showing successive enlargements.*

9-20   *South façade of the palace at Mshatta in Jordan, c. A.D. 743. Height: 5.54 m. Staaliche Museen zu Berlin. (Bildarchiv Preussischer Kulturbesitz, Berlin)*

Ferdinand and Isabella in 1492. The palace consists of two major units: the Court of Myrtles with its reflecting pool and surrounding apartments, and on axis and almost perpendicular to it the Court of the Lions, which is centered with a fountain supported on the backs of lions. It is believed that the former court and rooms were for more public use and the latter for private use, but the divisions are not absolute.

9-19   *Vestibule of the mihrab, Great Mosque of Cordoba, c. 10th century. (Alinari/Art Resource, NY)*

As it is described in literature and music, the Alhambra is an unearthly place, apparently designed to resemble paradise. The building focuses inward and its courts, column-filled halls, and carved, gilded, painted, and vaulted spaces induce a feeling of placidity and contemplation. The Court of the Lions is seen in Fig. 9-21 through a screen of columns and scalloped arches of the Hall of Justice (1394) with its three bays of equal size, each carrying a dome with a lantern. This space produces feelings similar to those of the infinite space suggested by the Great Mosque of Cordoba. The walls of the Hall of Justice (Fig. 9-22), carved and cut away, create lacy shadows while eliminating any feeling for the structure of the building.

The influence of the Muslims on the art and architecture of Europe can be found not only in architectural forms and techniques but also in the names of things. From Damascus came damask, a finely woven monochromatic patterned fabric combining linen and silk; from Mosul in Iraq came muslin. Muslim art also influenced metalwork, ceramics, and glassware because most Europeans imported, collected, and copied from the work that traveled east and west from Persia to Spain where the Prophet's power was felt.

Law and Doctrine

The evolution of Islamic doctrine contrasts with that of Christianity. Under persecution underground, Christians had early honed the rough edges of their religion. Muslims in their first century, on the other hand, were too involved with expansion and territorial consolidation to devote full attention to the

9-21   *Court of the Lions, the Alhambra, Granada, Spain, c.* A.D. *1354–91. (Alinari/Art Resource, NY)*

9-22   *Hall of Justice, the Alhambra, Granada, Spain, c.* A.D. *1354–91. (Bildarchiv Preussischer Kulturbestiz, Berlin)*

development of Islam as a religion. It was not until the eighth century that a corpus of specifically Islamic law began to be distinguished from traditional Arab custom. In this process the practice and words of Muhammad came to complement the modest legal content of the Quran itself. With obedience to God's will the primary commitment of the Muslim, the discovery of that will was a crucial prerequisite. Hence the evolution of the law was the earliest development of the religion. In this respect Islam appeared closer in spirit to Judaism than to Christianity.

As this evolution occurred during the second Islamic century, non-Arabs began to play a significant role in Muslim society, even while Arabic remained the dominant language. New converts to Islam asked the sorts of questions familiar to them in their former faiths: Does the human being have free will or are we predestined? How can a just God permit evil in this world? Do Quranic expressions such as "God's speech," "the hand of God," "in the sight of God," and so forth imply divine likeness to the human being?

In the emerging Islamic civilization the relationship between philosophy and religion produced nearly as much tension as it did in western Europe but with a different result. Greek philosophical texts were translated into Arabic and became influential, but the central position of the Quran as God's exact Word relegated human reason to the periphery. All Muslims, even the illiterate, recited the revelation as the core of their faith. No effort to rationalize it in a manner that modified revelation was generally acceptable.

Shi'ism, a Branch of Islam   One exception may be noted. Within the first generation of Islamic history a schism took root in the community over the question of leadership. A minority felt that the caliph should be a descendant of the prophet Muhammad, and they proved willing to fight for that concept. Their struggle, however, generally ended in defeat. This revolutionary faction became known as the Shi'ites, whereas the mainstream assumed the name of Sunnis. Among the small but important Shi'ite minority, philosophy retained an honored position throughout history, since it was often used to buttress their arguments for the legitimacy of the Prophet's heirs.

Sufism, or Islamic Mysticism   As the ideal of an Islamic society diverged with time from the reality of political power, and as Islamic law stressed the immense gulf between a transcendent God and forgetful humankind, some Muslims turned to an inner search for truth. The Sufis, as the Muslim mystics are called, seek to know God by devoting their whole being to the search for the divine essence within themselves. Grounded in Islam, Sufism nevertheless created a tension within it, for the mystics felt little need for the ritual and the law. Some even ostentatiously rejected the formalities of Islam and paid for their boldness with martyrdom. This dimension of Islam, this yearning of the mystic's soul for reunion with the divine, sought expression in deeply emotional poetry. The masterpieces of that Sufi poetry have long appealed to the devout of other faiths as well as Islam's own. In recent years, Sufi poetry has enjoyed a marked popularity among segments of American youth who seek spiritual experiences they seem unable to find through more mainstream religious traditions.

Political Decentralization

The vast extent of the Muslim world doomed any prospect of the centralized control that the caliphs of Baghdad initially desired. Even the caliph himself became a tool in the hands of his Turkish bodyguard and was soon to be relegated to a mere cipher under Turkish sultans, in essence military dictators. Elsewhere, governors asserted their independence, and in Spain even a rival caliph emerged. Yet the cultural and spiritual unity of the Muslim world remained vigorous despite political decentralization and internecine warfare among Muslim principalities.

The Impact of Islamic Civilization on Europe

From the early eighth century of the Christian era to the fifteenth century, Europe shared the Mediterranean Sea with Muslims in North Africa, the Iberian Peninsula, and Sicily. At first the contacts were sporadic and hostile, with Arab and Berber raiding parties seeking what booty they could find on the coasts of the barbarian kingdoms.

As Islamic governments consolidated their holds on the southern and western shores of the Mediterranean, however, raiding receded in favor of trade, most of it east-west commerce within the Muslim world but an increasing portion north-south as Europe slowly regained a level of prosperity sufficient to attract Muslim commerce.

It was not long before the dynamic cultural synthesis emerging in the central Islamic lands reached their Muslim coreligionists in the West. Cultural elements as diverse as Asian spices, fruits and grains,

Chinese paper, Indian numerals, and Greek thought were carried along trade routes to the Muslim courts of the West.

Congenial conditions for the cultivation of foods new to the West such as rice, sugarcane, watermelon, oranges, and lemons were found in the Mediterranean basin. The Arabic words for these foods soon found their way into local and then European languages. Cotton, too, was introduced as an industrial crop, ultimately affecting the clothing styles of Europeans. For several of these crops the development of irrigation works was necessary. Since the Arab conquerors of the Iberian Peninsula were originally from Syria, the extant waterwheels of Seville, for example, duplicate those today in Hama, Syria.

Mediterranean Islamic society sought to emulate Baghdad, the caliphal seat of Islam, and thus the cultural attainments of the central Islamic lands came within the reach of a Europe soon able to appreciate them. For instance, Ziryab, a musician and singer, fell out of the caliph's favor in early-ninth-century Baghdad and made his way to the rival Muslim caliphate in al-Andalus, as Muslim Spain is generally known. Until his death in 857, Ziryab was the arbiter of taste in the Islamic West not only in his profession as a musician but in fashion and the culinary arts as well. Quite as nineteenth-century Bostonians modeled their society on London fashion and culture, so the courts of al-Andalus recognized and sought the refined taste, standards of luxury, and intellectual attainments that emanated from the central Islamic lands.

Intellectual Life in the Iberian Peninsula   Andalusian society was a very mixed one in which cross-cultural diffusion was accentuated. It was made up of frequent Spanish converts to Islam as well as many Arabic-speaking Christians and prominent tricultural Jews fluent in Hebrew, Arabic, and a romance language. All were soon immersed in a milieu, known today as Hispano-Arabic culture, that by the tenth and eleventh centuries had become the intellectual, artistic, and literary peer of Baghdad's. Before it was extinguished by Christian reconquest, Hispano-Arabic culture had produced luminaries such as Ibn Rushd (died 1198), the philosopher known in the West as Averroes, whose commentaries on Aristotle heavily influenced the preeminent Roman Catholic philosopher Thomas Aquinas (died 1274; see Chapter 10) and Maimonides (died 1204), a Jewish philosopher and physician writing in Arabic whose *Guide for the Perplexed* likewise drew on the thought of Aristotle. In literature, Hispano-Arab poets applied local strophic forms to the

Arabic ode to create a unique genre, the *zajal*, that was in turn carried back to the central Islamic lands. This Hispano-Arabic culture was largely tolerant, and virtually all Arabic-speaking Andalusians, Muslim, Jew, and Christian, could identify with it.

Christian Spain, on the other hand, was culturally impoverished. Hostile to but economically dependent on al-Andalus, it was a relatively isolated backwater until French influence began to penetrate the northern kingdoms in the tenth century. Then as the eleventh-to fifteenth-century recovery of the Iberian Peninsula for Christendom—known as the Reconquista—proceeded, a second cross-cultural diffusion ensued even while warfare continued between Catholic and Muslim rulers. Mediated by Andalusian scholars of various backgrounds, the European acquisition of Hispano-Arabic culture was initiated by church leaders from north of the Pyrenees who appreciated the high civilization of al-Andalus even while disparaging its Islamic context.

Cultural Transmission in Spain   After it passed into Christian hands in 1085, the city of Toledo in the center of Spain became the most renowned of the hubs of cultural transmission. Arabs and Jews worked with European patrons to translate and edit Arabic texts, some of which were translations of Greek originals, while others were unique contributions. Although the names of certain translators, such as Herman of Dalmatia, Robert of Ketton, and Michael Scot, are well known, the attribution of specific works to them is debatable. More certain is the patronage of, for example, the abbot Peter the Venerable (died 1156) and the Castilian king Alfonso the Wise (reigned 1252–1284).

The Sicilian Milieu   Not all intellectual transmission was through Hispano-Arabic culture, however. Another route was through Sicily, conquered by North African Muslims in the ninth century. Although this Mediterranean island was retaken by the Christian Normans in the eleventh century, several of these kings admired the culture they found in Sicily and patronized Arabic scholars. The *Book of Roger*, commissioned by Roger II (1127–1154) and composed by al-Idrisi (died 1166), is a complete description of the world as known to Muslims and laid the basis for European knowledge of India, China, and the northern part of Africa. At Salerno in southern Italy, the medical lore of Islamic civilization was both taught and applied in its famous school. Both Salerno and a later medical school at Montpellier in southern France were the principal sites for European acquisition of Islamic medicine.

The Role of the Crusades in Cultural Transmission   The Levantine Crusades provided less opportunity for cross-cultural diffusion than might have been expected. Granted, the Europeans gained some knowledge of military architecture and technology from their two centuries' experience on the eastern shores of the Mediterranean Sea. From there as well as through Sicily and Spain they learned of new foods, clothing materials, and ways of caring for the sick and wounded. As opposed to mutual exchanges between the two cultures in Spain and Sicily, the religious passions of the Crusaders inhibited an extensive appreciation of Islamic civilization.

If the Crusades made only minor positive contributions to Western life, they generated a negative impression of Islam that has continued to deeply mark the western European mentality. Although initially conceived in religious terms, the Crusades were the product of new energies generated by a rapidly changing society, and Islam easily became identified as the enemy blocking the expansionist tendencies of this society and of its religion.

Indeed, it seemed that the Muslim world, covering more than half the known earth, was steadily pressing in on the Christian West. Tales of pilgrims to the Holy Land suffering from bedouin raids had been magnified, and the Byzantine emperor had appealed for aid against the Muslims. The initiative of the papacy for the crusading movement was soon expanded by church leaders writing enthusiastic tracts. These introduced or repeated crude errors about Islam, declaring it to be a deliberate perversion of the Christian truth, and Muhammad to be an imposter or an Antichrist. Dante, in his *Divine Comedy* (see Chapter 11), put Muhammad in the depths of hell. Muslims were also portrayed as violent people spreading their faith by the sword. Such tracts excused the Europeans' own resort to the sword as no more than a defense of their religion.

For a considerable period the Crusades hardly caused a ripple in the Muslim world. Muslim writers saw them initially as an extension of the Byzantine efforts to regain lost territory. But gradually, aided by the rebukes of the religious scholars, the Muslim attitude approached the diatribes of the Crusader propagandists. Muslim embitterment manifested in the East came to be matched in the West as the victorious forces of Spain and Portugal moved down to the tip of the Iberian Peninsula, forcing conversions of their Muslim subjects and finally, the conquest completed, compelling those who clung to their faith to leave the land. The era of Hispano-Arabic florescence was buried deep under the burnings and expulsions of the Inquisition.

In the long term it was the existence of this feared yet denigrated Islam, positioned to the south and east of Europe, that propelled the Portuguese in the fifteenth century to attempt the circumnavigation of the Muslim world. They hoped to reach by sea the spices the Europeans sought. Wedding crusade and commerce, however, proved in the end to be unprofitable for such a small kingdom, and the task of exploring and exploiting the world fell to others such as Spain, France, and eventually England. Nonetheless, the Por-

tuguese expedition was for Muslims the first instance of European colonialism that would so often join military occupation with efforts to undermine the social fabric of Muslim society and religion.

In summary, the impact of Islamic civilization on Europe has had three facets: first, the often unconscious adoption of foods, vocabulary, technology, and architecture through the Hispano-Arabic synthesis; second, the deliberate acquisition of the Islamic intellectual tradition through the translation into European languages of major scientific and philosophical works; and third, the negative interpretation of the religious tradition of the Muslim world, Islam, as an aspect of the Crusader mentality with consequences still with us today.

Reading Selections

Justinian

From *The Digest* or *Pandects*

Translation by S. P. Scott

The Emperor Caesar, Flavius, Justinianus, Pious, Fortunate, Renowned, Conquerer and Triumpher, Ever Augustus, to Tribonianus His Quæstor: Greeting.

With the aid of God governing Our Empire which was delivered to Us by His Celestial Majesty, We carry on war successfully, We adorn peace and maintain the Constitution of the State, and have such confidence in the protection of Almighty God that We do not depend upon Our arms, or upon Our soldiers, or upon those who conduct Our Wars, or upon Our own genius, but We solely place Our reliance upon the providence of the Holy Trinity, from which are derived the elements of the entire world and their disposition throughout the globe.

(1) Therefore, since there is nothing to be found in all things so worthy of attention as the authority of the law, which properly regulates all affairs both divine and human, and expels all injustice; We have found the entire arrangement of the law which has come down to us from the foundation of the City of Rome and the times of Romulus, to be so confused that it is extended to an infinite length and is not within the grasp of human capacity; and hence We were first induced to begin by examining what had been enacted by former most venerated princes, to correct their constitutions, and make them more easily understood; to the end that being included in a single Code, and having had removed all that is superfluous in resemblance and all iniquitous discord, they may afford to all men the ready assistance of their true meaning.

(2) After having concluded this work and collected it all in a single volume under Our illustrious name, raising Ourself above small and comparatively insignificant matters, We have hastened to attempt the most complete and thorough amendment of the entire law, to collect and revise the whole body of Roman jurisprudence, and to assemble in one book the scattered treatises of so many authors; which no one else has herebefore ventured to hope for or to expect, and it has indeed been considered by Ourselves a most difficult undertaking, nay, one that was almost impossible; but with Our hands raised to heaven, and having invoked the Divine aid, We have kept this object in Our mind, confiding in God who can grant the accomplishment of things which are almost desparate, and can Himself carry them into effect by virtue of the greatness of His power.

(3) We have also taken into consideration your marked integrity as disclosed by your labors, and have committed this work to you, after having already received the evidence of your talents in the preparation of Our Code; and We have ordered you in the prosecution of your task, to select as your assistants whomever you might approve of from among the most eloquent professors of law, as well as from the most learned men belonging to the bar of this great city. These, therefore, having been collected and introduced into Our palace, and accepted by Us upon your statements, We have permitted the entire work to be accomplished; it being provided, however, that it should be conducted under the supervision of your most vigilant mind.

(4) Therefore We order you to read and revise the books relating to the Roman law drawn up by the jurists of antiquity, upon whom the most venerated princes conferred authority to write and interpret the same; so that from these all the substance may be collected, and, as far as may be possible, there shall remain no laws either similar to or inconsistent with one another, but that there may be compiled from them a summary which will take the place of all. And while others have written books relating to the law, for the reason that their writings have not been adopted

by any authorities, or made use of in practice, We do not deem their treatises worthy of Our consideration....

(12) We desire Our compilation which, God willing, is to be drawn up by you, to bear the name of the Digest or Pandects, and no person learned in the law shall dare hereafter to add any commentaries thereto, and to confuse by his own prolixity the abridgement of the aforesaid work, as was done in former times, for almost all law was thrown into confusion by the opposite opinions of those interpreting it; but it is sufficient merely by indexes, and a skilful use of titles (which are called παράτιτλα), to give such warning that no change may take place in the interpretation of the same.

QUESTIONS

1. According to Justinian, what purpose does the law serve? To what extent would Cicero agree with the emperor's conception of law?

2. Why does Justinian highly prize the interpretations of the law found in ancient jurists but forbid modern jurists to make additions or commentaries on the text as he has had it codified?

3. How do you reconcile Justinian's reluctance to permit changes or commentaries on the three books making up the *Corpus* and his willingness to add a fourth book of new laws, *The New Constitutions,* which would expand over time?

Byzantine Poetry

MICHAEL ACOMINATOS (1140–1220)

Lament for Athens

Translation by Constantine A. Trypanis

This prose translation of a poem by Michael Acominatos of Athens reflects the nostalgia for the glories of ancient Greece felt by Byzantine intellectuals of the Middle Ages. Their sense of loss became only more intense in this period of Byzantine decadence. Acominatos lived to see the capture of both Constantinople and his native city by the Latin crusaders.

Love for Athens, a city once famous, wrote these words, a love that plays with shadows, that gives a little comfort to burning desire. Alas; it is impossible to see anything of that city famous in song, which has disappeared, hidden for long incalculable years in the depths of oblivion: and, to speak the truth, I suffer what lovers suffer. For they, when they cannot see the real shapes of their loves present, console the flame of longing, so to speak, by looking at their pictures. Thus, unhappy, I, a new Ixion, in love with Athens as he was with Hera,[1] miss her and embrace an image. Alas for what I suffer and say and write. Though I live in Athens I see Athens nowhere: only sad, empty, and blessed dust. Most unhappy city, where is your splendour? Everything has disappeared and is become as if it belonged to a myth: lawsuits, judges, the orators' stands, ballots, laws, speeches, the persuasive arguments of orators, councils, festivals, generals to lead your soldiers and your sailors, all the Muses, the very power of words. The entire glory of Athens is passed away; not even a dim trace of it can be seen. So, if I cannot see the city of Athens, famous in song, I must be forgiven for setting up an image of it in writing.

QUESTIONS

1. What aspects of life in the ancient city are singled out by the poet?

2. In what way is the poet's celebration of the ancient city comparable to what lovers do to console themselves for the lost beloved?

THEODORE PRODROMOS(?) (FL. 1140)

Promises Are Not to Be Kept

Translation by Constantine A. Trypanis

Leave me, leave me alone, now my heart is broken. I spoke to her and she turned away, and her caress was angry: what is this killing tenderness you inflict on me, murderess? "You said it once and you said it a second time; if you wish, you may repeat it. If you don't feel pity for your mouth, speak, and go on speaking. The trouble you take is for nothing, young man: my vows

---

[1]Ixion, king and father of the Centaurs, was punished for loving Hera, Zeus' wife, by being chained to an eternally revolving wheel in Hades.

are owed to another." "Vows can be broken, words spoken can be changed, and love too can pass from one man to another. As for the promises of love: do not bring them as an excuse. Ask anyone and he will tell you: it is no sin to break such vows."

QUESTIONS

1. What common elements can you find in this love poem and the love lyrics of ancient Egypt, Greece, and Rome?

2. What concept of love does the poet emphasize?

MANUEL PHILES (C. 1275–1345)

On an Icon of the Virgin

Translation by Constantine A. Trypanis

What is this? How, and through what art, did you find yourself, a faint and shadowy picture, gripped in the weaving of a humble woof? And how did the wax, melted by the flame, not burn the inflammable cloth upon which it fell, but skillfully paint this your image? Ah, Mary, you change the very nature of matter: you who once appeared in the guise of a bush the flames could not consume now depict yourself by means of this strange fire; and here Christ himself pours from above a secret moisture on the flame of the torch so that the believer may look on this picture and escape the ghostly flame of suffering.

QUESTIONS

1. Look again at the icon of the Virgin and Child (Fig. 9-11) after reading this poem. Does one illuminate the other in any way?

2. Describe the emotion that the poet feels for the icon. Could it be viewed as dangerous or heretical by iconoclasts?

FROM THE *Quran*

Translation by A. J. Arberry

The Quran, the holy scripture of Islam, is not meant to be translated. Muslims say, quite correctly, that in any language other than Arabic the revelations are not the Quran. They do indeed lose much of their force in English, since the rhythmic prose is lacking. These selections have been chosen to show the very different sorts of material to be found in the Quran: hortative, didactic, worshipful.

The first section is also the first *sura*, or chapter, one that is repeated by the devout Muslim at least fifteen times a day, since it forms an integral part of the five daily ritual prayers.

The second reading is evidently a very early sura, for it is clearly in response to Muhammad's discouragement as he is rejected by all but a handful of Meccans. The first word is a letter, the meaning of which is unknown.

The third reading is a verse from the longest sura in the Quran, the second. It is known as the "Throne Verse" and is often reproduced alone on placards to be hung in the home.

In the fourth selection Mary, the mother of Jesus, appears.

I
The Opening

In the Name of God, the Merciful, the
Compassionate

Praise belongs to God, the Lord of all Being,
the All-merciful, the All-compassionate,
    the Master of the Day of Doom.

Thee only we serve; to Thee alone we pray for
    succour.
    Guide us in the straight path,
the path of those whom Thou hast blessed,
not of those against whom Thou art wrathful,
    nor of those who are astray.

LXVIII
The Pen

In the Name of God, the Merciful, the
Compassionate

Nun

By the Pen, and what they inscribe,
thou art not, by the blessing of thy Lord,
    a man possessed.
Surely thou shalt have a wage unfailing;
surely thou art upon a mighty morality.
So thou shalt see, and they will see,
    which of you is the demented.

Surely thy Lord knows very well
those who have gone astray from
    His way, and He knows very well
    those who are guided.

So obey thou not those who cry lies. They
wish that thou shouldst compromise, then
    they would compromise.
And obey thou not every mean swearer,
backbiter, going about with slander,
hinderer of good, guilty aggressor,
coarse-grained, moreover ignoble,
because he has wealth and sons.
When Our signs are recited to him, he
says, "Fairy-tales of the ancients!"
We shall brand him upon the muzzle!

Now We have tried them, even as We tried
the owners of the garden when they swore
    they would pluck in the morning
and they added not the saving words.

Then a visitation from thy Lord visited
    it, while they were sleeping,
and in the morning it was as if it were
    a garden plucked.
In the morning they called to one another,
"Come forth betimes upon your tillage,
    if you would pluck!"
So they departed, whispering together,
"No needy man shall enter it today
    against your will."
And they went forth early, determined
    upon their purpose.
But when they saw it, they said, "Surely
    we are gone astray;
nay, rather we have been robbed!"
Said the most moderate of them,
"Did I not say to you, 'Why do you
    not give glory?'"
They said, "Glory be to God, our Lord;
    truly, we were evildoers."
And they advanced one upon another,
    blaming each other.
They said, "Woe, alas for us! Truly,
    we were insolent.
It may be that our Lord will give us
in exchange a better than it; to our
    Lord we humbly turn."

Such is the chastisement; and the chastisement
of the world to come is assuredly greater,
    did they but know.

Surely for the godfearing shall be Gardens of
    Bliss with their Lord.
What, shall we make those who have surrendered
    like to the sinners?

What ails you then, how you judge?
Or have you a Book wherein you study? Surely
    therein you shall have whatever you choose!
Or have you oaths from Us, reaching to the
Day of Resurrection? Surely you shall have
    whatever you judge!
Ask them, which of them will guarantee that!
Or do they have associates? Then
    let them bring their associates,
    if they speak truly.

Upon the day when the leg shall be bared, and they
    shall be summoned
        to bow themselves, but they cannot;
humbled shall be their eyes, and abasement shall
    overspread them,
for they had been summoned to bow themselves
    while they were whole.

So leave Me with him who
    cries lies to this discourse!
We will draw them on little by little
    whence they know not;
and I shall respite them—assuredly
    My guile is sure.

Or askest thou them for a wage, and so they
    are weighed down with debt?
Or is the Unseen in their keeping, and so
    they are writing it down?

So be thou patient under the judgment of thy Lord,
and be not as the Man of the Fish, when he called,
    choking inwardly.
Had there not overtaken him a blessing from his Lord
he would have been cast upon the wilderness,
    being condemned.
But his Lord had chosen him, and He placed him
    among the righteous.

The unbelievers wellnigh strike thee down
with their glances, when they hear the
Reminder, and they say, "Surely he is
    a man possessed!"
And it is nothing but a Reminder
    unto all beings.

II
The Throne Verse

God
there is no god but He, the
Living, the Everlasting.
Slumber seizes Him not, neither sleep;
to Him belongs
all that is in the heavens and the earth.
Who is there that shall intercede with Him
save by His leave?
He knows what lies before them
and what is after them,
and they comprehend not anything of His knowledge
save such as He wills.
His Throne comprises the heavens and earth;
the preserving of them oppresses Him not;
He is the All-high, the All-glorious.

XIX
Mary

... And mention in the Book Mary
when she withdrew from her people
to an eastern place,
and she took a veil apart from them;
then We sent unto her Our Spirit
that presented himself to her
a man without fault.
She said, "I take refuge in
the All-merciful from thee!
If thou fearest God...."
He said, "I am but a messenger
come from thy Lord, to give thee
a boy most pure."
She said, "How shall I have a son
whom no mortal has touched, neither
have I been unchaste?"
He said, "Even so thy Lord has said:
'Easy is that for Me; and that We
may appoint him a sign unto men
and a mercy from Us; it is
a thing decreed.'"
So she conceived him, and withdrew with him
to a distant place.
And the birthpangs surprised her by
the trunk of the palm-tree. She said,
"Would I had died ere this, and become
a thing forgotten!"
But the one that was below her
called to her, "Nay, do not sorrow;
see, thy Lord has set below thee
a rivulet.

Shake also to thee the palm-trunk,
and there shall come tumbling upon thee
dates fresh and ripe.
Eat therefore, and drink, and be
comforted; and if thou shouldst see
any mortal,
say, 'I have vowed to the All-merciful
a fast, and today I will not speak
to any man.'"
Then she brought the child to her folk
carrying him; and they said,
"Mary, thou hast surely committed
a monstrous thing!
Sister of Aaron, thy father was not
a wicked man, nor was thy mother
a woman unchaste."
Mary pointed to the child then;
but they said, "How shall we speak
to one who is still in the cradle,
a little child?"
He said, "Lo, I am God's servant;
God has given me the Book, and
made me a Prophet.
Blessed He has made me, wherever
I may be; and He has enjoined me
to pray, and to give the alms, so
long as I live,
and likewise to cherish my mother;
He has not made me arrogant,
unprosperous.
Peace be upon me, the day I was born,
and the day I die, and the day I am
raised up alive!"
That is Jesus, son of Mary,
in word of truth, concerning which
they are doubting.
It is not for God to take a son
unto Him. Glory be to Him! When He
decrees a thing, He but says to it
"Be," and it is.
Surely God is my Lord, and your
Lord; so serve you Him. This is
a straight path.

COMMENTS AND QUESTIONS

1. Is there anything in the first sura to which a monotheist other than a Muslim would take exception? Note that it does not even mention either Islam or Muhammad.

2. How would you characterize Allah in the second, early sura? What differences do you find between Allah and Yahweh, the God of the Jews (see Chapter 8)?

3. Do portions of the "Throne Verse" remind you of one of the biblical Psalms? If so, which one? Why do you suppose this verse is such a favorite with Muslims?

4. How does the fourth selection's account of Mary differ from that of the biblical Gospels? In what respects is it similar? From this account, what is the role of Jesus in Islam?

Sufi Poetry

Unlike the Quran, Sufism has found expression in virtually every language spoken by Muslim peoples, for it is a singularly individual devotional literature.

Here, for example, are the ecstatic utterances of the Persian eleventh-century mystic known as Baba Kuhi of Shiraz and a poem expressing the experience of the divine by al-Junayd of Baghdad, the greatest teacher of Sufism of the late ninth century.

BABA KUHI OF SHIRAZ

A Sufi Poem

Translation by Reynold A. Nicholson

In the market, in the cloister—only God I saw.
In the valley and on the mountain—only God I saw.
Him I have seen beside me oft in tribulation;
In favour and in fortune—only God I saw.
In prayer and fasting, in praise and contemplation,
In the religion of the Prophet—only God I saw.
Neither soul nor body, accident nor substance,
Qualities nor causes—only God I saw.
I opened mine eyes and by the light of His face
    around me
In all the eye discovered—only God I saw.
Myself with mine own eyes I saw most clearly,
But when I looked with God's eyes—only God I saw.
I passed away into nothingness, I vanished,
And lo, I was the All-living—only God I saw.

AL-JUNAYD OF BAGHDAD

Translation by A. J. Arberry

Now I have known, O Lord,
What lies within my heart;
In secret, from the world apart,
My tongue hath talked with my Adored.

So in a manner we
United are, and One;
Yet otherwise disunion
Is our state eternally.

Though from my gaze profound
Deep awe hath hid Thy face,
In wondrous and ecstatic grace
I feel Thee touch my inmost ground.

FROM THE *Epic of 'Antar*

This enormous epic tale about pre-Islamic Arabia stands in the Arab world at least on a par with the *Thousand Nights and a Night,* although it is less well known in the West. It is the tale of a black knight, originally a slave, who gains his freedom by his exploits and his chivalry. It tells of his loves and his achievements as a leader of men. Thus it reflects the values of that society, filtered, however, through those of medieval Egypt.

As we have it today, its style is of tenth- to fourteenth-century Egypt, and occasionally an Islamic anachronism creeps into the narrative. The selection is rewritten for an English-speaking audience by Diana Richmond from nineteenth-century translations.

The Fourth Story

'Abla

It was the custom in those far-off days that the Arab women should drink sheep's milk as they arose in the early morning, and this milk would be brought to the tents of the leaders of the tribe by a servant who had seen to it that the warm milk had been cooled in the dawn breeze. 'Antar performed this service for Samiya, wife of his father Sheddad, and for Sheriya, the wife of Malec, son of Karad, uncle of 'Antar. Malec was a man of suspicious nature, and one in whom envy and jealousy strove with arrogance for mastery of his soul. He lacked the graces of magnanimity so precious to the Arab people. His son, Amr, inherited his father's meanness, but his daughter, 'Abla, displayed in her person and in her personality all the gifts most admired in a daughter of the desert. Her merry humour, her kindness to the unfortunate and her respect for her elders rendered her a byword in the tribe; and as she emerged from childhood to womanhood her beauty was fast becoming legendary.

Yet, for all her good humour, there was little love between sister and brother, 'Abla and Amr. Indeed, he disliked what he considered to be her lack of dignity. For Amr was proud of the nobility of his family which he shared by birth, and he had not realized, as had his sister, that noble behaviour should accompany a high position. Moreover, as children, 'Abla had far excelled him as a rider of horses, for in those days she had sought to emulate Robab, and the Princess Zenobia, who led her father's men into battle in the days when Palmyra was still a fair city at the height of its beauty; and 'Abla would still recount the story of the conception of the mare, Dahis, the Thruster, and of the Great Race, but Amr did not like these stories.

And it happened at this time—and it was springtime—that when 'Antar entered the women's tent to serve the cool milk, he surprised his cousin 'Abla at her toilet, for she sat unveiled and only half-dressed while her mother combed and plaited her long black hair. 'Abla cried out in her embarrassment and fled across the tent, her hair flowing behind her as a silken pennant floats in the wind; and 'Antar, though almost bereft of his senses by her beauty, yet retained enough of them to observe the loveliness of her form—her ivory skin, and her firm breasts rising cleanly as do the desert dunes in the moonlight; and the rustle of her dress was soft as the wings of starlings flocking to the wadi in the evening hours. So 'Antar lost his heart to his cousin 'Abla, who was yet so far above him in rank that never could he aspire to marriage with her, being but a slave although of noble blood.

On the following morning, as he entered the tent again, he was overcome with embarrassment, for 'Abla cried in her merry way, "It seems, friend, that I must rise earlier than you to preserve my modesty! See how well I have done today, almost beating the dawn itself!" And she laughed, and her aunt and her mother laughed too; but as for poor 'Antar, his love and his confusion were so great that he offered the sheep's milk to his fair cousin before he had served it to the elder women. Then Samiya, wife of Sheddad, was furious, and drove him from the tent. But 'Abla smiled to herself and was not unaware of 'Antar's strength and comeliness for all that his colour was black as the pitch which oozes over the sand at the foot of the Persian mountains in the far desert.

In those days, as in our own, there were plots and intrigues among the slaves and servants, and among their masters too. Samiya's anger with 'Antar was exploited now by Zajir, slave of Rabia, who bore a grudge against 'Antar. Zajir told Samiya how 'Antar had learned his camel-riding and his horse-riding at the expense of the herds, and how he had injured the few and precious trees of the desert fringes by aiming at them his javelins and spears. And Samiya sought her husband and complained to him of the black slave who could not care for the animals in his charge nor appreciate the true position of an elder woman's rank compared to that of young 'Abla.

And Sheddad was angry, and seizing his son he beat him cruelly. But 'Antar, although he was already as strong as his father, suffered the beating in all humility because he respected his father and his father's position in the tribe. Zebeeba came also to her son and warned him to remember his lowly position. But 'Antar, who lay bound after the beating, burst his bonds simply by flexing his muscles, and seizing a horse he followed the slave Zajir into the desert, and there killed him for his treachery. "For," he said to himself, "a man should, if he have a grievance, speak openly to his opponent of the quarrel, nor should he secretly persuade a woman to speak for him."

Among the leaders of the tribe, too, there were feuds and dissension, for Rabia, clever and ambitious as he was, disliked the Prince and his brothers, and Sheddad and Malec swayed to one side or the other side, but all respected and feared, or loved, lord Zuhair.

Now when 'Antar had killed the second slave he sought protection from the Prince against Rabia's wrath, and the Prince made up his mind to settle the affair with no further bloodshed, for the Prince was a kindly man. He sought the elders in their assembly, and all rose as he entered, giving and receiving the greetings. And the Prince, still standing, turned to Rabia and said, "Cousin, I greet you, and if you love me I would ask a favour of you." "Indeed I love you," growled Rabia, who did no such thing, but to whom the courtesies were important as they are to all true Arabs. "Give me then, I pray, your slave Zajir," continued the Prince. Now Rabia valued Zajir, and thought he was still alive, and to give himself time to think he reproached the Prince, saying, "Sit down in your place, I beg of you, my cousin, for are we not all standing because you continue so?" "Do you wish I should sit down, and do you love me?" queried the Prince. "Then favour me with your slave, else I remain standing and may disbelieve your love." Rabia had no choice but to agree, and the company was seated, and when Zuhair joined them, then did the Prince reveal Zajir's death, and he explained to Rabia that this unfortunate fact was now of little consequence to the dishonest slave's former master. And Zuhair and his elders smiled at the Prince's trick, and Rabia appeared pacified by the gift of two new slaves.

But afterwards, Rabia sought out his brother, Amara the Coxcomb, who hated the Prince, and together they approached Sheddad, and they persuaded Sheddad that his Negro son was becoming a menace to the unity of the tribe, and Sheddad agreed, and a plot was laid to kill 'Antar when he was alone and unprotected in the desert. "For," said these uncles of his, and his father, "Lord Zuhair and the Prince think well of 'Antar, but may we not be overwhelmed by a veritable ocean of calamities and misfortunes if he continues to live among us? He must die."

Now 'Antar's flocks were grazing in a secluded valley far from the camp, and 'Antar was composing to himself a poem in praise of his beautiful cousin 'Abla, when an enormous lion burst through the bushes and confronted him. And behind the rocks, on the other side of the valley, 'Antar's father and his two uncles crept up in hiding, planning to murder him. But 'Antar thrust the crook he carried between the lion's teeth and, advancing, seized the animal's upper jaw in one hand and its lower jaw in the other hand, and tore the lion in two. Then he skinned the lion and burned its flesh, and started scraping its pelt for his own use; and as he scraped he sang:

> "O lion, father of lion cubs and king of the sandy
>   wastes and of the animals which dwell there,
> How strong thou art, how proud of thy strength.
>
>   But thou art brought low.
>
> And I—I did not use my sword or my lance,
> With my bare hands I brought about thy downfall.
> Of the two of us, is it not I that am the lion?"

And the men hidden behind the rocks shuddered and said, "Which of us would dare to attack this youth? Prudence demands we abandon our plan and return whence we came." And this they did, and when 'Antar returned with his flocks and his lion's skin, they joined in the rejoicing at his exploit and appeared as friendly and as deeply impressed as Zuhair himself.

So when, in a few days, the elders of the tribe and the fighting men went off upon a desert raid, Sheddad repented his harshness and left 'Antar, of whom he was secretly proud, in charge of his tents and of the flocks and of the women, and he warned 'Antar not to let any of them wander far, and 'Antar answered proudly, "O my master, should the smallest object be missing on your return, let me, for the remainder of my life, be kept in chains and bondage."

But when the warriors had departed, and after a few days constrained within the camp the women became bored, and Samiya, wife of Sheddad, proposed that a feast should be held on the shores of Dhat al Arsad's pools, not far from the camp, and 'Antar dared not hinder her, and indeed rejoiced with the women, for he would be for a whole day in 'Abla's company.

When the pleasure-seekers reached the lakeside on the following day, the sun sparkled upon the waters and was not too hot to hinder their preparations. The servants fanned the charcoal to a steady glow, and lambs were put to roast over it; and the two kids, which had been baking overnight buried in clay pots beneath the soil, were uncovered and distributed with rice and leben among the hungry children. Birds sang among the reeds, and the broad beaches of the lake were bright with flowers. Flushed with wine, some among the girls danced for their elders' delight, discarding their veils; and, among them all, 'Abla was the most beautiful.

Then suddenly a cry rang down the valley, "The Qahtan, the Qahtan!" And seventy horsemen armed to the teeth seemed to pour like a torrent from the crest of the eastern hill down to the waterside. Each horseman seized one of the girls or the women, and the children scattered, and the servants fled. And 'Antar? As he saw his beloved seized by one of the armed men and dragged to the saddle, 'Antar sprang like a panther and threw the marauder to the dust where death welcomed him as her own. 'Antar seized the warrior's arms and his horse, and pausing only to shelter 'Abla behind some rocks, outstripped the raiders and faced them, crying: "A curse upon you, evil ones, who dare only to attack women, the daughters and the wives of noble men. Now must you reckon with 'Antar!" Twenty men fell to his lance and sword, and the remainder fled, calling to each other, "If the slaves of this tribe display such strength and courage, what can the warriors be like!" So the women were saved and returned to camp, praising 'Antar with smiles and tears of gratitude, and 'Antar himself drove before him the arms and the horses of the twenty-one raiders he had slain, and he was elated, remembering 'Abla's heartfelt thanks at her rescue. Only Samiya feared the wrath of Sheddad, her husband, at having so wantonly exposed the tribeswomen to danger, so she swore all to secrecy; and only 'Abla and 'Antar remembered what looks had passed between them after the encounter.

But after a few days, when the warriors also had returned to the camp, Sheddad noticed the twenty-one new horses among his own horses, and he reproached

'Antar unjustly with having organized some raiding party of his own instead of minding the womenfolk—so winning for his tribe the slur of troublemaking. And 'Antar, bound by his promise, gritted his teeth and bore upon his body the whipping his father inflicted, and in his mind the humiliation he so little deserved. But Samiya's heart melted towards him, and in confessing all she saved him further punishment and, indeed, won for him Sheddad's good opinion, for he thought, In truth I have a noble son who has saved all the women of the tribe from rapine and who has allowed himself to suffer unjustly rather than betray a promise. Sheddad rewarded 'Antar with presents, as did the lord Zuhair. And Samiya praised 'Antar in poetry, saying:

> "It is right that I respect him, that I protect him,
> For did not his strength and valour preserve my
>   honour,
>   His courage preserve honour among us all?"

'Antar replied with a poem of gratitude, describing also his own steadfastness, for, he said:

> "Men are of two kinds—those whose hearts
> Crack with fear as a glass goblet crazes in the heat,
>   And those whose hearts are of rock."

So was Sheddad charmed, as 'Abla had been charmed by a poem on her gaiety and beauty on the day of the picnic by the lake.

QUESTIONS

1. What qualifies 'Antar as an epic hero?
2. What positive and negative social values do you find in this story?
3. What is the function of the poetry in the narrative?
4. What concepts of love are at work here?

USÂMA IBN MUNQIDH

An Appreciation of the Frankish Character

Translation by Philip K. Hitti

Usâma ibn Munqidh (1095–1188) was a Syrian gentleman and scholar who lived in close contact with the Crusaders for most of his life. His memoirs, a rare document because of their personal style, reveal his own view of the "Franks," as he knows all of them, whether French or otherwise.

Usâma: From Memoirs

An Appreciation of the Frankish Character

Their lack of sense.—Mysterious are the works of the Creator, the author of all things! When one comes to recount cases regarding the Franks, he cannot but glorify Allah (exalted is he!) and sanctify him, for he sees them as animals possessing the virtues of courage and fighting, but nothing else; just as animals have only the virtues of strength and carrying loads. I shall now give some instances of their doings and their curious mentality.

In the army of King Fulk, son of Fulk, was a Frankish reverend knight who had just arrived from their land in order to make the holy pilgrimage and then return home. He was of my intimate fellowship and kept such constant company with me that he began to call me "my brother." Between us were mutual bonds of amity and friendship. When he resolved to return by sea to his homeland, he said to me:

> My brother, I am leaving for my country and I want thee to send with me thy son (my son, who was then fourteen years old, was at that time in my company) to our country, where he can see the knights and learn wisdom and chivalry. When he returns, he will be like a wise man.

Thus there fell upon my ears words which would never come out of the head of a sensible man; for even if my son were to be taken captive, his captivity could not bring him a worse misfortune than carrying him into the lands of the Franks. However, I said to the man:

> By thy life, this has exactly been my idea. But the only thing that prevented me from carrying it out was the fact that his grandmother, my mother, is so fond of him and did not this time let him come out with me until she exacted an oath from me to the effect that I would return him to her.

Thereupon he asked, "Is thy mother still alive?" "Yes." I replied. "Well," said he, "disobey her not."

Their curious medication.—A case illustrating their curious medicine is the following: . . .

The king of the Franks[1] had for treasurer a knight named Bernard [*barnâd*], who (may Allah's curse be

---

[1]Fülk of Anjou, king of Jerusalem. (Tr.)

upon him!) was one of the most accursed and wicked among the Franks. A horse kicked him in the leg, which was subsequently infected and which opened in fourteen different places. Every time one of these cuts would close in one place, another would open in another place. All this happened while I was praying for his perdition. Then came to him a Frankish physician and removed from the leg all the ointments which were on it and began to wash it with very strong vinegar. By this treatment all the cuts were healed and the man became well again. He was up again like a devil. . . .

A Frank wants to show to a Moslem God as a child.—I saw one of the Franks come to al-Amîr Mu'în-al-Dîn (may Allah's mercy rest upon his soul!) when he was in the Dome of the Rock[2] and say to him, "Dost thou want to see God as a child?" Mu'în-al-Dîn said, "Yes." The Frank walked ahead of us until he showed us the picture of Mary with Christ (may peace be upon him!) as an infant in her lap. He then said, "This is God as a child." But Allah is exalted far above what the infidels say about him!

Franks lack jealousy in sex affairs.—The Franks are void of all zeal and jealousy. One of them may be walking along with his wife. He meets another man who takes the wife by the hand and steps aside to converse with her while the husband is standing on one side waiting for his wife to conclude the conversation. If she lingers too long for him, he leaves her alone with the conversant and goes away.

Here is an illustration which I myself witnessed:

When I used to visit Nâblus,[3] I always took lodging with a man named Mu'izz, whose home was a lodging house for the Moslems. The house had windows which opened to the road, and there stood opposite to it on the other side of the road a house belonging to a Frank who sold wine for the merchants. He would take some wine in a bottle and go around announcing it by shouting, "So and so, the merchant, has just opened a cask full of this wine. He who wants to buy some of it will find it in such and such a place." The Frank's pay for the announcement made would be the wine in that bottle. One day this Frank went home and found a man with his wife in the same bed. He

asked him, "What could have made thee enter into my wife's room?" The man replied, "I was tired, so I went in to rest." "But how," asked he, "didst thou get into my bed?" The other replied, "I found a bed that was spread, so I slept in it." "But," said he, "my wife was sleeping together with thee!" The other replied, "Well, the bed is hers. How could I therefore have prevented her from using her own bed?" "By the truth of my religion," said the husband, "if thou shouldst do it again, thou and I would have a quarrel." Such was for the Frank the entire expression of his disapproval and the limit of his jealousy.

Another illustration: . . .

Ordeal by water.—I once went in the company of al-Amîr Mu'în-al-Dîn (may Allah's mercy rest upon his soul!) to Jerusalem. We stopped at Nâblus. There a blind man, a Moslem, who was still young and was well dressed, presented himself before al-amîr carrying fruits for him and asked permission to be admitted into his service in Damascus. The amîr consented. I inquired about this man and was informed that his mother had been married to a Frank whom she had killed. Her son used to practice ruses against the Frankish pilgrims and coöperate with his mother in assassinating them. They finally brought charges against him and tried his case according to the Frankish way of procedure.

They installed a huge cask and filled it with water. Across it they set a board of wood. They then bound the arms of the man charged with the act, tied a rope around his shoulders and dropped him into the cask, their idea being that in case he was innocent, he would sink in the water and they would then lift him up with the rope so that he might not die in the water; and in case he was guilty, he would not sink in the water. This man did his best to sink when they dropped him into the water, but he could not do it. So he had to submit to their sentence against him—may Allah's curse be upon them! They pierced his eyeballs with red-hot awls. . . .

QUESTIONS

1. In what ways does the lifestyle of the Crusader differ from that of the Muslim, as revealed in these passages?

2. To what particular points does Usâma take exception?

---

[2] *Al-Sakhra,* the mosque standing near al-Aqsa in Jerusalem. (Tr.) Mu'în-al-Dîn Anâr was at that time the ruler of Damascus.

[3] Neapolis, ancient Shechem. (Tr.)

10

Medieval Europe:
Culture and the Cathedral

The continuity of political authority in Byzantium ensured the preservation of a high degree of antique culture in the areas under its control. Similarly, when Islam conquered a significant portion of the Eastern Empire's lands in the seventh century, the victors quickly incorporated the Greco-Roman culture into a high-level amalgam with their own religion and elements of advanced Persian culture. By comparison, in the western half of the Empire occupied by barbarian tribes, the heritage of antiquity survived largely in elementary forms. Only after 1000 did western Europe begin to make serious, permanent efforts to catch up with Byzantium and Islam, but by 1350 the gap had been closed.

The years between 1000 and 1350 are generally known in European history as the High Middle Ages. Within these centuries we can speak with some assurance of a civilization of the Middle Ages. Before 1000 medieval culture was still in formation; after 1350 new currents (which historians generally label as characteristic of the Renaissance) were becoming dominant. Medieval society was doubtless affected by survivals of primitive Germanic, Italic, and Celtic folk culture, together with admixtures of sophisticated pagan philosophy and literature, but the informing ideas centered on belief in a transcendent, all-powerful God who, through the God-man Christ, offered redemption to the sinful human race. Most cultural forms tended to be manifestations and expressions of this Christian conception of God and the human predicament.

Having characterized briefly the two other medieval cultures arising out of the wreckage of the Roman Empire, we are now in a position to focus on high medieval Europe, the medieval culture and society most directly the antecedent of our own. Prior to examining productions in the art and literature of this society, we will take up medieval developments in economics, in the Church, in political history, and in intellectual history generally. The early eleventh century in all these four areas initiated revivals that were interrelated. After five hundred years of progressive decline and relative stabilization at a low plateau, western Europe by 1000 began to stir with new life.

Medieval Revivals

Economic Revival

Already by the end of the tenth century the tempo of economic life was changing. The development of the castle had finally provided the population with a source of security. Agricultural techniques and inventions such as the horse collar, gradually came into widespread use, leading to an increase in agricultural productivity and ultimately to an enormous population rise between 1000 and 1250. The distribution of the population was also altered; because food was easier to produce, a portion of the population could be spared from direct employment in agriculture for other things. Established towns grew in size, and new ones were founded. By 1300 only about 10 percent of Europe's population lived in towns of more than 2000; nonetheless, the towns, serving as they did as focuses of economic and cultural life, played a role in medieval society much greater than this percentage would suggest. Silver deposits were exploited by mining; and when the bullion produced poured into the economy as currency, there was further expansion. International markets developed again, and large-scale production was encouraged.

Religious Revival

This renewed vitality in the economy was paralleled by a revival of religious interests. In the decades after 1050 the popes at Rome initiated a program to dislodge the churches and monasteries from the hands of secular powers and to make them independent. The whole present relationship of the Church to the secular power, they argued, was sinful. Men of the world dominated the men of God. The soul is superior to the body, yet those who by divine command are to control bodily things now dominate heavenly ones. The priest is in fact superior to the king because his realm is higher. The priest controls the sacraments, that is, rites such as baptism and communion, which are the channels through which divine, life-giving grace pours. The

pope, at the very pinnacle of the channels of grace, can let it flow or cut it off from whom he deems unworthy. The other priests act by his authority. For all his earthly power, the greatest monarch of Christendom will perish eternally if separated from the divine source; it depends on the priest and, first of all, the pope to decide whether the monarch is worthy to receive the sacraments.

On the basis of this theory the papacy from the mid-eleventh century embarked on a policy of removing secular rulers—kings and princes included—from power over the churches in their areas. Bishops, priests, abbots, and monks were to give ultimate obedience to the pope, the Vicar of Christ in Rome. Every Christian was commanded to follow divine law as it was interpreted by the papacy, and monarchs who disobeyed God's rule were to cease being monarchs. The result of the development was that by the early thirteenth century the Roman pope was the most powerful figure in Christendom. Not only did he effectively supervise all the churches and monasteries, but he also acted as the conscience of the secular rulers and their governments.

From the same eleventh century, however, as we have seen in discussing Byzantium (Chapter 9), the papacy lost whatever authority it had enjoyed over the eastern half of the Christian Church. The extension of the new reform movement south of Rome into Greek Italy so threatened the claim of the patriarch of Constantinople to control that area that it led to a break between East and West and the creation of two separate Christian churches.

Political Revival

These same centuries also witnessed a political revival. The economic revival intensified contact between the different regions of a realm and created a tendency for political integration. In the long run this served the cause of the secular rulers. Princes came increasingly to stress the public nature of political power and the obligations of subjects to obey them not on the basis of a personal oath but because the ruler was the prince in a given territory. In the course of the twelfth and thirteenth centuries the monarchies gradually asserted their authority at the local level and subordinated that of the nobility.

Increased central government, however, required money to pay for an army, a bureaucracy, and a royal court. This meant taxes. The king could not seize the money of his subjects. The Germanic conception of private political power founded on an oath was coupled with an implicit understanding that the leader would protect his follower's person and property. By the eleventh century there was a general recognition of the lord's right to demand aid from his followers in certain cases, but both the lord and his men had to agree in council when such circumstances existed and to work out the obligations of each man to his lord. Roman law, studied in Europe again from the eleventh century, also stipulated that "what touches all must be approved of by all." This was interpreted to mean that when levying a tax for the good of the country, the king had to consult with important individuals and with representatives of various segments of the population. Thus the desire of the monarchs to increase their power over the country led to the need for taxation, and this called into being consultative assemblies. Almost everywhere in Europe a tradition of consent of the people to taxation was developing.

By the fourteenth century the political revival would significantly hinder the effectiveness of papal intervention in international politics. Already in the twelfth, monarchies were diverting loyalties of their peoples to themselves not only away from local nobility but also away from the Christian republic led by the pope. But even by the first half of the thirteenth century this process was still only under way: if the glory was a fragile one, the papacy remained the most important political force in Europe.

Intellectual Revival

Along with the political, economic, and religious revivals beginning in the eleventh century came an intellectual revival. In its early stages in the eleventh and twelfth centuries, this revival can generally be described as a process of ordering knowledge in an effort to control experience. The initial step in this development around the year 1000 was the introduction of elementary texts of Aristotle's logic. Although these texts had been circulating separately for centuries, the study of them as a group was novel in the West and may have been introduced from Muslim Spain. Certainly the advanced texts of Aristotle's logic and his other works came to the west largely via Muslim Spain (see Chapter 9).

From the ancient Greek system of logic, Europeans learned the idea of subordinating one idea to another, the part to the whole. Logic instructed them in the process of arriving at new truth and of organizing their knowledge into categories. Trained in logic, Europeans were able to present systematically pieces of knowledge that before were a confused jumble. A great

European logician, Peter Abelard, wrote a book in the first half of the twelfth century called *Sic et Non* (Yes and No) in which he asked hundreds of central questions regarding human life and theology, such as "Is it right to murder another?" and "Does God exist?" After each question he placed the answers given by ancient great authorities, both pagan and Christian writers. Logic was also an aid in the reorganization of the highly confused laws of the Church. The scholars of the twelfth century gave an ordered form to Church or canon law, besides systematically presenting in concise fashion the fruits of numerous commentaries on the Holy Bible. All these endeavors gave people a confidence in the power of reason to understand the universe and offered them a possibility of eventually controlling it.

In the centuries between the fall of Rome and the eleventh century, learning was centered in cathedrals, monasteries, and a few princely courts of Europe. With the revival of the towns, however, the cathedral came to dominate intellectual life. Christianity was divided into hundreds of administrative units called dioceses. The major church of the diocese and the residence of the bishop was the cathedral. Almost without exception located in an urban center, the cathedral contained a school in which the young clergy of the diocese could learn Latin and the proper way of performing their future religious functions. The reinvigoration of town life was accompanied by a new concern for learning in these cathedral schools. The first organized teaching of Aristotle's basic logical works occurred around the year 975 in a cathedral school, that of Rheims. From this point until the twelfth century the initiative in education belonged to these schools. By the twelfth century the number of students had increased to such a degree that in places such as Paris and Oxford the cathedral was no longer able to contain the classes; then private teachers opened up their own schools in the vicinity. In the next century, as organization was given to this diversified instruction, the university was born.

The term *scholasticism* is usually applied to the scientific, theological, and philosophical learning taught in these schools and universities. First of all, this kind of learning was a monopoly of the schools, rather than of private scholars or secluded groups. The method, moreover, of presenting the thought in question-and-answer form was that followed in actual schoolroom teaching. But the term also applied to a common assumption of the thinkers of this three-hundred-year period. There was among them an implicit confidence that there was no conflict between the conclusions produced by reason and those accepted on faith, that the two sets of truth were compatible.

Initially, with the introduction of Aristotelian logic, the primary question became: to what extent could reason be employed to understand faith? As Christians, Europeans were committed to belief in the need of divine revelation to know certain truths. By the fifth century A.D. the basic doctrines of the Christian Church had been worked out on the basis of God's revealed word in the Bible, as follows: (1) the belief in a Trinity composed of Father, Son, and Holy Ghost, three persons in one divine substance. How this could be without making them three separate gods was acknowledged as divine mystery. (2) The belief in the creation of the universe out of nothing by an all-powerful God. (3) The doctrine of the fall of humans into evil through their own free will. (4) The belief in heaven as a final resting place for the good and in a hell as the place for punishment of the evil. (5) The belief in Christ, human and divine, as the redeemer of humanity. Because he was God, he could live on earth without sin, and by virtue of his humanity he could redeem sinful, fallen humankind. (6) The doctrine of eternal life for the soul in paradise and the resurrection of the body through redemption. (7) Redemption was promised to those who believed in Christ as lord and who did good works on earth. (8) The necessity of God's grace for salvation. Whether some people are predestined by God to believe in Christ and do good works with God's grace doing everything, or whether grace is offered to all and people must cooperate with it in the process of salvation, was a debated point. The overwhelming tendency in the Church, however, was to stress the power and responsibility of people to cooperate.

The most congenial philosophic school of antiquity for early Christian thinkers had been that of Plato and his followers. Christians were attracted by the Platonic doctrine of two levels of reality, the world of the Ideas and that of the senses. Plato embraced the idea of the immortality of the soul; and the negative attitude of Platonists to the body, which they considered a prison, also proved attractive to Christians eager to dominate bodily lusts. The Christians were so influenced by these ascetic impulses that they often overlooked their own doctrine that the body, too, would be raised to heaven with the soul. Plato seemed so close to Christianity in some things he wrote that many Christian scholars believed that he had written either under the influence of the Holy Ghost or with knowledge of the works of the Hebrew prophets.

Stoicism also proved attractive to Christians, at least in its moral doctrines. Stoic stress on indifference to worldly success or failure seemed to be helpful to believers in their efforts to turn to God from the false joys of the world. The late Stoic view of government as having largely negative functions of keeping order reappeared in the works of the Church Fathers. As reformulated by the latter, the duty of the state was to prevent sinners from killing one another while the Church went about saving human souls. The sword of kings was to be at the service of the Church: monarch and bishop were to work in harmony to bring people to seek righteousness.

The Church Fathers of the second to the fifth centuries, therefore, used the writings of Platonists and Stoics both as aids in elaborating Christian theological, philosophical, and moral ideas and as witnesses to the truth of Christian doctrine. Whereas the writings of ancient Latin Stoics such as Seneca survived in numbers between the fifth and the eleventh centuries, almost all of Plato was lost, and European knowledge of his thought came mainly from what the Church Fathers had written about him. Aristotle's thought had not been popular in late antiquity and had had little effect on Christian doctrine in its formative stages. However, the craze for Aristotelian logic beginning in the eleventh century added a third ancient Greek influence on Christian thought. Working with Latin translations of Aristotle's elementary logic texts and ancient commentaries on these, European scholars were eager to sharpen their newfound intellectual instruments on the Christian faith. The danger to divine mystery was clearly perceived by critics of such efforts. Pious Christians in the twelfth century were especially alarmed at what appeared to be the assumption of some theologians that God's mind, working by the same processes, was subject to the same rules and conditions in its operations as was the human mind and that it was thus possible for the human mind to understand why God had operated as he did. Did this not detract from God's all-powerful nature and will? But what, then, were the limits of reason?

In the course of the twelfth century Latin translations first of Aristotle's advanced logical writings and then of his philosophical, moral, and scientific works began to circulate in western Europe. Muslim Spain provided many of these translations, but areas in close contact with Islam and Byzantium, such as Sicily and the port city of Venice, also contributed a portion. Along with the Aristotelian texts came Latin translations of Arabic and Hebrew commentaries interpreting the philosopher's meaning.

The recovery of the whole Aristotelian corpus only further aggravated the problem of faith and reason.

Aristotle's logical works had been simply an introduction to this masterpiece of thought. Medieval Europe had been particularly weak in scientific knowledge, and, with the introduction of Aristotle's entire body of writings, Europeans became aware of a system of thinking, ultimately reducible to a few basic principles, that had something to say about almost everything in the universe. Aristotle answered questions that they had not even learned to ask.

In the course of the thirteenth century, however, as they came with the help of the Arabic and Jewish commentators to understand what Aristotle had written—his work was and is very difficult to read—Christian thinkers began to see that Aristotle believed in an eternal world and in a God who did not create the universe but who served only to explain why things in it moved. Moreover, he also seemed to believe that the human soul died with the human body. Aristotle appeared to be the culmination of the power of human reason; yet the results of his investigation, conducted according to the procedures of his logic (on which they too relied), seemed to point to some conclusions that contradicted the faith. Was the Christian faith therefore irrational? God was supposed to be truth, yet reason's conclusions apparently were not those of revelation.

Saint Thomas Aquinas   The most influential attempt to reconcile reason and revelation in the thirteenth century was that of Thomas Aquinas (died 1274), who showed, first of all, that Aristotle's proof for the eternity of the world was not a conclusive one. In fact, he maintained that there is no way by reason to prove either the eternity or the creation of the universe. We know that it was created, but that knowledge comes from faith. In the matter of Aristotle's position on the immortality of the human soul, Aquinas argued that Aristotle himself is ambiguous. Thus, he concluded, there is no proof that reason contradicts faith. Quite the contrary.

There are, according to Thomas Aquinas, many truths about the world that reason can discover: the causes of the rainbow, the source of locomotion in animals, and the like. More than this, there are certain truths revealed to us by God that could also be known by reason; for instance, that God exists and that he is one God. After all, some ancient pagans knew this through the use of their reason. Then there are truths about God that no pagan could have known, such as the existence of the Trinity. Thus for Aquinas the two spheres of truth, that established by reason and that by revelation, overlap.

If we follow reason according to the rules of logic, we can know many things about God and heaven; and, at the very pinnacle of this kind of truth, reason duplicates the lowest truths of revelation. Moreover, even the truths of revelation not open to human reason are not in themselves illogical, irrational. When reason examines them, in fact, they are quite reasonable. If people use reason according to the proper procedures of logic, they will gradually define a body of truth that at its greatest heights demands to be completed by the truths of faith.

Accordingly, Aquinas and thinkers like him were able to construct enormous systems of thought beginning with our awareness of ourselves and the world and integrating all aspects of our internal and external experience. Every natural phenomenon from the falling of the raindrops to the movement of the stars can be set within a framework of explanation that literally requires the truths of revelation to cap it with ultimate meaning. Just as these edifices of human thought presented a world where all truth pointed heavenward, so did the great stone cathedrals that dotted the landscape of western Europe in the thirteenth century.

Crusades

Beginning in 1095, Christian Crusades aimed at recovering the Holy Land continued sporadically into the sixteenth century, but the last serious enterprise was that of Saint Louis in 1248–1250 (see map). These warlike expeditions against the Muslims might generally be interpreted as signs of the rising self confidence of Europeans during these centuries of revival. Initially sparked by the religious zeal following the great reform movement of the eleventh century, the Crusades soon became determined by economic and political factors as well (for example, the capture of Constantinople in 1204, Chapter 9). Although deeply prejudiced against the foreign cultures they encountered, the Crusaders, and eventually western Europeans as a whole, were nonetheless much affected by the contact. To a significant degree the new pursuit of the upper classes for greater elegance in dress—silks and perfumes were introduced—and more refined forms of conduct stemmed from Eastern influences. Among technological innovations of Eastern origin were gunpowder ("Greek fire") for warfare and the astrolabe for sailing. Furthermore, the intellectual revival already under way at the time of the First Crusade was unquestionably invigorated by direct—even if often hostile—contact with intellectually superior cultures. If in the long run the repeated efforts of

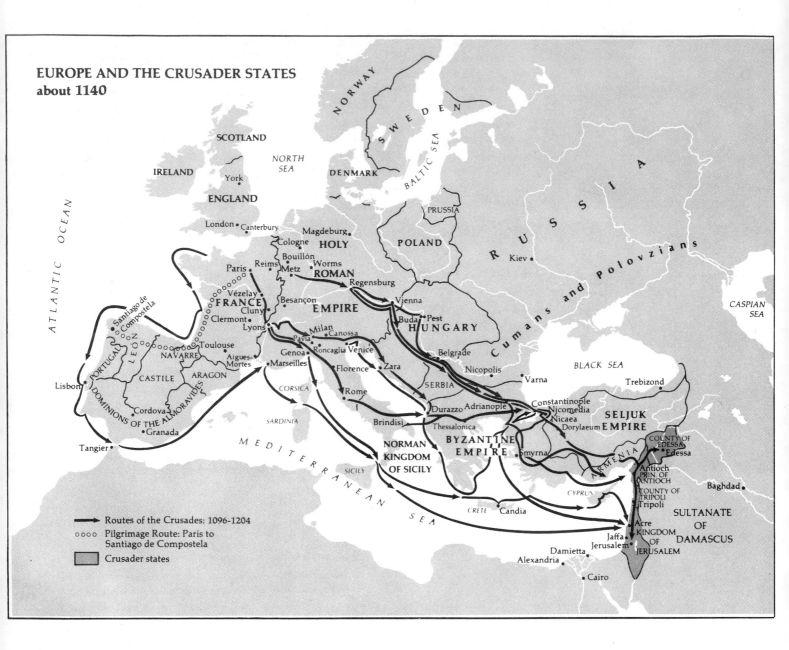

EUROPE AND THE CRUSADER STATES
about 1140

Routes of the Crusades: 1096–1204
Pilgrimage Route: Paris to Santiago de Compostela
Crusader states

western Europe to establish a Catholic Christian base on the eastern Mediterranean coast proved a colossal failure, European society had been helped to greater maturity by the experience.

Medieval Art and the Church: The Gothic Cathedral

Art in the ninth, tenth, and eleventh centuries, like learning, was centered in the court, the monastery, and the cathedral. These three institutions had the means, personnel, and time to produce creative work. Painting, sculpture, and architecture were viewed as ways to

enhance and explain Christian doctrine. It is also true that both monarchs and clergy realized the power of beauty and wealth to enhance their respective positions.

Along with the economic, religious, political, and intellectual revivals of Europe in the twelfth and thirteenth centuries, an artistic growth flourished. This gave rise to the Gothic style in art and architecture, a style whose forms and conventions would be practiced all over northern Europe and in the British Isles. Two particular occurrences were of great significance for this development: the pilgrimage and the Crusades. Both activities united people and provided them with profound new experiences.

10-1   *St. Sernin, Toulouse, east end. (Copyright 1992 ARS, NY/SPADEM, Paris)*

Pilgrimages

Since every Christian could not be a monk, nun, priest, or in some other way directly affiliated with the Church, it fell to the great numbers of lay Catholics to seek other ways to ensure their salvation. The immediate means open was the performance of good works, which usually meant contributions of time and wealth to the local church, cathedral, or monastery. Another was the route of penance—the undertaking of a pilgrimage to Rome, the Holy Land, or another shrine to seek the aid of a saint or saints. Along the route, the pilgrim could visit the relics and shrines of important local saints, who would then act on behalf of the sinner.

For the French and Germans one of the most favored pilgrimages was to Santiago de Compostela in northern Spain. This was the site of the tomb of Saint James, the son of Zebedee, one of Christ's chosen disciples. We know of it as a pilgrimage site as early as the mid-ninth century. By the mid-tenth century, clerics and laity were making the journey in increasing numbers. The map shows the route followed. Chaucer's *Canterbury Tales*, set on an English pilgrimage to

Thomas à Becket's shrine, reflects the spirit of comradeship that pilgrimages instilled (see Chapter 11).

Movement in a pilgrimage was slow, fifteen or twenty miles a day, mostly on foot. Monasteries and churches provided accommodations along the road and broke the monotony of the trip by their beauty. As pilgrims came from many directions to Santiago, churches and cathedrals began to develop specific regional types. In the great burst of building activity many architectural ideas were tried, discarded, and elaborated.

A brief look at one of the great pilgrimage churches in France will be of help in understanding the Gothic tradition that developed after the eleventh and twelfth centuries. Saint Sernin, located at Toulouse, in southern France, was one of many great churches built in the eleventh and twelfth centuries in response to the pilgrimages and to growing wealth, mobility, and ambition. All over France and Germany and in England, many builders employed the means of Roman architecture to create new feelings and form. We generally call this art *Romanesque* because of its relation to Roman architecture (Fig. 10-1).

The plan of Saint Gaul (Fig. 8-5) showed a church with rounded ends, *nave*, and two *apses*. Entrance was from the side, with no clearly defined *transepts*. Two round stair towers were located at one end outside the apse. Local parish churches were even simpler. They might have an apse; a crypt below ground for treasure, burial, and relics; and a simple nave with entry at the west end.

The plan of Saint Sernin at Toulouse (Fig. 10-2) represents a shape called a Latin cross. There is an entrance porch that opens into a *nave* with double aisles on each side. The *transept* and *apse* are sharply defined. On the east side of the transept and around the apse are separate small apses, which are called chapels. These are all related to each other by an aisle that goes all the way around the transept arms and around the apse itself. This passageway is called an *ambulatory*. It is comparable in some ways to the passage around the base of a dome or the passageway around the center of San Vitale in Ravenna, but the spaces are much more clearly separated.

From the outside we see that Saint Sernin is a brick and stone building with clearly defined roof forms. The nave roof is the highest, then lower down are the roofs over the aisles and the distinctly roofed apse and chapels.

On entering we would see a church meant to accommodate not only the monastery (of which it was a part) but also crowds of pilgrims. The arrangement

10-2 *Groundplan of St. Sernin, Toulouse, c. 1100.*

shops, and other buildings around it. Fantastic energy was put into the construction of these great stone works. Usually everyone in the village, from the lords and ladies down to the peasants, joined the professional stonemasons in doing their part to construct an edifice to the glory of God and to the representation of the Church on earth (Fig. 10-3).

Why did medieval people devote such time, energy, and money to the construction of these huge and complex buildings? It is hard to find anything comparable in the lives of modern people. We must try to remember that churches were not merely places to go on Sunday or decorations for a town; they represented a vital aspect of everyone's spiritual life. They were not only dwellings for God on earth but also a kind of bridge between the physical and spiritual realms. They began as heavy stone set on the ground, but they soared upward toward heaven. They contained something for everyone. For the common people, many of whom could neither read nor write, they offered a kind of visual religious education.

The stained-glass windows, the sculptures, and the architectural design of the churches built in the twelfth and thirteenth centuries tell us a great deal about the values and beliefs of the people who built them and worshiped in them. The term *Gothic*, used to describe their style, was coined in the Renaissance. Until the late eighteenth century it was a derogatory term,

of nave and aisles is comparable to that of Old Saint Peter's (Fig. 8-2), but the ceiling is composed of *barrel* and *groin vaults* like those used in the Colosseum (Fig. 7-10). Compare the plan of this church with that of the Great Mosque at Cordoba (Color Plate VI). What major differences do you observe? What accounts for those differences?

Effect of the Crusades

The Crusades afforded another opportunity for clergy and laity to gain wider knowledge of art forms, buildings, and building techniques. Just as the pilgrimages carried people to Spain with its important Islamic monuments, so the Crusaders became aware of spectacular buildings in Jerusalem, Constantinople, northern Africa, and other Eastern sites (see map). The forms and methods observed there fostered new ambitions and suggested new ways to achieve them, contributing to the rise of the Gothic style.

The Rise of Gothic Architecture

Many villages in France today still give the impression that an enormous church dominates the small houses,

10-3 *Cathedral of Chartres, aerial view. (Copyright 1992 ARS, NY/SPADEM, Paris)*

10-4 *Cathedral of Chartres, west front, exterior.* (Giraudon/Art Resource, NY)

10-5 *Cathedral of Chartres, nave. (Giraudon/Art Resource, NY)*

implying that a style created by the descendants of the Goths, one of the barbarian tribes that overran the Roman Empire, was uncivilized and greatly inferior to the classical style. (In a similar way, Westerners once considered African art barbaric until European artists in the early part of our century began to appreciate its originality.) Certainly, one can say that the aesthetic impression felt inside a Gothic cathedral is different from the impression one has inside a Roman building like the Pantheon, but most modern viewers would not at all agree with the Renaissance belief that this difference constitutes inferiority. Preference here is a matter of taste, temperament, knowledge, and experience. Formulate some of your own impressions of the interior and exterior of Notre Dame (Our Lady) of Chartres (Figs. 10-4 and 10-5) by comparing it with the Pantheon, Hagia Sophia, the Great Mosque at Cordoba, or the Hall of Justice at the Alhambra. Consider the actual size, the importance of the interior and exterior for the user, the purpose of each, the arrangement of interior spaces, the materials, and the way in which light comes into the buildings.

Now we will analyze some of the technical and artistic features of the Gothic cathedral. Gothic build-ings, like all other architecture, evolved from the technology, needs, and ideals of a particular time and place. The patrons and artisans who created these great churches drew on the current architectural solutions and skills while experimenting with and expanding both structural and formal capabilities. Masons, carpenters, and other artisans followed the routes of the Crusades and pilgrimages, learning from the great accomplishments of Muslim and Christian alike.

The monastery church of Saint Denis (Fig. 10-6), in the Ile-de-France, near Paris, and the cathedral of Notre Dame of Chartres, which we will consider in this chapter, document the origin and extraordinary capacities of the period for visual expression of metaphysical and deeply religious ideas.

Suger and Saint Denis

In 1120 a monk named Suger was named abbot of Saint Denis, one of the oldest and most venerable monastic foundations in France. Named for the founding saint of French Catholicism, it was also associated with the Capets, successors to Charlemagne, many of whom were buried there. Suger had been at Saint

Denis since childhood and had grown up with Louis VI, the Capetian king. A dynamic, ambitious, and highly intelligent individual, he had already distinguished himself as a diplomat for the papacy before becoming abbot. In 1147, when Louis VII left for the Second Crusade, Suger was made regent of the kingdom. But Suger did not seek power for its own sake. His association of the abbey with secular power came from his Christian desire to bring order and spiritual enlightenment to the poor and to the powerful. These beliefs, in combination with other factors (the church was in disrepair and crowded on feast days), caused Suger to begin to work on rebuilding the church at Saint Denis.

Descriptions of churches seen by Crusaders provided Suger with some ideas; but most important were those derived from his own theology, which developed in the years before the work at Saint Denis began. It was heavily Neoplatonic, for it was based on the writing of Dionysius, a sixth-century Greek mystic who was mistakenly associated with Saint Denis (A.D. 200s), the patron saint of France. Suger's ideas were also related to those of Aristotle and the scholastics. The two central themes with which he worked were harmony and light. Suger believed that all matter in some degree partakes of God and in some way reflects ultimate reality. Visible light is, therefore, the analogy for the light of God, and thus symbolic of the unity of all creation. As natural light infuses and transforms, so are we transformed by this heavenly light, illumination, knowledge. Suger also believed that the contemplation of the truly beautiful "worthy materials" of gold, gemstones, chalices, and altars could transport one from the world here below to the heavenly one. In 1144 he wrote:

> Thus, when out of my delight in the beauty of the house of God—the loveliness of the many-colored gems has called me away from external cares, and worthy meditation has induced me to reflect, transferring that which is material to that which is immaterial, on the diversity of the sacred virtues—then it seems to me that I see myself dwelling, as it were, in some strange region of the universe which neither exists entirely in the slime of the earth nor entirely in the purity of Heaven; and that, by the grace of God, I can be transported from this inferior to that higher world.

It became his ambition to make his church such a means of transcendence, to fill it with light and to give it a spiritual significance as great as that of its saint and the French kingdom.

We do not know how Suger conveyed his ideas to the expert builders who undertook the work. But we

10-6   *St. Denis, west front. (Giraudon/Art Resource, NY)*

do know that the combination of his visions and the hired technical skill produced a number of important changes in church design and construction that were absorbed at once by builders in the area around Saint Denis.

Perhaps the most significant innovation was a new system of *piers* and *vaults*, employing pointed arches that allowed the enlargement of the east end, creating a large *choir* (a rectangular space for the clergy between the transept and apse) surrounded by an aisle (ambulatory) with seven chapels spaced equidistantly on its outer edge (Fig. 10-7). These were roofed with vaults. Most important of all, however, the outside walls of the chapel and the *clerestory* above were now largely glass. This glass was richly colored—reds, blues, yellows, and some white. The small pieces of glass were arranged in patterns, figures, and stories. Joined together by lead strips, the panels were then set within a framework of stone. The east end of the church became a vessel for the transmission of divine, transforming light.

> Once the new rear part [east end] is joined to the part in front, the church shines with its middle part brightened. For bright is that which is brightly coupled with the bright. And bright is the noble edifice that is pervaded by the new light.

10-7   *Groundplan of the choir, St. Denis, near Paris, c. 1140.*

The church, filled with light, was a bridge to the ultimate reality of divine revelation, the harmonious and orderly world. The windows transformed light, as God's light transformed the dull heaviness of matter. Uplifted by this created light within the church, the worshipers' souls would rise to seek God, its uncreated source.

This new way of building will be explored further in the rebuilding of the Cathedral of Notre Dame of Chartres (Fig. 10-4), which is among the finest examples of Gothic design and construction.

The Cathedral at Chartres

The village of Chartres seems almost inundated by the fields of grain that spread out from the town, but the cathedral dominates the horizon. The church, dedicated to the Virgin, was founded before 743 (the first sure date associated with it). Its chief relic, the tunic of the Virgin, had been given by King Charles the Bald. This gift made Chartres the center of the veneration of the Virgin in western Europe, and the deep devotion it engendered is revealed by the successive buildings on the site. Documents tell of numerous fires, and we can follow successive rebuildings up to this great monument. A new basilica had been erected in the eleventh century. In the early twelfth century another fire occasioned the erection of the three entrances and tower bases at the west end. Then in June 1194 a fire devastated the basilica and town, leaving only the west front intact. From this anonymous account, written early in the thirteenth century, we can get a good idea of the role of this church in the life of the people.

> Therefore, in the year 1194 after the Incarnation of the Lord, since the church at Chartres had been devastated on the third of the Ides of June [June 10]

by an extraordinary and lamentable fire making it necessary later, after the walls had been broken up and demolished and leveled to the ground, to repair the foundations and then erect a new church. ... The inhabitants of Chartres, clerics as well as laymen, ... considered as their chief misfortune, the fact that they, unhappy wretches, in justice for their own sins, had lost the palace of the Blessed Virgin, the special glory of the city, the showpiece of the entire region, the incomparable house of prayer. ...

Indeed, when for several days they had not seen the most sacred reliquary of the Blessed Mary, the population of Chartres was seized with incredible anguish and grief, concluding that it was unworthy to restore the structures of the city or the church, if it had lost such a precious treasure, [which was] indeed the glory of the whole city. At last, on a particular holy day, when the entire populace had assembled by order of the clergy at the spot where the church had stood, the above mentioned reliquary was brought forth from the crypt. ... The fact must not be passed over that when, at the time of the fire, the reliquary frequently referred to had been moved by certain persons into the lower crypt (whose entrance the laudable foresight of the ancients had cut near the altar of the Blessed Mary), and they had been shut up there, not daring to go back out because of the fire now raging, they were so preserved from mortal danger under the protection of the Blessed Mary that neither did the rain of burning timbers falling from above shatter the iron door covering the face of the crypt, nor did the drops of melted lead penetrate it, nor the heap of burning coals overhead injure it. ... And after such a fierce conflagration, when men who were considered already dead from smoke or excessive heat had come back unharmed, all present were filled with such gladness that they rejoiced together, weeping affectionately with them.

... When, following the ruin of the walls mentioned above, necessity demanded that a new church be built and the wagons were at last ready to fetch the stone, all beckoned as well as exhorted each other to obey instantly and do without delay whatever they thought necessary for this construction or [whatever] the master workers prescribed. But the gifts or assistance of the laymen would never have been adequate to raise such a structure had not the bishop and the canons contributed so much money, as stated above, for three years from their own revenues. For this became evident to everyone at the end of the three-year period when all finances suddenly gave out, so that the supervisors had no wages for the workmen, nor did they have in view anything that could be given otherwise. But I recall that at that moment someone said—I know not by what spirit of prophecy—that the purses would fail before the coins needed

10-8 *Cathedral of Chartres, Royal Portal, exterior, west front. Left tympanum, Ascension of Christ; central tympanum, Second Coming of Christ; right tympanum, Incarnation of Christ. (Giraudon/Art Resource, NY)*

for the work on the church of Chartres [were obtained]. What is there to add? Since, in view of the utter failure of human resources, it was necessary for the divine to appear, the blessed Mother of God, desiring that a new and incomparable church be erected in which she could perform her miracles, stirred up the power of this Son of hers by her merits and prayers. When there was a large gathering of people there, she openly and clearly exhibited a certain new miracle, one unheard of for a long time past, seen by all for the first time. As a result, news of the miracle spread far and wide through the whole of Gaul and made it easier to give credence to succeeding miracles.

Out of despair the people, clerics, and nobility of Chartres created an enduring act of devotion by making this palace for the queen of heaven. The new church was occupied by 1220 and dedicated in 1260—an astonishingly short time given the technology of the age. Its form embraced the changes that Suger had made at Saint Denis, creating a harmonious, substantial expression of belief rendered into visible form.

Standing before the west front (Fig. 10-8), you feel that the building looks somewhat familiar. The central doors suggest that the nave and aisles lie behind, and at the end of the nave may be seen an apse. Turning to the right, moving across the front, and looking down the south side, you see a wing that joins the nave at right angles. The church has a transept that can be entered through a graceful three-part porch and doors. Standing before the porch of the transept, looking west, toward the front towers, you see the wall of the aisle, its roof sloping up slightly to meet the walls of the nave and clerestory that rise above it (Figs. 10-9 and 10-12).

Extension of the Building   Topping the aisle wall is a row of columns carrying arches and a lintel. This *parapet* partially conceals the aisle roof. The aisle wall is divided into seven regular intervals expressed by six large, single, pointed windows and a passageway. The wall of the nave rising above the aisle repeats the intervals, but the single window is replaced by pairs of tall pointed windows topped with a round one. These

10-9   *Cathedral of Chartres, south aisle, exterior. Windows of aisle are separated by wall buttresses that rise to the parapet. (Copyright 1992 ARS, NY/SPADEM, Paris)*

10-10 *Cathedral of Chartres, detail of nave, exterior, showing wall buttresses between aisle windows. These rise above aisle parapet as detached and flying buttresses of clerestory arcade. (Giraudon/Art Resource, NY)*

10-11 *Cathedral of Chartres, choir, exterior, west end. Aisle, clerestory and flying buttresses between windows. (Copyright 1992 ARS, NY/SPADEM, Paris)*

are the windows of the clerestory of the nave with its sharply pointed lead-covered roof. The exterior walls, however, seem less like walls than elaborate piers, and in the spaces between each window are carefully cut and laid towers of stone called *buttresses* (Fig. 10-10). Each buttress continues to rise vertically but becomes thinner and lighter as it is stepped in toward the clerestory wall. Beginning at the gabled opening with its figure, a section of stone arch reaches out to join the stone pier between the clerestory windows. Finally, as each buttress towers almost to the parapet of the nave roof, another arch reaches out to the clerestory pier. These are the *flying buttresses,* arches of stone reaching across space to help transfer the weight of wall and roof to the foundations. This is the building framework: a great skeleton of stone. Light and air pass over it freely, moving among the details of moldings, angles, and arches and over the surfaces of the great windows themselves. As you move around the apse (Fig. 10-11), you note that the walls and windows deflect in and out, responding to the location of the chapels around the apse. There are also flying buttresses around the apse, supporting its great windows that rise, like the nave clerestory, above the ambulatory below. The exterior of Saint Denis may have looked like this; Chartres resembles it in plan and, in all probability, idea. Walking around the choir to the north, you reach the other entrance to the transept. Both transept entrances are towered and columned, quite different from the west front, which was built before the fire of 1194, and therefore long before the north and south transepts. Completing the circuit of the church shows its familiar basilican plan (Fig. 10-12) but also demonstrates that it is realized in a new way: in a structure that seems to stand outside the walls of windows, windows that fill the interior with light.

To understand the physical achievement that made the building possible, we must remind ourselves of Roman vaulting and the pointed arches of Muslim architecture. The barrel and groin vaults of the Romans were semicircular in section, and the bay had to be regular (Fig. 10-13). Moreover, the tops of the arches had to be the same height. Piers, columns, and walls carried the vaults, and the windows were small. Centering was used to erect the vaults; and, as a basilica grew, bay by bay, it became a series of separate units of space.

Recall the interior of the Great Mosque of Cordoba (Color Plate VI). Study the plan of the apse of Chartres (Fig. 10-12). Pay particular attention to the dots and dark areas that indicate columns and piers. The diagonal lines on the plan indicate the joining of

10-12   *Groundplan, Chartres.*

been replaced by a greater unity—a whole greater than its parts, like but very unlike the space created within the Court of the Lions with its screens of columns (Fig. 9-22). The system of pointed arches, ribs, and flying buttresses made possible this accomplishment.

At the west front again, the towers seem to squeeze the portals between them, and the airy complexity of the south and north porches is replaced by a majestic weightiness, reinforced by the three round arched windows above the doors and the single huge, round window (Fig. 10-4). The south tower was finished about 1155, but the north tower spire was added only in the early sixteenth century. The three entrance doors are decorated with sculpted figures; and, as we examine the sculpture of the west front, we can begin to understand more about the church as a whole, this

10-13a   *Groin vaults normally require square bays. When a rectangular bay is needed, the arches on the shorter sides (1) must be raised to keep the four sides of the vault equal in height. This is not a very satisfactory solution.*

sections of the vaults. There are seven vaults of four sections each for the ambulatory, each of the side chapels contains vaults of five parts, but the bays of the ambulatory and chapels are irregular—they become larger as one moves from the apse out to the building wall. Regular Roman vaults would not permit this, nor would the system permit such irregularity in the size of pier and column. What permitted this new configuration in the plan? First, the arches of the vaults are not semicircular in section, but pointed; second, the vaults are joined by pointed ribs that act as a permanent centering for the vaults (Figs. 10-5 and 10-13).

Pointed arches, as we have seen, were already known in the architecture of Muslim countries. They have the advantage of being more self-supporting; the two sides lean on each other. Ribs had also been used before. What was new here was the combination of pointed arch and rib to make a vaulting system that was lighter and more flexible, permitting more and more wall to be opened for glass. The outward, downward thrust of the vaults is carried away from the walls by the piers and flying buttresses that rise above the roofs. The new system creates in Chartres spaces with no sharp delineations between ambulatory and chapel, or apse and aisle. The separate cells of space made by the chapels at Saint Sernin (Fig. 10-2) have

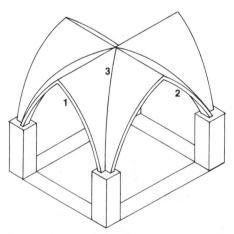

10-13b   *The pointed arch permits the arches of the short (1), long (2), and diagonal (3) spans to accommodate a rectangular bay with greater efficiency.*

palace for the Virgin, this place of transportation from earthly to heavenly life.

For the modern mind it is difficult to think of art as a teaching tool; but for medieval people, art, like everything else, had a purpose in the divine scheme of things. The cathedral, like the philosophical system of Thomas Aquinas, was concerned with God, the world, and humankind—with the accumulation of human knowledge and speculation and their relation to divine knowledge and revelation.

Exterior Sculptures The three doors of the west front, called the Royal Portal (Fig. 10-8), sit in round arches deep in the thick wall. The wall from the door to the outer wall face, the *jamb,* is slanted outward; these jambs are decorated with columns and figures. The columns have richly decorated bases, and their *capitals* are carved, providing a horizontal contrast to the jamb figures (Fig. 10-8). Above the doors are sculpted lintels, and above the lintel is the *tympanum,* the sculpture-filled panels that reach to the top of the opening. In the slanted area above the lintel from the arch to the wall's outer surface are stones called *archivolts,* also sculpted. All these sculptures, like Greek sculpture, would have been painted, gilded, and decorated to enhance and intensify the specific qualities of figure and setting.

The sculptures of the west front present the fundamentals of the Christian dogma with directness and clarity. Let us look more closely at each section to see how the sculptor presents images and relates them to each other and to the architectural framework. You might also ask how this sculpture differs from that we saw in Athens on the Parthenon and in Rome.

Beginning with the tympanum of the right door, we see a crowned, haloed Virgin seated on a throne, the Christ child in her lap (Fig. 10-14). On either side of the central figures is an angel swinging a censer, a container for burning incense. The Virgin and child face us directly; the folds of their garments fall symmetrically and emphasize this frontality. The angels, seen in profile, are almost identical, their poses giving the composition great repose. These heavenly attendants, the throne, and the pose tell us that we are before the Virgin as the queen of heaven.

The lintel below is divided into two registers containing the following scenes: lower register, left to right, the Annunciation (Gabriel visits Mary to tell her that she will conceive and bear a son, Jesus); the Visitation (Mary visits Elizabeth, the mother of John the Baptist); the Nativity and the angels announcing Jesus' birth to the shepherds; in the upper register, the Pre-

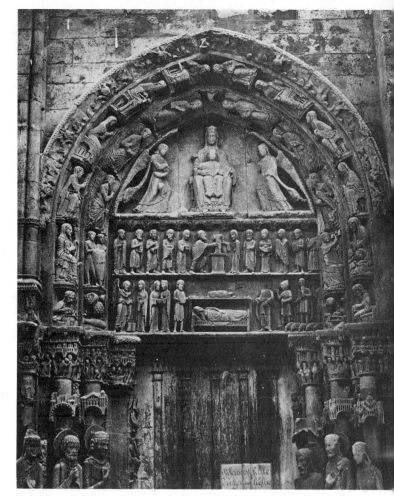

10-14 *Cathedral of Chartres, west front, right tympanum, Incarnation of Christ. (Giraudon/Art Resource, NY)*

sentation of Jesus in the Temple. All the figures in the scenes seem stocky and somewhat ill-proportioned; their clothes are simplified, and the faces all resemble each other. The figures in both rows share a simple rhythmical relation, spaced equidistantly apart and almost symmetrically. Was naturalism this artist's goal? What was the goal? Can we read the story with clarity and ease?

In addition to the apparent subjects, these representations were filled with much deeper meaning for medieval people—meanings that have been discovered in medieval treatises and sermons. For example, seeing Christ as a child and in young manhood reminds us that he was human and present with us, as well as being God. Mary, his mother, is human and divine also, the queen of heaven and the motherly intercessor for us. In the nativity scene we see Mary resting on what looks like a bed. A medieval person would have recognized it as an altar, and placing the

10-15   *Cathedral of Chartres, west front, left tympanum, Ascension of Christ. (Giraudon/Art Resource, NY)*

child in the manger on the altar's top edge alludes to Christ, the sacrifice, the Eucharist. The scene of the Presentation in the Temple repeats the idea; Christ stands in the center on an altarlike form. Thus the sculptures not only represent scenes from the life of Jesus, but they also serve as reminders of the complex nature of Christ, as God made humanity and as the sacrifice for humankind's salvation.

In the archivolts around the tympanum are personifications of the seven liberal arts: grammar, dialectic, rhetoric, arithmetic, music, geometry, and astronomy. The cathedral at Chartres was a seat of great learning, and the inclusion of the liberal arts in the sculptural program is a natural allusion to this and the major concern of the schools: to forge the links in knowledge from the human to the divine, from the systematic logic of Aristotle to the mystical transcendence of faith. These sculptures should also remind us that Christ is wisdom incarnate, the *logos*, the word of God made human.

The other two tympana expand the story begun in the right portal. In the left portal is the Ascension of Christ. In its tympanum, Christ, supported by angels, is drawn up into heaven on a cloud (Fig. 10-15). In the upper register of the lintel four angels announce his Second Coming to the apostles seated below. The archivolts are carved with signs of the zodiac and the labors of the months—Christ as man was in time;

Christ as God *is* time, the beginning and the end—seasons, labors, and life will stop at his coming again. Compare these figures to those on the right, Incarnation portal. Do words such as *simplicity, order, clarity, symmetry* apply? Look at the clouds and the angels' drapery. How do these figures compare with the Panathenaic festival? Those on the *Ara Pacis*?

The central tympanum shows Christ in majesty, one hand raised in blessing, surrounded by the four symbols of the Evangelists: Mark's lion, John's eagle, Matthew's man (or angel), and Luke's bull (Fig. 10-16). Angels and church elders in the archivolts and the apostles in the lintel witness the Second Coming—to judge the living and the dead. Christ is seated and crowned with a halo, his ultimate kingship emphasized by the two angels who hold the crown at the top of the archivolts.

The capitals on the columns below show scenes from the lives of Mary and Jesus. They connect the subjects of the three portals both narratively and visually. This is indeed a presentation of sacred history.

The remaining figures are the elongated columnar ones on the jambs. Only nineteen remain of the original twenty-four, male and female, crowned and uncrowned, neither ancient nor youthful. They share the stylized drapery and physical simplification of the other portal figures. But their scale and location give them a vibrating tension as they seem poised before the doors (Fig. 10-17).

10-16   *Cathedral of Chartres, west front, central tympanum, Second Coming of Christ. (Giraudon/Art Resource, NY)*

Plate VII
Chartres, stained glass
window (detail), 12th
century, Notre Dame
de la Belle Verrière.
(Scala/Art Resource, NY)

Plate VIII
Chartres, stained glass
window (detail), 12th
century, St. James
Major. Furriers and
drapers. (Giraudon/Art
Resource, NY)

Plate IX
Simone Martini,
Annunciation, 1333,
Galleria degli Uffizi,
Florence.
(Scala/Art Resource, NY)

Plate X
Gelede dancer, Meko.
(Frank Willett, Glasgow)

Plate XI
Gelede dance scene.
(Howard Wildman)

These great doors on the west, illuminated by the setting sun, must have been perceived as palatial, heavenly gates, the entry to the court of Mary, the queen of heaven, for one enters acutely aware of the majesty and presence of this person and her Son.

Interior   Passing from the exterior into the nave is like leaving one world to enter another. The nave arcade rises to support a row of shallow arched openings, and above these the clerestory rises to the vaults 118 feet above the floor (Fig. 10-5). The great piers that make up the nave arcade and separate the nave from the aisles are not single columns, like those of the Parthenon, but seem to be created from a collection of individual shafts. Each pier has a central shaft, and centered on each face is a smaller shaft: one faces the aisle, one faces the nave, and one faces the pier behind or in front of it. These are gathered at the base, rise to the capital, and then disperse in the nave and aisle vaults. The nave is seven bays long, the transept spreads left and right, and the choir, apse, and ambulatory seem distant and light-filled. As you move down the nave, radiant with the colored light spilling in from the stained-glass windows of the clerestory above, you remember the complex and weighty stone skeleton that supports this light-filled and awesome space. The interior is the final expression of the diversity and unity of a system of building with arches and ribs, piers and columns.

Look at one pier and one bay of the nave (Fig. 10-5). Compare it with a column of the Parthenon and the bay of the pilgrimage church, Saint Sernin. What is immediately different? The base of the Gothic pier has not one, but a variety of simple moldings that unite the small shafts attached to the central column. Because of the attached columns and their capitals, the pier does not seem to face squarely into the nave or aisle. The different locations of the attached columns cause your eyes to move across, around, and behind the pier so that the nave and aisle interlock. Follow the attached shafts as they rise upward. Those two that face each other and decorate the arch of the nave arcade carry a series of curved moldings (Fig. 10-5). The shaft facing the aisle carries smaller shafts that rise to become the aisle vault ribs. The shaft facing the nave bursts into five clearly articulated smaller shafts that rise to become the ribs of the nave vault. One shaft reaches the vault and crosses transversely; another crosses the vault diagonally to a pier on the other side of the bay. Where the two diagonal ribs meet, their flow is gathered into a circular *keystone*. Moreover, as each rib springs across the vault, it is multiplied into three

10-17   *Cathedral of Chartres, west front, Old Testament figures. (Giraudon/Art Resource, NY)*

The absolute identification of these figures has never been agreed on, but we think them to be kings and prophets of the Old Testament. It is as if these are the ancestors of the sacred history of the New Testament revealed above. In these figures we may also perceive the close ties between Church and state, kingship and priesthood. The crowned and uncrowned figures may refer to heavenly rule—earthly kingship and priesthood. The female figures may be the ancestors of the Virgin.

Our knowledge of the subject matter of the sculpture and windows and the architecture at Chartres derives not only from Chartres itself but also from the programs of decoration at numerous other cathedrals and churches. It is important to know that the work at Chartres is not an isolated phenomenon but reaches backward to earlier programs at other buildings and is subsequently influential in the creation of later programs, in both form and content. Chartres is a paradigm for many such buildings—the cathedrals at Rheims, Amiens, Paris, Rouen, Laon, Cologne, and Strasbourg and for churches in Paris and many other cities in France, Germany, and England.

or more curving ribs—not a flat rib. Between the ribs are the smooth surfaces of the vaults. Looking up, you see the vault of a single bay, which looks like this ✕ ; yet it merges into the next bay in a shape that looks like this ◇ . The experience produced is one of a constant fluid merging of separate but totally dependent units of space. The bays of the aisles, like those of the nave, melt into a whole. Reaching the light-filled apse, you experience an absorbing, objective order and consistency of building form that does not intimidate or overwhelm but absorbs you as an integral part of the whole, just as every base, shaft, capital, and molding is essential.

The structural knowledge and expertise that produced the cathedral are not a matter of speculation. They were the product of the guilds and lodges of masons who worked for the cathedral or monastery. These experts were conversant with the knowledge of engineering, stonemasonry, and mathematics necessary to make the building stand up. More specifically, we can say that the medieval mason proportioned a cathedral on a sure foundation of mathematics. The mason worked from a constant proportion, established in the beginning and capable of determining the measure of every member and element. This was not just a pragmatic tool; the mason, like the philosopher and theologian, believed that numbers and therefore harmony were reflections of the divine order of the world. From Aristotle and Pythagoras the mason drew knowledge of certain simple ratios as being the most sure reflections of that harmony, and applied them to plan and elevation. If we do not immediately see, we sense overriding appropriateness of height to width and of equal correctness of division within. Thus the Gothic cathedral is a concrete example of the use of reason in the service of faith, comparable to the philosophies of Abelard and Aquinas mentioned earlier in this chapter. The culture of the High Middle Ages was both practical and intellectual, but these two aspects were subordinated to humanity's primary purpose in life: the aspiration of the soul toward salvation by God, to be accomplished through the Church.

Stained-Glass Windows   Harmony and light, then, are the two binding physical motifs of Chartres: harmony of building—its spaces and forms—and light, the luminescence of the translucent window wall, stretching thin webs between the stones. These two values, harmony and light, are presented perhaps most completely in the stained glass of Chartres, where the art reached a level of unusual perfection. Unlike a painting, which reflects light, the windows transmit

and transform light. The varicolored light conceals, reveals, and warms the spare stone of the building. The jewel-like windows adorn the building as gold and gems adorn the vessels of the sacrament and cross of the altar. The Madonna herself is enthroned in the central window of the west front, and she is the subject of the windows of the north transept. But it is in a window in the south ambulatory, called *Notre Dame de la Belle Verrière* (Color Plate VII), that we sense the profound adoration that her people felt for her. This window is the oldest and was probably saved from the debris of the fire. Like the Virgin on the west front, she sits enthroned, holding her child on her knees. Angels bearing censers and candles fill the panels on either side. We see a loving and supporting intercessor. The deep ruby glass seems to fall slightly behind the blue of the Virgin's robe and warms the air around her. The deep, intense-blue side panels have ruby niches that house the angels. Their smaller scale, the more intricate gowns and poses give them an animation and vitality contrasting with the stable order that they surround. Mother and child, heavenly and earthly love are permanent images.

The other windows in the basilica organize and present all facets of medieval knowledge—Old and New Testament, lives of the saints, fundamentals of Christian doctrine, labors of the months, signs of the zodiac, vices and virtues, and the activities of the guilds. Like the sculpture on the west front, and that on the north and south transepts (which we will consider finally), the same events are repeated and elaborated—humanity and God in time and at the end of time.

Moreover, in the windows at Chartres we see once again the deep relationship between cleric and layperson. The townspeople depended for their economic vitality on the cathedral, the fairs, and the pilgrims who came because of the relics of the Virgin. They held meetings on the church's steps, sold wine from the crypt, gathered to seek jobs in the nave, attended plays presented before the west front, socialized, loved, and were baptized and buried from Our Lady's chapels. To these people we owe many of the windows. The five great windows of the apse honoring the Virgin were paid for largely by the butchers and bakers. The Saint James Major window was given by the merchant tailors who appear in the bottom corners in two scenes from a tailor's shop (Color Plate VIII). In another window a banner with a red stocking tells us that the hosiers gave it, while the Charlemagne window, which relates the origins of the French monarchy, was given by the furriers.

Perhaps it seems unfair to say so little about the glass at Chartres, particularly because the architectural arrangements seem to evolve in order to permit the creation of more and more windows. But it is the most magical of the aspects of the building and the least susceptible to reproduction, either visual or verbal. The subjects of the windows are high up and not easily read; rather, what is supremely important are the rich patterns of light that fall on the floors and play over the piers and ribs, transforming the entire space into a light-filled, unearthly one meant for contemplation and celebration. In the morning light the east end is filled with the new day, the church brightens with the noonday light, and the windows at the west end glow in the low setting sun. They reflect the passage of time, the Church triumphant in this world, and beyond this world.

Transept Door Sculptures   While it is not really possible to bring the experience of Chartres to a conclusion, it is appropriate to end with the latest sculpture (c. 1250–1270), that of the transept doors. The climactic scenes are found in the central tympana of each, and their meaning is enhanced by the subsidiary scenes in the doors on either side.

On the north portal concentration is on the Virgin's life, death, and assumption into heaven. The south portal presents the Christian Church on earth, in heaven, and ending in time on the day of the Last Judgment. The central portal shows the Last Judgment in the tympanum, the Twelve Apostles along the jambs, with Christ standing on the post between the doors. The left portal is dedicated to the *martyrs* (persons killed for their beliefs) and the right one to the *confessors* (persons who gave special witness to the faith).

Formally, the figures of both the north and south portals show a steady increase in the degree of humanization, naturalism, and individuality. Compared to the much earlier figures of the west front, they grow in bulk, gain weight and volume, and fill the space. The drapery articulates the forms of the body. Faces, hands, and feet become more convincing, yet a balance is always maintained between these figures and their architectural setting. Like the great stone framework itself, these figures are individual yet integral, separate parts of a great whole.

The complex of building, sculpture, and stained glass at Chartres is, for many who have experienced it, an almost perfect harmony between reason and emotion, order and complexity, the spiritual and the worldly.

Music and Drama in the Cathedral

The combined visual arts of the great Gothic cathedrals—architecture, painting, sculpture, and stained glass—exemplify the medieval Catholic belief (quite opposed to later, puritanical ones) that spiritual truths could be apprehended through physical, sensuous beauty. This same belief seems to underlie the service of the mass and the music developed for it. Earlier, in the monasteries, one-voiced (*monophonic*) chants called Gregorian chants (after Pope Gregory the Great) were sung at masses and at the monks' spiritual exercises during the day. In the Gothic period, individual singers were used along with a choir, and a many-voiced (*polyphonic*) type of music for the mass developed. The resonance provided by the soaring vaults of the cathedral gave this music a special richness that it would not have had in another setting. The performance of the mass, with its procession of priests and choirs, the play of light through the stained glass, the burning of incense, and the reverberations of music and oratory from the stones must have been an experience to delight both senses and spirit.

Each cathedral, as mentioned earlier, had a school for instructing the young clerics who sang in the choir and performed other services in the church. The school and the rest of the cathedral were administered and cared for by the chapter, a group of clergy associated with the cathedral and subject to a rule, or canon, that ordered their way of life. One of the duties of the chapter, and the boys in its school, was to provide music for the services of the church. Medieval musicians were always part of a community, either religious or secular; and the music they wrote and performed was composed for purposes other than a purely musical one, just as the purposes of medieval sculptors, painters, and architects were never purely artistic. In this regard they were unlike modern composers and performers who sell their wares as individuals to the public on an open market, for it was the community that imposed rules and requirements both on their daily lives and on their musical activities.

The demands of the community did not seem to restrict the musicians' creativity—on the contrary, medieval people seemed to be eager for more and more elaborate forms. It is perhaps because of this kind of demand that a type of drama developed out of the mass. This form, called *liturgical drama* because it was probably a part of the worship service, represented the same religious stories from the Old and New Testaments as were represented on the windows, walls, and niches of the cathedral; it acted on the imaginations of the faithful in much the same way. *The Play of Daniel,* which we will study here, is an example of liturgical drama; it must be understood both as music and as drama. This would, of course, ideally be true of Greek drama too, but at least we are fortunate enough to have manuscripts of medieval music (preserved in monasteries and cathedral schools) that give us some idea, if not a totally accurate one, of how it was performed. Medieval liturgical drama, in some ways stranger to the modern mind than Greek tragedy, is an important phenomenon in our cultural history because it developed at a time when the theater was all but dead in the Western world and thus made possible the growth of modern drama.

The theater, as it was known in the classical world, was in effect killed by the combined influence of barbarians and Christianity. The invaders of the Roman Empire had no idea what a theater was, and by the time of the fall of Rome, drama survived only in the form of bloody spectacles or rituals associated with pagan feasts. Seeing these survivals as corruptions of the body and spirit, Christians attempted to wipe them out; actors were, in fact, excommunicated from the Church. Nevertheless, it is a tribute to the human desire to participate in or to observe shows—to mime the outside world—that some form of dramatic activity continued throughout the early Middle Ages. Wandering minstrels, jugglers, tumblers, and other performers continued to entertain willing audiences in village squares.

Ironically, after centuries of hostility, it was within the Church itself that drama was reborn as an art form. It was as if the Church at last recognized the human need for imitation and spectacle and thus incorporated it for spiritual purposes. The mass itself is dramatic in character: it is a reenactment of the sacrifice of Christ. Processions, such as those held on Palm Sunday and Easter, added to its spectacular qualities. In line with the Gothic tendency to elaborate and enrich, evident in the art of the cathedral, the mass itself became more complex and decorative. Choirs began to sing in alternation with one another, a process called *antiphony* that is already somewhat dramatic. Then, in the early tenth century, lengthened musical passages and elaborations on the text of the mass were added. These *tropes,* as they were called, are credited with the rebirth of drama. A trope used in the Easter mass, referred to as "Quem Quaeritis?" (Whom do you seek?), is, as far as we know, the first "drama" ever to be performed within a church. Here (translated from Latin) is the entire text:

ANGEL: Whom do you seek in the tomb, O Christians?
THE THREE MARYS: Jesus of Nazareth, the crucified,
                                                O celestial ones.

ANGEL: He is not here, he is risen as he predicted.
            Go and tell that he is risen from the tomb.

Probably this text was sung by antiphonal choirs and did not involve actors. It is admittedly not much of a drama, but from it an entire new tradition was born. By the twelfth century, musical drama as part of the mass reached the point at which it involved characters, choruses, and real dramatic action.

The Play of Daniel

A good surviving example of medieval liturgical drama is *The Play of Daniel,* created in the twelfth century for the cathedral of Beauvais, a flourishing city of medieval France just northwest of Paris.

According to the prologue of *The Play of Daniel,* this music was written by the young scholars of Beauvais.

Ad honorem tui, Christe,	In your honor, Christ,
Danielis ludus iste,	This play of Daniel
In Belvaco est inventus,	Was created in Beauvais;
Et invenit hunc juventus.	The youth created it.

The language is Latin (with some phrases in Old French), and this is not surprising, for the affairs of the Church were conducted in Latin as, most likely, were the classes that these young men attended. At the end of the play appears the rubric, or performance instruction:

Hic auditis, cantores	After hearing this, the singers
incipient Te Deum	intone the "O God,
Laudamus.	We praise Thee."

This is the clue informing us that this play was probably performed at matins, a religious service celebrated daily by the chapter in the early hours of the morning before dawn. Matins is normally a long service, for it contains the chanting of nine complete Psalms and their antiphons as well as the reading of nine scriptural lessons and the singing of nine Responses and the Te Deum. Obviously, the addition of a complete drama would occur only for a special holiday; and, from references in the text, including the final prophecy of Daniel (which Christians interpret as foretelling the birth of Christ), we conclude that it was written for the Christmas season, probably performed at the end of matins for Christmas morning.

The Play of Daniel has many features that made it particularly attractive to twelfth-century Christians. Coming at the time of the first Crusades, the story includes the great historical personages of the Persian empire, King Belshazzar and King Darius, a subject most in keeping with current political interest. Then the story of the miracle of Daniel's salvation from the terror of the lions' den provides an opportunity for the dramatization of a spectacular event for people who fervently believed in the miraculous. The pageantry of the processions and the rituals of the Persian court were also affairs that could be related to the regular activities of the chapter but that were elevated to a higher level by being unusual or extraordinary. Lastly, the music itself had its own fascination. Each of these elements, when understood within the context of the whole, can speak to us directly when we listen to, and witness a performance of, *The Play of Daniel*.[1]

The music of the play is divided into nine sections, and it is possible that it substituted for, or replaced parts of, the nine sections of matins. The following divisions outline the Daniel story:

1. Prologue. Introduction of characters and synopsis of the story.

2. Belshazzar commands a feast and orders his wise men to interpret the riddle "Mene, Tekel, Peres," which a mysterious hand has written on the wall.

3. The queen arrives, suggests asking Daniel, and he is called before the king.

4. Daniel prophesies doom for Belshazzar but is rewarded for having spoken the truth.

5. The procession of Darius the Great arrives, Belshazzar is slain, and the musicians celebrate the ascendancy of the new ruler.

6. Darius calls for Daniel, raises him to high office, and Daniel pledges allegiance.

7. The jealous counselors find a way to force the king to condemn Daniel.

8. Daniel is saved from the lions by an angel, and he delivers his prophecy of the coming of the Son of Man.

9. Epilogue. An angel announces the birth of Christ, and the Te Deum is sung.

What about the music of the play? After all, it is radically different from current musical sounds. If we take the version recorded by the New York Pro Musica as a fair representation of the way it might have been performed during the twelfth century,[2] we are immediately struck by the presence of instruments no longer used in modern orchestras, a singing style that is cer-

tainly not common now, music that does not use *harmony*, and a language that is no longer spoken. Where does one begin in order to understand and enjoy? Perhaps first with the *dynamics*, the volume level of the performance.

Nothing in *The Play of Daniel* is loud. Europeans of the twelfth century were accustomed to a quiet unknown to us, and their hearing was sensitive to minute aural detail. The words of a solo voice at speaking level are much easier to understand and carry the excitement of the story line more effectively and intimately than an amplified voice artificially enhanced with electronic reverberation. Besides, the cathedral walls were reverberant enough. The listeners had no ear pollution from overamplified music, jet landings and freeway traffic, or background sounds of radio and television, vacuum cleaners, or dishwashers. Awareness of subtle variations in melody, in the *timbre* (or tonal color) of instruments, and in performer *inflection* is reflected in this music composed to glorify God and the world. Medieval people did not need volume to hear; they were more interested in finesse and detail.

Even the instruments play softly. The straight trumpet (fifteenth century!) used for this performance could in no way match the gross dynamics of a twentieth-century orchestral trumpet. What does play a significant role in medieval orchestration and replaces volume as an important factor of instrumental sonority is timbre, or tone color. Medieval musicians delighted in the variety, rather than the unity, of the instrumental sounds. The rebec is a little bowed fiddle with a thin nasal sound; the vielle a larger bowed string instrument with a more open tone; the minstrel's harp a stringed instrument that is plucked rather than bowed; and the psaltery another type of plucked string instrument. There were many different sounds from the percussion: jingles, triangles, finger cymbals, cymbals, tambourine, bells, and drums of varying size and pitch; likewise with the wind instruments: portative organ, recorders, and bagpipes. These instruments were not designed to blend but to stand apart and remain distinct. Medieval people heard and enjoyed the differences, and we can, too. Perhaps nineteenth-century America was striving for musical sameness, but late-twentieth-century America seems interested in cultivating, preserving, and appreciating individuality in a way much in keeping with that of medieval musicians and their audience.

In the same way that twelfth-century listeners would distinguish individual voices and separate timbres, they could also isolate different song types. Some kinds of music were appropriate for one action or emotion; other kinds were suitable for different

---

[1] The reader is advised to listen to *A Twelfth Century Music Drama: The Play of Daniel*, recorded by the New York Pro Musica directed by Noah Greenberg (Decca DL 9402). Specific listening assignments refer to this album. The text of the play (in Latin and in English) is included in the album.

[2] The scoring and editing are a modern reconstruction, for the original source does not indicate instruments, dynamics, voices, and so on.

situations. In *The Play of Daniel* two distinct musical types are easily discerned: songs and processionals. There are others, but let us study those two as the most important in this work. Daniel's lament, on being condemned to the lions, reads:

Heu, heu, heu!	Woe, woe, woe!
Quo casu sortis venit haec damnatio mortis?	By what chance of fate do I receive this condemnation to death?
Heu, heu, heu!	Woe, woe, woe!
Scelus infandum!	Unspeakable calamity!
Cur me dabit ad lacerandum	Why will this savage multitude
Haec fera turba feris?	Give me to be torn by wild beasts?
Sic me, Rex, perdere quaeris?	Thus, O King, do you seek to kill me?
Heu!	Woe!
Qua morte mori me cogis?	To what death do you compel me?
Parce furori.	Spare your fury.

The music is *through-composed* to emphasize the emotional intensity of each portion of the text. No repeated passages appear that would use the same music for different words, and, in this case, the beginning is nonmelodic (that is, it opens on a monotone) to underline the cry of despair, "*Heu, heu, heu!*"

As you listen to the recording, note that the composer further clarifies the text of this lament by basically setting the text one syllable to one pitch. In ecstatic passages of celebration and jubilation, it was customary to sing florid groups of notes, thus giving the music a sense of freedom and release. Here the opposite is true, for the sense of fear, uncertainty, and self-doubt calls for restraint and reflection.

A contrasting type of composition is a *conductus* or processional, and an excellent example is the procession of the queen coming to King Belshazzar: "*Cum doctorum.*"

Cum doctorum et magorum omnis adsit contio	All the throng of learned and wise men is present.
Secum volvit, neque solvit, quae sit manus visio.	They ponder, but cannot explain, the appearance of the hand.
Ecce prudens, styrpe cluens, dives cum potentia;	Behold the prudent, well-born, rich in power,
In vestitu deaurato coniunx adest regia.	Gold-clad spouse of the King is here.
Haec latentem promet vatem per cujus inditium	She will reveal the unknown prophet by whose information
Rex describi suum ibi noverit exitium.	The King will learn and know of his destruction.
Laetis ergo haec virago comitetur plausibus;	Let this heroine be accompanied with joyful applause;
Cordis, orisque sonoris personetur vocibus.	With strings and voices, let loud songs resound.

First notice that the Latin text is strophic; that is, it is written in verse form. The words are both metrical and rhymed, and so is the music. The meter for the first verse is

$$/\,\cup\,/\,\cup\,/\,\cup\,/\,\cup$$
$$/\,\cup\,/\,\cup\,/\,\cup\,/$$
$$/\,\cup\,/\,\cup\,/\,\cup\,/\,\cup$$
$$/\,\cup\,/\,\cup\,/\,\cup\,/$$

This is the basic meter of all the verses, but a few poetic changes in verses 3 and 4 are regularized by the music, which was probably composed with verse 1 in mind.

In listening, notice that the melody for "*Cum doctorum*" (the first stanza) is the same as that for the following three stanzas. In other words, the form is similar to some folk songs, modern hymns, a few "pop" songs, and many country and western tunes in which several verses are sung to the same melody. Music written this way is easily remembered; and, if it has a good beat (as this does), it carries the listener along in a forward movement of insistent rhythm. It cannot express the precise meaning of the text as well as a through-composed piece, but that is not important in this case, for this *conductus* was not written to express deep feelings and heighten a monologue but to accompany a parade. In other words, the medieval composer used different compositional means to accomplish quite different artistic ends.

It should be apparent by now that the music of this play is not just one long, continuous, undifferentiated monophonic song but a logical series of discrete artistic songs, balanced and blended into a recipe that produces effective music drama. The wedding of drama with music was certainly not new—we saw it with the Greeks, although their music is lost to us. (It is, rather, drama without music that is a recent form.) Both medieval liturgical drama and Greek drama have influenced modern drama, musical theater, and opera. Medieval music may, of course, still be found within the mass. But the music of the cathedral was only one side of the medieval contribution; the court would produce its own music.

READING SELECTION

TEXT OF *The Play of Daniel*

(*Prologue*)

BELSHAZZAR'S PRINCE:
In your honor, Christ,
This Play of Daniel
Was created in Beauvais;
The youth created it.

THE COURT:
To the Almighty One who holds the stars,
The crowd of men and mob of boys
Gives praise.

For they hear how faithful Daniel
Undergoes and bears many things
With constancy.

The King calls the wise men to him
That they may explain
The handwriting.

But they could not solve it,
And they fell silent, on the spot,
Before the King.

But to Daniel, upon reading the writing,
The words, which had been a mystery to them,
Soon became clear.

Because Belshazzar saw him surpass them,
He was exalted in the assembly,
It is told.

An insufficient case, brought to trial,
Delivered him to the lions' mouths
To be torn apart.

But you, O God,
Wanted Daniel's enemies
To be good to him.

Also, that he might not hunger,
You sent a prophet on wings
To give him food.

(*The Play Proper Begins*)

THE COURT:
O King, live forever!

BELSHAZZAR:
You who obey my voice,
Bring, for my use, the vessels
Which my father carried off from the temple
When he smote Judaea mightily.

THE COURT:
Let us rejoice in our King, great and powerful!
Let us sing his worthy praise in a suitable voice!
Let the joyous crowd resound with solemn odes!
Let them play harps, clap hands, make a thousand
     noises.

His father, who destroyed the temple of the Jews,
Did great things, and this one rules by his
     example.
His father despoiled the kingdom of the Jews;
This one celebrates, appropriately, with their
     vessels.

These are royal vessels, which were plundered
From Jerusalem to enrich royal Babylon.
Let us present them to Belshazzar our King,
Who has adorned his servants with purple.

He is mighty, he is strong, he is glorious,
Virtuous, courtly, handsome, and fair.
Let us rejoice in such a King with melodious
     voice;
Let all resound his loud praises in unison;
Babylon applauds, laughing, Jerusalem weeps.
The latter is despoiled; the former, triumphant,
     worships Belshazzar.
Let us all, therefore, exult in such a mighty one,
Offering the King's vessels to His Majesty.

Behold, here they are before you.

(*A hand writes* "MENE, TEKEL, PERES" *on the wall*)

BELSHAZZAR:
   Call the Chaldean mathematicians and astrologers.
   Find the soothsayers,
   And bring the wise men in!

TWO WISE MEN:
   O King, live forever!
   Here we are.

BELSHAZZAR:
   Whoever shall read this writing
   And disclose its meaning,
   Under his power
   Babylonia shall be placed,
   And he shall wear purple
   And a golden necklace.

THE TWO WISE MEN:
   We do not know, nor can we explain,
   What the writing is, nor what the hand means.

THE QUEEN AND HER ATTENDANTS:
   All the throng of learned
      and wise men is present.
   They ponder, but cannot explain,
      the appearance of the hand.

   Behold the prudent, well-born,
      rich in power,
   Gold-clad spouse
      of the King is here.

   She will reveal the unknown prophet
      by whose information
   The King will learn and know
      of his destruction.

   Let this heroine be accompanied
      with joyful applause;
   With strings and voices,
      let loud songs resound.

THE QUEEN:
   O King, live forever!

   That you may know the writer's meaning,
   King Belshazzar, hear my advice.
   With the captive people of Judaea,
   Daniel, learned in prophetic oracles,

Was brought from his country,
A prisoner of your father's victory.
He lives here under your rule,
And reason demands that he be called.
Therefore send for him without delay,
For he will show you what the vision conceals.

BELSHAZZAR:
   Seek Daniel and bring him here
   When he has been found.

THE COURTIERS:
   O Daniel, man and prophet of God
   Come to the King.
   Come, he wishes
   To speak to you.
   He is fearful and disturbed, Daniel,
   Come to the King.
   He wants to learn from you what is a secret to us,
   He will make you rich with gifts, Daniel,
   Come to the King.
   If he can learn from you the meaning of the writing.

DANIEL:
   I wonder greatly by whose advice
   The King's command seeks me out.
   I will go, however, and he shall know from me,
   At no cost, what is hidden.

THE COURTIERS:
   This is God's true servant,
   Whom all people praise,
   The fame of whose prudence
   Is known in the King's court.
   The King sends for him by us.

DANIEL:
   Poor, and an exile, I go to the King by your request.

THE COURTIERS:
   In the glory of youth,
   Full of heavenly grace,
   He greatly excels all men
   In virtue, in living, in his habits.
   The King sends for him by us.

DANIEL:
   Poor, and an exile, I go to the King by your request.

THE COURTIERS:
   This is he whose help
   Will explain that vision,

In which the writing of a hand
Disturbed the King deeply.
The King sends for him by us.

DANIEL:
Poor, and an exile, I go to the King by your request.

(DANIEL *appears before the* KING)

O King, live forever!

BELSHAZZAR:
Are you he who is called Daniel,
Brought here with the wretched of Judaea?
They say that you have the spirit of God,
And that you know whatever is hidden.
If, therefore, you can explain the writing,
Huge rewards will be given to you.

DANIEL:
King, I do not want your rewards.
The writings will be explained for no fee.
Now this is the solution:
Your destruction is at hand.
Your father was once mighty
Above all others.
Greatly puffed up with pride,
He was cast down from his glory.
For not walking with God,
But making himself like God,
He snatched the vessels from the temple
For his own use.
But after many excesses,
He finally lost his riches,
And divested of human form,
He ate grass for fodder.
You too, his son,
Are no less impious,
For you follow after his deeds
And use his vessels.
But whatever displeases God
Has a time for retribution,
And now the handwriting
Threatens a punishment.
And God says, MENE,
Your reign is at an end.
TEKEL means scales,
Which show you to be lacking.
PERES is distribution,
Your rule is given to another.

BELSHAZZAR:
Let him who thus has solved the mystery
Be clothed in a royal garment.
Take away the vessels, prince of the army,
Lest they be a source of misery to me.

THE QUEEN AND HER ATTENDANTS:
There is recorded, in the book of Solomon,
Fitting and proper praise of woman.
Her value is that of a strong man
From far and distant lands.
Her husband's heart trusts in her;
He possesses abundant riches.
Let this woman be compared
To one whose king is worthy of support.
For the eloquence of her words
Overcomes the wisdom of the learned.
Let us who are performing this play
On this solemn day
Give to her devout praise;
Let the ends of the earth come and sing.

THE MEN OF THE COURT:
Carrying the vessels of the King
Before whom the peoples of Judaea tremble,
And giving praise to Daniel,
Let us rejoice! Fitting praises
Let us bear him!
He foretold the King's downfall
When he explained the writing;
He proved the witnesses guilty
And freed Susannah.
Let us rejoice!
Fitting praises
Let us bear him!
Babylon exiled him,
When the Jews were taken captive
Whom Belshazzar honors.
Let us rejoice!
Fitting praises
Let us bear him!
He is a holy prophet of God.
Honored by Chaldeans
And Gentiles and Jews.
Therefore, making merry before him,
Let us rejoice!
Fitting praises
Let us bear him!

(KING DARIUS *and his soldiers and courtiers now enter, having overthrown* BELSHAZZAR)

DARIUS'S SOLDIERS AND COURT:
Behold! King Darius
Comes with his princes,
The noble one with his nobles.
And his court
Resounds with joy,
And there is dancing.
He is awesome,
Venerated by all.
Empires are
His tributaries.
All honor him as King
And worship him.
The land of Babylonia
Fears him, also.
With his armed troops,
Descending like a whirlwind,
He crushes armies
And destroys the strong.
Honesty and nobility
Are his endowments.
He is the noble King,
Darius of Babylonia.
Let this throng
Rejoice in him with dancing
And praise with joy
His mighty deeds,
So wondrous.
Let us all be glad together;
Let the drums sound,
Let harpists pluck their strings;
Let the musicians' instruments
Resound his praises.

(DARIUS *is seated on the throne. All acclaim him, saying*)

O King, live forever!

TWO COUNSELORS:
Hear us, you princes of the King's court,
Who administer the laws throughout the land.
There is a certain wise man in Babylonia,
Who by the gods' grace reveals secret things.
His advice pleased the King,
For he explained the writing to Belshazzar.
So quickly, let there be no delay—
We want to make use of his counsel.
If he will come, let him be made counselor
To the King, and he shall rank third in the kingdom.

(*Three* MESSENGERS *are sent to* DANIEL)

MESSENGERS:
Our embassy comes by command of the King,
O servant of God.

Your uprightness is praised to the King;
Your amazing skill commends you.
Through you alone was explained
The apparition of a hand which was a mystery to
everyone.
The King calls you to his court,
That he may acknowledge your discretion.
You shall be, according to what Darius says,
His principal adviser.
Therefore come, for the whole court
Is being readied for your pleasure.

DANIEL:
I will go to the King.

(DANIEL *is led before* DARIUS)

COUNSELORS, MESSENGERS, COURTIERS:
With great rejoicing let us celebrate the Christmas
solemnities;
God's Wisdom has now redeemed us from death.
He who created all things is born man, in the flesh;
His birth was foretold by the words of the prophet.
The old anointing of Daniel's time had ended;
The dispensation of the Jews is over.
On this Christmas,
With joy, O Daniel,
This crowd praises you.
You freed Susannah from a capital charge;
God inspired you by his holy spirit.
You proved the witnesses guilty by their own
accusations;
You destroyed the dragon Bel in the sight of the
people.
And God guarded you from the lions' pit.
Therefore, praised be the Word of God, born of a
Virgin.

DANIEL:
O King, live forever!

DARIUS:
Because I know your prudence,
Daniel, I give you responsibility
Over the entire kingdom
And award you the highest place.

DANIEL:
King, if you trust in me,
You will do no evil by following my advice.

TWO ENVIOUS ADVISERS:
O King, live forever!
It was decreed in your court

By the rulers who are glorious
That, by the power of your name,
Every god should be rejected
For the space of thirty days,
And that you should be adored as God by all, O
   King!
If anyone should be so rash
As to disregard your command
And to prefer another god above you,
The punishment should be
That he be delivered to the lions' pit;
Let this be proclaimed throughout your realm, O
   King!

DARIUS:
   I command and ordain
   That this decree be obeyed. Hear it!

(DANIEL *worships his own God in spite of the decree*)

TWO ENVIOUS ADVISERS:
   Do you remember, Darius, the observance you
      commanded,
   That whoever is guilty of praying to any god but you
   For anything will be given to the lions?
   This law was proclaimed by your princes.

DARIUS:
   It is true that I commanded
   All people to worship me.

TWO ENVIOUS ADVISERS:
   We saw this Jew, Daniel, worshiping
   And praying to his God in defiance of your laws.

DARIUS:
   May it never be granted you
   That that holy man should be so destroyed.

TWO ENVIOUS ADVISERS:
   The law of the Medes and the Persians in the annals
      commands
   That whoever scorns the King's decree be given to
      the lions.

DARIUS:
   If he has disobeyed the law that I made,
   Let him receive the punishment that I decreed.

(DANIEL *is seized and brought to the lions' den*)

DANIEL:
   Woe, woe, woe!
   By what chance of fate do I receive this
      condemnation to death?

Woe, woe, woe!
Unspeakable calamity!
Why will this savage multitude
Give me to be torn by wild beasts?
Thus, O King, do you seek to kill me?
Woe!
To what death do you compel me?
Spare your fury.

DARIUS:
   The God whom you worship so faithfully
   Will deliver you miraculously.

(DANIEL *is thrown into the lions' den*)

DANIEL:
   I am not guilty of this crime;
   God have mercy on me, eleyson.
   To this place, O God, send a defender
   Who will restrain the power of the lions, eleyson.

(*An* ANGEL *is sent to protect* DANIEL *from the lions.
Another* ANGEL *comes to* HABAKKUK, *far away*)

ANGEL:
   Habakkuk, pious old man,
   Bring food to Daniel,
   To the pit in Babylonia;
   The King of all commands it of you.

HABAKKUK:
   God in his wisdom knows
   That I know nothing of Babylon,
   Nor of the pit
   Into which Daniel has been put.

(*The angel leads him there*)

HABAKKUK:
   Arise, brother, and take food;
   God has seen your sufferings;
   God has sent me, give thanks to him
   Who made you.

DANIEL:
   You have remembered me, Lord;
   I accept this in your name, Alleluiah!

(DARIUS *approaches the pit*)

DARIUS:
   Do you think, Daniel,
   That he whom you revere and worship
   Will save you and rescue you
   From the death to which you are sent?

DANIEL:

O King, live forever!
With his accustomed pity, God sent an angelic
   protection
To close the lions' mouths for the time being.

DARIUS:

Bring Daniel out,
And throw the envious ones in.

(*His* PRINCES *proclaim the command*)

Bring Daniel out,
And throw the envious ones in.

TWO ENVIOUS ADVISERS:

We suffer this deservedly, for we have
Sinned against a holy man of God;
We have acted unjustly
And have done evil.

DARIUS:

I command all people to worship
Daniel's God, who rules the world.

DANIEL:

Behold, the holy one shall come,
The holiest of the holy,
Whom this king, powerful and mighty,
Commands us to worship.

Temples, anointings,
This kingdom shall cease;
The end of the Kingdom of Judaea,
And of its oppression, is at hand.

(*An* ANGEL *appears to announce the fulfillment of* DANIEL'S *prophecy*)

ANGEL:

I bring you a message from on high:
Christ, the ruler of the world, is born
In Bethlehem in Judah,
As the Prophet foretold.

(*The entire company sings the* "Te Deum laudamus")

We praise thee, O God;
We acknowledge thee to be the Lord.
All the earth doth worship thee,
The Father everlasting.
To thee all Angels cry aloud;
The Heavens and all the Powers therein;
To thee Cherubim and Seraphim continually do cry:

Holy, holy, holy,
Lord God of Sabaoth;

Heaven and earth are full of the Majesty of thy glory.
The glorious company of the Apostles praise thee.
The goodly fellowship of the Prophets praise thee.
The noble army of Martyrs praise thee.
The holy Church throughout all the world doth
   acknowledge thee;
The Father of an infinite Majesty;
Thine adorable true and only Son;
Also the Holy Ghost the Comforter.
Thou are the King of Glory, O Christ.
Thou art the everlasting Son of the Father.
When thou tookest upon thee to deliver man,
Thou didst humble thyself to be born of a Virgin.
When thou hadst overcome the sharpness of death,
Thou didst open the Kingdom of Heaven to all
   believers.
Thou sittest at the right hand of God, in the glory of
   the Father.
We believe that thou shalt come to be our Judge.
We therefore pray thee help thy servants,
Whom thou hast redeemed with thy precious blood.
Make them to be numbered with thy Saints in glory
   everlasting.
O Lord, save thy people
And bless thine heritage.
Govern them, and lift them up for ever.
Day by day we magnify thee;
And we worship thy Name ever world without end.
Vouchsafe, O Lord, to keep us this day without sin.
Have mercy upon us, O Lord, have mercy upon us.
O Lord, let thy mercy be upon us,
As our trust is in thee.
O Lord, in thee have I trusted;
Let me never be confounded.

COMMENTS AND QUESTIONS

1. Read the book of Daniel in the Old Testament, asking yourself what the author has done with the biblical story. Has he Christianized any of its specifically Jewish aspects? Has he added anything to the various characters or depicted them more clearly than they are in the story?

2. In noting the differences between the story of Daniel in the Bible and the way that it is handled in the play, you may be able to see something of the same process of transformation of myth into drama that was at work in Sophocles' creation of *Oedipus Rex*. Does the hero of *The Play of Daniel* show the same internal development or character transformations Oedipus does? Are the other characters as well defined? Why or why not?

3. From a comparison of these two plays, what inferences can you make concerning the differences between the classical and the medieval aesthetic, particularly concerning the view of the place of human beings held by each culture?

4. Could *Daniel* have been written as a tragedy? What keeps it from being a tragedy?

5. In what ways do the lack of harmony and orchestration affect the function of the melody in the *Daniel* play?

6. Even though you might not recognize distinctive melodies as such in *The Play of Daniel*, do you hear sounds that are more appropriate for one kind of action or emotion than for another?

11

Divine and Human Love

The Adoration of the Virgin Mary

*T*he cathedral of Notre Dame de Chartres, built as a palace for the queen of heaven, containing a relic of her tunic, full of images of her in stone and stained glass, is, among other things, a testament to the enormous importance that the mother of Jesus had in the spiritual and daily lives of medieval men and women. And Chartres was not the only such palace. Romanesque churches were dedicated to a variety of saints, but in the Gothic period the greatest cathedrals of France—Amiens, Reims, Laon, Rouen, and Paris—were named for the Virgin *Notre Dame* (Our Lady). Why did Mary play such an important part in medieval lives, and what were the effects of this worship of her?

The devotion to Mary was part of a general humanizing trend in religion that began in the eleventh and twelfth centuries. Monastic literature of this time began to emphasize the theme of tenderness and compassion for Jesus' sufferings. In art, Jesus was portrayed as more human. Whereas Byzantine portrayals of the Christ child had tended to be allegorical, making the baby look already like the king of the world, twelfth-century artists began to portray a more childlike child and with him a mother who could express the tenderness of human, as well as divine, love. The artists who represented this divine mother took care to represent her as a lady of great beauty, combining physical attractiveness with a more ethereal quality. In the language of Mary's devotees, the praise of spiritual and physical beauty was often intermingled. Mary was seen as a queen but also as a mother—a kind and warm woman full of compassion for human sufferings and shortcomings, able and willing to intercede between individuals and God and thereby to save souls. A great many stories about miracles done by the Virgin circulated orally in the twelfth century; some were written down. The following examples illustrate the common person's view of the Virgin's compassion and power.

> A clerk at Chartres led an unchaste life, but often prayed to the Virgin. When he died, he was buried outside the churchyard because of his bad reputation. The Virgin appeared to one of his colleagues, asked him why her "chancellor" had been so badly treated, and ordered that he be reburied in the churchyard.

> A certain thief named Ebbo was devoted to the Virgin, and even hailed her when he went out to steal. He was finally arrested and hanged [a common punishment for thieves] but the Virgin supported him for two days and when the hangmen tried to tighten the rope, she put her hands around his throat and prevented them. Finally he was let go.

One of the spiritual leaders most responsible for promoting the adoration of the Virgin in theology, as well as in popular devotion, was Saint Bernard (1090–1153). Bernard, abbot of Clairvaux and a close associate of the abbot Suger, was a Cistercian monk who emphasized in his teachings the value of the inner life and self-knowledge as part of a mystical ascension to God. Divine love, the essential attribute of the Virgin, could aid the soul in its progressive ascent from the love of bodily things, to the love of spiritual things, to the selfless love of God. The Virgin, human and yet the mother of God, could aid human beings in their progress from carnal to spiritual love. Saint Bernard's spiritual devotion to Mary would be immortalized by Dante Alighieri's representation of his hymn to the Virgin near the end of the *Divine Comedy*.

Representations of the Virgin Mary

The Virgin Mary was naturally a great subject for artists of all kinds. In the sculpture and glass at Chartres she is majestic and beautiful, portrayed as the mother of Christ and, therefore, the queen of heaven. Somewhat later, in the jamb sculptures on the west portal of Notre Dame de Reims (Fig. 11-1) she is depicted as a young, shy, innocent girl when visited by the archangel Gabriel. On the adjacent jamb she is the pregnant matron who greets her cousin Elizabeth, pregnant with the child who will be John the Baptist. Both women have a weight and gravity in their bearing, conveyed by pose and drapery, that is almost classical in feeling, and highly appropriate to the roles that God has assigned them.

11-1 Annunciation *and* Visitation, *jamb statues, west portal, Cathedral of Reims, c. 1225–45. (Giraudon/Art Resource, NY)*

The association of Mary with Christian and courtly love, and thus with majesty and divinity, provided the inspiration for Simone Martini's late-Gothic *Annunciation*, painted in 1333 (Color Plate IX). Martini (1283–1344) was born in Siena, but one of his chief patrons was Robert of Anjou, king of Naples (1278–1343). Through the Neapolitan court Martini was exposed to French art. The consequences of this contact are to be found in his stunning, glittering altarpieces executed in these years. The *Annunciation* is divided into panels that seem to echo the elaborate designs and proportions of the east portals of a French Gothic cathedral with its portals, finials, and carved, embossed, and double-curved arches. In this frame Martini has placed a most retiring, but nevertheless sinuous, sensuous Mary shrinking from the splendid beauty of the archangel Gabriel who has just alighted, his drapery still fluttering in the air.

This Mary annunciate is not a simple woman like the one depicted at Reims (Fig. 11-1), but rather a demure, decorous young princess with slender hands and delicate features. This is the Mary of the Court of Heaven, where she is seated on a marble throne, reads from a beautiful book, and is separated from her visitor by a gilded vase with unfading lilies, symbolic of her virtue and purity. Martini's careful attention to the things of the experienced world—the gold embroidered border of Mary's gown, the plaid pattern of Gabriel's drapery, the minute varicolored feathers of his wings—links us to the temporal world, which courtly love is to enlighten and inform with virtue like that of Mary's.

The Literature and Music of Courtly Love

The graceful reverence for Mary apparent in both painting and music reflect the tradition that has come to be known as "courtly love." Although it represented a literary vision of love rather than a reflection of contemporary reality, this style was associated with the new princely courts that first appeared in southern France in the early twelfth century and subsequently in northern France, England, and southern Germany. By this period, the economic revival had enriched rulers enough that they were able to maintain a modest group of friends and retainers around them. Like courts everywhere and at all times, these courts were marked by the effort to make an art of leisure and by the prominence of women in this attempt. The strong desire for entertainment and novelty was fulfilled either through the nobles' creativity and ingenuity or through attracting to the court someone endowed with these gifts.

One of the chief means of entertainment and artistic expression was literature, particularly songs and stories of love. Although the medieval nobles usually knew no Latin, both men and women were literate in the vernacular—that is, the modern European languages. Although stories about heroes, or epics, had been composed from as early as the seventh century in Anglo-Saxon and then in the other European tongues, the main literary language of the early Middle Ages was still Latin. By the twelfth century, however, the vernacular was increasingly the vehicle for literature, and love became the main theme. Formed primarily from classical expressions of ideal friendship (Cicero's *On Friendship*) and of destructive passion (Ovid's *Heroides* and *Metamorphoses*), combined with biblical expressions of mystical love (Song of Songs) and of charity (1 Corinthians), this courtly literature took a variety of forms.

The court of William of Aquitaine (1071–1137) was probably the first center for this new literature. Himself a poet, this prince of the southern French principality of Aquitaine encouraged the writing of vernacular literature in his entourage, as did his more famous daughter, Eleanor of Aquitaine (1122–1204). Surely one of the greatest women of the Middle Ages, Eleanor—beautiful, passionate, and willful—became first the wife of Louis VII, king of France, and then of Henry II, king of England. Patroness of a number of poets, including Bernart de Ventadorn, son of a mercenary soldier and a serving lady, she proved a significant influence in the diffusion of love literature to northern France and to England.

The Romance

One of the new genres of literature, the *romance*, a term originally signifying a composition in a romance (from Roman) language—French, Italian, or Spanish—was fast becoming the dominant form of narrative. In romances the main characters were knights and ladies, and the concerns were chivalry and love rather than heroic combat (as in the epic). But although the characters may have suggested ideals of courtesy and nobility, neither they nor their actions should be thought of as reflecting daily life at the time. They, their deeds of chivalry, and their loves were all fictions. And although the love that dominates these romances, as well as the new vernacular lyric poetry, is easily taken at face value, it was grounded more in fiction than in fact. The knight languishing in love for years and unable to bring himself to tell his lady of his feelings was a conventional literary figure. Around the fifteenth century, it is true that men started acting as they were described in the romances, but this was a case of life imitating art.

The medieval view of human nature, grounded in the classical and Christian insistence on the need to be guided by reason, would hardly permit an audience to find admirable a swooning lover, unable to act or even to think clearly. Such a figure would represent a ridiculous distortion of humans created in the image of God and provide a vivid example of the folly of allowing passion to overcome reason. Whereas the language of what has been popularly known as courtly love (although the term is a modern invention) was at times similar to that used to express love of God or devotion to the Virgin, the application of such language to earthly love, necessarily transitory and changing, served neither to elevate the earthly nor to lower the divine. Rather, instead of making the earthly lady appear like the Virgin Mary, this effusive praise emphasized the inappropriateness of the comparison. The use of religious language to describe a lady love could only seem like a strange, distorted overstatement. The fiction of courtly love, with the lady functioning as an object of adoration and the man acting as her humble servant, parodied not only the veneration of the Virgin but also the sacrament of marriage, in which the woman promised to love, honor, and obey her husband, who was properly her lord. For man to be controlled by woman was, in the medieval view, for him to give up his responsibilities, as asserted by his religion, and to create a situation that would have been regarded as inverted and perverted, hardly one to be taken seriously.

There exist several medieval handbooks on love. One of the most popular, by Andreas Capellanus (late twelfth century), contains two parts on seduction (with instructions and models). In the third and final part, however, Andreas writes that one concerned with salvation should forsake all such loves and turn to God. That even in the twelfth century people were not about to give up readily the pleasures of the flesh was clear to medieval writers: and one of the most important books of the Middle Ages, the thirteenth-century French narrative called *The Romance of the Rose,* shows in its dream *allegory* the lover ignoring the advice of Reason and continuing to pursue his earthly love. The final consummation—on the literal level a happy ending—is especially ironic, for the lover has allowed his passion to overcome his reason and has even jeopardized his salvation.

Even when the lover and the beloved are in accord, and even when their love seems good, it will fail—as medieval writings insist over and over—if they view it as the most important thing in their lives. As medieval Christianity emphasized, human love is properly a way of loving God and is good when it uses love of created things as a way of loving the Creator. If, on the other hand, the love is so consuming that it makes the lovers oblivious of anything outside themselves, including God, then it is what in Church tradition was called cupidity, wrong loving, not at all an expression of right loving, or charity.

Although from the twelfth century well into the Renaissance love provided the dominant subject of narratives and lyrics, the literature should not be viewed as celebrating this passion or sentiment. Rather, love provided a focal point for examining human folly and self-destruction; and the lover who regarded his own good ahead of what his religion taught him to be the common good was to be laughed at for his folly rather than pitied for his frustration.

The Troubadour Song

One of the most stylized expressions of courtly love is found in the poetry and the music of the troubadours. The troubadours were poet-composers who worked and entertained in the region of southern France known as Provence, and they wrote in the regional dialect, Provençal, or *langue d'oc.* The themes of troubadour love poetry are nearly always the same: they concern a beautiful, idealized lady for whom the poet languishes with love but who does not return his love. Like the poets of ancient Greece and the modern folk singer, these artists entertained their (usually aristocratic) audience with solo voice, accompanied by a stringed instrument, the lute.

Perhaps the most famous troubadour was Bernart de Ventadorn, son of a mercenary soldier and a serving lady in the castle of the earl of Ventadorn. As an adult, he worked as a member of the court of Eleanor of Aquitaine, so his presence was known in northern France as well. Bernart's travel surely contributed to the spread of the troubadour's art throughout France.

Although the poems of the troubadours concerned themselves with many subjects—morality, courtly love, politics—the preserved songs of Bernart seem to deal only with love. The stylized notions of chivalric love are matched by the stylized poetic and musical forms employed by the troubadours. The techniques of the troubadour, having originated in southern France, spread to many parts of Europe, and the musician became known by different names—*trouvère* and *Minnesinger.*

Islamic Origins?

The origins of the troubadour song, and of courtly love in general, remain a matter of speculation, but one theory is that their roots lie in the cosmopolitan world of eleventh-century Muslim Spain. An Arab tradition of innocent and pure love expressed in poetical form reached its fullest development there, perhaps because the mixed society of Muslims, Christians, and Jews offered relatively freer social relations than the more conservative Muslim East. A handbook on love from this culture resembles the twelfth-century manual by Andreas Capellanus. The eleventh-century *Ring of the Dove* by Ibn Hazm of Cordoba (in prose interspersed with poetry) dwells on the spiritual aspects of love while censuring sexual excesses and counseling continence. The themes of the courtly poetry from this period are indeed similar to those of the later troubadour songs. Normally an idealized, beautiful, and innocent lady is loved passionately but chastely and submissively by the poet. He expresses his willingness to endure endless anguish in vain hope of her favorable response to his plea. For example, in the following verses, the poet Ibn Zaydun lyrically proclaims his unreturned love for the princess Walladah:

> When shall I unfold what I feel for you
>   O my delight and suffering?
> When shall my tongue take the place
>   Of a letter to explain my love?
> God knows what
>   Has become of me because of you:
> My bedroom has become a void
>   And my drink tastless....
> Know that if you imposed on my heart what those
>   Of other people could not bear, mine can
>   withstand:
> Disdain me, I'll bear it; postpone, I'll be patient;
>   Be haughty, I'll be humble;
> Turn back, I shall follow; speak, I shall listen;
>   Order, I shall obey![1]

Such love poems were meant to be sung, although the music is unknown because there was no tradition of notation.

Whatever the origins of the troubadour song, this genre of extemporized vocal music surely had a history in Europe long before our earliest notated examples. By the time of Bernart, the courtly love song was a highly refined art, and it has had a deep and long-lasting influence on the secular songs of Europe and America.

Chaucer (c. 1342–1400) and the Comedy of Love

The love of noble knights for noble ladies was not the only aspect of passion that interested medieval people. They were also well aware of the comic aspects of romantic entanglements. Sex, as we saw with *Lysistrata*, has universal potential for comedy. Geoffrey Chaucer, writing in England at the end of the Middle Ages, was interested in a wide range of people and topics, among them the comic aspects of love and sex.

It has been said that if we possessed nothing of medieval literature other than Chaucer's narrative poem *The Canterbury Tales* (1390–1400), we would still have represented all the major types of medieval narrative. Representing three days of tale-telling by pilgrims on their way to Canterbury Cathedral, *The Canterbury Tales* develops by presenting apparent truths that are then undercut to seem not entirely valid. Chaucer's method enables him both to give *mirthe* and to provide *doctryne* or instruction. By insisting that his audience be aware of the complexities and ramifications of actions, especially those having moral significance, he forces them to participate in the creation of meaning and to look beyond the surface appearance of things.

Each of the tales is told by a different pilgrim, reflecting its narrator's personality in its tone and content. For instance, in "The Miller's Tale," on the surface a bawdy comedy, Chaucer uses an unlikely vehicle to undercut the noble appearance of courtly love, as brought out in "The Knight's Tale," which immediately precedes it. The situation of the piece is one typically ripe for sexual hanky-panky, with the old husband, John, married to a young woman, Alison. But even though John is jealous and worried about being cuckolded, he is apparently oblivious of their lodger, the young cleric Nicholas. In a sense John's unconcern is understandable, for clerics were supposed to be contemplatives, loving God and the Virgin, and being beyond the concerns of the flesh. But when Nicholas casts his eyes heavenward, it is only to deceive. Instead of using the things of this world as means of getting to eternal verities, Nicholas ironically reverses the process, using the other world as a means of obtaining his love in this world. The incongruous blend of contemplative and worldly may be seen when Nicholas embraces Alison and at the same time speaks to her as a subservient courtly lover and also when he

---

[1]Anwar G. Chejne, *Muslim Spain: Its History and Culture* (Minneapolis: University of Minnesota Press, 1974), p. 260.

uses a fictitious vision of the Second Deluge to effect his deception of the old husband. Although Noah's Flood was a traditional symbol of cleansing and purification, it is here ironically used as a vehicle for lechery. But John, the old husband, is so foolish that he cannot be pitied, for he does not even know God's covenant with humanity after the original Deluge that God would never again flood the earth.

The illicit love of Nicholas and Alison not only is contrasted with the inadequate but licit marriage but is also the basis for the love expressed by Absolon, another cleric. When Absolon sings outside the bedroom window urging Alison to love, he employs language clearly recognizable from the Song of Songs. Chaucer's point is far from burlesquing this mystical love; rather, by including it in an obviously inappropriate situation, he calls up the ideal love lacking in the bawdy sexuality at hand and makes the amorous passion of Absolon seem as inadequate as Absolon himself is ridiculous. It is at least as inappropriate for him to refer to Alison in terms of the imagery of mystical love as it is for Nicholas at the beginning of the tale to ask her for the "mercy" traditionally associated with prayers to the Virgin.

Dante Alighieri (1265–1321)

No study of the many varieties of love in the Middle Ages would be complete without at least mentioning what is undoubtedly the greatest love poem ever written, Dante Alighieri's *Divina Commedia* (*Divine Comedy*). Although human and divine love act as the impetus and the goal of this poem, the poem also encompasses a great deal more, especially politics and theology, and it is necessary to know something of Dante's life and times in order to approach it.

Thirteenth-Century Florence and Dante's Early Life

Although he was born seventy-five years before Chaucer, Dante was, like the English poet, the product of a society in transition from rural and courtly to urban and mercantile, from medieval to Renaissance. Although he was to know the bitterness of exile from his native city, Dante was, like Chaucer, a town dweller, profoundly urban and Florentine. The Florence of his youth was just entering into its period of greatness. In the course of his lifetime, the city on the Arno River established its international reputation as the producer of the finest woolen fabrics made. The soundness of its gold coin, the florin, made it the standard of

the Western world. By 1300, Florence's population of about one hundred thousand people equaled that of Venice, making them the two largest cities in Europe.

Legally, Florence, together with much of the upper half of Italy, formed the Kingdom of Italy, which in turn was part of the Holy Roman Empire. This empire, consisting of the kingdoms of Germany, Italy, and Arles (principally what is now eastern France), had, since the tenth century, been ruled by a German prince. The German emperor's capability to exert power over Italy had always been sporadic, so that Italian cities had, for long periods of time, found themselves, for all practical purposes, independent. Naturally, the stronger cities tended to expand and to create around themselves a ring of dependent little towns and cities over which they ruled, just as Athens and Sparta had done in ancient Greece. Although the governments of these city-states were not democratic, as those in Greece had been, by the thirteenth century most could be classified as republican—that is, they were ruled by a large body of citizens, although with the lower social elements excluded. In the Florence of Dante's time, the basis for citizenship and political participation in government was membership in one of the numerous guilds in the city.

The German emperors rarely exerted much real power over their Italian kingdom, but when they took their authority seriously and came into Italy with an army, the result was usually political chaos. At those times, the bulwark of Italian independence became the Roman papacy. A secular prince over a band of territories that straddled the central portion of the peninsula, the pope had good reason to fear the emperor's presence. Both pope and emperor had rival claims to certain areas, and friction between the two was almost inevitable. From the late twelfth century, when the German emperor Frederick Barbarossa had been exceptionally active in Italy, this struggle became institutionalized in Italian politics through the development of two political parties, the Guelf party, loyal to the pope, and the Ghibellines, loyal to the emperor. Within decades, the political life of every major Italian city-state was disrupted by a struggle between the two parties. Clearly, although the papal-imperial rivalry provided a kind of ideological umbrella for the parties throughout Italy, in each city-state local issues counted more in determining party loyalty.

The party struggle dividing Florence in the thirteenth century was particularly bitter. In 1267, the leaders of the Guelf party, who had been exiled by the Ghibellines, returned triumphantly to the city, drove

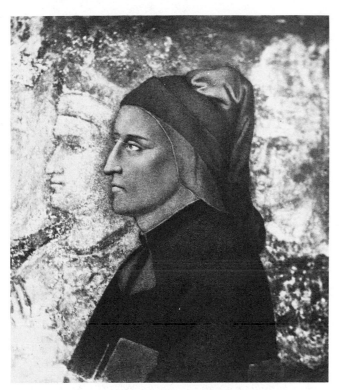

11-2 *Giotto's portrait of Dante as a young man included in the crowd in one of Giotto's frescoes. Museo Nazionale, Florence. (Alinari/Art Resource, NY)*

out their enemies, and established an enduring Guelf domination in Florence. But the Guelf victory did not bring peace, because within decades the Guelfs themselves divided into two parties called the White and Black Guelfs, and the struggle of parties resumed. Dante's involvement in this factional struggle was to change the course of his life, and his involvement in the political struggles of his time would also have a profound impact on his great work, the *Divina Commedia*.

Relatively little is known of the life of Dante. Born in 1265, he was the son of a family that, on his father's side, claimed descent from the Romans. Although the family was at the time in modest circumstances, Dante never had to seek gainful employment, and in early manhood managed to devote his time to study (Fig. 11-2). In an early work, the *Vita Nuova* (the New Life), Dante recounts the great influence on his life and on the *Commedia* of his love for a girl named Beatrice.

Dante tells us that he first met Beatrice when he was nine and she eight, and from that moment his heart was possessed by a passionate and enduring love. Nine years later he saw her again, dressed all in white,

walking in the street between two older ladies. On this occasion she turned and greeted him. Overjoyed, Dante promptly retired to the solitude of his bedroom where, thinking of Beatrice, he fell asleep and had a marvelous vision. When he woke, he composed the poem "To every captive soul, and gentle heart," his earliest known composition. To conceal his love for Beatrice, he paid attention to another lady, but this caused Beatrice to deny him her glance and plunged Dante into the deepest grief. When he saw her next at a wedding feast, perhaps her own in 1288, he could not keep from looking at her, whereupon Beatrice and the ladies about her began to whisper and make fun of him. Dante had to be led from the house by a friend.

Dante by this time was already married to a rich banking heiress to whom he had been betrothed since he was twelve. His wife, who ultimately bore him three or four children, could not have failed to notice her husband's utter desolation when in 1290 his beloved Beatrice died. Dante tells us that for a time he could do nothing, but finally, through the study of philosophy, he regained enough control to set down, in a mixture of prose and verse, the story of his love. Composed between 1292 and 1293, the *Vita Nuova* recounts Dante's moral regeneration through his pure love for Beatrice. At the end of this work, the author vows that he will write of her what has never yet been written of any woman, a resolve he was to carry out in the *Divina Commedia*.

The Sonnet and a New Vision of Love

From very early in his life, Dante had been one of a group of Florentine writers of poetry who wrote love poetry in the "vulgar" language—that is, in Tuscan Italian, Latin being still the official literary language of Italy. Influenced by the French and Provençal poets of courtly love, this *dolce stil nuovo* (sweet new style) celebrated the lofty, idealized figure of the beloved woman. Its poetry differed from the French, however, in placing heavier emphasis on the woman's redemptive role. Whereas the troubadours emphasized their ladies' social position and refinements, the Italian poets, in their less hierarchical urban society, tended to interpret "nobility" in terms of moral qualities and beauty. Perhaps the greatest contrast with the older courtly love tradition lay in the psychological sophistication of the Florentine poets, their concentration on the details of the effect of love on inner life.

The form most often used and indeed perfected by this group of poets, the *sonnet,* probably originated in Sicily, at the court of Frederick II, although some claim that its origins are Provençal. The sonnet, which we will study more extensively in Chapter 19, is practically the only fixed form of medieval poetry to continue to be used by modern poets. The many sonnets in the *Vita Nuova,* interspersed with the prose narrative of Dante's relationship with Beatrice, express a vision of love that seems to originate in the courtly praise of the beloved, and to extend beyond this to a religious awe resembling literature, praising the Virgin and preparing the religious role that Beatrice will play in the *Divine Comedy.* The following two sonnets, in the famous translation by the English poet Dante Gabriel Rossetti, illustrate this new vision of love. Rossetti has kept both the original rhyme scheme and the traditional division of the Italian sonnet—two quatrains, or the octave (eight lines), and two tercets, or the sestet (six lines).

Love and the gentle heart are one same thing,
   Even as the wise man° in his ditty saith:
   Each, of itself, would be such life in death
As rational soul bereft of reasoning.
'T is Nature makes them when she loves: a king   5
   Love is, whose palace where he sojourneth
   Is called the Heart; there draws he quiet breath
At first, with brief or longer slumbering.
Then beauty seen in virtuous womankind
   Will make the eyes desire, and through the
      heart   10
   Send the desiring of the eyes again;
Where often it abides so long enshrin'd
   That Love at length out of his sleep will start.
   And women feel the same for worthy men.

My lady carries love within her eyes;   15
   All that she looks on is made pleasanter;
   Upon her path men turn to gaze at her;
He whom she greeteth feels his heart to rise,
And droops his troubled visage, full of sighs,
   And of his evil heart is then aware: 20
   Hate loves, and pride becomes a worshipper.
O women; help to praise her in somewise.
Humbleness, and the hope that hopeth well,
   By speech of hers into the mind are brought,
   And who beholds is blessèd oftenwhiles.   25
   The look she hath when she a little smiles
Cannot be said, nor holden in the thought;
'T is such a new and gracious miracle.

---

²Guido Guinicelli, in the canzone that begins "Within the gentle heart Love shelters him."

Dante's Later Life

Because Dante, during the years immediately following his composition of the *Vita Nuova,* spent his time writing and studying, he played only a minor role in Florentine political life. Then in 1300 he was chosen to serve on the Signoria, the highest executive body of the Florentine Republic. Hardly a political partisan, Dante nevertheless felt that, in the tense situation created by rivalry between the Black and White Guelfs, the latter had the interests of the city more at heart. Dante's identification with the Whites led to his exile when in 1302 the Blacks, supported by a French prince and Pope Boniface VIII, took over the city by violence. Moving periodically from city to city in northern and central Italy, leading a life of poverty, he produced a remarkable series of works in prose and poetry.

Dante's one formal contribution to political theory, *On Monarchy,* was written between 1310 and 1313 in the period when Henry VII, the German emperor, was attempting to reassert control over the Italian kingdom in the name of peace. Dante's work reflects his thoughts on Italian politics after years of exile. Over the centuries the papacy had developed the doctrine that because the king ruled over the body and the Church over the soul, the ecclesiastical authority was not only morally superior but also had the prerogative to command the royal power. This position was closely linked to the view that the earth was a vale of tears and that the king's main task was to keep sinners from interrupting the Church as it went about the really important task of showing souls the way to the transcendent world. Essentially, royal power was negative, aimed at punishing evildoing. Given the central religious goal of the society, the Church expected Christian kings to look for guidance to the pope, who headed the great salvific enterprise.

Dante became convinced that the only way to stop factional divisions rending the fabric of Italian political and social life was to have a strong emperor, who would establish order. The arrival in Italy, in 1310, of Emperor Henry VII, who refused to recognize either the Guelf or the Ghibelline party, raised his hopes. Everywhere, however, the papacy was trying to thwart Henry's policies, justifying itself on the grounds that the emperor was disobedient to the pope. Consequently, Dante felt it necessary to attack directly the claim of the papacy for a supervisory role over the emperor. The two powers, the emperor and the pope, he declared, have authority in two separate realms, the worldly and the religious. The role of the emperor is to use his authority to help his subjects attain "terrestrial beatitude," whereas the pope seeks their "celestial beatitude." Thus there is no justification for one power to interfere with the other's work.

Clearly, what Dante has done is to reject the almost-unquestioned medieval assumption that the Church has a monopoly on moral and spiritual values. In contrast, Dante argues that life in this world, although of short duration, has its own integrity, significance, and rewards. Over this realm the secular power reigns supreme. The pope, on the other hand, rules the other sphere, that concerned with religious values, in which the goal can be reached only beyond the grave. This view of the separation of church and state was to have an impact on modern political ideas. The significance of the Roman Empire in God's design for humanity, and the importance of life on earth, are extremely important for an understanding of the *Divine Comedy.*

The Divine Comedy

Shortly before his death, Dante finished the work he called his "comedy" (the adjective "divine" was added by later admirers). This is certainly no comedy in the ordinary sense, but Dante so named it because it was written in the "vulgar" (Italian, rather than Latin) tongue and because, in contrast to tragedy, it begins in despair and ends in bliss. The work is also akin to comedy in its realistic view of human nature and in its inclusiveness of a wide variety of human types. It might best be described as a spiritual epic, for it is essentially the story of the poet's quest for salvation. In his "comedy," Dante developed in an entirely new way a motif that he knew from the sixth book of the *Aeneid* and from earlier medieval literature—a journey by a living man through the realm of the dead. As we saw in the *Epic of Gilgamesh* and in the *Odyssey,* the quest of the hero in the "other world" is central to the epic from its beginnings.

The *Divine Comedy* is composed of three books, or "canticles," each divided into thirty-three "cantos," with one introductory canto. In addition, the entire poem is composed in a verse scheme called *terza rima*—stanzas of three lines with interlocking rhymes. Multiples of three appear throughout the poem. The emphasis on the number three, symbol of the Holy Trinity, is quite intentional. Part of Dante's genius was to combine abstract forms of medieval symbolism with a new realism. In its overall design, the work is often compared to the philosophical system of Thomas Aquinas and to the great cathedrals, such as Chartres. Like them, it is an edifice that embraces and builds on almost every conceivable aspect of life, in this world and the next, with the whole pointing toward God. And yet Dante's graphic interest in individual human dilemmas and in the intricacies of Florentine politics reveals an artistic sensibility that goes beyond the medieval view.

Dante intended his readers to read his poetic journey on both a literal and an allegorical level. It is at the same time the story of Dante himself and of the people he meets during the course of his journey and the representation of Everyman's quest for salvation. The introductory canto begins with the poet's description of himself at age thirty-five on Good Friday in the year 1300, "midway in our life's journey" and "alone in a dark wood." The dark wood may symbolize the corruption in Florence that had so dismayed Dante, or his turning away from the pure love of Beatrice to baser loves, or a spiritual confusion resulting from neglect of religion. On a universal level, for the modern reader, the dark wood may signify something like a "midlife crisis" or any form of mental and spiritual confusion. In the depths of despair, Dante meets the shade of Virgil, who tells him that in order to find his way out of the dark wood he must first journey through the three parts of the Catholic afterlife—hell, purgatory, and paradise. Virgil will serve as his guide through the first two. Allegorically, Virgil represents human reason. Reason can understand the nature of sin, punishment, and purgation, but not the divine mysteries of faith. In paradise, therefore, Virgil will be replaced by the shade of Beatrice, at once Dante's long-lost love and a symbol of divine revelation.

In the first canticle, the *Inferno* (hell), Dante, guided by Virgil, witnesses the gamut of human sins and their punishments, suffering intensely himself. Dante's order of sins comes partly from classical sources, partly from other medieval texts, and is partly his own invention. Hell is shaped like a cone, with the lesser sins at the wide top and the gravest sins in the narrow bottom, where Satan resides (Fig. 11-3). The sins of passion are lighter than the sins of the intellect, and the worst sins of all are treachery to the two important powers in God's plan for earth, the Church and the Roman Empire. Thus the three heads of Satan, in the icy depths of hell, chew on the shades of Brutus and Cassius, traitors to the Roman Republic, and Judas, traitor to Christ. The law of punishment for sins in hell, as in purgatory, is defined by what Dante calls *contrapasso,* or retribution: sinners pay for their sins with a punishment of the same nature. Thus the lustful, who let themselves be carried away by stormy

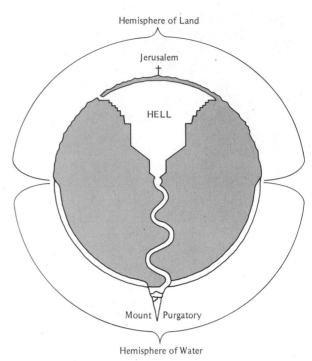

11-4 *Dante's Earth, showing Hell and Purgatory. (Reprinted with permission of David Higham Associates Limited, London, from Dante Alighieri,* The Divine Comedy, *trans. Dorothy L. Sayers, © 1949 by Dorothy L. Sayers.)*

11-3 *Cross-Section of Dante's Circular Hell. (Reprinted with permission of David Higham Associates Limited, London, from Dante Alighieri,* The Divine Comedy, *trans. Dorothy L. Sayers, © 1949 by Dorothy L. Sayers.)*

passions, are blown about by a violent wind; gluttons who "made pigs" of themselves wallow in mud; murderers are steeped in rivers of boiling blood, and so forth.

Once Dante has passed through the depths of hell, he must climb the mountain of purgatory (Fig. 11-4). Here, in the second book, *Purgatorio*, the sinners are not merely being punished; they are also purging themselves of sin for eventual entrance into paradise. On top of the mountain, in the earthly paradise, Beatrice comes to take Dante into heaven. The third book, *Paradiso*, recounts this final journey and assures Dante of his salvation (Fig. 11-5).

In the medieval worldview that Dante held, earth was believed to be at the center of the universe and the heavens a series of spheres around it from the closest sphere of the moon to the farthest empyrean sphere,

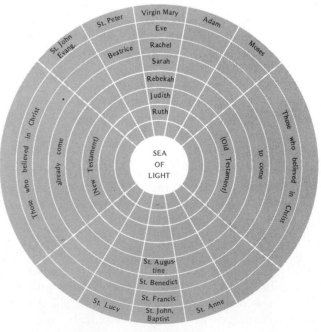

11-5 *Dante's Circular Heaven.*

the dwelling place of God. When Dante and Beatrice reach the empyrean, she prepares to leave the pilgrim to return to her place in heaven, entrusting him to Saint Bernard (Bernard of Clairvaux, devotee of Mary). Dante sings his final song of praise for Beatrice, conceding (although he praises his own poetic powers in the *Inferno*) that her heavenly beauty utterly undoes his art. Bernard promises Dante a vision of God, to be attained through the intercession of the Virgin Mary. Dante raises his eyes to the center of the mystic rose (a symbol of Mary, like the rose windows in the cathe-drals) and, while experiencing unearthly bliss, sees the queen of heaven herself enthroned. Saint Bernard then offers a prayer to the Virgin, asking her to intercede for Dante, and Dante experiences a final rapture as he gazes directly on God. God is the source of all love— "the Love that moves the Sun and the other stars" are the final words of the poem—and the Eternal Light. Light, bearing much the same significance as it did for Suger when he created his cathedral, is the dominant image in paradise. It is a tribute to Dante's genius that he was able to render the ineffable in human language.

READING SELECTIONS

FRANÇOIS VILLON (1431–AFTER 1463)

Ballade

Translation by William Frederic Giese

Written in the fifteenth century, the French poet François Villon's ballad about his mother vividly portrays the simple faith, in particular the devotion to the Virgin Mary, characteristic of the common people throughout the medieval period. In the latter part of the poem we observe how the wall paintings (probably of a Romanesque church) served to educate and to heighten religious emotion.

For His Mother to Our Lady

Queen of the skies and regent of the earth
And sovran empress of the realms of hell,
Receive me, Mary, though of little worth,
Yet heavenward bent, a child of Christian birth;
Through your grace only can I enter in—
For your great goodness, as I know full well,
Is greater than the burden of my sin.
O queen of heaven, your servitor am I,
And in this faith I mean to live and die.

Tell your blest Son I am His own, and thus,
Even as Egyptian Mary was forgiven
Or that most learnèd clerk, Theophilus,
Who once did seal a compact with the devil—
May God forbid I fall into like evil!—
So may I also be absolved and shriven;
For I hold true, howe'er unworthily,
Since I am weak, and sinful too alas,
The holy things that I have heard at Mass,
And in this faith I mean to live and die.

I am a woman poor and very old,
Who cannot read and nothing know at all,
But in the cloister, when my beads I've told,

I see God's paradise upon the wall,
All gay with harps and lutes, and, underneath,
A flaming hell where damned souls boil and seethe.
Hell frightens me, and heaven fills with joy:
O heavenly goddess, let the joy be mine,
For you to every sinner are benign
Whose faith is free of weakness and alloy—
And in this faith I mean to live and die.

Envoi

Virgin and blest princess without stain,
Thy Son was He who shall forever reign,
Jesus, who, wrought on by our feebleness,
Left His bright heaven to succor our distress
And offered on the cross His lovely youth.
Our Lord is He: this do I hold for sooth—
And in this faith I mean to live and die.

The "Ways of Love"

Translation by Edmund Reiss

The following medieval English poems, which appear here in a modern version, were found on the same page of a thirteenth-century manuscript. They illustrate well the interrelationship in medieval literature of the religious and the secular. Whatever the precise relationship between the two pieces—whether the first, urging love of God, provides a basis for understanding the earthly love of the second, or whether the complaint of earthly love is a parody of the overtly religious poem, simultaneously calling up ideal love and making clear the inadequacy of earthly passion—it is clear that the two together offer two sides of an issue, two perspectives that must be taken into account by the audience. Together, especially through their parallel language and verses, they create an ambiguous statement of love that demands solution or reconciliation.

The Way of Christ's Love

Little knows any man
The love by which he is bound,
Whose heart's blood for us ran
And who saved us with his wound.
His love for us has made us sound
And cast the devil to the ground.
    Ever and always, he has us in his thought;
    He will not lose what he so dearly bought.

He bought us with his holy blood,
What could he do more?
He is so meek and mild and good
That he never sinned therefore.
The sins we do we should rue sore,
And cry to Jesus, "Christ, thy ore!"
    Ever and always, he has us in his thought;
    He will not lose what he so dearly bought.

He saw his father full of pain
At man's most grievous fall.
With sad heart he swore again
That we should pay for all.
His sweet son he did call
And prayed him die for us all.
    Ever and always, he has us in his thought;
    He will not lose what he so dearly bought.

He brought us all out of death
And did a friend's good deed.
Sweet Jesus of Nazareth,
You give us heaven's meed.
Why do we not of him take heed?
His fresh wounds so grimly bleed.
    Ever and always, he has us in his thought;
    He will not lose what he so dearly bought.

His deep wounds bleed so fast,
We ought to care for him.
Out of hell he has us cast
And brought us out of sin.
For love of us his cheeks grow thin
His heart's blood he gave for his kin.
    Ever and always, he has us in his thought;
    He will not lose what he so dearly bought.

The Way of Woman's Love

Little knows any man
How secret love can be,
Until he desires a fair woman
Who has been loved previously.
The love of such does not last long;
She promises love but treats me with wrong.
    Ever and always sorrow weighs on me,
    I long for her whom I seldom see.

Today I would utter her name
If to say it I should dare.
She has by far the greatest fame
Of all those who are fair.
Unless she love me she will sin;
Woe is he who loves what he cannot win.
    Ever and always sorrow weighs on me,
    I long for her whom I seldom see.

Before her I fall on my knees
And cry, "Lady, thy grace!"
Lady, give my love some ease
And show me a fair face.
Unless you do, it will grieve me sore;
Love afflicts me so, I can live no more.
    Ever and always sorrow weighs on me,
    I long for her whom I seldom see.

Merry it is inside her tower
With knights and servants attending.
So it is in her bower
With mirth and pleasure unending.
Unless she love me, it will me rue;
Woe is he who loves a love untrue.
    Ever and always sorrow weighs on me,
    I long for her whom I seldom see.

Fairest creature of all such,
My good love, I salute you,
As many times and as much
As there are drops of dew,
Or stars in the sky, or grasses sweet and sour;
Whose love is untrue is seldom content an hour.
    Ever and always sorrow weighs on me,
    I long for her whom I seldom see.

Guiraut Riquier (fl. 1252–1294)

Song to the Virgin

William R. Trask

Representations of the Virgin Mary in medieval art and literature had many facets. Queen of heaven, loving mother, sister of the humble, she also appeared as a beautiful lady. The expression of mystical love for the Virgin began, in the twelfth century, to influence secular love poetry, so that poets began to write of their lady loves in terms more religious than amorous, as if they were worshiping them. In turn, love poetry had its influence on devotional poetry, so that the modern reader senses a confusion between the two realms. The following poem by the Provençal troubadour Guiraut Riquier may serve as a transition between the art of the cathedral and the art of the court.

Often in times past I thought that I was singing of love; yet I knew it not, for what I called love was my folly. But now love brings me to love such a lady that I can neither honor her nor fear her nor cherish her to the measure of her worth. But I hope that her love will hold me until the hope that I have in her is fulfilled.

For by her love I hope to increase in worth and honor and riches and joy. To nothing else, then, should I turn my thought or my desire. For, since all that I want I can have through her, I must do all that I can to serve her. For I have her love, if only I behave toward her as true love teaches me to do.

And so I must try my best: since she loves me, let me, too, love, for I could not love her if she did not give me the power. Hence it is only right that, for her love, I should give mine. For without her I am good for nothing. I can do nothing for her except to honor her. God, who has the power, grant that I may hold before my lady the banner of true lovers among whom love reigns.

I have neither wit nor knowledge to praise her; such is her honor that there is room for no more, such her virtue that nothing can increase it. How, then, can my praise honor her? The honor is mine, for I can only speak what is true. Hence I must do my best to tell the truth of her from morning to evening; for I can never fail in anything that I should do, if only I remember my lady.

So great is her beauty that it can never lessen, there is no imperfection in it, it shines night and day. So great is her power that it cannot fail. Such are her kindness and charity and wisdom and knowledge and pity and mercy that I hope her love—since she deigns to love me—will keep me joyful, if only I truly come to her.

Bernart de Ventadorn

Be m'an perdut

Translation by Carl Parrish

Bernart's chanson *Be m'an perdut* has only three musical *phrases*—that is, only three very short melodic ideas—and the first two are identical. This construction results in an *AAB* musical form, a common secular music pattern known in the Middle Ages as *barform*. Notice in the music that the end of the third phrase is repeated and that these are the same notes as the endings of the first two phrases. All this repetition creates easily remembered tunes, and, after all, we are dealing with song that is somewhat analogous to today's popular music. If the tune is not catchy, it will fail in its function of light and pleasant entertainment music.

The poet uses the same approach and care with the poetic devices of rhyme and *meter* in his composition. These qualities disappear in the translation, but their presence in the original allows an easy match of words and music as well as creating an ingenious and clever "way with words."

Be m'an perdut lai enves Ventadorn
    Tuih mei amic, pois ma domna no m'ama;
Et es be dreihz que jamais lai no torn,
    C'ades estai vas me salvatj' e grama.

The syllables in each line are grouped by units of length (short-long, short-long...), and this is matched to the metrical style of the day, the *modal* rhythm of long-short groupings.

Like many popular songs and folk songs of today that tell a story, this piece has several verses sung to the same melody. Notice in the translation that the male singer, the troubadour, sings about a rather unapproachable lady and refers to familiar images (the regions of Ventadorn and Provence as well as the lord of Beaucaire) in addition to fanciful creations of his imagination.

I am indeed lost from the region of Ventadorn
To all my friends, for my lady loves me not;
With reason I turn not back again,
For she is bitter and ill-disposed toward me.
See why she turns a dark and angry countenance
    to me:
Because I take joy and pleasure in loving her!
Nor has she aught else with which to charge me.

So, like the fish who rushes to the lure
And suspects nothing until caught upon the hook,
Once I rushed to the overpowering love
And was not aware until I was in the flame
That burns hotter than ever furnace did.
And yet I cannot free my hands from it,
So greatly does my love hold and chain me.

I marvel not that love holds me fast,
For a more entrancing form, I believe, was never
    seen;
Beautiful and white she is, and fresh and smooth,
And wholly as I wish and desire her.
I can say no ill of her, for there is none in her;
Yet gladly would I say it if I knew any,
But I know none, and so forbear to speak it.

Ever shall I wish her honor and good,
And shall be her aid, her friend and servant,
And shall love her whether it please her or not,

For one cannot gainsay one's heart without
    destroying it.
I know no lady, whether she will or nor,
Whom I could not love if I wished.
They all can bring one to grief, though.

To others, then, I am in forfeit;
Whichever will can draw me to her
On condition that what honor and benefit
She thinks to do me will not be sold too dearly,
For the seeking is grievous if sought in vain.
From experience I speak, for I have suffered,
And beauty has betrayed me badly.

To Provence I send joy and greeting
And more of good than I could speak.
And it is a wonder that I do this;
For I send that which I have not;
I have no joy save what is brought me
By my beauteous vision, and Sire Enchantment, my
    confident,
And Sire Pleasure, the Lord of Beaucaire.

Tornada
My beauteous vision, God works such wonder
    through you
That no one seeing you would not be enraptured
Who knew what to tell you and what to do.

BERNART DE VENTADORN

Be m'an perdut

es   be dreizh   que   ja - mais   lai ___   no   torn,   c'a -

des ___   e - stai   vas   me ___   sal - vatj' ___   e ___   , gra - ma.   Ve • us

per ___   quem _ fai   sem - blan ___   i - rat   e ___   morn: ___   car

en   s'a - mor ___   me   de - leih   e • m ___   so - orn! _____   Ni

de ___   ren   als   no • s   ran - cu - ra ___   ni • s _   cla - ma.

MARIE DE FRANCE

Equitan

Translation by Edmund Reiss

While the musician-poets of southern France excelled in the short lyric, those of Brittany, in northern France, specialized in longer narrative songs
called *lais*. These were probably composed orally,
and none of them has survived, but a woman of
exceptional education (for her time) and talent
made the *lai* into a written literary form. Her name
was Marie de France, and we know nothing more
about her except that she wrote in French at the
Norman court in England during the late twelfth
century. She probably derived the plots of her
twelve *lais* from those of the Breton singers. All
were written in verse, and they represent different
explorations of love and its effects on men and
women. "Equitan," which appears here in a modern prose translation, demonstrates especially vividly the destructiveness of illicit passion that was, as
mentioned earlier, a prime concern in this period.
By being so concerned with pleasure, the king in
this story is unable to rule justly. Not only does he
seek to murder his loyal seneschal, or field marshal,
he also ultimately brings about his own death as
well as that of his lady.

The tale also shows a blend of the courtly and
the ludicrous, especially at the end with the action
centering on the bath. Here what had seemed noble
and even beautiful is undercut so successfully that
the deaths of the lovers do not result in our feeling
any sense of tragedy. In fact, the fate of the two
lovers may be seen as a *parody* of the conventional
tragic ending of lovers who are ultimately ennobled
by being joined together in death.

Many noble lords have lived in Brittany. In times
past, through their prowess, courtesy, and nobility
they would compose lays of various adventures that
they had heard so that these could be held in mind and
not forgotten. They made one, which I have heard told
and which should not be neglected, about Equitan,
lord of Nantes, who was very courteous, just, and
royal.

Equitan was held in great esteem and loved much
in his country. He delighted in pleasure and love-
making, which to him constituted chivalry. Those who
love without sense or measure place their lives at
nought; such is the rule of love that no one who feels
passion can maintain his reason.

Equitan had a seneschal, a good knight, worthy
and loyal, who administered all his land and ruled it
justly, for the king was concerned only with hunting,
hawking, and love-making, and would not leave these
pursuits except to wage war.

The seneschal had married a woman from whom
great evil came to the country. The lady was exceptionally beautiful and of very good breeding. She had a
fine body and a lovely figure which Nature had taken
pains to fashion. Her eyes were clear and her face

beautiful, her mouth lovely, and her nose well shaped. There was none her equal in the entire kingdom. The king often heard her praised, and frequently he sent her his greetings as well as gifts. Even though he had never seen her, he desired her and wished that he could speak with her.

One day, to amuse himself, he secretly went hunting in the country where the seneschal lived. At night, when the king returned from his sport, he took his lodging at the castle where the lady was. There he could talk with her as much as he wished and reveal to her his heart and his desire. He found her to be very courteous and wise, beautiful of body and of face, well-mannered and cheerful. Love had taken him into His household. Love had shot an arrow at him, which made a great wound where it lodged in his heart. Love had no need for craft or subtlety. The king was so overcome by the lady that he became mournful and pensive. Now when he needed most to understand, he could not help himself. That night he neither slept nor rested, but blamed and accused himself.

"Alas!" he said. "What destiny has brought me into this country? Because of this lady whom I have seen I have an ache in my heart and all my body is trembling. I thought I would never fall in love, and if I love now I shall do evil. This is the wife of my seneschal. I should love and keep faith with him just as I wish him to do with me. If through some mishap he should learn of my passion, I know well that it would disturb him greatly. Nevertheless, it would be worse for me if I should go mad because of him. And it would be a shame if such a beautiful lady was without a lover. What would happen to her courtesy if she did not have a lover? There is no man on earth who would not benefit greatly from her love. Even if the seneschal should hear about it, he should not be too heavy-hearted. He should not have all of that treasure for himself alone; indeed, I wish to share it with him."

When he had said these things, the king sighed, then tossed and turned, and thought more. Finally he said, "Why am I so upset and so afraid? I still do not know, and have not tried to learn, whether she will have me for her lover. I will soon find out, and if she feels what I feel, I will be rid of this sorrow. God, it is so long until daylight! I still cannot sleep, and it has been so long since I went to bed last night."

The king stayed awake until dawn, which he awaited with great discomfort. He went out as though he planned to hunt, but soon he returned, saying that he felt ill. He went to his room and went to bed. The seneschal was concerned about him; he did not know what the sickness was that was causing the king to

tremble so. But his wife was the real cause of it. The seneschal had her go talk with the king in order to amuse and comfort him. The king opened his heart to her and let her know that he was dying because of her. She could either bring him comfort or give him death.

"Sir," the lady replied, "I must have some time to think. This is the first time I have been in this position. You are a king of great nobility. I am not so rich that you should approach me with love. If you do take your desire, I know truly that it will lead to nothing. You will soon leave me, and I will be ruined. If it should be that I love you and grant your request, love would not be equally divided between the two of us, for you are a powerful king, and my husband is one of your vassals. You would think to have mastery in this love, and love is not worthy if it is not among equals. A poor man who is honest, if he has sense and worth, is better than a prince or king who is not honest; the poor man will also have greater joy in love. She who loves above her station will be insecure in every way. The rich man believes that nothing can take away from him the love that he has acquired through his position."

Equitan replied, "Lady, please! Say no more to me! These words are not refined or courteous but are rather the business dealings of a merchant, who for gain or property devotes his efforts to an unworthy cause. There is no lady on earth, if she is wise, courteous, and generous of heart, provided she set a high value on her love and not be fickle, who, if she had nothing more than a rich prince of a castle under her mantel, would not suffer for him and love him loyally and well. Those who are fickle in love and who turn to deceit are in turn scorned and deceived. We have seen several of these false lovers; it is no wonder that they lose what they have earned through their efforts. My dear lady, I surrender myself to you. Do not take me as your king, but as your servant and your friend. I swear to you that I will do your pleasure. Do not cause me to die for you. You will be the lady and I the servant, you the proud lord and I the suppliant."

The king spoke to her so long and begged mercy so much that she finally assured him of her love and gave up her body to him. With their rings they pledged themselves to each other and swore their loyalty to each other. They desired each other greatly and loved each other fervently. Through their passion they died and came to their end.

For a long time their love affair lasted, for it was not known by anyone. At the time of their meetings—when they would speak together—the king told his people that he was to be bled privately. The doors of his chamber were closed, and you could not have found a man so daring as to enter unless summoned by the king. The seneschal held the court to hear the various pleas and petitions.

The king loved the lady for a long time and desired no other woman. He did not wish to marry anyone; indeed he did not wish to hear the subject spoken of. The people disliked this greatly, so much so that the wife of the seneschal often heard about it. It weighed on her heavily, and she feared losing the king. When she was able to speak with him—at a time when she should have been happy kissing, hugging, embracing, and playing with him—she wept sorely and expressed great sadness. The king asked what was wrong.

The lady answered, "Sir, I weep for our love which for me has turned to great sorrow. You will take a wife, the daughter of a king, and so you will leave me. I have heard it said often, and I know it well. And alas, what will become of me? Because of you I will die, for I know no other comfort."

The king said to her with great love, "Fair friend, do not be afraid. Indeed, I will not take a wife or leave you for another. Know this truly and believe it. If your husband were dead, I would make you my wife and queen. I swear, for no other will I leave you."

The lady thanked him and said he had made her very happy. And since he had assured her that he would not leave her for another, she would bring about the death of her husband right away. It would be easy to accomplish if the king would help her. He answered that he would do so. In fact there was nothing he would not do for her if it lay in his power, no matter whether it were wise or foolish.

"Sir," she said, "if it please you, come to hunt in the forest in the country where I live. Stay at the castle of my lord; there you will be bled and, three days later, bathed. My husband will be bled and also bathed along with you. Be sure to command him, without fail, to accompany you. And I will have the baths heated and the two tubs brought. His bath will be so boiling hot that no man on earth could sit in it without being scalded and killed. As soon as he is dead, call your men and his, and show them how he died suddenly in his bath."

The king agreed that he would do her will in everything.

Not three months passed before the king went hunting in the country. He had himself bled, on account of his illness. Along with him went his seneschal. On the third day the king said that he wished to bathe; the seneschal wished likewise.

"Bathe with me," said the king.

The seneschal said, "Gladly."

The lady had the baths heated and the two tubs brought and placed by each bed as planned. She had the boiling water poured in the seneschal's tub. That gentleman had arisen and gone out for his ease. The lady came to speak to the king who sat her down beside him. They lay on the bed of the seneschal and amused themselves playing with each other. They played together by the tub of scalding water which was in front of them. They had posted a servant girl to guard the door. The seneschal returned shortly and found his way blocked. He became so angry that he flung it open and discovered the king and his wife lying on the bed embracing each other. The king saw the seneschal as soon as he came in, and to cover up his villainy, he jumped into the tub with his feet together. There he was scalded and died. All his evil came back on them, and the seneschal remained safe and well. He had seen what happened to the king and immediately seized his wife and pushed her head first into the same bath. There both died, the king first and the lady after him.

Whoever wishes to understand the meaning of this can discover a lesson here. Those who pursue evil toward another will find all this evil returned on them. This happened as I have told you. The Bretons made a lay of it, about Equitan, how he and the lady whom he loved so much came to their end.

QUESTIONS

1. What feelings, as a reader, do you have toward the two lovers? Is the author's portrayal of them ambivalent in any way?

2. Do you find any contradiction between the story and the moral?

3. What elements of comedy or parody do you see in this story, and what do you think medieval people would have seen?

4. Could you write a modern version of this tale? How do you think the portrayal of love here might have influenced our ideas of love?

5. How did our term *romance* derive from such stories?

6. What meanings are attached to terms such as *refined* and *courteous,* and what have these values to do with the idea of courtly love?

GEOFFREY CHAUCER

The Miller's Tale

Translation by Neville Coghill

Some time ago there was a rich old codger
Who lived in Oxford and who took a lodger.
The fellow was a carpenter by trade,
His lodger a poor student who had made   105
Some studies in the arts, but all his fancy
Turned to astrology and geomancy,°
And he could deal with certain propositions
And make a forecast under some conditions
About the likelihood of drought or showers   110
For those who asked at favourable hours,
Or put a question how their luck would fall
In this or that, I can't describe them all.
   This lad was known as Nicholas the Gallant,
And making love in secret was his talent,   115
For he was very close and sly, and took
Advantage of his meek and girlish look.
He rented a small chamber in the kip°
All by himself without companionship.
He decked it charmingly with herbs and fruit   120
And he himself was sweeter than the root
Of liquorice, or any fragrant herb.
His astronomic text-books were superb,
He had an astrolabe to match his art
And calculating counters laid apart   125
On handy shelves that stood above his bed.
His press was curtained coarsely and in red;
Above there lay a gallant harp in sight
On which he played melodiously at night
With such a touch that all the chamber rang;   130
It was *The Virgin's Angelus*° he sang,
And after that he sang *King William's Note,*°
And people often blessed his merry throat.
And that was how this charming scholar spent
His time and money, which his friends had sent.   135
   This carpenter had married a young wife
Not long before, and loved her more than life.
She was a girl of eighteen years of age.
Jealous he was and kept her in the cage,
For he was old and she was wild and young;   140
He thought himself quite likely to be stung.
   He might have known, were Cato on his shelf,

107Divination.
118An inn.
131–132*The Virgin's Angelus . . . King William's Note:* Two popular
   religious songs.

A man should marry someone like himself;
A man should pick an equal for his mate.
Youth and old age are often in debate.   145
His wits were dull, he'd fallen in the snare
And had to bear his cross as others bear.
   She was a pretty creature, fair and tender,
And had a weasel's body, softly slender.
She used to wear a girdle of striped silk,   150
Her apron was a white as morning milk
To deck her loins, all gusseted and pleated.
Her smock was white; embroidery repeated
Its pattern on the collar front and back,
Inside and out; it was of silk, and black.   155
And all the ribbons on her milky mutch
Were made to match her collar, even such.
She wore a broad silk fillet rather high,
And certainly she had a lecherous eye.
And she had plucked her eyebrows into bows,   160
Slenderly arched they were, and black as sloes.
And a more truly blissful sight to see
She was than blossom on a cherry-tree,
And softer than the wool upon a wether.
And by her girdle hung a purse of leather,   165
Tasselled in silk, with metal droplets, pearled.
If you went seeking up and down the world
The wisest man you met would have to wrench
His fancy to imagine such a wench.
She had a shining colour, gaily tinted,   170
And brighter than a florin newly minted,
And when she sang it was as loud and quick
As any swallow perched above a rick.
And she would skip or play some game or other
Like any kid or calf behind its mother.   175
Her mouth was sweet as mead or honey—say
A hoard of apples lying in the hay.
Skittish she was, and jolly as a colt,
Tall as a mast and upright as a bolt
Out of a bow. Her collaret revealed   180
A brooch as big as boss upon a shield.
High shoes she wore, and laced them to the top.
She was a daisy, O a lollypop
For any nobleman to take to bed
Or some good man of yeoman stock to wed.   185
   Now, gentlemen, this Gallant Nicholas
Began to romp about and make a pass
At this young woman, happening on her one day,
Her husband being out, down Osney way.
Students are sly, and giving way to whim,   190
He made a grab and caught her by the quim
And said, "O God, I love you! Can't you see
If I don't have you it's the end of me?"
Then held her haunches hard and gave a cry

"O love-me-all-at-once or I shall die!"   195
She gave a spring, just like a skittish colt
Boxed in a frame for shoeing, and with a jolt
Managed in time to wrench her head away,
And said, "Give over, Nicholas, I say!
No, I won't kiss you! Stop it! Let me go   200
Or I shall scream! I'll let the neighbours know!
Where are your manners? Take away your paws!"
     Then Nicholas began to plead his cause
And spoke so fair in proffering what he could
That in the end she promised him she would,   205
Swearing she'd love him, with a solemn promise
To be at his disposal, by St Thomas,
When she could spy an opportunity.
"My husband is so full of jealousy,
Unless you watch your step and hold your breath   210
I know for certain it will be my death,"
She said, "So keep it well under your hat."
"Oh, never mind about a thing like that,"
Said he; "A scholar doesn't have to stir
His wits so much to trick a carpenter."   215
     And so they both agreed to it, and swore
To watch their chance, as I have said before,
When things were settled thus as they thought fit,
And Nicholas had stroked her loins a bit
And kissed her sweetly, he took down his harp   220
And played away, a merry tune and sharp.
     It happened later she went off to church,
This worthy wife, one holiday, to search
Her conscience and to do the works of Christ.
She put her work aside and she enticed   225
The colour to her face to make her mark;
Her forehead shone. There was a parish clerk
Serving the church, whose name was Absalon.
His hair was all in golden curls and shone;
Just like a fan it strutted outwards, starting   230
To left and right from an accomplished parting.
Ruddy his face, his eyes as grey as goose,
His shoes cut out in tracery, as in use
In old St Paul's. The hose upon his feet
Showed scarlet through, and all his clothes were
     neat   235
And proper. In a jacket of light blue,
Flounced at the waist and tagged with laces too,
He went, and wore a surplice just as gay
And white as any blossom on the spray.
God bless my soul, he was a merry knave!   240
He knew how to let blood, cut hair and shave,
And draw up legal deeds; at other whiles
He used to dance in twenty different styles
(After the current school at Oxford though,
Casting his legs about him to and fro).   245
He played a two-stringed fiddle, did it proud,
And sang a high falsetto rather loud;

And he was just as good on the guitar.
There was no public-house in town or bar
He didn't visit with his merry face   250
If there were saucy barmaids round the place.
He was a little squeamish in the matter
Of farting, and satirical in chatter.
This Absalon, so jolly in his ways,
Would bear the censer round on holy days   255
And cense the parish women. He would cast
Many a love-lorn look before he passed,
Especially at this carpenter's young wife;
Looking at her would make a happy life
He thought, so neat, so sweet, so lecherous.   260
And I dare say if she had been a mouse
And he a cat, she'd have been pounced upon.
     In taking the collection Absalon
Would find his heart was set in such a whirl
Of love, he would take nothing from a girl,   265
For courtesy, he said, it wasn't right.
     That evening, when the moon was shining
          bright
He ups with his guitar and off he tours
On the look-out for any paramours.
Larky and amorous, away he strode   270
Until he reached the carpenter's abode
A little after cock-crow, took his stand
Beside the casement window close at hand
(It was set low upon the cottage-face)
And started singing softly and with grace,   275
     "*Now dearest lady, if there pleasure be
     In thoughts of love, think tenderly of me!*"
On his guitar he plucked a tuneful string.
     This carpenter awoke and heard him sing
And turning to his wife said, "Alison!   280
Wife! Do you hear him? There goes Absalon
Chanting away under our chamber wall."
And she replied, "Yes, John, I hear it all."
If she thought more of it she didn't tell.
     So things went on. What's better than "All's
          well"?   285
From day to day this jolly Absalon,
Wooing away, became quite woe-begone;
He lay awake all night, and all the day
Combed his thick locks and tried to pass for gay,
Wooed her by go-between and wooed by proxy,   290
Swore to be page and servant to his doxy,
Trilled and rouladed° like a nightingale,
Sent her sweet wine and mead and spicy ale,
And wafers piping hot and jars of honey,

292Sang.

And, as she lived in town, he offered money.°   295
For there are some a money-bag provokes
And some are won by kindness, some by strokes.

Once, in the hope his talent might engage,
He played the part of Herod on the stage.
What was the good? Were he as bold as brass,   300
She was in love with gallant Nicholas;
However Absalon might blow his horn
His labour won him nothing but her scorn.
She looked upon him as her private ape
And held his earnest wooing all a jape.   305
There is a proverb—and it is no lie—
You'll often hear repeated: "*Nigh-and-Sly
Wins against Fair-and-Square who isn't there.*"
For much as Absalon might tear his hair
And rage at being seldom in her sight,   310
Nicholas, nigh and sly, stood in his light.
Now, show your paces, Nicholas you spark!
And leave lamenting to the parish clerk.

And so it happened that one Saturday,
When the old carpenter was safe away   315
At Osney, Nicholas and Alison
Agreed at last in what was to be done.
Nicholas was to exercise his wits
On her suspicious husband's foolish fits,
And, if so be the trick worked out all right,   320
She then would sleep with Nicholas all night,
For such was his desire and hers as well;
And even quicker than it takes to tell,
Young Nicholas, who simply couldn't wait,
Went to his room on tip-toe with a plate   325
Of food and drink, enough to last a day
Or two, and Alison was told to say,
In case her husband asked for Nicholas,
That she had no idea where he was,
And that she hadn't set eyes on him all day   330
And thought he must be ill, she couldn't say;
And more than once the maid had given a call
And shouted but no answer came at all.

So things went on the whole of Saturday
Without a sound from Nicholas, who lay   335
Upstairs, and ate or slept as pleased him best
Till Sunday when the sun went down to rest.

This foolish carpenter was lost in wonder
At Nicholas; what could have got him under?
He said, "I can't help thinking, by the Mass,   340
Things can't be going right with Nicholas.
What if he took and died? God guard his ways!
A ticklish place the world is, nowadays.
I saw a corpse this morning borne to kirk

That only Monday last I saw at work.   345
Run up," he told the serving-lad, "be quick,
Shout at his door, or knock it with a brick.
Take a good look and tell me how he fares."

The serving-boy went sturdily upstairs.
Stopped at the door and, standing there, the lad 350
Shouted away and, hammering like mad,
Cried, "Ho! What's up? Hi! Master Nicholay!
How can you lie up there asleep all day?"

But all for nought, he didn't hear a soul.
He found a broken panel with a hole   355
Right at the bottom, useful to the cat
For creeping in; he took a look through that,
And so at last by peering through the crack
He saw this scholar gaping on his back
As if he'd caught a glimpse of the new moon.   360
Down went the boy and told his master soon
About the state in which he found the man.

On hearing this the carpenter began
To cross himself and said, "St Frideswide bless
    us!
We little know what's coming to distress us.   365
The man has fallen, with this here astromy,
Into a fit, or lunacy maybe.
I always thought that was how it would go.
God has some secrets that we shouldn't know.
How blessed are the simple, aye, indeed,   370
That only know enough to say their creed!
Happened just so with such another student
Of astromy and he was so imprudent
As to stare upwards while he crossed a field,
Busy foreseeing what the stars revealed;   375
And what should happen but he fell down flat
Into a marl-pit. He didn't foresee that!
But by the Saints we've reached a sorry pass;
I can't help worrying for Nicholas.
He shall be scolded for his studying   380
If I know how to scold, by Christ the King!
Get me a staff to prise against the floor.
Robin, you put your shoulder to the door.
We'll shake the study out of him, I guess!"

The pair of them began to heave and press   385
Against the door. Happened the lad was strong
And so it didn't take them very long
To heave it off its hinges; down it came.
Still as a stone lay Nicholas, with the same
Expression, gaping upwards into air.   390
The carpenter supposed it was despair
And shook him by the shoulders with a stout
And purposeful attack, and gave a shout:
"What, Nicholas! Hey! Look down! Is that a
    fashion
To act? Wake up and think upon Christ's passion. 395
I sign you with the cross from elves and sprites!"

_____
²⁹⁵As one would to a whore.

And he began the spell for use at nights
In all four corners of the room and out
Across the threshold too and round about:
   Jesu Christ and Benedict Sainted   400
   Bless this house from creature tainted,
   Drive away night-hags, white Pater-noster,
   Where did you go St Peter's soster?°
   And in the end the dandy Nicholas
Began to sigh, "And must it come to pass?"   405
He said, "Must all the world be cast away?"
The carpenter replied, "What's that you say?
Put trust in God as we do, working men."
Nicholas answered, "Fetch some liquor then,
And afterwards, in strictest secrecy,   410
I'll speak of something touching you and me,
But not another soul must know, that's plain."
   This carpenter went down and came again
Bringing some powerful ale—a largeish quart.
When each had had his share of this support   415
Young Nicholas got up and shut the door
And, sitting down beside him on the floor,
Said to the carpenter, "Now, John, my dear,
My excellent host, swear on your honour here
Not to repeat a syllable I say,   420
For here are Christ's intentions, to betray
Which to a soul puts you among the lost,
And vengeance for it at a bitter cost
Shall fall upon you. You'll be driven mad!"
"Christ and His holy blood forbid it, lad!"   425
The silly fellow answered. "I'm no blab,
Though I should say it, I'm not given to gab.
Say what you like, for I shall never tell
Man, woman or child by Him° that harrowed
   Hell!"
   "Now, John," said Nicholas, "believe you me,   430
I have found out by my astrology,
And looking at the moon when it was bright,
That Monday next, a quarter way through night,
Rain is to fall in torrents, such a scud
It will be twice as bad as Noah's Flood.   435
This world," he said, "in just about an hour,
Shall all be drowned, it's such a hideous shower,
And all mankind, with total loss of life."
   The carpenter exclaimed, "Alas, my wife!
My little Alison! Is she to drown?"   440
And in his grief he very near fell down.
"Is there no remedy," he said, "for this?"
"Thanks be to God," said Nicholas, "there is,
If you will do exactly what I say

And don't start thinking up some other way.   445
In wise old Solomon you'll find the verse
'Who takes advice shall never fare the worse,'
And so if good advice is to prevail
I undertake with neither mast nor sail
To save her yet, and save myself and you.   450
Haven't you heard how Noah was saved too
When God forewarned him and his sons and
   daughters
That all the world should sink beneath the
   waters?"
"Yes," said the carpenter, "a long time back."
"Haven't you heard," said Nicholas, "what a
   black   455
Business it was, when Noah tried to whip
His wife (who wouldn't come) on board the ship?
He'd have been better pleased, I'll undertake,
With all that weather just about to break,
If she had had a vessel of her own.   460
Now, what are we to do? We can't postpone
The thing; it's coming soon, as I was saying,
It calls for haste, not preaching or delaying.
   "I want you, now, at once, to hurry off
And fetch a shallow tub or kneading-trough   465
For each of us, but see that they are large
And such as we can float in, like a barge.
And have them loaded with sufficient victual
To last a day—we only need a little.
The waters will abate and flow away   470
Round nine o'clock upon the following day.
Robin the lad mayn't know of this, poor knave,
Nor Jill the maid, those two I cannot save.
Don't ask me why; and even if you do
I can't disclose God's secret thoughts to you.   475
You should be satisfied, unless you're mad,
To find as great a grace as Noah had.
And I shall save your wife, you needn't doubt it,
Now off you go, and hurry up about it.
   "And when the tubs have been collected, three,   480
That's one for her and for yourself and me,
Then hang them in the roof below the thatching
That no one may discover what we're hatching.
When you have finished doing what I said
And stowed the victuals in them overhead,   485
Also an axe to hack the ropes apart,
So, when the water rises, we can start,
And, lastly, when you've broken out the gable,
The garden one that's just above the stable,
So that we may cast free without delay   490
After the mighty shower has gone away,
You'll float as merrily, I undertake,
As any lily-white duck behind her drake.

---

⁴⁰³*soster:* A medieval chant used to drive away evil spirits.
⁴²⁹Christ.

And I'll call out, 'Hey, Alison! Hey, John!
Cheer yourselves up! The flood will soon be
    gone.'   495
And you'll shout back, 'Hail, Master Nicholay!
Good morning! I can see you well. It's day!'
We shall be lords for all the rest of life
Of all the world, like Noah and his wife.

    "One thing I warn you of; it's only right.   500
We must be very careful on the night,
Once we have safely managed to embark,
To hold our tongues, to utter no remark,
No cry or call, for we must fall to prayer.
This is the Lord's dear will, so have a care.   505

    "Your wife and you must hang some way apart,
For there must be no sin before we start,
No more in longing looks than in the deed.
Those are your orders. Off with you! God speed!
To-morrow night when everyone's asleep   510
We'll all go quietly upstairs and creep
Into our tubs, awaiting Heaven's grace.
And now be off. No time to put the case
At greater length, no time to sermonize;
The proverb says, 'Say nothing, send the wise.'   515
You're wise enough, I do not have to teach you.
Go, save our lives for us, as I beseech you."

    This silly carpenter then went his way
Muttering to himself, "Alas the day!"
And told his wife in strictest secrecy.   520
She was aware, far more indeed than he,
What this quaint stratagem might have in sight,
But she pretended to be dead with fright.
"Alas!" she said. "Whatever it may cost,
Hurry and help, or we shall all be lost.   525
I am your honest, true and wedded wife,
Go, dearest husband, help to save my life!"

    How fancy throws us into perturbation!
People can die of mere imagination,
So deep is the impression one can take.   530
This silly carpenter began to quake,
Before his eyes there verily seemed to be
The floods of Noah, wallowing like the sea
And drowning Alison his honey-pet.
He wept and wailed, his features were all set   535
In grief, he sighed with many a doleful grunt.
He went and got a tub, began to hunt
For kneading-troughs, found two, and had them
    sent
Home to his house in secret; then he went
And, unbeknowns, he hung them from a rafter.   540
With his own hands he made three ladders after,
Uprights and rungs, to help them in their scheme
Of climbing where they hung upon the beam.

He victualled tub and trough, and made all snug
With bread and cheese, and ale in a large jug,   545
Enough for three of them to last the day,
And, just before completing this array,
Packed off the maid and his apprentice too
To London on a job they had to do.
And on the Monday when it drew to night   550
He shut his door and dowsed the candle-light
And made quite sure all was as it should be
And shortly, up they clambered, all the three,
Silent and separate. They began to pray
And *"Pater Noster*° mum," said Nicholay,   555
And "mum" said John, and "mum" said Alison
The carpenter's devotions being done,
He sat quite still, then fell to prayer again
And waited anxiously to hear the rain.

    The carpenter, with all the work he'd seen,   560
Fell dead asleep—round curfew, must have been,
Maybe a little later on the whole.
He groaned in sleep for travail of his soul
And snored because his head was turned awry.

    Down by their ladders, stalking from on high   565
Came Nicholas and Alison, and sped
Softly downstairs, without a word, to bed,
And where this carpenter was wont to be
The revels started and the melody.
And thus lay Nicholas and Alison   570
At busy play in eager quest of fun,
Until the bell for lauds had started ringing
And in the chancel Friars began their singing.

    This parish clerk, this amorous Absalon,
Love-stricken still and very woe-begone,   575
Upon the Monday was in company
At Osney with his friends for jollity,
And chanced to ask a resident cloisterer
What had become of John the carpenter.
The fellow drew him out of church to say,   580
"Don't know; not been at work since Saturday.
I can't say where he is; I think he went
To fetch the Abbot timber. He is sent
Often enough for timber, has to go
Out to the Grange° and ston° a day or so;   585
If not he's certainly at home to-day,
But where he is I can't exactly say."

    Absalon was a jolly lad and light
Of heart; he thought, "I'll stay awake to-night;
I'm certain that I haven't seen him stirring   590
About his door since dawn; it's safe inferring

----

555 Our Father.
585 Farm.
585 Stay.

That he's away. As I'm alive I'll go
And tap his window softly at the crow
Of cock—the sill is low-set on the wall.
I shall see Alison and tell her all   595
My love-longing, and I can hardly miss
Some favour from her, at the least a kiss.
I'll get some satisfaction anyway;
There's been an itching in my mouth all day
And that's a sign of kissing at the least.   600
And all last night I dreamt about a feast.
I think I'll go and sleep an hour or two,
Then wake and have some fun, that's what I'll
      do."
    The first cock crew at last, and thereupon
Up rose this jolly lover Absalon   605
In gayest clothes, garnished with that and this;
But first he chewed a grain of liquorice
To charm his breath before he combed his hair.
Under his tongue the comfit nestling there
Would make him gracious. He began to roam   610
To where old John and Alison kept home
And by the casement window took his stand.
Breast-high it stood, no higher than his hand.
He gave a cough, no more than half a sound:
"Alison, honey-comb, are you around?   615
Sweet cinnamon, my little pretty bird,
Sweetheart, wake up and say a little word!
You seldom think of me in all my woe,
I sweat for love of you wherever I go!
No wonder if I do, I pine and bleat   620
As any lambkin hungering for the teat,
Believe me, darling, I'm so deep in love
I croon with longing like a turtle-dove,
I eat as little as a girl at school."
"You go away," she answered, "you Tom-fool!   625
There's no come-up-and-kiss-me here for you.
I love another and why shouldn't I too?
Better than you, by Jesu, Absalon!
Take yourself off or I shall throw a stone.
I want to get some sleep. You go to Hell!"   630
"Alas!" said Absalon. "I knew it well;
True love is always mocked and girded at;
So kiss me, if you can't do more than that,
For Jesu's love and for the love of me!"
"And if I do, will you be off?" said she.   635
"Promise you, darling," answered Absalon.
"Get ready then; wait, I'll put something on,"
She said and then she added under breath
To Nicholas, "Hush . . . we shall laugh to death!"
    This Absalon went down upon his knees;   640
"I am a lord!" he thought, "And by degrees
There may be more to come; the plot may
      thicken."

"Mercy, my love!" he said, "Your mouth, my
      chicken!"
    She flung the window open then in haste
And said, "Have done, come on, no time to
      waste,   645
The neighbours here are always on the spy."
    Absalon starting wiping his mouth dry.
Dark was the night as pitch, as black as coal,
And at the window out she put her hole,
And Absalon, so fortune framed the farce,   650
Put up his mouth and kissed her naked arse
Most savorously before he knew of this.
    And back he started. Something was amiss;
He knew quite well a woman has no beard,
Yet something rough and hairy had appeared.   655
"What have I done?" he said. "Can that be you?"
"Teehee!" she cried and clapped the window to.
Off went poor Absalon sadly through the dark.
"A beard! a beard!" cried Nicholas the Spark.
"God's body, that was something like a joke!"   660
And Absalon, overhearing what he spoke,
Bit on his lips and nearly threw a fit
In rage and thought, "I'll pay you back for it!"
    Who's busy rubbing, scraping at his lips
With dust, with sand, with straw, with cloth,
      with chips,   665
But Absalon? He thought, "I'll bring him down!
I wouldn't let this go for all the town.
I'd take my soul and sell it to the Devil
To be revenged upon him! I'll get level.
O God, why did I let myself be fooled?"   670
    The fiery heat of love by now had cooled,
For from the time he kissed her hinder parts
He didn't give a tinker's° curse for tarts;°
His malady was cured by this endeavour
And he defied all paramours whatever.   657
    So, weeping like a child that has been whipped,
He turned away; across the road he slipped
And called on Gervase. Gervase was a smith;
His forge was full of things for ploughing with
And he was busy sharpening a share.   680
    Absalon knocked, and with an easy air
Called, "Gervase! Open up the door, come on!"
"What's that? Who's there?" "It's me, it's
      Absalon."
"What, Absalon? By Jesu's blessed tree
You're early up! Hey, *benedicite,*°   685
What's wrong? Some jolly girl as like as not

---

673 Gypsy's.
673 Whores.
685 A blessing.

Has coaxed you out and set you on the trot.
Blessed St Neot! You know the thing I mean."
    But Absalon, who didn't give a bean
For all his joking, offered no debate.   690
He had a good deal more upon his plate
Than Gervase knew and said, "Would it be fair
To borrow that coulter° in the chimney there,
The hot one, see it? I've a job to do;
It won't take long, I'll bring it back to you."   695
Gervase replied, "Why, if you asked for gold,
A bag of sovereigns or for wealth untold,
It should be yours, as I'm an honest smith.
But, Christ, why borrow that to do it with?"
"Let that," said Absalon, "be as it may;   700
You'll hear about it all some other day."
    He caught the coulter up—the haft was cool—
And left the smithy softly with the tool,
Crept to the little window in the wall
And coughed. He knocked and gave a little call   705
Under the window as he had before.
    Alison said, "There's someone at the door.
Who's knocking there? I'll warrant it's a thief."
"Why, no," said he, "my little flower-leaf,
It's your own Absalon, my sweety-thing!   710
Look what I've brought you—it's a golden ring
My mother gave me, as I may be saved.
It's very fine, and prettily engraved;
I'll give it to you, darling, for a kiss."
    Now Nicholas had risen for a piss,   715
And thought he could improve upon the jape
And make him kiss his arse ere he escape,
And opening the window with a jerk,
Stuck out his arse, a handsome piece of work,
Buttocks and all, as far as to the haunch.   720
    Said Absalon, all set to make a launch,
"Speak, pretty bird, I know not where thou art!"
This Nicholas at once let fly a fart
As loud as if it were a thunder-clap.
He was near blinded by the blast, poor chap,   725
But his hot iron was ready; with a thump
He smote him in the middle of the rump.
    Off went the skin a hand's-breadth round about
Where the hot coulter struck and burnt it out.
Such was the pain, he thought he must be dying   730
And, mad with agony, he started crying,
"Help! Water! Water! Help! For Heaven's love!"
    The carpenter, startled from sleep above,
And hearing shouts for water and a thud,

Thought, "Heaven help us! Here comes Nowel's°
    Flood!"   735
And up he sat and with no more ado
He took his axe and smote the ropes in two
And down went everything. He didn't stop
To sell his bread and ale, but came down flop
Upon the floor and fainted right away.   740
    Up started Alison and Nicholay
And shouted, "Help!" and "Murder!" in the
    street.
The neighbours all came running up in heat
And stook there staring at the wretched man.
He lay there fainting, pale beneath his tan;   745
His arm in falling had been broken double.
But still he was obliged to face his trouble,
For when he spoke he was at once borne down
By Nicholas and his wife. They told the town
That he was mad, there'd got into his blood   750
Some sort of nonsense about "Nowel's Flood,"
That vain imaginings and fantasy
Had made him buy the kneading-tubs, that he
Had hung them in the rafters up above
And that he'd begged them both for heaven's love   755
To sit up in the roof for company.
    All started laughing at this lunacy
And streamed upstairs to gape and pry and poke,
And treated all his sufferings as a joke.
No matter what the carpenter asserted   760
It went for nothing, no one was converted;
With powerful oaths they swore the fellow down
And he was held for mad by all the town;
Even the learned said to one another,
"The fellow must be crazy, my dear brother."   765
So to a general laughter he succumbed.
    That's how the carpenter's young wife was
    plumbed
For all the tricks his jealousy could try,
And Absalon has kissed her nether eye
And Nicholas is branded on the bum.   770
And God bring all of us to Kingdom Come.

QUESTIONS

1. How do you react to "The Miller's Tale"? Does it
   have appeal for modern readers?

2. How deeply do you become involved with each of
   the characters? Is it necessary to remain detached
   from them? Why or why not?

---

693 Plow blade.

735 Noah's.

3. Are these characters more or less realistic than those in earlier medieval literature, such as *The Play of Daniel*?

4. Compare the comedy of sex in this tale with that in *Lysistrata*. What differences are attributable to the differences in culture?

5. What impact does Chaucer's Christianity have on his comedy?

6. Compare the expressions of love in this tale with those in "Equitan." What justification can you find for the interpretation that this tale represents a parody of "courtly" love?

DANTE ALIGHIERI

FROM THE *Divine Comedy*

Translation by John Ciardi

Because the *Inferno* is the book most accessible to modern readers, we have chosen most of our selections from it. From the *Purgatorio* we have chosen Canto XXX, in which Dante is at last reunited with the long-lost Beatrice. The *Paradiso* is represented by the last canto, XXXIII, in which Saint Bernard leads Dante to a vision of the Virgin Mary, and at last to a vision of God. In addition to the translation, the introductions and notes are by the American poet John Ciardi. The note references refer to line numbers.

FROM THE *Inferno*

Canto I

The Dark Wood of Error

Midway in his allotted threescore years and ten, DANTE *comes to himself with a start and realizes that he has strayed from the True Way into the Dark Wood of Error (Worldliness). As soon as he has realized his loss, Dante lifts his eyes and sees the first light of the sunrise (the Sun is the Symbol of Divine Illumination) lighting the shoulders of a little hill (The Mount of Joy). It is the Easter Season, the time of resurrection, and the sun is in its equinoctial rebirth. This juxtaposition of joyous symbols fills Dante with hope and he sets out at once to climb directly up the Mount of Joy, but almost immediately his way is blocked by the Three Beasts of Worldliness: the* LEOPARD OF MALICE AND FRAUD, *the* LION OF VIOLENCE AND AMBITION, *and the* SHE-WOLF OF INCONTINENCE. *These beasts, and especially the She-Wolf, drive him back despairing into the darkness of error. But just as all*

seems lost, a figure appears to him. It is the shade of VIRGIL, *Dante's symbol of Human Reason.*

*Virgil explains that he has been sent to lead Dante from error. There can, however, be no direct ascent past the beasts: the man who would escape them must go a longer and harder way. First he must descend through Hell (The Recognition of Sin), then he must ascend through Purgatory (The Renunciation of Sin), and only then may he reach the pinnacle of joy and come to the Light of God. Virgil offers to guide Dante, but only as far as Human Reason can go. Another guide (*BEATRICE, *symbol of Divine Love) must take over for the final ascent, for Human Reason is self-limited. Dante submits himself joyously to Virgil's guidance and they move off.*

Midway in our life's journey, I went astray
   from the straight road and woke to find myself
   alone in a dark wood. How shall I say

what wood that was! I never saw so drear,
   so rank, so arduous a wilderness!
   Its very memory gives a shape to fear.   6

Death could scarce be more bitter than that place!
   But since it came to good, I will recount
   all that I found revealed there by God's grace.   9

How I came to it I cannot rightly say,
   so drugged and loose with sleep had I become
   when I first wandered there from the True Way.   12

But at the far end of that valley of evil
   whose maze had sapped my very heart with fear
   I found myself before a little hill   15

and lifted up my eyes. Its shoulders glowed
   already with the sweet rays of that planet
   whose virtue leads men straight on every road,   18

and the shining strengthened me against the fright
   whose agony had wracked the lake of my heart
   through all the terrors of that piteous night.   21

Just as a swimmer, who with his last breath
   flounders ashore from perilous seas, might turn
   to memorize the wide water of his death—   24

---

[1] *Midway in our life's journey:* The Biblical life span is three-score years and ten. The action opens in Dante's thirty-fifth year, i.e., 1300 A.D.

[17] *that planet:* The sun. Ptolemaic astronomers considered it a planet. It is also symbolic of God as He who lights man's way.

so did I turn, my soul still fugitive
    from death's surviving image, to stare down
    that pass that none had ever left alive.   27

And there I lay to rest from my heart's race
    till calm and breath returned to me. Then rose
    and pushed up that dead slope at such a pace   30

each footfall rose above the last. And lo!
    almost at the beginning of the rise
    I faced a spotted Leopard, all tremor and flow   33

and gaudy pelt. And it would not pass, but stood
    so blocking my every turn that time and again
    I was on the verge of turning back to the wood.   36

This fell at the first widening of the dawn
    as the sun was climbing Aries with those stars
    that rode with him to light the new creation.   39

Thus the holy hour and the sweet season
    of commemoration did much to arm my fear
    of that bright murderous beast with their good
        omen.   42

---

31 *each footfall rose above the last:* The literal rendering would be: "So that the fixed foot was ever the lower." "Fixed" has often been translated "right" and an ingenious reasoning can support that reading, but a simpler explanation offers itself and seems more competent: Dante is saying that he climbed with such zeal and haste that every footfall carried him above the last despite the steepness of the climb. At a slow pace, on the other hand, the rear foot might be brought up only as far as the forward foot. This device of selecting a minute but exactly-centered detail to convey the whole of a larger action is one of the central characteristics of Dante's style.

33–48 THE THREE BEASTS: These three beasts undoubtedly are taken from *Jeremiah* v, 6. Many additional and incidental interpretations have been advanced for them, but the central interpretation must remain as noted. They foreshadow the three divisions of Hell (incontinence, violence, and fraud) which Virgil explains at great length in Canto XI, 16–111. I am not at all sure but what the She-Wolf is better interpreted as Fraud and the Leopard as Incontinence. Good arguments can be offered either way.

38–39 *Aries...that rode with him to light the new creation:* The medieval tradition had it that the sun was in Aries at the time of the Creation. The significance of the astronomical and religious conjunction is an important part of Dante's intended allegory. It is just before dawn of Good Friday 1300 A.D. when he awakens in the Dark Wood. Thus his new life begins under Aries, the sign of creation, at dawn (rebirth) and in the Easter season (resurrection). Moreover the moon is full and the sun is in the equinox, conditions that did not fall together on any Friday of 1300. Dante is obviously constructing poetically the perfect Easter as a symbol of his new awakening.

Yet not so much but what I shook with dread
    at sight of a great Lion that broke upon me
    raging with hunger, its enormous head   45

held high as if to strike a mortal terror
    into the very air. And down his track,
    a She-Wolf drove upon me, a starved horror   48

ravening and wasted beyond all belief.
    She seemed a rack for avarice, gaunt and craving.
    Oh many the souls she has brought to endless
        grief!   51

She brought such heaviness upon my spirit
    at sight of her savagery and desperation,
    I died from every hope of that high summit.   54

And like a miser—eager in acquisition
    but desperate in self-reproach when Fortune's wheel
    turns to the hour of his loss—all tears and
        attrition   57

I wavered back; and still the beast pursued,
    forcing herself against me bit by bit
    till I slid back into the sunless wood.   60

And as I fell to my soul's ruin, a presence
    gathered before me on the discolored air,
    the figure of one who seemed hoarse from long
        silence.   63

At sight of him in that friendless waste I cried:
    "Have pity on me, whatever thing you are,
    whether shade or living man." And it replied: 66

"Not man, though man I once was, and my blood
    was Lombard, both my parents Mantuan.
    I was born, though late, *sub Julio,* and bred   69

in Rome under Augustus in the noon
    of the false and lying gods. I was a poet
    and sang of old Anchises' noble son   72

who came to Rome after the burning of Troy.
    But you—why do *you* return to these distresses
    instead of climbing that shining Mount of Joy   75

---

69 *sub Julio:* In the reign of Julius Caesar.

which is the seat and first cause of man's bliss?"
"And are you then that Virgil and that fountain
of purest speech?" My voice grew tremulous: 78

"Glory and light of poets! now may that zeal
and love's apprenticeship that I poured out
on your heroic verses serve me well!   81

For you are my true master and first author,
the sole maker from whom I drew the breath
of that sweet style whose measures have brought
    me honor.   84

See there, immortal sage, the beast I flee.
For my soul's salvation, I beg you, guard me from
    her,
for she has struck a mortal tremor through me."
    87

And he replied, seeing my soul in tears:
"He must go by another way who would escape
this wilderness, for that mad beast that fleers   90

before you there, suffers no man to pass.
She tracks down all, kills all, and knows no glut,
but, feeding, she grows hungrier than she was.   93

She mates with any beast, and will mate with more
before the Greyhound comes to hunt her down.
He will not feed on lands nor loot, but honor   96

and love and wisdom will make straight his way.
He will rise between Feltro and Feltro, and in him
shall be the resurrection and new day   99

of that sad Italy for which Nisus died,
and Turnus, and Euryalus, and the maid Camilla.
He shall hunt her through every nation of sick
    pride   102

till she is driven back forever to Hell
whence Envy first released her on the world.
Therefore, for your own good, I think it well   105

you follow me and I will be your guide
and lead you forth through an eternal place.
There you shall see the ancient spirits tried   108

in endless pain, and hear their lamentation
as each bemoans the second death of souls.
Next you shall see upon a burning mountain   111

souls in fire and yet content in fire,
knowing that whensoever it may be
they yet will mount into the blessed choir.   114

To which, if it is still your wish to climb,
a worthier spirit shall be sent to guide you.
With her shall I leave you, for the King of Time,
    117

who reigns on high, forbids me to come there
since, living, I rebelled against his law.
He rules the waters and the land and air   120

and there holds court, his city and his throne.
Oh blessed are they he chooses!" And I to him:
"Poet, by that God to you unknown,   123

lead me this way. Beyond this present ill
and worse to dread, lead me to Peter's gate
and be my guide through the sad halls of Hell."
    126

And he then: "Follow." And he moved ahead
in silence, and I followed where he led.   128

——————

110 *the second death:* Damnation. "This is the second death, even
the lake of fire." (*Revelation* XX, 14)

118 *forbids me to come there since, living, etc.:* Salvation is only
through Christ in Dante's theology. Virgil lived and died before
the establishment of Christ's teachings in Rome, and cannot
therefore enter Heaven.

125 *Peter's gate:* The gate of Purgatory. (See *Purgatorio* IX, 76 ff.)
The gate is guarded by an angel with a gleaming sword. The
angel is Peter's vicar (Peter, the first Pope, symbolized all Popes;
i.e., Christ's vicar on earth) and is entrusted with the two great
keys.

Some commentators argue that this is the gate of Paradise,
but Dante mentions no gate beyond this one in his ascent to
Heaven. It should be remembered, too, that those who pass the
gate of Purgatory have effectively entered Heaven.

The three great gates that figure in the entire journey are:
the gate of Hell (Canto III, 1–11), the gate of Dis (Canto VIII,
79–113, and Canto IX, 86–87), and the gate of Purgatory, as
above.

——————

95 *the Greyhound . . . Feltro and Feltro:* Almost certainly refers to
Can Grande della Scala (1290–1329), great Italian leader born in
Verona, which lies between the towns of Feltre and Montefeltro.

100–101 *Nisus, Turnus, Euryalus, Camilla:* All were killed in the war
between the Trojans and the Latians when, according to
legend, Aeneas led the survivors of Troy into Italy. Nisus
and Euryalus (*Aeneid* IX) were Trojan comrades-in-arms
who died together. Camilla (*Aeneid* XI) was the daughter of
the Latian king and one of the warrior women. She was
killed in a horse charge against the Trojans after displaying
great gallantry. Turnus (*Aeneid* XII) was killed by Aeneas in
a duel.

Canto III

The Vestibule of Hell: The Opportunists

The Poets pass the Gate of Hell and are immediately assailed by cries of anguish. Dante sees the first of the souls in torment. They are the OPPORTUNISTS, those souls who in life were neither for good nor evil but only for themselves. Mixed with them are those outcasts who took no sides in the Rebellion of the Angels. They are neither in Hell nor out of it. Eternally unclassified, they race round and round pursuing a wavering banner that runs forever before them through the dirty air; and as they run they are pursued by swarms of wasps and hornets, who sting them and produce a constant flow of blood and putrid matter which trickles down the bodies of the sinners and is feasted upon by loathsome worms and maggots who coat the ground.

The law of Dante's Hell is the law of symbolic retribution. As they sinned so are they punished. They took no sides, therefore they are given no place. As they pursued the ever-shifting illusion of their own advantage, changing their courses with every changing wind, so they pursue eternally an elusive, ever-shifting banner. As their sin was a darkness, so they move in darkness. As their own guilty conscience pursued them, so they are pursued by swarms of wasps and hornets. And as their actions were a moral filth, so they run eternally through the filth of worms and maggots which they themselves feed.

Dante recognizes several, among them POPE CELESTINE V, but without delaying to speak to any of these souls, the Poets move on to Acheron, the first of the rivers of Hell. Here the newly-arrived souls of the damned gather and wait for monstrous CHARON to ferry them over to punishment. Charon recognizes Dante as a living man and angrily refuses him passage. Virgil forces Charon to serve them, but Dante swoons with terror, and does not reawaken until he is on the other side.

I AM THE WAY INTO THE CITY OF WOE.
I AM THE WAY TO A FORSAKEN PEOPLE.
I AM THE WAY INTO ETERNAL SORROW. 3

SACRED JUSTICE MOVED MY ARCHITECT.
I WAS RAISED HERE BY DIVINE OMNIPOTENCE,
PRIMORDIAL LOVE AND ULTIMATE INTELLECT. 6

ONLY THOSE ELEMENTS TIME CANNOT WEAR
WERE MADE BEFORE ME, AND BEYOND TIME I STAND.
ABANDON ALL HOPE YE WHO ENTER HERE. 9

These mysteries I read cut into stone
  above a gate. And turning I said: "Master,
  what is the meaning of this harsh inscription?" 12

And he then as initiate to novice:
  "Here must you put by all division of spirit
  and gather your soul against all cowardice. 15

This is the place I told you to expect.
  Here you shall pass among the fallen people,
  souls who have lost the good of intellect." 18

So saying, he put forth his hand to me,
  and with a gentle and encouraging smile
  he led me through the gate of mystery. 21

Here sighs and cries and wails coiled and recoiled
  on the starless air, spilling my soul to tears.
  A confusion of tongues and monstrous accents
    toiled 24

in pain and anger. Voices hoarse and shrill
  and sounds of blows, all intermingled, raised
  tumult and pandemonium that still 27

whirls on the air forever dirty with it
  as if a whirlwind sucked at sand. And I,
  holding my head in horror, cried: "Sweet Spirit, 30

what souls are these who run through this black
    haze?"

7–8 *Only those elements time cannot wear:* The Angels, the Empyrean, and the First Matter are the elements time cannot wear, for they will last to all time. Man, however, in his mortal state, is not eternal. The Gate of Hell, therefore, was created

before man. The theological point is worth attention. The doctrine of Original Sin is, of course, one familiar to many creeds. Here, however, it would seem that the preparation for damnation predates Original Sin. True, in one interpretation, Hell was created for the punishment of the Rebellious Angels and not for man. Had man not sinned, he would never have known Hell. But on the other hand, Dante's God was one who knew all, and knew therefore that man would indeed sin. The theological problem is an extremely delicate one.

It is significant, however, that having sinned, man lived out his days on the rind of Hell, and that damnation is forever below his feet. This central concept of man's sinfulness, and, opposed to it, the doctrine of Christ's ever-abounding mercy, are central to all of Dante's theology. Only as man surrenders himself to Divine Love may he hope for salvation, and salvation is open to all who will surrender themselves.

8 *and beyond time I stand:* So odious is sin to God that there can be no end to its just punishment.

9 *Abandon all hope ye who enter here:* The admonition, of course, is to the damned and not to those who come on Heaven sent errands. The Harrowing of Hell (Canto IV) provided the only exemption from this decree, and that only through the direct intercession of Christ.

And he to me: "These are the nearly soulless
whose lives concluded neither blame nor praise.   33

They are mixed here with that despicable corps
of angels who were neither for God nor Satan,
but only for themselves. The High Creator   36

scourged them from Heaven for its perfect beauty,
and Hell will not receive them since the wicked
might feel some glory over them." And I: 39

"Master, what gnaws at them so hideously
their lamentation stuns the very air?"
"They have no hope of death," he answered me,   42

"and in their blind and unattaining state
their miserable lives have sunk so low
that they must envy every other fate.   45

No word of them survives their living season.
Mercy and Justice deny them even a name.
Let us not speak of them: look, and pass on."   48

I saw a banner there upon the mist.
Circling and circling, it seemed to scorn all pause.
So it ran on, and still behind it pressed   51

a never-ending rout of souls in pain.
I had not thought death had undone so many
as passed before me in that mournful train.   54

And some I knew among them; last of all
I recognized the shadow of that soul
who, in his cowardice, made the Great Denial.   57

At once I understood for certain: these
were of that retrograde and faithless crew
hateful to God and to His enemies.   60

These wretches never born and never dead
ran naked in a swarm of wasps and hornets
that goaded them the more the more they fled,   63

and made their faces stream with bloody gouts
of pus and tears that dribbled to their feet
to be swallowed there by loathsome worms and
maggots.   66

Then looking onward I made out a throng
assembled on the beach of a wide river,
whereupon I turned to him: "Master, I long   69

to know what souls these are, and what strange
usage
makes them as eager to cross as they seem to be
in this infected light." At which the Sage: 72

"All this shall be made known to you when we
stand
on the joyless beach of Acheron." And I
cast down my eyes, sensing a reprimand   75

in what he said, and so walked at his side
in silence and ashamed until we came
through the dead cavern to that sunless tide.   78

There, steering toward us in an ancient ferry
came an old man with a white bush of hair,
bellowing: "Woe to you depraved souls! Bury   81

here and forever all hope of Paradise:
I come to lead you to the other shore,
into eternal dark, into fire and ice.   84

And you who are living yet, I say begone
from these who are dead." But when he saw me
stand
against his violence he began again: 87

"By other windings and by other steerage
shall you cross to that other shore. Not here! Not
here!
A lighter craft than mine must give you passage."
                                                               90

---

⁵⁷*who, in his cowardice, made the Great Denial:* This is almost
certainly intended to be Celestine V, who became Pope in 1294.
He was a man of saintly life, but allowed himself to be convinced
by a priest named Benedetto that his soul was in danger since no
man could live in the world without being damned. In fear for his
soul he withdrew from all worldly affairs and renounced the
papacy. Benedetto promptly assumed the mantle himself and
became Boniface VIII, a Pope who became for Dante a symbol of
all the worst corruptions of the church. Dante also blamed
Boniface and his intrigues for many of the evils that befell Florence. We shall learn in Canto XIX that the fires of Hell are
waiting for Boniface in the pit of the Simoniacs, and we shall be
given further evidence of his corruption in Canto XXVII. Celestine's great guilt is that his cowardice (in selfish terror for his own
welfare) served as the door through which so much evil entered
the church.

---

⁸⁰*an old man:* Charon. He is the ferryman of dead souls across the
Acheron in all classical mythology.

^{88–90}*By other windings:* Charon recognizes Dante not only as a

And my Guide to him: "Charon, bite back your
　　　spleen:
　　this has been willed where what is willed must be,
　　and is not yours to ask what it may mean."　　93

The steersman of that marsh of ruined souls,
　　who wore a wheel of flame around each eye,
　　stifled the rage that shook his woolly jowls.　　96

But those unmanned and naked spirits there
　　turned pale with fear and their teeth began to
　　　chatter
　　at sound of his crude bellow. In despair　　99

they blasphemed God, their parents, their time on
　　　earth,
　　the race of Adam, and the day and the hour
　　and the place and the seed and the womb that
　　　gave them birth.　　102

But all together they drew to that grim shore
　　where all must come who lose the fear of God.
　　Weeping and cursing they come for evermore,　　105

and demon Charon with eyes like burning coals
　　herds them in, and with a whistling oar
　　flails on the stragglers to his wake of souls.　　108

As leaves in autumn loosen and stream down
　　until the branch stands bare above its tatters
　　spread on the rustling ground, so one by one　　111

the evil seed of Adam in its Fall
　　cast themselves, at his signal, from the shore
　　and streamed away like birds who hear their call.　　114

So they are gone over that shadowy water,
　　and always before they reach the other shore
　　a new noise stirs on this, and new throngs gather.　　117

"My son," the courteous Master said to me,
　　"all who die in the shadow of God's wrath
　　converge to this from every clime and country.　　120

And all pass over eagerly, for here
　　Divine Justice transforms and spurs them so
　　their dread turns wish: they yearn for what they
　　　fear.　　123

No soul in Grace comes ever to this crossing;
　　therefore if Charon rages at your presence
　　you will understand the reason for his cursing."
　　　　　　126

When he had spoken, all the twilight country
　　shook so violently, the terror of it
　　bathes me with sweat even in memory:　　129

the tear-soaked ground gave out a sigh of wind
　　that spewed itself in flame on a red sky,
　　and all my shattered senses left me. Blind,　　132

like one whom sleep comes over in a swoon,
　　I stumbled into darkness and went down.　　134

Canto V

Circle Two: The Carnal

The Poets leave Limbo and enter the Second Circle. *Here
begin the torments of Hell proper, and here, blocking the
way, sits* Minos, *the dread and semi-bestial judge of the
damned who assigns to each soul its eternal torment. He
orders the Poets back; but Virgil silences him as he earlier
silenced Charon, and the Poets move on.*

　　*They find themselves on a dark ledge swept by a great
whirlwind, which spins within it the souls of the* Carnal,
*those who betrayed reason to their appetites. Their sin was to
abandon themselves to the tempest of their passions: so they
are swept forever in the tempest of Hell, forever denied the*

---

living man but as a soul in grace, and knows, therefore, that
the Infernal Ferry was not intended for him. He is probably
referring to the fact that souls destined for Purgatory and
Heaven assemble not at his ferry point, but on the banks of the
Tiber, from which they are transported by an Angel.

100*they blasphemed God:* The souls of the damned are not permit-
　　ted to repent, for repentance is a divine grace.

123*they yearn for what they fear:* Hell (allegorically Sin) is what the
　　souls of the damned really wish for. Hell is their actual and
　　deliberate choice, for divine grace is denied to none who wish for
　　it in their hearts. The damned must, in fact, deliberately harden
　　their hearts to God in order to become damned. Christ's grace is
　　sufficient to save all who wish for it.

133–134DANTE'S SWOON: This device (repeated at the end of Canto
　　V) serves a double purpose. The first is technical: Dante
　　uses it to cover a transition. We are never told how he
　　crossed Acheron, for that would involve certain narrative
　　matters he can better deal with when he crosses Styx in
　　Canto VII. The second is to provide a point of departure for
　　a theme that is carried through the entire descent: the theme
　　of Dante's emotional reaction to Hell. These two swoons
　　early in the descent show him most susceptible to the grief
　　about him. As he descends, pity leaves him, and he even goes
　　so far as to add to the torments of one sinner. The allegory is
　　clear: we must harden ourselves against every sympathy for
　　sin.

light of reason and of God. Virgil identifies many among them. SEMIRAMIS *is there, and* DIDO, CLEOPATRA, HELEN, ACHILLES, PARIS, *and* TRISTAN. *Dante sees* PAOLO *and* FRANCESCA *swept together, and in the name of love he calls to them to tell their sad story. They pause from their eternal flight to come to him, and Francesca tells their history while Paolo weeps at her side. Dante is so stricken by compassion at their tragic tale that he swoons once again.*

So we went down to the second ledge alone;
    a smaller circle of so much greater pain
    the voice of the damned rose in a bestial moan.   3

There Minos sits, grinning, grotesque, and hale.
    He examines each lost soul as it arrives
    and delivers his verdict with his coiling tail.   6

That is to say, when the ill-fated soul
    appears before him it confesses all,
    and that grim sorter of the dark and foul   9

decides which place in Hell shall be its end,
    then wraps his twitching tail about himself
    one coil for each degree it must descend.   12

The soul descends and others take its place:
    each crowds in its turn to judgment, each
        confesses,
    each hears its doom and falls away through space.
        15

"O you who come into this camp of woe,"
    cried Minos when he saw me turn away
    without awaiting his judgment, "watch where you
        go   18

once you have entered here, and to whom you turn!
    Do not be misled by that wide and easy passage!"
    Any my Guide to him: "That is not your
        concern;   21

it is his fate to enter every door.
    This has been willed where what is willed must
        be,
    and is not yours to question. Say no more."   24

Now the choir of anguish, like a wound,
    strikes through the tortured air. Now I have come
    to Hell's full lamentation, sound beyond sound.   27

I came to a place stripped bare of every light
    and roaring on the naked dark like seas
    wracked by a war of winds. Their hellish flight   30

of storm and counterstorm through time foregone,
    sweeps the souls of the damned before its charge.
    Whirling and battering it drives them on,   33

and when they pass the ruined gap of Hell
    through which we had come, their shrieks begin
        anew.
    There they blaspheme the power of God eternal.   36

And this, I learned, was the never ending flight
    of those who sinned in the flesh, the carnal and
        lusty
    who betrayed reason to their appetite.   39

As the wings of wintering starlings bear them on
    in their great wheeling flights, just so the blast
    wherries these evil souls through time foregone.   42

---

[2] *a smaller circle:* The pit of Hell tapers like a funnel. The circles of ledges accordingly grow smaller as they descend.

[4] *Minos:* Like all the monsters Dante assigns to the various offices of Hell, Minos is drawn from classical mythology. He was the son of Europa and of Zeus, who descended to her in the form of a bull. Minos became a mythological king of Crete, so famous for his wisdom and justice that after death his soul was made judge of the dead. Virgil presents him fulfilling the same office at Aeneas' descent to the underworld. Dante, however, transforms him into an irate and hideous monster with a tail. The transformation may have been suggested by the form Zeus assumed for the rape of Europa—the monster is certainly bullish enough here—but the obvious purpose of the brutalization is to present a figure symbolic of the guilty conscience of the wretches who come before it to make their confessions. Dante freely reshapes his materials to his own purposes.

[8] *it confesses all:* Just as the souls appeared eager to cross Acheron, so they are eager to confess even while they dread. Dante is once again making the point that sinners elect their Hell by an act of their own will.

---

[27] *Hell's full lamentation:* It is with the second circle that the real tortures of Hell begin.

[34] *the ruined gap of Hell:* At the time of the Harrowing of Hell a great earthquake shook the underworld shattering rocks and cliffs. Ruins resulting from the same shock are noted in Canto XII, 34, and Canto XXI, 112 ff. At the beginning of Canto XXIV, the Poets leave the *bolgia* of the Hypocrites by climbing the ruined slabs of a bridge that was shattered by this earthquake.

[39] THE SINNERS OF THE SECOND CIRCLE (THE CARNAL): Here begin the punishments for the various sins of Incontinence (The sins of the She-Wolf). In the second circle are punished those who sinned by excess of sexual passion. Since this is the most natural sin and the sin most nearly associated with love, its punishment is the lightest of all to be found in Hell proper. The Carnal are whirled and buffeted endlessly through the murky air (symbolic of the beclouding of their reason by passion) by a great gale (symbolic of their lust).

Here, there, up, down, they whirl and, whirling,
    strain
    with never a hope of hope to comfort them,
    not of release, but even of less pain.   45

As cranes go over sounding their harsh cry,
    leaving the long streak of their flight in air,
    so come these spirits, wailing as they fly.   48

And watching their shadows lashed by wind, I cried:
    "Master, what souls are these the very air
    lashes with its black whips from side to side?"   51

"The first of these whose history you would know,"
    he answered me, "was Empress of many tongues.
    Mad sensuality corrupted her so   54

that to hide the guilt of her debauchery
    she licensed all depravity alike,
    and lust and law were one in her decree.   57

She is Semiramis of whom the tale is told
    how she married Ninus and succeeded him
    to the throne of that wide land the Sultans hold.   60

The other is Dido; faithless to the ashes
    of Sichaeus, she killed herself for love.
    The next whom the eternal tempest lashes   63

is sense-drugged Cleopatra. See Helen there,
    from whom such ill arose. And great Achilles,
    who fought at last with love in the house of
      prayer.   66

And Paris. And Tristan." As they whirled above
    he pointed out more than a thousand shades
    of those torn from the mortal life by love.   69

I stood there while my Teacher one by one
    named the great knights and ladies of dim time;
    and I was swept by pity and confusion.   72

At last I spoke: "Poet, I should be glad
    to speak a word with those two swept together
    so lightly on the wind and still so sad."   75

And he to me: "Watch them. When next they pass,
    call to them in the name of love that drives
    and damns them here. In that name they will
      pause."   78

Thus, as soon as the wind in its wild course
    brought them around, I called: "O wearied souls!
    if none forbid it, pause and speak to us."   81

As mating doves that love calls to their nest
    glide through the air with motionless raised wings,
    borne by the sweet desire that fills each breast—
      84

Just so those spirits turned on the torn sky
    from the band where Dido whirls across the air;
    such was the power of pity in my cry.   87

"O living creature, gracious, kind, and good,
    going this pilgrimage through the sick night,
    visiting us who stained the earth with blood,   90

---

[53] *Empress of many tongues:* Semiramis, a legendary queen of Assyria who assumed full power at the death of her husband, Ninus.

[61] *Dido:* Queen and founder of Carthage. She had vowed to remain faithful to her husband, Sichaeus, but she fell in love with Aeneas. When Aeneas abandoned her she stabbed herself on a funeral pyre she had had prepared.

According to Dante's own system of punishments, she should be in the Seventh Circle (Canto XIII) with the suicides. The only clue Dante gives to the tempering of her punishment is his statement that "she killed herself for love." Dante always seems readiest to forgive in that name.

[65] *Achilles:* He is placed among this company because of his passion for Polyxena, the daughter of Priam. For love of her, he agreed to desert the Greeks and to join the Trojans, but when he went to the temple for the wedding (according to the legend Dante has followed) he was killed by Paris.

---

[74] *those two swept together:* Paolo and Francesca (PAH-oe-loe: Frahn-CHAY-ska).

Dante's treatment of these two lovers is certainly the tenderest and most sympathetic accorded any of the sinners in Hell, and legends immediately began to grow about this pair.

The facts are these. In 1275 Giovanni Malatesta (Djoe-VAH-nee Mahl-ah-TEH-stah) of Rimini, called Giovanni the Lame, a somewhat deformed but brave and powerful warrior, made a political marriage with Francesca, daughter of Guido da Polenta of Ravenna. Francesca came to Rimini and there an amour grew between her and Giovanni's younger brother Paolo. Despite the fact that Paolo had married in 1269 and had become the father of two daughters by 1275, his affair with Francesca continued for many years. It was sometime between 1283 and 1286 that Giovanni surprised them in Francesca's bedroom and killed both of them.

Around these facts the legend has grown that Paolo was sent by Giovanni as his proxy to the marriage, that Francesca thought he was her real bridegroom and accordingly gave him her heart irrevocably at first sight. The legend obviously increases the pathos, but nothing in Dante gives it support.

were the King of Time our friend, we would pray
His peace
on you who have pitied us. As long as the wind
will let us pause, ask of us what you please.   93

The town where I was born lies by the shore
where the Po descends into its ocean rest
with its attendant streams in one long murmur.   96

Love, which in gentlest hearts will soonest bloom
seized my lover with passion for that sweet body
from which I was torn unshriven to my doom.   99

Love, which permits no loved one not to love,
took me so strongly with delight in him
that we are one in Hell, as we were above.   102

Love led us to one death. In the depths of Hell
Caïna waits for him who took our lives."
This was the piteous tale they stopped to tell.   105

And when I had heard those world-offended lovers
I bowed my head. At last the Poet spoke:
"What painful thoughts are these your lowered
brow covers?"   108

When at length I answered, I began: "Alas!
What sweetest thoughts, what green and young
desire
led these two lovers to this sorry pass."   111

Then turning to those spirits once again,
I said: "Francesca, what you suffer here
melts me to tears of pity and of pain.   114

But tell me: in the time of your sweet sighs
by what appearances found love the way
to lure you to his perilous paradise?"   117

And she: "The double grief of a lost bliss
is to recall its happy hour in pain.
Your Guide and Teacher knows the truth of
this.   120

But if there is indeed a soul in Hell
to ask of the beginning of our love
out of his pity, I will weep and tell: 123

On a day for dalliance we read the rhyme
of Lancelot, how love had mastered him.
We were alone with innocence and dim time.   126

Pause after pause that high old story drew
our eyes together while we blushed and paled;
but it was one soft passage overthrew   129

our caution and our hearts. For when we read
how her fond smile was kissed by such a lover,
he who is one with me alive and dead   132

breathed on my lips the tremor of his kiss.
That book, and he who wrote it, was a pander.
That day we read no further." As she said this,   135

the other spirit, who stood by her, wept
so piteously, I felt my senses reel
and faint away with anguish. I was swept   138

by such a swoon as death is, and I fell,
as a corpse might fall, to the dead floor of Hell.   140

102*that we are one in Hell, as we were above:* At many points of the *Inferno* Dante makes clear the principle that the souls of the damned are locked so blindly into their own guilt that none can feel sympathy for another, or find any pleasure in the presence of another. The temptation of many readers is to interpret this line romantically: i.e., that the love of Paolo and Francesca survives Hell itself. The more Dantean interpretation, however, is that they add to one another's anguish (a) as mutual reminders of their sin, and (b) as insubstantial shades of the bodies for which they once felt such great passion.

104*Caïna waits for him:* Giovanni Malatesta was still alive at the writing. His fate is already decided, however, and upon his death, his soul will fall to Caïna, the first ring of the last circle (Canto XXXII), where lie those who performed acts of treachery against their kin.

124–125 *the rhyme of Lancelot:* The story exists in many forms. The details Dante makes use of are from an Old French version.

126*dim time:* The original simply reads "We were alone, suspecting nothing." "Dim time" is rhyme-forced, but not wholly outside the legitimate implications of the original, I hope. The old courtly romance may well be thought of as happening in the dim ancient days. The apology, of course, comes after the fact: one does the possible, then argues for justification, and there probably is none.

134*That book, and he who wrote it, was a pander:* "Galeotto," the Italian word for "pander," is also the Italian rendering of the name of Gallehault, who in the French Romance Dante refers to here, urged Lancelot and Guinevere on to love.

LOWER HELL: The structure of Dante's Hell is based on Aristotle (as Virgil makes clear in his exposition), but with certain Christian symbolisms, exceptions, and misconstructions of Aristotle's text. The major symbolisms are the three beasts met in Canto I. The exceptions are the two peculiarly Christian categories of sin: Paganism and Heresy. The misconstructions of Aristotle's text involve the classification of "bestiality." Aristotle classified it as a different thing from vice or malice, but medieval commentators construed the passage to mean "another sort of malice." Dante's intent is clear, however; he understood Aristotle to make three categories of sin: Incontinence, Violence and Bestiality, and Fraud and Malice. Incontinence is punished in the Upper Hell. The following chart sets forth the categories of the Lower Hell.

THE CLASSIFICATIONS OF SIN IN LOWER HELL

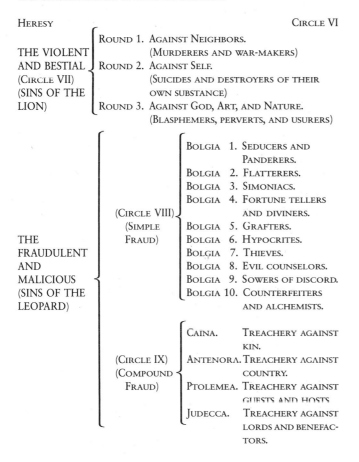

HERESY .... CIRCLE VI

THE VIOLENT AND BESTIAL (CIRCLE VII) (SINS OF THE LION)
- ROUND 1. AGAINST NEIGHBORS. (Murderers and war-makers)
- ROUND 2. AGAINST SELF. (Suicides and destroyers of their own substance)
- ROUND 3. AGAINST GOD, ART, AND NATURE. (Blasphemers, perverts, and usurers)

THE FRAUDULENT AND MALICIOUS (SINS OF THE LEOPARD)

(CIRCLE VIII) (SIMPLE FRAUD)
- BOLGIA 1. SEDUCERS AND PANDERERS.
- BOLGIA 2. FLATTERERS.
- BOLGIA 3. SIMONIACS.
- BOLGIA 4. FORTUNE TELLERS AND DIVINERS.
- BOLGIA 5. GRAFTERS.
- BOLGIA 6. HYPOCRITES.
- BOLGIA 7. THIEVES.
- BOLGIA 8. EVIL COUNSELORS.
- BOLGIA 9. SOWERS OF DISCORD.
- BOLGIA 10. COUNTERFEITERS AND ALCHEMISTS.

(CIRCLE IX) (COMPOUND FRAUD)
- CAINA. TREACHERY AGAINST KIN.
- ANTENORA. TREACHERY AGAINST COUNTRY.
- PTOLEMEA. TREACHERY AGAINST GUESTS AND HOSTS.
- JUDECCA. TREACHERY AGAINST LORDS AND BENEFACTORS.

Canto XXVI

Circle Eight
Bolgia Eight: The Evil Counselors

Dante turns from the Thieves toward the Evil Counselors of the next Bolgia (ditch), and between the two he addresses a passionate lament to Florence prophesying the griefs that will befall her from these two sins. At the purported time of the Vision, it will be recalled, Dante was a Chief Magistrate of Florence and was forced into exile by men he had reason to consider both thieves and evil counselors. He seems

prompted, in fact, to say much more on this score, but he restrains himself when he comes in sight of the sinners of the next Bolgia, for they are a moral symbolism, all men of gift who abused their genius, perverting it to wiles and stratagems. Seeing them in Hell he knows his must be another road: his way shall not be by deception.

So the Poets move on and Dante observes the EIGHTH BOLGIA *in detail. Here the* EVIL COUNSELORS *move about endlessly, hidden from view inside great flames. Their sin was to abuse the gifts of the Almighty, to steal his virtues for low purposes. And as they stole from God in their lives and worked by hidden ways, so are they stolen from sight and hidden in the great flames which are their own guilty consciences. And as, in most instances at least, they sinned by glibness of tongue, so are the flames made into a fiery travesty of tongues.*

Among the others, the Poets see a great doubleheaded flame, and discover that ULYSSES *and* DIOMEDE *are punished together within it. Virgil addresses the flame, and through its wavering tongue Ulysses narrates an unforgettable tale of his last voyage and death.*

Joy to you, Florence, that your banners swell,
  beating their proud wings over land and sea,
  and that your name expands through all of Hell!   3

Among the thieves I found five who had been
  your citizens, to my shame; nor yet shall you
  mount to great honor peopling such a den!   6

But if the truth is dreamed of toward the morning,
  you soon shall feel what Prato and the others
  wish for you. And were that day of mourning   9

already come it would not be too soon.
  So may it come, since it must! for it will weigh
  more heavily on me as I pass my noon.   12

We left that place. My Guide climbed stone by stone
  the natural stair by which we had descended
  and drew me after him. So we passed on,   15

and going our lonely way through that dead land
  among the crags and crevices of the cliff,
  the foot could make no way without the hand.   18

---

[7] *if the truth is dreamed of toward the morning:* A semi-proverbial expression. It was a common belief that those dreams that occur just before waking foretell the future. "Morning" here would equal both "the rude awakening" and the potential "dawn of a new day."

I mourned among those rocks, and I mourn again
  when memory returns to what I saw:
  and more than usually I curb the strain   21

of my genius, lest it stray from Virtue's course;
  so if some star, or a better thing, grant me merit,
  may I not find the gift cause for remorse.   24

As many fireflies as the peasant sees
  when he rests on a hill and looks into the valley
  (where he tills or gathers grapes or prunes his
      trees)   27

in that sweet season when the face of him
  who lights the world rides north, and at the hour
  when the fly yields to the gnat and the air grows
      dim—   30

such myriads of flames I saw shine through
  the gloom of the eighth abyss when I arrived
  at the rim from which its bed comes into view.   33

As he the bears avenged so fearfully
  beheld Elijah's chariot depart—
  the horses rise toward heaven—but could not see
                                                             36

more than the flame, a cloudlet in the sky,
  once it had risen—so within the fosse
  only those flames, forever passing by   39

were visible, ahead, to right, to left;
  for though each steals a sinner's soul from view
  not one among them leaves a trace of the theft.   42

I stood on the bridge, and leaned out from the edge;
  so far, that but for a jut of rock I held to
  I should have been sent hurtling from the ledge   45

without being pushed. And seeing me so intent,
  my Guide said: "There are souls within those
      flames;
  each sinner swathes himself in his own torment."
                                                             48

"Master," I said, "your words make me more sure,
  but I had seen already that it was so
  and meant to ask what spirit must endure   51

the pains of that great flame which splits away
  in two great horns, as if it rose from the pyre
  where Eteocles and Polynices lay?"   54

He answered me: "Forever round this path
  Ulysses and Diomede move in such dress,
  united in pain as once they were in wrath;   57

there they lament the ambush of the Horse
  which was the door through which the noble seed
  of the Romans issued from its holy source;   60

there they mourn that for Achilles slain
  sweet Deidamia weeps even in death;
  there they recall the Palladium in their pain."   63

"Master," I cried, "I pray you and repray
  till my prayer becomes a thousand—if these souls
  can still speak from the fire, oh let me stay   66

until the flame draws near! Do not deny me:
  You see how fervently I long for it!"
  And he to me: "Since what you ask is worthy,   69

34*he the bears avenged:* Elisha saw Elijah translated to Heaven in a fiery chariot. Later he was mocked by some children, who called out tauntingly that he should "Go up" as Elijah had. Elisha cursed the children in the name of the Lord, and bears came suddenly upon the children and devoured them. (2 *Kings* ii, 11–24.)

53–54*the pyre where Eteocles and Polynices lay:* Eteocles and Polynices, sons of Oedipus, succeeded jointly to the throne of Thebes, and came to an agreement whereby each one would rule separately for a year at a time. Eteocles ruled the first year and when he refused to surrender the throne at the appointed time, Polynices led the Seven against Thebes in a bloody war. In single combat the two brothers killed one another. Statius (*Thebaid* XII, 429 ff.) wrote that their mutual hatred was so great that when they were placed on the same funeral pyre the very flame of their burning drew apart in two great raging horns.

56–63*Ulysses and Diomede, etc.:* They suffer here for their joint guilt in counseling and carrying out many stratagems which Dante considered evil, though a narrator who was less passionately a partisan of the Trojans might have thought their actions justifiable methods of warfare. They are in one flame for their joint guilt, but the flame is divided, perhaps to symbolize the moral that men of evil must sooner or later come to a falling out, for there can be no lasting union except by virtue.

  Their first sin was the stratagem of the Wooden Horse, as a result of which Troy fell and Aeneas went forth to found the Roman line. The second evil occurred at Scyros. There Ulysses discovered Achilles in female disguise, hidden by his mother, Thetis, so that he would not be taken off to the war. Deidamia was in love with Achilles and had borne him a son. When Ulysses persuaded her lover to sail for Troy, she died of grief. The third count is Ulysses' theft of the sacred statue of Pallas from the Palladium. Upon the statue, it was believed, depended the fate of Troy. Its theft, therefore, would result in Troy's downfall.

it shall be. But be still and let me speak;
 for I know your mind already, and they perhaps
 might scorn your manner of speaking, since they
   were Greek." 72

And when the flame had come where time and place
 seemed fitting to my Guide, I heard him say
 these words to it: "O you two souls who pace 75

together in one flame!—if my days above
 won favor in your eyes, if I have earned
 however much or little of your love 78

in writing my High Verses, do not pass by,
 but let one of you be pleased to tell where he,
 having disappeared from the known world, went
   to die." 81

As if it fought the wind, the greater prong
 of the ancient flame began to quiver and hum;
 then moving its tip as if it were the tongue 84

that spoke, gave out a voice above the roar.
 "When I left Circe," it said, "who more than a
   year
 detained me near Gaëta long before 87

Aeneas came and gave the place that name,
 not fondness for my son, nor reverence
 for my aged father, nor Penelope's claim 90

to the joys of love, could drive out of my mind
 the lust to experience the far-flung world
 and the failings and felicities of mankind. 93

I put out on the high and open sea
 with a single ship and only those few souls
 who stayed true when the rest deserted me. 96

As far as Morocco and as far as Spain
 I saw both shores; and I saw Sardinia
 and the other islands of the open main. 99

I and my men were stiff and slow with age
 when we sailed at last into the narrow pass
 where, warning all men back from further voyage,
   102

Hercules' Pillars rose upon our sight.
 Already I had left Ceuta on the left;
 Seville now sank behind me on the right. 105

'Shipmates,' I said, 'who through a hundred
   thousand
 perils have reached the West, do not deny
 to the brief remaining watch our senses stand 108

experience of the world beyond the sun.
 Greeks! You were not born to live like brutes,
 but to press on toward manhood and recognition!
   111

With this brief exhortation I made my crew
 so eager for the voyage I could hardly
 have held them back from it when I was through;
   114

and turning our stern toward morning, our bow
   toward night,
 we bore southwest out of the world of man;
 we made wings of our oars for our fool's flight. 117

That night we raised the other pole ahead
 with all its stars, and ours had so declined
 it did not rise out of its ocean bed. 120

---

⁷²*since they were Greek.* Dante knew no Greek, and these sinners might scorn him, first, because he spoke what to them would seem a barbarous tongue, and second, because as an Italian he would seem a descendant of Aeneas and the defeated Trojans. Virgil, on the other hand, appeals to them as a man of virtuous life (who therefore has a power over sin) and as a poet who celebrated their earthly fame. (Prof. MacAllister suggests another meaning as well: that Dante [and his world] had no direct knowledge of the Greeks, knowing their works through Latin intermediaries. Thus Virgil stood between Homer and Dante.)

^{80–81}*one of you:* Ulysses. He is the figure in the larger horn of the flame (which symbolizes that his guilt, as leader, is greater than that of Diomede). His memorable account of his last voyage and death is purely Dante's invention.

⁸⁶*Circe:* Changed Ulysses' men to swine and kept him a prisoner, though with rather exceptional accommodations.

⁸⁷*Gaëta:* Southeastern Italian coastal town. According to Virgil (*Aeneid,* VII, 1 ff.) it was earlier named Caieta by Aeneas in honor of his aged nurse.

⁹⁰*Penelope:* Ulysses' wife.

⁹⁸*both shores:* Of the Mediterranean.

¹⁰¹*narrow pass:* The Straits of Gibraltar, formerly called the Pillars of Hercules. They were presumed to be the Western limit beyond which no man could navigate.

¹⁰⁴*Ceuta:* In Africa, opposite Gibraltar.

¹⁰⁵*Seville:* In Dante's time this was the name given to the general region of Spain. Having passed through the Straits, the men are now in the Atlantic.

¹¹⁵*morning . . . night:* East and West.

¹¹⁸*we raised the other pole ahead:* i.e., They drove south across the equator, observed the southern stars, and found that the North Star had sunk below the horizon. The altitude of the North Star is the easiest approximation of latitude. Except for a small correction, it is directly overhead at the North Pole, shows an altitude of 45° at North latitude 45, and is on the horizon at the equator.

Five times since we had dipped our bending oars
   beyond the world, the light beneath the moon
   had waxed and waned, when dead upon our
   course   123

we sighted, dark in space, a peak so tall
   I doubted any man had seen the like.
   Our cheers were hardly sounded, when a squall 126

broke hard upon our bow from the new land:
   three times it sucked the ship and the sea about
   as it pleased Another to order and command.   129

At the fourth, the poop rose and the bow went
   down
till the sea closed over us and the light was gone." 131

Canto XXXIII

Circle Nine
Cocytus: Compound Fraud
Round Two
Antenora: The Treacherous to Country
Round Three
Ptolomea: The Treacherous
to Guests and Hosts

*In reply to Dante's exhortation, the sinner who is gnawing
his companion's head looks up, wipes his bloody mouth on
his victim's hair, and tells his harrowing story. He is* Count
Ugolino *and the wretch he gnaws is* Archbishop Ruggieri.
*Both are in Antenora for treason. In life they had once
plotted together. Then Ruggieri betrayed his fellow-plotter
and caused his death, by starvation, along with his four
"sons." In the most pathetic and dramatic passage of the
Inferno,* Ugolino *details how their prison was sealed and
how his "sons" dropped dead before him one by one, weeping for food. His terrible tale serves only to renew his grief
and hatred, and he has hardly finished it before he begins to
gnaw Ruggieri again with renewed fury. In the immutable
Law of Hell, the killer-by-starvation becomes the food of his
victim.*

   The Poets leave Ugolino and enter Ptolomea, *so named
for the Ptolomaeus of* Maccabees, *who murdered his father-*

in-law at a banquet. Here are punished those who were
Treacherous Against the Ties of Hospitality. *They lie
with only half their faces above the ice and their tears freeze
in their eye sockets, sealing them with little crystal visors.
Thus even the comfort of tears is denied them. Here Dante
finds* Friar Alberigo *and* Branca d'Oria, *and discovers
the terrible power of Ptolomea: so great is its sin that the
souls of the guilty fall to its torments even before they die,
leaving their bodies still on earth, inhabited by Demons.*

The sinner raised his mouth from his grim repast
   and wiped it on the hair of the bloody head
   whose nape he had all but eaten away. At last   3

he began to speak: "You ask me to renew
   a grief so desperate that the very thought
   of speaking of it tears my heart in two.   6

But if my words may be a seed that bears
   the fruit of infamy for him I gnaw,
   I shall weep, but tell my story through my tears. 9

Who you may be, and by what powers you reach
   into this underworld, I cannot guess,
   but you seem to me a Florentine by your speech. 12

I was Count Ugolino, I must explain;
   this reverend grace is the Archbishop Ruggieri:
   now I will tell you why I gnaw his brain.   15

That I, who trusted him, had to undergo
   imprisonment and death through his treachery,
   you will know already. What you cannot know—
                                                        18

13—14 *Ugolino . . . Ruggieri:* (Oog-oh-LEE-noe: Roo-DJAIR-ee)
   Ugolino, Count of Donoratico and a member of the Guelph
   family della Gherardesca. He and his nephew, Nino de' Visconti, led the two Guelph factions of Pisa. In 1288 Ugolino
   intrigued with Archbishop Ruggieri degli Ubaldini, leader of
   the Ghibellines, to get rid of Visconti and to take over the
   command of all the Pisan Guelphs. The plan worked, but in
   the consequent weakening of the Guelphs, Ruggieri saw his
   chance and betrayed Ugolino, throwing him into prison with
   his sons and his grandsons. In the following year the prison
   was sealed up and they were left to starve to death. The law of
   retribution is clearly evident: in life Ruggieri sinned against
   Ugolino by denying him food; in Hell he himself becomes
   food for his victim.

18 *you will know already:* News of Ugolino's imprisonment and
   death would certainly have reached Florence. *What you cannot
   know:* No living man could know what happened after Ugolino
   and his sons were sealed in the prison and abandoned.

---

124 *a peak:* Purgatory. They sight it after five months of passage.
   According to Dante's geography, the Northern hemisphere is
   land and the Southern is all water except for the Mountain of
   Purgatory which rises above the surface at a point directly
   opposite Jerusalem.

that is, the lingering inhumanity
   of the death I suffered—you shall hear in full:
   then judge for yourself if he has injured me.   21

A narrow window in that coop of stone
   now called the Tower of Hunger for my sake
   (within which others yet must pace alone)   24

had shown me several waning moons already
   between its bars, when I slept the evil sleep
   in which the veil of the future parted for me.   27

This beast appeared as master of a hunt
   chasing the wolf and his whelps across the
      mountain
   that hides Lucca from Pisa. Out in front   30

of the starved and shrewd and avid pack he had
      placed
   Gualandi and Sismondi and Lanfranchi
   to point his prey. The father and sons had raced   33

a brief course only when they failed of breath
   and seemed to weaken; then I thought I saw
   their flanks ripped open by the hounds' fierce
      teeth.   36

Before the dawn, the dream still in my head,
   I woke and heard my sons, who were there with me,
   cry from their troubled sleep, asking for bread.   39

You are cruelty itself if you can keep
   your tears back at the thought of what foreboding
   stirred in my heart; and if you do not weep,   42

at what are you used to weeping?—The hour when
      food
   used to be brought, drew near. They were now
      awake,
   and each was anxious from his dream's dark
      mood.   45

And from the base of that horrible tower I heard
   the sound of hammers nailing up the gates:
   I stared at my sons' faces without a word.   48

I did not weep: I had turned stone inside.
   They wept. 'What ails you, Father, you look so
      strange,'
   my little Anselm, youngest of them, cried.   51

But I did not speak a word nor shed a tear:
   not all that day nor all that endless night,
   until I saw another sun appear.   54

When a tiny ray leaked into that dark prison
   and I saw staring back from their four faces
   the terror and the wasting of my own,   57

I bit my hands in helpless grief. And they,
   thinking I chewed myself for hunger, rose
   suddenly together. I heard them say: 60

'Father, it would give us much less pain
   if you ate us: it was you who put upon us
   this sorry flesh; now strip it off again.'   63

I calmed myself to spare them. Ah! hard earth,
   why did you not yawn open? All that day
   and the next we sat in silence. On the fourth,   66

Gaddo, the eldest, fell before me and cried,
   stretched at my feet upon that prison floor:
   'Father, why don't you help me?' There he died.   69

And just as you see me, I saw them fall
   one by one on the fifth day and the sixth.
   Then, already blind, I began to crawl   72

from body to body shaking them frantically.
   Two days I called their names, and they were
      dead.
   Then fasting overcame my grief and me."   75

---

22 *coop:* Dante uses the word *muda,* in Italian signifying a stone tower in which falcons were kept in the dark to moult. From the time of Ugolino's death it became known as the Tower of Hunger.

25 *several waning moons:* Ugolino was jailed late in 1288. He was sealed in to starve early in 1289.

28 *This beast:* Ruggieri.

29–30 *the mountain that hides Lucca from Pisa:* These two cities would be in view of one another were it not for Monte San Giuliano.

32 *Gualandi and Sismondi and Lanfranchi:* (Gwah-LAHN-dee...Lahn-FRAHN-kee) Three Pisan nobles, Ghibellines and friends of the Archbishop.

38 *my sons:* Actually two of the boys were grandsons and all were considerably older than one would gather from Dante's account. Anselm, the younger grandson, was fifteen. The others were really young men and were certainly old enough for guilt despite Dante's charge in line 90.

---

75 *Then fasting overcame my grief and me:* i.e., He died. Some interpret the line to mean that Ugolino's hunger drove him to

His eyes narrowed to slits when he was done,
  and he seized the skull again between his teeth
  grinding it as a mastiff grinds a bone.   78

Ah, Pisa! foulest blemish on the land
  where "si" sounds sweet and clear, since those
      nearby you
  are slow to blast the ground on which you stand,
                                                             81

may Caprara and Gorgona drift from place
  and dam the flooding Arno at its mouth
  until it drowns the last of your foul race!   84

For if to Ugolino falls the censure
  for having betrayed your castles, you for your part
  should not have put his sons to such a torture: 87

you modern Thebes! those tender lives you spilt—
  Brigata, Uguccione, and the others
  I mentioned earlier—were too young for guilt!   90

We passed on further, where the frozen mine
  entombs another crew in greater pain;
  these wraiths are not bent over, but lie supine.   93

Their very weeping closes up their eyes;
  and the grief that finds no outlet for its tears
  turns inward to increase their agonies: 96

for the first tears that they shed knot instantly
  in their eye-sockets, and as they freeze they form
  a crystal visor above the cavity.   99

And despite the fact that standing in that place
  I had become as numb as any callus,
  and all sensation had faded from my face,   102

somehow I felt a wind begin to blow,
  whereat I said: "Master, what stirs this wind?
  Is not all heat extinguished here below?"   105

And the Master said to me: "Soon you will be
  where your own eyes will see the source and cause
  and give you their own answer to the mystery."   108

And one of those locked in that icy mall
  cried out to us as we passed: "O souls so cruel
  that you are sent to the last post of all,   111

relieve me for a little from the pain
  of this hard veil; let my heart weep a while
  before the weeping freeze my eyes again."   114

And I to him: "If you would have my service,
  tell me your name; then if I do not help you
  may I descend to the last rim of the ice."   117

"I am Friar Alberigo," he answered therefore,
  "the same who called for the fruits from the bad
      garden.
  Here I am given dates for figs full store."   120

"What! Are you dead already?" I said to him.
  And he then: "How my body stands in the world
  I do not know. So privileged is this rim   123

---

cannibalism. Ugolino's present occupation in Hell would certainly support that interpretation but the fact is that cannibalism
is the one major sin Dante does not assign a place to in Hell. So
monstrous would it have seemed to him that he must certainly
have established a special punishment for it. Certainly he could
hardly have relegated it to an ambiguity. Moreover, it would be a
sin of bestiality rather than of fraud, and as such it would be
punished in the Seventh Circle.

79–80*the land where "si" sounds sweet and clear:* Italy.

82*Caprara and Gorgona:* These two islands near the mouth of the
Arno were Pisan possessions in 1300.

86*betrayed your castles:* In 1284, Ugolino gave up certain castles to
Lucca and Florence. He was at war with Genoa at the time and it
is quite likely that he ceded the castles to buy the neutrality of
these two cities, for they were technically allied with Genoa.
Dante, however, must certainly consider the action as treasonable, for otherwise Ugolino would be in Caïna for his treachery to
Visconti.

88*you modern Thebes:* Thebes, as a number of the foregoing notes
will already have made clear, was the site of some of the most
hideous crimes of antiquity.

91*we passed on further:* Marks the passage into Ptolomea.

105*Is not all heat extinguished:* Dante believed (rather accurately,
by chance) that all winds resulted from "exhalations of heat."
Cocytus, however, is conceived as wholly devoid of heat, a
metaphysical absolute zero. The source of the wind, as we discover in the next Canto, is Satan himself.

117*may I descend to the last rim of the ice:* Dante is not taking any
chances; he has to go on to the last rim in any case. The sinner,
however, believes him to be another damned soul and would
interpret the oath quite otherwise than as Dante meant it.

118*Friar Alberigo:* (Ahl-beh-REE-ghoe) Of the Manfredi of Faenza.
He was another Jovial Friar. In 1284 his brother Manfred struck
him in the course of an argument. Alberigo pretended to let it
pass, but in 1285 he invited Manfred and his son to a banquet
and had them murdered. The signal of the assassins was the
words: "Bring in the fruit." "Friar Alberigo's bad fruit" became
a proverbial saying.

of Ptolomea, that often souls fall to it
    before dark Atropos has cut their thread.
    And that you may more willingly free my spirit   126

of this glaze of frozen tears that shrouds my face,
    I will tell you this: when a soul betrays as I did,
    it falls from flesh, and a demon takes its place,   129

ruling the body till its time is spent.
    The ruined soul rains down into this cistern.
    So, I believe, there is still evident   132

in the world above, all that is fair and mortal
    of this black shade who winters here behind me.
    If you have only recently crossed the portal   135

from that sweet world, you surely must have known
    his body: Branca D'Oria is its name,
    and many years have passed since he rained
        down."   138

"I think you are trying to take me in," I said,
    "Ser Branca D'Oria is a living man;
    he eats, he drinks, he fills his clothes and his
        bed."   141

"Michel Zanche had not yet reached the ditch
    of the Black Talons," the frozen wraith replied,
    "there where the sinners thicken in hot pitch,   144

when this one left his body to a devil,
    as did his nephew and second in treachery,
    and plumbed like lead through space to this dead
        level.   147

But now reach out your hand, and let me cry."
    And I did not keep the promise I had made,
    for to be rude to him was courtesy.   150

Ah, men of Genoa! souls of little worth,
    corrupted from all custom of righteousness,
    why have you not been driven from the earth?   153

For there beside the blackest soul of all
    Romagna's evil plain, lies one of yours
    bathing his filthy soul in the eternal   156

glacier of Cocytus for his foul crime,
    while he seems yet alive in world and time!   158

Canto XXXIV

*Circle Nine
Cocytus: Compound Fraud
Round Four
Judecca: The Treacherous to Their Masters
The Center
Satan*

"On march the banners of the King," Virgil begins as the Poets face the last depth. He is quoting a medieval hymn, and to it he adds the distortion and perversion of all that lies about him. "On march the banners of the King—of Hell." And there before them, in an infernal parody of Godhead, they see SATAN *in the distance, his great wings beating like a windmill. It is their beating that is the source of the icy wind of Cocytus, the exhalation of all evil.*

All about him in the ice are strewn the sinners of the last round, Judecca, *named for Judas Iscariot. These are the* TREACHEROUS TO THEIR MASTERS. *They lie completely sealed in the ice, twisted and distorted into every conceivable posture. It is impossible to speak to them, and the Poets move on to observe Satan.*

He is fixed into the ice at the center to which flow all the rivers of guilt; and as he beats his great wings as if to escape, their icy wind only freezes him more surely into the polluted ice. In a grotesque parody of the Trinity, he has three faces, each a different color, and in each mouth he clamps a sinner whom he rips eternally with his teeth. JUDAS ISCARIOT *is in the central mouth:* BRUTUS *and* CASSIUS *in the mouths on either side.*

Having seen all, the Poets now climb through the center, grappling hand over hand down the hairy flank of Satan himself—a last supremely symbolic action—and at last, when they have passed the center of all gravity, they emerge from Hell. A long climb from the earth's center to the Mount of Purgatory awaits them, and they push on without rest, ascending along the sides of the river Lethe, till they emerge once more to see the stars of Heaven, just before dawn on Easter Sunday.

"On march the banners of the King of Hell,"
    my Master said. "Toward us. Look straight ahead:
    can you make him out at the core of the frozen
        shell?"   3

---

125 *Atropos:* The Fate who cuts the thread of life.
137 *Branca d'Oria:* (DAW-ree-yah) A Genoese Ghibelline. His sin is identical in kind to that of Friar Alberigo. In 1275 he invited his father-in-law, Michel Zanche (see Canto XXII), to a banquet and had him and his companions cut to pieces. He was assisted in the butchery by his nephew.

---

1 *On march the banners of the King:* The hymn (*Vexilla regis prodeunt*) was written in the sixth century by Venantius Fortunatus, Bishop of Poitiers. The original celebrates the Holy Cross, and is part of the service for Good Friday to be sung at the moment of uncovering the cross.

Like a whirling windmill seen afar at twilight,
   or when a mist has risen from the ground—
   just such an engine rose upon my sight   6

stirring up such a wild and bitter wind
   I cowered for shelter at my Master's back,
   there being no other windbreak I could find.   9

I stood now where the souls of the last class
   (with fear my verses tell it) were covered wholly;
   they shone below the ice like straws in glass.   12

Some lie stretched out; others are fixed in place
   upright, some on their heads, some on their soles;
   another, like a bow, bends foot to face.   15

When we had gone so far across the ice
   that it pleased my Guide to show me the foul
      creature
   which once had worn the grace of Paradise,   18

he made me stop, and, stepping aside, he said:
   "Now see the face of Dis! This is the place
   where you must arm your soul against all dread."
                        21

Do not ask, Reader, how my blood ran cold
   and my voice choked up with fear. I cannot write
      it:
   this is a terror that cannot be told.   24

I did not die, and yet I lost life's breath:
   imagine for yourself what I became,
   deprived at once of both my life and death.   27

The Emperor of the Universe of Pain
   jutted his upper chest above the ice;
   and I am closer in size to the great mountain   30

the Titans make around the central pit,
   than they to his arms. Now, starting from this
      part,
   imagine the whole that corresponds to it!   33

If he was once as beautiful as now
   he is hideous, and still turned on his Maker,
   well may he be the source of every woe!   36

With what a sense of awe I saw his head
   towering above me! for it had three faces:
   one was in front, and it was fiery red;   39

the other two, as weirdly wonderful,
   merged with it from the middle of each shoulder
   to the point where all converged at the top of the
      skull;   42

the right was something between white and bile;
   the left was about the color that one finds
   on those who live along the banks of the Nile.   45

Under each head two wings rose terribly,
   their span proportioned to so gross a bird:
   I never saw such sails upon the sea.   48

They were not feathers—their texture and their form
   were like a bat's wings—and he beat them so
   that three winds blew from him in one great
      storm: 51

it is these winds that freeze all Cocytus.
   He wept from his six eyes, and down three chins
   the tears ran mixed with bloody froth and pus.   54

In every mouth he worked a broken sinner
   between his rake-like teeth. Thus he kept three
   in eternal pain at his eternal dinner.   57

For the one in front the biting seemed to play
   no part at all compared to the ripping: at times
   the whole skin of his back was flayed away.   60

"That soul that suffers most," explained my Guide,
   "is Judas Iscariot, he who kicks his legs
   on the fiery chin and has his head inside.   63

Of the other two, who have their heads thrust
      forward,
   the one who dangles down from the black face
   is Brutus: note how he writhes without a word.   66

---

[38] *three faces:* Numerous interpretations of these three faces exist. What is essential to all explanation is that they be seen as perversions of the qualities of the Trinity.

[54] *bloody froth and pus:* The gore of the sinners he chews which is mixed with his slaver.

[62] *Judas Iscariot:* Note how closely his punishment is patterned on that of the Simoniacs (Canto XIX).

---

[17] *the foul creature:* Satan.

And there, with the huge and sinewy arms, is the
    soul
    of Cassius.—But the night is coming on
    and we must go, for we have seen the whole."   69

Then, as he bade, I clasped his neck, and he,
    watching for a moment when the wings
    were opened wide, reached over dexterously   72

and seized the shaggy coat of the king demon;
    then grappling matted hair and frozen crusts
    from one tuft to another, clambered down.   75

When we had reached the joint where the great
    thigh
    merges into the swelling of the haunch,
    my Guide and Master, straining terribly,   78

turned his head to where his feet had been
    and began to grip the hair as if he were climbing;
    so that I thought we moved toward Hell again.   81

"Hold fast!" my Guide said, and his breath came
    shrill
    with labor and exhaustion. "There is no way
    but by such stairs to rise above such evil."   84

At last he climbed out through an opening
    in the central rock, and he seated me on the rim;
    then joined me with a nimble backward spring.   87

I looked up, thinking to see Lucifer
    as I had left him, and I saw instead
    his legs projecting high into the air.   90

Now let all those whose dull minds are still vexed
    by failure to understand what point it was
    I had passed through, judge if I was perplexed.   93

"Get up. Up on your feet," my Master said.
    "The sun already mounts to middle tierce,
    and a long road and hard climbing lie ahead."   96

It was no hall of state we had found there,
    but a natural animal pit hollowed from rock
    with a broken floor and a close and sunless air.   99

"Before I tear myself from the Abyss,"
    I said when I had risen, "O my Master,
    explain to me my error in all this: 102

where is the ice? and Lucifer—how has he
    been turned from top to bottom: and how can the
    sun
    have gone from night to day so suddenly?"   105

And he to me: "You imagine you are still
    on the other side of the center where I grasped
    the shaggy flank of the Great Worm of Evil   108

which bores through the world—you *were* while I
    climbed down,
    but when I turned myself about, you passed
    the point to which all gravities are drawn.   111

You are under the other hemisphere where you
    stand;
    the sky above us is the half opposed
    to that which canopies the great dry land.   114

Under the midpoint of that other sky
    the Man who was born sinless and who lived
    beyond all blemish, came to suffer and die.   117

You have your feet upon a little sphere
    which forms the other face of the Judecca.
    There it is evening when it is morning here.   120

And this gross Fiend and Image of all Evil
    who made a stairway for us with his hide
    is pinched and prisoned in the ice-pack still.   123

On this side he plunged down from heaven's height,
    and the land that spread here once hid in the sea
    and fled North to our hemisphere for fright;   126

---

[67] *huge and sinewy arms:* The Cassius who betrayed Caesar was
more generally described in terms of Shakespeare's "lean and
hungry look." Another Cassius is described by Cicero (*Catiline*
III) as huge and sinewy. Dante probably confused the two.

[68] *the night is coming on:* It is now Saturday evening.

[82] *his breath came shrill:* Cf. Canto XXIII, 85, where the fact that
Dante breathes indicates to the Hypocrites that he is alive. Virgil's
breathing is certainly a contradiction.

---

[95] *middle tierce:* In the canonical day tierce is the period from about
six to nine A.M. Middle tierce, therefore, is seven-thirty. In going
through the center point, they have gone from night to day. They
have moved ahead twelve hours.

and it may be that moved by that same fear,
the one peak that still rises on this side
fled upward leaving this great cavern here.   129

Down there, beginning at the further bound
of Beelzebub's dim tomb, there is a space
not known by sight, but only by the sound   132

of a little stream descending through the hollow
it has eroded from the massive stone
in its endlessly entwining lazy flow."   135

My Guide and I crossed over and began
to mount that little known and lightless road
to ascend into the shining world again.   138

He first, I second, without thought of rest
we climbed the dark until we reached the point
where a round opening brought in sight the blest   141

and beauteous shining of the Heavenly cars.
And we walked out once more beneath the Stars.   143

FROM THE *Purgatorio*

(Dante and Virgil have climbed the mountain.)

Canto XXX

The Earthly Paradise: Beatrice
Virgil Vanishes

The procession halts and the Prophets turn to the chariot and sing "Come, my bride, from Lebanon." They are summoning BEATRICE, *who appears on the left side of the chariot, half-hidden from view by showers of blossoms poured from above by a* HUNDRED ANGELS. *Dante, stirred by the sight, turns to Virgil to express his overflowing emotions, and discovers that* Virgil has Vanished.

128*the one peak:* The Mount of Purgatory.

129*this great cavern:* The natural animal pit of line 98. It is also "Beelzebub's dim tomb," line 131.

133*a little stream:* Lethe. In classical mythology, the river of forgetfulness, from which souls drank before being born. In Dante's symbolism it flows down from Purgatory, where it washes away the memory of sin from the souls that are undergoing purification. That memory it delivers to Hell, which draws all sin to itself.

143*Stars:* As part of his total symbolism Dante ends each of the three divisions of the *Commedia* with this word. Every conclusion of the upward soul is toward the stars, God's shining symbols of hope and virtue. It is just before dawn of Easter Sunday that the Poets emerge—a further symbolism.

Because he bursts into tears at losing Virgil Dante is reprimanded by Beatrice. The Angel Choir overhead immediately breaks into a Psalm of Compassion, but Beatrice, still severe, answers by detailing Dante's offenses in not making proper use of his great gifts. It would violate the ordering of the Divine Decree, she argues, to let Dante drink the waters of Lethe, thereby washing all memory of sin from his soul, before he had shed the tears of a real repentance.

When the Septentrion of the First Heaven,
which does not rise nor set, and which has never
been veiled from sight by any mist but sin,   3

and which made every soul in that high court
know its true course (just as the lower Seven
direct the helmsman to his earthly port),   6

had stopped; the holy prophets, who till then
had walked between the Griffon and those lights,
turned to the car like souls who cry "Amen."   9

And one among them who seemed sent from Heaven
clarioned: "*Veni, sponsa, de Libano,*"
three times, with all the others joining in.   12

As, at the last trump every saint shall rise
out of the grave, ready with voice new-fleshed
to carol *Alleluiah* to the skies;   15

just so, above the chariot, at the voice
of such an elder, rose a hundred Powers
and Principals of the Eternal Joys,   18

1*the Septentrion of the First Heaven:* The Septentrion is the seven stars of the Big Dipper. Here Dante means the seven candelabra. They are the Septentrion of the First Heaven (the Empyrean) as distinct from the seven stars of the dipper which occur lower down in the Sphere of the Fixed Stars.

2*which does not rise nor set:* The North Star does not rise or set north of the equator, but the Septentrion, revolving around the North Star, does go below the horizon in the lower latitudes. This Septentrion of the First Heaven, however, partaking of the perfection and constancy of Heaven, neither rises nor sets but is a constant light to mankind. So these unchanging lights guide the souls of man on high, as the "lower Seven" (line 5), in their less perfect way, guide the earthly helmsmen to their earthly ports.

7*the holy prophets:* The twenty-four elders who represent the books of the Old Testament.

10*one among them:* The Song of Solomon.

11*Veni, sponsa, de Libano:* "Come [with me] from Lebanon, my spouse." (*Song of Solomon*, iv, 8.) This cry, re-echoed by choirs of angels, summons Beatrice, who may be taken here as revelation, faith, divine love, hence as the bride of the spirit, to Dante (man's redeemed soul).

17–18*a hundred Powers and Principals:* Angels.

all saying together: "*Benedictus qui venis*";
   then, scattering flowers about on every side:
   "*Manibus o date lilia plenis.*" 21

Time and again at daybreak I have seen
   the eastern sky glow with a wash of rose
   while all the rest hung limpid and serene, 24

and the Sun's face rise tempered from its rest
   so veiled by vapors that the naked eye
   could look at it for minutes undistressed. 27

Exactly so, within a cloud of flowers
   that rose like fountains from the angels' hands
   and fell about the chariot in showers, 30

a lady came in view: an olive crown
   wreathed her immaculate veil, her cloak was
      green,
   the colors of live flame played on her gown. 33

My soul—such years had passed since last it saw
   that lady and stood trembling in her presence,
   stupefied by the power of holy awe— 36

now, by some power that shone from her above
   the reach and witness of my mortal eyes,
   felt the full mastery of enduring love. 39

The instant I was smitten by the force,
   which had already once transfixed my soul
   before my boyhood years had run their course, 42

I turned left with the same assured belief
   that makes a child run to its mother's arms
   when it is frightened or has come to grief, 45

to say to Virgil: "There is not within me
   one drop of blood unstirred. I recognize
   the tokens of the ancient flame." But he, 48

he had taken his light from us. He had gone.
   Virgil had gone. Virgil, the gentle Father
   to whom I gave my soul for its salvation! 51

Not all that sight of Eden lost to view
   by our First Mother could hold back the tears
   that stained my cheeks so lately washed with dew. 54

"Dante, do not weep yet, though Virgil goes.
   Do not weep yet, for soon another wound
   shall make you weep far hotter tears than those!" 57

As an admiral takes his place at stern or bow
   to observe the handling of his other ships
   and spur all hands to do their best—so now, 60

on the chariot's left side, I saw appear
   when I turned at the sound of my own name
   (which, necessarily, is recorded here), 63

that lady who had been half-veiled from view
   by the flowers of the angel-revels. Now her eyes
   fixed me across the stream, piercing me through. 66

And though the veil she still wore, held in place
   by the wreathed flowers of wise Minerva's leaves,
   let me see only glimpses of her face, 69

---

[19]*Benedictus qui venis:* "Blessed is he who cometh." (*Matthew*, xxi, 9.)

[21]*Manibus o date lilia plenis:* "Oh, give lilies with full hands." These are the words of Anchises in honor of Marcellus. (*Aeneid*, VI, 883.) Thus they are not only apt to the occasion but their choice is a sweetly conceived last literary compliment to Virgil before he vanishes.

[31]*a lady:* Beatrice. She is dressed in the colors of Faith (white), Hope (green), and Charity (red).

[34]*since last it saw:* Beatrice died in 1290. Thus Dante has passed ten years without sight of her.

[36]*stupefied:* Dante describes the stupor of his soul at the sight of the living Beatrice in *La Vita Nuova*, XIV and XXIV. Then, however, it was mortal love; here it is eternal, and the effect accordingly greater.

---

[54]*washed with dew:* By Virgil. I, 124.

[55]*Dante:* This is the only point in the *Commedia* at which Dante mentions his own name. Its usage here suggests many allegorical possibilities. Central to all of them, however, must be the fact that Dante, in ending one life (of the mind) and beginning a new one (of faith) hears his name. The suggestion of a second baptism is inevitable. And just as a child being baptized is struck by the priest, so Beatrice is about to strike him with her tongue before he may proceed to the holy water.

[64]*that lady:* There are thirty-four Cantos in the *Inferno* and this is the thirtieth of the *Purgatorio*, hence the sixty-fourth Canto of the *Commedia*. This is the sixty-fourth line of the sixty-fourth Canto. In Dante's numerology such correspondences are always meaningful. Six plus four equals ten and ten equals the sum of the square of trinity and unity. Obviously there can be no conclusive way of establishing intent in such a structure of mystic numbering, but it certainly is worth noting that the line begins with "that lady." The Italian text, in fact, begins with *vidi la donna*, i.e., I saw the lady (who represents the sum of the square of trinity plus unity?). The lady, of course, is Beatrice.

[68]*wise Minerva's leaves:* The olive crown.

her stern and regal bearing made me dread
   her next words, for she spoke as one who saves
   the heaviest charge till all the rest are read.   72

"Look at me well. I am she. I am Beatrice.
   How dared you make your way to this high
      mountain?
   Did you not know that here man lives in bliss?"   75

I lowered my head and looked down at the stream.
   But when I saw myself reflected there,
   I fixed my eyes upon the grass for shame.   78

I shrank as a wayward child in his distress
   shrinks from his mother's sternness, for the taste
   of love grown wrathful is a bitterness.   81

She paused. At once the angel chorus sang
   the blessed psalm: "*In te, Domine, speravi.*"
   As far as "*pedes meos*" their voices rang.   84

As on the spine of Italy the snow
   lies frozen hard among the living rafters
   in winter when the northeast tempests blow;   87

then, melting if so much as a breath stir
   from the land of shadowless noon, flows through
      itself
   like hot wax trickling down a lighted taper—   90

just so I froze, too cold for sighs or tears
   until I heard that choir whose notes are tuned
   to the eternal music of the spheres.   93

But when I heard the voice of their compassion
   plead for me more than if they had cried out:
   "Lady, why do you treat him in this fashion?"   96

the ice, which hard about my heart had pressed,
   turned into breath and water, and flowed out
   through eyes and throat in anguish from my
      breast.   99

Still standing at the chariot's left side,
   she turned to those compassionate essences
   whose song had sought to move her, and replied: 102

"You keep your vigil in the Eternal Day
   where neither night nor sleep obscures from you
   a single step the world takes on its way;   105

but I must speak with greater care that he
   who weeps on that far bank may understand
   and feel a grief to match his guilt. Not only   108

by the workings of the spheres that bring each seed
   to its fit end according to the stars
   that ride above it, but by gifts decreed   111

in the largesse of overflowing Grace,
   whose rain has such high vapors for its source
   our eyes cannot mount to their dwelling place;   114

this man, potentially, was so endowed
   from eazly youth that marvelous increase
   should have come forth from every good he
      sowed.   117

But richest soil the soonest will grow wild
   with bad seed and neglect. For a while I stayed
      him
   with glimpses of my face. Turning my mild   120

and youthful eyes into his very soul,
   I let him see their shining, and I led him
   by the straight way, his face to the right goal.   123

80*his mother's sternness:* Beatrice appears in the pageant as the figure of the Church Triumphant. The Church is the mother of the devout and though she is stern, as law decrees, her sternness is that of a loving mother.

83–84*In te, Domine, speravi...pedes meos:* In mercy the angel chorus sings Psalm XXXI, 1–8, beginning "In thee, O Lord, do I put my trust" and continuing as far as "thou hast set my feet in a large room."

85–90*the spine of Italy:* The Apennines. *the living rafters:* The trees. *the land of shadowless noon:* Africa. In equatorial regions the noonday sun is at the zenith over each point twice a year. Its rays then fall straight down and objects cast no shadows.

101*compassionate essences:* The Angel chorus.

106*greater care:* For his understanding than for your intercession.

109–111*the working of the spheres:* The influence of the stars in their courses which incline men at birth to good or evil ends according to the astrological virtue of their conjunctions.

114*our eyes:* Beatrice is still replying to the plea of the Angel choir. Hence "our eyes" must refer not to mortal eyes, but to the eyes of the blessed. Not even such more-than-human eyes may mount to the high place of those vapors, for that place is nothing less than the Supreme Height, since Grace flows from God Himself.

The instant I had come upon the sill
  of my second age, and crossed and changed my
    life,
  he left me and let others shape his will.   126

When I rose from the flesh into the spirit,
  to greater beauty and to greater virtue,
  he found less pleasure in me and less merit.   129

He turned his steps aside from the True Way,
  pursuing the false images of good
  that promise what they never wholly pay.   132

Not all the inspiration I won by prayer
  and brought to him in dreams and meditations
  could call him back, so little did he care.   135

He fell so far from every hope of bliss
  that every means of saving him had failed
  except to let him see the damned. For this   138

I visited the portals of the dead
  and poured my tears and prayers before that spirit
  by whom his steps have, up to now, been led.   141

The seal Almighty God's decree has placed
  on the rounds of His creation would be broken
  were he to come past Lethe and to taste   144

the water that wipes out the guilty years
without some scot of penitential tears!"   146

FROM THE *Paradiso*

Canto XXXIII

The Empyrean

St. Bernard
Prayer to the Virgin
The Vision of God

ST. BERNARD *offers a lofty* Prayer to the Virgin, *asking her to intercede in Dante's behalf, and in answer Dante feels his*

---

^{125–126}*my second age . . . will:* When Beatrice had reached the full bloom of young womanhood Dante turned from her and wrote to his *donna gentile.* Allegorically, he turned from divine "sciences" to an overreliance upon philosophy (the human "sciences"). For this sin he must suffer.

¹⁴⁵*were he to come past Lethe:* In passing Lethe and drinking its waters, the soul loses all memory of guilt. This, therefore, is Dante's last opportunity to do penance.

---

soul swell with new power and grow calm in rapture as his eyes are permitted the Direct Vision of God.

    There can be no measure of how long the vision endures. It passes, and Dante is once more mortal and fallible. Raised by God's presence, he had looked into the Mystery and had begun to understand its power and majesty. Returned to himself, there is no power in him capable of speaking the truth of what he saw. Yet the impress of the truth is stamped upon his soul, which he now knows will return to be one with God's Love.

"Virgin Mother, daughter of thy son;
  humble beyond all creatures and more exalted;
  predestined turning point of God's intention;   3

thy merit so ennobled human nature
  that its divine Creator did not scorn
  to make Himself the creature of His creature.   6

The Love that was rekindled in Thy womb
  sends forth the warmth of the eternal peace
  within whose ray this flower has come to bloom. 9

Here, to us, thou art the noon and scope
  of Love revealed; and among mortal men,
  the living fountain of eternal hope.   12

Lady, thou art so near God's reckonings
  that who seeks grace and does not first seek thee
  would have his wish fly upward without wings. 15

Not only does thy sweet benignity
  flow out to all who beg, but oftentimes
  thy charity arrives before the plea.   18

---

^{1–39}ST. BERNARD'S PRAYER TO THE VIRGIN MARY. No reader who has come this far will need a lengthy gloss of Bernard's prayer. It can certainly be taken as a summarizing statement of the special place of Mary in Catholic faith. For the rest only a few turns of phrase need underlining. 3. *predestined turning point of God's intention:* All-foreseeing God built his whole scheme for mankind with Mary as its pivot, for through her He would become man. 7. *The Love that was rekindled in thy womb:* God. In a sense He withdrew from man when Adam and Eve sinned. In Mary He returned and Himself became man. 35. *keep whole the natural bent of his affections:* Bernard is asking Mary to protect Dante lest the intensity of the vision overpower his faculties. 37. *Protect him from the stirrings of man's clay:* Protect him from the stirrings of base human impulse, especially from pride, for Dante is about to receive a grace never before granted to any man and the thought of such glory might well move a mere mortal to an hybris that would turn glory to sinfullness.

In thee is pity, in thee munificence,
   in thee the tenderest heart, in thee unites
   all that creation knows of excellence!   21

Now comes this man who from the final pit
   of the universe up to this height has seen,
   one by one, the three lives of the spirit.   24

He prays to thee in fervent supplication
   for grace and strength, that he may raise his eyes
   to the all-healing final revelation.   27

And I, who never more desired to see
   the vision myself than I do that he may see It,
   add my own prayer, and pray that it may be   30

enough to move you to dispel the trace
   of every mortal shadow by thy prayers
   and let him see revealed the Sum of Grace.   33

I pray thee further, all-persuading Queen,
   keep whole the natural bent of his affections
   and of his powers after his eyes have seen.   36

Protect him from the stirrings of man's clay;
   see how Beatrice and the blessed host
   clasp reverent hands to join me as I pray."   39

The eyes that God reveres and loves the best
   glowed on the speaker, making clear the joy
   with which true prayer is heard by the most blest.   42

Those eyes turned then to the Eternal Ray,
   through which, we must indeed believe, the eyes
   of others do not find such ready way.   45

And I, who neared the goal of all my nature,
   felt my soul, at the climax of its yearning,
   suddenly, as it ought, grow calm with rapture.   48

Bernard then, smiling sweetly, gestured to me
   to look up, but I had already become
   within myself all he would have me be.   51

---

40 *The eyes:* Of Mary.

50 *but I had already become:* i.e., "But I had already fixed my entire attention upon the vision of God." But if so, how could Dante have seen Bernard's smile and gesture? Eager students like to believe they catch Dante in a contradiction here. Let them bear in mind that Dante is looking directly at God, as do the souls of Heaven, who thereby acquire—insofar as they are able to contain it—God's own knowledge. As a first stirring of that heavenly power, therefore, Dante is sharing God's knowledge of St. Bernard.

Little by little as my vision grew
   it penetrated further through the aura
   of the high lamp which in Itself is true.   54

What then I saw is more than tongue can say.
   Our human speech is dark before the vision.
   The ravished memory swoons and falls away.   57

As one who sees in dreams and wakes to find
   the emotional impression of his vision
   still powerful while its parts fade from his mind—   60

just such am I, having lost nearly all
   the vision itself, while in my heart I feel
   the sweetness of it yet distill and fall.   63

So, in the sun, the footprints fade from snow.
   On the wild wind that bore the tumbling leaves
   the Sybil's oracles were scattered so.   66

O Light Supreme who doth Thyself withdraw
   so far above man's mortal understanding,
   lend me again some glimpse of what I saw;   69

make Thou my tongue so eloquent it may
   of all Thy glory speak a single clue
   to those who follow me in the world's day;   72

for by returning to my memory
   somewhat, and somewhat sounding in these verses,
   Thou shalt show man more of Thy victory.   75

So dazzling was the splendor of that Ray,
   that I must certainly have lost my senses
   had I, but for an instant, turned away.   78

---

54 *which in Itself is true:* The light of God is the one light whose source is Itself. All others are a reflection of this.

65—66 *tumbling leaves...oracles:* The Cumean Sybil (Virgil describes her in *Aeneid,* III, 441 ff.) wrote her oracles on leaves, one letter to a leaf, then sent her message scattering on the wind. Presumably, the truth was all contained in that strew, could one only gather all the leaves and put the letters in the right order.

76—81 How can a light be so dazzling that the beholder would swoon if he looked away for an instant? Would it not be, rather, in looking at, not away from, the overpowering vision that the viewer's senses would be overcome? So it would be on earth. But now Dante, with the help of all heaven's prayers, is in the presence of God and strengthened by all he sees. It is by being so strengthened that he can see yet more. So the passage becomes a parable of grace. Stylistically it once more illustrates Dante's genius: even at this height of concept, the poet can still summon and invent new perceptions, subtlety exfoliating from subtlety.

And so it was, as I recall, I could
    the better bear to look, until at last
    my vision made one with the Eternal Good.   81

Oh grace abounding that had made me fit
    to fix my eyes on the eternal light
    until my vision was consumed in it!   84

I saw within Its depth how It conceives
    all things in a single volume bound by Love,
    of which the universe is the scattered leaves;   87

substance, accident, and their relation
    so fused that all I say could do no more
    than yield a glimpse of that bright revelation.   90

I think I saw the universal form
    that binds these things, for as I speak these words
    I feel my joy swell and my spirits warm.   93

Twenty-five centuries since Neptune saw
    the Argo's keel have not moved all mankind,
    recalling that adventure, to such awe   96

as I felt in an instant. My tranced being
    stared fixed and motionless upon that vision,
    ever more fervent to see in the act of seeing.   99

Experiencing that Radiance, the spirit
    is so indrawn it is impossible
    even to think of ever turning from It.   102

For the good which is the will's ultimate object
    is all subsumed in It; and, being removed,
    all is defective which in It is perfect.   105

Now in my recollection of the rest
    I have less power to speak than any infant
    wetting its tongue yet at its mother's breast;   108

and not because that Living Radiance bore
    more than one semblance, for It is unchanging
    and is forever as it was before;   111

rather, as I grew worthier to see,
    the more I looked, the more unchanging
      semblance
    appeared to change with every change in me.   114

Within the depthless deep and clear existence
    of that abyss of light three circles shown—
    three in color, one in circumference: 117

the second from the first, rainbow from rainbow;
    the third, an exhalation of pure fire
    equally breathed forth by the other two.   120

But oh how much my words miss my conception,
    which is itself so far from what I saw
    that to call it feeble would be rank deception!   123

O Light Eternal fixed in Itself alone,
    by Itself alone understood, which from Itself
    loves and glows, self-knowing and self-known;   126

that second aureole which shone forth in Thee,
    conceived as a reflection of the first—
    or which appeared so to my scrutiny—   129

seemed in Itself of Its own coloration
    to be painted with man's image. I fixed my eyes
    on that alone in rapturous contemplation.   132

109–114In the presence of God the soul grows ever more capable of perceiving God. Thus, the worthy soul's experience of God is a constant expansion of awareness. God appears to change as He is better seen. Being perfect, He is changeless within himself, for any change would be away from perfection.

130–144The central metaphor of the entire *Comedy* is the image of God and the final triumphant inGodding of the elected soul returning to its Maker. On the mystery of that image, the metaphoric symphony of the *Comedy* comes to rest.

In the second aspect of Trinal-unity, in the circle reflected from the first, Dante thinks he sees the image of mankind woven into the very substance and coloration of God. He turns the entire attention of his soul to that mystery, as a geometer might seek to shut out every other thought and dedicate himself to squaring the circle. In *Il Convivio*, II, 14, Dante asserted that the circle could not be squared, but that impossibility had not yet been firmly demonstrated in Dante's time and mathematicians still worked at the problem. Note, however, that Dante assumes the impossibility of squaring the circle as a weak mortal example of mortal impossibility. How much more impossible, he implies, to resolve the mystery of God, study as man will.

    The simultaneous metaphoric statement, of course, is that no man can lose his good in the vision of God, but only in looking away from it.

85–87The idea here is Platonic: the essence of all things (form) exists in the mind of God. All other things exist as exempla.

88*substance:* Matter, all that exists in itself. *accident:* All that exists as a phase of matter.

92*these things:* Substance and accident.

Like a geometer wholly dedicated
    to squaring the circle, but who cannot find,
    think as he may, the principle indicated—   135

so did I study the supernal face.
    I yearned to know just how our image merges
    into that circle, and how it there finds place;   138

but mine were not the wings for such a flight.
    Yet, as I wished, the truth I wished for came
    cleaving my mind in a great flash of light.   141

Here my powers rest from their high fantasy,
    but already I could feel my being turned—
    instinct and intellect balanced equally   144

as in a wheel whose motion nothing jars—
by the Love that moves the Sun and the other stars.

COMMENTS AND QUESTIONS

1. Describe the ordering of sins in Dante's vision of hell. How does this fit with your own religious or moral beliefs?

2. How does the law of *contrapasso* (retribution) work in the punishment of each sin?

3. Describe the portrayals of Virgil and of Beatrice, and Dante's relationship with them. Do they seem real as well as allegorical?

4. Compare the story of Paolo and Francesca (canto V of the *Inferno*) to Marie de France's *Equitan*. What seems to be Dante's attitude toward "courtly love"? How can Dante fall into a swoon out of sympathy for Francesca and still judge the lovers to be deserving of hell? Does he show this double attitude elsewhere?

5. Primo Levi, an Italian writer deported to Auschwitz during the Second World War, found that one means of survival was reciting the canto of Ulysses (*Inferno* XXVI) from memory (see Chapter 34). Do you see any relationship?

6. Describe Dante's portrayal of the depths of hell. Why is it made of ice rather than fire?

7. Describe the reunion of Dante and Beatrice. What understanding of love is communicated by each of them?

8. Give examples of the imagery Dante uses in the *Inferno* and that used in the *Paradiso*. Is Dante successful in the latter in portraying a mystical experience?

9. What points in common are there between Dante's visit to the "other world" and the visits of Gilgamesh, Odysseus, and Aeneas? What differences?

The mystery remains beyond Dante's mortal power. Yet, there in Heaven, in a moment of grace, God revealed the truth to him in a flash of light—revealed it, that is, to the God-enlarged power of Dante's emparadised soul. On Dante's return to the mortal life, the details of that revelation vanished from his mind but the force of the revelation survives in its power on Dante's feelings.

So ends the vision of the *Comedy*, and yet the vision endures, for ever since that revelation, Dante tells us, he feels his soul turning ever as one with the perfect motion of God's love.

Medieval Cultures

Intellectual Life and Religion

All three religions, Judaism, Christianity, and Islam, shared many of the same theological problems. If God is all-powerful, for example, how is the believer to understand the existence of evil in this world? Do people possess free will or is their destiny determined by God? In exploring such questions posed regarding their faith, all three medieval cultures, that of Islam, Byzantium, and western Europe, sought answers in Greek and Roman philosophical writings. Although many Muslim religious scholars rejected a rational approach to such questions, their explorations did serve to preserve the manuscripts for the benefit of western Europe. Generally more receptive to Greco-Roman philosophy, the Byzantines likewise played a crucial role in transmitting ancient philosophy to the Europeans.

Spiritual and Temporal Power

The Middle Ages witnessed the growth of two spheres of allegiance for every western European, the spiritual and the temporal. In his great synthesis of medieval thought, Dante outlined the proper sphere of each.

In the twelfth and thirteenth centuries, our focus of attention here, the Church claimed the right to act as the conscience of Christian rulers and their subjects, to determine proper Christian belief, and to judge offenses against the faith. While allowing discussion within broad limits, the Church permitted no questioning of basic doctrines. As it was, few had any desire to do so. Temporal rulers were advised not to interfere in matters of belief and morals and to support the judgment of the spiritual authority in such cases.

By the end of the thirteenth century, Church efforts to intervene in secular matters became so frequent that some thinkers reacted by insisting that the Church's domain was limited to religion proper and that civil morality, the dealings of people with one another, was in the control of secular rulers. Underly-ing this distinction was a new, more positive view of human existence on earth. Dante even dared speak of a "terrestrial beatitude."

This kind of distinction between spiritual and temporal was never clearly established in either Byzantine or medieval Islamic culture. The general subjection of the patriarch of Constantinople to the emperor prevented the former from clearly carving out a sphere of jurisdiction for himself into which the emperor could not intrude. In Islam, as in Judaism, religious law was so specific that it pervaded, at least in theory, most aspects of human life. Secular concerns certainly existed, but the dominance of the religious was at least rarely questioned in public.

In western Europe, moreover, recognition of a certain area of consciousness as off limits to temporal powers survived in later centuries, even after the Reformation, when religious authorities were no longer able to exercise close control over it. In the eighteenth and nineteenth centuries, thinkers came to define this spiritual sphere as within the province of the individual conscience and independent of the constraints of government action. Although the Reformation itself had, as we will see, a great deal of influence on this evolution, the origins of this demand for freedom of individual conscience really lie with the Church's medieval struggle to demarcate its sphere of authority.

Monarchy and the Modern State

By the twelfth and thirteenth centuries a new form of temporal power, the medieval monarchy, had developed; it was to serve as the basis for our modern state. There were essentially two kinds of states in the ancient period—the small, tightly knit city-state and the sprawling empire that controlled a variety of separate peoples by means of a relatively small elite. To expand as the city-states Athens and Rome had done was to become an empire, because the city-state had no means of integrating the new populations into its intensive political life. Thus it had to govern subject peoples with a corps of officials sent out from the mother city.

To the end of its existence the Byzantine state remained closely tied to the ancient Roman imperial ideal and the model of the autocratic Christian emperor represented by Constantine. While also an empire, medieval Islam was never able to establish a lasting form of government for its vast territories. The authority of the caliph as the ruler of the Muslim world was undermined by the vast extent of the realm and by the power of the military. The caliph became no more than a symbol of Muslim unity, whereas military commanders assumed the title of sultan, a term resonating with connotations of armed force.

The medieval European monarchy, on the other hand, was both larger than the city-state and more cohesive than the empire. Closely tied to the rise of the monarch's power was the development of representative institutions both at the local level and at the center, ultimately making subjects feel part of a greater whole. When a new area was incorporated into the country, *its* population too became involved in the political processes, and a sense of common identity arose. Using this sense of identity, the monarch could mobilize a far greater population than could the rulers of the city-state, demanding a greater degree of loyalty from them than could the emperor. In the centuries since the Middle Ages the supreme executive has become at least nominally an elected official; the European medieval monarchy with its representative element has served as the ancestor for the modern state adopted throughout the world.

Germanic Contributions

We have not emphasized the Germanic or "barbarian" contributions to our cultural roots, but we have at least mentioned their importance in the formation of medieval western European civilization. The personal sense of loyalty to the lord and the lord's responsibility to his people were essential ingredients in the rise of the medieval monarchy. The ruler could expect obedience, but the follower would normally be consulted in the decision-making process. Together with principles of Roman law, Germanic custom limited the ruler's freedom of action and encouraged cooperation with larger and larger groups of subjects in order to extend the operations and influence of the state.

Spiritual Centers

The great Byzantine churches, the Islamic mosques, and the medieval European cathedrals all represent centers not only of faith and religious ritual but also of the arts. Artisans, painters, craftspeople, builders, and architects worked under the patronage of their respective institutions to create a vocabulary of form and expression that met the needs of their culture and their faith. The contributions most characteristic of Byzantine Christianity are the Greek cross plan in architecture, the gold mosaic, and the icon. A highly formal and symbolic, rather than a naturalistic, style emphasized the predominance of the spiritual over the temporal. In spite of this, veneration of icons, or pictures of Christ or the saints, caused the iconoclasts to feel that believers were too attached to material objects and incited a century-long controversy. Saint Mark's Cathedral in Venice and the astounding mosaics in the churches of Ravenna attest to the influence of Byzantine art in Europe. Like Byzantine art, the literature of Byzantium shows a preference for the symbolic over the realistic. It also evokes another characteristic of this culture: a reverence for the classical Greek past that both reinforced and stood in conflict with the Christian present. Byzantium, it is important to remember, served as the transmitter of classical Greek culture to western Europe.

Like the vast Byzantine churches such as Hagia Sofia, great mosques such as the one in Cordoba, Spain, suggest by the magnificence of their architecture and decoration, along with the use of light, the presence of the world beyond in this one. Two developments characteristic of Islamic architecture—the pointed dome and the pointed arch—contribute to the sense of expansion and infinity. Since Muslim belief has tended to frown on the use of human figures in art, abstract symmetrical patterns drawn from floral, animal, and geometric forms tended to dominate decoration in mosques and palaces. In Europe, these became known as *arabesques*. These forms, along with the intricate Muslim calligraphy, finely woven textiles, ceramics, and other arts, were widely diffused in Europe and influenced European styles. Tales such as those in *The Thousand and One Nights* and other stories and poems of chivalry came to be widely read in Europe. Again, the presence of monuments such as the Great Mosque of Cordoba and the Alhambra palace testify to the impact of Islam on the West.

As the power of the Byzantine Empire waned and the Islamic empire withdrew from Europe, medieval Christianity established a cultural hegemony. Because it was such an important center for medieval life in western Europe, we have focused much attention on the cathedral. We looked at four cultural forms related to it: the schools and the philosophy taught there; the Gothic architecture, sculpture, stained-glass painting, and theory behind them; the music performed at worship services; and the adoration of the Virgin Mary, to whom the cathedrals were dedicated.

The art and thought in and around the cathedral show an extraordinary diversity and creativity and a love of elaboration quite different from the simplicity and restraint of classical art and thought. Three of the great systems of the European Middle Ages—the philosophy of Thomas Aquinas, Chartres Cathedral, and Dante Alighieri's *Divine Comedy*—seem to encompass everything in this world and the next in their province, while organizing each edifice so that the whole is directed toward God. The belief that the sensual and intellectual realms of being can serve as steps into the spiritual realm is at the heart of all three of these systems. This belief also explains the medieval love of *symbolism, allegory,* and suggestion. Modern art forms owe much to their medieval predecessors, both in their use of symbols (that is, the suggestion of "another world" through physical reality) and in their use of form to express feeling. The neoclassicists of the eighteenth century thought the distorted sculptures on medieval cathedrals much inferior to the naturalistic, proportioned Greek and Roman ones. In the twentieth century we are well aware that apparent distortion is one means of expression.

"Gothic" was a disparaging term given by the neoclassicists to medieval architecture. But the nineteenth century rediscovered its beauty to such an extent that the United States, like other Western countries, became dotted with neo-Gothic churches, cathedrals, and university buildings. Today, when most people think of a religious edifice, they think of some form of Gothic style. Our universities, not only those with neo-Gothic architecture, stand as testimonies that the roots in the cathedral schools have flourished.

Medieval and Modern Music and Drama

The vocal and instrumental music composed in the monasteries and cathedral schools was the first truly Western music. Much of it is still used in religious services today; and the great musical elaboration of medieval Europe, *polyphony,* is not only the basis of all modern music but also the distinctive feature identifying Western music from all other forms. While legend labels chant as the gift of God, history records polyphony as a human creation. The drama written along with medieval chant was also the first European drama, emerging within the cathedral at a time when the dramatic form in the Western world was almost dead.

Views of Women

The adoration of the Virgin Mary, a major element in medieval art and life and in Catholicism, has profoundly influenced our society's conception of women. We have seen how the Virgin was represented in twelfth- and thirteenth-century literature and art as a divine mother, an object of the highest form of spiritual love, an intercessor between humanity and God. The portrayal of earthly ladies in the same period, strongly influenced by the cult of the Virgin, and perhaps by Islamic courtly literature, became so etherealized that the lady became a symbol and the lover's feeling for her purely spiritual, or else she became a parody of the Virgin and the lover—an example of the destructiveness of earthly passion. Later centuries, however, took these parodies of swooning lovers worshiping their ladies quite seriously. As life began to imitate art, women became in a sense objects of veneration. To merit this attitude, they were supposed to be pure, chaste, and unattainable, not creatures of flesh and blood. Men developed the idea that women could be placed in two categories: pure (on a pedestal) and "fallen," so corrupted and irresponsible that they had to be controlled by men. We are only now changing the residues of this attitude.

Some of the gestures that stem from the courtly or chivalric tradition—men opening doors for women, holding out chairs for them, paying for their entertainment on dates—are still with us. So are some of our notions about love. Later centuries, as we shall see, took seriously the literary "courtly" type that presented love as an all-consuming, irresistible passion. From this came the "romantic" search for constant ecstasy and the resultant idea that adultery is necessarily more passionate than marriage. The idealization of the power and value of romantic love is very much a Western cultural value. More stable, traditional societies (as we will see in our study of Africa) view romantic love as exaggerated.

Transition to Renaissance

Although in the hierarchical vision of his great epic Dante faithfully reflected the integrated vision of the medieval universe and in his elaborate allegories captured the age's sense of its profound mysteries, he drew for his realistic description of many of the figures in his drama not from the culture of the cathedral or the court but from that of the city's marketplace. Whereas in Beatrice he elevated the ideal of spiritual love far beyond what it was in the work of the troubadour, the personalities he encountered on his journey to the depths of hell and his ascent through purgatory are men and women of flesh and blood.

Chaucer's tales remind us even more that medieval men and women were full, real people who enjoyed a good laugh and that "courtly" love viewed in a more earthly way could be an object of comedy. By Chaucer's time, the period we call medieval was also drawing to a close in the north. The fleshed-out characters in his stories mark the transition there as well to a more realistic, less symbolic vision of humanity and the universe.

PART FOUR

The Western African Cultural Root

12

African Backgrounds

As you saw in Chapters 1 and 2, the ancient civilizations of Mesopotamia and Egypt in the Nile valley gave rise to the world's earliest centralized states and cities. Texts from the dawn of history recount their trade and wars with one another. Ideas, religions, and technology flowed in multiple directions forming the ancient core of human achievement that preceded classical Greece and Rome. As we begin to examine the cultures of Africa when the histories of Africa, Europe, and the Americas become irrevocably entwined, it is useful to recall that one of the most ancient roots of Western civilization, as well as of our modern American one, was African.

The cultures of western Europe and those of Africa began to mingle and to affect each other during the fifteenth century. Since that time, and particularly with the beginning of the trans-Atlantic slave trade, European, American, and African civilizations have been inextricably intertwined. Our introduction of Africa into the humanities at this point anticipates the European age of exploration and expansion in the Renaissance, to be discussed in Volume II, and the subsequent interaction of these cultures over a five-hundred-year period.

Africa has influenced the West economically, as well as in the social and cultural realms. Profits from trade with Africa contributed to the development of northern Europe leading to the Industrial Revolution. Subsequently, the pursuit of markets for the goods produced by this revolution was an important economic motivation for the partition of Africa and the onset of colonial rule in the late nineteenth century. Patterns of economic relationships stimulated by colonialism, wherein Africa continued to provide raw materials or primary agricultural products to the industrialized West, remained little changed by the fact of independence for most of the African states in the 1960s and 1970s.

AFRICA TODAY

Images of Africa in the West

As Europe and America passed through the Enlightenment and into the age of democracy and nationalism, Africa remained a persistent symbol of "the other," of a civilization founded on principles of thought and religious behavior that were perceived to be fundamentally different from those of the West. The "noble savage" of the eighteenth century became the "primitive savage" at the bottom of the evolutionary ladder in the annals of social Darwinist thought. Social and religious movements springing from the latter spurred intense efforts to Christianize and to "civilize" Africans in the twentieth century. In America, it underlay missionary appeals and the Tarzan image, which, no longer as powerful as it once was, continued to influence American images of Africa well beyond the mid-twentieth century. Europeans and Americans involved in the effort to "tame" Africans, to make them more like themselves, often succumbed to the "heart of darkness" as it appears in the novel by Joseph Conrad and in the works of others such as Graham Greene. This image, a creation of the European mind, was rarely informed by substantive knowledge or the capacity to accept the legitimacy of different civilizations. Nevertheless, the idea of Africa and the African exercised a significant cultural influence on Western art and thought and will appear as a theme in Volume II of this book.

Africa and America

Perhaps more relevant to our purposes here is the direct role that Africa has played in the formation of

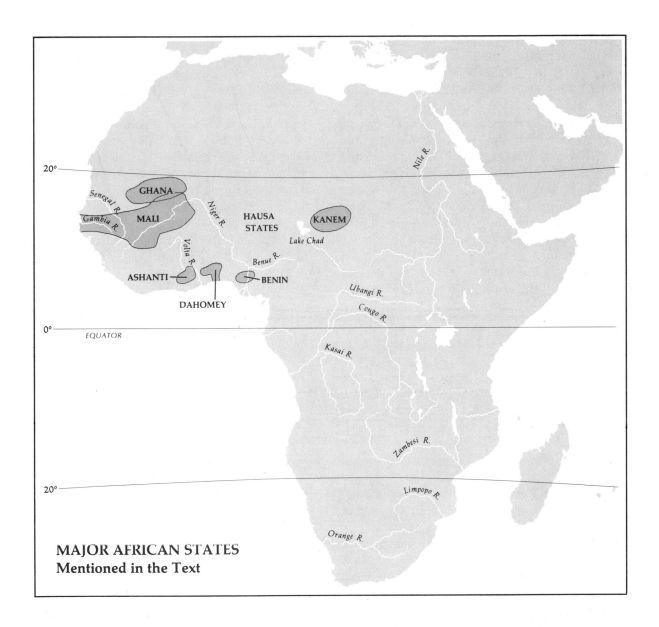

MAJOR AFRICAN STATES
Mentioned in the Text

American culture. Between the sixteenth and nineteenth centuries, more Africans came to the Americas than did people of other lands. Although the African slaves were put under great pressure to forget all aspects of their own, very diverse cultures, an amazing number of their customs were able to survive. We will look closely at the African "survivals" in African American culture (and their impact on the whole of American culture) at the end of this section and again in the chapter on African American culture in Volume II. Let us turn now to the study of Africa itself, both before and after the crucial contact with the West.

The continent of Africa is so large—and so diverse in its geographical, racial, linguistic, and cultural aspects—that it is almost impossible to speak of it generally, as a whole. Although we will need to make

some remarks about the entire continent, we will concentrate primarily on the area that was the homeland of most Africans sent to the New World: the western coast ranging from 20° north to 20° south of the equator and extending up to one thousand miles inland—roughly the areas comprising the coastline and the drainage basins of the two great rivers, the Niger and Congo (see map). We will look briefly at some important points in the history of this area, particularly the great empires that flourished around the time of the Renaissance in Europe. Our focus will then be on traditional arts, values, and systems of thought in the cultures of a few West African peoples. "Traditional" refers to non-Westernized, nonindustrialized Africa, as opposed to modern Africa, whose societies have been significantly transformed by the colonial experience. It is important to bear in mind that the concept of time in traditional African cultures is different from that in the West. Western art and thought, beginning with the Greeks, has been characterized by rapid change and a sense of evolution through time. African religions tend to emphasize the circularity, rather than the linearity, of time, and African artists put more value on community and tradition than on individuality and change. Thus, when we talk about a Yoruba style, we will not be particularly concerned with whether the work dates from the eighteenth or the twentieth century. In the case of oral poetry and tales, the dates of origin are usually not known. In the case of early African history, however, we will be interested in attempting to establish the times when the great civilizations flourished.

Stages in African History: The Great Empires

The systematic exploration of Africa by Europeans began in the fifteenth century. Europe had been in contact for hundreds of years with the north coast of Africa and in the fourteenth century had undertaken colonization of the Canary Islands off the mainland. But in the middle decades of the fifteenth century, under the sponsorship of Prince Henry the Navigator (1394–1460), son of John I of Portugal, a succession of ambitious expeditions was undertaken. By the time of the prince's death, Europe's knowledge of Africa extended far down the Guinea coast. By 1497 Vasco da Gama had successfully rounded the Cape of Good Hope, traveled up the east African coast, and made his way to Calicut on the west coast of India. His safe return to Lisbon in September 1499 marked the establishment of a sea route to the East, ushering in a major era in the history of Europe's relationship with Africa and Asia. Because of the significance of the European contact, the history of Africa for our purposes is divided into two periods with the fifteenth century as the point of demarcation.

Early Africa

The sources of knowledge of African history before the late fifteenth century are various. Most written evidence comes from travelers' accounts—primarily by Arabs who regularly traded with sub-Saharan peoples in West Africa and along the eastern coast of the continent. Few African peoples used writing, but a good deal is known from oral traditions transferred from generation to generation by specialists entrusted

with preserving the history of their people. Studies of these traditions have shown that they may contain biases and time distortions because of the social and political function they have in a society at a given time. But they are also likely to contain factual details, from the recent and sometimes from the remote past, that have been retained because of their importance. Recently, scholars have developed techniques for analyzing oral traditions more sophisticated than those available in the past. Coupled with the conclusions of modern research in archaeology, anthropology, botany, and linguistics, these written and oral accounts have enabled historians in recent years to establish the outlines of Africa's history before the fifteenth century.

For most archaeologists Africa is the cradle of humankind, although the relationship between the early forms of humanity discovered in the Olduvai Gorge in Kenya and the peopling of the continents remains an unsolved question. On the African continent itself human society in the course of its development evolved an incredible array of cultures characterized by divergent languages and beliefs, a wide range of technological levels, and many political and social organizations.

The varying development of Africa's people is closely related to the vast diversity of ecological settings found on the continent. The major areas include North Africa, dominated by the Sahara Desert in the west; the Nile valley; the savannah grasslands of eastern, central, and southern Africa; and the tropical rain forest of the West African coast and Congo River valley regions. The challenges of these different environments—their climates, soils, flora and fauna—have influenced the population growth, and the choices of economic, social, and political organization of Africa's peoples.

Stone Age groupings, characterized by hunting and gathering economies and small-scale bands as the principle of social organization, were the earliest form of society in evolutionary terms. The next major stage in human development led to the systematic cultivation of grains and root crops and the domestication of animals, known as the Neolithic Revolution. The significance of the Neolithic was that it created stable and sometimes surplus food supplies, enabling the expansion of population.

The lower Nile valley, where seasonal flooding inundated the nearby plains, was the first Neolithic site in Africa. Developing between the third and fourth millennia B.C., as we saw in Chapter 2, it nurtured the flowering of ancient Egypt. Spontaneous domestication of grains occurred in West Africa around the same time. The cultivation of crops such as the yam and the banana, introduced through ancient contacts between Malaysian peoples and those of the southeastern coast of Africa, spread to the rain forest areas of central and western Africa by the beginning of the Christian era.

In northern and western Africa pastoralism, often accompanied by nomadic forms of social organization, emerged in ancient times in the grasslands and the steppe areas where agriculture was marginally successful because of precarious rainfall. Agricultural and pastoral groups tended to be distinct, and relationships between sedentary farming and fishing communities and the pastoralists was a major factor in historical developments over the centuries for this area of Africa. Down the eastern half of the continent, however, techniques of agriculture and herding spread side by side within the same groups, and patterns of mixed farming evolved.

These stages in the development of African society can be dated only in the most general terms for most of the continent. With the introduction of metals, however, a more precise chronology of events is possible. The manufacture of metals meant more effective instruments for cultivating fields and better weapons. Greater production of food entailed population growth, and the military superiority of an army equipped with metal arms led to conquest and the creation of larger political organizations. Cities arose as political, religious, and economic centers; they were embellished with important buildings and a wealth of art objects.

Sub-Saharan Africa never produced either bronze or copper, but moved directly from the Stone Age into the Age of Iron. By the seventh or sixth century B.C., iron was being manufactured at Meroe. By the second century B.C., trade routes served as the medium for diffusing the techniques of metal making as far as western Nigeria. Recent discoveries in the area north of the juncture of the Niger and the Benue rivers indicate that between 200 B.C. and A.D. 200 a rich civilization, referred to as the Nok, dominated an area three hundred miles long in this river valley. Clay heads of animals and human beings, some of them going back as far as the ninth century B.C., testify to the artistic originality of the Nok peoples (Fig. 12-1).

Together with the Neolithic advances in the forested area, the production of iron triggered what is now referred to as the Bantu expansion. In the area of the Cameroons and western Nigeria agricultural, fishing, and iron-working peoples expanding in population and equipped with superior weapons spread out from their homeland toward the south and east, conquering or expelling the resident hunting and gathering peoples. Although the process endured for more than a thousand years, modern linguistic studies of peoples speaking Bantu languages show that gradually the Bantu speakers gained domination in the whole of central and southern Africa. Although each of the African peoples has its own language, they are all descended from Africans whose languages (like those of the Bantu speakers) ultimately derived from a common ancestral stock.

The secret of iron manufacture was only one of the items involved in African trade before the first century B.C. Trade between non-African peoples—Indians, Persians, and Arabs—and Africans along the eastern coast of the continent flourished in this period. At the same time Phoenician trading colonies in North Africa, centuries before the Roman conquest of this region, were active in exploring the Saharan oases and initiating commercial links with them. After the rapid spread of Islam across North Africa in the seventh century A.D., Arabs and Berber-speaking North Africans were the principal merchants engaging in trade with sub-Saharan Africa. Along the West African coast, Niger Delta peoples also traded in seagoing vessels with others as far west as modern-day Ghana. In the interior, cycles of regional markets extended the frontiers of contact, permitting the exchange of agricultural, craft, and some exotic products. Barter techniques—the exchange of one item for another—were widespread, but so were currencies. Some of the latter included cowrie shells, iron bars, salt, cloth, and gold. Such patterns of long-distance trade suggest the existence of other kinds of highly developed crafts in leather goods, iron implements, and cloth products.

Increasing complexity of social and political organization accompanied economic specialization. Complementarity of roles evolved between men and women as well as between whole subgroups within a given society. In contrast to the patterns of most Western societies, African women dominated agricultural production of subsistence economies. Men sometimes assisted in the preparation of fields for cultivation, but their main responsibilities lay in hunting and in the defense of their communities. Both men and women engaged in trade, although men tended to specialize in long-distance trade, including that with the Europeans when it began. These separate and complementary economic activities were buttressed by patterns of social organization sharply delineating men's and women's roles. In some societies descent was matri-

12-1 *Far left. Nok terra-cotta head. Jos Museum, Nigeria. (Photograph by Eliot Elisofon, Museum of African Art, Eliot Elisofon Archives) Center. Ife memorial bronze head from Nigeria, 13th century, Ife Museum, Nigeria. (Photograph by Eliot Elisofon, Museum of African Art, Eliot Elisofon* *Archives) Right. Commemorative head, Nigeria (Court of Benin), 16th century, bronze, height 9¼". (The Michael C. Rockefeller Memorial Collection, The Metropolitan Museum of Art, bequest of Nelson A. Rockefeller, 1979. 206.86)*

lineal; that is, inheritance of goods, access to land, and group leadership passed to children through the family of the mother. In these societies women themselves, while still under the daily dominance of men, had greater control over their own lives than did those in patrilineal societies.

Other kinds of social distinctions existed in addition to that between men and women. A few societies already had slavery, but the onset of the trans-Atlantic slave trade would expand its institutionalization in African societies of the west coast. Some groups, often those with specialist knowledge of ironworking or traditional medicines, operated as distinct castes: their members married only within the group and were set apart by special rules of dress, residence, and religious taboos that regulated their relationships with others. Such groups were not pariahs, however, and often occupied critical political and religious roles within the larger society.

Diversity in forms of political organization also characterized African societies. Two poles of political organization have traditionally been identified: "stateless societies" and state systems. Any one society, however, might lie at a point somewhere along the continuum between these two poles. "Stateless societies" were characterized by the predominance of kinship—family, lineage, and clan—as the basis of political organization. The units within which peoples interacted tended to be relatively small. There was little concentration of authority in the hands of any one person or group, spontaneous leadership emerging as the need arose. Residence patterns in "stateless societies" ranged from dispersed family homesteads to compact villages, but an important feature of such units was the equivalence of power between them; no one group could enforce its rules on another. There were some social institutions in "stateless societies" that extended across village boundaries. Age-group, religious, and initiation societies frequently were shared by others speaking the same language and sometimes by outsiders as well. The art and ideologies of ritual surrounding such organizations provided the potential for cultural unity of widely divergent groups despite the restricted range of political authority.

At the other extreme from the stateless societies lay the states characterized by a high degree of centralization of large territories; elaborate palace and government offices functioning in a wide range of economic and political tasks; court systems with constitutional and religious authorization to enforce their decisions; complex military organization; and close association between ritual and political authority, most often focused on the king.

We saw in Chapter 1 the complex of factors that archaeology has shown to be associated with the rise of states. For West Africa, the control of iron metallurgy and the sources of other minerals, a highly developed regional trade at the borderlands between savannah and rain forest, or savannah and desert, plus increased population were critical factors in the rise of states.

The Great Medieval Kingdoms

Ghana The ancient empire of Ghana (700–1230) owed its rise to its control of the gold supply so vital to Muslim merchants engaged in the trans-Saharan trade between Morocco and the far western Sudan. Although its kings and citizenry in the early days of the empire were not Muslim themselves, the kings worked closely with the Arab merchant community. They came to adopt techniques of trade and administration, facilitated by literacy in Arabic learned through contacts with the Muslim strangers. Trans-Saharan trade and Islam spurred the emergence of other West African states like Kanem, the Hausa states, and the greatest of the successor states to Ghana, Mali. We will discuss the Mali empire in connection with the epic *Sundiata* in the next chapter.

Benin One of the first African states to engage in trade with the Europeans was Benin, centered in the forested area just north of the Niger Delta, beyond the influence of the trans-Saharan trade and Islam. Historians believe that sometime between 900 and 1000 people from the kingdom of Ife to the northwest merged with those of the forested area. Ife itself reached the height of its power in the following centuries. Benin traditions claim that the founder of the major dynasty of Benin kings was Oranmiyan, the son of Oduduwa, ruler of the Ife.

After a time of troubles, the peoples of Benin had sent messages to Oduduwa requesting that he send a wise prince to rule them. After some time Oranmiyan, accompanied by courtiers and a medical specialist, settled in a palace at a place called Usama. He married a beautiful woman named Erinwinde, who gave birth to a son. Oranmiyan, as the traditions state, did not remain in Benin long; having established proper government, he resigned, saying that only a son of the land could rule such a troublesome people, and returned to Ife. His son by Erinwinde, named Eweka, was chosen by Oranmiyan to succeed him; and, at the time of Eweka's coronation, royal regalia and other symbols of office were sent by his father from Ife. Ruling many years, Eweka I strengthened the kingdom and probably began to extend Benin's influence over other peoples by settling colonies of his relatives and officers among them. Although Benin was probably never subject to Ife's political authority, the ancient city's spiritual authority is clear: the kings of Benin adopted the title *oba* from Ife. They also adopted Ife's technique of brass and bronze casting.

Art in Benin The Benin bronzes, illustrated in Figures 12-2 through 12-6, are among the master pieces of African art. The masks, heads, and plaques, reflecting prominent royal figures and scenes of the court, were closely associated with kingship and its rituals. For example, in Figure 12-6 can be seen the elaborate details of royal costume and paraphernalia, as well as the supreme power of the king in comparison to his subjects and servants (reflected in their relative degrees of prominence and position in the composition). Scenes of court life, including foreign visitors, were also portrayed, as illustrated by the figures of the merchant and the European soldier. These plaques were deliberate pictorial records of important events in Benin history. The naturalism of Benin art derived from its Ife heritage, and its representation of historical scenes sets it apart from other examples of traditional art.

Creation of the bronzes was the sole preserve of craftsmen appointed by the king. They were made by a technique called the *cire perdu* or "lost wax" method. Over a solid clay core a fine layer of wax was pressed and then carved in intricate detail. The wax layer was then encased in another clay mold provided with core holes for the wax to drain out when the entire piece was heated. Molten metal was poured into the open space between the inner core and outer layer of the mold. Finally, after cooling, the clay molds would be broken away, revealing the bronze object ready for fine sanding and polishing. The delicate details and regal simplicity of earlier Benin bronzes gave way in the late seventeenth and eighteenth centuries to heavier, more

12-2 *Mask from Wunmonijie, "Obalufon," bronze. (Reproduced by Courtesy of the Trustees of the British Museum)*

12-3 *Queen Mother of Benin, 16th century, bronze. (Reproduced by Courtesy of the Trustees of the British Museum)*

The Decline of Benin Other Europeans besides the Portuguese and the Dutch visited Benin, notably the English. William Hawkins first came to Benin in 1530. Thomas Windham in 1553 found that the king, "a Blacke moore," could easily converse in Portuguese. However, since the trading nations found more profitable sources of slaves elsewhere in Africa, Benin's direct contact with the Europeans diminished. The principal causes for the kingdom's decline remain unclear. It seems certain, however, that the trans-Atlantic slave trade engendered economic, political, and military rivals in Dahomey and Oyo in the seventeenth and eighteenth centuries. The monarchy at Benin nevertheless remained intact until the beginning of the colonial era.

Africa Since Contact with Europe

African history since the initial era of European contact in the fifteenth century has been one of uneven change and growth. The slave trade, followed by the shift to trade in natural products in the nineteenth century, affected those African peoples involved in it in many different ways. Kingdoms rose and fell, imported consumer goods replaced those of traditional manufacture, and the moral and social fabric was transformed by the loss of millions of individuals during their most productive years.

When powerful economic and political forces moved European countries to partition Africa in the late nineteenth century and to impose colonial rule, even those African peoples previously unaffected by Europe were now brought face to face with the West. Subjugated to the goals and needs of the colonial powers, African societies experienced much more intensive alteration of their political, economic, and social systems than in previous centuries. The science and technology of an industrialized Europe and a Christianity laden with Western interpretation and institutions were symbols of the Europeans' power over Africa. Some individuals and whole cultures adopted many Western forms in the hope of participating in that power; others resisted the new way. Both responses led to change in the ways that Africans perceived their world and acted in it. For the most part now independent, African countries that emerged in the twentieth century are attempting to overcome the colonial legacy of dependence and to combine material and technological progress with a nurturing of Africa's rich cultural heritage. It is to aspects of this traditional culture that we now turn.

elaborate, but still naturalistic objects. Some scholars believe that this apparent coarsening of the Benin style can be attributed to the surplus of casting metals acquired in greater abundance through the European trade.

At the apogee of its power and influence in the sixteenth and seventeenth centuries, Benin held authority over land and peoples in a triangle whose borders went deep into the delta in the east and as far as modern-day Benin (Dahomey) in the west (see map).

12-4 *European soldier with crossbow and ammunition, Benin bronze plaque. (Reproduced by Courtesy of the Trustees of the British Museum)*

12-6 *The Oba and his Assistants, bronze plaque, 17th century. (Reproduced by Courtesy of the Trustees of the British Museum)*

12-5 *Master Merchant, Benin bronze plaque, early 17th century. (Reproduced by Courtesy of the Trustees of the British Museum)*

The Culture of Benin

The traditions of the people of Benin and accounts by early European visitors, to which we now turn, illuminate the culture of a major African state as the worlds of Africa and Europe came together. The first three selections come from *A Short History of Benin,* containing the most famous collection of Benin oral traditions. The book was compiled in 1934 by Chief Jacob V. Egharevba, a member of a distinguished family in Benin and founder of the Benin Museum. Chief Egharevba's work itself is a synthesis of traditions from many groups within Benin: among others, the *oba*s themselves; the *ihogbe*, historians of deceased kings; the *ogbelaka*, royal bards; and the *iguneronmwo*, the royal brass smiths. Although most dates for the ancient period of Benin must remain relative, Chief Egharevba's work has been shown to be remarkably accurate when it can be compared to eyewitness accounts by travelers; it remains an indispensable source for the history of this African state. The fourth selection is a traditional poem extolling the oba and his office. It is taken from *African Poetry,* compiled and edited by Ulli Beier.

The Introduction of Brass-Casting from Ife

Oba Oguola wished to introduce brass-casting into Benin similar to various works of art sent him from Uhe Ife. He therefore sent to the Oghene of Uhe for a brass-smith and Igue-igha was sent to him. Igue-igha was very clever and left many designs to his successors and was in consequence deified and is worshiped to this day by brass-smiths. The practice of making brass-castings for the preservation of the records of events was originated during the reign of Oguola. He lived to a very old age.

Ewuare the Great

After the murder of Uwaifiokun, Ogus was crowned the Oba of Benin with the title Ewuare (Oworuare) meaning "It is cool" or "The trouble has ceased." (His reign traditionally began in about A.D. 1440.) Prior to his accession he caused a great conflagration in the city which lasted two days and nights as a revenge for his banishment.

Ewuare was a great magician, physician, traveler and warrior. He was also powerful, courageous and sagacious. He fought against and captured 201 towns and villages in Ekiti, Ikare, Kukuruku, Eka and the Ibo country on this side of the river Niger. He took their petty rulers captive and caused the people to pay tribute to him.

He made good roads in Benin City and especially the streets known as Akpakpaya and Utantan. In fact the town rose to importance and gained the name "City" during his reign. It was he who had the innermost and greatest of the walls and ditches made around the City and he made powerful charms and had them buried at each of the nine gateways to the city, to nullify any evil charms which might be brought by people of other countries to injure his subjects.

Ewuare was the first Oba of Benin to come into contact with Europeans, for Ruy de Sigueira visited the Benin area in 1472 although it is not known whether he actually reached the city.

The Coming of the Portuguese to Benin

Guns and Coconuts

A Portuguese explorer named John Affonso d'Aveiro visited Benin City for the first time in 1485–1486. He introduced guns and coconuts into this country.

Missionaries

It is said that John Affonso d'Aveiro came to Benin City for the second time during this reign (of Oba Esigie, which began in 1504). He advised the Oba to become a Christian, and said that Christianity would make his country better. Esigie therefore sent Ohenokun, the Olokun priest at Ughoton, with him, as an Ambassador to the King of Portugal, asking him to send priests who would teach him and his people the faith. In reply the King of Portugal sent Roman Catholic missionaries and many rich presents, such as a copper stool (*erhe*), coral beads and a big umbrella, with an entreaty that Esigie should embrace the faith. At the same time he also gave presents to the Ambassador and his wife. The King of Portugal also sent some Portuguese traders who established trading factories at Ughoton, the old port of Benin. They traded in ivory, Benin cloths, pepper and other commodities in the King of Portugal's interest. Owing to the unhealthy state of the country their commerce soon ceased.

But John Affonso d'Aveiro with the other missionaries remained in Benin to carry on the mission work, and churches were built at Ogbelaka, Idumwerie and Akpakpava (Ikpoba Road), the last named being the "Holy Cross Cathedral." ... The work of the Mission made progress and thousands of people were baptized before the death of the great explorer John Affonso d'Aveiro, who was buried with great lamentations by the Oba and the Christians of Benin City.

The missionaries went with Esigie to the Idah war which took place in 1515–1516.

QUESTIONS

1. Discuss the significance of metalworking and the origins of political power.
2. Note the characteristics of King Ewuare described in these selections: what values do they reflect?
3. What was the impression made by the early Portuguese visitors on their hosts?
4. How did Benin react to Christianity?

The Oba of Benin

He who knows not the Oba
let me show him.
He has piled a throne upon a throne.
Plentiful as grains of sand on the earth
are those in front of him.
Plentiful as grains of sand on the earth
are those behind him.
There are two thousand people
to fan him.
He who owns you
is among you here.
He who owns you
has piled a throne upon a throne.
He has lived to do it this year;
even so he will live to do it again.

QUESTIONS

1. What is the effect of *hyperbole* (figures of exaggeration) in this poem?
2. Compare the portrait of the oba in this poem with that of Ewuare the Great in the preceding excerpts.
3. Compare the portrayal of the oba's power in this poem with the suggestions of his power in Figure 12-6.

European Accounts of Benin

RUY DE PINA

FROM THE *Chronicle of John II*

Translation by J. W. Blake

Although the first European visitor was probably Ruy de Sigueira (who came, as noted in "Ewuare the Great," in 1472), John Affonso d'Aveiro was the first to engage Benin in sustained relationships with the Portuguese ruler and his subjects. Trading contact was initiated at Benin's port city of Gwato. The Portuguese description of the early period of contact is told in an excerpt from Ruy de Pina's *Chronicle of John II* (1792). Compare this version with Egharevba's: what are the differences and similarities between them?

The Discovery of the Kingdom of Benin

In this year [1486], the land of Beny beyond Myna to the Rios dos Escravos was first discovered by Joham Affom da Aveiro, who died there; whence there came to these kingdoms the first pepper from Guinee, whereof a great quantity was produced in that land; and presently samples of it were sent to Framdes [Flanders] and to other parts, and soon it fetched a great price and was held in high esteem. The king of Beny sent as ambassador to the king a negro, one of his captains, from a harbouring place by the sea, which is called Ugato [Gwato], because he desired to learn more about these lands, the arrival of people from them in his country being regarded as an unusual novelty. This ambassador was a man of good speech and natural wisdom. Great feasts were held in his honour, and he was shown many of the good things of these kingdoms. He returned to his land in a ship of the king's, who at his departure made him a gift of rich clothes for himself and his wife: and through him he also sent a rich present to the king of such things as he understood he would greatly prize. Moreover, he sent holy and most catholic advisers with praiseworthy admonitions for the faith to administer a stern rebuke about the heresies and great idolatries and fetishes, which the negroes practise in that land. Then also there went with him new factors of the king, who were to remain in that country and to traffic for the said pepper and for other things, which pertained to the trades of the king. But owing to the fact that the land was afterwards found to be very dangerous from sickness and not so profitable as had been hoped, the trade was abandoned.

WILLEM BOSMAN

FROM *New and Accurate Description of the Coast of Guinea*

The next selection describes some facets of Benin culture in the seventeenth century near the apogee of the kingdom's power, but at a time when rivals elsewhere, notably Oyo, were posing a challenge. The account is a letter written to Willem Bosman by David Van Nyendael and published in Bosman's *New and Accurate Description of the Coast of Guinea* (1705). Bosman was an employee of the Dutch West India Company; during his fourteen years in West Africa he served for a time as the chief factor at Axim in the Gold Coast.

Benin in 1700

The Inhabitants of this Country, if possessed of any Riches, eat and drink very well; that is to say, of the best. The common Diet of the Rich is Beef, Mutton or Chickens, and Jammes [yams] for their Bread; which, after they have boiled, they beat very fine, in order to make Cakes of it: they frequently treat one another, and impart a Portion of their Superfluity to the Necessitous.

The meaner Sort content themselves with smoak'd or dry'd Fish, which, if salted, is very like what we in *Europe* call Raf or Reekel; their Bread is also Jammes, Bananas, and Beans; their Drink Water and *Pardon-Wine*, which is none of the best. The richer Sort Drink Water and Brandy when they can get it. The King, the Great Lords, and every Governor, who is but indifferently rich, subsist several Poor at their Place of Residence on their Charity, employing those who are fit for any Work, in order to help them to a Maintenance, and the rest they keep for God's sake, and to obtain the Character of being charitable; so that here are no Beggars: And this necessary Care succeeds so well, that we do not see many remarkably poor amongst them. . . .

The King hath a very rich Income; for his Territories are very large, and full of Governors, and each knows how many Bags of Boesies (the Money of this Country [cowries]) he must annually raise to the King, which amounts to a vast Sum, which 'tis impossible to make any Calculation of. Others, of a meaner Rank than the former, instead of Money, deliver to the King Bulls, Cows, Sheep, Chickens, Jammes, and Cloaths; in short, whatever he wants for his Housekeeping; so that he is not oblig'd to one Farthing Expense on that account, and consequently he lays up his whole pecuniary Revenue untouch'd.

Duties or Tolls on imported and exported Wares are not paid here; but everyone pays a certain Sum annually to the Governor of the Place where he lives, for the Liberty of Trading; the Viceroy sends part of it to the King; so that his Revenue being determin'd and settled, he can easily compute what he hath to expect annually.

QUESTIONS AND COMMENTS

1. Compare Ruy de Pina's *Chronicle of John II* with Egharevba's account. What are the differences and similarities between them?

2. Look at Figure 12-3 for an African image of the European soldier. Compare this to the figure of

the master merchant or to that of the oba (Figs. 12-6 and 12-7). What strikes you about the images portrayed?

3. What is the evidence of social and political strat-ification in the letter to Bosman? Was the Benin monarchy an oppressive one in the seventeenth century? What qualities in Benin society appealed to its Dutch observer?

West African Literature: The Oral Tradition

African Languages

*T*he literary traditions of Africa are even more diverse than the literatures of Europe are. For one thing, the languages in which they are composed are more varied. Whereas nearly all European languages can be traced back to a common "proto" language (Indo-European) and thus belong to the same language family, Africa's languages not only are more than one thousand in number but also represent four major language families. These are (1) Afro-Asiatic, including among others Arabic, Berber, Hausa, and Cushitic; (2) Nilo-Saharan; (3) Khoisan, the languages of the hunting and gathering peoples of southern Africa; and (4) Congo-Kordofanian. Most of the languages in our area of concentration spring from the last family.

Written Literature in Africa

Apart from Arabic, which has a rich tradition of written literature including some works by black Africans, only a few African languages were written before the nineteenth or twentieth century. The hieroglyphic script of ancient Egyptian appears to have no written descendant, except possibly Meroitic. However, although Meroitic writing may have been based on a modified Egyptian system, its meaning remains elusive. Finding the key to Meroitic would open up a store of historical texts of great wealth and value that to date remain unusable. Ge'ez, the liturgical tongue of the Ethiopian Christian Church, and Amharic, for which the oldest documents date from the fourteenth century, are other examples with a long history. Works in Swahili and Hausa dating from the eighteenth and nineteenth centuries respectively can be found written in Arabic script. Modern African writers write either in their own languages in Arabic script or Roman script or, to reach a wider audience, in French, English, or Portuguese. Recent scholarship emphasizing the continuities between oral and written modes of expression and the decision recently by some African writers to write only in African languages only reinforce the importance of oral literature, to which we now turn.

Oral Literature

The rich body of oral literature permits us to understand the primary tradition of West Africa. A century ago the expression "oral literature" seemed a contradiction in terms. "Literature," to those educated in the Western humanistic tradition, meant something written down, a book in a library. Recent studies, however, have shown that European literature included many works composed orally, most notably, as we have seen, the epics of Homer. This fact has perhaps enabled Westerners to appreciate that poetry and prose of great beauty and complexity can be composed and passed down through the generations without being in written form.

The existence of an oral tradition implies a mentality very different from that of a society relying on documents. For one thing, the faculties of memory must be much more highly developed in an oral society. If the kingdom of Benin was able to rule a wide area without written documents, this was partly because it was able to rely on the extensive memories of its administrators. Most African societies have been

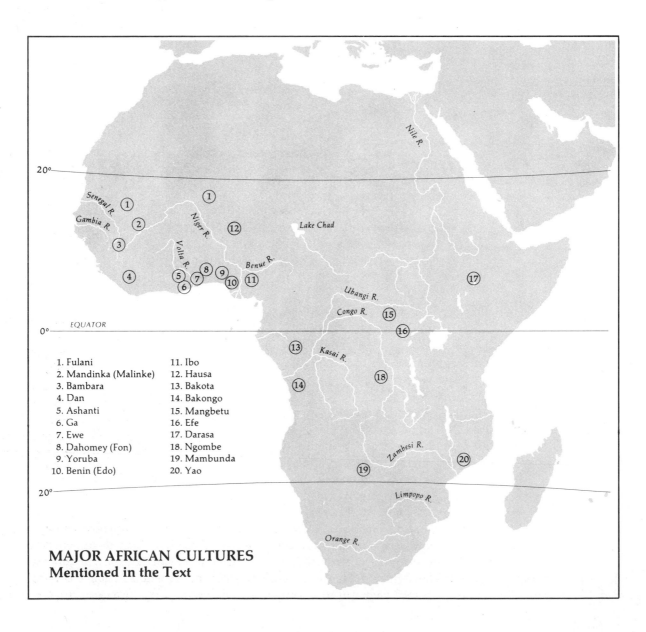

1. Fulani
2. Mandinka (Malinke)
3. Bambara
4. Dan
5. Ashanti
6. Ga
7. Ewe
8. Dahomey (Fon)
9. Yoruba
10. Benin (Edo)
11. Ibo
12. Hausa
13. Bakota
14. Bakongo
15. Mangbetu
16. Efe
17. Darasa
18. Ngombe
19. Mambunda
20. Yao

MAJOR AFRICAN CULTURES
Mentioned in the Text

able to preserve their histories through the *griot,* an official poet-historian whose job is to tell and transmit the history of the people. These histories may take the form of an epic poem, as we shall see in the excerpts from *Sundiata.*

In addition to history and the epic, oral literature in Africa includes *myths, tales, riddles, proverbs,* and *lyric* poetry. All of these *genres* are represented in the examples that follow.

It must be kept in mind that the texts in this book not only are translations from languages very different from English, but are also written transcriptions of an oral event. In the recitation of a tale or poem in Africa, the performer and the act of performance are as integral to the work as the arrangement of the words. Poetry and the epic histories are often the domain of specialists, but folk tales, riddles, and proverbs were and are available to all. Even with these forms, though, the skill of the teller is an important factor.

Appreciation of the written materials here will thus require some creative imagination on the part of the reader, yet, even divorced from performance and in translation, these works can be appreciated both for their literary qualities and for what they convey about African perceptions of the cosmos, creation, human dilemmas, and cultural priorities. We have included a few poems by modern African writers, written in English but drawing on the oral tradition. Several western and central African cultures are represented, but three major and distinct civilizations, from which we have taken several examples, deserve further introduction. These are the Mande complex (with specific reference to the Mandinka peoples), the Hausa, and the Yoruba (see map).

Mande

Mande is the name of a cultural complex and group of languages in western Sudan. Mande peoples were among the earliest to develop agriculture in sub-Saharan Africa. Mandinka (also called Mandingo or Malinke) is one of about twelve subgroups that make up the Mande group and that formed the core population of the Mali empire. Around the year 1200 several of them were joined together in revolt against the declining empire of Ghana. The remarkable leader of this revolt was a Mandinka man named Sundiata, the hero of the epic. As a result of his military victories, Mali flourished. With its economy based on the rich agricultural lands of the upper Niger and on secure control of the gold mines of Bambuk and Bure, Mali expanded to become the largest of the medieval African empires. Included within its boundaries were peoples and lands in parts of modern Guinea, Guinea-Bissau, Mali, Sierra Leone, Liberia, Ivory Coast, Senegal, northern Ghana, and Burkina Faso.

The fabulous wealth and high culture of Mali became known to the outside world through the pilgrimage of Mansa Musa in 1324 (Fig. 13-1). He and succeeding mansas, or kings, attracted scholars from North Africa and the Middle East to Timbuktu, Mali's principal port city of the trans-Saharan trade. These scholars, together with the local people, created a great center of Islamic learning around the famous mosque of Sankore. Muslim traders of various Mande groups spread Islam far beyond the core areas around Niani, the capital, and Timbuktu, some reaching as far east as Hausaland. Succession disputes and aggressive neighbors nurtured internal tensions in the empire, which, nevertheless, survived until the seventeenth century.

Hausa

Hausa is a linguistic term describing the several million peoples in West Africa who speak Hausa as their first language. Although their homeland is northern Nigeria and southern Niger, the Hausa have been engaged in long-distance trade for centuries; there are substantial Hausa-speaking communities in northern Ghana and in every major city in West Africa. Politically, the Hausa were long ago grouped into separate walled city-states to which the surrounding rural folk owed allegiance. From about the fourteenth century (perhaps stimulated by contact with Mande traders), Islam was the religion of the courts. In the early nineteenth century a holy war, or *jihad,* sparked a revolution that replaced the Hausa rulers with those from another group, the Fulani, and united them into a centralized state known as the Fulani empire. The Fulani empire included many non-Muslim groups from the lands north of the Benue and Niger rivers within its borders. By creating an area of unprecedented size within which trade, agriculture, travel, and communication could develop in relative peace, the empire imposed use of the Hausa language and Islamic values on many more peoples than before.

Yoruba

The Yoruba are an agricultural and trading people numbering several million who reside in southwestern Nigeria and the republic of Benin. Throughout most of the period of contact between Africa and Europe, the Yoruba were subjects of the Benin and Oyo empires.

13-1 *Catalan Map, 1375. (By permission of the British Library. BL Maps Ref. A.6.(3))*

The latter was a kingdom of far-flung boundaries that disintegrated in the early nineteenth century. Oyo and the successor kingdoms were constitutional monarchies in which the power of the king was balanced by a council of state and an institutionalized priesthood. The richness of the Yoruba aesthetic is better known to outsiders than, perhaps, that of any other African people. The traditions of poetry, sculpture, and dance are founded on an elaborate system of religious beliefs and practices. The hierarchy and ritual among the Yoruba gods mirror those of traditional Yoruba political structure. Yoruba religious beliefs have been remarkably successful in retaining their dynamism through accommodation with both Christian and Islamic practices. Perhaps one of the key reasons for this dynamism is the vitality of the poetry, myths, and proverbs (seen in the examples that follow) and their continued integration into social, political, and religious festivals of contemporary society.

The Epic

The original purpose of epic poetry, as we saw in the section on Homer in Chapter 3, was to "sing the famous deeds of men": to teach people in a pleasurable way about great heroes and historical events important to their culture. The epic hero, who exists or has existed in nearly all of the world's cultures, is a human being with certain superhuman qualities, someone who overcomes great obstacles and accomplishes both physical and spiritual triumphs for his people. Such a hero is Sundiata, whose legendary dimensions have informed the cultural identity of the Mande peoples down to the present time.

Myths

Myths, as we saw in the section on Greek mythology (Chapter 3), are intimately allied with the religious beliefs and the values of a particular culture. Unlike legends or epics, they are not based on historical events but attempt to explain or clarify the primal mysteries of nature, creation, and humanity's relationship with the gods. African myths are primarily oral; they are told and sung. They are often used in religious rituals; but, because there are a great many African religions, there is also a tremendous variety in African mythology. It is possible, nevertheless, to identify certain common features in the religions of the West African peoples under consideration here and to trace fundamental themes in their mythology. Since religion is such an important and unifying element of African culture, an understanding of some of the basic African beliefs will be useful in studying all aspects of that culture.

African Religions: Some Generalizations

All West African religions postulate the existence of a supreme God (whose name varies with the culture), associated with the creation of the universe. One of the great questions that the African myths ask is, Why is this God now so distant from the human world? The answer (as in the Judeo-Christian doctrine of the Fall) seems to lie in the fact of human imperfection. African myths show in a variety of ways how the supreme deity, exasperated with human perversity or troublesomeness, simply withdrew from his creation, leaving the administration of it to lesser gods, natural spirits, or ancestors of living humans. Unlike the Judeo-Christian God, the African supreme being did not return to intervene in human affairs. People in Africa rarely worship the high God by direct means; rather, they seek understanding and redress through lesser deities and spirits, each of whom represents an aspect of God. Communication between people and these highly charged spiritual forces is achieved through rituals in honor of them and through sacrifice.

Another important feature of African religion is the belief in the spiritual vitality of the natural world —as it is called in the West, animism. According to this belief, supernatural spirits or "souls" (Latin, *anima*) may inhabit the bodies of animals or even inanimate parts of nature such as trees, rocks, forests, mountains, and rivers. These spirits are often guardian spirits who must be acknowledged and appeased, for some of them are capable of causing or controlling events in the natural world. The blessings of resident spirits must be sought, for example, when a new settlement is built.

The spirits inhabiting the natural world are non-human in origin and therefore close to the realm of the gods. Nearer to the human world are the spirits of ancestors, the dead, whose souls are very much present in the everyday world and who may, for example, come to inhabit the body of a new baby. Although the ancestral souls do not have "power" like the spirits, they do have "awareness" and can be communicated with. They may act as mediators between the living and the spirits.

All of the spirits are believed to be inherently neither good nor evil—they can affect human lives in either positive or negative ways. The beautiful and beneficent natural world can also be malevolent and destructive. To live in it, one must acknowledge those powerful forces that are outside of, but intrinsically part of, the cycles of one's life. Because of this complex relationship of people to the phenomena of the world, there is a profound duality that pervades every aspect of African life. For example, one may believe in sky spirits and earth spirits, and they may contradict each other. Some spirits, such as the "tricksters," may embody contradictory traits. It is up to human wit and ingenuity to learn to appease the spirits and to determine what course to take.

Tales (Hausa)

Myths have to do with gods, spirits, and religious questions; but tales, the second type of oral prose literature, are more concerned with the social world of human beings. All African oral literatures contain a large body of tales, divided into distinct types according to their purpose, the context in which they are told, and the status of the teller.

The oral literature of the Hausa offers two main types of tales. *Tatsuniyoyi* are entertaining stories about animals and people, generally told by the older women to young children around the fire at night. They cloak lessons in social etiquette, morality, and personal values in amusing, memorable stories. The other type, *labarai*, are told by old men to each other and to young male adults. Their subject matter is most often cultural, family, and group history. While not to be taken literally, the labarai contain factual occurrences and represent for any given period of time the Hausa's view of their own past.

Riddles

Riddles, like folk tales, are most often told at night around the fire. They, too, form the early associations in the mind of the young person with the wisdom and style of elders. Frequently uttered as a statement rather than as a question, the essence of the idea and metaphors drawn instruct the young in the indirect but pithy aphorisms of life. In addition to allusions to the natural world that approach the poetic, riddles, like some poetry, allow explicit sexual references. The cleverness and wit of the stock phrases create the entertainment and memorability of the occasion.

Proverbs

Proverbs have a special place in oral literature. Rather than being told for entertainment like riddles and tales, they are most often used within conversation and, more formally, in the litigation of disputes within a community. The fluency with which a speaker can use proverbs is widely accepted as a measure of one's literary skill. Social relationships, philosophical observations, and ultimate moral values are illuminated in proverbs.

Poetry

Poetry is the most prolific and complex of the oral literature genres. In addition to being concerned with humanity's relationship to God and the spirits, all African poetry marks important experiences or transitions in the lives of people; birth, naming ceremony, death, love, work, initiation frequently provide the context for the creation of poetry. The most widespread type of poetry is the praise poem. Found nearly everywhere in Africa, praise poems extol kings, courtiers, and prominent personalities in the society as well as the gods. Sometimes called praise/abuse poetry, these poems also challenge leaders or the person praised to live up to the role their authority gives them. Popular poetry is composed and recited, often spontaneously, for the entertainment of the public.

Poetry, as with the ancient Greeks, is sung; and some types of poems are distinguished entirely by the style, pitch, and quality of voice associated with particular groups of singers. The merit of a poem is often judged not only by the skill of the artist-performer but also by the successful integration of works, music, and dance.

The Epic

FROM *Sundiata*

The oral epic *Sundiata* was told by the griot Mamadou Kouyaté to Djibril Tamsir Niane, who transcribed it and translated it into French in 1960. It has been translated into English by G. D. Pickett.

The Words of the Griot Mamadou Kouyaté

I am a griot. It is I, Djeli Mamadou Kouyaté, son of Bintou Kouyaté and Djeli Kedian Kouyaté, master in the art of eloquence. Since time immemorial the Kouyatés have been in the service of the Keita princes of Mali; we are vessels of speech, we are the repositories which harbour secrets many centuries old. The art of eloquence has no secrets for us; without us the names of kings would vanish into oblivion, we are the memory of mankind; by the spoken word we bring to life the deeds and exploits of kings for younger generations.

I derive my knowledge from my father Djeli Kedian, who also got it from his father; history holds no mystery for us; we teach to the vulgar just as much as we want to teach them, for it is we who keep the keys to the twelve doors of Mali.

I know the list of all the sovereigns who succeeded to the throne of Mali. I know how the black people divided into tribes, for my father bequeathed to me all his learning; I know why such and such is called Kamara, another Keita, and yet another Sibibé or Traoré; every name has a meaning, a secret import.

I teach kings the history of their ancestors so that the lives of the ancients might serve them as an example, for the world is old, but the future springs from the past.

My word is pure and free of all untruth; it is the word of my father; it is the word of my father's father. I will give you my father's words just as I received them; royal griots do not know what lying is. When a quarrel breaks out between tribes it is we who settle the difference, for we are the depositaries of oaths which the ancestors swore.

Listen to my word, you who want to know; by my mouth you will learn the history of Mali.

By my mouth you will get to know the story of the ancestor of great Mali, the story of him who, by his exploits, surpassed even Alexander the Great; he who, from the East, shed his rays upon all the countries of the West.

Listen to the story of the son of the Buffalo, the son of the Lion. I am going to tell you of Maghan Sundiata, of Mari-Djata, of Sogolon Djata, of Naré Maghan Djata; the man of many names against whom sorcery could avail nothing.

The First Kings of Mali

Listen then, sons of Mali, children of the black people, listen to my word, for I am going to tell you of Sundiata, the father of the Bright Country, of the savanna land, the ancestor of those who draw the bow, the master of a hundred vanquished kings.

I am going to talk of Sundiata, Manding Diara, Lion of Mali, Sogolon Djata, son of Sogolon, Naré Maghan Djata, son of Naré Maghan, Sogo Sogo Simbon Salaba, hero of many names.

I am going to tell you of Sundiata, he whose exploits will astonish men for a long time yet. He was great among kings, he was peerless among men; he was beloved of God because he was the last of the great conquerors.

Right at the beginning then, Mali was a province of the Bambara kings; those who are today called Mandingo, inhabitants of Mali, are not indigenous; they come from the East. Bilali Bounama, ancestor of the Keitas, was the faithful servant of the Prophet Muhammad (may the peace of God be upon him). Bilali Bounama had seven sons of whom the eldest,

Lawalo, left the Holy City and came to settle in Mali; Lawalo had Latal Kalabi for a son, Latal Kalabi had Damul Kalabi who then had Lahilatoul Kalabi.

Lahilatoul Kalabi was the first black prince to make the Pilgrimage to Mecca. On his return he was robbed by brigands in the desert; his men were scattered and some died of thirst, but God saved Lahilatoul Kalabi, for he was a righteous man. He called upon the Almighty and jinn[1] appeared and recognized him as king. After seven years' absence Lahilatoul was able to return, by the grace of Allah the Almighty, to Mali where none expected to see him any more.

Lahilatoul Kalabi had two sons, the elder being called Kalabi Bomba and the younger Kalabi Dauman; the elder chose royal power and reigned, while the younger preferred fortune and wealth and became the ancestor of those who go from country to country seeking their fortune.

Kalabi Bomba had Mamadi Kani for a son. Mamadi Kani was a hunter king like the first kings of Mali. It was he who invented the hunter's whistle; he communicated with the jinn of the forest and bush. These spirits had no secrets from him and he was loved by Kondolon Ni Sané. His followers were so numerous that he formed them into an army which became formidable; he often gathered them together in the bush and taught them the art of hunting. It was he who revealed to hunters the medicinal leaves which heal wounds and cure diseases. Thanks to the strength of his followers, he became king of a vast country; with them Mamadi Kani conquered all the lands which stretch from the Sankarani to the Bouré. Mamadi Kani had four sons—Kani Simbon, Kamignogo Simbon, Kabala Simbon and Simbon Tagnogokelin. They were all initiated into the art of hunting and deserved the title of Simbon. It was the lineage of Bamari Tagnogokelin which held on to the power; his son was M'Bali Nènè whose son was Bello. Bello's son was called Bello Bakon and he had a son called Maghan Kon Fatta, also called Frako Maghan Keigu, Maghan the handsome.

Maghan Kon Fatta was the father of the great Sundiata and had three wives and six children—three boys and three girls. His first wife was called Sassouma Bérété, daughter of a great divine; she was the mother of King Dankaran Touman and Princess Nana Triban. The second wife, Sogolon Kedjou, was the mother of Sundiata and the two princesses Sogolon Kolonkan and Sogolon Djamarou. The third wife was one of the Kamaras and was called Namandjé; she was the mother of Manding Bory (or Manding Bakary), who was the best friend of his half-brother Sundiata.

The Buffalo Woman

Maghan Kon Fatta, the father of Sundiata, was renowned for his beauty in every land; but he was also a good king loved by all the people. In his capital of Nianiba he loved to sit often at the foot of the great silk-cotton tree which dominated his palace of Canco. Maghan Kon Fatta had been reigning a long time and his eldest son Dankaran Touman was already eight years old and often came to sit on the ox-hide beside his father.

Well now, one day when the king had taken up his usual position under the silk-cotton tree surrounded by his kinsmen he saw a man dressed like a hunter coming towards him; he wore the tight-fitting trousers of the favourites of Kondolon Ni Sané, and his blouse oversewn with cowries showed that he was a master of the hunting art. All present turned towards the unknown man whose bow, polished with frequent usage, shone in the sun. The man walked up in front of the king, whom he recognized in the midst of his courtiers. He bowed and said, "I salute you, king of Mali, greetings all you of Mali. I am a hunter chasing game and come from Sangaran; a fearless doe has guided me to the walls of Nianiba. By the grace of my master the great Simbon[2] my arrows have hit her and now she lies not far from your walls. As is fitting, oh king, I have come to bring you your portion." He took a leg from his leather sack whereupon the king's griot, Gnankouman Doua, seized upon the leg and said, "Stranger, whoever you may be you will be the king's guest because you respect custom; come and take your place on the mat beside us. The king is pleased because he loves righteous men." The king nodded his approval and all the courtiers agreed. The griot continued in a more familiar tone, "Oh you who come from the Sangaran, land of the favourites of Kondolon Ni Sané, you who have doubtless had an expert master, will you open your pouch of knowledge for us and instruct us with your conversation, for you have no doubt visited several lands."

The king, still silent, gave a nod of approval and a courtier added, "The hunters of Sangaran are the best soothsayers; if the stranger wishes we could learn a lot from him."

---

[1]A Muslim term for invisible spirits, supernatural agencies.

[2]Honorific term for a great hunter; later applied to Sundiata.

The hunter came and sat down near Gnankouman Doua who vacated one end of the mat for him. Then he said, "Griot of the king, I am not one of these hunters whose tongues are more dexterous than their arms; I am no spinner of adventure yarns, nor do I like playing upon the credulity of worthy folk; but, thanks to the lore which my master has imparted to me, I can boast of being a seer among seers."

He took out of his hunter's bag twelve cowries which he threw on the mat. The king and all his entourage now turned towards the stranger who was jumbling up the twelve shiny shells with his bare hand. Gnankouman Doua discreetly brought to the king's notice that the soothsayer was left-handed. The left hand is the hand of evil, but in the divining art it is said that left-handed people are the best. The hunter muttered some incomprehensible words in a low voice while he shuffled and jumbled the twelve cowries into different positions which he mused on at length. All of a sudden he looked up at the king and said, "Oh king, the world is full of mystery, all is hidden and we know nothing but what we can see. The silk-cotton tree springs from a tiny seed—that which defies the tempest weighs in its germ no more than a grain of rice. Kingdoms are like trees; some will be silk-cotton trees, others will remain dwarf palms and the powerful silk-cotton tree will cover them with its shade. Oh, who can recognize in the little child the great king to come? The great comes from the small; truth and falsehood have both suckled at the same breast. Nothing is certain, but, sire, I can see two strangers over there coming towards your city."

He fell silent and looked in the direction of the city gates for a short while. All present silently turned towards the gates. The soothsayer returned to his cowries. He shook them in his palm with a skilled hand and then threw them out.

"King of Mali, destiny marches with great strides, Mali is about to emerge from the night. Nianiba is lighting up, but what is this light that comes from the east?"

"Hunter," said Gnankouman Doua, "your words are obscure. Make your speech comprehensible to us, speak in the clear language of your savanna."[3]

"I am coming to that now, griot. Listen to my message. Listen, sire. You have ruled over the kingdom which your ancestors bequeathed to you and you have no other ambition but to pass on this realm, intact if not increased, to your descendants; but, fine king, your successor is not yet born. I see two hunters coming to

your city; they have come from afar and a woman accompanies them. Oh, that woman! She is ugly, she is hideous, she bears on her back a disfiguring hump. Her monstrous eyes seem to have been merely laid on her face, but, mystery of mysteries, this is the woman you must marry, sire, for she will be the mother of him who will make the name of Mali immortal for ever. The child will be the seventh star, the seventh conqueror of the earth. He will be more mighty than Alexander. But, oh king, for destiny to lead this woman to you a sacrifice is necessary; you must offer up a red bull, for the bull is powerful. When its blood soaks into the ground nothing more will hinder the arrival of your wife. There, I have said what I had to say, but everything is in the hands of the Almighty."

The hunter picked up his cowries and put them away in his bag.

"I am only passing through, king of Mali, and now I return to Sangaran. Farewell."

The hunter disappeared but neither the king, Naré Maghan, nor his griot, Gnankouman Doua, forgot his prophetic words; soothsayers see far ahead, their words are not always for the immediate present; man is in a hurry but time is tardy and everything has its season. . . .

Summary   After some time the old man's prophecy came to pass. One day two hunters came from the land of Do to present to the king a young girl who, though she was shrouded in traveling clothes, was apparently a hunchback. They related to the king and his court how the king of Do Mansa-Gnemo Dearra had promised to reward anyone who killed an astounding buffalo that had been destroying the fields in the area. Having set out themselves to find the buffalo, the two hunters had befriended an old woman who confessed that she was the Buffalo of Do. She told them how to capture and kill it on the promise that when offered the reward of a beautiful young maiden, they choose an ugly girl who would be seated in the crowd.

Events transpired as the old woman had predicted, and the hunters were laughed out of town when they chose the ugly girl, Sogolon Kedjou. Unable to possess her, the hunters only later thought to present her to the king of Mali. Recognizing the fulfillment of what the old man had foretold, Naré Maghan married Sogolon.

The Lion Child

A wife quickly grows accustomed to her state. Sogolon now walked freely in the king's great enclosure and people also got used to her ugliness. But the first wife of the king, Sassouma Bérété, turned out to be unbearable. She was restless, and smarted to see

---

[3]The language of those who live in the savannah grasslands is, like their environment, clear and bright.

the ugly Sogolon proudly flaunting her pregnancy about the palace. What would become of her, Sassouma Bérété, if her son, already eight years old, was disinherited in favour of the child that Sogolon was going to bring into the world? All the king's attentions went to the mother-to-be. On returning from the wars he would bring her the best portion of the booty—fine loin-cloths and rare jewels. Soon, dark schemes took form in the mind of Sassouma Bérété; she determined to kill Sogolon. In great secrecy she had the foremost sorcerers of Mali come to her, but they all declared themselves incapable of tackling Sogolon. In fact, from twilight onwards, three owls came and perched on the roof of her house and watched over her. For the sake of peace and quiet Sassouma said to herself, "Very well then, let him be born, this child, and then we'll see."

Sogolon's time came. The king commanded the nine greatest midwives of Mali to come to Niani, and they were now constantly in attendance on the damsel of Do. The king was in the midst of his courtiers one day when someone came to announce to him that Sogolon's labours were beginning. He sent all his courtiers away and only Gnankouman Doua stayed by his side. One would have thought that this was the first time that he had become a father, he was so worried and agitated. The whole palace kept complete silence. Doua tried to distract the sovereign with his one-stringed guitar but in vain. He even had to stop this music as it jarred on the king. Suddenly the sky darkened and great clouds coming from the east hid the sun, although it was still the dry season. Thunder began to rumble and swift lightning rent the clouds; a few large drops of rain began to fall while a strong wind blew up. A flash of lightning accompanied by a dull rattle of thunder burst out of the east and lit up the whole sky as far as the west. Then the rain stopped and the sun appeared and it was at this very moment that a midwife came out of Sogolon's house, ran to the antechamber and announced to Naré Maghan that he was the father of a boy.

The king showed no reaction at all. He was as though in a daze. Then Doua, realizing the king's emotion, got up and signalled to two slaves who were already standing near the royal "tabala."[4] The hasty beats of the royal drum announced to Mali the birth of a son; the village tam-tams took it up and thus all Mali got the good news the same day. Shouts of joy, tam-tams and "balafons"[5] took the place of the recent silence and all the musicians of Niani made their way to the palace. His initial emotion being over, the king had got up and on leaving the antechamber he was greeted by the warm voice of Gnankouman Doua singing:

"I salute you, father; I salute you, king Naré Maghan; I salute you, Maghan Kon Fatta, Frako Maghan Keigu. The child is born whom the world awaited. Maghan, oh happy father, I salute you. The lion child, the buffalo child is born, and to announce him the Almighty has made the thunder peal, the whole sky has lit up and the earth has trembled. All hail, father, hail king Naré Maghan!"

All the griots were there and had already composed a song in praise of the royal infant. The generosity of kings makes griots eloquent, and Maghan Kon Fatta distributed on this day alone six granaries of rice among the populace. Sassouma Bérété distinguished herself by her largesses, but that deceived nobody. She was suffering in her heart but did not want to betray anything.

The name was given the eighth day after his birth. It was a great feast day and people came from all the villages of Mali while each neighbouring people brought gifts to the king. First thing in the morning a great circle had formed in front of the palace. In the middle, serving women were pounding rice which was to serve as bread, and sacrificed oxen lay at the foot of the great silk-cotton tree.

In Sogolon's house the king's aunt cut off the baby's first crop of hair while the poetesses, equipped with large fans, cooled the mother who was nonchalantly stretched out on soft cushions.

The king was in his antechamber but he came out followed by Doua. The crowd fell silent and Doua cried, "The child of Sogolon will be called Maghan after his father, and Mari Djata, a name which no Mandingo prince has ever borne. Sogolon's son will be the first of this name."

Straight away the griots shouted the name of the infant and the tam-tams sounded anew. The king's aunt, who had come out to hear the name of the child, went back into the house, and whispered the double name of Maghan and Mari Djata in the ear of the newly-born so that he would remember it.

The festivity ended with the distribution of meat to the heads of families and everyone dispersed

---

[4]Ceremonial drum.

[5]A type of xylophone in which the wooden keys are often mounted upon gourds.

joyfully. The near relatives one by one went to admire the newly-born.

Childhood

God has his mysteries which none can fathom. You, perhaps, will be a king. You can do nothing about it. You, on the other hand, will be unlucky, but you can do nothing about that either. Each man finds his way already marked out for him and he can change nothing of it.

Sogolon's son had a slow and difficult childhood. At the age of three he still crawled along on all fours while children of the same age were already walking. He had nothing of the great beauty of his father Naré Maghan. He had a head so big that he seemed unable to support it; he also had large eyes which would open wide whenever anyone entered his mother's house. He was taciturn and used to spend the whole day just sitting in the middle of the house. Whenever his mother went out he would crawl on all fours to rummage about in the calabashes in search of food, for he was very greedy.

Malicious tongues began to blab. What three-year-old has not yet taken his first steps? What three-year-old is not the despair of his parents through his whims and shifts of mood? What three-year-old is not the joy of his circle through his backwardness in talking? Sogolon Djata (for it was thus that they called him, prefixing his mother's name to his), Sogolon Djata, then, was very different from others of his own age. He spoke little and his severe face never relaxed into a smile. You would have thought that he was already thinking, and what amused children of his age bored him. Often Sogolon would make some of them come to him to keep him company. These children were already walking and she hoped that Djata, seeing his companions walking, would be tempted to do likewise. But nothing came of it. Besides, Sogolon Djata would brain the poor little things with his already strong arms and none of them would come near him any more.

The king's first wife was the first to rejoice at Sogolon Djata's infirmity. Her own son, Dankaran Touman, was already eleven. He was a fine and lively boy, who spent the day running about the village with those of his own age. He had even begun his initiation in the bush. The king had had a bow made for him and he used to go behind the town to practise archery with his companions. Sassouma was quite happy and snapped her fingers at Sogolon, whose child was still crawling on the ground. Whenever the latter happened to pass by her house, she would say, "Come, my son, walk, jump, leap about. The jinn didn't promise you anything out of the ordinary, but I prefer a son who walks on his two legs to a lion that crawls on the ground." She spoke thus whenever Sogolon went by her door. The innuendo would go straight home and then she would burst into laughter, that diabolical laughter which a jealous woman knows how to use so well.

Her son's infirmity weighed heavily upon Sogolon Kedjou; she had resorted to all her talent as a sorceress to give strength to her son's legs, but the rarest herbs had been useless. The king himself lost hope.

How impatient man is! Naré Maghan became imperceptibly estranged but Gnankouman Doua never ceased reminding him of the hunter's words. Sogolon became pregnant again. The king hoped for a son, but it was a daughter called Kolonkan. She resembled her mother and had nothing of her father's beauty. The disheartened king debarred Sogolon from his house and she lived in semi-disgrace for a while. Naré Maghan married the daughter of one of his allies, the king of the Kamaras. She was called Namandjé and her beauty was legendary. A year later she brought a boy into the world. When the king consulted soothsayers on the destiny of this son he received the reply that Namandjé's child would be the right hand of some mighty king. The king gave the newly-born the name of Boukari. He was to be called Manding Boukari or Manding Bory later on.

Naré Maghan was very perplexed. Could it be that the stiff-jointed son of Sogolon was the one the hunter soothsayer had foretold?

"The Almighty has his mysteries," Gnankouman Doua would say and, taking up the hunter's words, added, "The silk-cotton tree emerges from a tiny seed."

One day Naré Maghan came along to the house of Nounfaïri, the blacksmith seer of Niani. He was an old, blind man. He received the king in the anteroom which served as his workshop. To the king's question he replied, "When the seed germinates growth is not always easy; great trees grow slowly but they plunge their roots deep into the ground."

"But has the seed really germinated?" said the king.

"Of course," replied the blind seer. "Only the growth is not as quick as you would like it; how impatient man is."

This interview and Doua's confidence gave the king some assurance. To the great displeasure of Sassouma Bérété the king restored Sogolon to favour and soon another daughter was born to her. She was given the name of Djamarou.

However, all Niani talked of nothing else but the stiff-legged son of Sogolon. He was now seven and he still crawled to get about. In spite of all the king's affection, Sogolon was in despair. Naré Maghan aged and he felt his time coming to an end. Dankaran Touman, the son of Sassouma Bérété, was now a fine youth.

One day Naré Maghan made Mari Djata come to him and he spoke to the child as one speaks to an adult. "Mari Djata, I am growing old and soon I shall be no more among you, but before death takes me off I am going to give you the present each king gives his successor. In Mali every prince has his own griot. Doua's father was my father's griot, Doua is mine and the son of Doua, Balla Fasséké here, will be your griot. Be inseparable friends from this day forward. From his mouth you will hear the history of your ancestors, you will learn the art of governing Mali according to the principles which our ancestors have bequeathed to us. I have served my term and done my duty too. I have done everything which a king of Mali ought to do. I am handing an enlarged kingdom over to you and I leave you sure allies. May your destiny be accomplished, but never forget that Niani is your capital and Mali the cradle of your ancestors."

The child, as if he had understood the whole meaning of the king's words, beckoned Balla Fasséké to approach. He made room for him on the hide he was sitting on and then said, "Balla, you will be my griot."

"Yes, son of Sogolon, if it pleases God," replied Balla Fasséké.

The king and Doua exchanged glances that radiated confidence.

The Lion's Awakening

A short while after this interview between Naré Maghan and his son the king died. Sogolon's son was no more than seven years old. The council of elders met in the king's palace. It was no use Doua's defending the king's will which reserved the throne for Mari Djata, for the council took no account of Naré Maghan's wish. With the help of Sassouma Bérété's intrigues, Dankaran Touman was proclaimed king and a regency council was formed in which the queen mother was all-powerful. A short time after, Doua died.

As men have short memories, Sogolon's son was spoken of with nothing but irony and scorn. People

had seen one-eyed kings, one-armed kings, and lame kings, but a stiff-legged king had never been heard tell of. No matter how great the destiny promised for Mari Djata might be, the throne could not be given to someone who had no power in his legs; if the jinn loved him, let them begin by giving him the use of his legs. Such were the remarks that Sogolon heard every day. The queen mother, Sassouma Bérété, was the source of all this gossip.

Having become all-powerful, Sassouma Bérété persecuted Sogolon because the late Naré Maghan had preferred her. She banished Sogolon and her son to a back yard of the palace. Mari Djata's mother now occupied an old hut which had served as a lumber-room of Sassouma's.

The wicked queen mother allowed free passage to all those inquisitive people who wanted to see the child that still crawled at the age of seven. Nearly all the inhabitants of Niani filed into the palace and the poor Sogolon wept to see herself thus given over to public ridicule. Mari Djata took on a ferocious look in front of the crowd of sightseers. Sogolon found a little consolation only in the love of her eldest daughter, Kolonkan. She was four and she could walk. She seemed to understand all her mother's miseries and already she helped her with the housework. Sometimes, when Sogolon was attending to the chores, it was she who stayed beside her sister Djamarou, quite small as yet.

Sogolon Kedjou and her children lived on the queen mother's left-overs, but she kept a little garden in the open ground behind the village. It was there that she passed her brightest moments looking after her onions and gnougous. One day she happened to be short of condiments and went to the queen mother to beg a little baobab leaf.

"Look you," said the malicious Sassouma, "I have a calabash full. Help yourself, you poor woman. As for me, my son knew how to walk at seven and it was he who went and picked these baobab leaves. Take them then, since your son is unequal to mine." Then she laughed derisively with that fierce laughter which cuts through your flesh and penetrates right to the bone.

Sogolon Kedjou was dumbfounded. She had never imagined that hate could be so strong in a human being. With a lump in her throat she left Sassouma's. Outside her hut Mari Djata, sitting on his useless legs, was blandly eating out of a calabash. Unable to contain herself any longer, Sogolon burst into sobs and seizing a piece of wood, hit her son.

"Oh son of misfortune, will you never walk? Through your fault I have just suffered the greatest affront of my life! What have I done, God, for you to punish me in this way?"

Mari Djata seized the piece of wood and, looking at his mother, said, "Mother, what's the matter?"

"Shut up, nothing can ever wash me clean of this insult."

"But what then?"

"Sassouma has just humiliated me over a matter of a baobab leaf. At your age her own son could walk and used to bring his mother baobab leaves."

"Cheer up, Mother, cheer up."

"No. It's too much. I can't."

"Very well then, I am going to walk today," said Mari Djata. "Go and tell my father's smiths to make me the heaviest possible iron rod. Mother, do you want just the leaves of the baobab or would you rather I brought you the whole tree?"

"Ah, my son, to wipe out this insult I want the tree and its roots at my feet outside my hut."

Balla Fasséké, who was present, ran to the master smith, Farakourou, to order an iron rod.

Sogolon had sat down in front of her hut. She was weeping softly and holding her head between her two hands. Mari Djata went calmly back to his calabash of rice and began eating again as if nothing had happened. From time to time he looked up discreetly at his mother who was murmuring in a low voice, "I want the whole tree, in front of my hut, the whole tree."

All of a sudden a voice burst into laughter behind the hut. It was the wicked Sassouma telling one of her serving women about the scene of humiliation and she was laughing loudly so that Sogolon could hear. Sogolon fled into the hut and hid her face under the blankets so as not to have before her eyes this heedless boy, who was more preoccupied with eating than with anything else. With her head buried in the bed-clothes Sogolon wept and her body shook violently. Her daughter, Sogolon Djamarou, had come and sat down beside her and she said, "Mother, Mother, don't cry. Why are you crying?"

Mari Djata had finished eating and, dragging himself along on his legs, he came and sat under the wall of the hut for the sun was scorching. What was he thinking about? He alone knew.

The royal forges were situated outside the walls and over a hundred smiths worked there. The bows, spears, arrows and shields of Niani's warriors came from there. When Balla Fasséké came to order the iron rod, Farakourou said to him, "The great day has arrived then?"

"Yes. Today is a day like any other, but it will see what no other day has seen."

The master of the forges, Farakourou, was the son of the old Nounfaïri, and he was a soothsayer like his father. In his workshops there was an enormous iron bar wrought by his father Nounfaïri. Everybody wondered what this bar was destined to be used for. Farakourou called six of his apprentices and told them to carry the iron bar to Sogolon's house.

When the smiths put the gigantic iron bar down in front of the hut the noise was so frightening that Sogolon, who was lying down, jumped up with a start. Then Balla Fasséké, son of Gnankouman Doua, spoke.

"Here is the great day, Mari Djata. I am speaking to you, Maghan, son of Sogolon. The waters of the Niger can efface the stain from the body, but they cannot wipe out an insult. Arise, young lion, roar, and may the bush know that from henceforth it has a master."

The apprentice smiths were still there, Sogolon had come out and everyone was watching Mari Djata. He crept on all fours and came to the iron bar. Supporting himself on his knees and one hand, with the other hand he picked up the iron bar without any effort and stood it up vertically. Now he was resting on nothing but his knees and held the bar with both his hands. A deathly silence had gripped all those present. Sogolon Djata closed his eyes, held tight, the muscles in his arms tensed. With a violent jerk he threw his weight on to it and his knees left the ground. Sogolon Kedjou was all eyes and watched her son's legs which were trembling as though from an electric shock. Djata was sweating and the sweat ran from his brow. In a great effort he straightened up and was on his feet at one go—but the great bar of iron was twisted and had taken the form of a bow!

Then Balla Fasséké sang out the "Hymn to the Bow," striking up with his powerful voice:

"Take your bow, Simbon,
Take your bow and let us go.
Take your bow, Sogolon Djata."

When Sogolon saw her son standing she stood dumb for a moment, then suddenly she sang these words of thanks to God who had given her son the use of his legs:

"Oh day, what a beautiful day,
Oh day, day of joy;
Allah Almighty, you never created a finer day.
So my son is going to walk!"

Standing in the position of a soldier at ease, Sogolon Djata, supported by his enormous rod, was sweating great beads of sweat. Balla Fasséké's song had alerted the whole palace and people came running from all over to see what had happened, and each stood bewildered before Sogolon's son. The queen mother had rushed there and when she saw Mari Djata standing up she trembled from head to foot. After recovering his breath Sogolon's son dropped the bar and the crowd stood to one side. His first steps were those of a giant. Balla Fasséké fell into step and pointing his finger at Djata, he cried:

"Room, room, make room!
The lion has walked;
Hide antelopes,
Get out of his way."

Behind Niani there was a young baobab tree and it was there that the children of the town came to pick leaves for their mothers. With all his might the son of Sogolon tore up the tree and put it on his shoulders and went back to his mother. He threw the tree in front of the hut and said, "Mother, here are some baobab leaves for you. From henceforth it will be outside your hut that the women of Niani will come to stock up."

Sogolon Djata walked. From that day forward the queen mother had no more peace of mind. But what can one do against destiny? Nothing. Man, under the influence of certain illusions, thinks he can alter the course which God has mapped out, but everything he does falls into a higher order which he barely understands. That is why Sassouma's efforts were vain against Sogolon's son, everything she did lay in the child's destiny. Scorned the day before and the object of public ridicule, now Sogolon's son was as popular as he had been despised. The multitude loves and fears strength. All Niani talked of nothing but Djata; the mothers urged their sons to become hunting companions of Djata and to share his games, as if they wanted their offspring to profit from the nascent glory of the buffalo-woman's son. The words of Doua on the name-giving day came back to men's minds and Sogolon was now surrounded with much respect; in conversation people were fond of contrasting Sogolon's modesty with the pride and malice of Sassouma Bérété. It was because the former had been an exemplary wife and mother that God had granted strength to her son's legs for, it was said, the more a wife loves and respects her husband and the more she suffers for her child, the more valorous will the child be one day. Each is the child of his mother; the child is worth no more than the mother is worth. It was not astonishing that the king Dankaran Touman was so colourless, for his mother had never shown the slightest respect to her husband and never, in the presence of the late king, did she show that humility which every wife should show before her husband. People recalled her scenes of jealousy and the spiteful remarks she circulated about her co-wife and her child. And people would conclude gravely, "Nobody knows God's mystery. The snake has no legs yet it is as swift as any other animal that has four."

Sogolon Djata's popularity grew from day to day and he was surrounded by a gang of children of the same age as himself. These were Fran Kamara, son of the king of Tabon; Kamandjan, son of the king of Sibi; and other princes whose fathers had sent them to the court of Niani. The son of Namandjé, Manding Bory, was already joining in their games. Balla Fasséké followed Sogolon Djata all the time. He was past twenty and it was he who gave the child education and instruction according to Mandingo rules of conduct. Whether in town or at the hunt, he missed no opportunity of instructing his pupil. Many young boys of Niani came to join in the games of the royal child.

He liked hunting best of all. Farakourou, master of the forges, had made Djata a fine bow, and he proved himself to be a good shot with the bow. He made frequent hunting trips with his troops, and in the evening all Niani would be in the square to be present at the entry of the young hunters. The crowd would sing the "Hymn to the Bow" which Balla Fasséké had composed, and Sogolon Djata was quite young when he received the title of Simbon, or master hunter, which is only conferred on great hunters who have proved themselves.

Every evening Sogolon Kedjou would gather Djata and his companions outside her hut. She would tell them stories about the beasts of the bush, the dumb brothers of man. Sogolon Djata learnt to distinguish between the animals; he knew why the buffalo was his mother's wraith[6] and also why the lion was the protector of his father's family. He also listened to the history of the kings which Balla Fasséké told him; enraptured by the story of Alexander the Great, the mighty king of gold and silver, whose sun shone over quite half the world. Sogolon initiated her son into certain secrets and revealed to him the names of the medicinal plants which every hunter should know. Thus, between his mother and his griot, the child got to know all that needed to be known.

Sogolon's son was now ten. The name Sogolon Djata in the rapid Mandingo language became Sundiata or Sondjata. He was a lad full of strength; his arms had the strength of ten and his biceps inspired fear in his companions. He had already that authoritative way of speaking which belongs to those

---

[6]In Mandingo religion, the double of a spirit. The spirit may leave the body and incarnate itself in other persons or animals. In this case the mother's spirit became incarnate in the buffalo.

who are destined to command. His brother, Manding Bory, became his best friend, and whenever Djata was seen, Manding Bory appeared too. They were like a man and his shadow. Fran Kamara and Kamandjan were the closest friends of the young princes, while Balla Fasséké followed them all like a guardian angel.

But Sundiata's popularity was so great that the queen mother became apprehensive for her son's throne. Dankaran Touman was the most retiring of men. At the age of eighteen he was still under the influence of his mother and a handful of old schemers. It was Sassouma Bérété who really reigned in his name. The queen mother wanted to put an end to this popularity by killing Sundiata and it was thus that one night she received the nine great witches of Mali. They were all old women. The eldest, and the most dangerous too, was called Soumosso Konkomba. When the nine old hags had seated themselves in a semi-circle around her bed the queen mother said:

"You who rule supreme at night, nocturnal powers, oh you who hold the secret of life, you who can put an end to one life, can you help me?"

"The night is potent," said Soumosso Konkomba. "Oh queen, tell us what is to be done, on whom must we turn the fatal blade?"

"I want to kill Sundiata," said Sassouma. "His destiny runs counter to my son's and he must be killed while there is still time. If you succeed, I promise you the finest rewards. First of all I bestow on each of you a cow and her calf and from tomorrow go to the royal granaries and each of you will receive a hundred measures of rice and a hundred measures of hay on my authority."

"Mother of the king," rejoined Soumosso Konkomba, "life hangs by nothing but a very fine thread, but all is interwoven here below. Life has a cause, and death as well. The one comes from the other. Your hate has a cause and your action must have a cause. Mother of the king, everything holds together, our action will have no effect unless we are ourselves implicated, but Mari Djata has done us no wrong. It is, then, difficult for us to compass his death."

"But you are also concerned," replied the queen mother, "for the son of Sogolon will be a scourge to us all."

"The snake seldom bites the foot that does not walk," said one of the witches.

"Yes, but there are snakes that attack everybody. Allow Sundiata to grow up and we will all repent of it. Tomorrow go to Sogolon's vegetable patch and make a show of picking a few gnougou leaves. Mari Djata stands guard there and you will see how vicious the boy is. He won't have any respect for your age, he'll give you a good thrashing."

"That's a clever idea," said one of the old hags.

"But the cause of our discomfiture will be ourselves, for having touched something which did not belong to us."

"We could repeat the offence," said another, "and then if he beats us again we would be able to reproach him with being unkind, heartless. In that case we would be concerned, I think."

"The idea is ingenious," said Soumosso Konkomba. "Tomorrow we shall go to Sogolon's vegetable patch."

"Now there's a happy thought," concluded the queen mother, laughing for joy. "Go to the vegetable patch tomorrow and you will see that Sogolon's son is mean. Beforehand, present yourselves at the royal granaries where you will receive the grain I promised you; the cows and calves are already yours."

The old hags bowed and disappeared into the black night. The queen mother was now alone and gloated over her anticipated victory. But her daughter, Nana Triban, woke up.

"Mother, who were you talking to? I thought I heard voices."

"Sleep, my daughter, it is nothing. You didn't hear anything."

In the morning, as usual, Sundiata got his companions together in front of his mother's hut and said, "What animal are we going to hunt today?"

Kamandjan said, "I wouldn't mind if we attacked some elephants right now."

"Yes, I am of this opinion too," said Fran Kamara. "That will allow us to go far into the bush."

And the young band left after Sogolon had filled the hunting bags with eatables. Sundiata and his companions came back late to the village, but first Djata wanted to take a look at his mother's vegetable patch as was his custom. It was dusk. There he found the nine witches stealing gnougou leaves. They made a show of running away like thieves caught red-handed.

"Stop, stop, poor old women," said Sundiata, "what is the matter with you to run away like this? This garden belongs to all."

Straight away his companions and he filled the gourds of the old hags with leaves, aubergines and onions.

"Each time that you run short of condiments come to stock up here without fear."

"You disarm us," said one of the old crones, and another added, "And you confound us with your bounty."

"Listen, Djata," said Soumosso Konkomba, "we had come here to test you. We have no need of condiments but your generosity disarms us. We were sent here by the queen mother to provoke you and draw the anger of the nocturnal powers upon you. But nothing can be done against a heart full of kindness. And to think that we have already drawn a hundred measures of rice and a hundred measures of millet—and the queen promises us each a cow and her calf in addition. Forgive us, son of Sogolon."

"I bear you no ill-will," said Djata. "Here, I am returning from the hunt with my companions and we have killed ten elephants, so I will give you an elephant each and there you have some meat!"

"Thank you, son of Sogolon."

"Thank you, child of Justice."

"Henceforth," concluded Soumosso Konkomba, "we will watch over you." And the nine witches disappeared into the night. Sundiata and his companions continued on their way to Niani and got back after dark.

"You were really frightened; those nine witches really scared you, eh?" said Sogolon Kolonkan, Djata's young sister.

"How do you know," retorted Sundiata, astonished.

"I saw them at night hatching their scheme, but I knew there was no danger for you." Kolonkan was well versed in the art of witchcraft and watched over her brother without his suspecting it.

Summary Sogolon, knowing the danger that awaited her children in the court ruled by the jealous Sassouma, decided to leave until such time that Djata could return in safety to reign over Mali. In a parting act of malice Dankaran Touman sent Djata's griot, Balla Fasséké, on an embassy to the king of Sosso, Soumaoro Kanté, thereby depriving Djata of his friend and teacher. There Balla Fasséké remained along with Nana Triban until the eve of Soumaoro's major battle with Sundiata.

Vowing to return, Sogolon's son and his family began their seven years of exile during which Sundiata would grow to manhood. After brief stops in Djedeba and Tabon, they remained for a time at the court of the Cissés at Wagadou. There Sundiata learned much from the merchants and officials engaged in the trans-Saharan trade. After a time the Cisse king sent them on to the king of Mema, his cousin. The king of Mema's hospitality was generous, and Sundiata quickly became a favorite at the court. His first military campaigns were fought on behalf of the king of Mema, and so valorous were his exploits that he soon was named viceroy.

Soumaoro Kanté, the Sorcerer King

While Sogolon's son was fighting his first campaign far from his native land, Mali had fallen under the domination of a new master, Soumaoro Kanté, king of Sosso.

When the embassy sent by Dankaran Touman arrived at Sosso, Soumaoro demanded that Mali should acknowledge itself tributary to Sosso. Balla Fasséké found delegates from several other kingdoms at Soumaoro's court. With his powerful army of smiths the king of Sosso had quickly imposed his power on everybody. After the defeat of Ghana and Diaghan no one dared oppose him any more. Soumaoro was descended from the line of smiths called Diarisso who first harnessed fire and taught men how to work iron, but for a long time Sosso had remained a little village of no significance. The powerful king of Ghana was the master of the country. Little by little the kingdom of Sosso had grown at the expense of Ghana and now the Kantés dominated their old masters. Like all masters of fire, Soumaoro Kanté was a great sorcerer. His fetishes had a terrible power and it was because of them that all kings trembled before him, for he could deal a swift death to whoever he pleased. He had fortified Sosso with a triple curtain wall and in the middle of the town loomed his palace, towering over the thatched huts of the villages. He had had an immense seven-storey tower built for himself and he lived on the seventh floor in the midst of his fetishes. This is why he was called "The Untouchable King."

Soumaoro let the rest of the Mandingo embassy return but he kept Balla Fasséké back and threatened to destroy Niani if Dankaran Touman did not make his submission. Frightened, the son of Sassouma immediately made his submission, and he even sent his sister, Nana Triban, to the king of Sosso.

One day when the king was away, Balla Fasséké managed to get right into the most secret chamber of the palace where Soumaoro safeguarded his fetishes. When he had pushed the door open he was transfixed with amazement at what he saw. The walls of the chamber were tapestried with human skins and there was one in the middle of the room on which the king sat; around an earthenware jar nine heads formed a circle; when Balla had opened the door the water had become disturbed and a monstrous snake had raised its head. Balla Fasséké, who was also well versed in sorcery, recited some formulas and everything in the room fell quiet, so he continued his inspection. He saw on a perch above the bed three owls which seemed to be asleep; on the far wall hung strangely-shaped weapons, curved swords and knives with three cutting edges. He looked at the skulls attentively and recognized the nine kings killed by Soumaoro. To the right of the door he discovered a great balafon, bigger than he had ever seen in Mali. Instinctively he pounced upon it and sat down to play. The griot always has a weakness for music, for music is the griot's soul.

He began to play. He had never heard such a melodious balafon. Though scarcely touched by the hammer, the resonant wood gave out sounds of an infinite sweetness, notes clear and as pure as gold dust; under the skilful hand of Balla the instrument had found its master. He played with all his soul and the whole room was filled with wonderment. The drowsy owls, eyes half closed, began to move their heads as though with satisfaction. Everything seemed to come to life upon the strains of this magic music. The nine skulls resumed their earthly forms and blinked at hearing the solemn "Vulture Tune"; with its head resting on the rim, the snake seemed to listen from the jar. Balla Fasséké was pleased at the effect his music had had on the strange inhabitants of this ghoulish chamber, but he quite understood that this balafon was not at all like any other. It was that of a great sorcerer. Soumaoro was the only one to play this instrument. After each victory he would come and sing his own praises. No griot had ever touched it. Not all ears were made to hear that music. Soumaoro was constantly in touch with this xylophone and no matter how far away he was, one only had to touch it for him to know that someone had got into his secret chamber.

The king was not far from the town and he rushed back to his palace and climbed up to the seventh storey. Balla Fasséké heard hurried steps in the corridor and Soumaoro bounded into the room, sword in hand.

"Who is there?" he roared. "It is you, Balla Fasséké!"

The king was foaming with anger and his eyes burnt fiercely like hot embers. Yet without losing his composure the son of Doua changed key and improvised a song in honour of the king:

> There he is, Soumaoro Kanté.
> All hail, you who sit on the skins of kings.
> All hail, Simbon of the deadly arrow.
> I salute you, you who wear clothes of human skin.

This improvised tune greatly pleased Soumaoro and he had never heard such fine words. Kings are only men, and whatever iron cannot achieve against them, words can. Kings, too, are susceptible to flattery, so

Soumaoro's anger abated, his heart filled with joy as he listened attentively to this sweet music:

> All hail, you who wear clothes of human skin.
> I salute you, you who sit on the skins of kings.

Balla sang and his voice, which was beautiful, delighted the king of Sosso.

"How sweet it is to hear one's praises sung by someone else; Balla Fasséké, you will nevermore return to Mali for from today you are my griot."

Thus Balla Fasséké, whom king Naré Maghan had given to his son Sundiata, was stolen from the latter by Dankaran Touman; now it was the king of Sosso, Soumaoro Kanté, who, in turn, stole the precious griot from the son of Sassouma Bérété. In this way war between Sundiata and Soumaoro became inevitable.

Summary   The second half of the epic relates Sundiata's leave-taking of Mema in response to the pleas for rescue of a search party sent to find him, and tells of his triumphal series of battles against the terrible Soumaoro.

Allied with the armies of his childhood friends and with those who had offered him sanctuary during his exile, Sundiata led a massive force that included the cavalry of Mema and Wagadou; blacksmiths and the mountain Djallonkes; and groups under Fran Kamara of Tabon Wana. A victory at the valley of Tabon was followed by the first clash with Soumaoro's magic at Negueboria. The fame of Sundiata spread until all the sons of Mali were under his banner. But even a warrior like Sundiata was challenged to the limits by Soumaoro's sorcery. He was saved by the clever escape from Sosso of Balla Fasséké and Nana Triban; on the eve of the battle of Krina it was they who revealed Soumaoro's secret taboo. Reunited with his master, the griot Balla Fasséké sang the praises and history of Mali and challenged the assembled armies to prove themselves worthy of their heritage. At Krina, Soumaoro's power and magic were dissolved by Sundiata's mighty army and his destruction of Soumaoro's protective fetish. Despite hard-driven pursuit by Sundiata and Soumaoro's nephew Fakoli, Soumaoro avoided capture and ultimately disappeared into a mountain cave, never to be seen again. The city of Sosso was destroyed, and the rest of Soumaoro's allies, now in disarray, were vanquished.

The final sections relate the triumphal festival, the Kouroukan Fougan or the Division of the World, and the rebuilding of Sundiata's capital at Niani.

Kouroukan Fougan or the Division of the World

Leaving Do, the land of ten thousand guns, Sundiata wended his way to Ka-ba, keeping to the river valley. All his armies converged on Ka-ba and Fakoli and Tabon Wana entered it laden with booty. Sibi Kamandjan had gone ahead of Sundiata to prepare the great assembly which was to gather at Ka-ba, a town situated on the territory belonging to the country of Sibi. . . .

To the north of the town stretches a spacious clearing and it is there that the great assembly was to foregather. King Kamandjan had the whole clearing cleaned up and a great dais was got ready. Even before Djata's arrival the delegations from all the conquered peoples had made their way to Ka-ba. Huts were hastily built to house all these people. When all the armies had reunited, camps had to be set up in the big plain lying between the river and the town. On the appointed day the troops were drawn up on the vast square that had been prepared. As at Sibi, each people was gathered round its king's pennant. Sundiata had put on robes such as are worn by a great Muslim king. Balla Fasséké, the high master of ceremonies, set the allies around Djata's great throne. Everything was in position. The sofas,[7] forming a vast semicircle bristling with spears, stood motionless. The delegations of the various peoples had been planted at the foot of the dais. A complete silence reigned. On Sundiata's right, Balla Fasséké, holding his mighty spear, addressed the throng in this manner:

"Peace reigns today in the whole country; may it always be thus. . . ."

"Amen," replied the crowd, then the herald continued:

"I speak to you, assembled peoples. To those of Mali I convey Maghan Sundiata's greeting; greetings to those of Do, greetings to those of Ghana, to those from Mema greetings, and to those of Fakoli's tribe. Greetings to the Bobo warriors and, finally, greetings to those of Sibi and Ka-ba. To all the peoples assembled, Djata gives greetings.

"May I be humbly forgiven if I have made any omission. I am nervous before so many people gathered together.

"Peoples, here we are, after years of hard trials, gathered around our saviour, the restorer of peace and order. From the east to the west, from the north to the south, everywhere his victorious arms have established peace. I convey to you the greetings of Soumaoro's vanquisher, Maghan Sundiata, king of Mali.

"But in order to respect tradition, I must first of all address myself to the host of us all, Kamandjan, king of Sibi; Djata greets you and gives you the floor."

Kamandjan, who was sitting close by Sundiata, stood up and stepped down from the dais. He mounted his horse and brandished his sword, crying, "I salute you all, warriors of Mali, of Do, of Tabon, of Mema, of Wagadou, of Bobo, of Fakoli . . .; warriors, peace has returned to our homes, may God long preserve it."

"Amen," replied the warriors and the crowd. The king of Sibi continued.

"In the world man suffers for a season, but never eternally. Here we are at the end of our trials. We are at peace. May God be praised. But we owe this peace to one man who, by his courage and his valiance, was able to lead our troops to victory.

"Which one of us, alone, would have dared face Soumaoro? Ay, we were all cowards. How many times did we pay him tribute? The insolent rogue thought that everything was permitted him. What family was not dishonoured by Soumaoro? He took our daughters and wives from us and we were more craven than women. He carried his insolence to the point of stealing the wife of his nephew Fakoli! We were prostrated and humiliated in front of our children. But it was in the midst of so many calamities that our destiny suddenly changed. A new sun arose in the east. After the battle of Tabon we felt ourselves to be men, we realized that Soumaoro was a human being and not an incarnation of the devil, for he was no longer invincible. A man came to us. He had heard our groans and came to our aid, like a father when he sees his son in tears. Here is that man. Maghan Sundiata, the man with two names foretold by the soothsayers.

"It is to you that I now address myself, son of Sogolon, you, the nephew of the valorous warriors of Do. Henceforth it is from you that I derive my kingdom for I acknowledge you my sovereign. My tribe and I place ourselves in your hands. I salute you, supreme chief, I salute you, Fama of Famas.[8] I salute you, Mansa!"[9]

The huzza that greeted these words was so loud that you could hear the echo repeat the tremendous clamour twelve times over. With a strong hand Kamandjan struck his spear in the ground in front of the dais and said, "Sundiata, here is my spear, it is yours."

Then he climbed up to sit in his place. Thereafter, one by one, the twelve kings of the bright savanna

---

[7] Army troops, often of slave origin.

[8] King of kings.

[9] Emperor.

country got up and proclaimed Sundiata "Mansa" in their turn. Twelve royal spears were stuck in the ground in front of the dais. Sundiata had become emperor. The old tabala of Niani announced to the world that the lands of the savanna had provided themselves with one single king. When the imperial tabala had stopped reverberating, Balla Fasséké, the grand master of ceremonies, took the floor again following the crowd's ovation.

"Sundiata, Maghan Sundiata, king of Mali, in the name of the twelve kings of the "Bright Country," I salute you as 'Mansa.'"

The crowd shouted "Wassa, Wassa. . . . Ayé."

It was amid such joy that Balla Fasséké composed the great hymn "Niama" which the griots still sing:

Niama, Niama, Niama,
You, you serve as a shelter for all,
All come to seek refuge under you.
And as for you, Niama,
Nothing serves you for shelter,
God alone protects you.

The festival began. The musicians of all the countries were there. Each people in turn came forward to the dais under Sundiata's impassive gaze. Then the war dances began. The sofas of all the countries had lined themselves up in six ranks amid a great clatter of bows and spears knocking together. The war chiefs were on horseback. The warriors faced the enormous dais and at a signal from Balla Fasséké, the musicians, massed on the right of the dais, struck up. The heavy war drums thundered, the bolons gave off muted notes while the griot's voice gave the throng the pitch for the "Hymn to the Bow." The spearmen, advancing like hyenas in the night, held their spears above their heads; the archers of Wagadou and Tabon, walking with a noiseless tread, seemed to be lying in ambush behind bushes. They rose suddenly to their feet and let fly their arrows at imaginary enemies. In front of the great dais the Kéké-Tigui, or war chiefs, made their horses perform dance steps under the eyes of the Mansa. The horses whinnied and reared, then, overmastered by the spurs, knelt, got up and cut little capers, or else scraped the ground with their hooves.

The rapturous people shouted the "Hymn to the Bow" and clapped their hands. The sweating bodies of the warriors glistened in the sun while the exhausting rhythm of the tam-tams wrenched from them shrill cries. But presently they made way for the cavalry, beloved by Djata. The horsemen of Mema threw their swords in the air and caught them in flight, uttering mighty shouts. A smile of contentment took shape on Sundiata's lips, for he was happy to see his cavalry manoeuvre with so much skill.

In the afternoon the festivity took on a new aspect. It began with the procession of prisoners and booty. Their hands tied behind their backs and in triple file, the Sosso prisoners made their entry into the giant circle. All their heads had been shaved. Inside the circle they turned and passed by the foot of the dais. Their eyes lowered, the poor prisoners walked in silence, abuse heaped upon them by the frenzied crowd. Behind came the kings who had remained faithful to Soumaoro and who had not intended to make their submission. They also had their heads shorn, but they were on horseback so that everyone could see them. At last, right at the back, came Sosso Balla, who had been placed in the midst of his father's fetishes. The fetishes had been loaded onto donkeys. The crowd gave loud cries of horror on seeing the inmates of Soumaoro's grisly chamber. People pointed with terror at the snake's pitcher, the magic balafon, and the king of Sosso's owls. Soumaoro's son Balla, his hands bound, was on a horse but did not dare look up at this throne, which formerly used to tremble with fear at mere talk of his father. In the crowd could be heard:

"Each in his turn, Sosso Balla; lift up your head a bit, impudent little creature!" Or else: "Did you have any idea that one day you would be a slave, you vile fellow!"

"Look at your useless fetishes. Call on them then, son of a sorcerer!"

When Sosso Balla was in front of the dais, Djata made a gesture. He had just remembered the mysterious disappearance of Soumaoro inside the mountain. He became morose, but his griot Balla Fasséké noticed it and so he spoke thus:

"The son will pay for the father, Soumaoro can thank God that he is already dead."

When the procession had finished Balla Fasséké silenced everyone. The sofas got into line and the tam-tams stopped.

Sundiata got up and a graveyard silence settled on the whole place. The Mansa moved forward to the edge of the dais. Then Sundiata spoke as Mansa. Only Balla Fasséké could hear him, for a Mansa does not speak like a town-crier.

"I greet all the peoples gathered here." And Djata mentioned them all. Pulling the spear of Kamandjan, king of Sibi, out of the ground, he said:

"I give you back your kingdom, king of Sibi, for you have deserved it by your bravery; I have known you since childhood and your speech is as frank as your heart is straightforward.

"Today I ratify for ever the alliance between the Kamaras of Sibi and the Keitas of Mali. May these two people be brothers henceforth. In future, the land of the Keitas shall be the land of the Kamaras, and the property of the Kamaras shall be henceforth the property of the Keitas.

"May there nevermore be falsehood between a Kamara and a Keita, and may the Kamaras feel at home in the whole extent of my empire."

He returned the spear to Kamandjan and the king of Sibi prostrated himself before Djata, as is done when honoured by a Fama.

Sundiata took Tabon Wana's spear and said, "Fran Kamara, my friend, I return your kingdom to you. May the Djallonkés and Mandingoes be forever allies. You received me in your own domain, so may the Djallonkés be received as friends throughout Mali. I leave you the lands you have conquered, and henceforth your children and your children's children will grow up at the court of Niani where they will be treated like the princes of Mali."

One by one all the kings received their kingdoms from the very hands of Sundiata, and each one bowed before him as one bows before a Mansa.

Sundiata pronounced all the prohibitions which still obtain in relations between the tribes. To each he assigned its land, he established the rights of each people and ratified their friendships. The Kondés of the land of Do became henceforth the uncles of the imperial family of Keita, for the latter, in memory of the fruitful marriage between Naré Maghan and Sogolon, had to take a wife in Do. The Tounkaras and the Cissés became "banter-brothers" of the Keitas, while the Cissés, Bérétés and Tourés were proclaimed great divines of the empire. No kin group was forgotten at Kouroukan Fougan; each had its share in the division. To Fakoli Koroma, Sundiata gave the kingdom of Sosso, the majority of whose inhabitants were enslaved. Fakoli's tribe, the Koromas, which others call Doumbouya or Sissoko, had the monopoly of the forge, that is, of iron working. Fakoli also received from Sundiata part of the lands situated between the Bafing and Bagbé rivers. Wagadou and Mema kept their kings who continued to bear the title of Mansa, but these two kingdoms acknowledged the suzerainty of the supreme Mansa. The Konaté of Toron became the cadets of the Keitas so that on reaching maturity a Konaté could call himself Keita.

When Sogolon's son had finished distributing lands and power he turned to Balla Fasséké, his griot, and said: "As for you, Balla Fasséké, my griot, I make you grand master of ceremonies. Henceforth the Keitas will choose their griot from your tribe, from among the Kouyatés. I give the Kouyatés the right to make jokes about all the tribes, and in particular about the royal tribe of Keita."

Thus spoke the son of Sogolon at Kouroukan Fougan. Since that time his respected word has become law, the rule of conduct for all the peoples who were represented at Ka-ba.

So, Sundiata had divided the world at Kouroukan Fougan. He kept for his tribe the blessed country of Kita, but the Kamaras inhabiting the region remained masters of the soil.

If you go to Ka-ba, go and see the glade of Kouroukan Fougan and you will see a linké tree planted there, perpetuating the memory of the great gathering which witnessed the division of the world....

With Sundiata peace and happiness entered Niani. Lovingly Sogolon's son had his native city rebuilt. He restored in the ancient style his father's old enclosure where he had grown up. People came from all the villages of Mali to settle in Niani. The walls had to be destroyed to enlarge the town, and new quarters were built for each kin group in the enormous army.

Sundiata had left his brother Manding Bory at Bagadou-Djeliba on the river. He was Sundiata's Kankoro Sigui, that is to say, viceroy. Manding Bory had looked after all the conquered countries. When reconstruction of the capital was finished he went to wage war in the south in order to frighten the forest peoples. He received an embassy from the country of Sangaran where a few Kondé clans had settled, and although these latter had not been represented at Kouroukan Fougan, Sundiata granted his alliance and they were placed on the same footing as the Kondés of the land of Do.

After a year Sundiata held a new assembly at Niani, but this one was the assembly of dignitaries and kings of the empire. The kings and notables of all the tribes came to Niani. The kings spoke of their administration and the dignitaries talked of their kings. Fakoli, the nephew of Soumaoro, having proved himself too independent, had to flee to evade the Mansa's anger. His lands were confiscated and the taxes of Sosso were payed directly into the granaries of Niani. In this way, every year, Sundiata gathered about him all the kings and notables; so justice prevailed everywhere, for the kings were afraid of being denounced at Niani.

Djata's justice spared nobody. He followed the very word of God. He protected the weak against the strong and people would make journeys lasting several days to come and demand justice of him. Under his sun the upright man was rewarded and the wicked one punished.

In their new-found peace the villages knew prosperity again, for with Sundiata happiness had come into everyone's home. Vast fields of millet, rice, cotton, indigo and fonio surrounded the villages. Whoever worked always had something to live on. Each year long caravans carried the taxes in kind to Niani. You could go from village to village without fearing brigands. A thief would have his right hand chopped off and if he stole again he would be put to the sword.

New villages and new towns sprang up in Mali and elsewhere. "Dyulas," or traders, became numerous and during the reign of Sundiata the world knew happiness.

There are some kings who are powerful through their military strength. Everybody trembles before them, but when they die nothing but ill is spoken of them. Others do neither good nor ill and when they die they are forgotten. Others are feared because they have power, but they know how to use it and they are loved because they love justice. Sundiata belonged to this group. He was feared, but loved as well. He was the father of Mali and gave the world peace. After him the world has not seen a greater conqueror, for he was the seventh and last conqueror. He had made the capital of an empire out of his father's village, and Niani became the navel of the earth.

COMMENTS AND QUESTIONS

1. What is the griot Djeli Mamadou Kouyaté's conception of his role of historian? How would he define history? Does his definition differ from ours?

2. What is the Malinke view of fate or destiny as expressed here?

3. In the section "Soumaoro Kanté, the Sorcerer King," you read, "His fetishes had a terrible power...." *Fetish* means here an object believed to contain a supernatural power that may be used to protect the owner of the fetish or may be directed to harm another person. In this case Soumaoro used his fetishes to protect himself and to confuse his enemies. How does it appear that Soumaoro's power vanished when their secret was discovered?

4. What are the attributes of the hero as expressed in this Malian epic? How do they correspond with those in the *Epic of Gilgamesh*, the Homeric epics, and the *Aeneid*?

5. What are the ideals of government and of good leadership?

6. Seek out some *proverbs* from the text. How do they inform us in a capsulized way of Malinke values?

Two Yoruba Myths of Creation

The myths that follow address themselves, in the context of African religion, to three basic questions: (1) How did the world begin? (creation); (2) What caused God to withdraw from the human world? and (3) Why do people have to die? The two creation myths are Yoruba; they require a word of explanation on Yoruba religion, which will be discussed more fully in the poetry section. The highest God, named Oludumare or Olorun, has many aspects, which are represented by lesser deities called *orisha*. One of these is Obatala, god of creation.

The Creation of Land

At the beginning everything was water. Then Oludumare the supreme god sent Obatala (or Orishanla) down from heaven to create the dry land. Obatala descended on a chain and he carried with him: a snail shell filled with earth, some pieces of corn and a cock. When he arrived he placed the corn on the water, spread the earth over it and placed the cock on top. The cock immediately started to scratch and thus the land spread far and wide.

When the land had been created, the other Orisha descended from heaven in order to live on the land with Obatala.

The Creation of Man

Obatala made man out of earth. After shaping men and women he gave them to Oludumare to blow in the breath of life.

One day Obatala drank palm wine. Then he started to make hunchbacks and cripples, albinos and blind men.

From that day onwards hunchbacks and albinos and all deformed persons are sacred to Obatala. But his worshipers are forbidden to drink palm wine.

Obatala is still the one who gives shape to the new babe in the mother's womb.

QUESTIONS

1. How is the role of the supreme God, Oludumare, distinguished from that of the orisha Obatala?

2. What similarities and differences do you find in these creation myths and the story of creation in Genesis?

Myths on the Separation of Man from God

This myth comes from the Yao, one of a cluster of peoples speaking Bantu languages who live in northern Mozambique and adjacent lands in Tanzania.

Mulungu and the Beasts

In the beginning man was not, only Mulungu and his people, the beasts. They lived happily on earth.

One day a chameleon found a human pair in his fish trap. He had never seen such creatures before and he was surprised. The chameleon reported his discovery to Mulungu. Mulungu said, "Let us wait and see what the creatures will do."

The men started making fires. They set fire to the bush so that the beasts fled into the forest. Then the men set traps and killed Mulungu's people. At last Mulungu was compelled to leave the earth. Since he could not climb a tree he called for the spider.

The spider spun a thread up to the sky and down again. When he returned he said, "I have gone on high nicely, now you Mulungu go on high." And Mulungu ascended to the sky on the spider's thread to escape from the wickedness of men.

The following myth comes from the Ngombe, one of the many Mongo groups who live in the heart of the equatorial rain forest of Zaire. Their language and culture form part of the larger Bantu-speaking peoples of central and southern Africa.

The Withdrawal of God

Akongo was not always as he is now. In the beginning the creator lived among men; but men were quarrelsome. One day they had a big quarrel and Akongo left them to themselves. He went and hid in the forest and nobody has seen him since. People today can't tell what he is like.

The next two myths are from the Ashanti peoples of modern Ghana. They are one of the populous Akan cultural complex, one of whose characteristics is matrilineal descent. The Ashanti state, founded around 1680, became a principal political power on the Gold Coast during the eighteenth and nineteenth centuries. Its greatness resulted in part from European trade and in part from the fact that it integrated under its king (the *asantehene*) and ruling council many more of the Akan peoples into one state than had been achieved before. The Ashanti were also splendid craftspeople whose court art, textiles, and gold weights are among the highest achievements of West African art.

The Tower to Heaven

Long, long ago Onyankopon lived on earth, or at least was very near to us. Now there was a certain old woman who used to pound her mashed yams and the pestle kept knocking up against Onyankopon, who was not then high in the sky. So Onyankopon said to the old woman: "Why do you keep doing this to me? Because of what you are doing I am going to take myself away up in the sky." And of a truth he did so.

Now the people could no longer approach Onyankopon. But the old woman thought of a way to reach him and bring him back. She instructed her children to go and search for all the mortars they could find and bring them to her. Then she told them to pile one mortar on top of another til they reached to where Onyankopon was. And her children did so, they piled up many mortars, one on top of another, til they needed only one more mortar to reach Onyankopon.

Now, since they could not find another mortar anywhere, their grandmother the old woman said to them: "Take one out from the bottom and put it on top to make them reach." So her children removed a mortar from the bottom and all the mortars rolled and fell to the ground, causing the death of many people.

QUESTIONS

1. What generalization can you make from these myths about the basic cause of humanity's fall from its idyllic relationship with God?

2. What is the difference between the relationship between God and humanity and that between God and the animals in "Mulungu and the Beasts"?

3. What does "The Tower to Heaven" say about human ingenuity in relation to God? Compare the biblical story of the tower of Babel.

Myths on the Origin of Death

The Perverted Message

In primeval times, God had familiar intercourse with men and gave them all they needed. This state, however, came to an end when some women who were grinding their food became embarrassed by God's presence and told him to go away, and beat him with their pestles. God then withdrew from the world, and left its government to the spirits.

Afterward God sent a goat from heaven to the seven human beings on earth with the following message: "There is something called death. One day it will kill some of you. Even if you die, however, you will not be altogether lost. You will come to live with me in the sky."

On the way, the goat lingered at a bush in order to eat, and when God discovered this he sent a sheep with the same message. But the sheep changed the message to the effect that men should die, and that as far as they were concerned this would be the end of all things. When the goat then arrived with her true message, men would not believe it. They had already accepted the message delivered by the sheep. Shortly afterward the first case of death took place, and God taught men to bury their dead. He also told them that as a foil to death they should be given the capacity to multiply.

According to another version, God sent the sheep with eternal life as a gift to men. But the he-goat ran on ahead and gave them death as a gift from God. They eagerly accepted this gift, as they did not know what death was. The sheep arrived after a while, but it was too late.

The Efe are a small branch of the Mbuti hunting and gathering peoples who live in the Ituri forest of Zaire. They are seminomadic and often live in symbiotic relationships with nearby black African groups. This myth is from the Efe.

The Forbidden Fruit

God created the first human being Ba-atsi with the help of the moon. He kneaded the body into shape, covered it with a skin, and poured in blood. When the man had thus been given life, God whispered in his ear that he, Ba-atsi, should beget children, and upon them he should impress the following prohibition: "Of all the trees of the forest you may eat, but of the Tahu tree you may not eat." Ba-atsi had many children, impressed upon them the prohibition, and then retired to heaven. At first men respected the commandment they had been given, and lived happily. But one day a pregnant woman was seized with an irresistible desire to eat of the forbidden fruit. She tried to persuade her husband to give her some of it. At first he refused, but after a time he gave way. He stole into the wood, picked a Tahu fruit, peeled it, and hid the peel among the leaves. But the moon had seen his action and reported it to God. God was so enraged over man's disobedience that as punishment he sent death among them.

The following myth comes from the Darasa, one of a cluster of ancient Cushitic peoples who practice intensive agriculture by irrigation and terracing of mountain slopes in southern Ethiopia.

Man Chooses Death in Exchange for Fire

Formerly men had no fire but ate all their food raw. At that time they did not need to die for when they became old, God made them young again. One day they decided to beg God for fire. They sent a messenger to God to convey their request. God replied to the messenger that he would give him fire if he was prepared to die. The man took the fire from God, but ever since then all men must die.

Madagascar, the source of this next myth, lies in the Indian Ocean off the southeastern coast of Africa. Its peoples include descendants of both mainland Africans and Malayo-Polynesians who probably followed the seasonal trade winds from southeast Asia to settle on the island around the beginning of the Christian era.

Man Chooses Death in Exchange for Children

One day God asked the first human couple who then lived in heaven what kind of death they wanted, that of the moon or that of the banana. Because the couple wondered in dismay about the implications of the two modes of death, God explained to them: the banana puts forth shoots which take its place and the moon itself comes back to life. The couple considered for a long time before they made their choice. If they elected to be childless they would avoid death, but they would also be very lonely, would themselves be forced to carry out all the work, and would not have anybody to work and strive for. Therefore they prayed to God for children, well aware of the consequences of their choice. And their prayer was granted. Since that time man's sojourn is short on this earth.

COMMENTS AND QUESTIONS

1. Notice the closeness of animals to God in comparison to people. How do you interpret the significance of the "perverted message"?

2. Compare "The Forbidden Fruit" with the similar story in Genesis. Is the religious message of the two stories the same?

3. What is the cultural significance of fire? Why would people choose it over immortality? Look up the Greek myth of Prometheus to compare it with this.

4. How are the importance of children and continuity of the community over time expressed? Notice the expression of this value in other aspects of African culture.

A Labarai Tale

The labarai example below, "The Origin of All Kings"—sometimes called the Daura legend—relates the origin of the Hausa city-state political system. The legend probably developed in the eighteenth century at a time when Bornu, a kingdom to the east, exercised subtle political influence over the Hausa states. The attribution of Eastern origin (in this case Baghdad) is common among Islamic states in West Africa. The translator of this selection, and of the following tatsuniyoyi tales (with the exception of "The Kano Man," originally compiled by Frank Edgar), is Roberta Ann Dunbar.

The Origin of All Kings

This is the story of the first Kings of Daura, Kano, Katsina Gobir, Zazzau (Zaria) and Nuru (Rano), who descended from a man named Bayajibda, son of Abdullahi, King of Baghdad. Now the reason Bayajibda left Baghdad was that a heathen named Zidawa made war against them—a devastating war—and their land was divided into 40 parts.

Bayajibda went with twenty towards Bornu. Together with his soldiers they were a greater and more powerful force than the men of the King of Bornu. The Bornu king came from Syria. When Bayajibda's men realized they were more powerful than those of the King of Bornu they said to him, "Let's kill the King of Bornu so that you may succeed him."

But the King of Bornu hearing this was wary and could not be killed. The King of Bornu asked, "What is our plan for these intruders, my countrymen? The only plan I can see is to marry him off." So Bayajibda was given a daughter of the King named Magira to marry.

Peace and trust developed between them. When he went out on campaigns, Bayajibda would say to the King of Bornu, "Give me some of your men. I will take them to some villages and together we will conquer them." Sometimes he was given two thousand men; at others three thousand. But when he returned from war, he would not return with them. Rather, he set them up in towns in Bornu's territory.

After a time there were only two of Bayajibda's fellow countrymen left. He said to them, "Brothers, I want to look for a place for each of you to live." He set out with one of them and went to Kanem. He is King of Kanem. He set out with the other and went to Bagirmi. He is King of Bagirmi. Then Bayajibda, now alone, left, accompanied by his wife, the daughter of the King of Bornu, and his horse.

When the Bornu people saw that Bayajibda was alone, they kept trying to seek him out to kill him. Because of this he fled at great pace with his wife Magira who was pregnant. In this way they arrived at a certain town called Gabas. Bayajibda left his wife there as she was unable to travel further, and continued on his way. After his departure, she bore a son who was named Biram. He became King of Gabas, or as it was called Gabas of Biram.

When Bayajibda reached Daura, a queen was ruling there. Among the women who had ruled in Daura before, the first was Kufunu. After her the next was Gufunu, then Yakunu, Yakunya, Waizam, Waiwaina, Gidirgidir, Anagari, and Daura. It was she whom Bayajibda found ruling when he came.

When he arrived he alighted at the house of an old woman named Awaina and asked her to give him water. But she said to him, "Alas, my son, one can get water in this town only on Friday when people are gathered together." He replied, "I will draw water. Give me a bucket." She brought a bucket and gave him. It was nighttime when they spoke together about this.

When he had taken the bucket, he went to the well and dropped the bucket down inside. Now in the well lived a female snake. When the snake heard someone drop the bucket, she raised her head from the well and tried to kill Bayajibda. The name of the snake was Sarki. But he took out his sword, cut off her head and took the head and hid it. He drew water, drank and gave some to his horse. He took the rest to the old woman Awaina. He went into the house and lay down to rest.

At daybreak, people saw what this Arab from Syria had done. They were surprised at the size of what remained of the snake at the well. In a while the news reached Daura and she came with her warriors to the well site.

When the queen saw that the snake's head had been cut off and what remained behind, she was filled with wonder because this thing had so harassed the people. She said, "If I discover whoever has killed this snake, I will divide the kingdom in two and give him half." One man said, "I killed it." She asked, "Where is its head? If he doesn't show the head he is lying." So that man left. Another man came and exclaimed, "It was I who killed it." This one too was lying. Many men came forward, but each one was proclaiming himself falsely.

Then the old woman appeared and said, "Last night a stranger stopped at my house. He came with an animal, though whether it was an ox or a horse, I don't know. He took the bucket, drew water from the well, drank and gave some to his animal, bringing me the rest of it. Perhaps he is the one who killed the snake. We should find him and ask." So Bayajibda was summoned and Daura asked him, "Are you the one who killed the snake?" "It was I," he replied. She said, "Where is its head?" "Here it is," he said. Then the queen said, "I promised that for whoever did this thing, I would divide my town in two and give him half." He said, "Do not divide your town. As for me, I request your hand in marriage." So she married him and he lived in her house. She gave him a slave girl whom he took as a concubine. When people came to Daura's house they didn't say her name. Rather they said, "We are going to the house of Makas-Sarki, 'the killer of Sarki.'" Thus it happened that she assumed the name Sarki [the Hausa word for chief].

After some time, the concubine became pregnant although Daura did not. The concubine gave birth to a son. Bayajibda sought Daura's permission and she gave it to name him Makarabgari (Receiver of the town). After this Daura became pregnant and when she gave birth to a son, she sought her husband's permission to name him. They agreed and the child was called Bawugari. He was the first of the kings.

When Makas-Sarki, his father, died, Bawugari inherited his father's dwelling place and bore six children. The first named Gazaura, was King of Daura. Another of the same mother named Bagauda became King of Kano. Another son named Gunguma became King of Zazzau and another by the same mother named Dami became King of Gobir. The last two, also of the same mother, were Kumayau who became King of Katsina and Zamgugu who was King of Rano.

Thus ends the story of the kings.

COMMENTS AND QUESTIONS

1. The marriage between an indigenous queen and a newcomer is not an uncommon motif in legends of origin and may reflect the transition from an earlier matrilineal or matriarchal stage to a patrilineal and patriarchal stage in society. This kind of marriage is also a frequent way of explaining accommodation between foreign invaders and local people over whom they had established hegemony. Compare the story of Oedipus.

2. Political power was recognized not only because of military conquest, but also because of technological expertise. Bayajibda killed the snake that had restricted Daura's water supply; he also came with an animal, the horse, unfamiliar to the old woman who gave him shelter. Does this suggest anything to you about levels of technology or modes of warfare in pre-Bayajibda Hausa society?

3. Compare this tale with the epic *Sundiata*. Is Bayajibda a hero in the same sense that Sundiata is? What is the difference in the way in which an epic and a tale present a hero?

Tatsuniyoyi Tales

Dog, Hyena, and Lizard

Dog got up from his sickbed and was hungry. He saw Lizard stealing some beans, grabbed him, and headed for home. On the way he ran into Hyena. Dog dropped Lizard and took to his heels. Hyena said, "Let me take this thing in hand home first before I come back to take that thing in the bush." So she picked up Lizard and carried him to her hole. Then she came back looking for Dog, but couldn't find him. She went home and Lizard was gone. Poor Hyena said,

"Alas, whatever you manage to get hold of in this world, if it is not your fate to have it, having gotten it is useless—you'll lose it anyway."

Two Frogs

One day two frogs fell into a calabash of milk and couldn't get out. They swam around for a while, then one of them tired out and said,

"Today my days are finished."

So he gave up and sank to the bottom and died. But the other frog kept on swimming and swimming. He churned the milk so hard with all of his swimming, that it turned into butter. The frog climbed on top of the ball of butter and jumped out of the calabash.

God said, "Rise so that I may help you."

Squirrel and Hedgehog

One day it was raining. Hedgehog was wandering around when she came to the door of Squirrel's hole. She greeted him and said,

"I'm really cold. Is there any room there for me to take shelter?"

Squirrel said,

"There's a little space here, come on in."

They sat down together. After a while Squirrel said,

"Hey Hedgehog, our being together like this isn't very pleasant. Your body is all prickly. Why don't you go find another spot?"

Hedgehog said,

"Gee, this place is fine for me. Whoever doesn't find this place suitable, *he* should be the one to move!"

The Blind Man with the Lamp

A young man was strolling along one night when he caught sight of a man with a lamp. When he drew near he realized that the man was blind. The boy said,

"Hey blind man, have you lost your senses? What brings you to wandering around with a lamp? Aren't day and night all the same to you?"

The blind man said,

"Of course they are, stupid. Even at night I see better than you do. I don't carry this lamp for myself, but so that you silly people without eyes don't bump into me."

Life Is Better than Wealth

Once there was a man who was so poor he didn't know what to do. So he went to the king and said,

"I don't have anything to eat for today, or for tomorrow either. I don't have anything at all in the world save this loincloth. I'm tired of living. I want you to kill me."

The king said,

"All right."

He called some soldiers and told them to kill the man so that he could find rest. The soldiers were about to dispatch him when another came by and said,

"If you kill him, please give me his loincloth." When the poor man heard that he said,

"Stop! Take me back to the king. I have something to say."

So they took him back and the king asked them what happened. The poor man fell on his knees and said,

"Your highness, let me go. Today I have seen someone poorer than I am. Truly, life is great."

The king said,

"Be off with you and thank God that he has given you life and health."

Hasara and Riba

Hasara and Riba were sisters—same mother same father. Hasara was an extremely beautiful girl but poor Riba was ugly. Tinau and Sule sought their hands in marriage. Tinau was richer and better looking than Sule and he courted Hasara. So Sule proceeded to court Riba. The couples were married at the same time and each girl went to the home of her husband.

Now Hasara was proud and haughty. She liked elegant food, jewelry, and very expensive clothes. Riba, however, worked together with her husband. She helped him take goods to market and when they earned a profit, they put aside half of it, using the rest for their trading. Before a year was out Sule was a rich man. Tinau by that time was flat broke. To make a long story short, Tinau left Hasara with all her beauty. She married another and the same thing happened. Before the second year was past, Hasara had been married four times. But Riba is still there with her husband Sule. They are very prosperous and even have many cattle with shepherds to look after them. Whoever follows his heart's desire surely he will be wed to loss.

The Rivals

There were two boys who were courting the same girl. She couldn't decide which to accept, so she told them she would marry whichever one was the braver.

One day, the boys went to her place for a chat. When they got ready to go home, she accompanied them to the edge of the "bush." Suddenly, a leopard came upon them. The first boy hurled his spear at the leopard but missed it. The other did the same. They continued until all their spears were gone. Meanwhile the girl hid behind a tree. Then, one boy said to the other,

"Hurry home to my mother's house. There are some spears there near the bed. Gather them up and bring them back."

When the other boy departed, the one left behind fell on the leopard and wrestled with it. He got the leopard down and killed it. Then, he propped the leopard up, called to the girl, and told her to lie down in front of it. He then hid himself.

The other boy returned without any spears since they had already been borrowed by someone else. He came upon the leopard where he had left it and saw the girl lying on the ground in front of it. The boy said,

"Oh no, is that the way he is? He gets rid of me so that he can run off and lets the leopard kill the poor girl?"

Then he attacked the leopard with full force and grabbed it around the neck. The leopard's body fell over in a heap. The boy who had been hiding came out laughing.

So now, which one of them will the girl marry?

The Kano Man

This is the sharp fellow, the city slicker.

His character: A Kano man puts on a dark-blue gown, and a white Nupe one, and a black-and-white one; then he wears Kano-style trousers, either white or black-and-white; puts on a length of muslin for a turban; hangs a book over his shoulder and off he goes to school to recite the Koran; he takes a staff, a little gourd water-bottle, and away he goes. When he has finished at school, he returns home. When it is time for market he goes to market. Returning from there, when it is night, he puts on a leather loincloth, picks up a rope-ladder, and off he goes to steal. Sometimes he gets shot or wounded with a sword, and sometimes dies, and sometimes gets better.

The Kano character is also, if a rich visitor arrives, to receive him joyfully, and give him a gown, or a turban or a length of cloth. Then they get together with one of the household where he is staying and start bringing shoddy stuff to sell him. When the householder sees it, he praises its quality. They abuse his trust in them and trick him. But if the visitor is shrewd, he rejects all the stuff they bring him, saying, "I'm not buying it," and waits till he gets to the market and buys what he wants.

Trickery and fraud are Kano characteristics. Whoever you are, a Kano man will trick you—unless he thinks it can't be done. For there is no one so cowardly.

COMMENTS AND QUESTIONS

1. A major characteristic of African tales evident in the Hausa tatsuniyoyi is their realism and recognition of the flaws in human nature and in society. Some tales exhort people to good behavior; others express stereotypes about people from different places or walks of life as seen here in "The Kano Man." Kano was and is a major commercial center. Its markets attracted merchants from all over West and North Africa. How does this tale's image of the Kano man—the quintessential merchant—compare with our own image of the "city slicker"?

2. Hasara and Riba are not usual Hausa names as suggested in that story. Rather they are respectively the Hausa words for "loss" and "profit." What does this tale tell you about values of work and discipline?

3. What other Hausa values are expressed in these tales?

4. What shows you that these tales are well grounded in the socioeconomic realities of the Hausa people?

5. What model is suggested in the tales "Hasara and Riba" and "The Rivals" for a proper relationship between husband and wife?

6. Do the morals to these tales appear to be "tacked on," or are they woven into the fabric of the story? Give examples.

Yoruba Riddles

These riddles are reprinted from *Black Orpheus* and the *Journal of American Folklore*.

A round calabash in the spear grass.
Ans.: Moon and stars.

We cut its head, we cut its tail. It still insists on performing the ritual of its ancestors.
Ans.: A piece of cassava. However small a piece you cut—it will still grow.

We tie a horse in the house, but its mane flies above the roof.
Ans.: Fire and smoke.

We invited him to warm himself in the sun—he came. We asked him to take his bath. He said: death has come.
Ans.: Salt.

One cooked yam all over the world.
Ans.: The moon.

They cut off his head; they cut off his waist; his stump says he will inherit the title of his father's house.
Ans.: Yam.

Children walking; mother crawling.
Ans.: Gourd.

It bears fruit, we cannot pick it; the fruit falls, we cannot gather it.
Ans.: Dew.

Fat wife inside many thorns.
Ans.: Tongue and teeth.

Ancient will of my father, ancient will of my father; if a child gets into it, it reaches his neck; if an elder gets into it, it reaches his neck.
Ans.: A shirt or gown.

We seize hold of it; the child in its womb walks away.
Ans.: Gun.

Who is it that goes down the street past the king's house without greeting the king?
Ans.: Rainwater.

My father complained that I was late coming back from the farm. I said the road divided into three and I had to travel on three paths simultaneously.
Ans.: Putting on trousers.

People run away from her when she is pregnant. But they rejoice when she has delivered.
Ans.: A gun.

Yoruba Proverbs

Translation by Bakare Gbadamosi and Ulli Beier

The Yoruba proverbs included below are keys to the values of the Yoruba people. They sometimes express a surprising candor about political relationships, hospitality, and attitudes toward the elderly—areas where candor outside of proverbial speech would be impolitic and rude.

The egg eater does not think of the pain it cost the hen.

The dignified crawl of the earthworm arouses the envy of the cock.

A man has been beaten six times and is advised to be patient. What else is there for him to do?

When death is not ready to receive a man, it sends an expert physician at the right time.

A bachelor who asks for food too often will soon hear the price of vegetables.

The small hand of the child cannot reach the high shelf. The large hand of the adult cannot enter the neck of the calabash.

Only the man whom his child buries has really got a child.

It is the honour of the father that allows the son to walk about proudly.

We are talking about pumpkins. A woman asks what are we talking about. We say: this is a man's talk. But when we gather the fruit, who will break them and cook them?

Anger does not help. Patience is the father of character.

The river carries away an elderly person who does not know his own weight.

The thinking of a wolf is enough to tail a sheep.

What only stops a hawk from laughing will make the hen faint on her eggs.

The eagle makes the owner of the fowl go crazy.

The wisdom of others prevents a chief from being called a fool.

The god who favors a lazy man does not exist. It is one's hands that bring prosperity.

Everybody who comes to this world must become something. Only we don't know what.

The effort of forcing another man to be like oneself makes one an unpleasant person.

What causes a dog to bark is not sufficient to make a sheep gaze.

Having become king you prepare charms. Do you want to become a god?

One who takes another to court does not think that the other man has his own statement to make.

After the man has been cured, he beats the doctor.

The proud pond stands alone from the river, forgetting that water is common to both.

Mean people are common like trees in the forest.

An elderly man who cannot keep his mouth shut when he sees something strange, must use his mouth in court.

Do not be seen counting the toes of the man who has only nine.

QUESTIONS

1. What Yoruba social values and philosophical beliefs can you discern in the riddles? In the proverbs?
2. Attempt to define "riddle" as a literary genre. Which riddles here show evidence of a sophisticated wit?
3. Can you compare any of the proverbs here with those in the Bible?

Poetry

Most of the poems that follow have been taken from the rich oral tradition of the Yoruba language. They represent not only a wide variety of forms and subjects but also the intimate relationship that exists between poetry and everyday life in Africa. Two non-Yoruba poems illustrating this relationship are a Fulani love poem and the naming poem from the Ga people in Ghana. In addition, we have included three modern poems written in European languages but which make use of traditional themes.

The ritual character of the first four Yoruba poems calls for a further explanation of Yoruba religion and traditional forms of Yoruba poetry. We saw in the mythology section that in Yoruba belief the first, high God, Oludumare, is represented on earth by lesser deities called orisha. Orisha may also symbolize ancestor figures, ancient kings, and founders of cities. Each orisha is associated with some form of nature, or with a particular color or metal. Each of the four poems is a praise poem dedicated to one of the orisha. The first is about Obatala, god of creation (recall the Yoruba myths of creation); the second on Eshu, the unpredictable god of fate and the agent for change, good and bad. The subject of the third is Oshun, the mother goddess, protector of the town of Oshogbo and source of healing and fertility; and that of the

fourth, Ogun, whose association with iron and war is linked to survival, innovation, and technology. These poems are classified as *oriki* by the Yoruba—meaning poems based on names given to gods, places, rulers, and important persons. Oriki poetry is performed by professional singers or, in the case of poems about deities such as these, by the priests of the particular deity whose oriki is being sung.

Yoruba poetry is classified by the style of specific groups of performers more than by subject matter or poetic form. Whereas the oriki are sung by priests, *ijala* are sung by hunters, and the *iwi*, represented by "Children" and two Yoruba funeral songs, are poems sung by the *egungun*, the masqueraders. These have a specific religious function: they mediate between the community of the living and that of the recently dead. Masqueraders embody the spirit and imitate the voice of the person involved; during the ceremonial, dances are sacred. Reflecting the high degree of integration of religious beliefs with other aspects of social life, masqueraders may also entertain, sometimes offering social satires and commentaries.

In the Ga naming poem, as in the Yoruba iwi on children, the fragility of life, the desirability of children, and their symbolic importance as links between the living and dead appear as critical elements of belief. The poem, "The Beloved," was collected by Amadou Hampaté ba from the traditional literature of the Fulani, a nomadic group in West Africa.

The final three poems—written by Birago Diop, a Senegalese who writes in French, and Chinua Achebe and Wole Soyinka, two Nigerians who write in English—illustrate the fact that modern African writers continue to draw inspiration from traditional beliefs and from the themes and styles of oral literature. The Yoruba poetry is translated by Bakare Gbadamosi and Ulli Beier; the Ga poem by Neils Augustine Hesse.

Oriki—Yoruba Praise Poems
Oriki Obatala

He is patient, he is not angry.
He sits in silence to pass judgement.
He sees you even when he is not looking.
He stays in a far place—but his eyes are on the town.

The granary of heaven can never be full.
The old man full of life force.

He kills the novice.
And wakens him to let him hear his words.
We leave the world to the owner of the world.

Death acts playfully till he carries away the child.
He rides on the hunchback.
He stretches out his right hand.
He stretches out his left hand.

He stands by his children and lets them succeed.
He causes them to laugh—and they laugh.
Ohoho—the father of laughter.
His eye is full of joy,
He rests in the sky like a swarm of bees.

We dance to your sixteen drums that sound jingin,
    jingin,
To eight of the drums we dance bending down,
To eight of the drums we dance erect.
We shake our shoulders, we shake our hips,
Munusi, munusi, munusi,
We dance to your sixteen drums.

Those who are rich owe their property to him.
Those who are poor, owe their property to him.
He takes from the rich and gives to the poor.
Whenever you take from the rich—come and give it
    to me!

Obatala—who turns blood into children.
I have only one cloth to dye with blue indigo.
I have only one headtie to dye with red camwood.
But I know that you keep twenty or thirty children
    for me
Whom I shall bear.

Oriki Eshu

When he is angry he hits a stone until it bleeds.
When he is angry he sits on the skin of an ant.
When he is angry he weeps tears of blood.

Eshu, confuser of men.
The owner of twenty slaves is sacrificing,
So that Eshu may not confuse him.
The owner of thirty "iwofa" is sacrificing,
So that Eshu may not confuse him.
Eshu confused the newly married wife.
When she stole the cowries from the sacred shrine of
  Oya
She said she had not realized
That taking two hundred cowries was stealing.
Eshu confused the head of the queen—
And she started to go naked.
Then Eshu beat her to make her cry.
Eshu, do not confuse me!
Eshu, do not confuse the load on my head.

Eshu, lover of dogs.
If a goat gets lost in Ogbe,—don't ask me.
Do you think I am a thief of goats?
If a huge sheep is missing from Ogbe—don't ask me.
Do you think I am a thief of sheep?
If any fowl get lost in Ogbe—don't ask me.
Do you think I am a thief of birds?
But if a black dog is missing from Ogbe—ask me!
You will find me eating Eshu's sacrifice in a wooden
    bowl.

Eshu slept in the house.—
But the house was too small for him.
Eshu slept on the verandah—
But the verandah was too small for him.
Eshu slept in a nut—
At last he could stretch himself.

Eshu walked through the groundnut farm.
The tuft of his hair was just visible.
If it had not been for his huge size,
He would not have been visible at all.

Having thrown a stone yesterday—he kills a bird
    today.
Lying down, his head hits the roof.
Standing up he cannot look into the cooking pot.
Eshu turns right into wrong, wrong into right.

Oriki Oshun

We call her and she replies with wisdom.
She can cure those whom the doctor has failed.
She cures the sick with cold water.
When she cures the child, she does not charge the
    father.
We can remain in the world without fear.
Iyalode who cures children—help me to have my
    own child.
Her medicines are free—she feeds honey to the
    children.
She is rich and her words are sweet.
Large forest with plenty of food.
Let a child embrace my body.
The touch of a child's hand is sweet.

Owner of brass. Owner of parrots' feathers.
Owner of money.

My mother, you are beautiful, very beautiful.
Your eyes sparkle like brass.
Your skin is soft and smooth.
You are black like velvet.

Everybody greets you when you descend on the
world.
Everybody sings your praises.

Oriki Ogun

Ogun kills on the right and destroys on the right.
Ogun kills on the left and destroys on the left.
Ogun kills suddenly in the house and suddenly in the
field.
Ogun kills the child with the iron with which it
plays.
Ogun kills in silence.
Ogun kills the thief and the owner of the stolen
goods.
Ogun kills the owner of the slave—and the slave
runs away.
Ogun kills the owner of thirty "iwofa"—and his
money, wealth and children disappear.
Ogun kills the owner of the house and paints the
hearth with his blood.
Ogun is the death who pursues a child until it runs
into the bush.
Ogun is the needle that pricks at both ends.
Ogun has water but he washes in blood.

Ogun, do not fight me. I belong only to you.
The wife of Ogun is like a tim tim.
She does not like two people to rest on her.

Ogun has many gowns. He gives them all to the
beggars.
He gives one to the woodcock—the woodcock dyes
it indigo.
He gives one to the coucal—the coucal dyes it in
camwood.
He gives one to the cattle egret—the cattle egret
leaves it white.

Ogun is not like pounded yam:
Do you think you can knead him in your hand
And eat of him until you are satisfied?
Ogun is not like maize gruel:
Do you think you can knead him in your hand
And eat of him until you are satisfied?
Ogun is not like some thing you can throw into your
cap:
Do you think you can put on your cap and walk
away with him?

Ogun scatters his enemies.
When the butterflies arrive at the place where the
cheetah excretes,

They scatter in all directions.
The light shining on Ogun's face is not easy to
behold.
Ogun, let me not see the red of your eye.

Ogun sacrifices an elephant to his head.
Master of iron, head of warriors,
Ogun, great chief of robbers.
Ogun wears a bloody cap.
Ogun has four hundred wives and one thousand four
hundred children.
Ogun, the fire that sweeps the forest.
Ogun's laughter is no joke.
Ogun eats two hundred earthworms and does not
vomit.

Ogun is a crazy orisha who still asks questions after
780 years!
Whether I can reply, or whether I cannot reply.
Ogun please don't ask me anything.

The lion never allows anybody to play with his cub.
Ogun will never allow his child to be punished.
Ogun, do not reject me!
Does the woman who spins ever reject a spindle?
Does the woman who dyes ever reject a cloth?
Does the eye that sees ever reject a sight?
Ogun, do not reject me!

COMMENTS AND QUESTIONS

1. In "Oriki Obatala," note the dualistic nature of
   Obatala. He is the creator, a kindly deity, who can
   also kill (as in line 7). Refer to the myths of Obatala earlier in this chapter ("The Creation of Land"
   and "The Creation of Man"). What characteristics are portrayed in both the myths and this
   poem?

2. Eshu, as the poem "Oriki Eshu" states, is the
   "confuser of men." In Yoruba cosmology he symbolizes disorder, the unexpected—and yet this
   quality permits him to turn "wrong into right."
   How does the poem express the contradictions of
   his character?

3. Is the *tone* of the poem on the feminine deity,
   Oshun, different from those on the masculine
   deities? How so?

4. How does the poetic principle of *anaphora*, the
   successive repetition of words or phrases, operate
   in all of the oriki and especially in "Oriki Ogun"?
   What would be the effect and usefulness of this
   device in oral poetry?

Ijala—The Poetry of Yoruba Hunters

Adiye (Fowl)

One who sees corn and is glad.
The chicken wears its shin at the back.
We eat it with pounded yam.
Every fool will be buried in the cheek.
The foolish chicken has many relations:
Oil is its relative on the father's side.
Pepper and onion are its relatives on the mother's side.
If it does not see its friend salt even for a day
It will not sleep peacefully.

Etu-Duiker (Antelope)

Beautiful antelope with the slender neck.
Your thighs are worth twenty slaves.
Your arms are more precious than thirty servants.
Your neck is exquisite like a sacred carving.
You step out like a nobleman
Shaking the grass like bells.
Your facial marks are beautiful and bold
Even like those of the king of Ogbomosho.
You wash your body with white.
God has honoured you with white.
The hunter is happy when the owner of white
    appears.
I cannot be happy when I kill you,
Until I have found your body in the bush.
The pregnant woman demands your skin.
Lying on your skin she will bear a beautiful child.

New Yam

New yam causes the wife of yesterday to lose her
    manners,
New yam causes the head of the household to reject
    food.
It makes a rich person speak out.
Yam will pay its own debt.
"Lay me on a fine bed
And I will lay you on a fine lady."

COMMENTS AND QUESTIONS

1. What is the difference in tone between the poem on the chicken and the poem on the antelope? How do the poems render what the poets see as the essence of these two animals?

2. How is the antelope in "Etu-Duiker" personified? What dimension do *similes* give to the poem?

3. The yam, a root vegetable, is the staple food of many African peoples along the Guinea coast. Although yams are relatively easy to grow, they may be ravaged by drought or, to the contrary, rotted by untimely rains. The annual harvest of the new yams, often following a time of hardship and meager food supply, is the occasion for celebration. It is often signaled by religious rituals of thanks and communal solidarity.

4. Explain the relation of the last two lines of "New Yam" to the first part of the poem.

Iwi—The Poetry of Yoruba Masqueraders

Children

A child is like a rare bird.
A child is precious like coral.
A child is precious like brass.
You cannot buy a child on the market.
Not for all the money in the world.
The child you can buy for money is a slave.
We may have twenty slaves,
We may have thirty labourers,
Only a child brings us joy,
One's child is one's child.
The buttocks of our child are not so flat
That we should tie the beads on another child's hips.
One's child is one's child.
It may have a watery head or a square head,
One's child is one's child.
It is better to leave behind a child,
Than let the slaves inherit one's house.
A child is the beginning and end of happiness.
One must not rejoice too soon over a child.
Only the one who is buried by his child,
Is the one who has truly borne a child.
On the day of our death, our hand cannot hold a
    single cowrie.
We need a child to inherit our belongings.

COMMENTS AND QUESTIONS

1. Describe the style of this poem. What is the effect of the very short sentences?

2. What does this poem tell you about the importance of children in African society?

Funeral Poem I

Come nearer home,
Mother of Aina.
You knew how to produce children,
but never learned to chide them.
Come and receive the sacrifice
from your children.
You people of the road,
where did you meet her?
The mother of Kujusola
the mother of Alawede.
They met her on the road to Ede.
I thank the trees that did not fall on her.
I thank the river
that did not carry her away.
No one can bar her way
for she travels an underground path.
Like a new bride
She covers her head with a cloth.

Funeral Poem II

The hunter dies
and leaves his poverty to his gun.
The blacksmith dies
and leaves his poverty to his anvil.
The farmer dies
and leaves his poverty to his hoe.
The bird dies
and leaves its poverty to its nest.
You have died
and left me abandoned in the dark.
Where are you now?
Are you the goat
eating grass around the house?
Are you the motionless lizard
on the hot mud wall?
If I tell you not to eat earthworms
it's like asking you to go hungry.
But whatever they may eat in heaven
Partake with them.
A dead body cannot receive double punishment:
If there is not cloth to cover it—
There will always be earth to cover it.

COMMENTS AND QUESTIONS

1. What different emotions on the mourners' part
   are conveyed in these two poems, and how does
   the imagery express them?

2. How do the Yoruba beliefs that the dead live on as
   spirits or else are reincarnated appear in these
   poems?

Fulani Poetry

Amadou Hampaté ba

The Beloved

Diko,
of light skin, of smooth hair and long;
her smells sweet and gentle
she never stinks of fish
she never breathes sweat
like gatherers of dry wood.
She has no bald patch on her head
like those who carry heavy loads.
Her teeth are white
her eyes are like
those of a new born fawn
that delights in the milk
that flows for the first time
from the antelope's udder.
Neither her heel nor her palm
are rough; but sweet to touch
like liver; or better still
the fluffy down of kapok.

COMMENTS AND QUESTIONS

1. The Fulani, cattle-herding nomads, stem from the
   grasslands of the upper Senegal River, but have
   migrated over the centuries as far east as the Cameroons. How does the poet reflect here an intimate familiarity with nature and especially with
   the bush?

2. The romantic idea of love does not play an important social role in African society. Husbands and
   wives may, of course, love each other; but the
   existence of love is not a prerequisite for marriage.
   Love is not a major theme in African poetry,
   although beautiful love lyrics, like the above, do
   exist. Fulani women have a reputation for being
   especially beautiful and exciting. What image of
   Diko, the beloved, do you have from this poem?

3. Compare the way in which the poet here uses
   imagery to describe his beloved and his feelings
   about her to similar techniques in the poems of

Sappho (Chapter 3) and in the Song of Songs (Chapter 8).

Ga Poetry

Naming Poem

May good fortune come
May our stools be clean
May our brooms be clean
In a circle of unity
   have we met
When we dig a well
May we find water
When of this water we drink
May our shoulders find peace
The stranger who has come
On his mother's head be life
On his father's head be life
Behind his back may
   darkness be
Before his face may
   all be bright
May his head the world respect
And his brethren may he know
May we have forgiveness
   to forgive him
May he work and eat
When he sees he has
   not seen
When he hears he has
   not heard
In black he has come
In white may he return
May good fortune come

COMMENTS AND QUESTIONS

1. In many African societies the naming of a child is surrounded with ceremony; it is the public recognition of the personhood of the newborn and the acknowledgment of his or her full membership in the community. The "naming" or "outdooring" does not occur usually until one or two weeks following birth, when it seems certain that the child will survive its entry into the world. On the chosen day, significant members of the youngster's family may whisper the name into the child's ear before announcing it publicly. Special blessings and prayers follow, and the day is filled with gift-giving and celebration by the many relatives and guests invited to share in the occasion.

2. The Ga are a southern Ghanaian people of the Ewe linguistic subgroup of Twi speakers (just as the Ashanti, discussed earlier, are members of the Akan subgroup of Twi speakers). For many Ghanaian peoples there is a close link between the individual and the stool the individual customarily sits on (line 2); for some, a person's soul is said to reside in the stool. (See the discussion of art objects in Chapter 14.) Many rites of passage in the individual's life are carried out in connection with his or her stool, so it is appropriate that "stools" appear in connection with the naming.

3. How does the invocation of this poem illustrate by a shift in focus the link between the child and the community?

4. What are the values that the community wishes for the child?

5. What do *darkness*, *bright*, *black*, and *white* seem to signify?

BIRAGO DIOP (b. 1906)

Forefathers

Listen more often to things rather than beings.
Hear the fire's voice,
Hear the voice of water.
In the wind hear the sobbing of the trees.
It is our forefathers breathing.

The dead are not gone forever.
They are in the paling shadows
And in the darkening shadows.
The dead are not beneath the ground,
They are in the rustling tree,
In the murmuring wood,
In the still water,
In the flowing water,
In the lonely place, in the crowd;
The dead are not dead.

Listen more often to things rather than beings.
Hear the fire's voice,
Hear the voice of water.
In the wind hear the sobbing of the trees.
It is the breathing of our forefathers
Who are not gone, not beneath the ground,
Not dead.

The dead are not gone forever.
They are in a woman's breast,
A child's crying, a glowing ember.
The dead are not beneath the earth,
They are in the flickering fire,
In the weeping plant, the groaning rock,
The wooded place, the home.
The dead are not dead.

Listen more often to things rather than beings.
Hear the fire's voice,
Hear the voice of water.
In the wind hear the sobbing of the trees.
It is the breath of our forefathers.

CHINUA ACHEBE (b. 1930)

Generation Gap

A son's arrival
is the crescent moon
too new too soon to lodge
the man's returning.
His feast of re-incarnation
must await the moon's
reopening at the naming
ceremony of his
grandson.

COMMENTS AND QUESTIONS

1. Many African religions view human existence as a cyclical phenomenon wherein spirits may proceed through various phases of what we know as birth, life, and death in human, but sometimes animal form. This view, articulated in both traditional and modern poetry, reinforces humanity's sensitivity to, and awareness of, the natural world. Compare the metaphor of nature in "Forefathers" with that in the Yoruba funeral poems.

2. How is the cyclical nature of human existence conveyed in "Forefathers," Achebe's "Generation Gap," and the iwi on children?

WOLE SOYINKA (b. 1934)

Death in the Dawn

Traveller, you must set out
At dawn. And wipe your feet upon
The dog-nose wetness of the earth.

Let sunrise quench your lamps. And watch
Faint brush pricklings in the sky light
Cottoned feet to break the early earthworm
On the hoe. Now shadows stretch with sap
Not twilight's death and sad prostration.
This soft kindling, soft receding breeds
Racing joys and apprehensions for
A naked day. Burdened hulks retract,
Stoop to the mist in faceless throng
To wake the silent markets—swift, mute
Processions on grey byways.... On this
Counterpane, it was—
Sudden winter at the death
Of dawn's lone trumpeter. Cascades
Of white feather-flakes...but it proved
A futile rite. Propitiation sped
Grimly on, before.
The right foot for joy, the left, dread
And the mother prayed, Child
May you never walk
When the road waits, famished.

Traveller, you must set forth
At dawn.
I promise marvels of the holy hour
Presages as the white cock's flapped
Perverse impalement—as who would dare
The wrathful wings of man's Progression....

But such another wraith! Brother,
Silenced in the startled hug of
Your invention—is this mocked grimace
This closed contortion—I?

COMMENTS AND QUESTION

1. Wole Soyinka has consistently addressed human issues through the voice of Yoruba belief and expression. Although his works are masterpieces in English, and can be understood within the English reading of them, their power and subtlety are magnified for the reader who understands something of Yoruba culture. Ogun, the god of war and destruction, of the rains, of harvest, of disintegration and death, is a favorite although not always explicit subject of Soyinka's. In modern Nigeria, Ogun is god of the road, a claimant of countless lives on overcrowded highways; taxi and truck drivers are among those who worship him. He is the real subject of "Death in the Dawn." When the poet writes "May you never

walk / When the road waits, famished," it is Ogun that one fears may be famished. "Death in the Dawn" is not an oriki, but go back and reread "Oriki Ogun" after you have read Soyinka's poem. What traditional images of Ogun do you find in Soyinka's poem?

14

Visual and Musical Arts of West Africa

*J*ust as each African language has its own literary tradition, each African society has its own artistic and musical styles. We cannot hope to give even a bird's-eye view of the range and variety of African art and music in the present space. Rather, we will concentrate on the close observation of a few works in order to understand something of the African aesthetic. Since both African art and music have had a profound impact on their modern Western counterparts (see Chapter 34), we are already used to certain conventions, such as abstraction in art and the pentatonic (5-tone) scale in music, which shocked and puzzled earlier Western observers. We are not likely to view these arts, as did the European colonists, as awkward, tribal, or primitive. Nevertheless, there are characteristics of African art and music that make them significantly different from Western forms and that require our attention if we are to appreciate them. In spite of the great diversity of traditions and styles, even within West Africa alone, African art shares some common premises that we will examine first in the visual realm.

Visual Arts

Art and Communal Life

One of the basic differences between Western art and African art lies in the simple fact of classification. The art of the West is usually divided into "fine" and "applied" arts. In the first category are painting, sculpture, and architecture—the arts usually studied in the humanities. The second category includes more utilitarian objects such as furniture, ceramics, textiles, and clothing. This dichotomy does not exist in African art. For the African artist, the objects of everyday life may express beauty, harmony, and philosophical concepts as much as or more than something to hang on a wall. The museum or the gallery does not exist in traditional Africa. Although some Western and African arts are "useful" in the same way—palaces for kings, temples, objects for religious ceremonies—it must be kept in mind that *all* African art is in some way integrated into life in the community. At the same time, even the most humble object may manifest a complex relationship between people and society and their experiences and understanding of the world.

Understanding the world and interpreting one's experiences in it are the basis for art everywhere. The world of the traditional West African is one of close adherence to nature in all its manifestations: in the unchanging cycles of birth and death, planting and harvest, night and day, and the seasons. Yet circumstances may alter the seemingly permanent aspects of these events, and one is forced to assure their timely appearance. The seasonal migration of the herds that provide food and other staples of life, the natural cycles of fertility in animals, the beginning of the rainy seasons, the success of the planting and subsequent harvest, the normal, healthy birth of a child, are all subject to the vicissitudes of nature. This extraordinary awareness of inevitability and change in the face of natural phenomena is closely related to the *animism,* or belief in natural spirits, that characterizes African religions (see the "Myths" section of Chapter 13). The necessity to appease various spirits has been a motivating force for one type of African art. Objects, usually small statues, are created to invite a particular spirit, either "natural" or ancestor, to inhabit it. Great care is taken to make the object beautiful enough to entice the spirit to rest in it.

One might define the constant in African art and life as a tension between order and disorder, permanence and change. African societies place a great value on tradition, and ritual objects such as masks, costumes, and figurines pass on the values, laws, and beliefs of a people from one generation to another, as do the myths and tales of the oral tradition. This assures the permanence and the continuity of the community. On the other hand, the inevitability of change and the need to cope with it are reflected by the importance of *initiation* societies and the arts and rites associated with them. The process of the initiation is the passage of a boy or girl from childhood to adulthood, and the ritual takes place at the time of puberty. Women, in the case of girls, and men, in the case of boys, initiate the child by teaching certain practices, laws, and pieces of wisdom. The process recognizes that the young adults will be agents of

change within the community but assures that change will come about within the framework of tradition.

Much African art is religious in its orientation, not because it is all designed for cults or temples but because religion is so woven into the fabric of everyday African life. African plastic art contains multiple layers of meaning, and any one piece may contain elements in addition to religious ones that evoke commemoration of a ruler (as do the Benin bronzes seen in Chapter 12); regalia of office, such as pendants or staffs; or allusions to favorite mythical or tale characters, which may suggest ribaldry or even laughter. Although sculptural forms and symbolic elements often refer to the past, to beliefs or practices that are traditional, they may also incorporate the innovative and modern. Just as the objects of African art are intimately related to African life, so they are also related to one another. The many rituals and festivals in Africa, one of which we will study later in this chapter, use masks, costumes, music, poetry, and dance in the creation of a complete ensemble. The stylistic principles in a mask, for example, are closely related to those in the other arts. We will examine some of these aesthetic relationships when we look at the art of the festival.

We began this section on the visual arts by discussing the differences in classification between Western and African art and by pointing out that the West's distinction between "fine" and "applied" art does not exist. But how, then, has African art been classified? Africans designate their sculptures, masks, textile patterns, and dances with names appropriate to their function or style within a given culture. On the other hand, Westerners have been interested in a much broader scope—African art as a whole—and have therefore analyzed the relationship of art works across the continent, using ethnic group or formal stylistic criteria as the basis of their categorization. One of the most interesting systems of classification is that developed some years ago by Arnold Rubin;[1] it employs a combination of geographical, artistic, and cultural criteria to identify three major zones of African sculpture: the Sudanic, the Guinea Coast, and the Equatorial. Each zone is divided into style regions and, in some instances, subregions. The sculptural art of each of these regions or subregions has particular characteristics that distinguish it from the art forms of other regions. These characteristics may include, for

[1] Arnold Rubin, *The Sculptor's Eye* (Washington, D.C.: Museum of African Art, 1976).

example, a preference for certain types of masks, figures, or utilitarian objects over others; for emphasis on two-dimensional lines rather than on volume; for shared choice of color or medium in relation to sculpture; for the presence or absence of surface decoration; or for the degree of naturalism, as opposed to *abstractionism* or *expressionism,* in the sculpture. Art from the frontier areas of these regions is likely to show the influences of the adjacent region. The advantage of this system enables the observer to escape from rigid ethnic or formal classification to an understanding of African art that encompasses the aesthetic and the cultural; it also permits visualization of relationships on a broader scale, not only between art forms but also between art and other cultural features. Thus, it is interesting to note that the major sculpture-producing regions in Africa coincide with the area in which the Congo-Kordofanian languages, mentioned at the beginning of Chapter 13, are spoken.

Although we have chosen a simpler organization than Rubin's for the discussion of individual examples of African objects that follows (physical type and social function), the reader should bear in mind some of the ways, suggested earlier, in which sculptural forms may differ from region to region, in order to better appreciate the richness of the African plastic art tradition.

14-1 *Left. Mali. Bambara Chi Wara, Chi Wara headpiece, male antelope. Right. Chi Wara headpiece, female antelope. (Erle and Clyta Loran Collection)*

Masks and Headpieces

Masks and headpieces are usually worn by men in the context of the social and religious rituals of associations, sometimes referred to as secret societies. These societies function as the community's agents for social control, education (through initiation), and communication with the spirits of the ancestors. They are particularly important and powerful in ethnic groups that do not have centralized chieftaincies or kingships. Secret societies may be very specialized in their function, although some also operate in a variety of situations. Usually the associations consist of several grades or ranks through which individuals of skill and prestige may rise to positions of great influence. They are "secret" because their specialized knowledge is reserved to initiates of the societies and because the members are anonymous to the public when performing the masked rituals or acting on behalf of the association. When an individual dons the mask, he becomes the receptacle for the spiritual force of whatever essence is portrayed and is identified as that essence by those who behold him.

The Chi Wara headpieces are found among the Bambara (or, more properly, the Bamana), who live near the upper Niger in Mali, Senegal, and Guinea (Fig. 14-1). Chi Wara (sometimes also spelled Tyiwara) is a legendary figure who taught the Bamana to cultivate with digging sticks. It is also the name of one of a series of graded associations for Bamana men. In preparation for clearing the fields, two members of the association wear these headpieces in imitation of the male and female antelope—the antelope having become identified with the Chi Wara figure. They engage in ritual play to please the spirits of the earth and to ensure the earth's fertility.

These beautiful wooden forms display one of the major characteristics of much African sculpture. The artist has exaggerated those features of the animals that are most important for recognition by those who use or observe the ritual and that call attention to each animal's particular aspect. The female antelope's body is reduced to a simple flattened oval form, while the enlarged neck, head, and ears, which fit into tight curves, convey an impression of energy and strength.

14-2 *Above. Mali. Senufo. Kponiugo, fire-spitting mask. (Phoebe Apperson Hearst Museum of Anthropology, the University of California at Berkeley)*

14-3 *Right. Zambia, Western Province. Mambunda. Samahongo initiation mask. (Copyright Livingstone Museum)*

On her back rides a tiny young antelope whose form echoes that of the mother. The male antelope has a similar body; but his neck is formed of two curves with spiky extensions, his ears tilt backward, and his horns, stylized into a powerful upward thrust, tilt forward. The combination of curves with the antelope's spiky mane and the sharply contrasting direction of the ears and horns create a powerful sense of forward motion, whereas the female's representation seems to recoil slightly from his onslaught. The distinguishing features of heads, body color, and texture are reduced or ignored. It is the power of procreation that is emphasized.

Another characteristic frequently evident in African sculpture that is also present in the Chi Wara headpieces is the sense of reduction of a single piece of wood—the trunk of a tree perhaps—from which the objects were carved. This is part of the explanation for the polar, columnar aspects of these figures.

A mask that seems to represent qualities in opposition to the forceful flowing motion of the Chi Wara, however, is the *kponiugo,* or fire-spitting helmet (Fig. 14-2) of the Senufo. It is used by the Lo association, a group responsible for initiation schools among the

Senufo of the Côte d'Ivoire, Burkina Faso, and Mali regions. Its fearsome, expressionistic visage comprises the important features of equally important animals. The teeth are those of the crocodile; the tusks represent the warthog; the horns are those of the water buffalo or the antelope; and the chameleon, which perches on the head between the horns, is a symbol for the continuation of life. Sometimes these masks are also painted with leopard spots. Each of these animals represents a powerful spirit; and, combined in a powerful symmetry, they are said to represent the chaos of primordial times. As the wearer stalks through the night, tinder is struck under the chin to create the fire-spitting image. This wooden mask, probably cut from green wood for lightness, was blackened. Its wearer could both invoke and provoke powerful spirits.

Another initiation mask is that used by the Mambunda of Zambia, a people who share many common institutions, like the *Mukanda* schools (Fig. 14-3). During the instructional period of two to nine months, young boys between the ages of seven and fifteen are secluded. Among the dances performed and/or taught is one danced by the older men wearing these kinds of masks, which are used to evoke ancestral spirits and to drive away women and younger boys. It is a powerful mask that emphasizes the potential of facial curves for exaggeration. The pure symmetry of the form and the protruding mouth form sharp contrasts. The great expanse of forehead and the attached feathers across the scalp are another juxtaposition of opposites—smoothness with the ruffled feathers.

The white-faced masks, which may symbolize ancestor spirits or a young maiden, are worn by men of the Mmwo society of the northern Ibo peoples near Onitsha and Awka (Fig. 14-4). Those representing male ancestral spirits are used at funerals, festivals, and initiation rites to cause fear and awe among non-members of the society. These kinds of masks remind us again of the importance of the benign presence of the ancestors of the tribe. One of the important stylistic features of these, as of other, masks is the reduction of features and their orderly composition into a symmetrical whole. Since a spirit, not a person, is being evoked, naturalism of form, texture, and color are not prerequisites. We have here the principle of *abstraction* used for the representation of a being not of the natural world.

14-5 *Liberia. Dan mask. (Copyright Frank Willett)*

14-4 *Nigeria. Ibo, Mmwo mask. (The University Museum, University of Pennsylvania, neg. #S8-4994)*

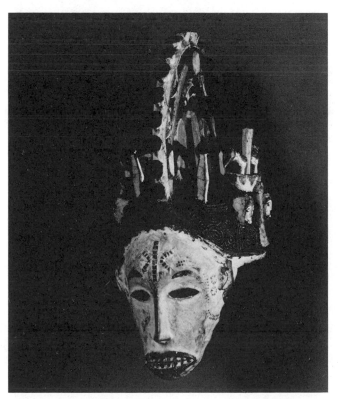

The Dan mask (Fig. 14-5) seems almost realistic when compared to the white-faced mask that we have just considered. The scale of the features and their realization seem much more human. But a brief consideration of the reduction of eyebrows to a single plane, the nose to perfect symmetry, the cheeks and chin to smooth planes, and the whole to this elegant oval shape contradicts the apparent naturalism. Like the masks of the Mmwo society and those of the Mambunda, masks of this type represent ancestral powers. They were often carried in miniature form by men as guardians and were also used to hide young boys in seclusion from the view of women.

Figurines

The possible artistic range of the transformation of the human visage is only hinted at by the masks that we have considered, but they do suggest how terribly exciting such forms must have been to Western artists when they first saw them. Pablo Picasso, one of the first European artists to be inspired by African art, used a Bakota reliquary figure (Fig. 14-6) for a series of studies. How little he understood of its real importance is

Another way in which powerful forces could be evoked or released is shown in the Bakongo *nkisi nkondi* (Fig. 14-8). Cavities in the head or stomach were the receptacles for magical substances. These *nkisi*—*fetishes* or objects embodying supernatural power—could be used for benevolent or malevolent effects. The pose sometimes reflected the purpose. A stiffened pose, upraised arm, and grimacing face were used to make the forms more menacing, while nails or sharp iron studs were driven into the body to release malevolent forces as in this nkonde. The fetishes used in voodoo have their origins in this kind of object.

14-7 *Nigeria. Northern Ibo ancestor figure, height 48". (The Strain Collection, New York)*

14-6 *Zaire. Bakota, reliquary figure,* mbulu-nugulu, *brass-covered wood. (Phoebe Apperson Hearst Museum of Anthropology, the University of California at Berkeley)*

emphasized by the use to which it was actually put, that is, to drive away evil from the remains of the dead. The "head" of the figure is exaggerated to enormous size in proportion to what Picasso, concentrating on the object as a figure in space, interprets as a body. Actually, the "body" is the base, intended to hold a basket containing a skull or bones and thus to protect the remains of an ancestor. Compare this rendition of the head with that of the Mambunda mask. Notice particularly the use of incising, the way in which facial features are stylized, and how one seems volumetric and the other two dimensional.

Human statues such as the one represented in Figure 14-7 from northern Iboland were carved for family shrines. Intended to house ancestral spirits, they served as a liaison between the human community and the deities of the spirit world. Through attention to shrines by the family or village, the spirits were honored and renewed. Figures of this type may be male or female; but, as is shown here, androgynous features often occur. The balanced frontal position, the opening of the hands in a gesture of reception, and the elaboration of facial decoration and coiffure are also typical features.

14-8 *Congo/Angola. Bakongo nail fetish figure,* nkisi nkondi. *(The University Museum, University of Pennsylvania, neg. #S8-70279)*

A final example of human figures serving as reservoirs of spirits are the Yoruba *ere ibeji* or twin statues. The Yoruba, among whom the incidence of twin birth is very high, believe that when one twin dies, the life of its surviving sibling is threatened because the twins share the same soul. Carved figurines such as those shown in Figure 14-9 are carried, fed, and clothed to keep the deceased spirit happy and to discourage it from forcing the living twin to join it in the spirit world. These various ways in which human figures are used as embodiments of spirit forces recall the use of *ushabti* figures in the tombs of ancient Egypt.

Divination Trays

Objects not representing the human figure and designed for specific, utilitarian purposes may also reflect religious principles. The Yoruba tray (Fig. 14-10) is used in the process of *divination,* foretelling the future or discovering secret knowledge. One of the features of Yoruba religion is the oracle of *Ifa,* a secret

body of wisdom that may be made available to a believer through the intervention of a *babalawo,* or priest. The priest then interprets the secret body of poems, called *odu,* in various combinations, using the Ifa divination tray.

Following initial discussion and ritual cleansing, the petitioner who has come to the priest is seated opposite him. Between them lies the divination tray, which has a light layer of sand on the surface. The priest takes a number of palm nut kernels, tosses them into the air, and marks on the tray the number of those that he catches. At the end of a series of tosses he uses the number and arrangement of marks on the tray to select those odu poems to be interpreted. The interpretations reflect the ordered intentions of the deities and the ancestors. But there is always the element of chance and disorder. The face of Eshu, the god of unpredictable fate and change, is inevitably present on the border of the tray. Placed opposite the priest during the divination process, the face reminds both priest

14-9 *Nigeria. Yoruba. Oyo, Saki area. Twin Memorial Figures* (Ere Ibeji). *Wood, beads, leather. Both 10⅞" high. (The Arnett Collection)*

14-10   *Nigeria. Yoruba. Ifa tray. (Copyright Frank Willett)*

and petitioner of the potential in human destiny for good or evil.

Stools

The manifestation of African spiritual and political principles in utilitarian objects is perhaps best exemplified by the Ashanti stools (Fig. 14-11). The Ashanti, like other Akan peoples of Ghana and the Côte d'Ivoire, believe that a person's spirit resides in his or her stool. When not in use, a stool is turned on its side so that no spirit other than the owner's will "sit" on the stool. Special stools are carved for an individual at important stages in his or her life, such as at puberty or marriage.

14-11   *Ghana. Ashanti. Wooden stool for a queen mother, decorated with silver sheeting. (Reproduced by Courtesy of the Trustees of the British Museum)*

This personal metaphor was extended to that of the state at the time of the founding of the Ashanti Confederacy by the king (*asantehene*) Osei Tutu in 1701. On a particular day when the king, subchiefs, and the Ashanti people were gathered together, Osei Tutu's chief priest summoned from the heavens a Golden Stool to enshrine and protect the soul of the new nation. The Golden Stool remains the single most important item of Ashanti court regalia: it stands for leadership and union. In this way stools also became symbols of political office for those with political authority delegated by the asantehene. The high status of members of the court, such as the queen mother, is reflected in the ceremonial stool, which is adorned with fine sculpture and a silver sheath overlay. The intricate surface designs frequently recall proverbs that the officeholder uses to convey a message or motto of his or her rule. Ceremonial stools like that pictured are reserved for state occasions; others are specially carved for domestic and personal use. At the death of an Ashanti ruler his ceremonial stool is blackened with soot and becomes the object of propitiation in the state ancestor cult.

Kente Cloth

A further example of artistic accomplishment and political authority manifest in utilitarian objects is the *kente* cloth of the Ashanti and Ewe peoples of Ghana. Kente is a large cloth, draped for ceremonial dress, made out of narrow strips sewn together that have been woven from cotton, silk, or wool threads. While strip weaving is common in Africa, what distinguishes kente is the elaboration of silk weft inlay designs that are geometric in character. There is a hierarchy of kente weavers and designs. At the pinnacle are the royal *asasia* cloths woven exclusively for the asantehene and his family, and for individuals granted a cloth as a symbol of loyalty or in return for services to the king. Pattern and color of the royal cloths carry special meanings appropriate to their owners. As do all kente, each asasia cloth has its name. The example shown here (Fig. 14-12) is called Everyone-Depends-on-Somebody. Its colors are gold, red, and blue. The gold and red are references to kingship and governmental power; blue refers to playfulness and humor. The equal intensity of the overall colors is coupled with the striking alternation of rectangles dominated by blue with those dominated by gold and red. The arrangement suggests the worth of both qualities in balance in the ideal society; power and authority must be matched by humor and simplicity.

14-12 *Ghana. Ashanti. Kente cloth (detail). (Reprinted from* African Art in Motion *by Robert Farris Thompson. Katherine Coryton White collection, UCLA Art Council, University of California, Los Angeles)*

Sculpture in Everyday Objects

While items of court regalia symbolize the authority of a ruler, other carved objects may commemorate a single person or group of persons, common and familiar. The Mangbetu of northeastern Zaire apply their excellent figurative sculpture to everyday objects rather than to statuary. Knife handles, harps, pipe bowls, and other containers are decorated with human heads and figures. Among them, the most famous of Mangbetu motifs are the pots carved to commemorate the bound heads and elaborate hairstyles of Mangbetu women (Figs. 14-13, 14-14). The coiffure itself is reminiscent of a woven basket. It consists of a fiber structure through which the hair is pulled, elongated with the addition of false hair, and then woven back through the fiber. The delicate woven lines of the coiffure are replicated in fine detail on the heads that sit atop the clay pots. The lower body of the pot reinforces the cylindrical shape of the head by curvilinear lines covering its surface.

14-14 *Zaire. Mangbetu woman. (Barbara W. Merriam)*

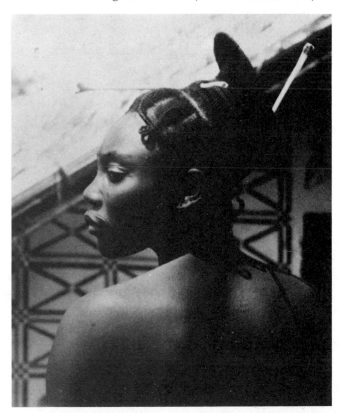

14-13 *Zaire. Mangbetu effigy pots. (Reproduced by Courtesy of the Trustees of the British Museum)*

COMMENTS AND QUESTIONS

1. How is exaggeration of natural features of human and animal forms used to stress spiritual or social principles? Give examples.

2. As has been stated above, masks may have varied purposes: some are intended to invoke powers of natural or supernatural forces. They represent mystery and the potential for good or evil. These often rely on images of the forest or bush to convey their meaning. Others symbolize civilization: human imposition of pattern and order on the natural world or idealized human values. Review the objects presented in this section and identify ones that seem to you to bear out each of these two purposes.

3. The nature-civilization contrast may be seen in statues and other sculpted objects as well. Compare the reliance on natural substance versus the reliance on human reference in the images of the Bakongo figure and the Ashanti stool. Identify the different images.

4. How does the form and placement during use of the Ifa divination tray suggest general principles of Yoruba cosmology?

5. There are many elements to consider in analyzing a work of sculpture: proportion, volume and dimension, compactness versus open space, surface texture (rough versus smooth, painted or unpainted). Of those objects that incorporate aspects of naturalism and stylized interpretation of the human form, which elements contribute to the effect of naturalism? Which to the effect of stylization?

6. Compare the Ibo *Mmwo* mask with the ancestor figure from northern Iboland. What design features do they share that might reflect an Ibo style?

African visual art may be utilitarian, decorative, symbolic, spiritual, or all of these at once. Masks and sculptures emphasize communication of spiritual forces and the interpretation of cosmic order to the human community; other objects symbolize or reinforce social relationships. In Benin (Chapter 12), bronze heads and plaques served to commemorate rulers and to record important historical events. There is, as we have seen, no dichotomy between "fine" and "applied" arts in Africa. Similarly, there is no division in African music between "concert" and "folk" music. Just as there are no museums in traditional Africa, there are no concert halls; music, like visual art ob-

jects, is intended to be used as part of the rituals and celebrations of everyday life.

African Music

The first observation that a careful observer of African music will surely make is some conclusion about the tremendous variety and complexity of the sounds emanating from this gigantic continent. The languages and cultures of the peoples of North Africa are closely related to those of the Arab world and the Middle East, traditions that differ—for geographic, economic, and political reasons—from those of southern, central, and West Africa. The music of this region, so oriental in its *modal, melodic,* and *improvisational* characteristics, although African for perhaps centuries, must be excluded from our consideration of indigenous African music, the music of black Africans. Likewise, one finds alongside the music of sub-Saharan Africa a tradition of Western music brought by the colonists from Europe, a practice that has its own traditions and has helped generate a new black African urban music called "high life," a chic modern music of the cities. Even when we dampen all the sounds that can be identified as "non-native" to the original peoples of Africa, we are still engulfed in an endless variety of musics and languages and peoples. The culture and the music of the Pygmy, Bushman, and Saharan peoples are not the same as those of the Yoruba, Ashanti, and Susu ethnic groups. Here, as in the literature and art sections, we will concentrate on the music of West African societies. After discussing some general characteristics shared by the music of these societies, we will move on to a more detailed study of one specific example: music from the Festival of the Tohossou, legendary princes of the royal family from the ancient kingdom of Dahomey.

Characteristics of West African Music: Similarities with Jazz

Most music performed by Africans is part of a social activity. Of course, individual music-making takes place in response to personal or ritual needs, but most musical performance accompanies the group activities of games, religious rites, feasts, festivals, and work. Music provides an opportunity for sharing in a communal creative experience. With the transferral of Africans to the New World, this West African music deeply influenced the development of jazz, with which, as we will see, it shares many characteristics. Because of a number of factors, black slaves in America were able to maintain much of their African musical heritage, all the while joining to it certain elements of the Euro-American musical tradition. The resulting hybrid had a markedly African base. The important points to keep in mind are these: the rich West African musical tradition; the comparative cultural isolation in which many black American slaves lived; the tolerance of musical activities among the slave communities accorded by white American masters; and the compatibility of the important elements of West African music with the current tradition of Euro-American music. As West African music is communal in its basic approach, jazz, too, is a shared creative experience: those in the normal small group of musicians, the combo, respond improvisationally to one another's musical signals and the social signals of the audience or dance crowd in a way different from the performance practice of a Western string quartet or a chamber orchestra. African musicians, when composing collectively, are part of a social interaction that often communicates a group sentiment or message, an extramusical consideration that is found only rarely in music of the West.

Depending on the event and local customs, the performing groups may be made up of young or old, male or female, or mixed. However, there is usually a hierarchical differentiation among the players—leading roles are played by professional musicians or specialists; secondary roles are performed by the others in both choruses and instrumental ensembles. As the *Sundiata* epic indicated, in Africa the griot, or praise singer, is a highly respected musician-poet, usually a professional, in many of these societies. The leading blues singers and jazz musicians of black America are often seen to be held in the same esteem by the regular members of the black community.

Elements of African Music

Little, if any, traditional African music takes any interest in *harmony* as we know it in the West, but most African sounds are compatible with European harmonies. The leading elements of African music are *melody, rhythm, timbre* (the distinctive sound of the instruments and voices), and text. Although verbal art is intertwined with African musical art, some societies are able to convey specific messages by instrumental sounds alone. That is, *pitch* and rhythm can be explicitly equated to textual messages, for speech in some languages is musical in the sense that pitch variations affect word meanings. But "talking drums" and "talking winds" are not characteristic of the music of most of the peoples who were brought to America from Africa as slaves. Even though there may be a tendency to overemphasize this particular feature of African music because it is so unique and fascinating, we might be well advised to consider that most music is communicative in a general way once we have learned the conventions. For example, we are all familiar with the sounds of military music, love songs, sad songs, happy dance music, and so on. We know that words for one variety cannot be properly set to sounds of another, or, if they are, then a joke is intended, a mistake has been made, or something is out of kilter. In other words, the sound of the music without the words conveys a somewhat specific message anyway. In like manner, it is accurate to say that most African music communicates messages and feelings, ideas that are extramusical. But to the degree that particular sounds are wedded to specific social functions, it is probably true that African music is more communicative than most Western music.

Rhythm

The complex rhythms of most African drumming depend on the use of a recurring rhythmic pattern within the totality of the ensemble. This time-line in African music is what the jazz drummer refers to as "time," that unwavering sense of beat that must prevail regardless of what else is happening in solo or in ensemble. In its simplest form, the time-line can be projected by a "beat" or metronomic pulse that sounds audibly and continuously. But it can also function as an unsounded, but understood, quantity of the time-line part, which the musicians perceive as an *ostinato* or regularly recurring rhythm pattern. Another obvious conclusion at which the impartial observer of African music will arrive is the distinct bias toward percussion that is a part of the aesthetic of African music. As in jazz, there is a tendency to include a rhythm section in every instrumental ensemble, and surely the close association of African music and jazz with dance—both as part of the dance and as accompaniment for the dance—explains, or at least accounts for, the importance of rhythm as a chief feature of both kinds of music. In fact, African drummers often perform on the move as part of the dance. Even when stationary, African drummers—and jazz drummers—have bodies in motion, with elbows flying, shoulders leaning, fingers tapping or pressing, and heads and mouths going.

Vocal Music: Call and Response

Although drumming and rhythm are probably preeminent in West African music, great stress is laid on vocal music. An exceptional variety may be found among the themes treated, such as war songs, hunting songs, play and work songs, religious and festival songs, and social commentary, a type not unlike the artifices of the American blues musician. Eileen Southern, renowned historian of the music of black Americans, cites the following as the earliest example of an African song text written down in a European language (1800):

> The winds roared, and the rains fell;
> The poor white man, faint and weary,
> Came and sat under our tree.
> He has no mother to bring him milk,
> No wife to grind his corn.
>
> *Chorus:*
> Let us pity the white man.
> No mother has he to bring him milk,
> No wife to grind his corn.

The leader-and-chorus format of much African vocal music often displays a call-and-response mode of performance; this, too, is another characteristic eagerly seized by jazz historians seeking stylistic parallels between jazz and native African music. The typical jazz performance of the vocal and instrumental blues has a singer or lead instrument perform the first half of each phrase, only to be answered by another instrumentalist or the ensemble itself. The tie between the jazz blues and the African responsorial performance may be tenuous, but the leader-chorus performance among African vocal ensembles is, in fact, the norm and a characteristic to be savored. Much is lost if the words are not understood, of course; but the virtuosity of the leader, in contrast to the solidity and enthusiastic response of the remaining performers, is a distinctive sound of the black African tradition. As we read more about the cultural traditions of black Africa, we would also do well to keep in mind these observations:

> From the first African captives, through the years of slavery, and into the present century black Americans kept alive important strands of African consciousness and verbal art in their humor, songs, dance, speech, tales, games, folk beliefs, and aphorisms. . . . Cultural diffusion between whites and blacks was by no means a one-way street with blacks the invariable beneficiaries. . . . Black relationship to the larger culture was complex and multidimensional.[2]

14-15   First Day of the Yam Custom in Dahomey, *from the 1819 edition of Edward Thomas Bowdich's* Mission from Cape Coast Castle to Ashantee. *(Courtesy of the Trustees of the Boston Public Library of the City of Boston and Frank Cass & Co., Ltd., London)*

Music from the Festival of the Tohossou

The princes of Dahomey are called the *tohossou,* descendants of a legendary king; their worship is the object of a cult whose ceremonies are performed in the twenty temples of the city of Abomey, capital of the ancient kingdom of Dahomey (Fig. 14-15). The music for portions of these ceremonies has been recorded.[3] We should prepare ourselves to hear, in addition to the sound of human voices, the music of three oblong drums, which are beaten by sticks on one side and the naked hand on the other; three iron bells struck with a short wooden stick; pairs of rattles contained in wicker baskets; and a small bell shaken by a priest. The festivities for one tohossou last four days, and the recorded excerpts sample music from morning to nightfall of one festival day. Five groups of people, the entire community, participate: the priests, the princes

---

[2] Lawrence J. Levine, *Black Culture and Black Consciousness* (London: Oxford University Press, 1977).

[3] *Anthology of the Music of Black Africa* (Everest 3254-3), Record 3, Sides A and B.

(descendants of the royal line), men, women, and musicians. Even children have a part to play, and this day's ceremony will have dancing, singing, and sacrifice. As the day progresses, the bull will be bound, its throat will be slit, and a lamb will later be sacrificed to appease the spirit of the bull. The mysteries of all these ceremonies and ritual acts are not all known and entirely understood; but, since the tohossou represent proud descendants of a warrior race, there are various songs, dances, and ritual acts dealing with the enemy, fallen brothers-in-arms, vengeance, and sacred deities. The first excerpt, "Song of Zomadonou," is sung by a young man portraying Zomadonou, a reincarnated prince, his words telling of the feats that made him famous. He is accompanied by one bell, struck in two places to obtain contrasting pitches, and the song of the bell creates the time-line ostinato: High (slow) High (slow) High (quick) Low (quick). Over and over again the pattern repeats as the prince sings his song to a *pentatonic* (five-note) *scale*. As Zomadonou sings, he is answered by the chorus, their response picking up the principal melodic figure of his solo song.

The second excerpt captures the voices of a male chorus grouped around the drums. It is basically a choral song meant to accompany a serpentine dance by the women as they snake their way three times around the sacred tree and sacrificial bull. The sound of the drums is not continuous, but the rattles keep a steady beat for the dance. Occasionally, a solo voice will interject a brief exclamation, but the pattern of the music is choral song, not call and response. The music of this example is similar to the first in that the melody employs an abbreviated scale, ostinato patterns prevail, and tone production by the vocalists is full-voiced, lusty, and somewhat strained.

Adomoussi, a priest devoted to the worship of the third tohossou, performs the third excerpt himself. Striking a bell in two places, he follows with a short declamatory phrase—"O thou, when thou raise the saber it is to kill...Thou panther which avenges itself...Thou shark in the water...An enemy..." The pattern is simple—bell, statement, bell, statement—and one can see the parallel in the country blues musician who strums a chord to arrange his thoughts and follows with the simply sung phrase. The priest has something to tell his people; his bell and method of delivery catch their attention.

The choir for the next recorded example, "The Way Is Free," is entirely composed of women. Using a piercing chest tone, the leader sings short phrases to be answered by the remaining choir members. The percussion accompaniment, which is not heavy, seems to be but loosely attached to the singing of the women. Since no dance is employed at this point in the ceremony, the drums seem to act more as background than accompaniment. Not so for the Nifossousso dance that follows. The regular beat is stately and dignified; it accompanies a procession of women who have shed their brightly colored costumes for white loincloths in a slow procession to the temple. Following this, the men call Botro, a woman, to come and perform her dance. In the seventh example the woman advances to dance and to sing a warlike and frightening ritual with a stick that she finally plunges into the earth.

Throughout the performance of each of these snippets of music and ceremony it is obvious that certain musical sounds relate to general feelings in the same way that certain musical sounds of the Western tradition do. The priest who shouted his exclamations to the accompaniment of a bell could not have been describing a quiet forest glade; the slow processional of the noble line of women moving to the temple would have been inappropriate to accompany the active dance of Botro. The sounds of African music, although different from those we are most accustomed to hear, open up to meaningful interpretation on careful listening and a little reflection. Then, as the similarities to our own music begin to surface, we see the heritage that has blended with Euro-American music to form that American music called jazz. Only recently have American jazz musicians begun to take a new look at African roots in a search for further inspiration and replenishment, and we will see in Chapter 15 and in Volume II how another transformation in American music has taken place as our sense of history draws us to new ideas from our past.

African Arts in Festival: The Efe/Gelede of the Western Yoruba

The unity of the arts with one another and with the values and lifestyle of a particular culture is nowhere so evident as in the ways in which people celebrate together. We have seen how the festival of Dionysus in ancient Greece brought together wine drinking, love-making, song, dance, mask, drama, and the architecture of the theater. The Romans honored Saturn, the god of agriculture, with a general feasting and unleashing of social restraints at the end of the year. Seeing that they could not do away with the Saturnalia, the Christians declared that Christmas would be celebrated at the end of December and retained certain pagan customs such as the yule log and the Christmas tree. Christian festivals also combined drama, music, visual effects, and dance, as we saw with *The Play of Daniel,* part of a Christmas celebration in the cathedral.

Western peoples continued to put on festivals and celebrations in the early modern period, and in some instances (witness Mardi Gras in New Orleans) they continue today; but modern industrialism and individualism have tended to wipe out what once seemed a communal necessity. Many of us are forced to "celebrate" our holidays by turning on the TV. In traditional African societies, however, and in countries (such as Brazil) where African influence is strong, festivals continue to be both a vital part of living and an important means of aesthetic expression. Even those Africans who are Christian or Muslim continue to participate in the festivals that have their roots in traditional religion.

The Yoruba culture, many aspects of which we have already studied, provides excellent examples of the synthesis of myth, poetry, dance, music, and visual arts in traditional festivals. One of these is the Efe/Gelede, celebrated by certain Yoruba subgroups in western Nigeria and the republic of Benin. The festival occurs annually before the beginning of the spring rains (between March and May) that will initiate the agricultural activities of the coming year. One of its purposes is thus to ensure the fertility of the earth. Women have always been symbols of fertility.

Significance of the Festival

In a patriarchal society where most ritual ceremonies reinforce the dominance of men over women, Efe/Gelede highlights the importance of women and serves as an occasion to recognize their spiritual powers. The specific context of Efe/Gelede derives from the importance of Iyanla, the Earth Mother or Great Mother, feminine counterpart of the supreme god Olorun or Oludumare.

Three Yoruba myths, all of which celebrate the mystical power and fertility of Iyanla, explain the background of the Efe/Gelede festival. The first tells that at the beginning of time when Oludumare sent

Obatala, Ogun, and Iyanla, the first three orisha, to earth, Iyanla complained that she, unlike the other two, had been given no special power. So Oludumare gave her the title "Mother of All," and presented her with a calabash containing a bird. The Great Mother promised to use her power by inflicting punishment on her enemies, but to those who appeased her she promised to grant wealth and children. In the second myth, the Great Mother, who had previously been blessed with many children, found that she could not bear any after her marriage to a man from Ketu (a Yoruba town in Benin). On consulting the oracle of Ifa, she was told to make sacrifices of corn and clay dishes and to dance with wooden figures on her head and metal anklets on her feet. She did so and promptly bore two children: a boy named Efe ("the Joker"), and a girl named Gelede. Her children found that when they grew up it was necessary for them, too, to dance with wooden images and iron anklets before they could have children. This dancing is reenacted in the festival.

The third myth recounts that another orisha, Orunmila, was told to sacrifice a wooden image, a waistcloth, and metal anklets before he undertook a visit to the haven of the witches. He performed the sacrifice, made his journey, and returned safely, proclaiming that he had made friends with Sickness and Death and that he would die no more. The Yoruba believe that the destructive power of Iyanla is manifested through the witches, symbolized by the bird in the calabash. Elements of the Gelede costume recall this myth.

By honoring the great mother Iyanla and her children Efe and Gelede, the celebrants hope that the mystical powers granted to women by Iyanla may be channeled into constructive behavior of use to the community rather than into activity destructive of it. The festival thus in a sense honors and celebrates all women, especially mothers. It is generally performed over a two-day period. The first, the day of Efe, is devoted primarily to poetry, the songs of Efe. The second, the day of Gelede, places more emphasis on costumes and dancing.

First Day: Efe

The Efe ceremony takes place in the market area, a setting of social, religious, and economic activity primarily involving women. At one end of the arena a small enclosure with double arches of palms is constructed. It serves as the entrance for the principal performer, Oro Efe, literally the word of Efe. As the audience gathers, masqueraders and dancers perform in anticipation of the Oro Efe, whose songs will last throughout the night.

Costume and Performance

The Oro Efe's elaborate costume, abounding in symbolism, includes leggings, iron gongs, and multicolored, appliquéd cloth over a bamboo hoop (Figs. 14-16, 14-17). The headdress consists of a veil and a frontal view of the human face in mask. It is topped by an elaborate superstructure containing symbolic animal figures, colors, and suspended knives. The lions, leopards, and snakes connote strength and royalty, while the knives are associated with Soponnon, god of smallpox, and Ogun, god of iron. The goddess of the rainbow, Osumare, is connected with the python. The crowning symbol on the headdress is the bird of the mothers, alluding to the belief that mothers, like witches, can transform themselves into birds at night to fly about their business (Figs. 14-17, 14-18).

The Oro Efe is veiled to enhance his spiritual remove from the audience, but the cult head who summons him by striking the sacred bells calls him by name. A flute player also summons the Oro Efe, and the crowd awaits him in silence. The Oro Efe appears, swaying and sounding his leg rattles, swinging the whisks in his hand. His first words honor deities, ancestors, mothers, and elders. The angle of his body and slow pace express recognition and reverence to the spiritual powers. In the second stage of the ceremony, a chorus and, gradually, the audience join in the Oro Efe's songs. The public's participation symbolizes agreement with the Oro Efe's words; it strengthens the spiritual and social communality of the occasion. The performance continues throughout the night with occasional interludes offered by the drummers, who present praise poems, proverbs, jokes, and riddles. The Oro Efe departs near dawn while the audience is distracted by a stilted dancer in hyena masquerade, and the night's activities are over.

Efe Poetry

The poetry recited by the Oro Efe and in choral repetition is based on the belief that *ase*—power, authority, potential energy—can be embodied in words as well as in deities, living men and women, and the ancestors. Women are perceived to have a special ase that can be used for the good or the ill of the community. The voicing of poetry also contains ase and may be used to help direct that of the women toward potential good.

14-16 *Right. Nigeria. Yoruba. Oro Efe. Dressing of dancer. Layers of embroidered and appliquéd cloth panels,* gberi, *are tied over a horizontally suspended bamboo hoop,* agboja. *(Henry John Drewal)*

14-17 *Far right. Nigeria. Yoruba. Oro Efe in full dress. (Henry John Drewal)*

14-18 *Benin. Yoruba. Oro Efe mask. Line drawing after a photograph of Oro Efe in performance at Ketu, April 24, 1971. (Henry John Drewal)*

The types of poetry recited include invocation, social comment or satire, history, and funeral commemoration. Several of each type may be sung throughout the night; examples of some of these follow.

Invocation

One segment of the invocation requests blessing for the community as a whole. The songs invariably mention smallpox and cholera, scourges on the population. They plead for agricultural success, which means wealth, and for progeny. Since the mothers are associated with both procreativity and fertility of the earth, these are not surprising themes. In this example the singer prays for the end of unexpected deaths caused by farming accidents. He protests in the first line that he (the community) has offered *orijio*—medicinal leaves—to placate the mothers. Shango, god of thunder, would never strike one of his shrines; why should the progenitors, *ose* and *aje*, strike down their own offspring? Agbojo and Onidofoi, the ancestral spirits of the town, have been duly honored. Making his points, the singer displays his respect for the mothers and acknowledges their power by summoning the support of onlookers to join in his prayers.

Social Comment

In social comment songs the Oro Efe uses praises, cajolery, and condemnation to highlight events that have occurred in the community. The tone is ribald, the poetry often sarcastic, the images satirical, posing the opposite to their traditional meaning. Even though the Efe ceremony is to appease the mothers, male dominance is lauded; women who have shown too great an independence from their husbands are ridiculed. The second poem bewails two outrages: not only did the man decried commit adultery against Ogunsola, but Ogunsola was in addition his elder. In the third poem the Oro Efe also stresses the theme of respect for elders by admonishing youth to remember that age, not wealth or Western education, brings wisdom.

Efe Poetry

Invocation

Orijio leaves charmed you to forgive my misdeeds.
Never have we suffered deaths from hoes, never
  from knives.
Have I lied?
Have I lied?
Never have we seen a thunderbolt strike a young *ose*
  tree.
Oso in the house were you not the one who gave
  birth to me?
Why do you not know us any longer?
Aje in the house, were you not the one who gave us
  birth?
Why do you not know us any longer?
Never have we seen a dog devour its child.
Never have we seen a dog devour its child.
Our mother, *opake*, forgive us our misdeed.
Our mother, do not allow me to falter
If a cult member has offended, expose him.
You joined our offering of thanksgiving to Agbojo,
Onidofoi was the one who saved us from death.
Young, old, households, and visitors, pray for my
  success.

Social Comment I

For a husband to grind pepper and grate cassava.
For a husband to grind pepper and grate cassava.
For a husband to cook *eba* and wash pots.
For a husband to cook *eba* and wash pots.
The wife you married, Sango, is wonderful.
She threatened her husband with a cutlass at the
  market.
She threatened her husband with a cutlass at the
  market.
I heard him shout to all around "help me!"
She threatened her husband with a cutlass at the
  market.

Social Comment II

The conceited man with all his money is teasing his
  elder.
The conceited man with all his money is teasing his
  elder.
Did Ogunsola marry his wife for you?
Did Ogunsola marry his wife for you?
Wretched person who pulls on the snake's tail.
Wretched person who pulls on the snake's tail.
If the snake bites you should I be concerned?
Wretched person who pulls on the snake's tail.

Social Comment III

Ah, truly young children are very wise.
However I say they are not as wise as their elders.
We called you to get the soup, but you went to add
  water to it.
But you are not as wise as the one who cooked it.
A goat is different from a horse, a white man is
  different from a Hausa.
You are not as wise as the one who did the cooking.

The Gelede Celebration

The Gelede is performed on the afternoon following the Efe festivities. Its purpose is to embody an approach to the mothers that appeals to their positive attributes. The priests and elders summon from the spectators attitudes necessary for the worship of the mothers: patience, indulgence, and composure. By upholding tradition and ridiculing those who offend it, the visual symbols, along with the music and dance of Gelede, attempt to please and honor the mothers.

The main performers for Gelede are masqueraders. Although they are all men, they traditionally

14-20 *Nigeria. Yoruba. Gelede mask: quadruped and snake. (Reproduced by Courtesy of the Trustees of the British Museum)*

14-21 *Nigeria. Yoruba. Male Gelede mask. Oya. (Courtesy of Roger Cte de la Burdé)*

14-19 *Nigeria. Yoruba. Female Gelede dancer with breastplate carved in the form of ibeji statues. Joga-Orile/Imasai, Northern Egbado, April, 1965. Regional Style Egbado. (Henry John Drewal)*

appear in pairs portraying males or females. The pairing probably alludes to the spiritual duality assigned to the mothers, and the males and females to the two children Efe and Gelede. The costumes, which consist essentially of mask, headwrap, and leg rattles (Fig. 14-19), exaggerate the sex characteristics of the male or female. Hoops and layers of cloth accentuate the chest of the male; a breastplate with elaborate carved breasts and wooden structures behind emphasize the female's physical attributes.

Masks consist of a head fitting over the upper portion of the masquerader's head and a superstructure above. The two components reflect different aesthetic values. The head is frontal, symmetrical, composed, and static, reflecting an ideal of patience, while the elaborate superstructure with its extended parts and asymmetrical design creates an effect of surprise. Colors in both parts are symbolic and frequently associated with the gods (Color Plate X).

The elaborate art of the Gelede masks touches on all aspects of Yoruba life. Some of the motifs frequently occurring in them are animals, deities, social roles, historical personalities, fashion, and foreign ele-

ments. More than one motif may appear in a given mask. The principal animals of Gelede are the snake, bird, mongoose, tortoise, and lizard. Animal compositions may embody qualities of personality and behavior, as in Figure 14-20, where the snake symbolizes patience and "coolness" but is attacked by a "hot" or vengeful quadruped, the mongoose.

14-22 *Nigeria. Yoruba. Female Gelede mask. Yemoja. (Reproduced by Courtesy of the Trustees of the British Museum)*

14-23 *Nigeria. Yoruba. Gelede mask. (The Strain Collection, New York)*

14-24 *Nigeria. Yoruba. Gelede mask. The Lorry. (Federal Department of Antiquities, National Museum, Lagos, Nigeria)*

Goddesses, such as Oya, goddess of the Niger River (Fig. 14-21), are frequently represented in the Gelede part of the festival. Certain masks proclaim the hierarchical ordering in Yoruba social roles and religion. The mask represented in Figure 14-22 has a superstructure dominated by Yemoja, another name for Iyanla. Before the priestess is a figure prostrate in traditional greeting and at her side a small boy seeking her protection and support. This reiterates Yemoja's praises, which proclaim her the protector of children. The relative proportion suggests the religious hierarchical ordering, while the balance creates the notion of stability.

Foreigners are often portrayed in masks that include features the Yoruba associate with different cultural groups. Thus Figure 14-23 portrays a Muslim man from northern Nigeria, as indicated by the distinctive cap with its diagonal bands. Europeans are shown with products of their culture: cameras, sewing machines, cars, and trucks often appear on the masks (Fig. 14-24). These elements of Western technology are used both for sheer entertainment and for satire, but they also imply a deeper spiritual message. Technological inventions are held by Yoruba commentators to be the result of the Europeans' spiritual power. Their appearance in Gelede masks may reflect a plea to the mothers to use their own spiritual powers in a positive way.

Dance

The visual imagery of the Gelede masks and costumes is enhanced by that of the dance, which is given great importance (Color Plate XI). Dance patterns in Africa, as elsewhere, evolve from habitual movements, posture, and gestures of work and play. Here the movements imitate qualities appropriate to the male or female sex, depending on the costume of the dancer. Like the words and performance of Efe and the dual composition of the masks, the dance heightens the tension inherent in this festival between male and female and between the perceived duality of the mothers. An example is the dance of the female masks performed by the young male dancer dressed as Tetede, wife of Efe. Tetede's costume with its pointed breasts emphasizes the male aggressive aspect of the feminine personality. The dance combines sequential deep knee bends, suggestive of a graceful curtsey, with a beating of shoulders and swaying of hips emphasizing female aggressivity. The dancer disguised as Efe also represents a male-female tension with both costume and mask. The heavy, layered costume suggests the ample figures of pregnant or mature women. Yet Efe's dance, accompanied by the explosion of ceremonial guns, vigorously approaches abandon as the tempo increases and the dance reaches its culmination. This abandon, although masculine in tone, implies caricature and exaggeration of movement and gesture associated with older women.

Through festival, as seen in both the tohossou cult ceremony of the Dahomean kings and the Efe/Gelede of the western Yoruba, we have witnessed the interplay of many facets of African aesthetic expression. Poetry, music, song, sculptured mask, costume, and dance create together an experience of high drama for participants and observers, enhancing the social, spiritual, and moral concerns of the community. Entertaining and at times ribald, the performers nevertheless establish the priority of the spiritual powers that energize life on earth. They reinforce old values and symbols and acknowledge new realities. Audience and performers in communion celebrate the continuity of the community over time and affirm its vitality. While specific to certain groups of western Nigeria and Benin, these festivals evoke an essentially African mode of perception—the integration and wholeness of life.

COMMENTS AND QUESTIONS

1. African festivals—combining as they do music, costume, plastic art, and dance—confront all the senses with images and symbols of beliefs about human society and about spiritual forces. In reviewing this section, identify some of these in the case of Yoruba society by answering the following:
   a. What elements of the masks are symbols of the Yoruba deities?
   b. How is color used symbolically in mask and costume?
   c. How does the organization of both Efe and Gelede segments of this festival illustrate the tension in Yoruba society between the roles of men and those of women? Who are the dancers? How do their costumes and dance styles convey the tension?

2. Think of other festivals that you have studied or know about from Western traditions. Can you identify similar components and purposes in them?

3. How does Gelede incorporate new experiences of cross-cultural contact of the Yoruba and integrate them into traditional Yoruba belief systems?

15

African Roots and Continuities

General Characteristics of the African Humanities

While a great diversity characterizes the many cultures on the continent of Africa and even within the area of West Africa studied here, there are certain modes of perception and cultural forms that may be characterized as African. These include, in the social realm, the veneration of elders, ancestors, and kinship ties generally, as well as the importance given to secret societies and initiation rites. We have seen that traditional religion, sometimes even among Muslim or Christian Africans, acts as a binding communal force. The close relationship with nature and the belief in a spirit world influencing it are primary motivating forces in the African arts and in the multifaceted art of the festival. African oral literature is devoted not only to religious ritual but also to moral instruction of the young and to the perpetuation of the history and traditions of a people. The griot, or oral historian–poet, plays a vital role in the latter aspect.

The traditional character of African art and culture makes the stylistic periodization that we have used in the study of Western culture somewhat irrelevant in terms of Africa. Aside from the tomb paintings and figures of ancient Egypt and Kush, the Nok sculptures, and the arts of Ife and Benin, which can be dated, our examples of literature, art, and music have been drawn from several centuries of African experience, including the present one. The festivals performed in the 1990s include modern elements although they derive from ancient forms and ideas. Similarly, the poems of Diop, Achebe, and Soyinka express this continuity between ancient and modern.

Certain fundamental ideas and beliefs are shared across traditional African cultures. These include the commitment to a holistic view of life; the definition of community as the living, the dead, and the unborn; and a sensibility to the delicate balance between human society and natural forces in the universe—sometimes visible, sometimes invisible. If human beings must recognize the importance of natural and supernatural forces, their intelligence nevertheless is responsible for affecting their destiny. African ideas share with Western humanism a respect for the dignity of human beings and an acceptance of the foibles of human nature.

The African humanities exhibit perhaps even more than those of classical Greece a profound aesthetic and philosophical unity. Robert Farris Thompson, in his study *African Art in Motion,* has attempted to describe some of the basic principles that unite African arts and thought, particularly around the central art of dance. His conclusions, presented in brief form below, are well worth our consideration.

1. Age and wisdom are venerated in African society. African art nonetheless shows a particular dynamic of age that would not in the West be associated with advanced years, for the elder is supposed to retain a certain youthful vitality. Even the terra cotta mask from the ancient Nok culture (see Fig. 12-1), although representing a high official who would necessarily be someone of advanced years, does not show the face of an aged man. The elder dancer who executes his performance with disciplined vitality is highly regarded.

2. In dance, plastic art, and music, great attention is given to proportion and balance. Silence, or the "suspended beat" in music, and open space in art are not passive qualities but active components of the rhythmic flow. Balance is vitalized in perceiving the individual qualities and motions of body parts integrated into a whole. The ability to imagine and perform multiple rhythms in dance is an extension of this principle.

3. Sharpness of line and a crisp beginning and ending characterize both dance and sculpture. The Mmwo mask (Fig. 14-4) demonstrates the clear boundaries of pattern that the carver's knife establishes.

4. African arts portray an ideal of *resemblance* rather than *identity*. Sculptors, in particular, seek to represent a moral or spiritual force rather than to make an individual portrait. Although African art runs a gamut from the rather naturalistic Benin bronzes to abstract masks, it is never totally realistic or totally nonfigurative, but rather seeks a balance somewhere between the two poles.

5. *Ancestorism,* which Thompson defines as "the belief that the closest harmony with the ancient way is

the highest of experiences, the force that enables a man to rise to his destiny," is a powerful motivation in the African arts. The sculpture of the mask, mythology, music, and dance are used in rites to establish links between living sons and daughters and the community of ancestors.

6. A final principle of "coolness," a word that has equivalents in many African languages, unites all the preceding ones. Aspects of "coolness" are visibility and openness, luminosity, and smoothness coupled with clarity. A dance, for example, may be characterized by extreme vitality but also by extreme control and by facial composure, the "mask of the cool." The belief in rebirth and reincarnation, which unites living vitality with orientation toward the ancestral, is an important component of "coolness." This unison of energy and balance, of "hot" movement and "cool" composure in African art, music, and dance is perhaps the most unique feature of African aesthetics.

African Survivals in African American Culture

The fact that almost one million Africans, originating primarily in the western regions that we have studied, were imported to North America as a result of the slave trade has had profound effects on American culture. These effects have been transmitted to American culture as a whole by means of the continuities or "survivals" of African culture in African American culture.

The term "African survival" is used by scholars to denote a specific form or function of an institution, ritual, belief, language, or art that is clearly identifiable with an African origin, although adapted to the New World situation. Such survivals have always been noticeable among black populations in South America and the Caribbean. North Americans of European origin, however, as well as many of African origin, tended until recently to deny that there was anything African about black American culture. Thus it was said that the American Negro had no past; his or her culture was purely a product of the slaves' adaptation to white America. In the early twentieth century, the black scholars W. E. B. DuBois and Carter Woodson were among the first to point out African survivals in the religious, social, and aesthetic life of African Americans. An anthropologist, Melville H. Herskovits, continued the investigation of this question in his work *The Myth of the Negro Past,* published in 1941. Herskovits challenged the popularly held assumption that African Americans had no cultural past. Outlining principal features of a "cultural complex" based on common patterns of behavior of the African cultures in the regions of slave origin, he identified certain features of African American culture in the Americas and the Caribbean that evolved from African cultural institutions. Aspects of African American culture that differed from comparable institutions of the European-based society would thus be explained by the different cultural heritage of black Americans rather than by their failure to imitate white behavior properly.

Other scholars, such as E. Franklin Frazier, argued that conditions of oppression were the real cause of the distinctive features of black culture, especially in regard to family structure. For example, the sale of family members to different masters during slavery and the need for black men to seek work away from home after emancipation resulted in an apparent predominance of single-parent and matriarchal households.

Numerous recent studies of both the African and the African American past have defined more precisely both the types of African survivals to be found in African American culture and the means by which they may have survived. The formation of African American culture was a complex process indeed; but certain features of its social institutions, religious organizations, and beliefs, as well as its arts and letters, can now be identified as having distinctly African origins.

The Extended Family

Identification with the extended (as opposed to the nuclear) family, the great importance of children to the sense of a community's continuity over time, and the special roles played by men and women in family life are African features that have persisted in African American social life. Coupled with the latter is the acceptability of the economic independence of women. African women, unlike their European counterparts, could have rights in land and property. In certain circumstances, children born outside marriage were welcome additions to the woman's family. In many African societies children are often raised by people other than their own parents: sometimes grandparents, sometimes friends of their parents' generation. Although preferences of these types may have been reinforced by the conditions of slavery and the plight of freed slaves, they provided adaptable models for a "normal" African American family life, if different from those of the majority culture.

Groups and Associations

Types of bonding and grouping characteristic of traditional African societies reappear in various ways in African American society. At the time of initiation, African boys and girls form close bonds with their age-mates that continue, in the form of a society, throughout their lives. Age or initiation mates treat each other as brothers and sisters, granting reciprocal rights and obligations. Such groups are often the focus of festival, entertainment, and mutual support activities. Related to these groups are "titled" societies in which individuals can display their wealth and enhance their status by the purchase of a succession of "titles" bringing them recognition and respect. Titled societies also encourage cooperation in economic activities through the use of fees for insurance, burial, or investment purposes. Aspects of both the age-grade and titled societies may be seen in the structure and vitality of men's and women's groups, brotherhoods, and so on, among African Americans. Even the organization of black American churches and their auxiliary societies reflects these African patterns of association.

Importance of Oral Eloquence

The African American church, where permitted to develop independently, incorporated other social norms and roles of African society. Among these were leadership by elders and/or by individuals who were gifted speakers. In those African societies where leadership was informal or officially vested in a group of elders, individual influence and leadership were exercised through one's knowledge of custom and traditions as well as through sound judgment and rhetorical skill. Since the New World experience rarely permitted free and open public expression to black people, especially to men, these highly valued skills were developed in the single largest institution that the blacks had to themselves, the churches. Preachers in African American churches have traditionally been political leaders in a society within a society. It is significant that many of the civil rights movement's leaders were first of all ministers in black churches. Martin Luther King, Jr., for example, was a gifted politician noted as well for his eloquence and his sense of history. As such, his leadership role in African American society is reminiscent of that of the griot. In highly centralized states, the griots were important officials of the court. They exhorted troops to battle and counseled the ruler by recalling past heroes and events of their people's history. Their fate, as we have seen in the epic *Sundiata,* was closely bound to that of the king, who symbolized his people.

Oral Literature

The importance of the oral tradition in African life appears, as we have seen, not only in political and historical rhetoric but also in the tales used to transmit the wisdom of elders to the young. Some of the animal and human characters in African tales—notably Hare, Tortoise, and Spider—found their way to the New World in the tales told by African nursemaids to their children and to those of their masters. The transfer of animal characters was not the only African pattern to appear in this setting. The performance of the "uncle" and "auntie" figures who recited the tales was important. These stories used the theme of the trickster hare, common in African folklore, who outwitted those of superior physical strength (or social position) by his swiftness and cunning. The language of the tales was often replete with proverbs, riddles, and double meaning. They also sustained the pedagogical purpose of African tales: to impart a moral lesson or model of behavior.

Other kinds of African American tales also reflect an African origin. For instance, there is a predominance of tales concerned with questions about the origin of the cosmos or, more generally, about how things came to be as they are. Religious tales containing plots about conjuring, voodoo, and natural phenomena reflect African religious practices that have been adapted to the New World setting. "Preacher" tales—ones by and about ministers—may combine elements of the trickster character with the primacy of the performance element. In the folk genre of the "black sermon" it is the preacher's skill in heightening the spiritual experience of the congregation through poetic use of the popular language that, more than the substance of the words, creates the popularity of the teller. Spirituals, Christian religious songs created in the context of slavery, often included actual hidden messages or codes. The importance of rhythm and verse is characteristic of African American field hollers, riddles, and proverbs, as well as of some of the tales.

Written Literature

Many of the themes and stylistic devices of African American folk literature mentioned above—trickster, animal, preacher subjects; moralistic purpose; the use of exaggeration, double meaning, hidden messages, rhythm, and verse—have been used by black American writers in their short stories, poetry, and novels.

One of the earliest examples is Charles Waddell Chesnutt's *The Conjure Woman*, published in 1899, and widely read by white as well as black Americans. In this work a series of short stories develops around an elderly former slave named Uncle Julius. Uncle Julius, the epitome of deference and helpfulness toward his employer, frequently "explains things" to him through stories strongly reminiscent of the folk tale. The strange ways of nature, conjuring, and animals are common subjects. Irony and satire provide the tales with various levels of meaning that belie Uncle Julius's innocence and simplicity. James Weldon Johnson's *God's Trombones: Seven Negro Sermons in Verse* is an excellent early example of the use of the black folk sermon in literature. The themes and literary techniques explored by Jean Toomer in *Cane*, Ralph Ellison in *The Invisible Man*, and Richard Wright in *Native Son* are more recent examples of literature reflecting a great sensitivity to their African and African American folk heritage by black American writers. We will explore this connection more fully in Chapter 33 of Volume II.

Language

African languages themselves have left their mark on the speech of African American communities. Lorenzo Turner was the first to point out specific words from a variety of African languages in the speech of the Gullah communities off the South Carolina coast. More subtle—and, because of that, more persistent—linguistic influences were patterns of sentence construction. The speech of black Americans, long thought to be merely bad English, has been shown in recent years to be the result of an English vocabulary superimposed on grammatical and syntactical patterns common to related African languages. It is strikingly similar to contemporary African dialects derived from contact with European languages. Other African linguistic influences are even more widespread.

Beliefs

African beliefs about the nature of the universe, about humankind's relationship to the world of nature, and about humanity's relationship to humanity have also survived in African American cultures of the New World. Embodying what could be called aspects of religion, these survivals appear both within and without established black churches. Blacks in Latin America and the West Indies (and some influenced by them in the United States) worship and venerate numerous African deities, particularly those of the Yoruba. Often their names have been joined with those of the Christian saints whose personalities are perceived to be similar. In some instances the body of worshipers follow African patterns of cult organization, leadership, and ritual, although most have been altered by Christian forms.

We have seen how the spiritual vitality of the natural world and the belief in resident spirits influence all aspects of traditional African life. Acknowledgment of the spiritual power of water remains a recognizably African feature of African American religion. It is not without reason that the Baptist Church, which baptizes by immersion in water, is the most populous black American church. The spiritual potential of plants or of objects controlled by powerful spirits appears in the New World practices of "working roots" and of voodoo. Here a human agent, using herbs or objects as an intermediary, may direct powerful spirits to hinder or assist another person, often at the request of a third party. Inveighed against as superstitions or regarded more positively as folk medicine, such skills involve closely guarded secret knowledge and have rarely been studied in a systematic way. Credible witnesses testifying to the psychic power of such skills or forces at work have in recent years led modern scientists in the fields of pharmacology and psychiatry to study these phenomena in both Africa and the New World.

Music

African music and dance are the most well known African influences on African American and American culture in general. In Africa, the two arts are not easily distinguished from poetry and song, and none of these from the pervasive quality of ritual. Above all is the predominant role in African and African American music of rhythm. It is varied and multiple in composition, often emphasizing the unexpected by the coincidence of otherwise differing rhythms on a normally unaccented beat, called *syncopation*. Jazz music was founded on this predominance of rhythm. In addition to rhythm, jazz musicians preferred harmonic scales, intervals of thirds, and the call-and-response pattern of solo instrument or voice with a chorus, all features widely used in Africa. Generally speaking, the African and African American singing style uses the voice like an instrument, placing greater emphasis on

its percussive role and on particular *timbres* of voice than European music does. The call-and-response pattern of leader and chorus was a distinctive feature of African American spirituals, of course, before it was extended to the secular realm by jazz musicians.

Dance

Although less studied than music, African American dance can be seen to bear African characteristics of form, composition, and body stance. Preferences for group dancing in lines or in circles, with movement running counterclockwise in the latter, are typical in African dance throughout the continent. A frontal pose of the face and the vigorous use of separate parts of the body to accent different rhythms of the dance were readily marked by early European visitors to Africa. The survival of these features is generally, if not always precisely, noted by observers of African American dance.

Interrelation of Arts

In traditional Africa, poetry, song, music, and dance are always integrated into patterns of work and ritual as well as into those of sheer entertainment. Nothing is too sacred or too profane to be celebrated in art. Moreover, the participation in celebration, as we saw with the Efe/Gelede festival, serves to unite the community, to restore balance, and to reaffirm values. It seems likely that African American artistic values and expression drew on African content, form, occasion, and style; moreover, they also served to develop and sustain the slaves' self-conscious sense of community. Their extension and elaboration since slavery have created a distinctive African American aesthetic and have greatly enriched American culture as well as Western culture as a whole.

The Influence of Africa on the Western Humanities

The most direct impact of the African humanities on those of the West beyond black America has been in the fields of music and art. Artists such as Picasso who "discovered" African sculpture in the early part of this century brought a vibrant, shocking, and refreshing set of aesthetic norms to Western art. Similarly, the African rhythms that African Americans developed in jazz revitalized a tradition of Western music. Other aspects of African American culture—dance, language and poetry, religion—that have their roots in Africa have been adopted or imitated by others in the West. More indirectly, Africa has influenced the humanities in Europe and America as theme or symbol. Black people appear in Western literature and art as evil, mysterious, savage, passionate, or inherently noble. Europe's contact with Africa was a source of the important idea of cultural relativity that began in the sixteenth century. The enormous burden of guilt that slavery left to the Western mind had its impact on the humanities. In later chapters we will see some examples of poets and philosophers in the eighteenth and nineteenth centuries who spoke out against the slave trade in various ways. The inhumaneness of such an institution called into question the very foundations of the humanities, and humanists were among the first to decry it. It is nonetheless true that the great flourishing of European culture that was to dominate the world in the modern era was made possible in part by the exploitation of Africa.

Glossary

Italics are used within the definitions to indicate terms that are themselves defined elsewhere in the glossary and, in a few cases, to distinguish titles of works or foreign words.

ABA Form MUSIC: A particular organization of parts used in a musical *composition* in which there are three units, the first and third of which are the same. See *Da capo aria.*

Abbey Religious body governed by an abbot or abbess, or the collection of buildings themselves, also called a monastery.

Absolutism The theory that all political power in a society is derived from one authority, normally a monarch.

Abstract VISUAL ARTS: Not representational or *illusionistic.* Describes painting or sculpture that simplifies or distills figures from the material world into *forms,* lines, *colors.*

Affect MUSIC: The production of emotional reactions in the listener by certain musical sounds, according to a theory from the baroque period. For example, sorrow should be characterized by slow-moving music, hatred by very repulsive harmonies.

African Survival A specific form or function of an institution, ritual, belief, language, or art that is clearly identifiable with an African origin, although adapted to the situation of African descendants in the New World.

Allegory LITERATURE, VISUAL ARTS: The technique of making concrete things, animals, or persons represent abstract ideas or morals. A literary allegory usually takes the form of a *narrative* which may be read on at least two levels; for example, Dante's *Divine Comedy.* Medieval sculptures often have allegorical significance.

Altarpiece VISUAL ARTS: A painted or sculptured decoration on canvas or panels placed behind or above an altar.

Ambulatory ARCHITECTURE: A covered passageway for walking. In a church, the semicircular passage around the main altar.

Anaphora (ah-na′fo-rah) LITERATURE: A rhetorical figure which uses the repetition of the same word or phrase to introduce two or more clauses or lines of verse.

Animism The belief that parts of nature, such as water, trees, etc., have souls and can influence human events. The term is used by Westerners to describe African religions.

Antiphon MUSIC: In Gregorian chant, a short text from the Scriptures or elsewhere set to music in a simple *style,* and sung before and after a Psalm or a canticle.

Antiphonal MUSIC: See *Antiphony.*

Antiphony (an-ti′fo-ny) MUSIC: The sound produced by *choirs* or instruments "answering" one another. For instance, one choir will sing, and then it is "answered" by another choir.

Antithesis LITERATURE: The balance of parallel word groups conveying opposing ideas.

Apse (aap′ss) ARCHITECTURE: A large semicircular or polygonal *niche, domed* or *vaulted.* In a Roman *basilica* the apse was placed at one or both ends or sides of the building. In a Christian church it is usually placed at the east end of the *nave* beyond the *choir.*

Arcade ARCHITECTURE: A covered walk made of *arches* on *piers* or *columns,* rather than *lintels.*

Arch ARCHITECTURE: 1. Commonly, any curved structural member that is used to span an opening. 2. Specifically, restricted to the spanning members of a curved opening that are constructed of wedge-shaped stones called *voussoirs.* Arches may be of many shapes, basically round or pointed. See Roman Architecture (Ch. 7) and Gothic Architecture (Ch. 10).

Archaic 1. Obsolete. 2. In its formative or early stages.

Architrave (ahr′kuh-trave) ARCHITECTURE: A *beam* that rests directly on the *columns;* the lowest part of the *entablature.*

Aria (ah′ree-ah) MUSIC: An elaborate *composition* for solo voice with instrumental accompaniment.

Aristocracy Form of government from Greek word meaning "rule by the few for the common good."

Arpeggiated MUSIC: Describes a rippling effect produced by playing the notes of a chord one after another instead of simultaneously. See *Chord.*

Asantehene (a-sahn′tee-hee-nee) The Akan term for the King of the Ashanti state.

Ase (ah say′) Yoruba word meaning power, authority, potential energy.

Atmospheric Perspective See *Perspective.*

Atonal MUSIC: Describes music written with an intentional disregard for a central keynote (or tonal center). This style of composition was developed after World War I by Arnold Schoenberg and his followers.

Aulos (ow′los) MUSIC: The most important wind instrument of the ancient Greeks. It is not a flute (as is often stated), but a shrill-sounding oboe. It originated in the Orient and was associated with the orgiastic rites of the god Dionysus.

Axis VISUAL ARTS: The imaginary line that can be passed through a building or a figure, around which the principal parts revolve. See *Balance.*

Balance VISUAL ARTS: The creation of an apparent equilibrium or *harmony* between all the parts of a *composition,* be it a building, painting, or sculpture.

Ballad A narrative poem or song in short stanzas, usually with a refrain, often handed down orally.

Balustrade ARCHITECTURE: A rail or handrail along the top edge of a roof or balcony, made up of a top horizontal rail, a bottom rail, and short *columns* between.

Baptistry ARCHITECTURE: The building or room for performing the rite of baptism. Contains a basin or pool.

Baroque Term first applied to the visual arts and later to the music and literature of the 17th and 18th centuries to designate a style characterized by energy, movement, realism, and violent contrasts. The baroque style is often set in opposition to the orderly and formal "classical" style of the High Renaissance.

Barrel Vault See *Vault.*

Base ARCHITECTURE: 1. The lowest visible part of a building. 2. The slab on which some *column* shafts rest. See *Orders.*

Basilica (bah-sil'i-cah) ARCHITECTURE: A large, rectangular hall with a central space surrounded by aisles on the sides and an *apse* at one or each end or side. The basilica was used as a court of justice by the Romans and adopted by the early Christians as a church.

Bay ARCHITECTURE: One of a series of regularly repeated spaces of a building marked off by vertical elements.

Beam ARCHITECTURE: A large piece of squared timber, long in proportion to its breadth and thickness, used for spanning spaces. A *lintel* is a specific kind of beam.

Blank Verse LITERATURE: Unrhymed lines in *iambic pentameter.* A common form for dramatic verse in English. See Shakespeare (Ch. 19).

Boss ARCHITECTURE: The circular *keystone* at the crossing of diagonal *ribs.* May be richly carved and decorated.

Buttress ARCHITECTURE: The vertical exterior mass of masonry built at right angles into the *wall* to strengthen it and to counteract the lateral *thrust* of a *vault* or *arch.* Architecture of the Gothic period developed this *form* into the flying buttress, which is a combination of the regular or *pier*-like buttress and the arched buttress. See *Chartres* (Ch. 10).

Cadence MUSIC: A formula or cliché that indicates a point of repose. The cadence is one of several possible melodic, rhythmic, or harmonic combinations that signal a slowing down or stopping of the forward motion.

Candace Title of the Queen Mother in Nubia.

Cantilever ARCHITECTURE: 1. A horizontally projecting member, sometimes called a bracket, used to carry the cornice or eaves of a building. 2. A beam or slab, projecting beyond the wall or supporting column, whose outward thrust or span is held down at one end only. See Robie House (Ch. 31).

Capital ARCHITECTURE: The uppermost or crowning member of a *column, pilaster,* or *pier* that forms the visual transition from the post to the *lintel* above. See *Orders.*

Caryatid (kahr'ee-ah-tid) ARCHITECTURE: The name given a *column* when it is disguised as a female figure.

Casting SCULPTURE: A method of reproducing sculpture through the use of a mold that is the receptacle for a liquid which hardens when cooled. The method may be used to produce solid or hollow cast *forms.*

Cathedral Principal church of a diocese, literally the location of the bishop's throne, or cathedra.

Cella ARCHITECTURE: The principal chamber of a Greek or Roman temple, housing the cult image.

Centering ARCHITECTURE: The temporary wooden *structure* that supports an *arch* or dome while it is being erected.

Chapel ARCHITECTURE: 1. A small church. 2. A separate compartment in a large church that has its own altar.

Choir ARCHITECTURE: The part of the church reserved for clergy and singers, usually the space between the crossing and the *apse.* MUSIC: A group of singers in a church.

Chord MUSIC: The simultaneous sounding of three or more usually harmonious *tones.*

Chordal MUSIC: Characterized by the employment of *chords* in a logical progression of harmonies.

Choreographer DANCE: Person responsible for the *choreography* of a dance.

Choreography DANCE: The design and arrangement of the movements of a ballet or modern dance.

Chromatic MUSIC: Describes a scale progressing by half-tones instead of the normal degrees of the scale; e.g., in C major: c-c#-d-d#-e instead of c-d-e. VISUAL ARTS: Refers to the visual spectrum of hues. See *Color.*

Cire Perdu (seer pehr-doo') SCULPTURE: French expression meaning "lost wax." Technique for making bronze sculpture that involves molding wax over a clay mold, encasing it with another clay mold, heating the mold, then allowing the wax to drain out and replacing it with molten bronze.

Classic, Classical ALL ARTS: Recognized generally to be excellent, time-tested. LITERATURE AND VISUAL ARTS: 1. From ancient Greece or Rome. 2. From "classical" (fifth century B.C.) Greece or having properties such as *harmony, balance,* moderation and magnitude characteristic of art of that period. MUSIC: The musical *style* of the late 18th century. Leading composers in the classical style are Haydn, Mozart, and the early Beethoven.

Clerestory (clear'story) ARCHITECTURE: An upper story in a building that carries windows or openings for the transmission of light to the space beneath.

Coda MUSIC: A passage of music added to the end of a piece to confirm an impression of finality.

Coffer, Coffering ARCHITECTURE: Originally a casket or box, later, a recessed ceiling panel. Coffering is a technique for making a ceiling of recessed panels.

Collage (kohl-lahzh') VISUAL ARTS: From the French, *coller,* "to glue." A technique for creating *compositions* by pasting or in some way attaching a variety of materials or objects to a flat surface or canvas.

Colonnade ARCHITECTURE: A series of regularly spaced *columns* supporting a *lintel* or *entablature.*

Color VISUAL ARTS: A quality perceived in objects by the human eye that derives from the length of the light waves reflected by individual surfaces. The visible spectrum is divided into six basic hues: red, orange, yellow, green, blue, and violet. Red, yellow and blue are called the *primary colors;* the others, which result from mixing adjacent primary colors, are called *secondary colors.* White, black, and grays result from mixing these six hues and are not *chromatic:* they cannot be distinguished by hue, only by value. Value is the property of a color that distinguishes it as light or dark. Colors that are "high" in value are light colors; those that are "low" in value are dark colors. Adding white to a color will raise its value to make a *tint;* adding black to a color will lower its value to make a *shade.* Saturation is the property of a color by which its vividness or purity is distinguished. See also *Complementary Colors, Cool Colors, Warm Colors.*

Column ARCHITECTURE: A cylindrical, upright post or pillar. It may contain three parts: *base, shaft,* and *capital.*

Comedy LITERATURE: A drama that ends happily, intended to provoke laughter from its audience. Comedy often includes *satire* on types of characters or societies.

Complementary Colors VISUAL ARTS: Hues that form a neutral gray when mixed but, when juxtaposed, form a sharp contrast. The complementary of any *primary color* (red, yellow, or blue) is made by mixing the other two primaries. Example: The complementary of red is green, obtained by mixing yellow with blue.

Composition VISUAL ARTS: The arrangements of elements within the work in order to create a certain effect based on a variety of principles and conventions: e.g., *balance, color, contour, focal point, proportion, scale, symmetry, volume.* MUSIC: The putting together of elements such as *melody, harmony, rhythm,* and orchestration into a musical *form.* The term may be used similarly to denote a putting together of elements in a dance or film. LITERATURE: The act of composing an oral or written work.

Compound Pier ARCHITECTURE: A *pier* or post made up of attached *columns.* See *Chartres* (Ch. 10).

Concerto (con-chair'toe) MUSIC: A composition for one or more solo instruments and an orchestra, each competing with the other on an equal basis.

Content ALL ARTS: What the *form* contains and means. Content may include subject matter and theme. The quality of a work of art is often judged by the appropriateness, or apparent inseparability, of form and content.

Continuo MUSIC: In the scores of baroque composers (Bach, Handel) the bass part, performed by the harpsichord or organ, together with a viola da gamba or cello. The continuo, during the baroque era, provided the harmonic structure of the pieces being performed.

Contour PAINTING, DRAWING: The visible edge or outline of an object, *form* or shape, used especially to suggest volume or mass by means of the distinctness, thickness, or color of the edge or line.

Contrapuntal (con-tra-pun'tal) MUSIC: In a *style* that employs *counterpoint.*

Cool Colors VISUAL ARTS: Blues, greens, and associated hues. Cool colors will appear to recede from the viewer in a picture, while *warm colors* will tend to project.

Cornice ARCHITECTURE: 1. The horizontal projection that finishes the top of a *wall.* 2. In classical architecture, the third or uppermost horizontal section of an *entablature.* See *Orders.*

Counterpoint MUSIC: Music consisting of two or more *melodies* played simultaneously. The term is practically synonymous with *polyphony.*

Couplet LITERATURE: Two lines of poetry together, of the same meter and rhyme.

Crossing In a church, the intersection of the *nave* and *transept* in front of the *apse.*

Cuneiform Writing system used in Mesopotamia, based on wedge shapes.

Da Capo Aria (dah cah'poh ahr'ee-ah) MUSIC: A particular type of *aria* that developed in the baroque period (17th and 18th centuries). It consists of two sections, the first of which is repeated after the second. The result is the *ABA form.* See *Aria, ABA Form.*

Deduction PHILOSOPHY: Reasoning from a general principle to a specific fact or case, or from a premise to a logical conclusion.

Democracy From the Greek word meaning "rule by the people." A form of government in which the electorate is coincident with the adult population (sometimes only the adult males) of a community.

Demotic The most simplified, "popular" Egyptian writing system.

Despotism Government by a ruler with unlimited powers.

Dialectic PHILOSOPHY: 1. Platonic—A method of logical examination of beliefs, proceeding by question and answer. 2. Hegelian and Marxian—A logical method that proceeds by the contradiction of opposites (thesis, antithesis) to their resolution in a synthesis.

Dome ARCHITECTURE: A curved or hemispherical roof structure spanning a space and resting on a curved, circular, or polygonal *base.* Theoretically, a dome is an *arch* rotated 360 degrees around a central *axis.* See *Pantheon* (Ch. 7).

Drapery SCULPTURE: The clothing of a figure or *form* in a usually nonspecific but *tactile* and responsive material.

Drum ARCHITECTURE: The cylindrical or polygonal *structure* that rises above the body of a building to support a *dome.*

Duration MUSIC: The time-value assigned to a musical note; that is, how long it is to be played or sung.

Dynamics MUSIC: Words or signs that indicate the varying degrees of loudness in the music. For instance, *forte* (loud), *piano* (soft, quiet), *diminuendo* (decrease *volume* gradually).

Ego In Freudian theory, one of the three parts of the mind. The ego is the conscious, controlling, self-directed part.

Egungun (eh-goon-goon) Yoruba masqueraders concerned with mediating between the community of the living and that of the recently dead.

Elevation ARCHITECTURE: 1. Generally, a term that refers to one of the sides of a building. 2. Specifically, a drawing or graphic representation showing one face or side of a building. It can be of the interior or exterior.

Empiricism PHILOSOPHY: The theory that knowledge is derived from observation of nature and by experiment.

Entablature ARCHITECTURE: The upper section of a classical *order* resting on the capitals of the columns and including architrave, frieze, *cornice,* and pediment.

Epic LITERATURE: A long *narrative* poem that recounts an event of importance in a culture's history and presents a hero of that culture. See section on Homer (Ch. 3).

Episode LITERATURE: In Greek tragedy, a section of action between two choruses. In drama and fiction generally, a group of events having unity in itself. A story is created from a series of related episodes. A fiction is said to be episodic if the episodes fall into no logical relationship.

Epithet LITERATURE: A short phrase used to modify a noun by pointing out a salient characteristic. Epithets (e.g., Homer's "swift-footed Achilles") are often used in epic poetry.

Eros In Greek mythology, son of Aphrodite and god of sexual love, called "Cupid" by the Romans.

Ethics PHILOSOPHY: The branch of philosophy dealing with problems of good and bad, right and wrong, in human conduct.

Façade (fa-sahd') ARCHITECTURE: A face of a building.

Fetish Statue or other object believed to embody supernatural power.

Figurative VISUAL ARTS: Describes painting or sculpture in which the human body and the objects of habitual visual experience are clearly recognizable in the work.

Fluting ARCHITECTURE: The grooves or channels, usually parallel, that decorate the shafts of *columns*. Fluting may run up and down a shaft or around the shaft in various directions.

Focal Point VISUAL ARTS: The place of major or dominant interest on which the eyes repeatedly focus in a painting, drawing, or architectural arrangement.

Foreshortening PAINTING: The method of representing objects or parts of objects as if seen from an angle so that the object seems to recede into space instead of being seen in a frontal or profile view. The technique is based on the principle of continuous diminution in size along the length of the object or figure. See *Perspective* and *Vanishing Point*.

Form ALL ARTS: The arrangement or organization of the elements of a work of art in space (visual arts) or time (literary, musical, performing arts). A form may be conventional or imposed by tradition (the Greek temple, the sonnet, the sonata, the five-act play) or original with the artist. In the latter case, form is said to follow from, or adapt itself to, *content*.

Free Verse LITERATURE: Poetic lines with no conventional meter or rhyme.

Fresco PAINTING: The technique of making a painting on new, wet plaster. Fresco painting was particularly favored it Italy from Roman times until the eighteenth century. See Ch. 17.

Frieze ARCHITECTURE: 1. Middle horizontal element of the classical *entablature*. See *Orders*. 2. A decorative band near the top of an interior wall that is below the *cornice* molding.

Frontality (adj. frontally) Artistic device used by the Egyptians whereby part of the body appears frontally and part in profile.

Fugal MUSIC: Characteristic of the *fugue*.

Fugue (fewg) MUSIC: A *composition* based on a *theme* (known as the *subject*) that is stated at the beginning in one voice part alone and is then restated by the other voice parts in succession. The theme reappears at various places throughout the composition in one voice part or another in combination with forms of itself.

Gable ARCHITECTURE: The triangular space at the end of a building formed by the slopes of a pitched roof, extending from the *cornice* or eaves to the *ridge*. In classical architecture the gable is called a *pediment*.

Gallery ARCHITECTURE: A long, covered area, usually elevated, that acts as a passageway on the inside or exterior of a building.

Genre (john'ruh) LITERATURE: A literary type or form. Genres include *tragedy, comedy, epic, lyric, novel*, short story, essay.

Greco-Roman Belonging to the cultures of ancient Greece and Rome.

Grid VISUAL ARTS: A pattern of vertical and horizontal lines forming squares of uniform size on a chart, map, drawing, etc.

Griot (gree-oh') African oral poet, musician, and historian.

Groin Vault See *Vault*.

Groundplan ARCHITECTURE: A drawing of a horizontal *section* of a building that shows the arrangement of the *walls*, windows, supports and other elements. A groundplan is used to produce blueprints.

Ground Plane PAINTING: In a picture, the surface, apparently receding into the distance, on which the figures seem to stand. It is sometimes thought of as comparable to a kind of stage space.

Harmonic Modulation MUSIC: The change of key within a composition. Modulations are accomplished by means of a *chord* (or chords) common to the old key as well as the new one.

Harmony MUSIC: The chordal structure of music familiar to most Western listeners in popular music accompanied by guitars, in Romantic orchestral music, etc.

Hebraic Belonging to the Hebrews, Jews, or Israelites. Refers primarily to the culture of the ancient Hebrews of biblical times.

Hebraism Hebrew culture, thought, institutions.

Hellenic Greek. Usually refers to the "classical" period of Greek culture; i.e., the fifth and fourth centuries B.C.

Hellenism The culture of ancient Greece.

Hellenistic Literally, "Greek-like." Refers to Greek history and artistic style from the third century B.C.

Hieratic Egyptian writing system; a simplified cursive form of hieroglyphics. See *Hieroglyphic*.

Hieroglyphic Egyptian writing system, originally based on pictures.

Homophonic (hawm-o-fon'ic) Characteristic of *homophony*.

Homophony (hoh-maw'foh-nee) MUSIC: A single *melody* line supported by its accompanying *chords* and/or voice parts. See *Monophony, Polyphony, Chord,* and Texture.

Hubris (hyoo'bris) A Greek word meaning arrogance or excessive pride.

Hue See *Color*.

Hyperbole (high-purr'boh-lee) LITERATURE: A figure of speech that uses obvious exaggeration.

Iamb (eye′amb) LITERATURE: A metrical "foot" consisting of one short (or unaccented) syllable and one long (or accented) syllable. Example: hĕllō.

Iambic Pentameter (eye-am′bic pen-tam′eh-ter) LITERATURE: The most common metrical line in English verse, consisting of five *iambs*. Example, from Shakespeare: "Shăll Ī cŏmpāre thĕe tō ă sūmmĕr's dāy?"

Id In Freudian theory, one of the three parts of the mind. The id is the instinctive, non-controlled part.

Ifa (ee′fah) A Yoruba system of divination in which a priest advises his clients of proper courses of behavior based upon the casting of palm kernels and the interpretation of poems chosen for their numerical links to the patterns of thrown kernels.

Illusionism VISUAL ARTS: The attempt by artists to create the illusion of reality in their work. Illusionism may also be called realism. It is important to remember that illusionism is not the motivating intention of all works of art.

Image ALL ARTS: The representation of sense impressions to the imagination. Images are a fundamental part of the language of art. They differ from the abstract terminology of science and philosophy in that they are a means whereby complex emotional experience is communicated. Images may be tactile, auditory, olfactory, etc., but the word is ordinarily used for visual impressions.

Imagery LITERATURE: Patterns of images in a specific work or in the entire works of an author. May refer to a specific type (animal imagery, garden imagery). VISUAL ARTS: The objects, *forms* or shapes depicted by the artist in a particular work.

Impasto (em-pah′stoh) PAINTING: Paint that has the consistency of thick paste, used for bright highlights or to suggest *texture*. Examples: Rembrandt and Van Gogh.

Improvisation MUSIC: The art of performing spontaneously rather than recreating written music.

Induction PHILOSOPHY: Reasoning from particular facts or cases to a general conclusion.

Inflection MUSIC: The shaping or changing of a musical passage in a way that is unique to the individual performer of the music.

Initiation Ceremonies or rites by which a young person is brought into manhood or womanhood, or an older person is made a member of a secret society, brotherhood, etc.

Inquisition A former tribunal in the Roman Catholic Church directed at the suppression of heresy.

Irony LITERATURE: A manner of speaking by which the author says the opposite of what he means, characteristically using words of praise to imply scorn. Dramatic or tragic irony means that the audience is aware of truths which the character speaking does not understand.

Iwi (ee′wee) Yoruba poems sung by Egungun masqueraders.

Jamb ARCHITECTURE: A vertical member at either side of a door frame or window frame. When sculpture is attached to this member it is called a jamb sculpture or jamb figure. See *Chartres* (Ch. 10).

Kente (ken′teh) Large ceremonial cloth from Ghana made of narrow strips sewn together and distinguished by elaborate, multicolored geometric designs of silk.

Keystone ARCHITECTURE: The central wedge-shaped stone of an *arch* that locks together the others.

Komos Greek word for a revel. Root of the word *comedy*.

Kouros (koo′rohs), **Kore** (koh′ray) SCULPTURE: Greek for a male nude votive figure, female votive figure.

Labarai (lah-bah-rye′) Hausa tales told by old men, involving cultural, family, and group history.

Lantern ARCHITECTURE: The windowed turret or tower-like form that crowns a *dome* or roof.

Libretto (lih-bret′toe) MUSIC: The text of an opera, *oratorio*, or other dramatic musical work.

Linear Perspective See *Perspective*.

Lintel ARCHITECTURE: The horizontal member or *beam* that spans an opening between two upright members, or posts, over a window, door, or similar opening.

Lyric LITERATURE: A short poem or song characterized by personal feeling and intense emotional expression. Originally, in Greece, lyrics were accompanied by the music of a lyre.

Matrilineal System of descent in which inheritance of goods, access to land, and group leadership pass to the children through the family of the mother.

Medium (pl. media) ALL ARTS: 1. The material or materials with which the artist works. Examples from VISUAL ARTS: paint, stone, wood, bronze, plaster, concrete. MUSIC: sound. LITERATURE: language. CINEMA: film. DANCE: human body. DRAMA: language, costume, lighting, actors, sound, etc. 2. Modern means of communication (television, radio, newspapers). 3. PAINTING: A substance such as oil, egg, or water with which *pigment* is mixed.

Melodic Elaboration MUSIC: The ornamentation of *melody* by one or more of a number of possible musical devices, such as added notes, interval changes, etc.

Melody MUSIC: A succession of musical *tones*. Often the melody is known as the "tune," and is not to be confused with the other accompanying parts of a song. See *Homophony*.

Metaphor LITERATURE: A figure of speech that states or implies an analogy between two objects or between an object and a mental or emotional state. Example: "My days are in the yellow leaf;/The flowers and fruits of love are gone" (Byron) makes an analogy between the poet's life and the seasonal changes of a tree.

Metaphorical Describing statements or representations to be taken as analogy, not to be taken literally.

Meter POETRY: A regularly recurring rhythmic pattern. Meter in English is most commonly measured by accents, or stresses, and syllables. The most common metric "foot" in English is the *iamb*. The most common verse line is the *iambic pentameter* (five iambs). MUSIC: A pattern of fixed temporal units. For example, 3/4 meter means one beat to a quarter note and three beats to a measure. In a musical *composition* meter is the basic grouping of notes in time.

Metope (meh'toh-pay) ARCHITECTURE: The blank space of block between the *triglyphs* in the Doric *frieze*, sometimes sculpted in low *relief*. See *Orders*.

Modal MUSIC: Describes a type of music conforming to the scale patterns of the medieval Church *modes*. See *Modes*.

Modeling VISUAL ARTS: 1. The creation of a three-dimensional *form* in clay or other responsive material, such as wax, soap, soft bone, ivory, etc. 2. By analogy, in painting and drawing, the process of suggesting a three-dimensional *form* by the creation of *shade* and shadow.

Modernism Generic name given to a variety of movements in all the arts, beginning in the early 20th century. Promotes a subjective or inner view of reality and uses diverse experimental techniques.

Modes MUSIC: Melodic scales used for church music of the Middle Ages. The modes are organized according to *pitches* similar to our modern major and minor scales, yet different enough to set them apart from the modern scales.

Molding ARCHITECTURE: A member used in construction or decoration that produces a variety in edges or contours by virtue of its curved surface.

Monastery The dwelling place of a community of monks. See *Abbey*.

Monasticism A way of life assumed by those who voluntarily separate themselves from the world to contemplate divine nature. See *Monastery*.

Monophonic (mo-no-fohn'ic) Characteristic of *monophony*.

Monophony (mo-nof'o-nee) MUSIC: A simple *melody* without additional parts or accompaniment, such as the music of a flute playing alone or of a woman singing by herself. See *Homophony, Polyphony, Texture*.

Mosaic VISUAL ARTS: A *form* of surface decoration made by inlaying small pieces of glass, tile, enamel, or varicolored stones in a cement or plaster matrix or ground.

Motet (moh-tette') MUSIC: Usually an unaccompanied choral composition based on a Latin sacred text. The motet was one of the most important forms of *polyphonic* composition from the thirteenth through the seventeenth centuries.

Motif (moh-teef'), **Motive** (moh-teev') LITERATURE: A basic element that recurs, and may serve as a kind of foundation, in a long poem, fiction, or drama. A young woman awakened by love is the motif of many tales, such as *Sleeping Beauty*. VISUAL ARTS: An element of design repeated and developed in a painting, sculpture, or building. MUSIC: A recurring melodic phrase, sometimes used as a basis for variation.

Mural PAINTING: Large painting in oil, fresco, or other *medium* made for a particular *wall*, ceiling, or similar large surface.

Myth Stories developed anonymously within a culture that attempt to explain natural events from a supernatural or religious point of view.

Mythology The body of myths from a particular cultural group.

Naos (nah'ohs) ARCHITECTURE: Greek word for the *cella* or main body of a Greek temple.

Narrative LITERATURE: 1. (noun) Any *form* that tells a story or recounts a sequence of events (novel, *tale*, essay, article, film). 2. (adj.) In story form, recounting.

Narthex ARCHITECTURE: The entrance hall or porch that stands before the *nave* of a church.

Naturalism LITERATURE, VISUAL ARTS: Faithful adherence to the appearance of nature or outer reality.

Nave ARCHITECTURE: In Roman architecture, the central space of a *basilica;* in Christian architecture, the central longitudinal or circular space in the church, bounded by aisles.

Nave Arcade ARCHITECTURE: The open passageway or screen between the central space and the *side aisles* in a church.

Nemesis (neh'ma-sis) Greek goddess of Fate. Word means retribution, punishment.

Neoclassicism ALL ARTS: A movement that flourished in Europe and America in the late seventeenth and eighteenth centuries, heavily influenced by the classical style of Greece and Rome. Neoclassical art and literature is characterized by sobriety, balance, logic, and restraint. The corresponding musical style (18th century) is usually called *classical*.

Neolithic The stage in the evolution of human societies when peoples began systematic cultivation and the domestication of animals.

Niche (nish) ARCHITECTURE: A semicircular or similarly shaped recess in a wall designed to contain sculpture, an urn, or other object. It is usually covered by a half*dome*.

Nonobjective VISUAL ARTS: Not representing objects in the material world.

Novel LITERATURE: A lengthy prose narrative, traditionally spanning a broad period of time, containing a plot and developing characters. The modern European novel took form in the eighteenth century.

Oba Name for the chief ruler of Benin.

Oculus (ock'you-luhs) ACHITECTURE: Circular opening at the crown of a *dome*. See *Pantheon* (Ch. 7).

Odu (oh'doo) A secret body of poetry used in the Yoruba *Ifa* divination process.

Oil Painting The practice of painting by using *pigments* suspended in oil (walnut, linseed, etc.).

Oligarchy (oh'lih-gar-key) Greek word meaning "rule by the few." Rule by the few where the state is primarily utilized to serve the interest of the governors. Traditionally contrasted with *aristocracy*, rule by the few for the common good.

Olorun (oh-low'roon), **Oludumare** (oh-loo-doo-mah'ray) The Yoruba term for the supreme high deity.

Open Fifths MUSIC: *Chords*, normally made of three sounds, with the middle *pitch* absent.

Oratorio MUSIC: An extended musical setting for solo voices, chorus, and orchestra, of a religious or contemplative nature. An oratorio is performed in a concert hall or church, without scenery, costumes, or physical action. One of the greatest examples is Handel's *Messiah*.

Orchestration MUSIC: Orchestration is the art of writing music for the instruments of the orchestra that will bring out desired effects of the various instruments. Indeed, it is the art of "blending" the voices of the orchestra so that a pleasing sound is the end result.

Orders ARCHITECTURE: Types of *columns* with *entablatures* developed in classical Greece. The orders are basically three: Doric, Ionic, and Corinthian. They determine not only the scale and therefore dimensions of a temple but also the experience generated by the building, or its *style*. See section on Greek Architecture and diagram of the orders (Ch. 4).

Oriki (ohr-ee'key) Yoruba term meaning praise poems based on names given to gods, places, rulers, and important persons.

Orisha (ohr-ee'sha) In Yoruba religion, lesser gods (below the chief god) and sometimes ancestor figures, ancient kings, and founders of cities who have been deified.

Ostinato (aw-stee-nah'stoe) MUSIC: Italian for obstinate or stubborn; the persistent repetition of a clearly defined *melody*, usually in the same voice. This device is often used in a bass part to organize a *composition* for successive variations.

Oxymoron (ock-see-mohr'on) LITERATURE: A figure of speech that brings together two contradictory terms, such as "sweet sorrow."

Palazzo (pa-laht'so) ARCHITECTURE: Italian for palace, or large, impressive building.

Palladian ARCHITECTURE: Designating the Renaissance architectural style of Andrea Palladio.

Panel Painting A painting made on a ground or panel of wood, as distinguished from a *fresco* or a painting on canvas.

Parapet ARCHITECTURE: In an exterior *wall,* the part entirely above the roof. The term may also describe a low wall that acts as a guard at a sudden edge or drop, as on the edge of a roof, battlement, or wall.

Parody LITERATURE: A work that exaggerates or burlesques another, serious one. Often a parody pokes fun at an author and his style. The parody may be compared to a visual caricature or cartoon.

Pathos (pay'thaws) ALL ARTS: A quality that sets off deep feeling or compassion in the spectator or reader.

Patrilineal System of descent in which inheritance of goods, access to land, and group leadership passes to the children through the family of the father.

Pediment ARCHITECTURE: In classical architecture the triangular space at the end of a roof formed by the sloping ridges of the roof. The pediment was often filled with decoration which could be painted or sculpted or both.

Pentatonic Scale MUSIC: Five-note scale that occurs in the music of nearly all ancient cultures. It is common in West African music and is found in jazz.

Perspective VISUAL ARTS: Generally, the representation of three-dimensional objects in space on a two-dimensional surface. There are a variety of means to achieve this. The most familiar is that of "linear perspective" developed in the fifteenth century and codified by Brunelleschi, in which all parallel lines and edges of surfaces recede at the same angle and are drawn, on the picture plane, to converge at a single *vanishing point*. The process of diminution in size of objects with respect to location is very regular and precise. Other techniques, often used in combination with linear perspective, include: (a) vertical perspective—objects further from the observer are shown higher up on the picture, (b) diagonal perspective—objects are not only higher but aligned along an oblique *axis* producing the sensation of continuous recession, (c) overlapping, (d) *foreshortening,* (e) *modeling,* (f) *shadows,* and (g) atmospheric perspective, the use of conventions such as blurring of outlines, alternation of hue toward blue, and decrease of *color* saturation.

Philosophe (fee-low-soph') Eighteenth-century French intellectual and writer; not usually a systematic philosopher.

Phrase MUSIC: A natural division of the *melody;* in a manner of speaking, a musical "sentence."

Picture Plane PAINTING: The surface on which the picture is painted.

Picture Space PAINTING: The space that extends behind or beyond the picture plane; created by devices such as *linear perspective*. Picture space is usually described by foreground, middleground, and background.

Pier ARCHITECTURE: A *column,* post, or similar member designed to carry a great load; may also refer to a thickened vertical mass within the *wall* designed to provide additional support.

Pigment PAINTING: The grains or powder that give a *medium* its *color.* Can be derived from a variety of sources: clays, stones, metals, shells, animal and vegetable matter.

Pilaster (pih'lass-ter) ARCHITECTURE: A flattened engaged *column* or *pier* that may have a *capital* and *base.* It may be purely decorative or it may reinforce a *wall.*

Pitch MUSIC: A technical term identifying a single musical sound, taking into consideration the frequency of its fundamental vibrations. Some songs, or instruments, are pitched high and others are pitched low.

Plan See *Groundplan.*

Plane A flat surface.

Plasticity VISUAL ARTS: The quality of roundness, palpability, solidity, or three-dimensionality of a *form.*

Plinth A block or slab on which a statue, pedestal, or column is placed, and, by extension, the base on which a building rests or appears to rest.

Podium ARCHITECTURE: The high platform or *base* of a Roman temple, or any elevated platform.

Polis (poh'liss) The ancient Greek city-state.

Polyphonic (paul-ee-fon'ick) Characteristic of *polyphony.*

Polyphony (paul-if'o-nee) MUSIC: Describes *composition* or *improvisations* in which more than one *melody* sounds simultaneously—that is, two or more tunes at the same time. Polyphony is characterized by the combining of a number of individual melodies into a harmonizing and agreeable whole. See *Homophony, Monophony,* and *Texture.*

Portico ARCHITECTURE: Porch or covered walk consisting of a roof supported by *columns.*

Post-and-Lintel ARCHITECTURE: an essential system of building characterized by the use of uprights—posts—which support horizontal *beams*—lintels—in order to span spaces. Used as supports for a window or door, the posts are the *jambs* and the *lintel* is the window head.

Primary Colors Red, Yellow, Blue—the three primary hues of the spectrum. See *Color.*

Pronaos (pro′nah-ohs) ARCHITECTURE: In classical architecture, the inner *portico* or room in front of the *naos* or *cella.*

Prose LITERATURE: Generally, may mean any kind of discourse, written or spoken, which cannot be classified as poetry. More specifically, prose refers to written expression characterized by logical, grammatical order, *style,* and even *rhythm* (but not *meter*).

Proverb A saying that succinctly and effectively expresses a truth recognized by a community or a wise observation about life. Proverbs are most often transmitted orally.

Rationalism PHILOSOPHY: The theory that general principles are essentially deductive; i.e., deducible from an examination of human reason. Reason, not the senses, is the ultimate source of basic truths.

Realism LITERATURE, VISUAL ARTS: A movement which began in the mid-nineteenth century and which holds that art should be a faithful reproduction of reality and that artists should deal with contemporary people and their everyday experience.

Recitative (reh-see-tah-teev′) MUSIC: A vocal style used to introduce ideas and persons in the musical *composition,* or to relate a given amount of information within a short period of time. The recitative has practically no melodic value. This device is employed extensively in Handel's *Messiah.*

Relief Sculpture Sculpture that is not freestanding but projects from a surface of which it is a part. A slight projection is called low relief (bas-relief); a more pronounced projection, high relief.

Republic A form of government in which ultimate power resides in the hands of a fairly large number of people but not necessarily the entire community. This power is exercised through representatives. The word derives from Latin meaning "public thing."

Response MUSIC: A solo-chorus relationship in which the soloist alternates performance with the chorus. The response is a particularly noteworthy device in traditional African music as well as in Gregorian chant.

Responsorial MUSIC: Describing the performance of a chant in alternation between a soloist and a chorus. (It is unlike antiphonal music, where alternating choruses sing.)

Rhythm ALL ARTS: An overall sense of systematic movement. In music, poetry, and dance this movement may be literally felt; in the visual arts it refers to the regular repetition of a *form,* conveying a sense of movement by the contrast between a form and its interval.

Rib ARCHITECTURE: Generally a curved structural member that supports any curved shape or panel.

Ribbed Vault ARCHITECTURE: A *vault* whose sections seem to be supported or are supported by slender, curved structural members that also define the sections of the vault. The ribs may run either transversely, that is from side to side, or diagonally, from corner to corner of the vault.

Riddle A form of popular, usually oral, literature that asks an answer to a veiled question. Riddles often make use of striking *images* and *metaphors.*

Ridge ARCHITECTURE: The line defined by the meeting of the two sides of a sloping roof.

Romance LITERATURE: A long narrative in a *Romance language,* presenting chivalrous ideals, heroes involved in adventures, and love affairs from medieval legends.

Romance Language One of the languages that developed from popular Latin speech during the Middle Ages, and that exist now as French, Italian, Spanish, Portuguese, Catalan, Provençal, Romanic, and Rumanian.

Romanesque An artistic movement of the eleventh and twelfth centuries, primarily in architecture. The name comes from similarities with Roman architecture.

Romanticism A movement in all of the arts as well as in philosophy, religion, and politics that spread throughout Europe and America in the early nineteenth century. The romantics revolted against the Neoclassical emphasis on order and reason and substituted an inclination for nature and imagination. See Ch. 27.

Rose Window ARCHITECTURE: The round ornamental window frequently found over the entrances of Gothic cathedrals.

Sarcophagus (sahr-cough′a-gus) A large stone coffin. It may be elaborately carved and decorated.

Satire A mode of expression that criticizes social institutions or human foibles humorously. The Roman invented the verse satire, but satire may appear in any literary *genre,* in visual art, in film, mime, and dance.

Satyr (say′ter) **Play** LITERATURE: A light, burlesque play given along with *tragedies* and *comedies* at the festival of Dionysus in ancient Athens.

Scholasticism PHILOSOPHY: A way of thought that attempted to reconcile Christian truth with truth established by natural reason. Originating in the early Middle Ages, it reached its height in the thirteenth century in response to the recovery of Aristotle's scientific and philosophical writings.

Secondary Colors See *Color.*

Section ARCHITECTURE: The drawing that represents a vertical slide through the interior or exterior of a building, showing the relation of floor to floor.

Shade PAINTING: A *color* mixed with black. Mixing a color with white produces a *tint.*

Shading VISUAL ARTS: The process of indicating by graphics or paint the change in *color* of an object when light falls on its surface revealing its three-dimensional qualities. Shading can be produced not only by a change of color, but also by the addition of black, brown, or gray, or by drawing techniques.

Shadow VISUAL ARTS: The *form* cast by an object in response to the direction of light.

Shed Roof ARCHITECTURE: A roof shape with only one sloping *plane,* such as the roof of a lean-to, or that over the *side aisle* in a Gothic or Romanesque church.

Side Aisle ARCHITECTURE: The aisles on either side of, and therefore parallel to, the *nave* in a Christian church or Roman *basilica.*

Simile (sim′eh-lee) LITERATURE: A type of *metaphor* which makes an explicit comparison. Example: "My love is like a red, red rose."

Sonata MUSIC: An important form of instrumental music in use from the baroque era to the present. It is a *composition* usually with three or four movements, each movement adhering to a pattern of contrasting tempos. Example: Allegro, Adagio, Scherzo, Allegro.

Sonnet LITERATURE: A *lyric* poem of fourteen lines, following one of several conventions. The two main types of sonnet are the Italian (Petrarchan) which divides the poem into octave (eight lines) and sestet (six lines) and the English (Shakespearean) which divides the poem into three quatrains of four lines each and a final rhyming couplet.

Span ARCHITECTURE: The interval between two posts, *arches, walls,* or other supports.

Stained Glass ARCHITECTURE: Glass to which a *color* is added during its molten state, or glass which is given a hue by firing or otherwise causing color to adhere to the glass.

Stele (stee′lee) ARCHITECTURE: In classical Greece a stone upright or slab used commemoratively; it may mark a grave or record an offering or important event.

Stretto MUSIC: The repetition of a *theme (subject)* that has been collapsed by diminishing the time values of the notes. As a result, the listener is literally propelled to the dramatic end or climactic conclusion of the music. Handel used this *fugal* device effectively in the last chorus of his *Messiah.*

Structure ALL ARTS: The relationship of the parts to the whole in a work of art. A structure may be mechanical (division of a play into acts, a symphony into movements) or may be more concealed and based on such things as the inter-relationships of *images, themes, motifs, colors,* shapes. In a *narrative* the structure usually refers to the arrangement of the sequence of events. In architecture structure may refer either to the actual system of building or to the relationships between the elements of the system of building.

Style ALL ARTS: Characteristics of *form* and technique that enable us to identify a particular work with a certain historical period, place, group, or individual. Painters in Florence in the 15th and 16th centuries used *perspective, color,* etc., in ways that allow us to identify a Renaissance style, but within that group we may distinguish the individual style of Leonardo from that of Raphael. The *impressionist* painters in France at the end of the nineteenth century used light and *color* in a particular way: a painting in which this technique is followed has an impressionistic style. But the use of certain *forms, colors,* design and *composition* enables us to distinguish within this group the style of Renoir from that of Monet. Afro-European *rhythms* and *improvisation* distinguish a jazz style, but within that general category are many schools of jazz or even different styles of one individual, such as Duke Ellington. Literary style is determined by choices of words, sentence *structure* and syntax *rhythm,* figurative language, rhetorical devices, etc. One may speak of an ornate, simple, formal, or colloquial style; of a period style such as *Neoclassical, romantic, realist;* or of an individual's style. Style is sometimes contrasted with *content.*

Subject ALL ARTS: What the work is about. The subject of the painting "Mont Ste Victoire" is that particular mountain; the subject of Richard Wright's *Native Son* is a young black man in Chicago. MUSIC: The *melody* used as the basis of a *contrapuntal composition* (e.g., the subject of a *fugue*).

Suite MUSIC: An important instrumental form of baroque music, consisting of a grouping of several dancelike movements, all in the same key.

Superego In Freudian theory, one of the three parts of the mind. The superego is the censuring faculty, replacing parents or other authorities.

Symbol VISUAL ARTS, LITERATURE: An *image* that suggests an idea, a spiritual or religious concept, or an emotion beyond itself. It differs from *metaphor* in that the term of comparison is not explicitly stated. Symbols may be conventional; i.e., have a culturally defined meaning such as the Christian cross or the Jewish star of David. Since the nineteenth century, symbols have tended to denote a variety or an ambiguity of meanings.

Symbolism 1. The use of symbol in any art. 2. A literary school which began in France in the late nineteenth century, characterized by the use of obscure or ambiguous *symbols.*

Symmetry VISUAL ARTS: The balance of proportions achieved by the repetition of parts on either side of a central *axis.* The two sides may be identical, in which case we can speak of bilateral symmetry.

Syncopation MUSIC: A rhythmic device characterized as a deliberate disturbance of a regularly recurring pulse. Accented offbeats or irregular *meter* changes are two means of achieving syncopation.

Tactile VISUAL ARTS, LITERATURE: Refers to the sense of touch. In the visual arts, tactile *values* are created by techniques and conventions that specifically stimulate the sense of touch in order to enhance suggestions of weight, *volume* (roundness), visual approximation, and therefore three-dimensionality. Writers may also create tactile effects, as in the description of cloth or skin.

Tale LITERATURE: A simple *narrative,* whose subject matter may be real or imaginary, and whose purpose is primarily to entertain. Tales may also make use of "morals" to instruct.

Tatsuniyoyi (taht-soon-yoh′yee) Hausa tales about animals and people told by old women to entertain and instruct young children.

Tempera (tehm′per-ah) PAINTING: Technique in which the *pigment* is suspended in egg, glue, or a similar soluble *medium,* like water. Tempera paint dries very quickly and does not blend easily, producing a matte (flat, nonreflective) surface, because, unlike *oil paint,* it is essentially an opaque medium.

Texture VISUAL ARTS: Surface quality (rough, smooth, grainy, etc.) LITERATURE: Elements such as *imagery,* sound patterns, etc. apart from the *subject* and *structure* of the work. MUSIC: The working relationship between the *melody* line and the other accompanying parts, or the characteristic "weaving" of a musical *composition*. There are three basic musical textures: *Monophonic* (a single line), *Homophonic* (a melody supported by *chords*), and *Polyphonic* (multiple melodic lines).

Thanatos Greek word for death. For Freud, the death-wish or death-force, opposed to Eros, the life force.

Theme VISUAL ARTS: A *color* or pattern taken as a subject for repetition and modification. Example: a piece of sculpture may have a cubical theme. MUSIC: A *melody* which constitutes the basis of variation and development. Example: "The Ode to Joy" song in the last movement of Beethoven's *Ninth Symphony*. LITERATURE AND PERFORMING ARTS: An emotion or idea that receives major attention in the work. A novel or film may contain several themes, such as love, war, death. A dance may be composed on the theme of struggle, joy, etc. Theme is sometimes used in this sense for visual arts and music as well.

Threnody (threh'no-dee) MUSIC: A song of lamentation, a very mournful song.

Through-Composed MUSIC: Describes a type of song in which new music is provided for each stanza. A through-composed song is thus unlike most modern hymns, folk, and popular songs, which use the same tune for each stanza.

Thrust ARCHITECTURE: The downward and outward pressure exerted by a *vault* or *dome* on the *walls* supporting it.

Timbre (taam'bruh) MUSIC: The quality of "color" of a particular musical *tone* produced by the various instruments. For instance, the very "nasal" sound of the oboe is markedly different from the very "pure" sound of the flute.

Tint VISUAL ARTS: The *color* achieved by adding white to a hue to raise its *value*, in contrast to a *shade*, which is a hue mixed with black to lower its value.

Tonal MUSIC: Organized around a pitch center. A tonal *composition* is one in which the *pitches* of all the various *chords* and *melodies* relate well to one another. Tonal music has a recognizable beginning, middle, and end. See *Chord, Melody, Pitch*.

Tonality MUSIC: The specific *tonal* organization of a composition.

Tone ALL ARTS: The creation of a mood or an emotional state. In painting, tone may refer specifically to the prevailing effect of a *color*. Thus, a painting may be said to have a silvery, bluish, light, or dark tone as well as a wistful, melancholy, or joyful tone. The term may also refer to *value* or *shade* (see *Color*). In literature, tone usually describes the prevailing attitude of an author toward his material, audience, or both. Thus a tone may be cynical, sentimental, satirical, etc. In music, "tone color" may be used as a synonym for *timbre*. Tone in music also means a sound of definite *pitch* and duration (as distinct from noise), the true building material of music. The notes on a written page of music are merely symbols that represent the tones that actually make the music.

Tornada (tore-nah'dah) MUSIC: In troubadour songs, a short stanza added at the end as a "send-off."

Tracery ARCHITECTURE: The curvilinear or rectilinear pattern of open stonework or wood that supports the glass or other transparent or translucent material in a window or similar opening. May also be used generally to refer to decorative patterns carved similarly on wood or stone.

Tragedy LITERATURE: A serious drama that recounts the events in the life of a great person which bring him or her from fortune to misfortune. Tragedies usually meditate on the relation between human beings and their destiny. Tragedies first developed in ancient Greece; other great periods of tragedy include Elizabethan England and France under Louis XIV. The word is sometimes used to describe a novel or story.

Transept ARCHITECTURE: The transverse portion of a church that crosses the central *axis* of the *nave* at right angles between the nave and *apse* to form a cross-shaped (cruciform) planned building.

Triglyph (try'glif) ARCHITECTURE: The block carved with three channels or grooves that alternates with the *metopes* is a classical Doric *frieze*. See *Orders*.

Triumphal Arch ARCHITECTURE: The monumental urban gateway, invented by the Romans, set up along a major street to commemorate important military successes. It may have one or three arched openings and is usually decorated with inscriptions, *reliefs*, and freestanding sculpture on the top.

Trope MUSIC: Lengthened musical passage or elaboration on the Mass used during the Middle Ages. LITERATURE: 1. Verbal amplification of the text of the Mass. 2. A figure of speech.

Troubadour A lyric poet and singer, including wandering minstrels, originating in Provence in the eleventh century and flourishing throughout southern France, northern Italy, and Eastern Spain during the twelfth and thirteenth centuries.

Truss ARCHITECTURE: Originally a wooden structural member composed of smaller, lighter pieces of wood joined to form rigid triangles and capable of spanning spaces by acting as a *beam*.

Tympanum (tihm'pah-nuhm) ARCHITECTURE: The triangular or similarly shaped space enclosed by an *arch* or *pediment*.

Tyranny In ancient Greece, meant "rule of the strong man." Historically, came to mean arbitrary rule of one, but generally taken to mean arbitrary political rule of any kind.

Value See *Color*.

Vanishing Point PAINTING: The point or points of convergence for all lines forming an angle to the *picture plane* in pictures constructed according to the principles of linear *perspective*.

Vault ARCHITECTURE: The covering or spanning of a space employing the principle of the *arch* and using masonry, brick, plaster, or similar malleable materials. The extension of an arch infinitely in one plane creates a barrel or tunnel vault. The intersection of two barrel vaults at right angles to each other produces a cross or groin vault. *Ribs* are sometimes placed along the intersections of a groin vault to produce a *ribbed vault*.

Veneer VISUAL ARTS: A thin layer of precious or valuable material glued or otherwise attached to the surface of another, less expensive, or less beautiful material. The Romans, for example, applied thin layers of marble to the concrete and rubble fill surfaces of their buildings to produce a more splendid effect. In this century, valuable woods like walnut or mahogany are applied as veneers to the surfaces of plywood.

Verisimilitude Literally, "true-seeming." LITERATURE: A doctrine prevalent in the *Neoclassical* period, which hold that elements in a story must be so arranged that they seem to be true or that they could actually occur. VISUAL ARTS: The effect of near-perfect emulation or reproduction of objects in the visual world. Not to be confused with *realism*.

Vernacular The common daily speech of the people; non-literary language. During the Middle Ages, any language that was not Latin.

Viewpoint The position or place from which the viewer looks at an object or the visual field.

Vizier A chief administrator.

Volume ARCHITECTURE: Refers to the void or solid three-dimensional quality of a space or *form* whether completely enclosed or created by the presence of forms which act as boundaries. Compare the "volume" of the *Parthenon* with the "volume" of the *Pantheon*.

Volute A spiral or scroll-like ornamental form, which may be used either as a purely decorative or as a supporting member in an architectural ensemble. The curvilinear portion of an Ionic capital is a volute, and by extension a portion of such a shape is a volute.

Voussoir (voo-swahr') ARCHITECTURE: The wedge-shaped stone or masonry unit of an *arch,* wider at the top and tapering toward the bottom.

Wall ARCHITECTURE: A broad, substantial upright slab that acts as an enclosing *form* capable of supporting its own weight and the weight of *beams* or *arches* to span and enclose space.

Warm Colors VISUAL ARTS: The hues commonly associated with warmth—yellow, red, and orange. In *compositions* the warm colors tend to advance, in contrast to the *cool colors,* which tend to recede from the viewer.

Watercolor PAINTING: Technique using water as the *medium* for very fine *pigment.* Watercolor dries very fast and can be extremely transparent.

Ziggurat ARCHITECTURE: The Mesopotamian temple-tower.

Credits

Index

Page numbers in boldface type indicate black and white illustrations.

Aachen, 268
Abelard, Peter, *Sic et Non (Yes and No)*, 295
Abraham, 226
Abu Temple [Tell Asmar], statuettes from, 7, **7**
Achebe, Chinua, *Generation Gap*, 427
Achilles, 70
Acominatos, Michael, *Lament for Athens*, 284
Acropolis [Athens] 72, 99, **100**; Erechtheum, 107, **107**; Propylaea, 106–107, **107**
Action, of epic poetry, 72, 73–74
Adiye (Fowl) (Yoruba poem), 424
Aeneid (Virgil), 73, 200–224
Aeschylus, 115; *Agamemnon*, 115; *The Libation Bearers*, 115; *Oresteia*, 115; *The Persians*, 98, 115; *Prometheus Bound*, 115; *Seven Against Thebes*, 115; *The Suppliants*, 115
Africa, 379–387; American culture and, 380–382; Catalan map of, **396**; contact with Europe and, 382, 386; diversity of, 381; early, 382–385; Islamic expansion into, 273, 274; Kushite influence on, 51–52; major cultures of, Map 394; major states of, Map 381; medieval kingdoms of, 385–386; modern, Map 380; religions of, 382, 397, 430, 449; sub-Saharan, 383; Western images of, 380. *See also* African art; African music; Efe/Gelede festival; West Africa
African American culture: African survivals in, 450–453; dance in, 453; language and, 452; music in, 438–439, 440, 442, 452, 453–454; religion and, 452–453
African art, 429–438; classification of, 430–431; communal life and, 429–431; divination trays, 435–436, **436**; figurines, 433–435, **434**, **435**; interrelation of, 453; kente cloth, 436, **437**; masks and headpieces, 431–433, **431–433**; sculpture in everyday objects and, 437, **437**; stools, 436, **436**. *See also* Efe/Gelede festival

African Art in Motion (Thompson), 450
African music, 438–442; call and response, 439–440; elements of, 439; from festival of the tohossou, 440–442, **441**; rhythm and, 439; similarities with jazz, 438–439; songs, 444–445
African Poetry (Beier), 389
Afro-Asiatic languages, 393
Agamemnon, king of Mycenae, 69–70
Agamemnon (Aeschylus), 115
Age of Iron, in Africa, 383
Agriculture: African, 383; Egyptian, 28; Mesopotamian, 3–4, during Middle Ages, 294
Aisles, of churches, 230, 300
Akhenaton IV, pharaoh of Egypt. *See* Amenophis IV, pharaoh of Egypt
Akkadian kingdom, 13, **13**
Akkadian language, 11, 12, 13
Alcaeus, 75
Alexander the Great, 41, 181; empire of, 183, Map 182
Alfonso the Wise, 281
Alhambra [Granada, Spain], 277–278, **279**
Al-Junayd of Bagdhad, *Epic of 'Antar*, 288–291
Allegory, 326
Allegory of the Cave, The (Plato), 168–170
Altar of the Peace of Augustus, The (Ara Pacis Augustae), 186–187, **188**
Altar of Zeus [Pergamon], 108, **109**, 181
Amarna Period, 38–40
Ambo, 263–264
Ambulatory, 266, 299
Amenemhat III, pharaoh of Egypt, 36
Amenhotep IV, pharaoh of Egypt. *See* Amenophis IV, pharaoh of Egypt
Amenophis III, pharaoh of Egypt, 38–39
Amenophis (Akhenaton; Amenhotep) IV, pharaoh of Egypt, 38, 39, **39**, 40; art under, 39, 39–40, **40**; *The Great Hymn to the Aten*, 57–59
Amharic language, 393
Amon, Egyptian god, 38, 45
Amon-Ra, Egyptian god, 32, 36
Amon Temple [Kawa], 48–49, **49**
Amos, book of, 243–244
Andalusia, intellectual life in, 280–281

Anglo-Saxon language, 325
Animism, African religions and, 397, 430
Ankhhaf, bust of, 35, **35**
Anlamani, 44
Annunciation (Martini), 325, Color Plate IX
Antelope (Etu-Duiker) (Yoruba poem), 424
Anthemius of Tralles, Hagia Sophia, 263–264, **264**, **265**
Antigone (Sophocles), 115, 117
Antiphony, 312
Apedemek, Egyptian god, 45, 46
Aphrodite of Cnidos (Praxiteles), 107, **108**, 181
Aphrodite of Cyrene, 108, **108**
Appreciation of the Frankish Character, An (Ibn Munqidh), 291–292
Apse, 231, 263, 267–268, 299
Aqueducts, Roman, 188, **190**
Aquinas, Thomas, 280–281, 297; *Guide for the Perplexed*, 280–281
Arabic language, 273, 279, 280, 393; African literature in, 394
Ara Pacis Augustae (The Altar of the Peace of Augustus), 186–187, **188**
Arcadius, 232
Archaic period, of Greece, 70–71
Arches: Islamic, 276, **277**; pointed, 276, **277**, 302, 305, **306**, 306; Roman, 187–188, **189**, 190, **191**; true, 187–188, **189**
Archetypes, 8
Archilochos, 75
Archimedes, 182
Architecture: Byzantine, 263–264, **264–267**, 266–269, **268**; classical Greek, 99–102, **100–102**, 106–107, **107**, 256; of Crete, 68–69, **70**; Egyptian, 33, **33**, **34**, 35; Islamic, 275–278, **276–279**, Color Plate VI; medieval, 298–311, **299–309**, Color Plate VII, Color Plate VIII; Mesopotamian, 4; Mycenean, 70, **70**; Roman, 187–188, **189–193**, 190, 192, 256; Sumerian, 5–7, **6**
Archivolts, 307
Aristophanes: *The Birds*, 118; *The Frogs*, 118; *Lysistrata*, 118, 140–161, 196
Aristotle, 117, 229, 296; *On the Generation of Animals*, 166; *The*

469